PROFESSIONAL SECRETARY'S ENCYCLOPEDIC DICTIONARY

Fourth Edition

By the
PRENTICE HALL EDITORIAL STAFF

Revised by
MARY A. De VRIES

PRENTICE HALL
Englewood Cliffs, New Jersey 07632

Prentice-Hall International (UK) Limited, *London*
Prentice-Hall of Australia Pty. Limited, *Sydney*
Prentice-Hall Canada, Inc., *Toronto*
Prentice-Hall Hispanoamericana, S.A., *Mexico*
Prentice-Hall of India Private Limited, *New Delhi*
Prentice-Hall of Japan, Inc., *Tokyo*
Simon & Schuster Asia Pte. Ltd., *Singapore*
Editora Prentice-Hall do Brasil, Ltda., *Rio de Janeiro*

© 1989 *by*

PRENTICE-HALL, INC.

Englewood Cliffs, NJ

10 9 8 7 6 5 4 3 2

Printed in the United States of America

Previous editions of this book were published
as *Private Secretary's Encyclopedic Dictionary*.

Library of Congress Cataloging-in-Publication Data

Professional secretary's encyclopedic
dictionary.

Rev. ed. of: Private secretary's encyclopedic
dictionary.   3rd ed.   c1984.
Includes bibliographical references and index.
1. Business—Dictionaries.   I. De Vries,
Mary Ann.   II. Prentice-Hall, inc.
III. Private secretary's encyclopedic
dictionary.   IV. Title.
HF1001.P78 1989   651'.03'21   88-22474
ISBN 0-13-725417-2

ISBN 0-13-725417-2

PRENTICE HALL
BUSINESS & PROFESSIONAL DIVISION
A division of Simon & Schuster
Englewood Cliffs, New Jersey 07632

HOW TO USE
THIS FOURTH EDITION

The *Professional Secretary's Encyclopedic Dictionary* does more than provide definitions of key terms that you should know; when appropriate, it explains what to do at work and illustrates the pertinent form, technique, or procedure to follow in performing both routine and occasional tasks. In this respect the book serves as a valuable training tool as well as a useful book of definitions and a source of essential information about some of the major fields of professional and business activity.

Although most of the entries in this edition were heavily revised in light of wide-ranging changes in the working world, the presentation follows the same format as that of the previous edition. So that you can select a specific topic of concern, without wading through the entire book, the entries are collected in chapters about specific individual topics. The fourth edition has seventeen such chapters (or fields of activity), that are divided into six parts:

I. *Office Procedures and Practices*: Office Procedures; Communications: Telecommunications, Electronic Messages, and Postal Service; Conferences and Meetings; Travel; Office Supplies and Equipment

II. *Written Communication*: Grammar and Vocabulary; Correspondence; Writing, Editing, and Publishing

III. *Business Law and Organization*: Business Law; Business Organization and Management

IV. *Accounting and Finance*: Accounting and Bookkeeping; Taxes; Business Mathematics, Investments, and Finance; Banking.

V. *Real Estate and Insurance*: Real Estate; Insurance

VI. *Reference Section*: Tables, Weights, and Measures

Some overlap is inevitable in certain chapters; for example, an entry about traveler's checks would be pertinent in both the chapter on travel and the one on banking. Rather than use duplicate entries in such cases, cross-references are employed extensively throughout the book. Sometimes it is helpful when reading about one topic to be able to expand your knowledge by reviewing related topics. After reading about a "title" in real estate, you might also want to read about "title insurance." Therefore, the entry Title includes the cross-reference "See Chapter 16/Title insurance." This enables you quickly to find the chapter where the entry will be found. The term Title insurance, in capital and small capital letters, refers to an entry about title insurance located in Chapter 16, "Insurance." However, not all cross-references are made to an entry in another chapter. For instance, in the first chapter the entry Index and indexing has this sentence: "The folders or cards are then arranged according to the Filing systems being used." The term in capital and small capital letters refers to the entry Filing systems located in the *same* chapter. In all cases, if the cross-reference does not contain a chapter number, the entry is in the same chapter. Because cross-referencing is so important to those who need additional information, 99 new cross-references were added in this edition.

New information was often incorporated into the entries that were carried over from the previous edition. The former entry Erasures and corrections on typed material, for example, is now titled Erasures and corrections and has been expanded to include corrections by computer and word processor as well as by typewriter. In some cases, the previous discussion may have been adequate but more illustrations or examples were needed. For instance, the entry *Lay, lie* under the main entry Words, commonly misused (Chapter 6, "Grammar and Vocabulary"), included a discussion of these confusing words, so often used incorrectly, but had no examples of how they are actually used in a sentence. The revised and expanded entry in the fourth edition now provides ten sample sentences using both *lie* and *lay* and their principal parts.

A survey of the various fields of activity in this book revealed some gaps in the coverage of the previous edition. To plug any such weak spots, 106 new entries were added, bringing the total number of major entries to nearly 1,100. With hundreds of subentries in addition, the number of actual topics in this edition ranges well into the thousands. The following are a few examples of the important new entries:

Word processing (Chapter 1)
Electronic message systems (Chapter 2)

Secretarial staff meetings (Chapter 3)

Travel security (Chapter 4)

Office paper (Chapter 5)

Prefix (Chapter 6)

Continuation page (Chapter 7)

Research (Chapter 8)

American Law Reports (Chapter 9)

Management by objectives (Chapter 10)

T-account (Chapter 11)

Depreciation (Chapter 12)

Discount (Chapter 13)

Electronic transfer of funds (Chapter 14)

Trust deed or deed of trust (Chapter 15)

Government insurance programs (Chapter 16)

If you are just beginning your career, you can use this book as a learning guide; if you are a veteran office employee, you can use it as a refresher guide or simply as a quick and easy way to expand your knowledge in selected areas. To find the specific topics of interest to you, check the detailed table of contents, where each chapter's entries are listed alphabetically, or refer to the index at the back of the book, which includes both entries and other terms, all arranged alphabetically without regard to the chapter in which they appear.

More and more each year, secretar-ies, administrative personnel, and other office employees are being called upon to widen their horizons of skills and knowledge. For example, many secretaries who used to type reports for their employers now perform some or all of the research and edit or even draft the copy. To cope with this increasing pressure to know and to do more, employees must become familiar with terms and procedures in other areas of activity outside the office or business in which they are employed. The *Professional Secretary's Encyclopedic Dictionary* is designed to fill this need, to give you a practical, easy-to-use reference source for some of the major areas of business and professional activity so that you can increase your familiarity with different terminology and know how to perform a wide variety of tasks, step by step, when required.

Like the previous edition, this one also can be used to help you solve problems, save time at work, and answer the many questions that arise each day in a busy office. At the same time, it can be the cornerstone of an ongoing program of self-education. To receive maximum benefit, however, you should keep it on your desk and use it often. Make it a habit, in fact, to consult it on a daily basis.

Mary A. De Vries

ACKNOWLEDGMENTS

Assistance in preparing the fourth revised edition of *Professional Secretary's Encyclopedic Dictionary* came from many sources. Numerous companies, schools, and libraries supplied current literature on office practices and procedures, particularly in the area of advanced technology such as modern communications equipment and techniques. Many state and federal governmental agencies and departments as well as private services and businesses responded to requests for information and willingly gave time and attention to questions and other requests. I especially want to thank those individuals named below who directly contributed to the book by reviewing, correcting, and updating selected portions of the text. Without their time, concern, and invaluable expertise, the project could not have been completed successfully.

Although each chapter in the book was subject to my own preliminary and final research and editing, many of the chapters were revised further by various experts until we were satisfied that coverage was as thorough as time and resources would allow. For example, all chapters in the book were read and corrected by Jean McCormack, writer, research consultant, and real estate consultant. Moreover, all chapters in the first part were also reviewed and corrected by Brenda Hobbs, owner, Centralized Secretarial Services. The chapter on real estate was reviewed, corrected, and updated by McCormack; by Carol Springer, owner, Springer Realty; and by Veronica Tyler, research consultant. The chapter on insurance was reviewed, corrected, and updated by Don Risk, partner, Mahoney/Risk Insurance, and by Tyler. The chapter on grammar, the library reference material in Chapter 8, and the tables in the concluding chapter were also corrected and updated by Tyler, who additionally helped greatly in preparing the final manuscript for submission. The chapters on law and on business organization and management were reviewed, corrected, and updated by Carolyn Baldwin, attorney at law, Baldwin & Dunn; the chapter on law was also reviewed by John Sears, attorney and counselor at law, Kiger & Sears. The chapters on accounting and bookkeeping; taxes; business mathematics, investments, and finance; and banking were reviewed, corrected, and updated by Becky Arterbury, accountant, Sigafoos and Arterbury; the chapter on business mathematics, investments, and finance was also reviewed by T. R. Merry, consultant to business. Portions of the forms-of-address chart in Chapter 7 were reviewed, corrected, and updated by Sister Anne Vaccarest, director of communications, Sisters of Mercy of New Hampshire. The work of these professionals has made the book more current and accurate and more useful to all readers, for which I am deeply grateful.

In addition, I sincerely appreciated the current information on travel that I received from Robert Preston, travel agent, Kachina Travel Agency; on current forms of address in the military provided by SFC Daniel J. Donahue, U.S. Army; and on advanced communications procedures supplied by Clare Gorman, advertising and promotion, MCI International. My thanks also go to Jerome Heitman, executive director, Professional Secretaries International, who sent the study outline for the Certified Professional Secretaries exam, and to Heitman and Clifford Gallo, associate director of public relations, New Hampshire College, for their assistance in providing materials for the book.

The extent of assistance and information contributed by these authorities was enormous, and I am indebted to every one of them. However, most of the new or revised information in the majority of chapters represents my own contribution, and the final version of each entry in all chapters is my own; I am therefore responsible for any errors or shortcomings that may have escaped us.

Mary A. De Vries

CONTENTS

Alphabetizing and indexing · Assistants · Automation (office) · Callers · Chain feeding · Character count · Chinese copy · Collating · Color coding · Combing-back · Conforming · Data processing · Dictation, taking and transcribing · Draft · Enclosure · Erasures and corrections · Etiquette in the office · Filing systems · Follow-up system · Guest list · Incoming mail · Index and indexing · Information storage and retrieval · Job evaluation · Mail record · Mass card · Merit rating · Microfilming · Office management · Outgoing mail · Personnel · Presents · Professional Secretaries International · Purchasing · Records management · Screening calls · Social matters · Spacing between typewriter characters · Statistical typing · Suggestion system · Sympathy, expressions of · Tabulated material · Theater tickets · Tickler file · Time management · Training an assistant · Typing · Underscoring · Word processing · "Z" ruling

memo calendar · Printed law blank · Punched-card equipment · Ribbons · Stationery · Stencils · Typesetting equipment · Window envelope · Writing paper

Abbreviations · Adjective · Adverb · Agreement of verb with subject · Alternate subject · Apostrophe · Appositive · Capitalization · Collective noun · Colon · Comma · Compound personal pronoun · Compound subject · Compound term · Dash · Diacritical marks · Division of words · Double negatives · Ellipsis points · Exclamation point · Future tense · Gerund · Hyphen · Indefinite pronoun · Infinitive · Intervening noun · Language · Noun · Omission of words · Parentheses · Participle · Past tense · Perfect tense · Period · Possessives · Predicate nominative · Prefix · Preposition at the end · Present tense · Pronoun · Punctuation · Question mark · Quotation marks · Section sign · Semicolon · Sequence of tenses · Subjunctive mood · Suffix · Trite expressions · Verb · Virgule · Voice · Words, commonly misused

Acknowledgment letters · Addressing officials (chart) · Adjustment in account, letters making · Appointment letters · Attention line · Body of letter · Business cards · Complimentary close · Copy-distribution notation · Continuation page · Credit and collection letters · Dateline · Enclosure notation · Envelopes · Follow-up letters · Form letters · Holiday card lists · Identification line · Idention · Information, letters that process · Inside address · Invitations · Layout · Letters · Mailing notation · Memo · Model letters · Notation · Personal notation · Postscript · Reference line · Refunds, letters requesting · Sales promotion letters · Salutation · Signature · Social-business letters · Subject line · Transmittal letter · Visiting cards

Advertising · Agate line · Appendix · Associated Press (AP) · Backbone (of book) · Back matter · Ben Day process · Bibliography · Blueprinting ·

Contents

Boldface (bf) · Cold type · Copy · Copy editing · Copyright · Cropping · Cut · Dummy · Duplicating processes · Extract · Footnotes · Front matter · Full measure · Galley proof · Gravure · Hot type · Index and indexing · Information sources · Italic · lc · Layout · Letterpress · Lightface (lf) · Linecuts and halftones · Linotype · Logo · Lowercase · Ludlow · Manuscript · Mat · Mechanical · Monotype · News release · Offset · Page proof · Pica · Plate · Point · Preface to a book · Proofreaders' marks · Proofreading · Public domain · Publicity · Query · Quoted material · Report · Repro proof · Research · Roman · Running head · Stet · Superior figure · Table of contents · Type face · Type measurements · Typemarking · United Press International (UPI) · Uppercase · Widow · Word count

AFL-CIO · Acceleration clause · Accounting · Acknowledgment · Affidavit · Agent · American Digest system · American Jurisprudence · American Law Reports · *Amicus curiae* · Answer · Antitrust laws · Appeal · Arbitration · Assessment · Assignment · Attachment · Attestation · Bailment · Bankruptcy · Bill of sale · Blue law · Blue sky laws · Books and records (corporate) · *Bona fide* · Boycott · Breach of contract · Breach of warranty · Brief · Bulk sales law · Capital · *Caveat emptor* · *Certiorari* · Chose in action · Citations to legal authorities · Class action · Codicil · Collection agency · Commerce clause · Commodity Exchange Act · Common law · Complaint · Consent decree · Constructive receipt · Contracts · Cooling-off period · Corpus Juris Secundum · Courts · Covenants · Default · Department of Labor · Derivative Action · DIALOG · Disability benefit laws · Disaffirm · Discharge of contract · Docket · Eminent domain · Estoppel · Execution · Fair employment practices · Fair-trade acts · Federal Trade Commission Act · Fiduciary · Franchise · Fraud · Garnishment · Guaranty · Holder in due course · Indemnification of directors and officers · Indemnity · Indenture · Independent contractor · Injunction · Interstate Commerce Commission · Interstate commerce, intrastate commerce · Judgment · Jurat · Laches · Legal tender · LEXIS · Libel and slander · Lien · Liquidated damages · Lockout · Monopoly · Monopoly price · National Labor Relations Act · National Labor Relations Board · National Reporter System · Negotiable instrument · Nonnegotiable instrument · Notarize · Notary public · Novation · Official reports · Open shop · Option · Patent · Personal property · Piercing the corporate veil · Pledge · Power of attorney · Preemptive rights · Pricing practices · Principal · Protest · Quasi · Ratification · Regulation of business · Representative action · Rescind · Right-to-work laws · Sale · Seal · Securities Act of 1933 · Securities Exchange Act of 1934 · Service of process · Social Security Act · Statute of frauds · Statute of limitations · Statutory law · Stipulation · Subpoena · Summons · Testimonium clause · Tort · Trademark · Trespass · Trust · Trust deed · Unemployment insurance · Unfair employment practice · Uniform Commercial Code · Usury · Void; voidable · Wage-Hour Law · Waiver · Warranty · WESTLAW · Without recourse · Worker's compensation laws · Writ

10. BUSINESS ORGANIZATION AND MANAGEMENT 346

Abstract company · Advertising agency · Affiliated companies · Affirmative action · Agency · Agribusiness · Alien corporation · Annual report · Backlog · Bill of lading · Board of directors · Budget · Business corporation · Business organization, forms of · Bylaws · Capital · Capital structure · Cartel · Certificate of incorporation · Chairperson of the board · Charitable corporation · Close corporation · Closed shop · Collections · Committee · Common carrier · Conglomerate · Consignment · Consolidation · Consortium · Controller (comptroller) · Corporate entity · Corporate seal · Corporation · Corporation service company · Cumulative voting · De facto corporation · De jure corporation · Directors' fees · Docket · Domestic corporation · Dummy incorporators · Dun & Bradstreet · Economy of scale · Equal-opportunity employer · Ergonomics · Executive committee · Featherbedding · Finance committee · First-in, first-out (FIFO) · Foreign corporation · Foreign trade · General contractor · Goodwill · Holding company · Incorporated partnership · Incorporators · Interested director · Interlocking directorates · Internal reports · Inventory · Investment company · Job lot · Joint venture · Joint stock company · Junior board of directors · LCL · LTL · Last-in, first-out (LIFO) · Limited partnership · Liquidation · Management guide · Management by objectives · Markdown · Markup · Massachusetts trust · Merchandising, retail · Merger · Merit rating · Moneyed corporation · Nonprofit corporation · Nonstock corporation · Officers of a corporation · Parent corporation · Partnership · President · Promoters · Proprietorship, sole · Public corporation · Public utility corporation · Pyramiding · Quasi-public corporations · Registered office · Reorganization · Reservation of corporate name · Resident agent · Resolution · Resolutions book · Rights · Secretary (corporate) · Seniority · Silent partner · Sole practitioner · State of incorporation · Stock ·

Stock certificate · Stock corporation · Stock insurance company · Stock ledger · Stockholder · Subchapter S corporation · Subsidiary · Syndicate · Task force · Transfer agent · Treasurer · Vice president · Voting at stockholders' meetings · Voting trust

Accounting · Accounting records · Accounts · Accounts payable · Accounts receivable · Accrual accounting · Accrued assets · Accrued expenses · Accrued income · Accrued liabilities · Adjusting entries · Assets · Audit · Auditor · Bad debt losses · Balance sheet · Book value · Books of final entry · Books of original entry · Capital · Capital asset · Capital expenditure · Capital stock · Capitalization · Cash · Cash account · Cash accounting · Cash disbursements journal · Cash journal · Cash receipts journal · Closing entries · Comparative balance sheet · Comparative income statement · Control account · Cost accounting · Credit · Current assets · Current capital · Current liabilities · Current ratio · Debit and credit · Deficit · Depletion · Depreciation · Double-entry bookkeeping · Equity capital · Expense account · Financial statement · Fiscal period · Fixed assets · Fixed costs · Footing · Funded debt · Goodwill · Gross income · Gross revenue · Income · Income statement · Intangible assets · Journal · Ledger · Liabilities · Natural business year · Net assets · Net income · Net working capital · Net worth · Notes payable · Notes receivable · Obsolescence · Operating expenses · Overhead · Owner's equity · Paid-in capital · Paid-up capital · Payroll · Payroll journal · Petty cash · Posting · Prepaid expenses · Profit · Profit and loss · Quick assets · Replacements · Retained earnings · Revenue · Selling expenses · Semivariable cost · Single-entry bookkeeping · Statement of changes in financial position · Statement of revenue and expenditures · T-account · Tax accounting · Trial balance · Variable costs · Wasting asset · Work sheet · Working capital · Working papers · Write-off

Ad valorem taxes · Adjusted gross income · Alternative minimum tax · Assessment · Basis · Capital gain and loss · Carry-back, carry-over · Casualty loss · Child- and dependent-care credit · Contributions · Credits, tax ·

Deductions · Deferred-compensation agreement · Deficiency · Dependent · Depreciation · Direct tax · Estate tax · Estimated tax · Excise taxes · Exclusions · Franchise tax · Gift tax · Graduated (progressive) tax · Head of household · Income · Income tax · Income tax files · Individual retirement programs · Information return · Interest · Joint return · Meals and entertainment expenses · Medical and dental expenses · Merit rating · Miscellaneous deductions · Multiple-support agreement · Payroll taxes · Penalties · Property taxes · Real estate records · Real estate taxes · Return · Royalties · Sales and use taxes · Self-employment tax · Sick pay · Social security taxes · Stamp tax · Standard deduction · State income taxes · State unemployment insurance tax · Surtax · Surviving widow or widower · Tax lien · Tax sale · Taxable income · Taxes other than federal income · Taxes, the secretary's duties · Withholding · Withholding deposits

Acid-test ratio · Addition, shortcut · Aliquot part · Amortization · Amortization schedule · Amortized loan · Annuity · Arabic numerals · Assessment · Assignment · Assumed bonds · At the opening · Averages · Baby bond · Basing-point system · Basis point · Bearer instrument · Bearish · Bears · Bid and asked prices · Big board · Bill of exchange · Bill of sale · Black market · Blue-chip stocks · Bond · Bond discount and bond premium · Bond transaction · Broad market · Broker · Broker's monthly statement · Broker's purchase and sale confirmation · Bullish · Bulls · Business arithmetic · Carrying charge · Cash discount · Charge-account credit · Closing price · Collateral · Collateral trust bonds · Commission · Commodity exchanges · Commodity Exchange Commission · Conditional sale · Contingent interest · Contingent rent · Cost-plus pricing · Coupon bonds · Cumulative dividends · Day order · Debentures · *Del credere* · Delivery of securities · Discount · Dishonor · Dividends · Division, shortcut · Dow Jones averages · Earnest (earnest money or binder) · Equipment trust bonds · Equity · Escrow · Ex-dividend · Face value · Fidelity bond · Finance charge · Finance and investments · Fractional share · GTC order · General mortgage bond · Growth stock · Guaranteed bonds · Hedging · Income and adjustment bonds · Industrials · Insolvency · Insolvent · Installment sale · Interest · Investment · Joint annuity · Joint bonds · Limit order · Line of credit · Listed securities · Loan on real estate · Long sale · Margin · Market order · Mathematical signs and symbols · Money market · Mortgage bond · Multiplication, shortcuts · Mutual fund ·

Note · Odd lot · Over-the-counter market · Paper profits · Par value stock and no-par stock · Partial payment of debts · Participating bonds · Percentage · Pledge · Point · Portfolio · Price-earnings ratio · Prime rate · Purchase money mortgage · Puts and calls · Pyramiding · Qualified stock option · Qualifying shares · Ratio · Rebate (refund) · Redemption · Registered bond · Restricted stock option · Retirement plans · Revolving account · Roman numerals · Savings bonds · Secured bonds · Secured loan · Securities and Exchange Commission · Securities markets · Securities record · Security-transaction files · Serial bonds · Series bonds · Shortcuts · Short sale · Sinking fund · Split-coupon bonds · Spread · Stock · Stock exchanges · Stock (or bond) power · Stock purchase warrant · Stock split · Stock transaction · Stop-loss order · Straddle · Straight loan · Surety bond · Term loan · Transfer of securities · Treasury notes and bonds · Underwriter · Underwriting · Unlisted securities · Variable annuity · Wash sale · Watered stock · When-issued · Yield

Automatic teller · Bank accounts · Bank discount · Bank draft · Bank by mail · Bank money order · Bank note · Bank reserves · Bank statement · Branch banking · Cashier's check · Certificates of deposit · Certified check · Check · Checking credit · Clearinghouse · Commercial bank · Computer services · Credit cards · Credit union · Debit memo · Deposits · Direct deposits · Electronic transfer of funds · Federal Deposit Insurance Corporation · Federal Reserve Act · Federal savings and loan associations · Federal Savings and Loan Insurance Corporation · Finance companies · Foreign exchange · Foreign money · Instant loan service · Interest checking · Joint bank account · Kiting · Loans · Money management · Money market certificates · Mutual savings banks · Night depository · Rediscount rate · Safe deposit box · Savings account · Savings bonds · Stop payment · 24-hour banking

Abstract of title · Adverse possession · Air rights · Appraisal · Appurtenances · Assessed valuation · Beneficiary · Binder · Broker · Certificate of

plans · Rider · Risk · Salvage · Single-premium insurance · Subrogation ·
Supplemental insurance · Term insurance · Title insurance · Underwriter ·
Underwriting · Whole-life contracts · Worker's compensation insurance

Birthstones · Flower calendar · Wedding anniversary presents · State information · Greek alphabet · Metric system of weights and measures · Tables
of weights, measures, and values

PART I

OFFICE PROCEDURES AND PRACTICES

CHAPTER 1

OFFICE PROCEDURES

Alphabetizing and indexing. When individual names are indexed, the last name comes first, then the first name or initial, and then additional names or initials. If the name of a business concern contains the name of an individual, it is indexed in the same order as the name of the individual. Otherwise, each word comprising the name, with the exception of articles, prepositions, and conjunctions (see below), is considered in the order in which it appears.

NAMES

Robert A. Morris
Robert A. Morris & Son
R. L. Jones, Inc.
National Building Company

INDEX AND FILE AS

Jones, R. L., Inc.
Morris, Robert A.
Morris, Robert A., (&) Son
National Building Company

Names are alphabetized according to the first word in the name *as indexed*. When the first word of two or more names is the same, the names are alphabetized according to the second word, then according to the third, and so on.

NAMES

John Lewis Harper
Adam O. Harper
John K. Harper

INDEX AND FILE AS

Harper, Adam O.
Harper, John K.
Harper, John Lewis

In addition to the foregoing basic rule for indexing and alphabetizing, the following rules also apply:

Names of unequal length. When two or more names are of unequal length but contain the same word or words and are spelled the same up to and including the last word of the shorter name, index and file the shorter name first.

ORDER

Davis, A.
Davis, Annette
Davis, Annette R.
Davison, A.
First National Bank
First National Bank (and) Trust

Precedence of letters. 1. *Letters used as words.* One or more single letters (other than abbreviations such as *Inst.* or hyphenated letters such as *T-R*), such as *ABC*, are each considered as a separate unit. (Some secretaries file all letter names in alphabetical order before the word names. Follow the preferred practice in your office.

ORDER

AA Club
A B C Cleaners
AWACS
A-M Drugstore
Arnold's Deli
Astor Insurance Co.

2. *Ampersand symbol.* The ampersand symbol (&) is not considered a letter and is disregarded in determining alphabetical sequence.

ORDER

D (&) O Sporting Goods
Dexter Furniture Company
Donaldson, T. R.
Donaldson (&) Samuels, Inc.

Hyphenated names. Treat names composed of letters, words, or syllables joined by one or more hyphens as one word. When the hyphen is used instead of a comma in a firm name, the individual parts of the name are treated as separate words. The hyphen sometimes replaces the comma when the names of two individuals make up the firm name.

NAMES

Down-Stairs Art Gallery
Downers-Grove Boat Dock
Miles-Sloane (&) Co.
   (hyphen used instead of comma)
Miles, Winston M.
Mile-High Tower

INDEX AND FILE AS

Downers-Grove Boat Dock
Down-Stairs Art Gallery
Mile-High Tower
Miles-Sloane (&) Co.
   (hyphen used instead of comma)
Miles, Winston M.

Abbreviations. Abbreviations, such as *Chas., Co., Geo., Jas., St., Wm.,* are alphabetized in the same sequence as if spelled in full. Spell out when indexing for ease in filing.

NAMES

Walter Snow
Jas. Anderson
St. Peter's Cathedral
Wm. Snow
Jane Anderson

INDEX AND FILE AS

Anderson, James
Anderson, Jane
Saint Peter's Cathedral
Snow, Walter
Snow, William

3

Compound firm names. 1. When a firm name consists of a compound word that is sometimes spelled as one word, sometimes as two or more words, index as written but treat as one word in alphabetizing.

ORDER

Last Chance Hotel
Las Vegas Guides
Newport Boat Dock
New Port Rentals
New York Transit
Newark Stationers
South, J. M.
Southwest Distributors
South West Shipping, Inc.

2. Authorities differ about whether compound geographic names, such as *New York*, should be treated as one or two words in alphabetizing. Adopt a rule and follow it uniformly. In the example above, compound English geographic names (e.g., New York) are treated as two words.

Sr., Jr., II, and III. Many offices disregard seniority titles in indexing and alphabetizing. If you retain such titles, alphabetize according to the designation. The order is as follows: *II* (Second), *III* (Third), *Jr., Sr.*

ORDER

McKay, John, II
McKay, John, III
McKay, John, Jr.
McKay, John, Sr.

Surnames and prefixes. When individual surnames are compounded with prefixes, such as *D', De, Del, De La, Di, Fitz, L', La, Las, Los, M', Mc,*

Mac, O', San, Santa, Ten, Van, van Der, von, and *von Der,* index as written and treat as one word in alphabetizing, disregarding the apostrophe, the space, or the capitalization, if any.

ORDER

Damata, J.
D'Amato, P.
De Lamara, A. D.
De La Mare, A. D.
McIntyre, A. C.
Mead, Robert A.
Tenants' Committee, Inc.
Ten Eyck, E. M.

Articles, prepositions, and conjunctions. Disregard articles, prepositions, and conjunctions in determining alphabetical sequence. The words in parentheses in the following examples are disregarded.

NAMES

D. S. Baker
Geo. Billings
The Bicycle Club
Society for the Preservation of
    Forests
Society of Arts and Sciences

INDEX AND FILE AS

Baker, D. S.
Bicycle Club (The)
Billings, Geo.
Society (of) Arts (and) Sciences
Society (for the) Preservation (of)
    Forests

Articles, prepositions, and conjunctions in foreign languages. Consider an article in a name in a foreign language as part of the word that

4

immediately follows it; treat prepositions and conjunctions as separate words in determining alphabetical sequence.

NAMES

Der Amerikaner
Société des Auteurs, Musiciens et
  Compositeurs
C. H. Deramer
Société des Auteurs et Peintres

INDEX AND FILE AS

Deramer, C. H.
Der Amerikaner
Société des Auteurs et Peintres
Société des Auteurs, Musiciens et
  Compositeurs

Words ending in s. When a word ends in *s*, index and file as spelled regardless of what the *s* denotes, whether possession, with or without the apostrophe, or a singular or plural ending.

ORDER

Women Executive's Association
Women's Action Group
Womens Auxiliary
Womens Trade Alliance
Women's United Committee

NOTE: Some authorities hold that the *'s* should be disregarded in filing. The logic behind the rule illustrated here is that from the sound of the name it is usually impossible to tell what the *'s* denotes. For example, a person looking for the file on *Womens Auxiliary* would not know whether to look before or after *Women Executive's Association*.

Names containing numbers. When a name contains a number, alphabetize as if the number were spelled out in full. Spelling out the names when indexing facilitates the filing. If the number as spelled out contains more than one word, alphabetize according to the first word; if the words are joined by hyphens, treat as one word. For example, *twenty* comes before *twenty-eight*, but *twenty-eight* comes before *twenty-one*.

NAMES

28 Sutton Place, Inc.
2059 Third Ave. Corp.
The 21 Club

INDEX AND FILE AS

Twenty Fifty-Nine Third Ave. Corp.
Twenty-Eight Sutton Place, Inc.
Twenty-One Club (The)

Some authorities treat an entire numerical unit as one word regardless of hyphens. In that case, the number *twenty-eight* would precede *twenty fifty-nine*.

EXCEPTION: Numbered streets and branches of organizations numbered consecutively should be arranged in numerical sequence. Thus *Branch Number 4* precedes *Branch Number 5*, although if the numbers were spelled out and alphabetized, *Branch Number Five* would precede *Branch Number Four*.

Government offices. Index and file names of government offices under the names of the governing body, with the names of the departments, bureaus, or institutions as subtitles.

FEDERAL

United States Government
Treasury (Dept. of)
Accounts (Bur. of)

STATE

Mississippi (State of)
Education (Dept. of)
Rural Education (Div. of)

COUNTY

Suffolk (County of)
County Clerk

CITY

Memphis, Tennessee
City Planning Commission

Titles. 1. Titles are disregarded in indexing and filing but are usually written in parentheses at the end of the name.

EXCEPTION: If the name of an individual contains a title and a first name, without a last name, consider the title as the first word.

NAMES

Madame Celeste
Count Henri Dizonni
Dr. J. C. Astor
Miss Lois Chandler
Sister Mary Bennett

INDEX AND FILE AS

Astor, J. C. (Dr.)
Bennett, Mary (Sr.)
Madame Celeste
Chandler, Lois (Miss)
Dizonni, Henri (Count)

2. If a firm name contains a title, consider the title as the first word.

ORDER

Lord Bentley's Apparel
Queen Anne's Tea Shop
Sir Benjamin Hook's Seafood

Married women. Index and file names of married women according to their maiden or married last names, depending upon their preference, followed by their first names. Show the husband's initial or name in parentheses on the file label when it is convenient or important to have this additional information.

NAMES

Mrs. Albert S. (Mary L.) Jenson
Mrs. Robert E. (Ada R.) Brown

INDEX AND FILE AS

Brown, Ada R.
    (Mrs. Robert E. Brown)
Jenson, Mary L.
    (Mrs. Albert S. Jenson)

Phonetic indexing. Indexing according to the sound of the name. This method of indexing, also known as *soundex*, is used in insurance companies and other organizations that have large name files. Names that sound alike but are spelled differently are reduced to phonetic essentials and then coded.

EXAMPLE

CODE NUMBERS	Sound Equivalents
1	b, f, p, v
2	c, g, j, k, q, s, x, z
3	d, t
4	l
5	m, n
6	r

The letters *a, e, i, o, u, h, w,* and *v* are disregarded. Each code is made up of the first letter of the name and three numbers from the code. If there are less than three numbers, zeros are added. For example, the code for the names *Muller, Moeller, Moller, Mueller,* is M-460. All of the names in the M-460 group are alphabetized.

Alphabetical filing. See FILING SYSTEMS.

Applicants. For sources of applicants, see PERSONNEL, 2. *Recruiting.*

Assembling mail. See OUTGOING MAIL.

Assistants. Some secretaries are responsible for selecting and training their own assistants (see PERSONNEL). In addition, secretaries often have other personnel duties, especially when they work in a small office or are secretaries to department heads in large organizations.

The assignment of duties to an assistant secretary depends upon his or her position in the office—whether the person is a stenographer and second secretary or the secretary's assistant. Executives often give all of their dictation to assistant secretaries, except the part they put on a dictating machine, and also assign other duties to the assistant. In that case, a secretary should assign to the assistant only those duties that can be done between assignments from the executive.

Many employees prefer to work with, or through, only one secretary and leave it to that secretary to assign duties to an assistant. In that case, here are some of the duties that might be assigned when the assistant first begins to work.

1. Open and partially route mail.
2. Transcribe dictation.
3. Do copy work.
4. File marked material.
5. Take dictation.
6. Do routine, follow-up correspondence, without dictation.
7. Assemble factual material from reference books or files.
8. Run miscellaneous time-consuming errands.

As assistants become proficient in the duties first assigned to them, they should be given more responsibilities. For example, an assistant might mark the filing material, write letters that are not routine follow-ups, handle telephone calls, and keep the appointment calendar.

Association for secretaries. See PROFESSIONAL SECRETARIES INTERNATIONAL.

Automation (office). Process of making clerical functions partially or wholly automatic. Automatic data processing (ADP) is a fast and efficient way to handle large volumes of routine, repetitive work. The term *automation* is widely used in connection with electronic systems. Electronic data processing (EDP) frees personnel from time-consuming work and creates many new types of jobs, but the electronic computer is only one of the tools of automation. Office machines from the lowest to the highest level are all tools of automation, thus making it possible for any office to be automated to a degree consistent with its size and work load. A small office, for example, might have an electronic typewriter and a conventional telephone and intercom system. A larger office might have one or more word processors and a computerized telephone exchange and use some form of high-speed transmission such as telex. Offices of all sizes commonly have electric or electronic typewriters and computers or word processors, copying machines, advanced communications equipment, accounting equipment, addressing and mailing machines, and numerous other machines designed to handle a great variety of functions. For a description of each machine, see Chapter 5, "Office Supplies and Equipment."

Bring-up files. See FOLLOW-UP SYSTEM.

CPS. Certified Professional Secretary. See PROFESSIONAL SECRETARIES INTERNATIONAL.

Callers. In the secretary's contact with callers, all of the qualities essential for success in the profession are brought into play: poise, tact, social adaptability, judgment, and good manners. Often the secretary is the first person visitors meet, so the secretary's role as a representative of the entire company is highly important to good public relations.

Secretaries are always conscious of a double duty in relations with callers:

first, to assist their employers, and second, to assist the visitor. Executives rarely tell their secretaries what they expect of them as receptionists. Sometimes they will give explicit instructions about a particular caller, but generally they expect their secretaries to do the following without instructions.

1. Find out the caller's name, company affiliation, and the purpose of the visit.

2. Maintain goodwill by making the caller's contact with the firm pleasant and satisfactory.

3. Greet any caller appropriately and know what to say and what not to say.

4. Judge which callers the executive will welcome, which he or she wants to avoid, which should be seen by someone else in the organization, and which the secretary should take care of.

5. Make explanations to anyone the executive will not see, without antagonizing the caller.

In addition, employers expect a secretary to keep appointment records on the calendar (see Chapter 5/ CALENDARS); write appointment letters (see Chapter 7/LETTERS), and furnish them with reminders of appointments.

The secretary's duties toward callers are (1) to give them prompt attention, (2) to greet them graciously, (3) to display genuine interest in them and a desire to help, and (4) to make them comfortable while waiting.

Formality is appropriate in greeting

an office caller. The secretary should say, "How do you do?" or "Good morning," or "Good afternoon"—not "Hello"—and should let the caller make the first gesture toward shaking hands.

If the secretary's desk is at the entrance of the office, or in a convenient or conspicuous location, he or she need not rise to speak to a caller unless the person is someone of considerable importance or much older.

The secretary should show callers where to leave their hats, coats, briefcases, and other articles. The secretary should not offer to assist a man with his coat but may help a woman remove her coat and should hang it up for her.

When the callers have to wait, the secretary should ask them to have a seat, indicating a chair. If they have to wait any length of time, they should be offered a newspaper or magazine. If callers deserve special attention, the secretary should ask if there is anything he or she can do while they are waiting. Frequently, callers will say they would like to look up something in the telephone directory, or make a call, or see someone else in the organization. The secretary should offer to look up the number but should not insist. If they want to telephone someone, the secretary should show them to a private phone if one is available.

The secretary should not begin a conversation with waiting visitors but should respond if they show an inclination to talk. The conversation should be on topics in which they are likely to be interested—a trip they

have recently taken, or current topics, but never on controversial issues. A secretary should not tell his or her employer's friend a story the employer would enjoy telling personally—a story about a hole-in-one at golf or news about the employer's family. If visitors ask questions about the business, replies should be in generalities.

Introducing a business caller. A secretary mentions the names of the caller and his or her employer upon bringing the caller into the executive's office. The order of mentioning the names is the same as in a social introduction. The name of the person who is being honored is always mentioned first. When older persons, women, or dignitaries are announced, they are customarily mentioned first—for example, "Bishop Davis, this is Mr. Orlando." When the executive's position is considered more important than the caller's, the order is reversed—for example, "Mr. Orlando, this is Joey Stevens from our Mailing Department."

Telephone calls for the visitor. When there is a telephone call for a visitor, the secretary should ask the person calling if it is possible to leave a message. If so, the secretary types the message on a sheet of paper, addressing it to the visitor, and also types his or her own name, the date, and the time at the bottom of the sheet. No visitor should be required to decipher strange handwriting.

If the person calling insists upon speaking to the visitor, the secretary should go into the conference room, and with a glance that takes in both employer and visitor, apologize for

9

the interruption: "Pardon me for interrupting, Mr. Gray [looking at the visitor], Ms. Smith is on the phone and wants to speak to you. Do you want to take it here [indicating which telephone he should use]?" If he or she says yes, the call is put through. Often, however, the visitor will prefer to call back, in which case the secretary gives this message to the person calling and types the telephone number as a reminder for the visitor.

If several people are in conference with the executive and the secretary must deliver a message to one of them, he or she should type it and take it to that visitor. If the person is wanted on the phone, the secretary should also type on the card: "Do you want to take the call in my office?" The visitor can then leave the conference without disturbing the others. (But ask your employer if he or she would prefer to have you interrupt the conference through the intercom.)

Calls by office personnel. In many business organizations today, top officials keep an open door to the office personnel. The secretary usually must make the appointment but, if the open-door policy prevails, does not inquire about the purpose of the appointment. The secretary should always treat officers and executives of the company with deference and respect, but it is not necessary to rise every time an officer enters the office. However, the secretary should offer a chair if the person has to wait.

Interrupting conferences. The secretary should try to avoid interrupting a conference (see Chapter 3/CONFER-ENCE) but, if it is essential to enter a room where an executive is in conference, should do so quietly and unobtrusively, without knocking at the closed door. Any message that must be delivered to someone in the conference room should be typed on a slip of paper. If the secretary wants instructions, he or she should type the questions. The secretary's employer can then handle the matter with a minimum of interruption. If it is essential to announce a caller while the executive is occupied with someone, the secretary simply takes in the visitor's card or types the name on a slip of paper.

Problem callers. When it is your job not to disturb your employer, or when he or she does not want to see a visitor, tell the caller you are sorry that you are not authorized to interrupt your employer or that you are not authorized to make any appointments at that time. Suggest that the caller write a letter and offer to see that the letter is promptly passed along to your employer. When a caller is threatening, ring for security or quietly step into your employer's office and explain the situation. A female secretary might want to ask for male assistance in handling an emotional male caller, but a female secretary may have more success in calming an emotional female caller herself.

Refreshments. If visitors arrive while you are having refreshments and your desk is near the area where they are waiting, it is usually appropriate to offer them something also. If guests are already waiting in your office, postpone having your own refreshments. In large reception rooms, no effort is made to offer refreshments to numerous callers. However, follow the custom in your office.

Seeing a caller out. You may find it necessary to remind your employer that it is time for the next appointment—a cue to visitors that it is time to leave. Or if your employer warns you in advance that your assistance will be needed in cutting a visit short, you might interrupt politely with a reminder that it is time for him or her to leave or to attend some meeting. As visitors prepare to leave, hand them their coats and other articles left in your office (if a caller is a woman, you may help her put on her coat), and show the visitors to the door, saying "Good-bye" with a pleasant smile. If your building is large and the visitors are strangers, you should, in most cases, point out directions to the elevator or the lobby.

Carbon papers. See Chapter 5/ CARBON PAPER.

Certified Professional Secretary. See PROFESSIONAL SECRETARIES INTERNATIONAL.

Chain feeding. Inserting a second card, envelope, or other typing material into the typewriter before the first is removed. The turn of the platen that removes the first item from the typewriter brings the second into typing position. Chain feeding may be backward or forward.

Envelopes. If numerous envelopes are to be addressed, feed one after another into the typewriter before removing the typed envelope.

Cards. See TYPING, *Typing small cards.*

Character count. Method of estimating the length of typewritten copy by counting the letters, figures, and symbols, that is, the characters. In counting characters, punctuation marks and spaces between words count as characters; a short line at the end of a paragraph counts as a full line.

(1) Measure the length of a line in inches. (2) Multiply the result in step (1) by ten if the type is pica; by twelve if it is elite. This step gives the number of characters to the line. (3) Multiply the number of characters in a line, step (2), by the number of lines on a page of copy. (4) Multiply the number of characters to a page, step (3), by the number of pages.

Computers and word processors automatically determine the length of each page of copy, and many software programs display the current number of pages stored while work is in progress. See WORD PROCESSING.

Chinese copy. An exact copy, not a reproduction, of an executed document, signed letter, quoted material, extract from a book, and the like. The copy purports to be a "true and exact" copy and includes even obvious errors. Although successive exact original copies can be printed out in computer or word processor preparation, and although photocopies are commonly accepted in many professions as exact copies, this is how a Chinese copy should be prepared using a typewriter:

1. Type the word *COPY* in the upper left-hand corner.

2. Copy exactly, even obvious errors.

3. Indicate obvious errors copied from the original as follows: (a) Underline an incorrect letter or figure. (b) Put the designation *sic* in parentheses or brackets after apparently or obviously incorrect words or phrases. (c) Show an omission by a caret. If the typewriter does not have a caret, use the slanting bar and underscore key. (/).

agreement entered into the <u>31th</u> day of April. . . .

upon reciept. . . .

I give, devise and bequest [sic] unto. . . .

meeting of the United ¯/ Assembly in New York. . . .

4. Copy page for page and line for line as far as practicable.

See Chapter 8/QUOTED MATERIAL for an illustration of Chinese copy.

Chronological filing. See FILING SYSTEMS.

Collating. Process of checking a set of typed pages for correct numerical sequence. After a typing job consisting of more than one page is completed, the material is separated into sets consisting of the original of each page, the first carbon of each page, the second carbon of each page, and so on. Each set is then checked for correct sequence. The task of compiling the sets of copies and collating them is facilitated by the use of a rubber finger or pencil eraser. Collating aids are available, from simple, inexpensive trays or racks to complex, high-speed, automatic machines with up to 100 stations (bins that hold the sets of papers). See also Chapter 5/ COLLATING EQUIPMENT.

Color coding. In both folder tabs and containers, *color coding* is a filing system that uses color as the key to organization and identification. Quick storage and retrieval and ease in spotting misfiles are two of the more obvious benefits of this technique. Many offices also use different colored carbon copies for different purposes. For example, white copies may be intended for the correspondence files and yellow copies for the accounting files.

Color can be applied numerically (e.g., black = 10; red = 20; green = 30) or by subject (e.g., black = Insurance; red = Real Estate; green = Investments). Some offices are using color to make evaluations as well (e.g., black = a promising prospective customer; red = a potential, but difficult customer; green = an unlikely prospect). The uses of color are almost limitless. Manufacturers of supplies and cabinets have complete systems already designed, and sales literature describing them is available free—or you can devise your own system.

Column of figures, typing. See STATISTICAL TYPING.

Combing-back. The process of moving forward from week to week reminders of matters that require attention at an indefinite date until a definite date is established or until the matter is completed. See FOLLOW-UP SYSTEM.

Conferences. See Chapter 3/CONFERENCE.

Conforming. Writing or typing on a photocopy, or a carbon copy, something that was inserted in or added to the original after the copy was made. After the original of a document is signed, the copies should be conformed, that is, made like the original. Conforming includes writing in, or typing in, signatures, dates, recording data, and notarial data inked or stamped on the original. In typing the signature, there is no need to type *Signed* in front of the typed signature. When conforming an executed document bearing an official or a corporate seal, write in brackets at the left of the official or corporate signature the words [*CORPORATE SEAL*] if the seal is a corporate seal; [*NOTARIAL SEAL*] if the seal is that of a notary public; or [*OFFICIAL SEAL*] if the seal is that of any officer other than a notary public. Seals of individuals are indicated by *SEAL* (see Chapter 9/SEAL) unless written otherwise on the original.

Contributions. See Chapter 12/CONTRIBUTIONS.

Corrections on typed material. See ERASURES AND CORRECTIONS.

Correspondence. See Chapter 7, "Correspondence."

CPS exam. See PROFESSIONAL SECRETARIES INTERNATIONAL.

Cross-references in filing. See FILING SYSTEMS.

Daily mail record. See MAIL RECORD.

Data processing. The process by which data (e.g., payroll reports, sales forecasts) are collected or received, converted into machine-readable form, stored, rearranged, and transmitted as required. Computers and other machines are commonly employed to process this information systematically and rapidly, with a minimum of human effort.

A *data-processing system* refers to the computer hardware (equipment) and software (set of instructions) required to perform the operations. The processing operation requires that incoming information be converted into a common "language" that can be transmitted from one machine to another. Data to be fed into a computer (*input*) for processing are prepared by keyboard on a punched card or tape or, more commonly, on magnetic tape or disk. After processing, the data (*output*) may be printed directly on paper (hard copy) by a printer, or they may first be produced in coded form (e.g., a punched card), or they may appear directly on a computer monitor (screen) for viewing. See AUTOMATION (OFFICE); Chapter 5/BUSINESS MACHINES; DATA-PROCESSING EQUIPMENT; PUNCHED-CARD EQUIPMENT.

Decentralized filing. See FILING SYSTEMS.

Decimal system of filing. See FILING SYSTEMS.

13

Dewey decimal system. See FILING SYSTEMS.

Dictation, taking and transcribing. *Taking dictation.* Although some persons write their letters in longhand, taking dictation is a daily or at least a frequent occurrence for many secretaries. Whether dictation is handled by machine or person to person, observing a few simple rules will simplify the entire process.

1. If you use shorthand, make it a practice right away in the morning to sharpen pencils (preferably medium soft lead) and have one or more shorthand notebooks ready, with rubber bands to secure completed pages. Have paper clips handy to clip certain pages together if desired. Finally, have special files or other pertinent material ready to take with you when your employer calls.

2. Use a colored pencil to write or mark special instructions in your notebook.

3. Use a separate notebook for each dictator and leave space between letters or somehow keep them separate in each notebook. There may be changes or copy to insert later, and space will be needed then. Use only the left column if the dictator makes a lot of changes.

4. If the dictator does not specify, ask about the type of item—letter, memo, or other; the number of carbon copies and to whom; the addressee's name and address; any other special instructions, such as if there is a subject line or enclosures.

5. During dictation, face the dictator if possible and place your notebook on the desk or rest it in a comfortable position for writing and flipping filled pages over without pausing. Date the first page at the bottom where it is easy to see when paging through the notebook later. Do not hesitate to speak up if the dictator is talking too fast or if you do not understand something. But wait until the end of the letter to ask for clarification of something minor. Most of the material you will record in shorthand, but an unfamiliar word can best be written out in longhand. Remember that accuracy is of the utmost importance.

6. After taking the dictation, put the dictator's initials at the close; double-check spelling of names, addresses, and unusual words; and correct grammatical errors.

7. If you are having difficulty, it may be necessary to take a refresher course or at least work on troublesome words and symbols after hours.

Transcribing dictation. Transcribing the notes or tapes is just as important as taking the dictation. Most secretaries will want to begin as soon as possible, while everything is fresh in mind. If a transcription machine is used, it is necessary to be thoroughly familiar with it before beginning. Observing a few basic rules will simplify the entire process of transcribing the notes or tapes:

1. Clear your desk and organize the materials needed for transcription—stationery, envelopes, erasers, and so on. A copyholder or some support should be set up for the shorthand notebook, and the type-

writer should be checked for a fresh ribbon and clean keys.

2. Reread all dictation (or listen to the tapes, disks, or belts), organize it in order of importance, and solve problems such as paragraphing or missing punctuation or errors in spelling before you begin typing. Most executives expect their secretaries to polish and rephrase awkward passages.

3. Estimate the length of the letter so that it is positioned attractively on the stationery; this will take practice before you know how much typed copy comes from one of your notebook pages or from a transcription belt or tape.

4. If you cannot find a time of day to transcribe without interruption, have a colored pencil ready to mark the spot on your notebook where you stop each time. A transcription machine will automatically remain at the point where you stop it. When you complete a letter, draw a diagonal line through your notes or on the identification strip that accompanies a transcription belt or tape. Do not discard old notebooks, belts, disks, or tapes. File and retain them according to the retention schedule your office requires.

5. Place addressed envelopes over the typed letters, along with carbon copies and enclosures, and leave them face up on your employer's desk for his or her signature. (Some people prefer to have the letters only. In that case, you can present the letters for signature immediately and type the envelopes later, taking the addresses from the carbon copies of the letters.) After the letters are signed, proceed with filing and mailing, as described in Chapters 2 and 4. See also Chapter 5/BUSINESS MACHINES, *Dictating machines*.

Donations. See Chapter 12/CONTRIBUTIONS.

Draft. A first copy of material that is to be revised. The word *Draft* should be written across the top of every page of a draft to avoid mistaking it for the final copy. Drafts usually should be double- or triple-spaced for convenience in making changes. In retyping a draft, the following should be carefully noted: (1) portion marked for omission; (2) additional material to be inserted; (3) transpositions; (4) corrections in spelling, punctuation, and the like; (5) correct word choice and clarity; (6) completeness of various material, such as table of contents, appendixes, tables, charts, and so on; and (7) placement of footnotes and consistency with bibliography. See Chapter 8/MANUSCRIPT.

Duplicating and copying. See Chapter 8/DUPLICATING PROCESSES.

Electronic mail. See Chapter 2/ELECTRONIC MESSAGE SYSTEMS.

Electronic storage and retrieval. See INFORMATION STORAGE AND RETRIEVAL.

Enclosure. *Outgoing mail.* When it is necessary to fasten enclosures together or to a letter, staples should be used rather than pins or metal clips to avoid damaging Postal Service or company mail-room machines.

1. *Enclosures the size of the letter.* If the enclosure consists of two or more sheets, they should be stapled together but not fastened to the letter. The enclosure and the letter should be folded separately and the enclosure slipped inside the last fold of the letter.

2. *Enclosures larger than the letter.* Enclosures too large to fit into a commercial envelope of ordinary size may be handled in one of several ways.

(a) The letter is inserted with the enclosure in the large envelope, which is sealed. First-class postage is charged for both the letter and the enclosure. The material will be dispatched as first-class mail.

(b) A letter may be enclosed with a parcel if postage is paid for the letter at the first-class rate and for the package at the parcel-post rate. The postage for the letter may be placed on the parcel separately or included with the postage for the parcel. The material will be dispatched as fourth-class mail. Beneath the postage and above the address, "First-Class Mail Enclosed," is written. If practical, the letter should be placed on top of the other items that make up the parcel.

(c) A combination envelope is used. This is a large envelope with a flap that is fastened by a patent fastener of some kind *but not sealed.* A smaller envelope of commercial size is affixed on the front of this envelope in the process of manufacture. The letter is inserted into the small envelope,

and the flap is sealed. Postage is affixed to the large envelope at the third-class rate and to the small envelope at the first-class rate. The mail will be dispatched as third-class mail.

3. *Enclosures smaller than the letter.* Small enclosures should be stapled to the letter in the upper left-hand corner, on top of the letter. If two or more such enclosures are sent, the smaller one should be placed on top. Enclosures such as coins that cannot be stapled should be taped to a card or placed in a small, marked envelope, which is then stapled to the letter.

Incoming mail. When an incoming letter contains an enclosure, the enclosure should be fastened to the accompanying letter. If the enclosure referred to is missing, a notation to that effect should be made on the letter and the omission called to the attention of the sender of the letter. See Chapter 7/MODEL LETTERS.

Equipment. See Chapter 5, "Office Supplies and Equipment."

Erasures and corrections. With a computer or word processor, corrections and changes in text are made by pressing the appropriate keys rather than by applying an eraser or correction product to an actual sheet of paper. Usually, you can observe the changes as you make them on the monitor (display screen). With some software you might highlight the text to be corrected (on the screen) with a tiny mark called a *cursor.* Then by pressing a key(s), the erroneous letters, words, sentences, and so on would be deleted automatically, and you would be ready to type the correct material in its place. As you would type, the computer would automatically readjust all other words, sentences, and paragraphs to accommodate the new text. Electronic typewriters, too, often have similar (although usually much more limited) display and automatic-correction capabilities.

An electric typewriter with a built-in correcting key is another option. A device feeds a roll of coated correction paper, and the erasure is made in a manner similar to the use of KO-REC-TYPE® (see below). Correcting typewriters lift an error from the page, allowing for corrections that are scarcely—if at all—noticeable.

Corrections on carbon copies. Corrections on carbon copies are often much fainter than the rest of the typing. To maintain equal density of color on both original and carbon, make the correction as follows: After erasing, adjust the ribbon control indicator to stencil position. Put the carriage in the proper position and strike the proper key. This will leave an impression on the carbon copies, but the original will still be blank. Then switch the control indicator back to the ribbon, place the carriage in position, and again strike the proper key.

Erasures near the bottom of a page. To erase on a line near the edge of the page, feed the sheet back until the bottom of the paper is free of the platen. Erase and turn the page back into position for typing.

Corrections on bound pages. Corrections can be made on pages that are bound at the top. Insert a blank sheet of paper in the typewriter, as though for typing. When it protrudes about an inch above the platen, insert between it and the platen the unbound edge of the sheet to be corrected. Turn the platen toward you until the typewriter grips the sheet to be corrected. You can then adjust the bound sheet to the proper position for making the correction. Correction cannot be made on pages that are bound at the side without unstapling them.

For noncorrecting electric typewriters, products such as KO-REC-TYPE® and Liquid Paper make this job easy. The former is a special paper with a white ink backing. Use it by backspacing to the error and placing a strip of the coated paper over it. Restrike the original error, which will disappear. Then remove the paper, backspace, and strike the correct character. Correction paper is also available for use on carbon copies.

Liquid Paper, which comes in various colors, is a correction fluid that is daubed on the error. Wait a few seconds for it to dry and then type over it.

To use a standard typewriter eraser, move the carriage as far to the side as possible and rub with short, light strokes. A steel eraser guard or celluloid shield between carbon paper and copies is preferable to pieces of paper, which one might forget to remove afterwards. An eraser made of glass fibers permits erasures on the original without the impression going through to the carbon. Electric erasers, some battery operated, are also available.

Etiquette in the office. Common sense dictates most of the basic rules of etiquette in an office.

1. It is always courteous to say "Good morning" or "Good night," whether or not you know someone personally. This courtesy does *not* mean you should try to promote a conversation with the company president. Nor should you describe personal matters or respond in detail to the greeting "How are you today?"

2. Give newcomers a friendly reception, introduce them to coworkers and offer a helping hand with their work. If you are the newcomer, however, use some restraint at first and do not be overly friendly or try too hard to impress others.

3. Use of first names is common in the informal atmosphere of many modern offices. Follow the practice in effect, but whenever in doubt always use a title such as *Mr., Mrs., Miss,* or *Ms.* Whenever appropriate, use a formal title instead, such as *Doctor* or *Professor.* Never address a supervisor or executive by his or her first name unless you are requested to do so.

4. Observe common table manners when having refreshments, and do not let this practice interfere with your work. Be certain that company policy permits employees to have refreshments in the office or at a desk. Personal grooming should be attended to in the washroom, never at your desk or while having refreshments.

5. Latecomers are never appreciated. It is important to be on time for work, for meetings, and in any other situation. Similarly, it is rude and dangerous to make a wild exit from your office and the parking lot at the end of the day.

6. Gossip is to be avoided at all times. It can be serious and harmful and is always a breach of good etiquette.

7. Personnel problems should be dealt with as discreetly and carefully as possible. You are not expected to solve the personal problems of others, although courtesy and compassion dictate that a referral to outside professional assistance is always in order.

8. Try to avoid both borrowing and lending. If you must borrow, be certain to return the money promptly. If someone owes you money and is late in repaying the loan, tactfully remind the person but do not complain about it to other coworkers.

9. Do not allow a dishonest or otherwise unethical coworker to push you into similar questionable practices. Keep your employer fully informed—daily if necessary—of your own work and practices so that it will be clear to everyone that any misdeeds are not yours.

10. Respond to injured and ill coworkers instantly. When conditions warrant, call an ambulance, company nurse or doctor, or other professional assistance. Offer to help take over some of the duties of a recuperating coworker.

11. Deal with performance problems of assistants immediately. Review their qualifications and discuss the problem directly. Watch for areas where more training is needed, areas of confusion to the employee, and personal factors, such as boredom, inadequate motivation, and interference from outside sources.

See also TRAINING AN ASSISTANT; PERSONNEL; SYMPATHY, EXPRESSIONS OF.

Exact copy. See CHINESE COPY.

Filing equipment. See Chapter 5, "Office Supplies and Equipment."

Filing systems. The basic conventional filing systems are alphabetical, geographical, numerical, decimal, and chronological. Electronic filing (e.g., document filing on diskettes, labeling and storage of printouts, and electronically coded indexes for large automatic storage and retrieval systems) also may apply the principles of any of these systems.

Alphabetical filing system. Most filing is alphabetical, although numerical filing is becoming increasingly popular in offices of all sizes, particularly with the use of computers. See 1. *Name files* and 2. *Subject files* for the use of an alphabetical system in name and subject files.

1. *Name files.* The easiest and quickest method of filing is to classify material according to name and to file it alphabetically. This system should be used wherever possible, because no cross-index or list of files is necessary. See the rules under ALPHABETIZING AND INDEXING.

(a) *Folders.* Open a folder for each correspondent or name, if sufficient material justifies a separate folder. From three to ten papers justify starting a folder. Arrange papers within the folder by date, with the most recent date on top.

(b) *Miscellaneous folder.* Open a miscellaneous folder for each letter of the alphabet and place it in back of the last name folder under the particular letter. File material for which there is no separate name folder in the miscellaneous folder, alphabetically rather than by date. This keeps all papers relating to a particular name together. When they reach the required number, three to ten, make a separate folder.

(c) *Voluminous correspondence with the same person.* If correspondence with the same person or firm is voluminous, separate it into date periods. You can obtain folders with printed date headings (Figure 1) or type the dates on the labels.

(d) *Correspondents with the same name.* Folders for correspondents with the same name have a different colored label. The distinctive color is a signal to use extra precaution in filing or in looking for filed material. Thus if blue labels are used generally and there is a folder for Abernathy, Edgar, Sr., with a salmon label, the file clerk knows immediately that there is also a folder for another Abernathy, Edgar, with a salmon label.

2. *Subject files.* Some material does not lend itself to classification by name and must be classified by sub-

FILING SYSTEMS: FIGURE 1: Alphabetical name file arranged in four positions

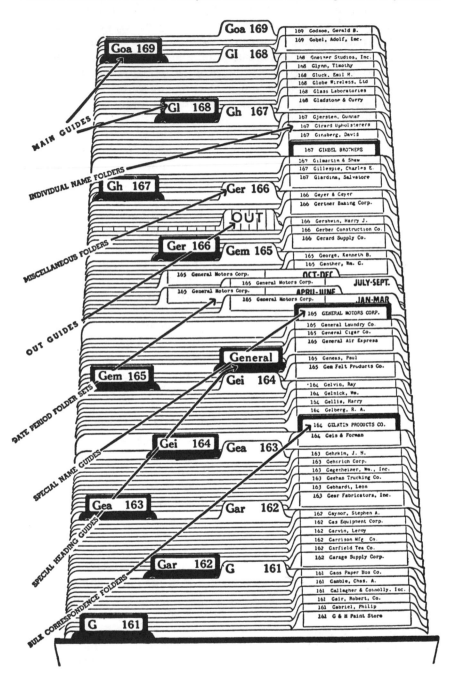

ject. The installation of a subject file requires great care. The secretary should not attempt to choose the subject headings until he or she is thoroughly familiar with the material that is to be filed. The list should be comprehensive and yet simple enough to avoid confusion. Subject headings must be specific, significant, and technically correct. Nouns are chosen whenever possible, for they are more specific than other parts of speech, such as adjectives.

Subject files are expanded by adding other main subjects or by subdividing those already in use. If necessary, subheadings may be further subdivided, but for a secretary's purpose, a breakdown into main headings and subheadings is generally adequate.

(a) *Arrangement of subject files.* Subject files may be filed alphabetically, or they may be arranged in any logical order and filed according to a numbering system. (In a standard classification adopted by the American Institute of Architecture, the subjects are arranged according to the order of procedure in building. Thus *excavation* comes ahead of *acoustics.*) Secretaries generally prefer the alphabetical system. All subject folders are arranged alphabetically under each main heading.

In a subject file that has main and subheadings, there is a three-position arrangement as follows: *Alphabetical guides* are cardboard separators with the letter of the alphabet at the left. *Main subject guides* are cardboard separators with metal or transparent plastic tabs into which the names of the main subjects can be inserted.

These tabs should be in the center. Or a "miscellaneous folder," may be used as a main subject guide, as described below. *Subheading folders* are right-position tabs. Folders with precut tabs are available with tabs of varying widths (e.g., half cut, one-third cut).

Miscellaneous folders for main headings are labeled like the guide and have a label different in color from that on the regular folders. A miscellaneous folder is placed in back of all other folders. It may be used instead of a main subject guide. In that case, the folder should have a center-position tab and should be placed in front of the subheading folders.

If the subject file has main headings, subheadings, and further breakdowns, guides instead of folders are used for the subheadings, and a four-position, instead of a three-position, arrangement is used.

(b) *Folders in the subject file.* The papers in a subject folder are arranged by date, with the most recent date on top. In the miscellaneous folder, material is filed alphabetically by subject rather than by date. When three to ten papers on a particular subject are accumulated in the miscellaneous folder, a separate subject folder is added as a subheading.

Both the main heading and the subheading are typed on the file labels. For convenience in filing and finding, the subheading is typed on the first line and the main heading on the second line, indented two spaces or in parentheses. The main heading may be typed in red to distinguish it more readily from the subheading.

(c) *Index to subject file.* For subject

files, it is generally advisable to keep either an alphabetical list (typewritten or computer prepared) or a card index of the subjects (1) to avoid filing material under a new heading when there is already a folder for the subject and (2) to enable a person who is not familiar with the files to locate filed material.

If an *alphabetical list* is used as an index, the main headings are typed in solid caps and the subheadings with initial caps. After each subheading, the main heading under which the subheadings are classified is typed in parentheses. There should be sufficient space between the items to permit additions of new subjects. (If a list is prepared by computer this is not necessary since the computer automatically rearranges all other copy to accommodate an insertion.) *The list must be kept up to date.* An alphabetical list will usually be adequate when the files are not extensive and additions are infrequent. Here is the arrangement of an alphabetical list of subject files:

Applications (Personnel)
CONTRACTS
EXPENSE ACCOUNTS
FORM LETTERS
Holidays (Personnel)
Hotels, Reservations (Travel)
INSURANCE
INVESTMENTS
Itineraries (Travel)
Leases (Contracts)
MEETINGS
Minutes (Meetings)
PERSONNEL
TRAVEL

If a *card index* is used, there should be an index card for each subject heading and for each subheading. The card for each subheading shows the main heading under which it is classified. When a subject heading is not self-explanatory, the card describes the material covered by it. There are also cross-reference cards for subjects on which there is insufficient material to justify a separate folder and for subjects under which material might logically have been classified but for which another heading was chosen. Thus the secretary to a department head might have a main heading "Personnel." Since there are only a few papers relating to "Lunch Hour," this material might be filed in the miscellaneous "Personnel" folder. An index card for the subject "Lunch Hour" indicates that material relating to it is filed in the miscellaneous "Personnel" folder. All cards are filed alphabetically. The card index or a computer-prepared alphabetical list is usually preferable for extensive, growing files because either one is easily kept up to date.

3. *Combined name and subject file.* If a name file is in general use and occasionally there is material that should be filed by subject, or if a subject file is in general use and occasionally there is material that should be filed by the name of the individual, the occasional folders are combined with the main file. For example, a name file might include a folder labeled "Applications" to receive the few applications that are kept in the files. A cross-reference

sheet is put under the name of the applicant in the miscellaneous folder for the letter with which the name begins. Or a subject file might include a folder labeled with a person's name, which would actually be a subject.

4. *Subject-duplex file.* When additional coding is necessary, material may be identified by a combination of subjects and numbers. This is often necessary when files are expanding rapidly, with numerous subdivisions. Main subject headings have a base number, such as 100, and subheadings have auxiliary numbers (or letters), such as 100.1. Folders are then put in numerical sequence. This type of system requires the additional maintenance of a computer-prepared list or a cross-index card file, with all subjects arranged alphabetically to show what the numbers stand for.

5. *Cross-reference.* Frequently material may be filed logically under one or more names or subjects. In those cases, the material is filed under one name or subject and is cross-referenced under the other. For example, a letter from Joel Remsen might relate to Sammuel Abernathy. The logical place to file the letter is under *Abernathy*, but a cross-reference should be made under *Remsen*. If Remsen has a regular folder, the cross-reference sheet is placed in it; if not, it is put in the miscellaneous folder under *R*. A permanent cross-reference is usually maintained when a name or subject can be filed under more than one designation. For example, a permanent cross-reference

should be maintained under *Simon, Franklin & Company* to *Franklin Simon & Company*. When a permanent cross-reference is desirable, a guide inserted in its proper alphabetical position among the regular file folders serves as a cross-reference signal. The back of an old file folder may be used. Colored cross-reference sheets in pads, about eight and one-half by eleven inches, may be purchased at any store carrying office supplies.

Many offices have odd-sized material or bulk objects (blueprints, film, and so on) that must be stored in a special place. A cross-reference sheet in the regular files may be desirable in such cases.

Cross-reference labels should be in a color different from the color of the labels used on the regular folders. Use cross-reference sheets freely.

There are instances, however, when frequent references or the need for full information immediately may preclude the use of a standard cross-reference procedure. A photocopy of the document in question placed in the regular files would be preferable for such situations.

6. *Out guides.* Guides the same height as the file folders but of different colored stock with the word *Out* printed on the tab are used to control material removed from the files. The out guide has space on which to make an entry of the date, the material taken, who has it, and the date it should be returned. See Figure 2. The guide is placed in the files where the removed material was located.

FILING SYSTEMS: FIGURE 2: Out card

			OUT		
DATE	**MATERIAL**	**DATE REMOVED**	**TO BE RETURNED**	**CHARGE TO WHOM**	**REMARKS**

Secretaries in a private office do not put an out guide in the file every time they withdraw material for their employers. They use the guide under these circumstances: (1) Someone outside the immediate office wants the material. (2) An employer expects to take the material out of the office, for example, when he or she goes on a trip. (3) The secretary expects the employer to keep the material a week or so, for example, to prepare a report.

Numerical filing system. Under the numerical system, numbers are used on the file folders, which are arranged numerically. This is an indirect method of filing because it must be used in connection with a cross index that shows what the number stands for; an alphabetical list is maintained by computer or an index card is made for each folder, and the cards are arranged alphabetically. The advantages of the system are the rapidity and accuracy of refiling and the opportunity for indefinite expansion. The numerical system is used in files where each of the jobs, clients, or subjects has a number that acts as an identification mark (e.g., requisitions, invoices); for the filing of confidential records (e.g., job applications, insurance policies); for handling a rapidly growing file; and in files where extensive, permanent cross-reference is necessary.

1. *Consecutive number file.* With this system, guides and folders in a consecutive file are arranged in ascending order (1, 2, 3, etc.). However, with this system all new folders pile up at the end of the files.

2. *Terminal digit file.* With this system, a number such as 345678 is divided into units (34-56-78) and then reversed to 78-56-34. The far right digits (34) might be the file drawer number; the far left digits (78) might refer to the order of papers in the folder, for example, 78-56-34, 79-56-34, and so on, and the center digits (56) might refer to the folder number. This system insures that new folders are scattered throughout the files.

3. *Coded-number file.* With this system, numbers and letters identify a person or product, such as a charge

account number or an application number.

Geographical filing system. Under the geographical system, material to be filed may be classified first according to the name of the state, then according to cities or towns, and last according to the names of companies and correspondents in each city or town. Some offices also use a breakdown including countries or regions. Equipment houses supply standard sets of guides. This type of file also requires a cross index. A computer-prepared list or name cards are prepared showing the geographical location; cards are filed alphabetically by name. If the location is not known, reference is made to the name in the cross index to determine the location. This system is used principally by sales organizations where a review of the activity in any given territory is of more importance than the name of a company or individual.

Decimal filing system. The decimal system of filing is based on the Dewey decimal system used in some public libraries and in some highly specialized businesses. All records in an office are classified under ten or fewer principal headings, which are numbered 000 to 900. Each heading is divided into ten or fewer subheadings, which are numbered from 10 to 90, preceded by the applicable hundreds digit. Each subheading may be subdivided into ten or fewer headings, which are numbered from 1 to 9, preceded by the appropriate hundreds and tens digits. If necessary, these headings may be further subdivided and numbered from .1 to .10,

and so on, under the appropriate full number. The following example illustrates a breakdown of books on "Useful Arts" under the Dewey classification used in libraries:

Useful arts	600
Engineering	620
Canal engineering	629

The secretary is seldom called upon to install a decimal system of filing. Should it become necessary, he or she should consult books describing the Melvil Dewey system, which can be obtained at most public libraries.

Chronological filing system. The chronological file is used *in addition to* one of the other systems. It contains photocopies or carbon copies, in chronological order, of outgoing correspondence and other material. It is useful in finding something when you recall the approximate date but not the name or subject of previously filed material. It is also useful in studying events during a particular period and as a means for an executive to review activity in the office while he or she was away.

Electronic filing system. Although massive amounts of material can be transferred from computer memory to permanent storage on an internal hard disk or various small floppy disks (diskettes), this system is seldom satisfactory by itself. To secure a paper copy, the document must be located on the hard disk or the appropriate diskette and the printer must then print out the desired material. Usually, filing or storage on such magnetic media is considered supplementary to conventional filing. However, computers are used to prepare and maintain coded indexes to use in large centralized filing departments. See INFORMATION STORAGE AND RETRIEVAL. For storage in reduced form, see MICROFILMING.

Preparing material for conventional filing. Be certain the material has been released for filing; if it has, separate papers into categories, for example, personal correspondence, business correspondence, reports, and purchase orders. Arrange individual items alphabetically or code them numerically. Some secretaries circle key words with a yellow marker or a nonreproducible blue pencil (on material that may have to be photocopied later). Many offices prefer that self-sticking, removable notes be used instead of writing on the actual document. Watch for stapled items that should be removed; mend torn papers; and remove all paper clips. Finally, fill out cross-reference sheets before filing. If you have a lot of filing, with numerous categories, you may want to purchase some trays or racks to speed the process of separating material into appropriate categories.

File-retention schedule. Your company may have a firm file-retention program that all offices are required to observe. If not, ask your employer whether a schedule should be developed. Often legal advice is required to determine state and federal requirements concerning the retention of business material. An excellent guide to records retention is available free from Electric Wastebasket Corporation, 145 West 45th Street, New York, NY 10036.

Folding letters. See OUTGOING MAIL.

Follow-up system. A method of filing material whereby it will be brought to the attention of the interested person on a certain date. The follow-up file is a check on whether correspondence has been answered or other desired action taken. If not, a follow-up request is in order.

Equipment for follow-up system. Numerous styles of equipment for follow-up purposes are available, but the only equipment necessary is a file drawer and file folders. You can make a set of file folders consisting of (a) 12 folders labeled from January through December, (b) 31 folders labeled from 1 through 31, and (c) 1 folder marked "Future Years." If the volume of follow-up material is heavy, it is advisable to have two sets of folders labeled by days—one for the current month and one for the succeeding month. Tabbed guides marked 1 through 31 and removable separators tabbed with the months will make it easier to locate a particular folder, but they are not necessary for the efficient functioning of the system.

Arrangement of folders for follow-up. The folders labeled by days are arranged in numerical order in the front of the file. The follow-up material for the current month is put in these folders. The folder labeled for the current month is at the back of the other monthly folders ready to receive any material to be followed up in the same month next year.

Immediately following the numerical daily folders is the folder for the forthcoming month, followed by the folder for the succeeding month, and so on. Figure 1 is a diagram of the folders when Friday, April 15, is the current day.

Operation of the follow-up system. 1. A notation or reminder of material that is to come up for action must be placed in the follow-up file while the material itself remains in its proper place in the regular files. An extra copy of correspondence that requires a follow-up is made, preferably on paper of a different color. The date on which the item is to be followed up is marked on the extra copy. When there is no copy of material for follow-up, a brief memo is written for the follow-up file. The memo should indicate where the material is filed.

2. Material to be followed up in the current month is placed in the proper date folders. Each day the empty daily folder is transferred to the back of the folder for the forthcoming month. Thus there are always 31 daily folders for follow-ups, part of them for the remaining days in the current month and part of them for the first part of the forthcoming month. Material to be followed up more than 30 or 31 days in the future is put in the proper month folder, regardless of the day of follow-up. See Figure 1, which is a diagram of the arrangement of folders on April 15. On that day, material to be followed up from April 18 through May 13 is placed in daily folders; material to be followed up after May 13 is placed in the proper month folder.

FOLLOW-UP SYSTEM: FIGURE 1: Diagram of follow-up lines

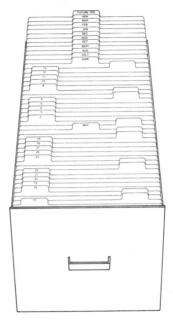

3. On the first of each month, the material from the folder for that month is transferred into the folders labeled by days. To avoid filing material for follow-up on Saturdays (if the office closes), Sundays, or holidays, reverse the folders for those days so that the blank side of the label faces the front of the file. Notice in Figure 1 that the folders for April 16, 17, 23, 24, and 30 and May 1, 7, and 8 are blank. The empty folder for the current month is then transferred to the rear of the other month-by-month folders.

Follow-ups on a small scale. When only a small amount of correspondence or other matters need follow-up, a set of follow-up folders is not necessary. Copies are marked with the follow-up date and are filed chronologically in one folder, with those marked for the earliest follow-up on top.

Material calling for follow-up. Items usually placed in the follow-up file are (1) matters referred to other executives or department heads for information or comment; (2) correspondence or memos awaiting an answer; (3) orders for future delivery; (4) items that come up for periodic consideration, such as company reports of various kinds, tax matters, and contract renewals; (5) promises to be carried out in the future; (6) regular receivables for which there is no invoice (e.g., a rental payment). A card tickler file is as useful as follow-up file folders for any type of material except correspondence, but it is a waste of time to make a card notation of correspondence when an extra carbon can be made at the time of transcription.

Follow-up files are sometimes called "bring-up files" and "future files." See also TICKLER FILE.

Future files. See FOLLOW-UP SYSTEM.

Geographical filing. See FILING SYSTEMS.

Gifts. See PRESENTS.

Guest list. A list of persons invited to an entertainment should be kept by an executive's secretary. It should be typed in alphabetical order, double spaced, with two columns, each an inch wide, on the right hand side of the sheet. One column is headed *Accepts*, the other *Regrets*. As the replies to invitations are received,

accepts or *regrets* is written in the appropriate column opposite the respective names. Writing the word eliminates errors that might be caused by putting a check mark in the wrong column.

Each day after the mail is received, a recapitulation of the replies should be attached to the first page of the guest list.

		10/15/__
Number invited		100
Acceptances	30	
Regrets	5	
No reply	65	100

The recapitulation changes every day, but it enables the secretary to tell the executive the exact status of the invitation list at any time.

Some occasions, such as dinners or luncheons, require arrangements for a definite number of guests. Three or four days before the event, the secretary might telephone or wire the invited guests from whom no reply has been received. This is permissible because one assumes that the invitation would have been answered if it had been received.

A follow-up telegram might read:

Please let me know whether you plan to attend dinner honoring Mr. Edwards on the fifteenth.

Notice the use of the expression "let me know" instead of the businesslike "advise" or "inform." The name of the person who issued the invitation should be signed to the wire.

Holidays. See Chapter 3/SUNDAY OR HOLIDAY MEETINGS.

Incoming mail. Mail received in a business office. Messages may arrive conventionally from the U.S. Postal Service or a private delivery service. They also may be received as a telegram or cable, by facsimile machine, through a telex exchange, or via an electronic-mail system or a voice-data system. See Chapter 2/ DELIVERY SERVICES; ELECTRONIC MESSAGE SYSTEMS; INTERNATIONAL COMMUNICATIONS; POSTAL SERVICE; TELEGRAPH SERVICE, DOMESTIC. The following procedure is recommended for handling conventional incoming mail:

Sorting. Sort the mail into piles of (1) correspondence, (2) bills and statements (if they are distinguishable at a glance from the correspondence), (3) advertisements and circulars, and (4) newspapers and periodicals. Further separate personal from business items into outside and interoffice material. If you receive a moderate or heavy mail load, use one of the sorting racks or trays, available from office suppliers, to speed and simplify the process of separating into categories.

Opening. Open correspondence first, taking care not to cut the contents with the letter opener. For rapid opening, have the flaps of the envelopes facing upward. Slit all the envelopes and then remove the contents, making certain that no enclosures are left in the envelopes. Open packages carefully and save address labels if a letter is not enclosed with the address on it. Attach the enclosures to the letters. If the address of the sender is on the envelope but not on the letter, attach the envelope to the letter. Write "Not at this address" on mail delivered to you in error (only first-class mail is returned to the sender without applying additional postage).

Letters marked *Personal* or *Confidential* should never be opened unless your employer has given instructions to that effect.

Routing the mail. Letters and memos should be sorted into three piles: (1) those that require your employer's attention, (2) those that require the attention of someone else in the organization, and (3) those that require your attention.

If possible, the mail should be on your employer's desk when he or she arrives at the office. When the file or previous correspondence relating to a current letter will facilitate action, the incoming letter should be attached to the file.

Your employer may want the mail annotated. If so, jot appropriate comments and reminders in the margins of letters, underscore key phrases, and so on. Use a nonreproducible blue pencil that will not show if the document has to be copied. Since many offices do not permit any writing on incoming mail, you may want to use self-sticking, removable notes.

If several people should see the correspondence, the name of each is written on a slip attached to the correspondence, the names being numbered in the order in which each person should receive the mail. If mail is frequently routed to the same people, their names may be printed or mimeographed on a routing slip. (See Figure 1.)

INCOMING MAIL: FIGURE 1: Routing slips

		Date: 3/5/--	
	(To be routed in the order numbered)		
2	Mrs. Jacobs	M.	3/7
1	Mr. Hartwell	RW	3/6
4	Mr. Smith	J.S.	3/10
3	Mr. Dennison	E.D.	3/8
	Mr. Snow		
5	File		
	Please initial, date, and forward.		

Newspapers and periodicals. The ones your employer likes to read are put in a folder labeled *Newspapers and Periodicals* and placed on his or her desk or in a briefcase to take home. The other newspapers and periodicals are sent to persons in the organization who need them, or they are put on the shelves for reference. If your employer is paying for a periodical he or she does not want, that is not needed by someone in the organization, or that is not valuable as reference material, ask about canceling the subscription.

Advertisements and circulars. These items are often useful as a free source of information on new products, services, meetings, and other news. They should not be thrown away until they have been examined. Some of them might interest your employer or some department in the organization. If an order blank is enclosed with an advertisement, it should be clipped to the advertisement.

Bills and statements. These items are filed until a certain time of the month. It is not necessary to open them until the other mail has been opened and routed to the proper places. (See also MAIL RECORD.)

Index and indexing. The arrangement of the names on the folder tabs or on cards for filing purposes. The folders or cards are then arranged according to the FILING SYSTEMS being used. (For basic rules of indexing for filing purposes, see ALPHABETIZING AND INDEXING.) See also Chapter 8/INDEX AND INDEXING.

Information storage and retrieval. A system for filing documents or graphic records and selecting and retrieving them rapidly on demand (e.g., classification, indexing, and machine-searching systems). These systems are common when massive amounts of information must be stored and retrieved. Some data-retrieval machines are electronically coded to locate and convey regular files in a matter of minutes or seconds.

Computers are commonly used to maintain an index that identifies file material and its location. In large file departments, operators may use a numerical keyboard to enter the location of the file (as specified on the index). A mechanical or electronic transportation device is then activated to find the material and physically move a shelf or storage container in and out.

Large storage and retrieval systems are needed when a company has a filing department that must transport containers to and from a central storage area. But offices also use systems with automatic features that do things such as move a tray in and out.

Some material is stored on magnetic tapes or disks or on punched cards or tapes. *Micrographics* is a method of filing information on microfilm or microfiche. Material stored in a computer is retrieved by illumination on a television-type screen, by printing the information on paper (hard copy), or by releasing it in some coded form for further interpretation. One type of videodisk system that serves as an electronic filing cabinet allows you to retrieve images such as pages or photos from a disk in less than half a second.

See also MICROFILMING; Chapter 5/ BUSINESS MACHINES; FILING EQUIPMENT; PUNCHED-CARD EQUIPMENT.

Integrated voice-data terminals. See Chapter 2/ELECTRONIC MESSAGE SYSTEMS.

Itemized material. See TABULATED MATERIAL.

Job evaluation. The determination for payroll purposes of the value of one job in comparison with all other jobs in an organization. This method eliminates the difficulty of comparing dissimilar jobs in terms of pay. Job analysis and job description precede and form the basis for job evaluation and job specification. These definitions are essential to job evaluation: (1) *Job:* the task with its duties and responsibilities. Job evaluation gauges the job, not the person. (2) *Job standardization:* determines how jobs should be done; time and motion study and plant layout are used to arrive at the most economical way to do a job. This phase is usually done by

industrial engineers. (3) *Job analysis:* determines the facts about a job and uncovers the various components. (4) *Job specification:* lists the abilities and qualities that an employee must have to fill the job.

See also MERIT RATING; PERSONNEL.

Job specification. See PERSONNEL, 1. *Job specification.*

Mail record. The secretary should keep a simple daily record of all mail sent *out* of her office for action by another person. This applies to telegrams, telex and facsimile messages, electronic-mail messages, and reports, as well as traditional letters and memos. The purpose of the record is twofold: it serves as a check on the receipt and disposition of mail that gets misplaced and for follow-up, if necessary.

For the daily mail record, you may use looseleaf sheets with vertical columns. See Figure 1. If the record is kept with pencil or pen instead of on the typewriter, the sheet should be lined horizontally. Use a double space between each entry on the typewriter.

The *Date* column shows the date on which the material is sent out of the office. *Description* shows the date of the communication, name of the sender, and the subject matter. *To Whom Sent* obviously refers to the person to whom the material is sent. The *Action to Be Taken* column shows the action that was checked on the slip attached to the communication before forwarding it. The deadline date for disposition should be writ-

MAIL RECORD: FIGURE 1: Daily mail record

DAILY MAIL RECORD				
Date	Description	To Whom Sent	Action to Be Taken	Follow-up
3/5	Johnson, Preface to Corp. Sec'y, 3/3	L. Pershing	Approval	3/8
3/5	Sloane of U. of Neb., request for free copy of Credits & Collections 3/3	McDermitt	Reply	

ten in the follow-up column if it is necessary to follow up to see that proper action is taken. When the matter has had the necessary attention, draw a line through the entry.

In some organizations, certain department heads receive all of the mail of the department so that they can assign the correspondence to the proper person for reply. In such cases, the daily mail record is particularly important.

Mass card.   A written statement signed by a Roman Catholic priest that a mass will be said for the repose of a soul. See SYMPATHY, EXPRESSIONS OF.

Meetings, arranging.   See Chapter 3/CONFERENCE.

Merit rating.   Whereas JOB EVALUATION gauges the job, *merit rating* gauges the jobholder. It is used for appraising employees for promotion and for correction of shortcomings. Actually, the job specification provides a frame of reference that merit rating fits into. It sets the outer limits of advancement for a particular job and specifies the qualifications and characteristics that the employee should possess to do his or her job properly.

Rating consists essentially of (1) judging employees on certain characteristics that have been found to be essential, (2) putting the judgments on paper, and (3) scoring the results. There is no standard rating sheet. The nature of the business and the type of job influence the form.

Microfilming.   One of the microform processes (microfilm, microcard, microfiche, and ultrafiche). Of these four, microfilming is the best-known method of transferring documents onto a roll of film (the other three processes simply refer to cards or sheets of film rather than rolls). After microfilmed documents are reduced and stored on film, they can be viewed on a screen when desired, and with certain equipment, they can be photocopied at the same time. Depending on company policy and legal requirements, original, full-size files can then be destroyed, and only the film retained, with a savings in storage space of up to 98 percent. Material can also be shipped in reduced form at a substantial savings over the cost to transmit full-size, original documents. Moreover, the film is noncombustible, reducing the danger of loss through fire. Microfilm has special benefits in the storage and retrieval of extensive or continuous records, such as mailing lists, accounts receivable, personnel forms, and stock certificates or bulky items such as engineering drawings. The need to control or reduce storage space is a prime consideration in the purchase of these systems. Also, the need to retrieve massive amounts of data rapidly may be a key factor.

See also INFORMATION STORAGE AND RETRIEVAL.

Minutes, taking. See Chapter 3/ MINUTES.

Money presents. See PRESENTS.

Numerical filing. See FILING SYSTEMS.

Office management. Office management is essentially a service function. It involves (1) the supervision of all clerical work and the personnel who perform it; (2) the supervision of telephone, telegraph, conventional mail processing, telex, facsimile, electronic-mail, and other transmission systems; dictation and transcription; bookkeeping and other record keeping; and filing; (3) the specification of all office equipment, such as chairs,

desks, filing equipment, and calculating machinery; (4) the control of the physical layout—lighting and furniture arrangement; (5) the coordination of office functions with other offices and with external organizations; (6) the planning function, including both short-term scheduling of time and activities and long-range planning for handling special programs and projects; and (7) the quality-control activities, that is, establishing standards and monitoring to see that the work meets basic requirements in appearance, accuracy, and so forth.

Office papers. See Chapter 5/ OFFICE PAPER.

Out guides. See FILING SYSTEMS.

Outgoing mail. Mail sent out by a business office. Messages may be sent conventionally by the U.S. Postal Service or by a private delivery service. They also may be sent as a telegram or cable, by facsimile machine, through a telex exchange, or via an electronic-mail or voice-data system. See Chapter 2/DELIVERY SERVICES; ELECTRONIC MESSAGE SYSTEMS; INTERNATIONAL COMMUNICATIONS; POSTAL SERVICE; TELEGRAPH SERVICE, DOMESTIC. In preparing outgoing letters for conventional mailing, secretaries (1) get their employers' signatures on the letters, (2) assemble them for mailing, and (3) fold and insert the letters in the envelopes.

Getting signatures on outgoing letters. When letters are given to someone to be signed, those that the person dictated should be separated from those that someone else wrote. The most usual method of giving letters to someone for signature is to remove the carbon copy and insert the flap of the envelope over the original letter and its ENCLOSURES. Many executives are interested only in the letters, however, and consider envelopes a nuisance. If you do not include the envelopes with the letters to be signed, you can submit the letters as soon as they are typed and then type the envelopes from the addresses on the copies.

Assembling the mail. After the mail is signed, it is assembled for actual mailing. Before the letters are folded and inserted in the envelopes, each letter should be checked for the following: (1) Has the letter been signed? (2) Are all the enclosures included? (3) Are the inside address and the envelope address the same? (4) Did the dictator make any revisions that involve retyping? (Since this happens, it makes sense not to file copies until you are certain no letters have to be retyped.)

Folding letters. Letters written on full-size letterheads for insertion in no. 9 or no. 10 envelopes should be folded as follows: one fold from the bottom, about one-third of the way up; a second fold from the bottom to within one-sixteenth of an inch of the top. Insert in the envelope, top up.

Letters written on full-sized letterheads for insertion in smaller envelopes should be folded as follows: one fold from the bottom to within one-quarter of an inch of the top; a second fold from right to left, about one-third of the way across; a third fold from left to right within one-

quarter of an inch of the right edge. Insert with the right edge up.

Letters written on half-size letterheads should be folded as follows: one fold from right to left, about a third of the way across; a second fold from left to right, leaving about one-sixteenth of an inch between the edges at the right. Insert in a small envelope with the right edge up.

No matter how they are folded, letters should be inserted into envelopes without turning them over; that is, in such a manner that when the letter is removed from the envelope and unfolded the type side is facing the reader. An exception occurs when you must use paper clips to fasten enclosures. Since clips may damage postal equipment, you should insert the letter upside down so that the clip falls at the bottom of the letter, not where the postage is applied. See also ENCLOSURE.

Personnel. There is no "recommended" personnel organization or personnel approach. An owner-manager of a business may perform all personnel functions. He or she may have a personnel manager or may let the office manager do the hiring. Regardless of the formal setup, in addition to training personnel, one is concerned with these problems: (1) preparing job specifications; (2) recruiting personnel; (3) interviewing, selecting, and hiring; and (4) keeping records.

1. *Job specification.* Before candidates are recruited, a description of the job the employee will be expected to fill should be prepared. The de-

scription is called a "job specification"; it is essentially a list of qualifications for the job. What skills, what physical strength, what personal characteristics are needed? If the personnel department does the recruiting for the office manager, the job specification gives this department a yardstick to go by and helps it to use more accurate screening.

2. *Recruiting.* Recruits may be obtained from many sources. Experience and the job will indicate the best one. The usual sources, although not listed in the order of their importance, are (1) commercial employment agencies; (2) public employment agencies; (3) placement offices in schools and colleges; (4) employment bureaus in charitable and social organizations; (5) calls from casual applicants, applications on file, unsolicited letters; (6) newspaper advertisements placed by the applicant or by the employer; (7) blind advertisements placed in news papers by the employer; and (8) applicants recommended by employees and friends.

3. *Selecting personnel.* Many factors will help in deciding whom to employ: interviews, answers on employment application blanks, and specially prepared standard tests. Often they are used in combination. An interview is usually the first step in selecting office personnel. Depending on the nature of the available job, points to appraise in a preliminary interview are (1) appearance—neatness and cleanliness of dress; (2) speech—pronunciation and choice of words; (3) accuracy—organization and presentation of facts; (4) ade-

quacy of educational background as related to the available position; (5) bearing—manner of approaching and leaving the interview; (6) adequacy of previous experience; (7) ambitions and desires as expressed during the interview; (8) physical condition—deformities or apparent physical handicaps that might endanger or prevent the employee from performing certain tasks; however, keep in mind that the Rehabilitation Act of 1973, as amended in 1974, prohibits discrimination based on handicap—check with your firm's attorney if you have any questions; and (9) general attitudes—antagonistic, subservient, friendly, confident. The employment application is essential to record background and the name-address-relatives type of information. It gives the source for verification of applicant's statements.

Several kinds of preemployment tests are used, and they are known by many names, but they are all for the purpose of determining the applicant's present ability, aptitude for doing a certain job, general intelligence, and personality characteristics. The selection and use of scientific tests is a specialized study, and it requires experience and knowledge to adapt them to practical use. No training is required to give simple tests of mechanical skill, such as typing. Most experts agree that about one-third weight should be given to the test and two-thirds to the application blank and interview. See Chapter 9/FAIR EMPLOYMENT PRACTICES.

4. *Keeping personnel records.* Records are used to compile *useful*

information. Many of the large manufacturers of forms maintain advisory services that aid employers in designing efficient personnel forms. An employment application, a form verifying application blank statements, and a payroll data sheet are essential. The use of additional forms depends on the size and type of the business and the nature of the personnel organization. See JOB EVALUATION; MERIT RATING.

Handling personnel problems. Every office, large or small, is a potential trouble spot as far as human relations are concerned. Even in the highly automated office, where tasks involve person-machine contact more than person-to-person interface, personnel problems may confront the secretary. Problems sometimes arise among fellow workers—conflicts or disagreements that may set one person at odds with another or individual troubles that may prompt one person in need to seek help from another. Other difficulties concern working for more than one person, romantic involvements at work, and competitive office politics. See also ETIQUETTE IN THE OFFICE; TIME MANAGEMENT; TRAINING AN ASSISTANT.

1. *Avoiding serious conflicts.* How do you handle a situation where you and another worker are in strong disagreement? First, you should remember that it is necessary to continue working each day with your coworkers. Arguments seldom solve anything. The sensible route is to take time to listen and try to understand the other side—before the disagreement becomes a conflict. If you still disagree, do not change your opinion, but do not let it anger you that someone else has a different viewpoint. If you are in charge, you are entitled to put your decision into effect if it concerns office procedures. If it is a matter of concern to your employer, let him or her render the final decision. The important thing to remember is that patience, understanding, and a friendly attitude will go a long way in preventing disagreements from becoming battles.

2. *Dealing with the problems of others.* One of the most difficult situations arises when a secretary either is asked for personal help or is in a situation where it seems necessary to offer assistance. If the person in trouble is a coworker, and possibly a good friend as well, the secretary will doubtless feel compelled to offer help and comfort. There is a dangerous point that may be reached. A good rule to remember is that you never really help someone by covering for his or her errors or problems. If someone has a drinking problem, for instance, or some emotional problem affecting his or her work, do not play doctor or psychologist, and do not help to hide it from your employer. However, if someone specifically asks for your assistance, you can help the person find *professional* guidance *outside.*

If the individual with a problem is your employer, and you are asked to offer suggestions, do the same thing—recommend qualified *professional* assistance. If the problem is extremely serious and is clearly jeopardizing the company's welfare, you should carefully consider advising your employer's immediate superior that a threatening problem exists. But this is a step that should be taken only under extreme conditions. In all other cases, keep a private written record of times, dates, and events for possible later reference, but otherwise, attempt to remain neutral. If your employer's problem is minor, or at least is not a threat to the company, what you do depends upon how much it disturbs you. You can try to ignore it or ask for a transfer to another office.

Every situation that presents itself is different, and your response will have to be dictated by the seriousness of it and your own involvement. Certainly, you should not seek out individuals with problems and attempt to involve yourself as an amateur psychiatrist or counselor.

3. *Office politics.* Fair, ethical competition is healthy in most instances, and you can justifiably improve your position by taking on extra duties, making useful suggestions, and working hard to benefit your company and your boss. But irrational, unethical behavior is damaging to the people who are involved. Sometimes overly ambitious employees bend rules and principles without concern for the consequences to themselves and others. If this happens in your office, do not feel pressured to compete with a person who uses questionable tactics to get ahead or accomplish a goal. Instead, continue to perform your duties honestly and responsibly. But there is nothing wrong with offering your own ideas, asking for promotions and raises, and so on.

When you suspect that someone is dealing unfairly in your office, try to keep your employers and coworkers informed of your own activities. Document your actions and accomplishments, sending memos to your employer from time to time to keep him or her completely informed. This will help you to ward off the threat of having an unethical coworker claim credit for your accomplishments or having someone intentionally sabotage your efforts. A responsible, rational, ethical attitude toward your work and toward others is the only acceptable position to take in any situation.

4. *Romantic involvements.* Office romances can pose problems when they distract employees and interfere with work. Should you become involved with a coworker, adopt a firm rule that you will not use company time to pursue your personal interests. However, some companies have a "no fraternization policy." You could then be fired for having a romantic relationship on or off the job. If you are the object of unwanted attention from a coworker or your employer, flatly state that it is your firm policy *never* to get involved with someone in your office. Be as firm as necessary. If that doesn't work and the problem is serious, keep a written record (time, date, place) of unwanted actions or remarks and your efforts to discourage them. If the harassment continues, consult your supervisor. If he or she is the guilty party, you may have to consult your boss's supervisor. (In view of the obvious risks with this

step, proceed with caution.) If you still are unsuccessful in stopping unwanted advances, you can also ask the personnel director to file a complaint with the Equal Opportunity Commission—or you can file it yourself. If you believe you are in physical danger, go to the police and consult an attorney if you need further representation. Remember that sexual harassment is a crime, and no one should *ever* submit to any form of annoyance, harassment, or intimidation.

5. *Working for more than one person.* When you have more than one boss, it is extremely important to treat the combination as a team of persons serving the same company. Adaptability is a key factor in making this type of arrangement work. You will find it much easier if you can adjust to the different pace, demands, and attitudes of each person. In particular, avoid favoritism. When time conflicts occur, make a point of discussing the matter with each person. Meanwhile, learn how to schedule your work and time requirements to accommodate the needs of each person and develop your organizational and planning abilities to the highest degree possible.

6. *Working with other departments.* You may find occasions when you need the assistance and cooperation of other departments. Naturally, you should also offer to be helpful to others when that situation is reversed Conflicts may occur in working with other departments if two people need something at the same time. To cope

with this problem, try developing and maintaining good relations with your principal contact in each department. Keep the channels of communication open and be appreciative when someone grants you a favor. If you need the help of another department in handling a rush job, discuss the problem with your contact. If another person's work is ahead of yours, discuss it with that person. Most people are reasonable and will gladly try to help when they understand your needs and problems. See also ETIQUETTE IN THE OFFICE; TIME MANAGEMENT; TRAINING AN ASSISTANT.

Postal regulations. See Chapter 2/ POSTAL SERVICE.

Presents. Secretaries may have certain responsibilities with respect to Christmas and other holiday presents that their employers give to friends and business associates. Some secretaries also purchase and mail them. You should have a notation on your calendar to bring such gift lists to your employer's attention. Figure 1 is a suggested form of a list; it is self-explanatory. See also Chapter 7/HOLIDAY CARD LISTS. Your employer makes additions or deletions, approves the presents suggested by you or decides on something else, and indicates the price range. To avoid duplication, you should keep a card record of presents given at other times of the year as well as at Christmas.

Money presents. Make a list of those to whom your employer gives money and ask him or her to indicate the amount. The list may include household employees, elevator op-

PRESENTS: FIGURE 1: Christmas list

Name	Gift yr. before last	Gift last yr.	Amt. spent	Suggestion	Amt. to spend?
	CHRISTMAS LIST (Mr. Palmer)			19____	
Mr. & Mrs. Watson	cocktail glasses	silver bowl	$50	bronze vase	
Bill Thompson	humidor	manicure kit	$18	leather address book	

erators, door attendants, janitors, and building superintendents (but not building managers) of apartment houses and office buildings; mail carriers; and any others who perform services throughout the year and are not tipped. The amount given to apartment house employees is usually based on the rent; the amount given others, on length of service.

If the amount of money is small—twenty dollars or less—crisp, new bills should be used; for a larger amount, write checks. No matter what the amount or to whom it is given, the money should be inserted in an envelope printed for that purpose, for example, Christmas.

Professional Secretaries International. Secretaries and executives recognize that successful secretaries today not only must be proficient typists and stenographers but also must be experts in a variety of business fields and human relations.

Professional Secretaries International has played an important role in furthering this position. The association sponsors the Institute for Certifying Secretaries, which certifies secretaries who meet specific qualifications and pass a certifying examination. A secretary who is interested in becoming a CPS (Certified Professional Secretary), thereby demonstrating her superior secretarial abilities, should write to Committee on Qualifications, Institute for Certifying Secretaries, 301 East Armour Boulevard, Kansas City, Missouri 64111-1299.

Study outline for CPS exam. Applicants must fall within one of four categories: secretary (experience completed); secretary (employed full time, experience to be completed); business educator (secretarial experience completed); or student (now enrolled, experience to be completed). The following outline, reprinted with permission from *Capstone,* 1987, summarizes examination content in six key areas:

I BEHAVIORAL SCIENCE IN BUSINESS tests the principles of human relations and organizational dynamics in the work place. It focuses on needs, motivation, nature of conflict, problem-solving techniques, essentials of supervision and communication, leadership styles, and understanding of the informal organization.

At Martinez Aerospace, employees actively participate in the decision-making process. Skills and interests are considered in suggesting courses of action. Ideas presented to the group are evaluated on the basis of merit and relevance to the goal. This is an example of which type of group?

A. Autocratic

B. Democratic

C. Laissez-faire

D. Oligarchic

II BUSINESS LAW measures (1) the secretary's knowledge of the principles of business law and (2) knowledge of the effect of governmental controls on business. Understanding of the historical setting in which these controls developed should be emphasized in preference to names and dates.

Maple Leaf Petroleum Corporation, a refinery, orally agreed to supply Charlton, a dealer, with one million gallons of gas per month. Because of the oil shortage, Maple Leaf refused to deliver the gas as promised to Charlton. Charlton sued. The result was judgment for

A. Charlton, as an order for future goods is valid.

B. Charlton, as the offer was accepted.

C. Maple Leaf, as an oral contract for more than $500 is not enforceable.

D. Maple Leaf, as consideration was not paid.

III ECONOMICS AND MANAGEMENT consists of 35% economics and 65% management. Emphasis is placed on understanding of the basic concepts underlying business operations. Key economic and management principles as well as the latest governmental regulations in business are included.

The balance of trade computation includes

A. all payments between countries for trade, consultants, and investments.

B. capital outflows to foreign countries for investments and foreign investments in the U.S.

C. the dollar value of all merchandise imported and exported during a one-year period.

D. U.S. government grants to other nations.

IV ACCOUNTING measures (1) knowledge of the elements of the accounting cycle; (2) ability to analyze financial statement accounts; (3) ability to perform arithmetical operations associated with accounting and computing interest and discounts; and (4) ability to summarize and interpret financial data.

If a company earned $2.30 a share on its common stock, and the stock is selling at $30 a share on the market, what is the price/earnings ratio?

A. 5.76

B. 7.60

C. 13.04

D. 13.40

V OFFICE ADMINISTRATION AND COMMUNICATION measures proficiency in subject matters unique to the secretary's position: (50% office administration) execu-

tive travel, office management, records management, and reprographics; and (50% written business communication) editing, abstracting, and preparing communications in final format.

A question at the opening of a persuasive request letter

A. can legitimately force the reader to commit to a position.

B. should enable the reader to answer yes or no.

C. should indicate the attitude of the writer.

D. should start the reader thinking and get the reader to continue reading.

VI OFFICE TECHNOLOGY covers the secretary's responsibilities created by data processing, communications media, advances in office management, technological applications, records-management technology, and office systems.

Due to the high costs of creating, storing, retrieving, reproducing, and disseminating paper documents, a "paperless" information system is emerging, relying on such alternative information carriers as

A. computer-based accounting systems.

B. magnetic-coated and photosensitive recording materials.

C. movable workstations.

D. word processing equipment.

Correct Answers:

I-B, II-C, III-C, IV-C, V-D, VI-B

Purchasing. Many secretaries purchase the supplies used in their offices. If your company has a purchasing department, you may be required to fill out a requisition form and present it to the person who does the purchasing. Or you may be required to fill out a purchase order and deliver it to a local office supply store. Small offices may not require either a requisition form or purchase order. Follow the practice in your company. If you pick up supplies in person, or order them by telephone, you probably will charge them to your employer's account at that store. No matter what practice you follow, double-check your supplies against the copy of the invoice you receive before storing any of the material.

Use some form of inventory control in maintaining your storage area, even if it is no more than a shelf in the office's coat closet. A list of supplies and quantities taped to the inside of the door may suffice. Be certain to cross off the old quantity and write in the new quantity whenever you remove something. It also helps to mark the remaining number of copies on the front of each package. This type of record keeping will be your best guide to reordering supplies in sufficient time before they are exhausted. You will have better control if only one person distributes the supplies, but if it is office policy to let employees help themselves, put a large sign on one of the shelves to remind everyone to change the quantities listed on the inventory sheet taped to the door whenever supplies are removed.

Records management. The creation and disposition of records. The secretary is always involved in records management, primarily through the typing and filing of documents. But

41

many decisions must be made in the overall process of records management: (1) How will the records be produced? (2) What filing systems will be used for active files? (3) What process will be used to transfer and store inactive or seldom-used files? (4) What methods of retrieval are required? (5) What type of retention schedule is needed? (6) Which company policies affect management decisions? (7) What types of safeguards are needed to protect records? (8) How will responsibility for each function be assigned? (9) What types of controls will be effective?

As a general rule, never dispose of anything without permission. Most companies have a program determined by state and federal legal requirements for record retention. For further information, consult a guide such as the guide to records retention available free from the Electric Wastebasket Corporation, 145 West 45th Street, New York, NY 10036.

Before you put files into storage, type a storage control schedule for the active files (standard forms are available in office-supply stores). Your schedule should show the storage box's contents, location of the box, date to destroy the contents, date destroyed, and the person who authorized disposal.

See also Typing of various documents; Filing systems; Information storage and retrieval; Microfilming; and maintenance of various records described in Chapter 15, "Real Estate"; Chapter 16, "Insurance"; and Chapter 12, "Taxes."

Recruiting. See Personnel, 2. *Recruiting.*

Reminder systems. See Tickler file; Follow-up system; Chapter 5/ Calendars.

Routing mail. See Incoming mail.

Routing slip. See Incoming mail, *Routing the mail.*

Screening calls. Procedure to protect your employer from the inconvenience of answering unimportant or undesirable telephone calls. The secretary asks who is calling and decides whether the call should be put through or perhaps transferred to someone else. When your employer is away, try to handle as many calls as possible yourself before offering to have your employer return the call later.

An executive usually expects his or her secretary to screen calls; otherwise the calls do not go through the secretary but are put through directly to the executive. A polite way of asking who is calling is, "May I tell Ms. Owens who is calling?" Or "May I ask who is calling?" Legitimate callers seldom object to giving their names. Almost all callers not only volunteer their names but also briefly state their business.

In a new position, the secretary is not familiar with the names of people who have legitimate business with an executive. It is better to err by putting through a few unnecessary calls than by delaying or rejecting important ones. If the caller insists upon withholding his or her name, the secretary might say very politely, "I'm sorry, but Ms. Owens has someone with her at the moment. Since you can't tell me who's calling, I'd suggest you write to her and mark your letter 'personal.' I'll be glad to see that she gets it right away."

Screening personnel. See PERSONNEL, 3. *Selecting personnel.*

Secretary's assistant. See ASSISTANTS; TRAINING AN ASSISTANT.

Side captions, typing. See STATISTICAL TYPING, *Side captions.*

Social matters. Whether an executive is meticulous about the amenities or indifferent to them, when secretaries act for their employers in social matters, they must follow established rules of etiquette. Among the amenities frequently left to secretaries are sending and acknowledging invitations (see also Chapter 7/INVITATIONS); attending to holiday remembrances (see PRESENTS; Chapter 7/ HOLIDAY CARD LISTS); recording taxes (see Chapter 12/CONTRIBUTIONS); and sending expressions of sympathy at the time of death (see SYMPATHY, EXPRESSIONS OF).

Spacing between typewriter characters. In nonjustified text, usage has established the following standard rules for spacing between typewriter characters:

One space:

After a comma

After a semicolon

After a period following an abbreviation or an initial but not between initials forming a single abbreviation

After an exclamation mark used in the body of a sentence

Before and after "x" meaning "by," for example, 3" x 5" card

Two spaces:

After a colon

After every sentence

After a period following a figure or letter at the beginning of a line in a list of items

No spacing:

Before or after a dash, which is two hyphens

Before or after a hyphen

Between quotation marks and the matter enclosed

Between parentheses and the matter enclosed

Between any word and the punctuation following it

Between the initials that make up a single abbreviation—for example, COD

Before or after an apostrophe, unless it begins or ends a word

Punctuation should never be separated from the word it follows—for example, a dash should never be placed at the beginning of a line.

Statistical typing. Every secretary has the occasional task of typing papers that contain columns of figures, tabulations, lists, and other items typed in a special style. When a computer or word processor is used, the procedure is greatly simplified. Depending on the software used, format instructions (e.g., column width) can be specified in advance, and the computer will automatically determine the proper arrangement of data. Some software will also perform minor operations such as aligning columns of figures at the decimal point. Other software is designed to perform complex mathematical calculations as well.

When statistical material is prepared by typewriter, however, it is necessary to make a number of manual calculations. Certain techniques improve the appearance of the typed material. The suggestions that follow for typewriter preparation are arbitrary but are used in the offices of many executives who take pride in the appearance of their work. These same guidelines can be used in preparing format instructions for your computer or word processor.

Columnar headings. Statistical material usually consists of a column of descriptive items on the left and one or more columns of figures. The column on the left is variously referred to as *side headings, particulars, descriptive column, the stub,* and the like. Columns of figures usually have a heading; frequently, the descriptive column also has a heading. Suggestions for typing the columnar headings follow:

1. Center the heading over the longest line of type in the column. (See Illustrations 1 and 2.)

2. Underscore the last line of the heading. (See Illustration 3.) The underscoring extends the length of the longest line in the column, including the dollar mark and any reference that follows the figure. (See Illustration 1.) If the longest line of the column heading is longer than the longest line of figures, the underscoring extends the length of the longest line of the heading. (See Illustration 2.)

Net Sales

$20,142,453

Illustration 1

Depreciation

$80,003

Illustration 2

Net Profit
Before Federal
Income and
Excess Profits
Taxes

$10,169,353

Illustration 3

3. Underscore the descriptive column heading the length of the heading only. (See Illustration 4.)

Expenses

Salaries, wages, and bonuses
Entertainment
Research and development
Insurance

Illustration 4

If the heading is much shorter than the column, try leaving space between the letters of the heading, thus: E x p e n s e s.

4. Capitalize the headings as though they were titles—begin each word, except the short prepositions, articles, and conjunctions, with a cap-

ital. (See Illustrations 3, 4, 5, and 6.) Generally, begin only the first word with a capital in the left column of descriptive items. (See Illustration 7.)

5. Double-space between the underscoring and the first item in the column. See the preceding illustrations.

6. The last lines of all column headings should be parallel. Before beginning to type the headings, look at all of them and determine how many lines the longest will take. Drop other headings accordingly. (See Illustration 5.)

12 Months Ending	Gross Operating Revenue	Federal and State Income Taxes	Net Income	Net Income Before Income Taxes
12/31/—	$1,696,138	$74,000	$147,727	$221,727
12/31/—	1,953,522	101,900	189,456	291,356
12/31/—	2,217,902	87,000	160,402	247,402
12/31/—	2,247,018	138,100	259,354	397,454
12/31/—	2,185,942	144,300	229,203	373,503
12/31/—	2,406,014	162,500	191,347	353,847
12/31/—	2,429,753	177,000	188,889	365,889

Illustration 5

7. If a heading extends over two or more subheadings, underscore the top heading the length of the subheadings. (See Illustration 6.) Single-space between the headings and subheadings.

	Cash Dividends Paid		
Year	Total	Preferred	Common
19—	$285,507	$ 66,000	$219,507
19—	386,837	114,367	272,470

Illustration 6

Dollar marks. 1. Place a dollar mark in front of the first figure in a column and in front of the totals and subtotals. (See Illustrations 8 and 9.) Or you may omit the dollar marks in front of subtotals. (See Illustration 10.) The manuscript from which the typed copy is made is a guide in this respect. A dollar mark always precedes a figure that is double-underlined and, also, the figure immediately following a double underline. (See Illustration 8.)

	December 31, 19—			
	Gross Book Value	Depreciation, etc.		Net Book Value
		Total	Percent	
Oil lands and leases	$ 160,472	$ 85,003	53	$ 75,469
Tangible development	233,276	139,268	60	94,008
Intangible development	398,886	398,886	100	—
Total properties for oil production	792,634	623,157	79	169,477
Pipe lines and other transportation facilities	167,351	76,943	46	90,408
Oil refineries and chemical plants	488,276	285,987	59	202,289
Marketing and miscellaneous facilities	155,349	89,564	58	65,785
	1,603,610	1,075,651	67	527,959
Land	37,410	—	—	37,410
TOTALS	$1,641,020	$1,075,651	66	$565,369

Illustration 7

45

$1,656,895
338,510
$1,318,385
239,167
27,515
$1,585,067

$2,821,745

$299,055
221,483
$77,572
273,813
$315,385

Illustration 8

2. The dollar marks in a column of figures are aligned with reference to the figure having the greatest number of digits. Before typing the first dollar mark, count the number of digits, including commas and decimal point, in the amount with the largest number of digits and place the first dollar mark accordingly. Thus if the column has an amount of $10,000,000 in it, and the first figure in the column is $10,000, there will be four spaces between the dollar mark and 10,000.

3. If the column does not have a total, the dollar mark is placed in front of the first figure only. (See Illustration 5.)

Underlining and double-underlining in columns of figures. 1. Underline to indicate points of addition and subtraction.

2. Double-underline the grand total at the end of a column or tabulation. Or subtotals might also be double-underlined. (See Illustration 9.) The manuscript copy will be the guide.

GROSS SALES, net of returns, allowances, and discounts	$20,223,663
COST OF SALES	14,384,161
GROSS PROFIT	$ 5,839,502

Selling, shipping, and delivery expenses	$ 2,818,095
General and administrative expenses	997,104
Engineering, general research, and development expenses	528,851
	$ 4,344,050

| PROFIT FROM OPERATIONS | $ 1,495,452 |

OTHER INCOME:

Royalties	$ 55,811
Profits on disposals of fixed assets	3,508
Miscellaneous	9,665
	$ 68,984
	$ 1,564,436

Illustration 9

3. Extend the underlining or double-underlining the entire length of the figure, including the dollar mark but not including any reference, such as a footnote reference, that might follow the figure.

4. When double-underlining, be careful about the spacing between the lines. The underlines should not appear as one broad line, nor should there be a wide space between them. (A typewriter may be equipped with a double-underscore key, which quickly pays for itself in time saved if there is a volume of statistical typing.)

A comparison of illustrations 7 and 10 will clarify the use of underlining. In Illustration 10 the total of each group of figures is underlined. These totals are not included in the succeeding totals but are all added to arrive at the final total ($113,463,467). In Illustration 7 the total of the first group of figures (Total properties for oil production) is not underlined because it is added with the figures that produce the next subtotal. In other words, the subtotals in Illustration 7 are not underlined because they are cumulative, whereas those in Illustration 10 are underlined because they are not cumulative.

CURRENT ASSETS:

Cash	$ 13,256,364
U.S. government obligations, at cost	24,288,014
Receivables	8,625,711
LESS—Provision for doubtful accounts and allowances	(922,011)
Inventories, at lower of standard or actual cost or market (Note 1) ..	18,599,312
Prepaid expenses	863,472
Total current assets	64,710,862

INVESTMENTS:

Associated companies (Note 2) ...	4,617,293
Foreign subsidiary companies, not consolidated (Note 3)	921,959
Miscellaneous	894,053
	6,433,305

PLANT AND EQUIPMENT, AT COST:

Land	929,058
Buildings, machinery, and equipment	67,062,431
LESS—Depreciation and amortization	(26,048,626)
	41,942,863

OTHER ASSETS	376,437
	$113,463,467

Illustration 10

Double-underlining is often used after subtotals that are not cumulative. For example, the subtotals in Illustration 10, if this practice were followed, would be double-under-

lined. Figures that are double-underlined are always preceded by a dollar mark. See all of these illustrations.

Side captions. The side captions in a financial statement or schedule tell what the figures parallel to it represent. These captions are longer than the columns of figures and have certain peculiarities, such as carryover lines and indentations, that are usually typed in a specified style.

1. Indent each carryover line in an item at least two spaces from the beginning of the item. See Illustration 11.

2. Begin each item with a capital letter.

3. Indent each item under a caption, or group heading, at least two spaces from the beginning of the last line of the group heading. Note from Illustration 11 that this practice results in the alignment of all items under a group heading, but items of equal position under different headings are not necessarily aligned if a heading has a carryover line.

4. The most common practice is to follow the caption or group heading with a colon, as in Illustration 11, but the colon may be omitted.

5. The side caption to a total or subtotal is indented about eleven to thirteen spaces.

6. Frequently, the principal side captions are written in solid caps. (See Illustration 10.) When the caption is unusually long, the first part of it might be written in solid caps and

Current assets:	
Cash in banks and on hand	$ 2,628,948
United States government securities—at cost plus accrued interest	700,114
Recoverable taxes on income	34,214
Accounts receivable, less allowance for bad debts, discounts, etc. of $20,877 in 1953 and $21,971 in 1952	1,405,936
Inventories, at the lower of "first-in, first out" cost or market (note 1):	
Raw materials, goods in process, finished goods, etc.	1,525,818
Merchandise in transit	95,522
Supplies	18,508
Total inventories	$ 1,639,848
Total current assets	$ 6,409,060
Other assets:	
Cash surrender value of life insurance (note 2)	84,073
Investment, at cost, in Cardinal Supply & Manufacturing Company, wholly owned Subsidiary not consolidated (note 3)	25,000
Total other assets	$ 109,073
Plant and equipment—at cost, less allowance for depreciation and amortization (note 4):	
Land	113,156
Buildings	1,074,003
Machinery and equipment	4,175,150
Office equipment and automobiles	263,550
Construction in progress	94,788
	5,720,647
Less allowance for depreciation and amortization	1,596,229
	4,124,418
Spare equipment and repair parts	408,644
	4,533,062
Fully amortized emergency facilities, at cost, $359,282, less allowance for depreciation, $145,615, at September 30, 1953 and $131,022 at September 30, 1952	213,667
Plant and equipment—net	$ 4,746,729
Prepaid expenses and deferred charges:	
Insurance, rent, and other items	116,518
Leasehold costs, less amortization of $34,028 at September 30, 1953 and $16,012 at September 30, 1952 (note 5)	415,685
Total prepaid expenses and deferred charges	532,203
	$11,797,065

Illustration 11

the last part in lower case. (See Illustration 12.)

TAXES ON INCOMES, less United States
  Treasury savings notes at December
  31, 19—, of $1,503,900—estimated   4,257,447

Illustration 12

7. Unless a side caption is written in solid caps, capitalize only the first word. (See Illustration 13.)

8. When an item is more than one line long, try to group the words or phrases that are closely related; also

avoid hyphenating a word. The italicized words in the following examples obviously belong together and should be typed on the same line. Examples:

Fifteen year 3⅜% sinking fund debentures
  due May 1, 1963,
  less $140,000 in current liabilities
Earned surplus ($12,522,830
  restricted as to payment dividends
  under terms of debenture agreement)
Less estimated additional sinking fund
  requirements for year
  shown among current liabilities

Columns consisting of figures other than dollars. When a column consists of items made up of a mixture of dollars, percentages, and other numbers, place a dollar mark in front of every number that represents a dollar amount and place the percentage symbol after percentages. The dollar marks are not aligned. The percentage symbols are aligned with the right margin of the column; they are placed beneath the last digit in the column. (See Illustration 13.)

Sales	$19,033,933
Net income	$1,061,863
Net income per dollar of sales	5.58%
Number of common shares	533,752
Net income per common share	$1.99
Dividends per common share	$0.90
Income taxes paid per common share	$2.24
Stockholders' equity per common share	$18.03
Long-term debt, December 31	$770,000
Net current assets—working capital	$6,295,798
Current ratio	5.3–1
Number of stockholders, December 31	3,318
Number of employees, December 31	1,828

Illustration 13

Series of columns. In financial statements, the total of a group of figures is frequently carried to the next column, rather than placed beneath the tabulation. (See Illustration 14.)

1. Underline the last figure in the tabulation and type the total in the next column on a line with it. The double underline may be used instead of the single.

2. Place a dollar mark in front of the first figure in each column, aligning it with the longest figure in the column. Also place a dollar mark in front of the grand total in the last column.

3. Double-underline the grand total in the last column. (See Illustration 14.)

4. When the total has a descriptive side caption of its own, it is necessary to drop the total one space beneath the last item in the tabulation, but the total is typed in the next column. (See Illustration 15.)

As an alternative, the dollar mark may be placed in front of the first figure after every underlining, whether the figure represents a total or the first item in a new group of figures. (See Illustration 16.)

Percentages. 1. If a column heading contains *percent* or abbreviation of it, the percentage amounts in the column are not followed by the percentage sign (%).

2. If the column heading has some other designation, such as *Increase*, and the amounts in the column are percentages, follow the same practice in the use of the

CURRENT ASSETS:

Demand deposits in banks and cash on hand		$2,441,064	
U.S. government obligations, at cost plus accrued interest (substantially at quoted market)		1,045,126	
Accounts receivable:			
Trade	$2,257,349		
Other	5,733		
	2,263,082		
Reserve for doubtful accounts	15,323	2,247,759	
Inventories, at substantially the lower of cost or market:			
Finished goods and work in process	1,310,840		
Raw materials	2,102,550	3,413,390	
PREPAID TAXES, INSURANCE, AND SUPPLIES		172,278	$ 9,319,617
CASH VALUE OF LIFE INSURANCE			126,477
PROPERTY, PLANT, AND EQUIPMENT, AT COST:			
Land		53,814	
Land improvements	38,589		
Buildings	1,855,576		
Machinery and equipment	3,462,313		
	5,356,478		
Reserves for depreciation	2,155,852	3,200,626	3,254,440
			$12,700,534

Illustration 14

Cash in our vaults and in banks		$1,557,597,136.69
United States government securities and securities guaranteed by the government	$1,669,423,368.98	
Federal agency securities	185,205,454.83	
State, county, and municipal securities	557,704,312.06	
Other securities	108,772,485.48	
Stock in Federal Reserve Bank	10,500,000.00	
TOTAL SECURITIES		2,531,605,621.35
Loans guaranteed or insured by the United States Government or its agencies under the National Housing Act, the "G.I. Bill," the Defense Production Act, or some other provision of law	$1,171,843,741.90	
Other loans to our customers for use in their businesses for building, buying, or modernizing their homes, for financing automobile or household equipment purchases, etc.	2,976,869,992.59	
TOTAL LOANS AND DISCOUNTS		$4,148,713,734.49

Illustration 15

percent sign that is followed in the use of the dollar mark. Generally, the percent sign comes after the first figure and after each figure before and after double-underlining. (See Illustration 17.)

3. Percent may be abbreviated to *Pct.* or *Pctge.* in column headings to save space.

4. Do not use the percent sign in a column heading; use only when it

LIABILITIES

Current liabilities:
Note payable to bank—installment due within one year		$ 51,500.00
Accounts payable		333,436.46
Taxes withheld for taxing authorities		50,716.21

Accrued expenses:
Payroll	$ 86,887.77	
Taxes on payrolls and transportation	11,104.97	
Insurance	33,948.81	
Other	9,766.43	141,707.98
Federal taxes on income—estimated		168,687.74
Total current liabilities		$ 746,048.39

Long-term debt:
Notes payable to bank, unsecured	$636,000.00	
Less installment due within one year	51,500.00	584,500.00

Stockholders' equity:
$5.00 cumulative preferred stock of $100.00 par value per share: redeemable at $105.00 per share plus accrued dividends authorized and outstanding 1,500 shares	$150,000.00	
Common stock of $1.00 par value per share		
Authorized 100,000 shares, outstanding 50,600 shares	50,600.00	
Reduction surplus (arising from retirement of prior issue of preferred capital stock)	21,750.00	
Surplus of predecessor companies to September 19, 1947	988,504.93	
Earned surplus since September 19, 1947	617,452.26	1,828,307.19
		$3,158,855.58

Illustration 16

follows an amount. (See Illustration 17.)

Percentage of Sales	Increase
15	19.3%
20	13.0
35	32.3%
15	
50	8.4%
	11.9
35	20.3%
20	
55	

Illustration 17

Cents. 1. In dollar figures, omit the decimal point if no cents are included in the column. (See Illustration 14.)

2. If cents appear in some of the figures, add two ciphers to all the other figures. (See Illustration 15.)

Dates. 1. In tabulating a number of dates for the *same* year, abbreviate the months and align both left and right margins. Three-letter abbreviations are shown in Illustration 18. Notice that no period is required after the abbreviations.

2. In tabulating a number of dates for *different* years, indicate the month by number and separate month, date, and year by virgules. Align the right margin of the column. (See Illustration 5.)

19—

Jan	23
Feb	2
Mar	19
Apr	11
May	12
Jun	5
Jul	31
Aug	23
Sep	9
Oct	25
Nov	4
Dec	31

Illustration 18

3. When a date is a column heading, it should be written according to the width of the column beneath it. Any one of the examples in Illustration 19 is permissible.

December 31, 19—	Dec. 31, 19—

Dec. 31, 19—	December 31, 19—

Illustration 19

Fractions. In typing fractions, use the individual numbers with the virgule. They are more legible in copies. Separate the fraction from the whole number by a hyphen, thus, 4-⅔.

Commas in figures. 1. Use commas to set off thousands, hundreds of thousands, and so forth in amounts and quantities. (See Illustration 20.)

Tons	Amount
28,356	$15,687,432.98

Illustration 20

2. Certificate and check numbers and other serial designations are written without commas, thus, *No. 3847.*

Abbreviations. Generally, abbreviations are not used in tabulations. However, it is sometimes necessary to abbreviate to save space or to improve the appearance of the setup of a statement. We have indicated above how dates and *percent* may be abbreviated. The ampersand (&) also may be used in column headings to save space.

Use of dittos to indicate repetition. When one or more words are repeated in the same column, without intervening word or words, type *Do* below the center of the word or words for each repetition. Some typists use double quotation marks (") in place of *Do*. If the company name takes more than one line and is repeated in the next item, both lines must be repeated; no ditto is used. If various dates appear in the same column, type the first three letters of each month, thus aligning the column of dates at right and left margins. (See Illustration 21.)

		To be
Pig'n Whistle	Jun 30, 19—	returned
Do	Sep 15, 19—	Do
Merriman- Broadcasting Systems, Inc.	Do	Do
Merriman- Broadcasting Systems, Inc.	Mar 30, 19—	Do

Illustration 21

Vertical lists in tabulations. When typing a vertical list of years, companies, cities, products, and the like, you may separate them by an extra space after every fifth item to make the list easier to read. When months are listed vertically, an extra space may be left after every third month, thus separating quarters.

Blank amounts in statements and tabulations. When a statement or tabulation consists of several columns and some of the amounts are blank, type a single or double hyphen in the center of the column where no amount appears. The hyphens make it easier for the reader to trace an item across the page, and they indicate that the amounts were not omitted in error.

See also Typing.

Suggestion system. The procedure of encouraging employees by financial awards to make suggestions that will improve management, cut costs, or save money. Suggestion systems have been called employee "imagineering." They are just that: a simple means of permitting labor to participate in management. The installation of a suggestion system is a four-step process. A company must (1) provide a means for soliciting and collecting suggestions—usually a "suggestion box," (2) establish a committee of one or more to evaluate the suggestions that are submitted, (3) establish a schedule of awards for ideas that are accepted and a means for providing suitable explanations for rejections, and (4) develop a means for putting the suggestions into practice.

Supervision of assistants. See Training an assistant.

Sympathy, expressions of. Sympathy to the family of a deceased friend or acquaintance is usually expressed by (1) flowers, (2) a letter of sympathy, (3) mass cards, or (4) contributions.

Flowers. It is customary to send flowers to a bereaved family, except an Orthodox Jewish family. It is appropriate to send them fruit baskets. A visiting card, with the engraved name struck out in ink and bearing a few words of sympathy, may accompany flowers. Usually, however, the secretary orders flowers by telephone and the florist supplies the card, on which he or she writes the name of the person sending the flowers. The florist will ask the name of the deceased, where the funeral is to be conducted, and the date and time of the service. Flowers are appropriate at a memorial service—as for someone lost at sea—and when the deceased is to be cremated. Cut flowers are not appropriate for a funeral service. Some kind of floral piece, a spray or a wreath, is preferable.

Letters of condolence. These letters may be sent to a family of any faith. See Chapter 7/Social-business letters, 2. *Letters of condolence or sympathy.*

Mass cards. Mass cards may be sent to a Roman Catholic family by a Catholic or a non-Catholic. They may be obtained from any priest. It is customary to make an offering to the church at the time of asking for the card. Although a Roman Catholic might ask a priest to say a mass for a non-Catholic, it is not in good taste to send a mass card to a non-Catholic family.

Charitable contributions. Friends often send contributions to charities or other organizations in which the deceased was interested, instead of flowers. (See Chapter 12/CONTRIBUTIONS.) The organization usually sends the family of the deceased a notice of the contribution.

Tabulated material. 1. *Text*. When text is tabulated or itemized in the body of a letter, the items are usually preceded by a number or letter in parentheses or followed by a period. Each line of the tabulated text should begin two spaces to the right of the number. (See Figure 1.)

2. *Statistical*. A statistical tabulation frequently occurs within the body of a letter, report, or other typed material. It is preferable to type it on the same page with the paragraph or sentence that introduces it and should not be broken and continued on the next page. Before typing the statistical material, gauge the probable space required for the tabulation to see if there is enough space on the page for the entire tabulation. In the case of computer preparation you may need to adjust the normal

TABULATED MATERIAL: FIGURE 1: Tabulated textual material

I have revised the affidavit you returned, in accordance with your recommendations. If you find it satisfactory as now drawn, please:

1. Swear to it before a notary and have him or her affix the notarial seal and stamp

2. Fill in the last column of Schedule B concerning the months for which payments are in default on each vehicle

3. Return the affidavit with five forms of the conditional sale contract

page break that the computer determines automatically. If it is necessary to break the introductory paragraph, carry at least two lines to the page on which the tabulation is typed.

Leave a double space between the tabulation and the *preceding* text and a double space or three spaces between the tabulation and the *following* text. (If the text is written with one and one-half spaces between lines, leave one and one-half before the tabulation and one and one-half or two spaces after it.) Items of more than one line may be separated with a little more than a single space by releasing the typewriter platen. In the case of computer preparation, format specifications for spacing can be modified as desired.

Center all tabulations horizontally with relation to the portion of the sheet that will not be bound. Or use an indentation equal to or greater than the paragraph indentation. If possible, leave at least five spaces between the longest item and the first digit in a column of figures. Figure 2 illustrates a statistical tabulation in the body of a report. (See also STATISTICAL TYPING.)

Telegraph services. See Chapter 2/ TELEGRAPH SERVICE, DOMESTIC; INTERNATIONAL COMMUNICATIONS.

Telephone, using. See Chapter 2/ TELECOMMUNICATIONS SERVICES.

Theater tickets. The secretary's chief responsibility when an executive entertains at the theater is reserving the tickets. That is a difficult chore unless the tickets are ordered far in

TABULATED MATERIAL: FIGURE 2: Tabulated statistical material in body of report

Bankers' acceptances were confirmed by correspondence with the respective institutions in the following amounts:

The Safety Trust Company:		
Due 19—:		
April 15	$2,500	
April 20	8,600	$11,100
Anycity Bank & Trust Co.:		
Due 19—:		
February 1		15,000
ABC National Bank:		
Due 19—:		
February 15	15,000	
March 1	4,500	19,500
		$45,600

The acceptances are secured by trust receipts pledging merchandise or proceeds therefrom to be first applied to the satisfaction of such acceptances.

advance. Theaters, telephone services, and ticket agencies are listed in the telephone directory, and newspapers carry advertisements of current plays. Many hotels also have information on and facilities for the purchase of theater tickets, tours, and other forms of entertainment. Upon short notice, a ticket agency may be helpful. An account at an agency simplifies the problem somewhat. Establish a contact at the agency and make all purchases through the same person. Specify the event and the date, and the agent will deliver the tickets to you or at the theater box office. An additional charge by the agency is sometimes added to the original cost of each ticket. Many agencies will allow you to charge the tickets with one of the major credit cards. You can also purchase tickets at the box office—if seats are still available—and many box offices accept credit cards. Large cities have telephone services, such as Ticket Central in New York, where you can specify the area (but usually not seat or row) desired and charge the amount to a credit card. Tickets then can be picked up at the box office. (Inquire about a service charge.) Tickets sent through the mail should include the numbers of the seats in your letter of transmittal (with the information on your carbon copy in case the tickets are lost). When you give the tickets to your employer, enclose them in an envelope with this information typed on it: (1) day of the week and date of performance, (2) curtain time, (3) name and address of the theater, (4) name of show, and (5) seat numbers.

Tickler file. A reminder system. A tickler file has a tabbed guide for each month of the year and thirty-one tabbed guides, one for each day of the month. The guides come in various sizes, but the preferable size for a tickler is three by five inches. The daily guides are placed behind the current month guide. Memos are made on cards or slips, which are filed behind the daily guide according to the date on which the matter is to be brought up.

Among the numerous uses of a tickler file are (1) its use with a calendar or diary (see Chapter 5/ CALENDARS), (2) its use as a FOLLOW-UP SYSTEM, (3) tax-return reminders, and (4) insurance-expiration reminders.

Time management. Better management of time usually means developing better working habits. Set priorities and organize your work schedule according to those priorities. Establish goals and write down everything you want to do. Use calendars or any other form of reminder to help you follow the schedule you draw up and to help you meet deadlines. Delegate routine work to assistants to create more free time to handle important matters. Discourage unnecessary time-consuming intrusions and interruptions. Schedule work that requires long periods of concentration during the least hectic hours. Improve communications to prevent misunderstandings and backtracking. Group activities such as filing and running errands to save time and energy. Streamline your work to eliminate unnecessary steps. Use moments when you are waiting for someone or something to plan future work. Avoid procrastination by starting the day with something you like to do. If practical, consider asking your employer to send you to a time-management seminar.

Training an assistant. Some secretaries are asked to interview and train new full- or part-time employees. For example, your employer may think it is time to add a clerk-typist who will assist you in many of your duties. Your office, or the personnel office in a large company, will advertise and arrange for the interviews.

Interviewing. You must plan ahead for the interviews, to find out what you want to know about the applicant and also to provide information to the applicant—all within the time set aside for the meeting. These are the basic steps involved:

1. Set a mutually convenient time.

2. Prepare a detailed, written description of the company and the job, listing specific tasks the applicant will have to perform.

3. Devise skills tests if applicable, such as a typing test, when prepared tests are not available.

4. Draw up a list of specific questions you want to ask (your company may have a standard application form, but this list is necessary in addition) and take notes throughout the interview.

5. Make certain the applicant is comfortable and at ease and try to encourage him or her to volunteer information and indicate relative interest in skills and job duties.

6. Summarize and type the results, and present them to your employer along with any recommendations or comments you have, after all the interviews are completed.

Once the new worker is hired, the job orientation and training begin. The new employee should be made to feel at home and acquainted with not only the immediate office but also the general company policy and facilities.

Training will require (1) careful instruction and explanation of duties, presented at a pace the employee can digest, and (2) practice sessions in which actual tasks are first completed under your direct supervision, often with step-by-step explanations as work proceeds. It will become evident when direct, constant supervision on the spot can be relaxed.

Once the worker is functioning independently—with the exception of occasional questions—you should still check work occasionally for errors and general quality, as well as checking for efficiency and overall performance. If further guidance or discipline is required, do not hesitate to provide it. Remain alert to dissatisfaction and encourage open communication that will prevent such problems.

It is important throughout the worker's employment to provide motivation. An employee who has no incentive to do better probably will not. Remember, too, throughout your instruction and supervision that a compliment is just as important as constructive criticism. Job satisfaction is essential in any position. For instance, instead of telling someone, "You made three errors in this letter, so you'll have to do it over," say, "With a little more prac-

tice, Linda, I think you'll be typing error-free letters. For now, let's try this one again—I circled the three typos I noticed."

In spite of all your efforts to find and select the right candidate and train him or her properly, there is always the chance that it will not work out. The employee may be unable to adjust to the work pace or may be unable to produce work of adequate quality. If further training will not solve the problem, you will be forced to advise your employer, and he or she may ask you to discharge the employee. It will be necessary to tell the employee as gently as possible that he or she is being released. You could suggest further training or education or that the individual might be more suited for a different type of job or office. Be as tactful, but direct, as possible and wish him or her well upon leaving.

The following chart shows points on which a secretary should train an assistant and methods to use. (Instruction for some things may not be necessary if the trainee has previous experience.)

Basic Training for the Secretary's Assistant

ITEM	METHOD
1. Supplies, where they are kept and how they are stored	a. Show trainee where each item is kept. b. Give trainee a diagram (if available) of the supply cabinet that shows where each item is stored.
2. Stationery supplies and use of each	a. Show trainee each type of stationery. b. Explain how each is used. c. Give trainee a stationery folder con-

taining each type of stationery on which is typed instructions for its use (including computer/word processor and typewriter format specifications), number of copies to make, and distribution of copies.

3. Forms
   a. Show trainee samples of each form he or she will have to fill in.
   b. Explain the use of the form.
   c. Give trainee sample of each form properly filled out.
   d. Attach to each form a typed memo about the number of copies to make and the distribution of the copies, unless this information is evident from the form itself.

4. Company practice in writing letters and memos
   a. Have trainee study manual if there is one. (The manual will contain sample letters on company letterhead.)
   b. Mark in this handbook the parts that apply to practice in the company, including computer/word processor and typewriter preparation. Have trainee study them.
   c. Give trainee sample letters prepared on company letterhead if there is no manual. Include computer/word processor and typewriter format specifications.

5. Special typing techniques:
   Feeding small cards
   Chain feeding
   Decimal tabulation
   Making special characters
   Typing narrow labels
   a. Refer trainee to appropriate item in this book and other secretarial publications as need for each operation arises.
   b. Have trainee apply procedure explained there.
   c. Demonstrate if necessary.

6. Neat arrangement of typed work, especially the setup of tables
   a. Show trainee samples.
   b. Explain setup process on typewriter and computer/word processor format procedures.
   c. Refer trainee to TABULATED MATERIAL and STATISTICAL TYPING in this chapter.

7. Inserting carbon paper and numerous copies in typewriter
   a. Show trainee how a folded sheet of paper can help as starter.

      b. Have trainee apply procedure after you explain it.

      c. Demonstrate again if necessary.

---

8. Improvement of text preparation

      a. Point out defects in trainee's work.

      b. Demonstrate operations of parts of computer/word processor or typewriter that aid in text preparation.

      c. Remember to compliment trainee on work well done.

---

9. Text-correction procedure

      a. Review correction steps with typewriter and computer/word processor.

      b. Refer trainee to ERASURES AND CORRECTIONS in this chapter.

      c. Have trainee apply suggestions made there.

      d. Demonstrate if necessary.

---

10. Operation of dictaphone transcriber

      a. Explain mechanical operation.

      b. Demonstrate.

      c. Have trainee use the machine while you watch.

      d. Correct any inaccurate use, demonstrating again if necessary.

---

11. Operation of reproduction and photocopy equipment, when to use each, and difference in cost

      a. Demonstrate operation of each machine as need arises.

      b. Explain each step as you perform it.

      c. Have trainee take each step while you watch.

      d. Explain to trainee when particular machine is used and why.

      e. Tell trainee the number of copies that can be made by each machine and the comparative cost of reproduction by each.

      f. Give trainee booklets from manufacturers.

---

12. Care of equipment:
    Typewriter
    Computer/word processor
    Dictaphone transcriber
    Reproduction equipment
    Photocopier
    Facsimile
    Teleprinter
    Other equipment

      a. Explain and demonstrate the care that should be given each piece of equipment.

      b. Set an example by the proper care of your own equipment.

      c. Give trainee booklets from manufacturers.

      d. Give trainee chart showing costs of

machines to emphasize the necessity of proper care.

13. Filing	a. Point out to trainee the types of paper and nonpaper material filed in each cabinet or group of cabinets, including computer diskettes and printouts and miscellaneous odd-sized material such as blueprints. b. Open each drawer and explain the arrangement of the files. c. Give trainee chart or list of file cabinets and their contents. d. Demonstrate, step by step, explaining each step. e. Refer trainee to FILING SYSTEMS in this chapter. f. Mark material for trainee to file. g. Watch trainee file some material, correcting any misconceptions. h. After assistant is thoroughly familiar with system, let him or her mark material. i. Check material marked by assistant before it is filed. j. Point out to trainee any inaccurately marked material, explaining inaccuracy. k. When assistant learns to mark all material correctly, it will not be necessary to check the material before it is filed. l. Explain procedures for using central filing department, if there is one.
14. Telephone facilities and their use	a. Explain and demonstrate use of office telephone facilities, such as voice-data terminals. b. Have trainee practice operation of any unusual facilities. c. Give trainee directory of officers, department heads, and key employees. d. Refer trainee to Chapter 2/TELECOMMUNICATIONS SERVICES in this book. e. Explain to trainee how to handle each type of incoming call. f. If an out-of-the-ordinary call comes in, show trainee how to handle it. g. Have trainee place outgoing calls. h. Have trainee take incoming calls.
15. Office facilities, such as telegraphic and messenger	a. Enumerate and explain to trainee when and how each facility is used.

    b. As need arises, have trainee make use of facilities.
(Any forms used in connection with the facilities should have been given to trainee with other forms. See No. 3, of chart.)

16. Company products and nomenclature

    a. Take trainee on tour of company plant or offices, pointing out different products.
    b. Refer trainee to company manual if there is one.
    c. Give trainee list or dictionary of technical terms.
    d. Point out to trainee any misuse or misspelling of technical terms in his or her work.

17. Improvement of grammar

    a. Point out errors in work prepared by trainee.
    b. Point out the rules of grammar in Chapter 6, "GRAMMAR AND VOCABULARY," and under various items in this book that are applicable to errors made by trainee.

18. Improvement of spelling, syllabication, punctuation, capitalization

    a. Refer trainee to Chapter 6, "GRAMMAR AND VOCABULARY," and the rules for DIVISION OF WORDS as well as for various punctuation marks in this book.
    b. Point out errors in work prepared by trainee.
    c. Make sure that trainee makes frequent use of the dictionary and doesn't guess, especially for correspondence.
    d. Remember to compliment trainee for work well done.

19. Handling incoming mail

    a. Refer trainee to INCOMING MAIL in this chapter.
    b. Explain any practices different from the usual procedure followed in your office.
    c. Explain the procedure for nontraditional postal mail such as electronic mail and telex.
    d. Refer trainee to directory of officers, department heads, other key employees, and branch offices.
    e. Give trainee routing lists for any mail

or periodicals received and routed by your office.

---

20. Handling outgoing mail	a. Refer trainee to OUTGOING MAIL in this chapter. b. Explain any practices different from the usual procedure followed in your office. c. Explain the procedure for nontraditional postal mail such as electronic mail and telex.

---

21. Preparing reports	a. Give trainee sample report. b. Point out any specific points to follow, such as numbering of headings and subheadings and other typewriter or computer/word processor format requirements. c. Refer trainee to Chapter 8/REPORT in this book for study.

---

22. Correspondence without dictation	a. Refer trainee to various applicable items in this book. b. Point out sample letters of type that trainee is to write without dictation. c. Suggest improvements that can be made in letters written by trainee. d. Refer to item 4 in this chart.

---

23. Specific duties of trainee's position	a. Prepare for trainee a job breakdown of each specific duty. b. If necessary, explain the procedure followed in each specified duty. c. Point out errors made by trainee in any step of a procedure. d. Commend trainee on accomplishments.

Transcription. See DICTATION, TAKING AND TRANSCRIBING.

Travel arrangements. See TRAVEL.

Typing. Whether you use a typewriter or a computer/word processor, modern equipment and good typing skills are the essentials for efficient processing of information in a busy office. (See also Chapter 5/BUSINESS MACHINES for a description of electric and electronic typewriters.) Typing speed and accuracy come with practice, whether you use an ordinary electric typewriter, an electronic typewriter, or an advanced word processor. (See WORD PROCESSING.) In addition to typing letters and memos (see Chapter 7, "Correspondence"), secretaries must also type telegrams, forms with ruled lines, small cards, all kinds of manuscripts, and—in some offices—legal documents.

Typing on ruled lines. In typing on ruled lines, the horizontal spacing should be adjusted so that the bases of letters that extend below the line of the type (*y*, *g*, and *p*) just touch the ruled line. The proper adjustment is particularly important for filling in printed forms.

Typing small cards. It is easier to type a series of small cards by chain feeding them from the *front* of the platen. After typing the first card, feed backwards until the card has a top margin of about three-quarters of an inch. Insert the next card between the platen and the typed card. Each succeeding card will be held in place by the card preceding it. The cards automatically pile up against the paper table in the order in which they are inserted in the machine.

Typing telegrams. Procedure in typing and sending telegrams varies with the company, but many of them issue instructions similar to the following: (1) Make four copies of every telegram. Send the *original* to the mail desk for pickup by the telegraph messenger. Send Copy 1 with the letter of confirmation. Keep Copy 2 for your file. Send Copy 3 to the purchasing department and mark it *Purchasing Department*. (2) Omit the salutation and complimentary close. (3) Double-space. (4) Do not divide words at the end of a line. (5) Use solid caps only for code words. (6) Type and punctuate as you would any other material.

Type the following information in the lower left-hand corner of each telegram: how sent (fast telegram, night letter, mailgram); sent by (name of person and department); charge (name of department to which telegram is to be charged); date; time message is sent; and number of chargeable words.

It is not necessary to remove a letter or other work from the typewriter when a "rush" telegram has to be typed. This is the procedure:

1. Back-feed the paper and carbons in the machine until the paper shows a top margin of about two inches.

2. Insert the first sheet of the telegram behind the material being typed, against the paper table, as if nothing were in the typewriter.

3. To make carbons of the telegram, insert the second sheet of the telegram against the coated side of the carbon paper already in the machine. Thus the second sheet of the telegram is between the carbon and the second sheet of the letter. Do the same for each carbon in the typewriter. (A sheet must be inserted for each carbon in the machine to prevent the typing from showing on the carbon copies of the work that is in the machine.) For additional copies, add carbon sheets in the usual manner.

4. Turn the platen knob until the telegram blanks are in position for typing.

5. After typing the message, back-feed until the telegram can be removed from the machine.

6. Forward-feed to the point at

which typing of the letter or other work had stopped and continue typing.

Typing manuscript. Manuscript should be typed neatly and legibly, on sheets of uniform size, preferably white bond, eight and one-half by eleven inches, the type commonly used in offices. A copy should be made for reference purposes, but the original is always sent to the printer. The following suggestions should be followed in typing the manuscript (see also Word Processing):

1. Keep the length of the typewritten line down to six inches.

2. Use double or triple spacing.

3. Keep the right-hand margin as even as possible, to help in estimating the length of the copy.

4. Indicate paragraph indentations clearly. Five or six spaces are sufficient, but there should be consistency throughout the manuscript in whatever number of spaces is adopted.

5. Type headings and subheadings in the position they are to occupy on the final printed page and be uniform in capitalization.

6. Use only one side of the sheet.

7. Leave a margin of at least one and one-half inches on all four sides.

8. Keep the pages as nearly uniform in length as possible, to help in estimating the length of the copy.

9. See Chapter 8/FOOTNOTES for the proper method of typing footnotes to a manuscript.

10. If references are made to material appearing in other parts of the manuscript, instruct the printer (on the manuscript) to carry a query on each successive proof as a reminder or put in the correct page reference numbers when the final page proofs are received. (See Chapter 8/QUERY; PAGE PROOF.)

11. Type extracts of quoted material just like the main text, double spaced, full measure. To indicate that an extract is to be printed in a smaller size of type, draw a vertical line in the left margin, beginning exactly where the extract begins and ending where it ends. (See Chapter 8/EXTRACT; QUOTED MATERIAL; FULL MEASURE.)

12. Identify lists, examples, problems, and other material of subordinate importance that is to be set in smaller type or indented and draw a vertical line next to them in the left margin.

See also STATISTICAL TYPING; DRAFT; Chapter 8/MANUSCRIPT; BIBLIOGRAPHY; REPORT; TABLE OF CONTENTS; Chapter 3/MINUTES; Chapter 15/LAND DESCRIPTION.

Typing legal documents. Some secretaries regularly or occasionally type legal documents. For a professional job, these suggestions should be followed:

1. Paper. In jurisdictions where legal paper is still allowed, legal documents may be typed on white letter-size paper (eight and one-half by eleven inches) or legal-size paper (eight by thirteen or eight and one-half by fourteen inches).

2. *Margins.* There should be a two-inch margin at the top and a

one-inch margin at the bottom. If paper without ruled margins is used, the left-hand margin should be one and one-fourth or one and one-half inches, depending on where the paper is bound, and the right-hand margin about one inch. The typing should never extend beyond the ruled margins on legal paper.

3. *Spacing.* Legal documents are usually double-spaced, with a triple space between numbered articles or items and between paragraphs with side headings. Quoted material and description of land may be single-spaced. (See Chapter 8/QUOTED MATERIAL; Chapter 15/LAND DESCRIPTION.)

4. *Punctuation and capitalization.* Legal documents use the same punctuation in the same way as other material, such as correspondence. Capitalization rules differ slightly. Names, for example, are typed in all capitals. Often the first letter of a specific paper (e.g., *Deed*) is capitalized. Court and venue names are typed in all capitals, as are titles of legal papers, such as *AGREEMENT*. Key words and phrases, such as *IN WITNESS WHEREOF* and *WHEREFORE*, are also typed in all capitals.

5. *Paragraphs.* Paragraphs are usually indented ten spaces. A legal document should *never* be typed in block style. The margins of indented material should be five to ten spaces from the margins of the document itself, with an indentation of an additional five spaces for paragraphing the indented material. The right margin of an indentation may be flush with the margin of the document instead of being indented.

A paragraph should never end with the last line of the page. At least one or two lines should be carried over to the next page. This is particularly important in typing wills as a check against omission of pages.

6. *Numbered pages.* Pages should be numbered about one-half inch from the bottom of the sheet, in the center, the number being preceded and followed by a hyphen, thus, -5-. Some attorneys and other professionals require that the total number of pages be given, thus, *5 of 12*, meaning the fifth page in a document of twelve pages.

7. *Signature.* The line for signature should never be on a page by itself. At least two lines of the document in addition to the testimonium clause should appear on the page with the signature. An acknowledgment or an attestation clause following the signature does not obviate this requirement. (See Chapter 9/TESTIMONIUM CLAUSE; ACKNOWLEDGMENT; ATTESTATION.)

8. *Copies.* Duplicate originals (copies that are signed) are typed on the same kind of paper as the original. Other carbon copies may be made on onionskin paper. After the original and duplicate originals are signed, the copies are conformed. (See CONFORMING.)

9. *Erasures and interlineations.* If an error is made involving more than a few letters of a word, the paper should be retyped. The signer of the document must initial interlineations.

10. *Numbers.* Numbers are written in words and repeated in numer-

als in parentheses, for example, *five thousand (5,000)*.

11. *Amounts of money.* Amounts of money are spelled out and repeated in parentheses, the figures in parentheses following the word *dollars*. Each word, except conjunctions, begins with a capital—for example, *Eight Hundred Fifty and 80/100 Dollars ($850.80)*.

12. *Dates.* Dates may be expressed in figures or spelled out. Even if the day of the month is spelled out, the year may be written in figures, thus—the *twenty-first day of August, 1985*.

See also "Z" RULING.

Underlining. See UNDERSCORING.

Underscoring. Underscoring, or underlining, in typed material is equivalent to italics in printed material but is used less freely, probably for appearance' sake. Generally, the underlining is continuous and not broken at the spacing between words, but it may be broken in report headings and title pages for a decorative effect. (See Chapter 8/REPORT.) The following uses of underscoring are recommended:

1. Underscore for emphasis. The dictator indicates when underscoring is to be used for emphasis.

2. Underscore material that is in italics in the original or that you want to appear in italics in typeset and printed material.

3. Underscore to indicate unfamiliar foreign words and phrases or abbreviations of them.

EXCEPTIONS. Do not underscore foreign words that have become a part of English speech through continuous use. If in doubt, consult Webster. Some words are in roman when standing alone but are in italics when used in certain phrases. For example, the word caveat is not italicized but the phrase *caveat emptor* is.

Word processing. The term *word processing* generally refers to all forms of text processing, whether by electric, electronic, or automatic (e.g., magnetic tape) typewriter or by computer or word processor (i.e., a computer dedicated to the task of text production). Specifically, the term is associated with computer handling of text.

Computers and word processors differ in physical appearance, memory capacity, and peripheral equipment. A typical *stand-alone system* would likely have a keyboard, central processor, disk drive(s), storage device, monitor (video-display screen), printer, and perhaps optional equipment such as a modem (to send and receive messages over the telephone lines). *Shared systems* are connected to a larger central computing source, and an operator might work at a terminal having only a keyboard and a monitor. See Chapter 5/BUSINESS MACHINES for a description of the basic components of various types of systems.

Computers are operated with software, often provided on a magnetic diskette the size of a small phonograph record, which is inserted into the system's disk drive(s). *System software* is the program, or instructions, that tell the computer what to do. *Program software* enables you to do certain things such as prepare text or work on an accounting spreadsheet. For example, *word processing software* enables you to type letters, reports, tables, and so on. *Spell-checking*, or *proofreading, software* checks spelling and alerts you to typographical and spelling errors.

Software capabilities. Precisely which operations (e.g., moving a block of copy) you can perform and the steps you must take to accomplish a specific task (e.g., select the text, press a delete key, select the new location, press an insert key) depend on the particular equipment you are using and your word processing program's particular capabilities. Basically, however, a word processing program will enable you to enter text (type a document), change it (edit: delete, insert, move around, or otherwise modify words, sentences, paragraphs, sections, or even whole documents), view your typing on a monitor, print it out on a machine that looks like a typewriter without a keyboard, and file (store) what you typed on a magnetic disk or tape.

Depending on your software, you may be able to format your documents automatically. This means that before you type a letter, for instance, you can type a set of instructions such as space between paragraphs, top and bottom margins of each page, amount of paragraph indentation, and left and right margin settings. Once you have typed those instructions, you can continue typing each new item without figuring out and setting up the same format each

time. Some software will locate a word repeated throughout a document (a *search* feature) and automatically change it to something else if you so specify (a *replace* feature). Perhaps you would want to change all occurrences of *utilize* to *use* but would not want to read the entire document yourself to locate each one.

Operating procedure. Your hardware (equipment) and software (word processing program, proofreading program, and so on) will come with detailed sets of instructions (although you may find it necessary to discover many editing procedures by trial and error). Often to start your equipment, you must insert a systems diskette and then a program diskette, or a combined diskette, followed by a blank diskette on which you will store the new document you want to type. Label the diskette with a felt-tip pen so that you don't damage the highly sensitive surface, and keep magnetic materials away from both equipment and diskettes.

Once the software identification and a blank window appear on the monitor, you can begin typing. You may decide simply to type the text and worry about format (margins and so on) later, or you may want to key in your specific instructions so that as you type the computer will automatically arrange the text as you specify. To delete or insert a word, sentence, or larger block of copy, your software may require that you highlight it on the screen by moving a tiny mark (cursor) over it, after which you press a delete key and then type the corrected material in its place. You can move the cursor around on the monitor by pressing keys with arrows or, depending on your hardware and software, by rolling a hand-held device called a "mouse" over a flat surface such as a desk. As you delete or insert copy, the computer will automatically rearrange the rest of your material accordingly. In other words, you don't have to retype a page or more—only the specific letter, word, or section(s) that you want to revise. Moreover, you don't have to use a carriage return at the end of each line of text. The computer will automatically decide when it is time to begin each new line (a *wrap* feature), although you can intervene and start a new line earlier if you wish by pressing the required key(s) for that operation.

Special keys enable you to jump to the beginning, middle, or end of a document and review what you typed on the screen. If you want to see it on paper, you can press the required keys and activate the printer, which will print out (type) the document according to your initial format specifications. Most keyboards have other special-function keys that you can program yourself. Perhaps you want to repeat some operation throughout a report simply and quickly by pressing a single key each time rather than going through a series of steps with each occurrence.

You should save what you have typed every few pages or every ten to fifteen minutes—in case of a malfunction, then, there will not be a lot of material to retype. The typed material goes into the computer's random-access memory (RAM). Once you

shut down the computer or an electrical jolt interrupts it, the text in RAM is wiped out. So periodically, you must press the required keys to transfer your text from RAM to permanent storage on an internal hard disk or a removable document diskette. In the future, whenever you want to work further on that document, you can insert it and type the name that you gave to it (follow your instruction booklet for naming files), press the required key(s), and the document will appear on the monitor, ready for you to edit it as you wish.

Once you have finished your work for the day, it is important to shut down the printer, monitor, and processing unit in the order specified in your instruction booklet. Remove the diskettes carefully and lock them in a dust-free, secure diskette file or cabinet. If your equipment has a hard disk, you may have a key that locks the central processing or separate disk-drive unit in a case. Or perhaps your document disk can be accessed only by a password known just by authorized personnel. Observe the procedure in your office, and if you have any doubts, be certain to ask your employer for further instructions.

"Z" ruling. Inked ruling placed in a printed law blank when the fill-ins typed on the form do not fill the space provided. The ruling is made to protect the instrument from alteration, as shown here. _____

CHAPTER 2

COMMUNICATIONS:
TELECOMMUNICATIONS,
ELECTRONIC MESSAGES,
AND POSTAL SERVICE

Area codes. The telephone areas identified by three-digit numbers that precede local telephone numbers. See LONG-DISTANCE CALLS and the map of area codes, Figure 1.

Business communication. Any form of communication about business matters. Letters (see Chapter 7/ LETTERS), telex messages (see ELECTRONIC MESSAGE SYSTEMS; see also TELEGRAPH SERVICE, DOMESTIC; INTERNATIONAL COMMUNICATIONS), memos (see Chapter 7/MEMO), and reports (see Chapter 8/REPORT) are forms of business communication. The telephone is one of the media of business communication. (See TELECOMMUNICATIONS SERVICES.)

COD mail. See POSTAL SERVICE.

Cablegram. See INTERNATIONAL COMMUNICATIONS.

Certified mail. See POSTAL SERVICE.

Code address, registered. See INTERNATIONAL COMMUNICATIONS.

Computer communications. See ELECTRONIC MESSAGE SYSTEMS; Chapter 5/BUSINESS MACHINES.

Conference calls. See LONG-DISTANCE CALLS, *Conference calls.*

Delivery services. International, national, and local private delivery services, such as United Parcel Service

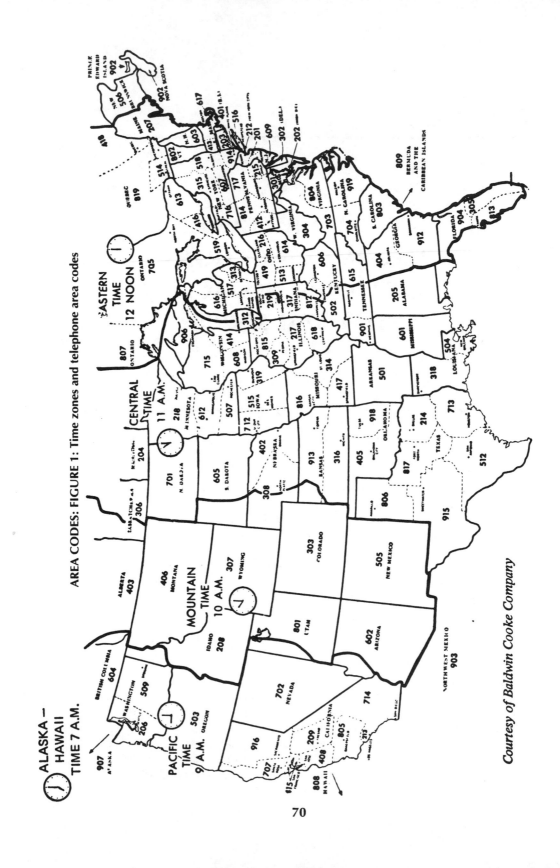

AREA CODES: FIGURE 1: Time zones and telephone area codes

Courtesy of Baldwin Cooke Company

70

and Federal Express, deliver letters and packages, often by both air and ground transportation. In addition to the companies that are devoted exclusively to message and package delivery, other organizations such as bus lines and airlines provide letter and package delivery as a supplementary service. Some services additionally offer other forms of message delivery such as electronic mail and facsimile transmission. (See ELECTRONIC MESSAGE SYSTEMS.) Rate schedules, size and weight restrictions, delivery networks, and services in general vary from one company to another. Delivery time may vary from within an hour locally to one- to two-day service elsewhere.

Pick-up and delivery service is available with many of the private delivery companies. Most also maintain offices locally or in certain cities where you may deliver your letters or packages in person. Some of the organizations provide free kits containing mailing envelopes and boxes. Usually, you can open an account with the company and charge your mailings.

Fast delivery services are usually more expensive than conventional mail delivery. (See POSTAL SERVICE.) To avoid unnecessary expense, secretaries should consider the urgency for delivery. A letter that would usually take several days in transit does not need overnight service if it is mailed on Friday and would simply have to wait at the destination anyway until business offices opened again on Monday. To make the best decisions, compare rates, regulations (size and weight limits, amount of insurance

coverage, and so on), and delivery time of the various companies servicing your area as well as the options available through the U.S. Postal Service.

Domestic postal service. See POSTAL SERVICE.

Domestic telegraph service. See TELEGRAPH SERVICE, DOMESTIC.

Electronic message systems. Generally, systems with the capability of communicating between two points or over a network via terminals; specifically, electronic communications capabilities such as electronic mail.

Electronic Mail (E-mail). A form of message transmission whereby a sender creates (types) a message on a computer terminal or word processor and sends it to a receiver at another terminal, generally over the telephone lines. Users of E-mail can send any type of message or material—letters, reports, graphics, and so on—that can be prepared by computer or word processor.

The E-mail systems in use today are still evolving, and the use of E-mail depends upon the existence of terminals at both the source and the destination. For example, you can transmit only to someone who also has a communicating terminal where your message can be received. Messages in E-mail systems are transmitted to computer "mailboxes," or "files" in a computer, where the messages are held for receivers. An E-mail system may be *centralized* (individual terminals are linked to, or function through, a large central computer) or in the form of a *network* (each individual terminal is capable of transmitting and receiving messages on its own). With computer-based E-mail, multiple users can access the same message.

In addition to private E-mail systems, including local-area networks (LANs) in which computers are wired to one another, public data networks such as MCI offer third parties access to large databases; such a service acts as a clearinghouse for its subscribers' electronic messages.

Although transmission procedures vary depending on the type of equipment and terminal(s) you have, as well as your software, you usually can create (type) a message of any length at any time and, following the instructions in your software, send it to another terminal over the telephone lines. A subscriber service will issue its own additional instructions for accessing its network. By typing the required words and codes on your computer or word processor keyboard, you can learn if there are any messages waiting for you. You also may be able to receive preliminary information such as who sent the message and how long it is. A receiver can read a message, store it, or immediately send a reply.

Since messages are prepared on a computer or communicating word processor keyboard, you can edit them and print out your own hard (paper) copy with your printer. But editing with E-mail software is much more limited than it is with most word processing software. However, firms can design their own E-mail programs.

Messages may be classified according to access by others. A *private electronic "mailbox"* means that only the designated recipients can read their own mail. A *bulletin-board system* means that messages are available for all users to read. Passwords may be used for security, although some E-mail systems have no security measures. Users should determine their particular requirements before subscribing to a service or purchasing E-mail software.

Voice mail. Like E-mail, *voice-mail systems* can also transmit, receive, and store messages and can be accessed from almost any telephone worldwide. With a voice system, however, an operator must intervene to transcribe the message onto paper, whereas a computer-based E-mail system can print out a hard copy when needed. A *voice-data system* is simply an integrated form of system combining the capabilities of both data exchange and voice transmission.

Facsimile. Commonly known as "fax," facsimile is the simplest form of E-mail. Exact copies of material—text or graphics—are transmitted from one machine to another. (The term *transceiver* refers to a machine that can both send and receive.) Thus there is no keyboard or editing capability. The document must be prepared on other equipment such as a word processor and then physically placed on the fax machine. By pressing the required buttons, depending on your particular equipment, the document is scanned, and images are converted into signals that can travel over the telephone lines to a receiving terminal.

Fax machines are classified as *Group I*, older machines that use slower analog (continuous-wave) transmissions of four to six minutes a page; *Group II*, machines built after 1976 that still use the analog technique but transmit at two to three minutes a page; *Group III*, machines standardized in 1980 that use the faster digital technique whereby messages are converted to code and are transmitted at twenty seconds to a minute per page; and *Group IV*, machines being developed now that will use the digital technique and will transmit a page in mere seconds.

For users who purchase their own machines or lease them, facsimiles are simple to use and relatively inexpensive—a page usually costs less than a first-class letter. Also, the machines can be programmed to send and receive when no operator is there. For those who do not want to purchase or lease a machine, fax services are available to transmit documents. Some services provide high-volume users with their own machines; occasional users can deliver a copy to any organization offering fax transmission and have it sent. Large communications services such as ITT World Communications offer not only fax service but telex and other forms of data transmission on a subscription basis.

See also Chapter 5/BUSINESS MACHINES.

Telex. A keyboard-to-keyboard, or terminal-to-terminal type of transmission. The machines designed for telex transmission are commonly known as "teleprinters" or "teletypewriters." (However, various interfaces can convert your computer or word processor into a full telex center, and you can connect your machine to the telephone lines with a modem.) With telex, like E-mail but unlike facsimile, you can prepare and send the message at the same machine. Depending on your equipment, you press the required buttons, or dial in, and send the prepared message over the telephone lines. It is then printed out on a teleprinter at the receiving telex terminal. Telex is considered slower than some of the other forms of transmission (see *Teletex*, below); also, messages must be prepared in all capital letters on a teleprinter keyboard, and the printout quality is inferior to an E-mail computer printout, for example.

Telex I is the original telex. The new Telex II (formerly TWX) uses a different code in transmission and transmits about one hundred words a minute compared to about sixty-seven with Telex I. Both, however, are standard worldwide, and someone who subscribes to Telex I service can communicate with someone else who subscribes to Telex II service. Users must follow the instructions supplied by their particular subscriber service in typing and formatting a message and in sending it. Usually, you press a "call" button to activate service, and you then receive an answerback (identification) exchange. Then the system will prompt you, line by line, what to type. The instructions you receive from your subscriber service will give you a number of codes and abbreviations to use in preparing the message (e.g., CFM = confirm).

Teletex. This service, designed for high-volume users, was first developed and introduced in West Germany in 1981, and Western Union introduced it in the United States in 1983. Teletex users can transmit messages to both teletex and telex subscribers.

Teletex transmission operates about forty-five times the speed of standard telex, and the format and typeface of a teletex message resemble those of a traditional business letter rather than the all-capital letters and inferior print quality of telex. Teletex also has other features such as accents and diacritical marks. The much greater speed of teletex over standard telex often means greater savings as well. (Contact Western Union for current page rates and monthly subscription fees.)

Word processors or computers that are equipped to send and receive messages automatically are used with teletex. Therefore, the system has the editing capability of a word processor or computer.

Leased channel. A service intended for very high-volume users who need more than standard telex or regular telephone service. Some services will lease an exclusive, private communications line between an organization and its overseas office, for example, to transmit telex, voice, facsimile, E-mail, and other messages. Such a line may be leased for a monthly charge regardless of the time or volume usage, or there may be an additional message-unit charge. *Private-line switching* is used when a private line is needed to link a number of company offices. With various switching mechanisms, service companies can interconnect a user's private lines and also connect the private lines with other networks such as telex. Such a system can usually accept and switch messages from any location in the subscriber's communications network to any combination of other locations. A *packet-switching* service interconnects computers or other data terminals and connects data terminals with computing facilities. With this type of service, incompatible systems can communicate with one another, and one can use a wide variety of databases and other services. *Tie lines*, leased from a common carrier such as AT&T, are direct wire links between two points. They may, for example, connect two or more private branch exchanges or provide a link between a firm and Western Union.

Express mail. See POSTAL SERVICE.

FCC. See FEDERAL COMMUNICATIONS COMMISSION (FCC).

Facsimile. See ELECTRONIC MESSAGE SYSTEMS; Chapter 5/BUSINESS MACHINES.

Federal Communications Commission (FCC). An independent government body whose members are appointed by the president and charged with the regulation of all common carriers engaged in interstate or foreign communication by wire or by radio. The commission grants licenses and regulates rates.

Although profane language and lottery-type offers are not permitted by radio transmission, the commission does not have censorship powers.

First-class mail. See POSTAL SERVICE.

Forwarding mail. See POSTAL SERVICE.

Fourth-class mail. See POSTAL SERVICE.

INTELPOST. See POSTAL SERVICE.

I-SAL. See POSTAL SERVICE.

Incoming mail. See Chapter 1/ INCOMING MAIL.

Insured mail. See POSTAL SERVICE.

International cable or radio. See INTERNATIONAL COMMUNICATIONS.

International carriers. Companies that send messages from one country to another, for example, ITT World Communications, RCA Global Communications, and MCI International. In addition to traditional international messages, some of the services offered by these carriers are shore-to-ship and ship-to-shore communication and radio photo service. See INTERNATIONAL COMMUNICATIONS.

International communications. Messages to foreign countries can be sent by a variety of methods: E-mail, facsimile, telex, cablegram, radio, satellite, and conventional mail. If the message is to be sent by telex, it may be sent over a private leased channel or it may be sent through a public subscriber network. A cablegram (international telegram) can be sent through Western Union or any of the international carriers providing this service. The name of the desired carrier should be written or typed on each message immediately after the destination (e.g., Via ITT). A duplicate copy of a typed cablegram can also be sent by facsimile. (See ELECTRONIC MESSAGE SYSTEMS.)

Cablegrams sent through Western Union or one of the international carriers are charged according to words. See *Registered code address,* below. Since each carrier has its own rates and typing instructions, you should request details from the one of your choice. Cablegrams sent through Western Union are classified as follows:

Full-rate messages (FR). This is the standard fast service for messages in plain or secret (coded or ciphered) language. The charge per word varies according to the destination. There is a minimum charge of seven words. Both the address and the signature are counted in the charge. Consult a time chart such as INTERNATIONAL TIME CHART, Figure 1, to determine whether the less expensive letter telegram would arrive in time.

Letter telegrams (LT). Letter telegrams (sometimes known as night letters) provide an overnight service (to certain countries) designed for messages of some length that need not arrive before the next day. They may be written in plain language only; however, registered code ad-

75

dresses may be used (see below). The minimum charge for letter telegrams is for twenty-two words. The address and signature are counted in the charge as well as the indicator *LT*, which must be inserted after the address.

Special classes. One service, *reply prepaid (RP),* allows you to pay in advance for a reply from your overseas addressee. Another service, *paid confirmation (PC),* accepted in some countries, provides for notification of date and time of delivery. Confirmation costs the equivalent of seven extra words at the full-rate message price. To request forwarding, type *FS* before the person's name. To have the message delivered after business hours, type *NUIT* before the person's name.

Radiogram. To send a full-rate cablegram to a ship at sea, type the name of the passenger (in full since there may be more than one with the same last name aboard), his or her stateroom (if known), the ship, the location (e.g., North Atlantic), and the radio station (e.g., use one word such as SANFRANCISCORADIO) in the address. Addresses and signatures are counted as in other international messages. Messages may be filed with an international carrier or Western Union. Type *INTL* above the addressee's name and type the routing indicator (e.g., Via RCA) after the destination.

Radio photo service. This service covers the transmission of photographs by radio. Among the types of material suitable for transmission are financial statements, machine drawings, production curves, fashion designs, architectural designs,

typewritten matter, printed matter, affidavits, contracts, signatures, and business and legal papers of all kinds. Photo service is available to the public through some international carriers such as RCA Global Communications.

Registered code addresses. A charge is made for both the address and the signature in all messages sent to foreign countries. However, a registered code address and signature may be used. They obviate the expense incurred in using full addresses and signatures. You can register through one of the major international carriers or Western Union.

Direct international services. 1. *Networks.* Businesses are linked to numerous countries all over the world by a vast international network of channels. Subscribers to services such as telex can send messages from their own terminals to one of the international carriers and from there have it instantly transmitted to its destination overseas. Companies without equipment can also use an international service such as ITT or Western Union to transmit their messages.

2. *International leased-channel service.* Leased-channel service, rented from the international carriers, offers companies the daily use of a private line between two points. High-volume users can thus enjoy greater speed and economy because a large quantity of information can be sent at a relatively low cost.

3. *Satellite communications.* Messages beamed to a satellite in space are rebeamed to their destination faster

and at less cost than they can be transmitted by telephone. Because this means of transmission is relatively new, it is not as popular as the older technologies, but the speed and economy features should make satellite communications more prominent in future business communications. Like other network communications such as standard telex, satellite transmission service is offered by subscription, and companies can send and receive a variety of communications, such as digital data, facsimile, and digital voice. The largest satellite communications system today is INTELSAT. The marine version, used for contacts with ships or offshore oil rigs, is INMARSAT.

International mail. See POSTAL SERVICE, *International mail.*

International radio. See INTERNATIONAL COMMUNICATIONS.

International telex service. See INTERNATIONAL COMMUNICATIONS, *Direct international services.*

International time chart. Chart showing time differentials throughout the world. (See Figure 1.) Consult TIME ZONE, Figure 1, on time differentials when sending messages to foreign countries.

Interoffice communication. Communication between persons in different offices in the same organization.
Written. See also Chapter 7/ MEMO.
Oral. Communication systems for interoffice use include privately owned equipment as well as inter-

communicating features built into the regular telephone system. Systems vary, depending upon size and sophistication. Some telephones have an inside line that is used for interoffice conversations. Other systems do not use the regular office telephones but provide a separate intercom system for communications between offices. Some of the advantages to be gained with the proper installation are: (1) One can speak to an associate instantly. On some systems, the conversation can be completely private. (2) Information can be obtained from any part of the organization while one is telephoning on outside lines. (3) Intermittent but important dictation can be given to secretaries over the system without waste of time. (4) Throughout the organization, better coordination is secured; delays are eliminated; errors are reduced; executive supervision is increased as interior communication is used to weld the organization together, to eliminate walking and visiting, and to encourage instant follow-through on all work.

Leased-channel service. See ELECTRONIC MESSAGE SYSTEMS; INTERNATIONAL COMMUNICATIONS, *Direct international services.*

Letter telegram. See INTERNATIONAL COMMUNICATIONS.

Long-distance calls. Companies such as AT&T and MCI that provide long-distance telephone service by subscription are called "other common carriers" (OCCs) or "specialized common carriers" (SCCs). Under the

INTERNATIONAL TIME CHART: FIGURE 1: Time differentials throughout the world

Aleutian Islands, Tutuila, Samoa	Hawaiian Islands, Alaska	Tahiti	San Francisco & Pacific Coast	Chicago, Central America (except Panama), Mexico, Winnipeg	Bogota, Havana, Lima, Montreal, Bermuda, New York, Panama	Buenos Aires, Santiago, Puerto Rico, Lapaz, Asuncion	Rio, Santos, Sao Paulo	Iceland	Algiers, Lisbon, London, Paris, Madrid	G.M.T.	Bengazi, Berlin, Oslo, Rome, Tunis, Tripoli, Warsaw, Stockholm	Cairo, Capetown, Istanbul, Moscow	Ethiopia, Iraq, Madagascar	Bombay, Ceylon, New Delhi	Chungking, Changtu, Kunming	Calebes, Hong Kong, Manila, Shanghai	Korea, Japan, Adelaide	Brisbane, Guam, Melbourne, New Guinea, Sydney	Solomon Islands, New Caledonia	Wellington, Auckland*
1:00pm	2:00pm	2:00pm	4:00pm	6:00pm	7:00pm	8:00pm	9:00pm	11:00pm	MIDNIGHT	0000	1:00am	2:00am	3:00am	5:30am	7:00am	8:00am	9:00am	10:00am	11:00am	11:30am
2:00pm	3:00pm	3:00pm	5:00pm	7:00pm	8:00pm	9:00pm	10:00pm	MINUIT	1:00am	0100	2:00am	3:00am	4:00am	6:30am	8:00am	9:00am	10:00am	11:00am	MIDI	12:30pm
3:00pm	4:00pm	4:00pm	6:00pm	8:00pm	9:00pm	10:00pm	11:00pm	1:00am	2:00am	0200	3:00am	4:00am	5:00am	7:30am	9:00am	10:00am	11:00am	Mediodia	1:00pm	1:30pm
4:00pm	5:00pm	5:00pm	7:00pm	9:00pm	10:00pm	11:00pm	Medianoche	2:00am	3:00am	0300	4:00am	5:00am	6:00am	8:30am	10:00am	11:00am	NOON	1:00pm	2:00pm	2:30pm
5:00pm	6:00pm	6:00pm	8:00pm	10:00pm	11:00pm	MIDNIGHT	1:00am	3:00am	4:00am	0400	5:00am	6:00am	7:00am	9:30am	11:00am	MIDI	1:00pm	2:00pm	3:00pm	3:30pm
6:00pm	7:00pm	7:00pm	9:00pm	11:00pm	MINUIT	1:00am	2:00am	4:00am	5:00am	0500	6:00am	7:00am	8:00am	10:30am	Mediodia	1:00pm	2:00pm	3:00pm	4:00pm	4:30pm
7:00pm	8:00pm	8:00pm	10:00pm	Medianoche	1:00am	2:00am	3:00am	5:00am	6:00am	0600	7:00am	8:00am	9:00am	11:30am	1:00pm	2:00pm	3:00pm	4:00pm	5:00pm	5:30pm
8:00pm	9:00pm	9:00pm	11:00pm	1:00am	2:00am	3:00am	4:00am	6:00am	7:00am	0700	8:00am	9:00am	10:00am	12:30pm	2:00pm	3:00pm	4:00pm	5:00pm	6:00pm	6:30pm
9:00pm	10:00pm	10:00pm	MIDNIGHT	2:00am	3:00am	4:00am	5:00am	7:00am	8:00am	0800	9:00am	10:00am	11:00am	1:30pm	3:00pm	4:00pm	5:00pm	6:00pm	7:00pm	7:30pm
10:00pm	11:00pm	11:00pm	1:00am	3:00am	4:00am	5:00am	6:00am	8:00am	9:00am	0900	10:00am	11:00am	NOON	2:30pm	4:00pm	5:00pm	6:00pm	7:00pm	8:00pm	8:30pm
11:00pm	Medianoche	MINUIT	2:00am	4:00am	5:00am	6:00am	7:00am	9:00am	10:00am	1000	11:00am	MIDI	1:00pm	3:30pm	5:00pm	6:00pm	7:00pm	8:00pm	9:00pm	9:30pm
MIDNIGHT	1:00am	1:00am	3:00am	5:00am	6:00am	7:00am	8:00am	10:00am	11:00am	1100	Mediodia	1:00pm	2:00pm	4:30pm	6:00pm	7:00pm	8:00pm	9:00pm	10:00pm	10:30pm
1:00am	2:00am	2:00am	4:00am	6:00am	7:00am	8:00am	9:00am	11:00am	NOON	1200	1:00pm	2:00pm	3:00pm	5:30pm	7:00pm	8:00pm	9:00pm	10:00pm	11:00pm	11:30pm
2:00am	3:00am	3:00am	5:00am	7:00am	8:00am	9:00am	10:00am	MIDI	1:00pm	1300	2:00pm	3:00pm	4:00pm	6:30pm	8:00pm	9:00pm	10:00pm	11:00pm	MINUIT	12:30am
3:00am	4:00am	4:00am	6:00am	8:00am	9:00am	10:00am	11:00am	1:00pm	2:00pm	1400	3:00pm	4:00pm	5:00pm	7:30pm	9:00pm	10:00pm	11:00pm	Medianoche	1:00am	1:30am
4:00am	5:00am	5:00am	7:00am	9:00am	10:00am	11:00am	Mediodia	2:00pm	3:00pm	1500	4:00pm	5:00pm	6:00pm	8:30pm	10:00pm	11:00pm	MIDNIGHT	1:00am	2:00am	2:30am
5:00am	6:00am	6:00am	8:00am	10:00am	11:00am	NOON	1:00pm	3:00pm	4:00pm	1600	5:00pm	6:00pm	7:00pm	9:30pm	11:00pm	MINUIT	1:00am	2:00am	3:00am	3:30am
6:00am	7:00am	7:00am	9:00am	11:00am	MIDI	1:00pm	2:00pm	4:00pm	5:00pm	1700	6:00pm	7:00pm	8:00pm	10:30pm	Medianoche	1:00am	2:00am	3:00am	4:00am	4:30am
7:00am	8:00am	8:00am	10:00am	Mediodia	1:00pm	2:00pm	3:00pm	5:00pm	6:00pm	1800	7:00pm	8:00pm	9:00pm	11:30pm	1:00am	2:00am	3:00am	4:00am	5:00am	5:30am
8:00am	9:00am	9:00am	11:00am	1:00pm	2:00pm	3:00pm	4:00pm	6:00pm	7:00pm	1900	8:00pm	9:00pm	10:00pm	12:30am	2:00am	3:00am	4:00am	5:00am	6:00am	6:30am
9:00am	10:00am	10:00am	NOON	2:00pm	3:00pm	4:00pm	5:00pm	7:00pm	8:00pm	2000	9:00pm	10:00pm	11:00pm	1:30am	3:00am	4:00am	5:00am	6:00am	7:00am	7:30am
10:00am	11:00am	11:00am	1:00pm	3:00pm	4:00pm	5:00pm	6:00pm	8:00pm	9:00pm	2100	10:00pm	11:00pm	MIDNIGHT	2:30am	4:00am	5:00am	6:00am	7:00am	8:00am	8:30am
11:00am	Mediodia	MIDI	2:00pm	4:00pm	5:00pm	6:00pm	7:00pm	9:00pm	10:00pm	2200	11:00pm	MINUIT	1:00am	3:30am	5:00am	6:00am	7:00am	8:00am	9:00am	9:30am
NOON	1:00pm	1:00pm	3:00pm	5:00pm	6:00pm	7:00pm	8:00pm	10:00pm	11:00pm	2300	Medianoche	1:00am	2:00am	4:30am	6:00am	7:00am	8:00am	9:00am	10:00am	10:30am
1:00pm	2:00pm	2:00pm	4:00pm	6:00pm	7:00pm	8:00pm	9:00pm	11:00pm	MIDNIGHT	2400	1:00am	2:00am	3:00am	5:30am	7:00am	8:00am	9:00am	10:00am	11:00am	11:30am

rules of *equal access,* all carriers will have the same access so that you can dial 1 plus long distance with any carrier you choose without adding other numbers representing access codes. However, some carriers may offer other services that involve additional codes. You may, for example, have to dial a customer code to have the cost of a call assigned to a particular customer account on your telephone bill.

Station-to-station and person-to-person calls. A station-to-station call is made when the caller is willing to speak with anyone who answers; a person-to-person call, placed through the operator, is necessary when the caller must speak with a particular person, department, or extension. Although a station-to-station call is usually less expensive, in some cases it is more economical to make a person-to-person call. If the person with whom you wish to speak at the called point is usually difficult to locate, use the person-to-person call, for the time spent in locating the person may run up the cost of a station-to-station call higher than the cost of a person-to-person call. For information on WATS calls, see TELE-COMMUNICATIONS SERVICES.

Messenger calls. If it is necessary to reach someone who does not have a telephone, the operator at the called point may be authorized to send a messenger for the person desired. Whether or not the call is completed, the caller pays the cost of the messenger's service, which is in addition to the regular person-to-person charge for the call.

Appointment calls. In placing a person-to-person call, you may specify a certain time that you will talk with a person. The telephone operator will try to put the call through at the exact time. The charge is the same as for a person-to-person call. The advantage of an appointment call is that it saves time.

Conference calls. Conference service makes it possible for a person to be connected simultaneously with a number of other stations. No special equipment is required. For example, if your employer needs to discuss a contract provision with three other people (or any number up to ten) who are in different cities, by means of a conference call, he or she and the other persons can talk back and forth via long distance as though they were grouped around a conference table.

An executive also can speak to a gathering of employees in different cities instead of to individuals by having the telephone company install loudspeaker equipment appropriate for the number of listeners.

In arranging a conference call, ask the long-distance operator to connect you with the conference operator and explain the setup you want. You will be billed at the person-to-person rate for *each* number to which you are connected.

IDDD (International direct-distance dialing). This service is available from most cities in the United States to numerous countries overseas. To place a call to any of the participating countries, dial the international access code, country code, city code, and then the local telephone number, which could be a two- to seven-digit number.

Mobile calls. You can make local and long-distance calls to automobiles, trucks, aircraft, boats, and ships. Ask the operator for the mobile, marine, or high-seas operator and give the number and party you want to reach. See MOBILE AND SHIP-TO-SHORE CALLS. See also TELECOMMUNICATIONS SERVICES; AREA CODES.

Mailgram. See TELEGRAPH SERVICE, DOMESTIC.

Messenger service. See LONG-DISTANCE CALLS, *Messenger calls.*

Mobile and ship-to-shore calls. This service makes it possible to interconnect mobile units—such as cars, trucks, passenger trains, aircraft, boats, and ships—with the general telephone system. Direct telephone communication with mobile air and marine units eliminates mileage and time required by special trips, thus saving operational costs. Radio equipment is installed on the unit. Equipment may be rented from the telephone company or provided by the owner of the mobile unit. A new cellular technology accommodates more network subscribers and has eliminated the overloaded channels and long waits of precellular mobile transmission. Mobile numbers are listed in the regular telephone directory. To reach an offshore number, ask the operator for the marine or high-seas operator and give the number and party you want to reach.

Money orders. Telegraph. Money may be telegraphed to any place in the United States and to almost any place in the world. The sender fills out a short form provided by the telegraph company. Unless the telegraph company has been instructed to waive identification, the person to whom the money is sent must identify himself or herself to the company. A fee is charged for the service.

Multiple addresses. See TELEGRAPH SERVICE, DOMESTIC, *How to type a telegram.*

Night letter. Class of domestic telegraph message. See TELEGRAPH SERVICE, DOMESTIC.

OCR addressing. See Chapter 7/ ENVELOPES.

Outgoing mail. See Chapter 1/ OUTGOING MAIL.

Overseas calls. It is possible to call almost all important cities throughout the world from any telephone. Rates for this service can be obtained from the long-distance operators. (See also LONG-DISTANCE CALLS, *IDDD (International direct-distance dialing)*; INTERNATIONAL COMMUNICATIONS; MOBILE AND SHIP-TO-SHORE CALLS.)

Overseas telex service. See INTERNATIONAL COMMUNICATIONS.

Parcel post. See POSTAL SERVICE.

Person-to-person telephone calls. See LONG-DISTANCE CALLS.

Postal service. The *Domestic Mail Manual* contains regulations and information about rates and postage, classes of mail, special services, wrapping and mailing requirements, and collection and delivery services. The manual and looseleaf supplementary service help purchasers keep up to date with current information and changes as they occur. The manual and suppplementary service are sold on a subscription basis only. The *National Five-Digit Zip Code and Post Office Directory* lists all post offices arranged alphabetically by states. International mail regulations are described in the *International Mail Manual*, a manual and looseleaf supplementary service sold on a subscription basis. Except for free booklets available at your local post office, publications and subscriptions concerning postal rates and regulations are sold by the Superintendent of Documents, U.S. Government Printing Office, Washington, D.C. 20402.

Domestic postal service. 1. *Classes of mail and special services.* The U.S. Postal Service offers express, first-class, second-class, third-class, and fourth-class mail. Some of the special services, or forms of handling, that the U.S. Postal Service provides are registered mail, certified mail, insurance, collect on delivery, special delivery, special handling, money orders, mailgrams, self-service postal centers, post office lockbox and caller service, philatelic mail order service, first-day cover service, and business-reply mail.

2. *Mailable items and how to dispatch them.* The following list shows the class of mail by which to send each item.

Item	*How to Send*
Bills and statements of account	First class
Birth announcements	First class
Bonds	
Negotiable	Registered first class
Nonnegotiable	First class or certified first class
Books	Fourth class
(Special rates apply to books. The book may be autographed. Mark the package "Special Fourth-Class Rate: Books.")	
Catalogs	Third, fourth class
(Special rates apply to printed catalogs individually addressed and not weighing more than ten pounds. Each piece must be clearly marked "*Catalog.*")	
Checks:	
Filled out	First class
Cancelled	First class
Certified	Registered first class
Endorsed in blank	Registered first class
Circulars	Third class
Currency	Registered first class
Documents:	
No intrinsic value	Certified mail

With intrinsic value:

 Signed originals .... Registered first class

 Copies .... First class

Drawings .... Third class

Form Letters .... Third class

 (Check with the post office for the category of third-class mail best suited to your needs.)

Greeting cards .... First class

Jewelry .... Registered first class

 (Limit of liability is twenty-five thousand dollars. Consult postmaster on limits if other insurance is carried.)

Letters:

 Carbon copies .... First class

 Duplicate copies .... First class

 For delivery to addressee only .... Registered or certified first class

 Form (see Form letters)

 Handwritten or typed .... First class

Magazines .... Second class

Manuscript:

 Without proof sheets .... Fourth class, insured

 (Mark the package "*Special Fourth-Class Rate.*")

 Accompanied by proof sheets .... Third or fourth class, depending on weight

 (Corrections on proof sheets may include insertion of new matter, as well as marginal notes to the printer. The manuscript of one article may not be enclosed with the proof of another unless the matter is mailed at the first-class rate.)

Merchandise (see Packages)

Money Orders .... First class

Newspapers .... Second class

Packages:

 Up to sixteen ounces .... Third class

 Sixteen ounces and over .... Parcel post

 (Packages may be sealed if they bear an inscription authorizing inspection by the postmaster. Packages containing articles valued at not more than five hundred dollars may be insured, but if they contain articles valued at more, they should be sealed and registered. First-class postage will then apply, and the liability limit is twenty-five thousand dollars.)

 Containing personal messages (See ENCLOSURE, 2. *Enclosure larger than the letter.*)

Periodicals .... Second class

Photographs .... Third class

 (Wrap with a cardboard protection and mark the envelope "*Photograph—Do Not Bend.*" Photographs may be autographed.)

Postal Cards .... First class

Postcards .... First class

 (To be mailed at postcard rates, cards cannot be smaller than three and one-half by five inches or four and one-half by six inches. If the card is enclosed in an envelope, it cannot be mailed at the postcard rate. Cards carrying a statement of a past-due account cannot be mailed at the card rate because they must be enclosed in an envelope.)

Plants, seeds, cuttings, scions, bulbs, roots ...	Third class or parcel post depending on weight
Printed matter:	
Less than sixteen ounces	Third class
Sixteen ounces and over	Fourth class
Stock certificates	
Negotiable	Registered first class
Nonnegotiable	First class or certified
Tapes, cassettes, and diskettes:	
Nonpersonal	Special fourth class
Personal	First class

(Mark packages for contents to avoid damage to magnetic surfaces. Mark fourth-class sound packages "SOUND RECORDING.")

Typewritten material	First class

(See also Manuscript.)

3. *Minimum-size standards.* The following minimum-size standards apply to all mailable matter: All mailing pieces must be at least .007 inch thick, and all mailing pieces (other than keys and identification devices) that are one-fourth-inch thick or less must be (1) rectangular, (2) at least three and one-half inches high, and (3) at least five inches long. Anything less than the minimum size is prohibited from the mails.

4. *Nonstandard mail.* First-class mail weighing one ounce or less, single-piece rate third-class mail, and certain international mail weighing one ounce or less are nonstandard and subject to a surcharge in addition to the applicable postage and fees unless they meet the following size standards: (1) length not greater than eleven and one-half inches, (2) height not greater than six and one-eighth inches, (3) thickness not greater than one-fourth inch, and (4) an aspect ratio (ratio of height to length) be-

tween 1:1.3 and 1:2.5 inclusive. Length must not be less than 1.3 or greater than 2.5 times the height.

5. *Classes of mail.* (a) *Express Mail.*® Express service offers reliable expedited delivery of high-priority shipments within the United States and to selected foreign countries. The fastest service, it provides several options for both private and business customers who require reliable overnight delivery of letters and packages.

To use *Express Mail Next Day Service,* take your shipment to any designated Express Mail Post Office by the time designated at the facility. Your mailing will be delivered by 3 p.m. the next day, or it can be picked up by the addressee at a designated post office as early as 10 a.m. the next business day.

Express Mail Custom Designed Service is available only on a scheduled basis between designated locations. Mailers must complete a service agreement (Form 5631) that sets up the place and date of shipment. *Express Mail Same Day Airport Service* is available between designated airports for same-day delivery. Mail must be delivered at an airport facility during times specified by the Postal Service. For more information on requirements and on cities served, consult your postmaster or customer service representative.

(b) *First-class mail.* Letters and cards (under twelve ounces) receive expeditious handling and transportation and free forwarding (for one year) and return and may not be opened for postal inspection. Any mailable matter may be sent as first-class mail. Postcards (commercial), postal cards (Postal Service), personal correspondence, matter wholly or partially in writing or typewriting, bills, and statements of account must be mailed as first-class mail. When first-class matter is included with second-, third-, or fourth-class matter, postage at the first-class rate is required for the letter. The package should be marked "Letter Enclosed."

First-class mail usually will be delivered overnight locally and to certain designated areas if it is properly addressed (including zip code) and deposited in time. The designated overnight delivery area is dependent on transportation accessibility and scheduling. Second-day delivery is scheduled for locally designated states nationwide to which transportation is available for consistent achievement of two-day delivery. Third-day delivery encompasses all remaining outlying areas nationwide.

(c) Presort first-class mail. The Postal Service offers a presort rate that is less than the regular rate for letters and postcards. The presort rate is charged on each piece that is part of a group of ten or more pieces sorted to the same five-digit zip code or a group of fifty or more pieces sorted to the same three-digit zip code prefix. To qualify, a mailing must consist of at least five hundred pieces. Mail that cannot be separated to five or three digits is counted toward the minimum volume but does not qualify for the lower rate. Carrier-route rates apply to each piece that is part of a group of ten or more pieces properly sorted to the same carrier route, rural route, highway contract route, post office box section, or general delivery unit. Each mailing must have a minimum of five hundred pieces. Customers are required to pay an annual fee to take advantage of the presort rate.

(d) *Zip + 4 first-class mail.* This category of postage discounts consists of letters and postcards that are part of a mailing of at least five hundred pieces of a zip + 4 presort mailing or at least two hundred fifty pieces of a zip + 4 nonpresort mailing. The city-state-zip + 4 code line of the address must be located within an area one inch from the left edge of the mailing piece and one inch from the right edge. The bottom line of the address must be at least five-eighths inch from the bottom edge, and the top line must be no more than two and one-fourth inches from the bottom edge. Ask at your local post office for details on having your hard-copy (paper) diskette mailing lists converted to zip + 4 free of charge.

(e) *First-class zone-rated (priority) mail.* First-class zone-rate (priority) mail is first-class mail weighing more than twelve ounces, and rates are based on zoned distances. Except to APOs and FPOs, the maximum weight limit is seventy pounds. The maximum size is 108 inches, length and girth combined. Priority mail may be registered or insured or sent COD or special delivery if the charges for these services are paid in addition to the regular priority mail rate.

(f) *Second-class mail (newspapers and other periodicals).* Second-class mail includes newspapers and other periodicals issued at least four times a year. A publisher or registered news agent who mails at the second-class rate must have a second-class permit obtained from the post office.

To qualify for second-class rates, publishers and news agents must normally distribute primarily to paid subscribers. (For additional information, contact your local post office.) Second-class publications may not be designed primarily for advertising purposes. They must be formed of printed sheets and may not be reproduced by stencil, mimeograph, or hectograph processes. The regular second-class postage rate varies depending on the distance mailed, the advertising portion of the publication's content, and whether the publication is mailed to an address within the county of publication.

Requester publications, whether free or by paid subscription must have at least twenty-four pages but no more than 75 percent advertising.

Mailers must produce a legitimate list of persons who requested the publication.

(g) *Third-class mail (advertising mail and merchandise weighing less than one pound).* Third-class mail consists of circulars, booklets, catalogs, and other printed materials not required to be sent as first-class mail. It also includes merchandise, farm products, and keys. Each piece is limited in weight to less than sixteen ounces. There are two subcategories: single-piece rate and bulk rate.

Third-class mail is subject to postal inspection but may be sealed if clearly marked "Third Class" on the outside. It is advisable to designate the contents on the wrapper, such as "Merchandise" or "Printed Matter." Writing, except something in the nature of an autograph or inscription, is not permitted on third-class matter. "Do not open until Christmas," or a similar legend, may be written on the wrapper; other directions or requests may not. Corrections of typographical errors may be added. Bulk rate requires a bulk-mail permit and is applicable to mailings of pieces separately addressed to different locations in quantities of not less than two hundred pieces or fifty pounds. The pieces must be zip coded, presorted, and bundled or sacked. Ask at your post office for sacking requirements for the various categories (e.g., carrier route) and the requirements for nonprofit organizations.

(h) *Fourth-class mail (parcels).* Parcels weighting one pound or more (except special or library rate) are mailable as fourth-class mail. Generally, parcels weighing a maximum of seventy pounds and measuring up to 108 inches in girth and length combined can be mailed anywhere in the United States (ask at your post office about exceptions).

When mailing larger parcels, you should contact your local post office for appropriate mailing instructions. Be certain that packages are securely prepared for rough handling. Do not seal the package unless it bears an inscription that it may be opened for postal inspection. No communication may be enclosed with a parcel unless additional postage is paid. Invoices and customer's orders that relate entirely to the articles may be enclosed. When articles are being returned for repair, exchange, or credit, no communication, such as "Please credit my account," may be included unless additional postage is paid, but the sales slip may be enclosed. Seasonal greetings may be enclosed. A letter may be enclosed with a parcel if postage is paid on the letter at the first-class rate and on the package at the parcel-post rate. The mail will be dispatched as fourth-class matter. Beneath the postage and above the address, write the words "First-Class Mail Enclosed." Special-handling postage entitles fourth-class mail to the same handling as is given to first-class mail, but not to special delivery by the office of destination. Nor does special handling insure the safe delivery of the mail.

6. *Special services.* (a) *Business-reply mail.* Senders who want to encourage responses by paying the postage for those responses may use the business-reply service. Application is made by filling out U.S. Postal Service Form 3614, for which there is no charge. Mailers pay a fee and guarantee they will pay the postage for all replies that are returned. Two options are available: (1) If an advance deposit is made at the post office, the mailer must pay an accounting charge plus a nonimal amount per piece returned. (2) If no deposit is made, there is no accounting charge; however, the mailer must pay for each piece returned.

Business-reply mail must be identified as such in large letters on the address side of the envelope. Also appearing on the same side must be the permit number, the name of the post office issuing the permit, and the words "No Postage Stamp Necessary if Mailed in the United States." The envelope must also carry the words "Postage Will Be Paid by Addressee" or the inscription "Postage Will Be Paid by" over the name and address of the person or business firm to which the mail is being returned.

(b) *Registered mail.* A high-security service is available for all items mailed as first-class mail, and it is the safest way to send valuable and irreplaceable articles. Registered mail is accounted for during each phase of mail processing and delivery. Registry fees include proof of mailing and proof of delivery, indemnity protection up to twenty-five thousand dollars, and are based on the value of the article. A return receipt showing delivery information is available for an additional nominal fee. Restricted delivery service is also available for an additional fee. Registered mail must be sealed. Mail without intrinsic value may be registered for the minimum fee or certified. See *Certified mail*, below. Priority mail may be registered, and registered mail may be sent COD.

(c) *Certified mail*. Certified mail service is available for all mailable matter of no intrinsic value mailed as first-class mail and provides proof of mailing and delivery. A return receipt showing delivery information is available for an additional fee. Restricted delivery service is also available for an additional fee. Certified mail does not offer indemnity protection and is not available for international mail.

(d) *Insurance*. Most first-, third-, and fourth-class mail may be insured (for the actual value of the article; do not overinsure). Insurance service provides indemnity protection against loss and damage up to five hundred dollars for merchandise. Indemnity levels are based on a graduated fee schedule. Return receipt and restricted delivery services are available for those parcels insured above twenty-five dollars.

(e) *Collect on delivery*. COD is a merchandise payment system that permits postal customers to mail an article for which they have not been paid and have the price of the article as well as the postage collected from the addressee. COD service includes indemnity and is available for first-, third-, and fourth-class mail. Fees are graduated and are based on the amount to be collected or indemnity protection desired. COD service is not available for international mail.

The sender of a COD parcel must guarantee return and forwarding postage. COD mail may be sent special delivery or special handling if fees applying to these services are paid in addition to postage and COD charges.

(f) *Special delivery*. Special delivery is available for all classes of mail except bulk third class and Express Mail. It is available at offices served by city carriers and within a one-mile radius of any post office, station, or branch, except contract stations, branches, or community post offices. This mail is given immediate delivery during prescribed hours. Consult your local post office on its availability at the destination office. It receives preferential handling in processing and fast delivery at the destination post office. It is also delivered on Sundays and holidays. Special delivery fees vary depending on the class of service used and the weight of the article.

Special delivery mail bearing the correct postage and fees can be deposited at all points that first-class mail can be deposited. However, it is recommended that special delivery be deposited at postal facilities to insure the best service. Customers should use special delivery sticker labels, which can be obtained free from the local post office, to identify the mail properly.

(g) *Special handling*. Special handling provides expeditious handling in dispatch and transportation for third-and fourth-class mail but does not provide special delivery. It is available for a fee based on weight and the class of mail.

(h) *Domestic money orders.* Postal Service money orders are a safe and convenient way to send money through the mail and may be purchased at all post offices. They are available in amounts up to seven hundred dollars nationwide. Should your money order be lost or stolen, it will be replaced. Money orders can be redeemed at many banks, stores, and businesses, as well as at all post offices.

(i) *Mailgram service.* Mailgram is a service that enables you to send a message to virtually any address in the continental United States and Canada for delivery on the next business day. You simply call Western Union's toll-free number and dictate your message to the operator. Your message is transmitted electronically to a serving post office close to the recipient where it is delivered by a regular carrier the next business day.

(j) *Self-service postal centers.* Self-service postal centers are customer-operated vending and mailing equipment located in U.S. Postal Service post office lobbies, shopping centers, college campuses, and so on. These centers provide complete mailing information and services for letters and parcels as well as sales of stamps, envelopes, postal cards, stamp booklets, parcel insurance, and individual stamps. Most centers are open twenty-four hours a day, seven days a week. All postal items in U.S. Postal Service machines are sold at face value. Contact your local postmaster for the location of the nearest U.S. Postal Service self-service equipment.

(k) *Post office lockbox and caller service.* Post office lockbox and caller services are premium services provided for the convenience of the public at an addition charge. These two services, provided in additional to available carrier or general delivery, afford customers privacy and permit customers to obtain their mail at their convenience. Lockboxes are accessible during the hours the lobby is open, and caller service is accessible during the hours that window service is available. Both services make use of the traditional post office box number as the address.

(l) *Philatelic mail order service.* The Philatelic Sales Branch provides mail order service for current postage stamps, postal stationary, and other philatelic products, such as commemorative mint sets and *Stamps and Stories.* A free catalog of all items available can be obtained by writing to the Philatelic Sales Branch, Washington, D.C. 20265-9998.

(m) *First-day cover service.* To obtain first-day issue cancellations, customers should send self-addressed envelopes to the postmaster of the official first-day city. Customers may purchase their own new stamps from their local post offices, affix them in the upper right-hand corner of the envelopes, and submit them for cancellation service. Or customers may request the post office to affix the stamps (limit of fifty covers); such requests must enclose a check or money order to cover the value of the postage affixed. Cash will not be accepted. Covers bearing customer-affixed stamps will be given preferential service. Cancelled covers will not be returned in protective envelopes even when furnished by the customer. All requests must be postmarked no later than fifteen days after the date of issuance for stamps and no later than the date of issuance for stationery items. A schedule of upcoming issuances can be obtained by writing to the Philatelic Sales Branch, Washington, D.C. 20265-9998.

Zip Codes. To speed delivery of your mail, use the following tips on the envelope address:

1. Always use the two-letter abbreviation of a state plus the zip code. Capitalize both letters of the abbreviation; do not put periods between the letters; thus, New Jersey—NJ. Do not use any punctuation between the state abbreviation and the zip code or, for OCR addressing, between the city designation and the state abbreviation (see Chapter 7/ENVELOPES).

2. Use only two spaces between the state abbreviation and the zip code. Place the zip code on the same line as the state abbreviation.

3. Use only approved city, street, and place-name abbreviations. See Figure 1 for a list of the traditional state abbreviations and the two-letter state abbreviations used with zip codes.

4. Use zip + 4 (the nine-digit zip code) to facilitate automation. Inquire at your post office about free zip + 4 updating of mailing lists by the Postal Service.

A zip code directory is available for reference in every post office. Copies also may be purchased from Five-Digit Zip Code Directory Orders, Address Information Center, 6060 Primacy Parkway, Suite 101, Memphis, TN 38188-9980. For information about post office sorting, including the optical character reader (OCR), ask at your post office for a copy of *Addressing for Automation.* Also ask for a copy of *A Guide to Business Mail Preparation,* which explains OCR addressing requirements.

International mail. Foreign or international mail is mail deposited for dispatch to points outside the United States and its territories and possessions. Foreign mail is classified as postal union mail, parcel post, and Express Mail International Service.

1. *Postal union mail.* Postal union mail is divided into LC mail and AO mail. *LC mail* (letters and cards) consists of letters, letter packages, aerogrammes, postcards, and postal cards. *AO mail* (other articles) includes printed matter, matter for the blind, and small packets.

(a) *Letters and letter packages.* Personal handwritten or typewritten communications having the character of current correspondence must be sent as LC mail. Do not use envelopes of weak or insubstantial paper. Write the words "LETTER (LETTRE)" on the address side of letters or letter packages that may be mistaken for other articles by reason of their volume or packing. Airmail should be clearly designated by "PAR AVION" in writing or in label form.

The rate for letters and letter packages varies according to the country of destination and for surface or air transport. Merchandise that is liable to customs duty may be for-

POSTAL SERVICE: FIGURE 1: State abbreviations

Traditional and U.S. Postal Service Two-Letter Abbreviations

State	Traditional Abbrev.	Postal Abbrev.	State	Traditional Abbrev.	Postal Abbrev.
Alabama, State of	Ala.	AL	Nebraska, State of	Nebr.	NE
Alaska, State of	Alas.	AK	Nevada, State of	Nev.	NV
Arizona, State of	Ariz.	AZ	New Hampshire, State of	N.H.	NH
Arkansas, State of	Ark.	AR	New Jersey, State of	N.J.	NJ
California, State of	Calif.	CA	New Mexico, State of	N.M.	NM
Canal Zone	CZ	CZ	New York, State of	N.Y.	NY
Colorado, State of	Colo.	CO	North Carolina, State of	N.C.	NC
Connecticut, State of	Conn.	CT	North Dakota, State of	N.D.	ND
Delaware, State of	Del.	DE	Ohio, State of	Ohio	OH
District of Columbia	D.C.	DC	Oklahoma, State of	Okla.	OK
Florida, State of	Fla.	FL	Oregon, State of	Oreg.	OR
Georgia, State of	Ga.	GA	Pennsylvania, Commonwealth of	Pa.	PA
Hawaii, State of	Hawaii	HI	Puerto Rico	P.R.	PR
Idaho, State of	Ida.	ID	Rhode Island and Providence Plantations, State of	R.I.	RI
Illinois, State of	Ill.	IL	South Carolina, State of	S.C.	SC
Indiana, State of	Ind.	IN	South Dakota, State of	S.D.	SD
Iowa, State of	Iowa	IA	Tennessee, State of	Tenn.	TN
Kansas, State of	Kans.	KS	Texas, State of	Tex.	TX
Kentucky, Commonwealth of	Ky.	KY	Utah, State of	Utah	UT
Louisiana, State of	La.	LA	Vermont, State of	Vt.	VT
Maine, State of	Maine	ME	Virgin Islands	V.I.	VI
Maryland, State of	Md.	MD	Virginia, Commonwealth of	Va.	VA
Massachusetts, Commonwealth of	Mass.	MA	Washington, State of	Wash.	WA
Michigan, State of	Mich.	MI	West Virginia, State of	W.Va.	WV
Minnesota, State of	Minn.	MN	Wisconsin, State of	Wis.	WI
Mississippi, State of	Miss.	MS	Wyoming, State of	Wyo.	WY
Missouri, State of	Mo.	MO			
Montana, State of	Mont.	MT			

warded in letters or letter packages to many countries, prepaid at the letter rate of postage, if the importation of the article is permitted by the country of destination. Check with the post office regarding the appropriate form to be filled out and labels to be affixed. Consult the post office for restrictions and requirements in the country of destination.

(b) *Aerogrammes.* Sheets that can be folded in the form of an envelope and sealed. They can be sent to all foreign countries at a uniform rate. Messages are to be written on the inner side of the sheets, and no enclosures are permitted. Aerogrammes manufactured by private concerns, if approved by the U.S. Postal Service, are also accepted for mailing after the required postage has been affixed. Aerogrammes may be registered.

(c) *Postcards and postal cards.* Only single cards are acceptable in international mail; reply-paid cards and folded (double) cards are not accepted. The maximum size is six by four and one-half inches, and the minimum size is five and one-half by three and one-half inches. The rate varies according to country of destination, with surface or air rates applying. Add "PAR AVION" to the left side of the front of the card.

(d) *Printed matter.* Paper on which letters, words, characters, figures or images, or any combination thereof, not having the character of a bill or statement or actual or personal correspondence, have been reproduced in several identical copies by any process other than handwriting or typewriting. Computer-prepared material is considered printed master. In addi-

tion, manuscripts of literary works or of newspapers and scores or sheets of music in manuscript are accepted as printed matter. *Regular printed matter* consists of all printed matter other than books, sheet music, and publisher's second-class publications. The rate for printed matter varies according to the country of destination, with surface and air rates applying. Printed matter may be sealed if postage is paid by permit imprint, postage meter stamps, precancelled stamps, or second-class indicia. Write "PRINTED MATTER" on the wrapper and specify the type of printed matter, such as "BOOKS" or "SHEET MUSIC," since special rate apply to these categories. Write "PAR AVION" for air service. Customs forms may be required in some countries (inquire at your post office).

(e) *Matter for the Blind.* Material admissible in international mail as matter for the blind includes books, periodicals, and other matter in Braille or special type; embossing plates; and voice recordings and special paper for the blind. The weight limit is fifteen pounds. The package should not be sealed. Rates vary according to country of destination and for air transport. The surface rate for this type of matter is free. Write "MATTER FOR THE BLIND" in the upper right corner and add "PAR AVION" for air service.

(f) *Small packets.* A class of postal union mail designed to permit the mailing of small items of merchandise, commercial samples, or documents that do not have the character of current and personal correspondence. Tapes, cassettes, and similar items may be sent as small packets. Philatelic items may be mailed under the small packet classification only to Canada. The postage rates are lower than for letter packages or parcel post and vary according to country of destination and for surface and air transport. Mark the address side of the packet "SMALL PACKET" or its equivalent in a language used in the country of destination. Small packets, whether or not they are subject to customs inspection, must bear the green customs label, Form 2976.

You may enclose in small packets a simple invoice and a slip showing the names and addresses of the sender and addressee. Small packets may not contain any letter, note, or document having the character of actual personal correspondence; coins, bank notes, paper money, postage stamps (cancelled or uncancelled), or any values payable to the bearer; platinum, gold, or silver (manufactured or unmanufactured); precious stones, jewelry, or other precious articles. Some countries will not accept small packets. Consult the post office for restrictions and requirements in the country of destination.

2. *Parcel post.* Parcel post may be sent to almost every country in the world, either by direct or indirect service. The parcels are sent from the United States by surface vessel or by airplane to a port in the country of destination or to a port in an intermediate country to be sent from there to the country of destination. In the latter case, the parcels are subject to transit charges in the intermediate country. Merchandise is permitted but not written communication having the character of current and personal correspondence. Customs and other restrictions and regulations vary with the country of destination. Add "PAR AVION" to the back side of the parcel and label 19 to the address side. Before preparing a parcel to be sent to a foreign country, consult postal authorities.

Pack items in canvas or similar material, double-faced corrugated card-board boxes, solid fiber boxes or cases, thick cardboard boxes, or strong wooden boxes at least half an inch thick. Do not pack in ordinary pasteboard containers. It is permissible to use heavy wrapping paper or water-proof paper as the outside covering of a carton or box, but it may not be used as the only covering of the contents. Boxes with lids screwed or nailed on the bags sewed at the openings may be used, provided they conform to the special provisions of the country of destination.

3. *Express Mail International.* A high-speed class of mail exchanged with forty-nine countries by mutual agreements. One- to two-day delivery is provided, with two types of basic service. *Custom Designed Service* may be picked up from any address or mailed at designated postal facilities. *On Demand Service* is available at designated facilities for nonscheduled expedited service to certain countries. Insurance is available for both services.

4. *Special services. Insurance* and *air service* are available to some coun-

tries. *Special handling* entitles surface parcels, printed matter, matter for the blind, and small packets to preferential handling between the mailing point and the U.S. point of dispatch. COD and certified mail are not available for international mail but *certificates of mailing* furnish evidence of mailing without insurance. *Special delivery* is available to most countries for postal union mail. *Registration* is available to most countries for letters, letter packages, small packets, matter for the blind, and printed matter. *Return receipts* may be purchased at time of mailing. *Restricted delivery* is available to many countries for registered articles only. Other services are *reply coupons* to prepay mail from other countries and *money orders* for safe transmission of money to certain countries. *Recall* and *change of address* services enable a sender to ask for an item to be returned or its address changed. *INTELPOST* is a means of sending exact copies of documents electronically to many countries for pickup within an hour or delivery by regular mail. *I-SAL* (International Surface Air Lift) is a fast bulk-mail system for printed materials to many countries. *International priority airmail* is available anywhere except Canada and saves one day over the usual four- to seven-day delivery of regular air mail. For more information, consult your post office.

Priority mail. See Postal service.

Private delivery services. See Delivery services.

Radio photo service. See International communications.

Registered mail. See Postal service.

Second-class mail. See Postal service.

Ship-to-shore calls. See Mobile and ship-to-shore calls.

Shore-to-ship and ship-to-shore communication. See International communications.

Special delivery mail. See Postal service.

Station-to-station calls. See Long-distance calls.

Telecommunications services. Although the office manager usually is responsible for administering efficient telephone service at minimum cost, the secretary must know how to use—and sometimes help to select—telecommunications services and equipment.

Whereas "other common carriers" or "specialized common carriers" provide service for Long-distance calls, seven regional Bell operating companies (BOCs) provide local service: U.S. West, Pacific Telesis, Southwestern Bell, Bell South, Bell Atlantic, Nynex, and Ameritech. The BOCs offer local and short-distance toll calls and 800/WATS service.

Telephone systems. Two common telephone systems in business offices are the pushbutton, or key, desk telephones and the telephone exchanges, or switching devices.

1. *Pushbutton system.* Pushbutton desk telephones are usually intercon-

nected among various offices as well as connected to outside lines. A variety of accessories may be selected, depending upon office needs, such as *buzzer buttons* to signal others to pick up and take incoming calls or *intercom buttons* that one must push before dialing certain digits to contact someone. Pushbutton desk telephones in an office usually have hold buttons, and many have other features such as programming for *automatic* and *speed dialing*, whereby certain numbers can be called merely by pushing a button or dialing an abbreviated code rather than redialing the full number each time. A *routing capability* means that calls can be transferred automatically from a remote location to another telephone. Some systems have a *message feature* such as a light on the telephone to signal people that the receptionist or secretary has a message for them. Some secretaries use lightweight *headsets* so that their hands will be free while they are talking on the telephone or taking telephone dictation. *Dial safeguards* are small devices that prevent unauthorized persons from making outside calls. *Call sequencers* may indicate which is the next call in line, process unanswered calls after a certain number of rings, or monitor incoming traffic to alert management if more operators are needed. *Speakerphones* channel sound through a speaker so that one or more persons can talk without using the telephone receiver. *Picturephones* enable you to see the person who is calling on a televisionlike screen.

2. *Telephone exchanges.* An exchange, or switching device, also interconnects office telephones and provides access to outside lines. Technology ranges from the early plug-in switchboards, handled by an operator, to the modern computerized systems and the digital equipment that integrates both voice and data. PBX (private branch exchange) systems include the *PMBX* (*private manual branch exchange*), in which the exchange is manually operated; the *PABX* (*private automatic branch exchange*), in which the switching is accomplished automatically; and the *CBX* (*computerized branch exchange*), in which the switching is achieved by computer. Depending on the system you have, you may have to dial a code (such as "g") before placing a call to an outside location. In an exchange, unlike in a pushbutton, or key, system, the switching occurs in a central mechanism that is activated by dialing codes instead of by pushing a button. Also, an exchange can usually accommodate many more telephones than a pushbutton system.

Answering machines. Answering devices, similar to a tape recorder, record messages from callers when you are away. A remote feature enables you to call your number from another location and activate the machine so that it will play the recorded messages for you. Other possible features include a message light indicator, fast forward or backward, quick erase, remote announcement change, message date-time indicator, and telephone recording capability. An *answering service* may be a staffed organization or an automatic device. Usually, the service is connected to your telephone line so that service operators can receive and answer your telephone if it rings a certain number of times while you are away.

Remote call forwarding. This feature means that, through the use of a special code, your calls can be forwarded automatically to ring at another telephone. Some businesses want customers to be able to call a number locally even though the business actually answers the forwarded call in a different location. By having calls forwarded, it may be possible to serve customers in another area without having an office or representative physically located there.

Paging. Sometimes called "beepers" because of the sound they make, paging devices are activated when you have a telephone call, alerting you to go to another telephone and call your office. However, they operate only within a certain area and must be kept with you at all times when you are away from your telephone.

Voice mail. Voice-mail equipment enables callers to leave voice messages or reply with their own voice messages. (See ELECTRONIC MESSAGE SYSTEMS.) In a voice-mail network of subscribers, nonsubscribers can call and leave messages for subscribers even though the nonsubscribers cannot receive or respond to messages through the system. A message can be sent to one or more persons and can be left at any time of the day or night.

Mobile systems. Cellular radio transmission is an improved version of traditional wireless mobile telephone equipment used in cars, planes, trains, and ships. This newer technology will accommodate more network subscribers and has overcome the overloaded channels and long delays characteristic of pre-cellular transmission. Both new and old mobile telephones function with a small radio-computer mounted on the vehicle. Numbers can then be dialed the same as they would from another telephone as long as the vehicle is within the coverage area of a mobile telephone company. Callers can also access the public telephone network with a mobile telephone, so calls can be made worldwide from a mobile unit. Mobile telephone numbers are listed in the regular telephone directory.

Private lines. Private lines can be leased from one of the "other common carriers," such as AT&T, for exclusive use by a company that has a heavy volume of calls to a designated geographic area nationally or internationally. *Tie lines* connect exchanges of a firm in two locations, which means that offices of a company in different locations can communicate without toll calls. A *foreign-exchange line (FX)* enables one to place or receive calls as if one were in another location. A company might, for example, appear to have an office somewhere when it really has a leased line to handle calls to and from that location without toll charges.

WATS. Wide-area telephone service, or WATS, may be inbound or outbound. The necessary lines are installed in a company's offices. Depending on your telephone system, you may first have to dial a code such as "8" and then dial the desired number. When a large number of calls are made to a designated area, an outbound WATS line may be more economical. When a large number of calls come in from a wide area, an inbound WATS line may be more cost effective. Inbound calls are made on a number with an 800 prefix, and these numbers are listed in a special WATS directory. Callers can dial an 800 number long distance at no charge to them. Hence 800 numbers are common in telemarketing or any other business activity in which customer contact is desired and encouraged.

Teleconferencing. Teleconferences, or audioconferences, are simultaneous telephone connections whereby you can talk with more than one person in different locations at the same time. Some firms install special equipment to conduct conferences by telephone. But you can also dial the long-distance operator and explain the simultaneous connections you want. Each connection is billed as a separate person-to-person call. Teleconferences are most successful for short discussions. One to two days of travel time, for instance, would be impractical just for a thirty-minute or one-hour conference. However, as with any meeting, with a teleconference, participants should be notified in advance to avoid delays or absences. A transcript of the meeting can be sent later to the participants. See Chapter 3, "Conferences and Meetings," for details concerning meeting arrangements.

Videoconferencing. Videoconferences use cameras and transmission equipment so that participants can see one another on a televisionlike screen. Firms that use this type of conference may rent or purchase the equipment and facilities, but since they are very expensive, occasional users commonly rent what is needed. A videoconference can be transmitted either by satellite or by terrestrial means. A large conference might involve numerous participants in conference rooms with wide-screen monitors and several cameras. A very small conference might involve only two offices, each with a picturephone, so that the participants in each office could see the others as they would talk by telephone. Videoconferences, like other meetings, require proper planning and conduct during the meeting. Participants should be given advance notice as well, and a paper copy or a videotape of the proceedings can be sent later to the attendees. See Chapter 3, "Conferences and Meetings," for details concerning meeting notices, agendas, and other arrangements.

Telephone calling card. You can obtain a calling card from the telephone company that will permit you to charge your call to your office or home telephone number while you are at another telephone. Follow the instructions you receive with your calling card. Often you are required to dial 0 and next the number you want to reach; you then must wait for a dial tone and enter your calling-card number. To dial another number, you usually do not hang up but simply press # and dial the next number without reentering your calling-card number.

Teleconference. See TELECOMMUNICATIONS SERVICES.

Telegram. See TELEGRAPH SERVICE, DOMESTIC; Chapter 1/TYPING, *Typing Telegrams.*

Telegraph service, domestic. Includes Western Union messages sent by wire to any point in the continental United States, Canada, Mexico, and Saint Pierre and Miquelon Islands. Messages sent to Hawaii and other points overseas are classified as cablegrams. (See INTERNATIONAL COMMUNICATIONS.)

Classes of domestic service. The three principal classes of domestic telegraph service are (1) fast telegram, (2) mailgram, and (3) night letter.

1. *Fast telegram.* The fast telegram is quicker than any other class of service and may be hand delivered two to five hours after being called in. The charge is based on a minimum of fifteen words, with an additional charge for each word in excess of fifteen. Nothing is gained by condensing the message to fewer than fifteen words. The address and signature are not counted as words. Code may be used. Call Western Union for current rates.

2. *Mailgrams.* Mailgrams are sent electronically from Western Union to the post office nearest the addressee and printed out individually. Prefer-ential treatment is given to mailgrams, insuring their delivery in the next regular mail after being received at the destination post office either the same day or the next morning, depending on time of arrival and schedule of mail deliveries.

3. *Night letter.* A night letter is the least expensive message service. Delivery is made on the morning of the next day or the morning of the next business day in the case of a business message. A night letter may be filed with the telegraph company at any time up to 2 a.m. The charge is based on a minimum of one hundred words, with an additional charge for each group of five words in excess of one hundred. The cost of a one hundred-word night letter is less than the cost of a fifteen-word fast telegram. Nothing is gained by condensing the night letter to fewer than one hundred words. The address and the signature are not counted as words. Code may be used.

Money orders. Money orders can be sent through Western Union. The sender may call in and charge the order to Visa or MasterCard or take cash, a check, or money order to the local Western Union office. There is no limit on amount sent if cash is used. Call Western Union beforehand to determine the amount currently accepted by check.

Data-Phone. This service enables users to send photographs, maps, punched cards and tape, and other documents from one machine to another. Units are connected to the business telephone and can instantly transmit material at high speed from one location to another over regular telephone lines. For telex and facsimile messages, see ELECTRONIC MESSAGE SYSTEMS.

How to type a telegram. Most companies simply telephone their messages to Western Union. However, if you prepare typed copy for delivery to Western Union or for transmission by facsimile or some other means, the following guidelines are useful:

1. The number of copies depends on the requirements of your company. Four is the usual number if the telegram is to be picked up by a messenger.
   a. The original for pickup by the telegraph messenger
   b. A copy for confirmation by mail
   c. A copy for your file
   d. A copy for the accounting department (or for your telegraph account file if you pay your employer's telegraph bill)

2. Check the class of service in the form provided on the telegraph blank—domestic service in the upper-left corner, international service in the upper-right corner. Also type the class of service two spaces above the address.

3. Type the date and hour in the upper-right corner, two spaces above the address.

4. Omit the salutation and complimentary close.

5. Double-space the message.

6. Do not divide words at the ends of line.

7. Type as you would any other material. Use caps only for code words.

8. In the lower-left corner type:
   a. Reference initials
   b. How the message is to be sent—*Charge, Paid,* or *Collect*
   c. Address and telephone number of the sender, unless printed on the blank

9. If the telegram is to be charged, type the name of the charge account in the space provided on the blank.

How to send a telegram to multiple addresses. If the same message is to be sent to a number of people, the message is typed only once. All names and addresses are listed on a separate sheet with this notation: "Please send attached message to the following 12 (whatever the number is) addresses."

How to send a telegram to traveling passengers. 1. *Passenger on a train.* A telegram to a passenger on a train is sent in care of the conductor. The address includes the name of the passenger, train name or number, direction in which it is traveling, car and reservation number, station and arrival time, city and state.

2. *Passenger on a plane.* A message may be sent to an airport for delivery to a plane passenger. The address includes the name of the passenger, the name of the airline, flight number and direction in which the plane is traveling, airport and arrival time,

city and state. It is not possible for a plane passenger to receive a message while the plane is in transit.

3. *Passenger on a ship in port.* Treat the location as a land-based destination. Include the full name of the passenger, the name of the port and pier, the steamship line and name of the ship, the stateroom number, and the departure time.

How charges for telegrams are counted. 1. *Addresses.* No charge is made for essential material in one complete address. A charge is made for alternate names or addresses. No charge is made for notations, such as *personal* or *will call.* The telegram may be addressed to the attention of a specific individual without charge.

2. *Signature and address of sender.* No charge is made for the name of the sender. The city and state from which the message is sent are included in the dateline free of charge, but a charge is made for the sender's street address if it is to be transmitted. The signature may include the company name and the name of the individual sending the telegram without charge, but a charge is made for the name of a department added to such a signature.

3. *States, countries, and cities.* In the message itself names of states, countries, and cities are counted according to the number of words they contain. For example, *New York City* is three words, *United States* is two. Running the words together as *Newyork* does not affect the count. If the names are abbreviated, they

count as one word. Thus *NYC* is one word.

4. *Abbreviations.* Abbreviations that do not contain more than five letters are counted as one word. They should be written without spaces or periods—*COD, UN, FOB.*

5. *Initials.* If separated by a space, initials are counted as separate words, but if written without spaces, they are counted as one word for each five letters or fraction thereof. Thus *R L* is counted as two words, but *RL* is one word.

6. *Personal names.* Personal names are counted in accordance with the way they are usually written. Thus *Van der Gren* is counted as three words; *Van Dorn,* as two words; and *O'Connell,* as one word.

7. *Mixed groups of letters and figures.* Mixed groups of letters, figures, and the characters $\$,/,\&,\#,'$ (indicating feet or minutes) and " (indicating inches or seconds) are counted at the rate of five characters, or fraction thereof, to the word in messages between points in the United States and between points in Mexico. Thus *one hundred* is counted as two words, but *100* is counted as one word; *$34.50,* as one word (the decimal is not counted); *44B42,* as one word; but *100th* (six characters), as two words. In messages sent to Canada and Saint Pierre and Miquelon Islands, each figure, affix, bar, dash, and sign in a group is counted as a word.

8. *Punctuation marks.* Punctuation marks are not charged for, but the

words *stop, comma,* and the like are counted.

9. *Compound words.* Compound words that are hyphenated in the dictionary are counted as one word. Thus *son-in-law* is one word. Combinations of two or more dictionary words are counted according to the number of words of which they are composed. Thus *highschool* and *Newyears* are each counted as two words.

How to economize on telegrams and cablegrams. When trying to be economical in the use of telegraphic service, consider three things:

1. The urgency of the message
2. Time differentials
3. The wording of the message

1. *Urgency of message.* In some cases, delivery on the same day may be essential; in others, delivery on the morning of the following day would be satisfactory. The fastest service is, of course, the most expensive; it should therefore be used where speed is necessary.

2. *Time differentials.* Consider the variations in standard time in different parts of the United States and in different countries in choosing the class of service by which to send a message. (See TIME ZONE, Figure 1.)

3. *Wording of message.* Much money can be saved by exercising a little care and ingenuity in the wording of a message. Although terseness should not be carried to the point where the message is not clear, complete sentence structure is not necessary. Verbs, nouns, and adjectives are the important words.

See INTERNATIONAL COMMUNICA-

TIONS for instructions on sending messages to foreign countries.

Telephone. See TELECOMMUNICATIONS SERVICES; LONG-DISTANCE CALLS, *Conference calls, IDDD (International direct-distance dialing);* MOBILE AND SHIP-TO-SHORE CALLS; OVERSEAS CALLS; TELEPHONE LIST.

Telephone directory. The *telephone directory* lists all the business and personal phones in your community, except unlisted numbers and newly installed telephones. The listings include the names of the individuals or companies, their street addresses, and their telephone numbers. They are arranged alphabetically.

The telephone directory also helps you by suggesting alternate spellings of a name. At the beginning of the list of telephone subscribers named *Swaringen,* for example, you will find a note reading, "See also Swearingen, Swearingin."

If you make frequent calls to cities other than those listed in your local telephone directory, you can obtain directories for those areas by calling your local telephone business office and requesting them. Also, many libraries have various telephone books that you can consult for occasional reference.

The yellow pages are especially helpful in locating suppliers of office materials, transportation and meal services, and organizations that may have information you need to collect in the course of your work.

Telephone list. List of frequently called numbers that the secretary keeps in a small directory on the desk. In addition to numbers called frequently on company business, the telephone numbers of the following should be listed: airlines, car rental agencies, building manager or superintendent, emergency calls (fire, police, ambulance, and so on), express office, messenger service, telex and other message services, post office, railroads, travel agency, stationer (office supplies), time of day, typewriter repairs, weather. Personal numbers for your employer that should be listed include: bank, dentist, doctors, family (residence and business), florist, friends whom your employer calls frequently, garage, organizations to which your employer belongs, services (dry cleaner, tailor, and so on), stores, theater ticket agency.

Teleprinter. See Electronic message systems; Chapter 5/Business machines.

Teletex. See Electronic message systems.

Telex. See Electronic Message Systems; International communications.

Third-class mail. See Postal service.

Time differentials. Variations in standard time in different parts of the world. If one Time Zone is on daylight savings time, the normal differential that exists between the zone and another when both are on standard time is increased or de-

creased by one hour. See International time chart, Figure 1.

Time zone. Area to which a particular standard time applies. There are twenty-four time zones in the world. In each zone, the time is uniform and changes by one hour in passing from one zone to the next. The time zones in the United States are eastern, central, mountain, and Pacific, the time being one hour slower in each zone from east to west. (See Area codes, Figure 1.) Thus when it is 8 o'clock in the eastern zone, it is 5 o'clock in the Pacific zone. Figure 1 shows how to calculate the time in foreign countries when eastern standard time is known. To determine standard time overseas, add to or subtract from eastern standard time as indicated.

Typing telegrams. See Chapter 1/ Typing, *Typing telegrams.*

Videoconference. See Telecommunications services.

Voice mail. See Electronic message systems.

Written communication. See Chapter 7, "Correspondence."

Zone, postal. Units of area measured by distance into which the United States is divided for the purpose of calculating parcel post and priority mail rates. There are eight such zones for priority mail and eight zones plus a local zone for fourth-class mail. (See Postal service, 1. *Classes of mail and special services.*

TIME ZONE: FIGURE 1: Chart to determine standard time overseas

To determine STANDARD TIME overseas
add (+) to or subtract (-) from
EASTERN STANDARD TIME as indicated:

	E.S.T.		E.S.T.		E.S.T.
Afghanistan	+9½	Finland	+7	Norway	+6
Albania	+6	Formosa	+13	Pakistan	+10 (5)*
Algeria	+6	France	+6	Panama	0
Argentina	+2	Germany	+6	Paraguay	+1
Aruba	+½	Ghana	+5	Peru	0
Australia	+15 (1)*	Great Britain	+5	Philippines	+13
Austria	+6	Greece	+7	Poland	+6 (6)*
Azores	+3	Guatemala	-1	Portugal	+5
Belgian Congo	+6 (2)*	Haiti	0	Puerto Rico	+1
Belgium	+6	Hawaii	-5	Rhodesia	+7
Bermuda	+1	Hungary	+6	Roumania	+7
Bolivia	+1	Iceland	+4	Salvador (El)	-1
Borneo (Br)	+13	India	+10½	Saudi Arabia	+8 (7)*
Brazil	+2 (3)*	Iran	+8½	Singapore	+12½
Bulgaria	+7	Iraq	+8	Spain	+6
Burma	+11½	Irish Republic	+5	Surinam	+1½
Canal Zone	0	Israel	+7	Sweden	+6
Ceylon	+10½	Italy	+6	Switzerland	+6
Chile	+1	Japan	+14	Syria	+7
China	+13 (4)*	Korea	+13½	Thailand	+12
Colombia	0	Lebanon	+7	Tunisia	+6
Costa Rica	-1	Luxembourg	+6	Turkey	+7
Cuba	0	Madagascar	+8	Union of South Africa	+7
Curacao	+½	Malaya	+12½	USSR	+8 (8)*
Czechoslovakia	+6	Morocco	+5	Uruguay	+2
Denmark	+6	Netherlands	+6	Venezuela	+½
Dominican Republic	0	Netherlands Antilles	+½	Vietnam	+12
Ecuador	0	Newfoundland	+1½	Virgin Islands	+1
Egypt	+7	New Zealand	+17	Yugoslavia	+6
Ethiopia	+8	Nicaragua	-1		

Note: (1)* Brisbane, Canberra, Melbourne,
New South Wales, Sydney, Queensland.
(2)* Leopoldville.
(3)* Rio de Janeiro, Sao Paulo, Santos.
(4)* Hong Kong, Peiping, Shanghai, Tientsin.
(5)* Karachi   (6)* Warsaw   (7)* Djeddah   (8)* Moscow

102

CHAPTER 3

CONFERENCES AND MEETINGS

Adjourned meeting. Continuation of a MEETING that was originally postponed (adjourned), because a QUORUM was not present or for some other reason that prevented action from being concluded until a later date. If the necessary quorum fail to attend a STOCKHOLDERS' MEETING, for example, the meeting must adjourn to another time, in the manner fixed by the statute, charter, or bylaws. This is the only legal action that can be taken. At any adjourned meeting, new transactions are permitted only if all of the stockholders consent to them.

The chair may disregard that the meeting is a continuation meeting and allow new stockholders of record and stockholders who were not present or represented at the original meeting to vote.

The principles governing adjourned meetings of stockholders, as explained above, apply to directors' meetings and other formal organizational meetings as well. See ADJOURNMENT.

Adjournment. The act of postponing a meeting until another time (see ADJOURNED MEETING) or indefinitely. The adjournment may be to a certain day or SINE DIE—that is, without naming a day and finally terminating the meeting—or subject to the call of the chair. In a committee, a motion "to rise" has the same effect as an adjournment in an assembly. The motion to adjourn specifies which form of adjournment will be taken, and if none is specified, the adjournment is final and puts an end to all unfinished business. Such business, however, can be introduced again at another meeting as if it had not been brought up previously.

A *recess* is an adjournment for a limited time, such as a thirty-minute coffee break.

Agenda. (pl). Digests of matters to be treated or upon which action is to be taken at a meeting; sometimes termed the ORDER OF BUSINESS. The following form illustrates an agenda prepared for a directors' meeting.

Agenda of Directors' Meeting

AGENDA OF BOARD MEETING

————————, 19———,

at the Company

Offices————————————City

1. Read minutes of last meeting. (Attached to the agenda will be a typewritten copy of the minutes of the previous meeting.)

2. Submit the following statements: (Here enumerate the reports to be presented to the meeting. Copies of the reports may be attached to the agenda.)

3. Adopt resolution approving minutes of the Executive Committee meetings. (If minutes are long, copies may be made and attached to the agenda. See Chapter 13/EXECUTIVE COMMITTEE.)

4. Adopt resolution authorizing transfer agent and register to issue certificate of stock in place of lost certificate of ————————. (*The action to be taken may be sufficiently well described to indicate the nature of the resolution that will be drafted by the secretary or the resolution may be framed in advance by the secretary and attached to the agenda.*)

(*Here follows an enumeration of other new business to be acted upon, each item being indicated by a summary of the resolution that is required.*)

Type the agenda on eight-and-one-half-by-eleven-inch paper. Follow the practice in your office concerning the number of drafts to prepare. You will be expected to prepare at least one rough draft for the chairperson and perhaps several if the agenda is revised a number of times before it is final.

The exhibits and supporting papers, statements, reports, and so forth that contain the information necessary to supply the groundwork for discussion are usually attached to the agenda. One plan is to prepare for each director a binder with numbered tabs, each tab corresponding with the numbered item on the agenda. Copies of all pertinent papers, reports, statements, or other material are placed behind the proper tabs.

The agenda may be prepared several days before the meeting. Some matters of a confidential nature should be omitted and presented at the meeting at some suitable time, thereby breaking the order of the agenda. Some executives request items for the agenda in advance. Often such a request accompanies the NOTICE OF MEETING.

Annual meeting. In corporation affairs, the yearly meeting of stockholders for the election of directors. (See STOCKHOLDERS' MEETINGS.) In other organizations, the annual meeting may refer to the combined annual meeting and CONFERENCE, with presentation of lectures, workshops, and so on.

Appointment. A prearranged meeting. The date, time, and purpose of all business appointments should be entered on a calendar or appointment book. (See Chapter 5/CALENDARS.) Each morning the secretary should place on his or her employer's desk a typed schedule of appointments, showing where and with whom each appointment is to be held, the purpose of it, and any additional pertinent information. Memo paper, about six by nine inches, is desirable for this purpose. At the time of each appointment, the secretary should give his or her employer any material that will be needed for the meeting.

Appointments for a month. Many executives like to see the month's engagements at a glance. Figure 1 illustrates a calendar designed for this purpose. It is made of cardboard and is about nine by eleven inches.

Under the arrangement of dates on this calendar, every Sunday in the month is on the top row, every Monday on the next row, and so on.

See Chapter 4/TRAVEL APPOINTMENT SCHEDULE for form of appointment schedule when an executive travels.

For model letters requesting appointments and replies to letters asking for appointments, refer to Chapter 7/APPOINTMENT LETTERS.

Appointment calls. See Chapter 2/ LONG-DISTANCE CALLS.

Call of directors' meetings. The bylaws of the corporation generally indicate who has authority to call meetings of the board of directors,

APPOINTMENT: FIGURE 1: Appointment calendar for a month

NOVEMBER 1988				
	Sunday, 6th	Sunday, 13th	Sunday, 20th	Sunday, 27th
	Monday, 7th	Monday, 14th	Monday, 21st	Monday, 28th
Tuesday 1st	Tuesday, 8th	Tuesday, 15th	Tuesday, 22nd	Tuesday, 29th
Wednesday 2nd	Wednesday, 9th	Wednesday, 16th	Wednesday, 23rd	Wednesday, 30th
Thursday, 3rd	Thursday, 10th	Thursday, 17th	Thursday, 24th	
Friday, 4th	Friday, 11th	Friday, 18th	Friday, 25th	
Saturday, 5th	Saturday, 12th	Saturday, 19th	Saturday, 26th	

although sometimes this subject is covered by statute. The meeting must be called by the person authorized, but if the designated officer does not send the notices, another officer may do so. The duty of calling a meeting is frequently delegated to the chairperson of the board, or in the chair's absence, to the president. Provision is also generally made that meetings may be called upon written direction of a certain number of directors.

The manner of calling directors' meetings is controlled by the charter, or articles of incorporation, and bylaws, not by an agreement among corporate stockholders or organizational members. In the absence of other provisions in the statute or bylaws of the organization, the meeting need not be called in any particular manner. If all of the directors receive proper notice, the meeting will be valid. Such notice may consist of a typed (e.g., typewriter or computer-word processor) letter, memo, or telegram or a printed or photocopied form. The one-paragraph form below, if prepared on regular business stationery, may be double-spaced.

Call of Regular Meeting of Directors by President

_____, 19 ____

To the Directors of _____ Corporation:

The undersigned, President of the _____ Corporation, hereby calls the regular monthly meeting of the Board of Directors of said Corporation, to be held at the office of the Corporation, _____ (Street), _____ (City), _____ (State), on the _____ day of _____ , 19 ___, at ___ o'clock in the ___ noon.

_____ President

Follow the provisions of the charter, or articles of incorporation, or of the bylaws concerning the number of days of advance notice required to call a meeting. If no formal requirements exist, mail a call or notice in sufficient time for out-of-town directors to make travel and hotel arrangements. When time permits, reply slips may be enclosed for participants to use in acknowledging the call or notice and indicating whether they will attend. Other material also may be enclosed, such as a preliminary agenda and various reports. The mailing may also include a request for agenda topics, that is, matters to be discussed at the meeting.

Call of stockholders' meeting. A person with the power to bring a meeting into being may issue a call that ordinarily consists of written direction to the corporate secretary or other officer authorized to notify the stockholders. It is proper practice to have the call signed by the president or other authorized officer. In some instances, it is required that a copy of the call be posted on a bulletin board in the main office of the corporation. See Notice of meeting.

It is a common irregularity in corporate procedure for the call and notice of a meeting to be combined, and care should be taken to avoid this.

The bylaws generally indicate who may call regular and special meetings of stockholders. Occasionally, the provisions governing the calling of meetings are found in the certificate of incorporation. In many states, the manner of calling meetings is fixed by statute. If there is a conflict between the bylaws and the statute about who shall make the call, the statute controls. If neither the bylaws nor the statute designates who shall call meetings of the stockholders, the directors, acting as a board, are the proper officers to do so, and they may call a meeting whenever they deem it necessary.

Prepare the call on the appropriate business letterhead. A form, such as the following example, of more than one paragraph is usually single-spaced with a double space between paragraphs the same as any other business letter or memo.

Call of Regular Annual Meeting of Stockholders by President

To _____ ,
Secretary of _____ Corporation:

The regular annual meeting of stockholders of the _____ Corporation is hereby called for _____ (*Day of Week*), the ____ day of _____ , 19 ____, at _____ o'clock in the _____ noon, to be held at the principal office of the Corporation at _____ ____ (*Street*), _____ (*City*), ____ ____ (*State*), for the following purposes:
(*Insert purposes.*)

You are hereby directed, as Secretary of said Corporation, to give proper notice of said meeting to the stockholders of said Corporation, as prescribed by the bylaws thereof.

_____
President
Dated _____ , 19____.

Called meeting.   A synonym for a corporation's SPECIAL MEETING, or special purpose meeting, as distinguished from its periodically scheduled REGULAR MEETING. See STOCKHOLDERS' MEETINGS.

Conference.   A meeting for discussion and interchange of opinions, views, and ideas. Conferences among the executives of a company are essential to modern business management. Although useful, they are undoubtedly time consuming and in some companies are carried to the extreme. To eliminate time-wasting conferences and committees, some companies appoint a conference manager; no conference can be called without the conference manager's approval. Most companies prefer informal conferences in which executives feel free to speak out. (See also LOADED CONFERENCE.)

Conferences are also held among top executives of various companies. Hundreds of top executives spend between twenty and thirty days a year at conferences for the exchange of information, knowhow, and ideas. These conferences, also called conventions, are arranged and sponsored by associations, such as the American Management Association, and a registration fee is charged.

Conference preparations.   The manager may be in charge of conference preparations or at least some aspect of planning activities. His or her secretary may thus be involved in making arrangements for meeting rooms, speakers' invitations, meals, registration, programs and mailing lists, special events, and equipment rentals.

1. *Room reservations.* After the conference site and hotel, motel, or convention center have been selected, the facility will designate a representative to work with the conference planners in reserving meeting rooms of adequate size, with proper acoustics, and able to accommodate audiovisual and other equipment that speakers may use.

2. *Speakers.* Invitations to speak at a conference are generally extended by letter or by combination letter and phone call from the person in charge of these arrangements. Standby speakers are common since someone inevitably drops out at the last minute. Even when speakers are not compensated, it is customary to give each one a small gift or conference memento.

3. *Meals.* The facility where the conference will be held will designate a representative to work with the planning committee in selecting menus and projecting the number of meals required and the size of room for service. Usually a certain number must be guaranteed, that is, paid for even if fewer persons arrive for each meal. Therefore, estimating attendance at mealtime is very important to control costs.

4. *Registration.* This is the area of activity in which the secretary is most often involved. After registration forms are printed and mailed, the actual registrations begin arriving; some may be made by telephone. The secretary must keep careful records, both of the registrations and the checks that accompany them. If the completed forms indicate which sessions the registrant wants to attend, a tally should be supplied to the manager daily, so that he or she will know when a particular session has reached maximum allowable attendance. The amount of monies received must also be reported daily, to allow the manager to determine pending budgetary matters. Registrants who have not paid must be billed promptly. All registrations must be acknowledged and refunds on cancellations made. Preprinted confirmation slips are almost essential if there are more than a hundred registrants. Some registration forms have a tab that can be detached and returned to the registrant. All forms should be filed, usually alphabetically, so that they can be retrieved instantly. Usually, all forms and necessary records are transported to the conference site for use by registration clerks at the registration desk as registrants check in. A copy of the forms, or a list of registrants, with name, address, and pertinent information, must be kept in the office, however, as a safeguard should the other be lost in transit or at the conference. If a list is maintained by computer, additions, deletions, and other changes can be edited in and an updated list printed out each day or as needed.

5. *Programs and mailing lists.* The program committee must collect enough information on speakers, sessions, and other conference activity to organize a program, which must be typeset and printed—all in adequate time for mailing. Programs should reach prospective registrants four to six weeks in advance, to allow them

time to make travel plans, request travel expense funds from their companies, and so on. A decision must be made whether to mail programs first class (faster, but more expensive) or third class (more economical, but at least three weeks, preferably four, of mail time should be allowed if the mailing is nationwide). It is rarely possible to delay the preparation of the program until the name of every speaker is known. Typesetting, printing, addressing, and mailing time must be considered in making all deadlines.

Mailing lists often come from many sources—associations, trade publications, directories, mailing houses, and in-house lists of previous conference attendees, customers, and prospects. There may be a charge for use of certain lists. In addition to the mailing of the programs, other types of promotion are essential—news releases, radio or TV announcements, flyers for company bulletin boards, and so on. An airline will sometimes contribute to printing and mailing costs or provide free mailings if the sponsoring organization will designate it the official airline for the conference or will allow the airline to include advertising in the program package.

6. *Special events.* Many conferences include special events, such as a dinner-dance, especially if both husbands and wives attend. These events require room reservations, meal planning, arrangements for speakers and entertainment, and the printing and sale of tickets or the preparation and mailing of invita-

tions. Preconference publicity should include mention of special events.

7. *Equipment rental.* Invitations to speakers often include a form for them to complete and return that specifies equipment needs. Audiovisual equipment, for instance, is almost always a must. If the facility does not provide required equipment, it must be rented, with arrangements for rental and delivery and pickup made in advance. The representative at the conference facility should be consulted first about such arrangements. Most facilities provide extensive service of all kinds and are happy to assist in making nearly all arrangements. However, even the best possible service should be monitored closely so there are no embarrassing slipups during the meeting.

Other secretarial duties. 1. Note all important deadlines (printing, mailing, etc.) on your calendar and your employer's calendar.

2. Put the names of registrants on the mailing list (e.g., three-by-five-inch card file or computer list) that you maintain for conference mailings.

3. Make up a detailed checklist of things you and your employer want to do before the conference, another of things to take along to the conference, and one of things to do at the conference.

Convention. See CONFERENCE.

Directors' meetings. Formal meetings or assemblies of the individual directors of a corporation for the purpose of taking joint action on business of the corporation. The board of directors, acting as a body, has sole authority to manage the corporation in those matters not reserved for action by stockholders.

A casual and informal meeting of all the directors, without a record of the meeting, is not a legal meeting, except in three cases: (1) If by usage or custom the directors have managed the affairs of the corporation without formal meetings, and the corporation and its stockholders have by long practice acquiesced in an informal manner of doing business, the acts of the directors, if they are within the scope of their powers, are valid, for otherwise great injury might be done to third persons relying on this course of conduct. (2) If the stockholders or directors with knowledge of the facts acquiesce in informal action taken by the directors, they are bound by that action. (3) If the directors are themselves the only stockholders, action taken by all of them informally and without a meeting is corporate action.

Kinds of directors' meetings. Meetings of directors may be either regular or special. The only difference is in the matter of notice. If there is no evidence that the meeting was regular, it will be presumed to have been special. *Regular meetings* are called at the time and place and in the manner provided for in the bylaws or in the statutes. *Special meetings* may be called at any time as provided in the bylaws. The manner of calling special meetings may be fixed by the bylaws or by statute.

Place of directors' meetings. The directors' meetings should be held at the place and time designated in the NOTICE OF MEETING, which should not conflict with the requirements of the statute, charter, or bylaws.

Preparations. The corporate secretary, who usually is responsible for preparation for a directors' meeting, ordinarily takes the following steps.

1. He or she gathers data to be presented at the meeting.

When the corporate secretary is almost entirely responsible for the program of meetings, he or she may confer with the various officers who have business to submit, gather from them the material that will be referred to at the meeting, and examine the papers to determine what further steps can be taken to facilitate action at the meeting.

In addition, the corporate secretary should accumulate in advance all necessary notes and material, and keep them in a board basket or meeting folder. (See Chapter 5/BOARD BASKET.)

2. The corporate secretary also sends a notice of the meeting to the directors. (See NOTICE OF MEETING.)

3. He or she writes the directors' meeting agenda.

4. The corporate secretary arranges for payment of fees to directors whenever they are to receive fees for attending the meeting, by requisitioning the required funds from the corporation treasurer.

5. He or she makes preparations for recording the minutes of the meeting.

Preliminary approval of business to be transacted. In some organizations, the rule is adopted that before any matter can be brought to the attention of the directors, it must have the unanimous approval of all officers, meeting as an executive cabinet. In others, it is the custom to hold meetings of executives in advance of the meetings of the board of directors, at which matters to be brought before the board are discussed. These meetings are sometimes formal, and the views of each executive are noted. When the opinion for a given proposal is unanimous, the matter is referred to either the corporate secretary or the legal department for preparation of resolutions. Otherwise the subject is dropped or is held for further discussion.

In some large corporations, special committees are appointed to confer with the officer or department head who advocates the consideration of a certain question by the board of directors. In some cases, after the special committee has recommended action, the matter must then be passed upon by the executive committee before it may be placed in the order of business. The usual practice seems to be not to hold formal meetings of executives or officers for the discussion of resolutions but to have the president or the chairperson of the board discuss them informally with the interested officers. Frequently, the office secretary is called into such conferences to take notes and prepare a memo on the views expressed.

Matters to be passed upon by the board of directors of large corporations are frequently discussed at meetings of the executive committee or the financial or other committee. The action of the board is then based entirely on the action of the committee.

Quorum. It should be understood that the presence of a QUORUM at a meeting is necessary to enable the directors to transact business.

Conduct of directors' meetings. In the case of small corporations, meetings of the board of directors are usually conducted in an informal manner. Larger corporations, however, often conduct their directors' meetings with considerable formality. The president usually presides at meetings of the directors, unless some other provision is made by the bylaws.

Votes are usually taken in an informal manner, generally by a call for yes and no answers. The ORDER OF BUSINESS varies, but the following order is followed in many organizations:

1. Call to order

2. Announcement of a quorum present

3. Reading and approval of the minutes of the previous meeting

4. Reports of officers and committees

5. Old business

6. Declaration of dividend, if one is to be declared

7. New business

8. Nomination and election of new officers
9. Committee appointments
10. Announcements
11. Adjournment

Docket. In corporation terminology, the AGENDA, or list of matters to be taken up at a meeting. The term is seldom used today. See instead Chapter 9/DOCKET.

First meeting of stockholders. The meeting of prospective stockholders for the purpose of organizing and incorporating a corporation; an INCORPORATORS' MEETING. This meeting must be held in the state of incorporation.

Incorporators' meeting. The formal organizational meeting of the incorporators for the purpose of complying with state statutes or laws governing the completion of organization of a corporation.

Loaded conference. A CONFERENCE called after the executive calling it has talked informally with the conferees and thus assured himself or herself that they are in agreement about some matter to be resolved. The time-wasting formal conference is called to protect the executive from criticism if the action decided upon is not successful.

Meeting. A gathering or assembly of persons, such as a corporation's STOCKHOLDERS' MEETING, or a committee meeting, usually for the purpose of discussing and deciding a particular matter or matters. At least two kinds of meetings must be held by every corporation organized for profit: (1) STOCKHOLDERS' MEETINGS, often called "corporate meetings," and (2) DIRECTORS' MEETINGS. Meetings of committees, such as the Executive Committee and Finance Committee, may also be held, particularly in large corporations. See Chapter 10/EXECUTIVE COMMITTEE; FINANCE COMMITTEE.

Schedule of meetings. The list of stockholders' and directors' meetings to be held during the year is prepared in advance by the corporate secretary in order that preparations for each particular meeting may begin in time. If no definite time has been fixed by the bylaws or by resolution for all of the meetings that will be held, the schedule may be made up on the basis of tentative dates. (See Chapter 10/RESOLUTION.) Figure 1 illustrates a form in which the schedule may be prepared.

Consult your office copy of the bylaws for the required dates of meetings. Your employer will give you the meeting dates not specified in the by-laws. Type them in the appropriate monthly column. Information for other columns pertaining to date, place, and notice requirements can also be taken from the bylaws. Fill in the information about business to be discussed, who calls the meeting, and remarks at the time each meeting is called.

Meeting file. The permanent file of essential material needed for corporate meetings. In many organizations, the office secretary helps prepare and maintain this file. In it are

MEETING: FIGURE 1: Schedule of meetings

CHART OF MEETINGS FOR THE YEAR

Company	Meeting	Specified Date as per Bylaws	Jan	Feb	Mar	Apr	May	June	July	Aug	Sep	Oct	Nov	Dec	Time	Place Specified		Notice Required	Business Spec'f'd	Called By	Remarks
																Bylaws	Call				
....Co., Inc.	Stockholders' Annual																				
Ch. of Bd.	Directors' Annual																				
Pres.	Directors' Regular																				
Secy.	Directors' Special																				
	Stockholders' Special																				
.... Corp.	Stockholders' Annual																				
Ch. of Bd.	Directors' Annual																				
Pres.	Directors' Regular																				
Secy.	Directors' Special																				
	Stockholders' Special																				

kept a pamphlet copy of the corporation laws of the state in which the corporation is organized, a copy of the corporation's charter and bylaws; with amendments, and other papers of a similar nature that may be needed at any corporate meeting. In addition, the file contains other data that both the office secretary and the corporate secretary or the manager accumulate as preparations for a particular meeting are being made. After the particular meeting has taken place, the papers in the meeting file pertaining to the particular meeting are removed, and only the documents mentioned as necessary for all meetings remain in the file.

Meeting folder. A file folder in which the office secretary helps collect notes and material to be used at a forthcoming corporation meeting, such as a board of directors' meeting. Similar to a meeting file.

The meeting folder, as its name implies, is merely a bound folder. The particular meeting to which it applies is indicated on the cover. In this folder are placed all documents and papers pertaining to matters to be discussed at the meeting, as well as a copy of the call of the meeting and of the notice of meeting, a form of report to the cashier of directors' fees, a skeleton of the minutes, any proposed votes or other business received at the corporate secretary's office before the meeting, and a form of memo for mailing extracts of minutes. A similar folder might be prepared for any executive who will be attending a meeting. If several folders are needed, use different colored labels or in some way mark

them so your employer can find material quickly and easily during the meeting.

Envelope file of memos. This method is similar to the meeting folder method in that the envelope contains the material that will be referred to at the meeting. It is somewhat different, however, in that the face of the envelope constitutes a page for entries of material received and at the same time furnishes a list from which the corporate secretary will make up a schedule of business to be taken up at the meeting.

Meetings held by proxy. When meetings of stockholders must be held at the principal office in the state in which the organization is organized, because either the statute or charter so provides, or for reasons of expediency, and the corporation is merely represented in the state by a resident agent (see Chapter 10/RESIDENT AGENT), the meetings of the stockholders may be held entirely by PROXY and conducted by the resident agent.

The minutes of such a meeting are prepared in advance of the meeting, with the names of the persons present as proxies omitted so that they may be inserted after the meeting has been held. Ordinarily, the minutes are prepared by a corporation service company and examined and approved by the corporation's attorney. (See Chapter 10/CORPORATION SERVICE COMPANY.)

This method of holding meetings is generally used only in instances in which the corporation is small, a close corporation, or a subsidiary corporation entirely owned by a parent corporation. (See Chapter 10/ Close corporation; Subsidiary; Parent corporation.) The preparations for a meeting held entirely by proxy should be left to the attorney of the corporation and should not be undertaken by the corporate secretary. As far as the corporate secretary is concerned, he or she has no preparation to make for such a meeting beyond that of furnishing the attorney with any data requested. After the meeting has been held, the secretary will receive the proxies for filing, together with a complete copy of the minutes of the meeting.

As far as the attorney is concerned, his or her preparations depend on the extent of the services to be rendered by the outside organization. The attorney may leave the preparation of notices, proxies, list of stockholders, and minutes of the meeting to the outside organization and merely check the work done, or the attoney's office staff may attend to these matters.

See also Conference; Secretarial staff meetings.

Minutes. The official record of proceedings at a meeting. Specifically, in the plural, the word *minutes* means the official record of the proceedings at a meeting of an organized body, such as the stockholders or directors of a corporation.

Generally, the corporate secretary acts as secretary of all corporate meetings and keeps the minutes of those meetings. The office secretary may be asked to take the minutes in shorthand during the meeting in addition to transcribing a recorded version.

When you are given this task, compile a seating chart to help you recognize persons who are speaking. Figure 1 is a form you can use to record resolutions. In addition, keep handy copies of reports and other material so that you can quickly doublecheck facts and figures in your notes. Since minutes are legal evidence of action taken, they should be clear, concise, and unambiguous. The general form of minutes is fairly well standardized. (See the example below.) After a heading designating whether the meeting is a stockholders,' directors', committee, or other meeting, the minutes usually (1) begin with the time and place of meeting; (2) establish that the meeting was properly called; (3) show that notice was given or waived (see Waiver of notice); (4) give the names of the chairperson and secretary of the meeting; (5) in a stockholders' meeting, state the amount of stock represented in person or by Proxy, thus indicating whether a Quorum was present; in a directors', committee, or other meeting, list those present; and (6) state that the minutes of the previous meeting were read.

The additional subject matter of the meeting consists of a clear, accurate, and complete report of all business transacted. The names of proposers and seconders of Motions are sometimes omitted unless required for legal purposes. In most cases, it is not necessary that the names of those voting for or against a proposition be recorded, but if special request is made for the recording of dissenting votes by a minority, the entries should be so made by the secretary taking the

MINUTES: FIGURE 1: Secretary's memo form for entering notes of minutes at a meeting

	SECRETARY'S MEMO *MEETING OF BOARD OF DIRECTORS*
	Stated Reg. Notice Annual Personal
ORGANIZATION	Special Waiver
DATE	19— Hour Standard
PRESENT	No. present Necessary for quorum
CHAIR	
SECRETARY	
MINUTES	
STATEMENTS	
RESOLUTIONS	
#1	Proposed by Seconded by For Votes Against
#2	Proposed by Seconded by For Votes Against
#3	Proposed by Seconded by For Votes Against
#4	Proposed by Seconded by For Votes Against
#5	Proposed by Seconded by For Votes Against
#6	Proposed by Seconded by For Votes Against
#7	Proposed by Seconded by For Votes Against
NOTES	
ADJOURNMENT	Fees Per member present
DISBURSEMENT	Expenses Per member present Sundries Total
	(Signed) . . . . Secretary

minutes. See STOCKHOLDERS' MEET-INGS and *Minute book,* below.

Preparation for taking minutes. The preparation of materials for taking the minutes usually is the responsibility of the corporate secretary. The office secretary often assists with some or all of these steps:

1. Prepare in advance a statement of the order of business and the AGENDA. The *agenda* is a digest of action to be taken at the meeting. Often a copy of the agenda of a directors' meeting is given to each director as well as to the presiding officer. Sometimes preliminary agendas are sent along with the NOTICE OF MEETING.

2. If important matters are to be considered, indicate the names of those who are to present the business to the meeting.

3. Have ready all books, papers, contracts, and reports that are likely to be called for at the meeting.

4. Draft in advance MOTIONS or resolutions of the business to come before the meeting, if the subject has been thoroughly worked out and is ready for the vote of the directors or stockholders. (See Chapter 10/RES-OLUTION.) Resolutions prepared in advance save time, clarify the propositions, and simplify the entries in the minute book.

5. If payment is to be made immediately to the directors for attendance at the meetings, the corporate secretary should have available the necessary funds.

6. Bring to the meeting a preprinted form for entering the notes of the minutes of the meeting. (See Figure 1.)

Skeleton form of minutes. After a meeting has been held, minutes are prepared in a form similar to the one shown below if a formal format is required. For meetings that do not observe this degree of formality, the minutes also may be prepared without following a rigid pattern, although even less formal minutes should follow the order of business at the meeting and should contain essential facts and figures.

Minutes of Special Meeting of Stockholders

[*Note:* The headings in brackets sometimes appear in the minute book as marginal notes.]

[*Time and place of meeting*]

A special meeting of the stockholders of _____ Corporation was held at the office of the Corporation at _____ (*Street*), _____ (*City*), _____ (*State*), on the _____ day of _____, 19 ____, at _____ o'clock _____ M.

[*Presiding officer: Secretary*]

_____, President of the Corporation, presided at the meeting, and _____, Secretary of the Corporation, acted as Secretary of the meeting, as provided by the Bylaws.

[*Roll call*]

The Secretary called the roll of stockholders, and all stockholders were found present either in person or by proxy. (*If not all stockholders are present, insert statement as in minutes of annual meeting, in the preceding form.*)

The following notice of the meeting was read by the Secretary and ordered spread upon the minutes of this meeting:

117

(Insert notice of meeting.)

[*Proof of notice of meeting*]

The Secretary then presented an affidavit, showing that the notice of meeting aforesaid had been duly mailed to each stockholder at his or her last known address, more than _____ (___) weeks (or days) preceding this meeting.

[*Proof of publication of notice of meeting*]

The Secretary also presented an affidavit of publication of the aforesaid notice of meeting in the _____ , a newspaper published and having a circulation in the county where the principal business office of the Corporation is located, on the _____ day of _____, 19 ___, and on the _____, _____, and ___ days of _____ , 19 ___, as required by law and by the Bylaws of this Corporation. (*If publication is not required, omit this clause.*)

[*Inspectors of election*]

The President stated that the Board of Directors had heretofore chosen two Inspectors, _____ and _____, and that it was desirable that their appointment be confirmed at the meeting.

Upon motion duly made and seconded, the appointment of _____ and _____ as Inspectors was unanimously confirmed, and they and each of them took and subscribed to the prescribed oath.

The Inspectors thereupon took charge of the proxies and, upon examination thereof and of the stock books, reported that there were present in person or by proxy stockholders of record owning _____ (_____) shares of stock, being the entire outstanding capital stock of the Corporation.

[*Vote on resolutions*]

On motion duly made and seconded, and after due deliberation, the following resolution was voted upon:

(Insert resolutions covering matters considered at meeting.)

The Inspectors of Election canvassed the votes and reported that the aforesaid resolution had been adopted by the affirmative vote of all the stockholders of the Corporation.

[*Adjournment*]

No other business coming before the meeting, the meeting was thereupon adjourned.

———————————————
President

———————————————
Secretary

Preparing minutes. The following is a suggested list of rules relating to the form to be followed by those who prepare the minutes for the minute book:

1. The heading designating the meeting should be capitalized and centered.

2. Paragraphs may be block style or indented about ten spaces.

3. Names of attending directors and absentees, or similar lists, should be indented about fifteen spaces.

4. The text of the minutes should be double-spaced, although portions may be single-spaced (e.g., list of attendees).

5. An extra space should be left between each paragraph; a triple space may be left between each item in the order of business.

6. Resolutions should be indented about fifteen spaces and single-spaced.

7. The words *Board of Directors* and the word *Corporation*, when reference is made to the corporation whose minutes are being written, should be capitalized.

8. Captions in margin should be in capitals.

9. A margin of one and one-half or two inches should be left on the

left- or right-hand side of the page, depending on whether it is a left- or a right-hand page, for captions and indexing. (See *Index to minutes*, below).

10. The minutes should be summarized in marginal headings.

11. The words *WHEREAS* and *RESOLVED* should be all capitals and followed by a comma, and the word *That* should begin with a capital letter (e.g., *RESOLVED That*).

12. Sums of money, when mentioned in a resolution, should be written first in words and then in figures in parentheses.

Correction of errors in minutes. The minutes of a meeting are usually approved at the next meeting. The chairperson informally directs correction of simple errors. If the error can be corrected immediately, the correction should be made at the meeting and the minutes, as changed, offered for approval. If the error involves a revision of the minutes, the corrections of the minutes of the previous meeting are reported in the minutes of the current meeting.

Excerpt of Minutes Showing Adoption of Minutes of Previous Meeting as Corrected

RESOLVED, That the minutes of the meeting of _____ , held on the ____ day of _____, 19 ____, be and they are hereby adopted and approved in their entirety, except that the words " _____ " be eliminated from the resolution _____ _____ (*specify subject matter of resolution for identification*) contained therein.

Inserting corrections in the minute book.

Erroneous material should be crossed out by drawing a red line through each line of the incorrect material. The correct minutes should be written in between the red lines. Reference should be made in the margin of the corrected minutes to the minutes of the following meeting, to show where the correction was ordered.

When it is impractical to make the correction this way, the erroneous material should be crossed out in red and a note made in the margin showing where the revised minutes appear. The corrected minutes should be inserted behind the original minutes. The original pages are retained and indication that they are obsolete is made by reference to the minutes of the meeting at which the errors were corrected.

Minute book. A record book in which the corporate secretary keeps the meeting minutes and other pertinent material. As a rule, the minutes of stockholders' meetings and those of the directors' meetings are kept in separate books. Small companies, however, sometimes use one book for both, dividing the book into two distinct parts. Naturally, there are many more pages devoted to directors' meetings than to stockholders' meetings, since the latter usually occur only once a year. A form used by many small corporations is to have a single minute book containing minutes of both directors' and stockholders' meetings run in consecutive order, without separation of one class of meeting from the other. This is particularly helpful in small corporations where joint meetings are held because the stockholders and directors are identical.

The first pages of the minute book generally contain a copy of the charter, or articles of incorporation, of the corporation. A certified copy is often actually bound or pasted in the book. If it is your job to help maintain the minute book, leave a few blank pages after the charter, or articles, for the insertion of amendments. Following these blank pages, and beginning at the top of a right-hand page, are the bylaws of the corporation. Again, leave a few blank pages for new bylaws or amendments. Occasionally, when amendments are brief, they are interlined in the bylaws themselves. After the bylaws, the minutes of the first meeting appear. It is customary to begin each set of minutes at the top of a new page.

Index to minutes. An alphabetically arranged system of references, by key word and page, to the contents of the minute book of a corporation, or the contents of the minutes of any particular meeting.

Large corporations usually have their minutes carefully indexed, so that any business passed upon at a formal meeting, however remote in time, may be referred to and reviewed easily and quickly. Some corporations do not index the directors' meetings, but keep a complete index of the minutes of the executive committee. The index can be maintained by computer, with additions edited in and a revised copy printed out after each meeting. Card indexes, looseleaf binder indexes, or bound books also may be used for the purpose. Many large corporations have a separate index at the beginning of each minute book.

Preparing the index is facilitated by the use of captions in the minutes. The index card contains the subject matter taken from the captions and a reference to the page on which the caption appears. If a more detailed index is desired, the captions appearing on the page may bear a number, and reference on the card may be made to the number rather than to the page. The numbers run consecutively through the minute book.

Type a card for each topic (first check to see if a card already exists) as soon as you finish typing the minutes. Use cross-references if topics might be described in more than one way. The topic heading usually goes in the upper-left corner. The date and location are centered on the card (e.g., 8/17/83——Book 4——p. 61). If the same topic comes up later, simply add the new date and location on the same card.

Motion. Formal proposal or suggestion of a measure made in accordance with the requirements of the rules of PARLIAMENTARY PROCEDURE for the consideration and action of those present at a meeting.

Most matters of business that come before a meeting are introduced by a motion recommending that the assembled body express an opinion, take certain action, or order that certain action be taken. A motion, in other words, is a proposal, and the expression "I move" is equivalent to the statement "I propose." A resolution is adopted by a motion, made and seconded, that the resolution be adopted. (See Chapter 10/RESOLUTION.) Every motion need not be followed by a resolution. For example, someone may move that the meeting be adjourned, that a particular discussion be postponed, or that the report of a committee be accepted. The motion is or is not seconded, as the case may be, and a vote is taken. MINUTES, Figure 1, illustrates a convenient form to use in recording motions made during a meeting.

Motions are classified in ROBERT'S RULES OF ORDER in this way: (1) *principal or main motions*; (2) *subsidiary or secondary motions*, for example, those applied to other motions for the purpose of disposing of them; (3) *incidental motions*, that is, those that arise out of other questions; and (4) *privileged motions*, or those taking precedence over all other questions, such as a motion to fix the time of adjournment.

Notice of meeting. An informal meeting notice—for example, about a sales staff meeting or a budget committee meeting—may be handled by telephone, letter, memo, or printed form. For a small meeting, the notice can be prepared by computer with individual copies printed out; for a large meeting, the notice will likely be typed, prepared by computer, or typeset and then duplicated in large quantities by some method such as offset printing. Whether or not a notice follows a specific format and wording, it should nevertheless be specific about time, place, date, and purpose of the meeting. Corpora-

tions must observe the formalities specified in the bylaws.

Directors' meeting. The notice of directors' meeting is the writing by which the directors of a corporation are informed that a directors' meeting will be held and of the time and place of holding such meeting. The provisions of the bylaws should be followed in sending notices of meetings to directors. Even if notice of a regular meeting is not required by the bylaws, it is advisable to notify the directors of the meeting. If a special meeting is to be called, the directors should be telephoned or telegraphed (e.g., telex, facsimile, conventional telegram) to determine whether the time is convenient for all of them. A written notice should be sent after the time of the meeting is definitely fixed.

The list of directors kept in the current meeting folder should be tabulated, with columns showing the date each was notified, the date a follow-up notice, if any, was sent, and the replies. See also CALL OF STOCKHOLDERS' MEETING.

Form and content of notice. Notices of directors' meetings are usually prepared on the corporation's letterhead. Printing the notice on cards or paper slips, in advance, with blanks for filling in the date, time, and place of the meeting, saves time over individually typing each notice. A light stock for card notices is preferable, since heavy stock is not suitable for insertion in a typewriter to fill in necessary information. The notice is sent in the name of the corporate secretary. It should specify the date, place, and hour at which the meeting is to be held. It is advisable, although not obligatory unless required by statute or bylaw, for the notice of a special meeting to state the purpose for which it is held.

Notice of Special Meeting of Directors, Specifying Purposes

————(City) ——— (State)

To ———— , ———— , and ———— ,
Directors of ———— Corporation:

NOTICE IS HEREBY GIVEN That, in accordance with the provisions of Article ____, Section ———— , of the Bylaws of the ———— Corporation, and in accordance with the requirements of the laws of the State of ———— , a special meeting of the Board of Directors of the said Corporation will be held at its office and principal place of business, ———— (*Street*), ————(*City*), ———— (*State*), on the ———— day of ———— , 19 ____, at ———— o'clock in the ———— noon, for the purpose of:
1. (*Insert particular purposes of meeting.*)
2. To transact such other business as may lawfully come before said meeting.

————————
Secretary

Stockholders' meeting. The notice of a stockholders' meeting is the writing by which a corporation's stockholders are informed that a meeting will be held and of the time and place of holding such meeting.

The bylaws tell how and when notices of stockholders' meetings, both annual and special, shall be sent. The corporate secretary must follow those provisions closely. Notices are in writing, usually duplicated by printing press for large quantities, and they are mailed to the stockholders a certain number of days before the meeting, *as specified in the bylaws.*

Form and content of notice. The notice of a stockholders' meeting may be in the form of a postcard or an announcement sent in a sealed envelope. The notice should specify the date, place, and hour at which the meeting is to be held, and, in the case of a special meeting, the purpose of the meeting. (See PROXY, Figure 1, for an example of a notice combined with a proxy.)

Notice of Special Meeting of Stockholders, Indicating Purpose of Meeting

NOTICE IS HEREBY GIVEN that a special meeting of the stockholders of the ———— Company, a corporation of the State of ————, has been called and will be held on ———— , 19 ____, at ———— o'clock ____ M., at the registered office of the Company, (*address*) ———— , City of ———— , State of ———— , for the following purposes:
1. (*Insert purpose of meeting.*)
2. To transact any other business that may come before the said meeting.

If you are unable to be present in person, please sign the enclosed form of proxy and return it in the enclosed stamped envelope.

By order of the Board of Directors.

————————
Secretary

Dated ———————— , 19 ____ .

Letters replying to notice of meeting. Stockholders do not usually reply to a notice of meeting. If they do not plan to attend, they give someone their

PROXY. But directors and committee members should reply to notices of meeting. Letters in reply to the notice should (1) repeat the time, date, and place of meeting; (2) state whether or not the executive plans to attend; and (3) give a reason if he or she does not plan to attend.

Letter 1

Mr. Mason plans to be present at the meeting of the Finance Committee to be held on Tuesday, October 26, at 9:30 A.M., in your office.

Letter 2

Ms. Jackson received the notice of the meeting of the Finance Committee to be held on Tuesday, October 26, 9:30 A.M. Unfortunately, previous business appointments will prevent her from attending the meeting. Enclosed is her proxy.

Order of business. The order in which items of business are brought before a meeting. The business to be transacted at a meeting need not follow any particular order, even though one is prescribed by the bylaws. A logical order of business, however, expedites the conduct of the meeting. The following order is usually pursued at an annual stockholders' meeting.

1. Call to order
2. Election of the chair and the appointment of a temporary secretary, if necessary
3. Presentation of proofs of the due calling of the meeting.
4. Presentation and examination of proxies
5. Announcement of a quorum present.
6. Reading and settlement of the minutes of the previous meeting.
7. Presentation of list of stockholders
8. Reports of officers and committees
9. Ratification of directors' and executive committee's acts
10. Appointment of inspectors of election
11. Opening of polls
12. Election of directors
13. Closing of polls
14. Report of inspectors
15. Declaration of election of directors
16. New business
17. Adjournment

The reading and settlement of the minutes of the previous meeting is often eliminated. As a substitute, the chair or the corporate secretary announces at the outset that minutes of the previous meetings are available for the inspection by any person who cares to examine them. If any stockholders indicate a desire to make such an examination, they should be given ample opportunity to do so. See DIRECTORS' MEETINGS, *Conduct of directors' meetings*, for order of business at directors' meetings.

Other types of meetings, such as the directors' meeting of a professional society, might follow a different order of business, for example:

1. Call to order
2. Reading and approval of previous meeting's minutes
3. Treasurer's report
4. Other reports
5. Old business
6. New business
7. Nominations and election of officers
8. Committee appointments
9. Announcements
10. Adjournment

The order of business dictates the order in which various AGENDA topics will be discussed.

Parliamentary procedure. Formal rules of conduct governing the holding of meetings, usually based on the rules developed and followed by the British Parliament. If a corporation's bylaws require its meetings to be conducted according to the rules prescribed by a manual of parliamentary procedure, the requirement is binding on all members of the corporation. Parliamentary procedure is ordinarily not necessary at stockholders' meetings, but some adherence to its elementary principles is always to be recommended.

Figure 1, a table of motions, may be used for ready reference by participants in meetings as well as by the chair. The motions down to and including the main motions are arranged in the order of their priority. See also ROBERT'S RULES OF ORDER.

Proxy. Authority to vote at a meeting for an absent stockholder, director, or other organizational member. The term is also applied to the person or persons holding the authority. Although the statutory provisions concerning voting by proxy vary from state to state, the usual provisions for stockholders are (1) that the proxy shall be in writing, (2) that the person giving it can revoke it at any time, (3) that it will expire after a certain number of months or years from its date unless the stockholder executing the proxy indicates the length of time it is to continue in force, and (4) that the term of the proxy shall be limited to a definite period. The usual procedure is to check the proxy signature with the name on a stock certificate.

As a stockholders' meeting usually cannot be held unless a QUORUM (a certain portion) of the stock is represented, it is usually necessary to get proxies when the stockholders are widely scattered. The Securities and Exchange Commission (SEC) regulates the solicitation of proxies in respect to registered securities. (See Chapter 13/SECURITIES AND EXCHANGE COMMISSION.) A proxy for a stockholders' meeting need not be in any particular form, as long as it meets statutory requirements and requirements of the SEC. It need not be witnessed, but a witness can prove the authenticity of the signature. The form for proxies for other types of meetings also varies. Figure 1 illustrates a combined notice and proxy form that could be used for an annual meeting.

PARLIAMENTARY PROCEDURE: FIGURE 1: Table of motions

(Y = Yes; N = No; ? = Depends upon circumstances or necessity; † = If put to vote; M = Majority)

	Recognition of Chair Required	In Order if Another Has the Floor	Second Required[1]	Requires Immediate Decision	Debatable[2]	Debate May Extend to Main Question	Amendable	Two-Thirds Vote Required[5]	May Be Reconsidered
To fix the time to adjourn	Y	N	Y	N	N[3]	...	Y	M	N
To adjourn	Y	N	Y	N	N	...	N	M	N
Questions of privilege	N	?	N	Y	N	...	N	...	...[7]
Order of the day	N	Y	N	Y	N	...	N	Y	Y
To lay on the table	Y	N	Y	Y	N	...	N	M	N
Previous question	Y	N	Y	Y	N	N	N	Y	Y
To postpone to a certain time	Y	N	Y	N	Y	N	Y	M	Y
To commit	Y	N	Y	N	Y	N	Y	M	Y
To amend	Y	N	Y	N	Y	Y	Y	M	Y
To postpone indefinitely	Y	N	Y	N	Y	N	N	M	N[8]
Appeals	N	Y	N	Y	N	...	N	M	Y
Objection to consideration	N	N	Y	Y	N	N	N	Y	Y
Withdrawal of a motion	N	N	Y	N	Y[4]	...	Y	M	N[8]
Division of a question	Y	N	Y	Y	N	N	Y	M	N
Suspension of the rules	Y	N	Y	N	N	...	N	Y	N
To fill blanks	Y	N	Y	Y	Y	N	Y	M	N
To read papers	Y	N	Y	N	N	...	N	M	Y
To reconsider	Y	N	Y	N	Y[4]	Y[4]	N	M	N
To rescind	Y	N	Y	N	Y	Y	Y	M	N[9]
To substitute	Y	N	Y	N	Y	N	Y	M	Y
Main, or principal, motion	Y	N	Y	N	Y	N	Y	M	Y
Point of order	N	Y	N†	Y	N	...	N	M†	N†
Inquiry	N	?	Y†	Y†	N	...	N	M†	N†
Division of house	N	Y	Y	Y	N	...	N	M	N

[1] It may be advisable in stockholders' meetings to eliminate entirely requirements for a seconding of motions, since practically every stockholder, except a holder of a single share, has more than one vote and in effect, therefore, has the right to second his or her own motion.

[2] Even when a question is not debatable, the chair may desire debate or tolerate it to facilitate business or to preserve unity, but the chair is always justified in terminating debate; the chair should terminate it if a point of order is raised as to the propriety of debate. Under parliamentary procedure, the minority has the right to deliberate and, if possible, to convince those not in agreement; this right the majority cannot take away. It would seem, however, that this applies only to questions that are debatable.

[3] If no other question is on the floor, it is debatable.
[4] This motion is debatable only if all or any part of the original question is debatable.

[5] In spite of what may be said in the table as to a majority being sufficient, special rules of the corporation or of the statutes may require a two-thirds or any other vote. Unless otherwise stated in a rule or in a statute, a percentage required to carry a question means a percentage of the voting strength present.

[6] A question of privilege is decided by the chair, but the decision is subject to appeal.   [8] If previous notice of intent to rescind has not been given, a two-thirds vote is required.
[7] A negative vote may be reconsidered.
[9] The answer applies to negative vote on the question only.

PROXY: FIGURE 1: Proxy form combined with notice

NOTICE

You are hereby notified that the Annual Meeting of the stockholders of (company) will be held in (location), on (date), at (time). If you do not expect to attend, please sign this proxy card and mail it promptly. No postage is required.

PROXY

I hereby constitute (name), (name), and (name), who are officers or directors of the Company, or a majority of such of them as actually are present, to act for me in my stead and as my proxy at the Annual Meeting of the stockholders of (company), to be held in (location), on (date), at (time), and at any adjournment or adjournments thereof, with full power and authority to act for me in my behalf, with all powers that I, the undersigned, would possess if I were personally present.

Effective Date: _____

Signed _____
                                                 Stockholder

_____
          City   State   Zip Code

PLEASE MAKE SURE YOU HAVE COMPLETED WITH YOUR SIGNATURE AND ADDRESS BEFORE MAILING. NO POSTAGE REQUIRED.

Proxy committee. Committee appointed by management of a corporation to represent and vote at meetings for stockholders who authorize it to do so. The proxy committee votes for the directors whom management itself has nominated. Thus management selects and elects the directors and, because of the apathy of stockholders, is able to perpetuate its control of the corporation. However, any opposing interest may form its own proxy committee, send out its own proxy forms, and solicit proxies for itself. (See PROXY.)

Quorum. The number of persons who must legally be present at a meeting to transact corporate business or the business of any assembly of persons. When the membership of the assembling group or body consists of a *definite* number of persons as required by law—for example, a board of directors or the United States Senate—a majority (more than half) of the members are required to make a quorum, unless the controlling law expressly states that another number constitutes a quorum. At common law, when the membership of the assembling body consists of an *indefinite* number of persons (that is, the law requires no definite number)—as the stockholders of a corporation—any number constitutes a quorum; however, the bylaws, and frequently the statutes or charter, customarily make an express provision concerning a quorum. In the case of a stockholders' meeting, the designated quorum usually relates to the amount of stock represented at the meeting and not to the number of stockholders.

A quorum, as specified in the statute, charter, or bylaws, must be present not only to begin a meeting but to transact business. Thus if during the meeting a number of stockholders depart, leaving less than a quorum present, the meeting must be discontinued by adjournment. However, if a meeting is once organized and all parties have participated, no person or faction, by withdrawing capriciously and for the sole purpose of breaking a quorum, can then render the subsequent proceedings invalid. If stockholders have withdrawn for the purpose of breaking a quorum, because of whim, caprice, or chagrin, the law will consider the action as unavailing and will permit the meeting to proceed.

Recess. See ADJOURNMENT.

Regular meeting. A routine, periodically scheduled meeting for the transaction of ordinary business, such as the ANNUAL MEETING of stockholders for the election of directors. The time or schedule of such meetings, for corporations, usually is fixed by the bylaws. Regular meetings often are called general meetings or stated meetings. (see STOCKHOLDERS' MEETINGS.)

Robert's Rules of Order. A classic manual describing parliamentary procedure. The book, available in many bookstores, covers methods of organizing and conducting meetings, responsibilities of officers, and procedures in regard to motions. It describes the commonly accepted procedures for conducting meetings of all sizes and types, from a small committee meeting to a large stockholders' meeting.

Secretarial staff meetings. Secretaries may schedule regular or occasional meetings with trainees, assistants, and other coworkers to deal with specific projects or general office practices.

Preparation. Such meetings may be brief and relatively informal, but they will still benefit from adequate preparation by both those conducting and those attending the meeting. The person calling the meeting should send the others an agenda or give them a general ideas of the topics to be discussed. The members attending the meeting should review the preliminary information and prepare notes to help them contribute to the discussion. They should bring these notes to the meeting along with pencil, paper, and any other relevant material.

The person conducting the meeting should notify the others of the date, place, and time of the meeting.

In small offices the notice of these meetings and follow-up reminders are usually given in person or by telephone rather than in writing. The choice of time and location will need to take account of the patterns of business activity peculiar to the individual offices. Often such meetings will be scheduled early in the day or during the lunch hour so that normal office activity will not be interrupted. Secretaries should arrange to have their incoming calls handled and visitors greeted during the meeting.

Meeting procedure. Formal procedural rules are usually not required for informal staff meetings. An informal check that all members are present is sufficient for the meeting to begin. However, the person conducting the meeting should initiate and guide the discussion. Topics should be dealt with in order, and discussion confined to the prepared subjects. Members should have the opportunity to speak in turn. Minutes are usually not required, but everyone should take notes especially in regard to decisions reached and assignments made. The person conducting the meeting, however, should keep a prepared summary for future reference, especially in regard to decisions and assignments. Rather than taking formal votes on issues, members may simply agree on solutions or decisions. At the end of the meeting the discussion and decisions should be summarized orally for the attendees.

Seminar. A meeting of individuals with similar professional interests for the purpose of exchanging and discussing information. Unlike conferences, seminars usually have fewer attendees, do not include the more extensive activities and events of a conference (e.g., product displays, dinner-dance), and may be of shorter duration. See also CONFERENCE.

Sine die. Without day; without a specified day being assigned for a future meeting or hearing.

Special meeting. A corporate meeting that is not one regularly scheduled pursuant to corporate bylaw or statutory provisions; any meeting that is not an ANNUAL MEETING or a REGULAR MEETING; an out-of-routine, special-purpose meeting. In general, unless all the stockholders are present in person or by proxy, only the special business for which the meeting was called may be transacted at a special meeting. Special meetings sometimes are referred to as *called meetings.* See STOCKHOLDERS' MEETINGS; NOTICE OF MEETING.

Stockholders' meetings. Gatherings or meetings of STOCKHOLDERS for the purpose of joint exercise by them of the rights guaranteed to them by statute, charter, and by-laws.

A valid meeting cannot be held unless the amount of stock necessary to constitute a QUORUM is represented. Every owner of capital stock has the right to vote each share of stock he or she owns at all meetings of stockholders unless the right is denied by statutory or charter provision, or by an agreement under which the stockholder holds the shares. Absent stockholders may vote by PROXY. See also MINUTES and Chapter 10/VOTING AT STOCKHOLDERS' MEETINGS; CUMULATIVE VOTING; VOTING TRUST.

Stockholders' consent to a particular transaction may be given (1) in writing, (2) in writing expressed at a special meeting, (3) at any meeting called to consider the question, or (4) at any meeting.

Kinds of stockholders' meetings. Meetings of stockholders are either regular or special. The REGULAR MEETING is usually the annual meeting required to be held for the election of directors, and the time for holding this meeting is generally fixed by the bylaws. Regular meetings are frequently called "general meetings" or "stated meetings." SPECIAL MEETINGS are sometimes known as "general extraordinary meetings" or "called" meetings.

A corporation may not transact any extraordinary business at a regular meeting of the stockholders without proper notice having been given to the stockholders, but it may transact any ordinary business that may come before the meeting. The corporation cannot transact at a general meeting any business that the statute requires to be transacted at a special meeting. At a special meeting of the stockholders, no business other than that specified in the call for the meeting may be considered or transacted unless all stockholders entitled to vote are present in person or represented by proxy and unless all consent to the transaction of the business.

Call of meeting. See CALL OF STOCKHOLDERS' MEETING.

Time of meetings. The general rule is that a meeting, to be legal, must take place at the time and place designated in the bylaws or the charter. (See *Omission of stockholders' meeting* below.)

Place of meetings. Meetings of stockholders, both annual and special, must be held within the state, unless otherwise provided by statute.

In the absence of statutory provisions, the place at which a stockholders' meeting and an INCORPORATORS' MEETING (sometimes called the FIRST MEETING OF STOCKHOLDERS) is to be held is determined by common law principles. The common law rule is that both stockholders' and incorporators' meetings must be held within the state of incorporation.

If the charter or statute makes no specific provision that the meeting must be held within the state, action taken at a meeting held outside the state will be valid if all the stockholders participate in the meeting. All transactions concluded at the meeting may subsequently be ratified at a meeting held within the state by dummies acting on stockholders' proxies. (See MEETING, *Meetings held by proxy.*) When a corporation is chartered in more than one state, a meeting in any one of the states is valid for all of them, and there is no necessity for a repetition of the meeting in any other of the states.

Preparation for meetings. A checklist of preparations required for a stockholders' meeting is often kept by corporate secretaries in the meeting file (see MEETING, *Meeting file; Meeting folder*), each item being checked off as it is attended to. The office secretary frequently assists in such preparations and often maintains the list in a tickler file and brings the item to the corporate secretary's attention on the days when some action must be taken—such as preparing a notice, sending a notice to the press for publication or to the mailing department, and making up the list of stockholders.

Conferences. Premeeting, individual discussion of matters to be taken up at a stockholders' meeting is an indispensable part of the preparations for the meeting. The corporate secretary is responsible for most of these matters, particularly the briefing of the chair. Similarly, possible nominees for designation as inspectors of election and the like should be sounded out in advance concerning their willingness to serve.

Material to take to meetings. The office secretary should help collect the following material for the corporate secretary to take to any meeting of stockholders: (1) pamphlet copy of the corporation laws of the state in which the corporation is organized; (2) copy of the certificate of incorporation, with marginal notations of amendments and copies of them; (3) copy of the bylaws, with marginal notations of amendments and copies of them; (4) separate sheet for order of business; (5) rules and regulations of the corporation, if any, governing the conduct of meetings; (6) proof of the mailing of notices of the meeting and, where necessary, of publication; (7) the original call for the meeting and, if there has been a demand for a call, the original of the demand; (8) the minute book; (9) the corporate

seal; (10) current papers pertaining to the meeting; (11) blank affidavits, oaths, and the like.

Order of business. See ORDER OF BUSINESS.

Conduct of a meeting. In the absence of express regulation by statute or bylaw, stockholders' meetings, including those for the election of directors, are controlled largely by accepted usage and custom. The fundamental rule is that all who are entitled to take part shall be treated with fairness and good faith. Most corporations conduct their meetings with considerable informality. If the bylaws provide that the meetings shall be conducted according to the rules prescribed by a manual of parliamentary procedure, the requirement must be enforced. Although formality is not essential, some method of obtaining the assent of the stockholders is necessary to bind the corporation. See PARLIAMENTARY PROCEDURE; ROBERT'S RULES OF ORDER.

It is advisable to have an executive officer present at the meeting, but there is no requirement that the directors or officers attend. In large corporations, general counsel usually attends the meetings to act as adviser to the chair. Several clerks (or sometimes the inspectors) act as ushers.

Omission of stockholders' meeting. The statutes of many states indicate what will happen if no meeting takes place. Generally, if an annual meeting was not held at the time specified for its holding, the directors may call a meeting within a reasonable time thereafter. If a meeting has not been held at the regular time, they should call it whenever it is demanded by any stockholder.

Under statutory provision, but more often under bylaw provision, meetings that cannot be held at the time noted because a QUORUM is not present may be adjourned and may be held at the adjourned hour without subsequent notice. See ADJOURNED MEETING.

Reconsideration of action by stockholders. Stockholders at a corporation stockholders' meeting, while they are still in session, may alter or change any resolution or MOTION adopted by them at the meeting. (See Chapter 10/ RESOLUTION.) They also may reconsider and repeal any vote or resolution after the meeting, by subsequent vote or resolution, unless such action will disturb rights that have become vested as a result of the prior action.

Adjournment. Meetings may be adjourned to a day certain, or they may be adjourned SINE DIE—that is, without naming a day and finally terminating the meeting—or they may be adjourned subject to the call of the chair. The motion to adjourn specifies which form of adjournment will be taken, and if none is specified, the adjournment is final. (See ADJOURNED MEETING.)

Sunday or holiday meetings. Since the date set for regular meetings may occasionally fall on a Sunday or holiday, provision should be made in the bylaws or by resolution for such a contingency. In the absence of statute or bylaw prohibiting a meeting on a holiday, the meeting cannot be held without notice on any day other than that appointed in the bylaws. Thus an action at a meeting held without notice the day after the regular date, which was a holiday, was void. A meeting of directors on Sunday is valid if affirmed at a weekday meeting. When agreements and contracts entered into on Sunday are void under the statute, a board of directors cannot amend or rescind a legal contract at a Sunday meeting.

Teleconference. See Chapter 2/TELECOMMUNICATIONS SERVICES; TELECONFERENCING.

To rise. See ADJOURNMENT.

Videoconference. See Chapter 2/ TELECOMMUNICATIONS SERVICES, VIDEOCONFERENCING.

Waiver of notice. By signing a waiver of notice, stockholders may indicate they do not require the corporation to notify them of meetings. Such waiver is recorded on the list of stockholders until rescinded.

CHAPTER 4

TRAVEL

ASTA. American Society of Travel Agents, Inc. See Travel agency.

Air travel. Plane reservations are usually made through a company travel department or a Travel agency but also may be made by telephoning the reservations desk at the desired airline. Information necessary to make a reservation includes (1) point of departure and destination, (2) date desired, (3) time of departure, (4) airline and flight number, (5) class of accommodation desired, and (6) special needs (e.g., wheelchair, nonsmoking section). The secretary to an executive usually does not leave the selection of flight, route, and the like to the airline representative or travel agent but might ask for suggestions if it is not possible to get the desired reservation. The airline representative or travel agent making the reservation at the point of departure will follow through on reservations for the entire trip. If part of a trip is to be made by train, car, or shuttle, the agent will also make such reservations.

Shuttle service. To make connections for another flight, it is sometimes necessary to travel from one airport to another. Although buses and taxis are available in large cities, air-shuttle service (e.g., helicopter) is sometimes recommended. The agent making the other reservations will include this type of connecting service between airports or nearby cities not connected by a major airline.

Payment. Travelers may use one of the major credit cards accepted by most airlines and travel agencies or open an account with an airline or at an agency, thus eliminating the trouble of having to pay every time a ticket is purchased. Some companies have a company account to be used by individuals in the organization. (See Travel funds, 3. *Credit cards.*)

Some travel agencies and airlines mail or deliver tickets when time permits; otherwise, the secretary or a messenger has to pick them up from the airline's ticket office or at the travel agency. See TICKETS, PAYMENT FOR AND DELIVERY OF.

Cancellation of reservation. Goodwill of the transportation companies is kept by prompt cancellation of any space that is not going to be used. Some airlines will not provide a refund if a reservation is not cancelled by a certain date. Since the reservation is usually made locally, it may be cancelled by telephone. A reservation for a return flight or for stages of an interrupted flight may not be held if the traveler does not confirm the reservation within a certain number of hours before the flight is to be resumed.

Planning the trip. When planning a business trip by airplane, an executive is interested in (1) airlines that can be used for the trip, (2) time schedules, (3) whether meals are served on the flight, (4) cost, and (5) BAGGAGE facilities. (see ITINERARY; TRAVEL SECURITY.) The information can be obtained from the following sources:

1. *Travel agents.* See TRAVEL AGENCY.

2. *Guides.* The best known publication that includes timetables of domestic and foreign airlines and other pertinent information is the *Official Airline Guide,* published twice monthly by Reuben H. Donnelley, 2000 Clearwater Drive, Oak Brook, IL 60521, and available by subscription or by the purchase of single copies. However, schedules change frequently, and only a travel agency with up-to-the-minute computerized data or the airlines reservation desk can provide the latest information.

3. *Flight schedules of specific airlines.* Again, printed schedules can give one a general idea of routes and schedules but not up-to-the-minute information.

4. *Airlines.* Any necessary information may be obtained over the telephone from the airlines that might be used for a specific trip by calling the airline (use the free 800 number listed in the Yellow Pages) and asking for "Information."

5. *Airline clubs.* Major airlines often offer membership in airline clubs for an annual fee. Members are provided with information, special lounges at airports, conference rooms with telephones, travel discounts, and other services.

Airline clubs. See AIR TRAVEL.

Appointment schedule. See TRAVEL APPOINTMENT SCHEDULE.

Automobile travel. Car rental—domestic and foreign—may be made in advance either through a company travel department, a TRAVEL AGENCY, or one of the major car-rental agencies. Payment may be made by check or, more commonly, by credit card. See TRAVEL FUNDS, 3. *Credit cards.* Some companies establish accounts with a particular car-rental agency and are billed monthly.

Information necessary to arrange for a rental car includes (1) places where a car or limousine is needed, (2) the traveler's preferences for make and size of car, (3) method of payment, (4) dates and times car is needed, and (5) whether drop-off in another city is desired. Some car-rental agencies provide a computer printout of directions to local destinations; a travel agent can suggest rental agencies that do this.

Persons who travel by automobile a great deal will find it advantageous to be a member of an auto club such as the American Automobile Association, which has a travel service available to plan any trip a member wants to take. (The AAA headquarters is located at 8111 Gatehouse Road, Falls Church, VA 22042.) To secure travel service, telephone or mail your request to the nearest branch of the auto club, and routings will be forwarded to you, or you may contact them in person by visiting the nearest branch. A club's travel department usually assists its members in some or all of these ways:

1. Advises them what route to use, where to stop, and what to see.

2. Prepares a special route map.

3. Provides last-minute information on weather and highway conditions.

4. Assists in selecting and securing motel and hotel accommodations in advance of the trip.

5. Provides emergency road service.

6. Provides bail and arrest bonds.

7. Provides accident insurance.

8. Offers an auto-theft reward (see TRAVEL SECURITY).

9. Offers discounts on car-rental and other travel services.

Members of some clubs also receive a number of maps, travel guides, and directories covering outstanding points of interest.

Airlines, railroads, and hotels also offer assistance in arranging car rentals.

Cancellation of reservation. Reservations may be cancelled by calling the travel agent, car-rental agency, or other organization through which the arrangements are made. As always, reservations should be cancelled promptly whenever plans change.

Baggage. Persons planning a business trip, especially if traveling by plane, are interested in knowing the number of pounds of baggage that can be checked on the ticket without additional charge and also the limitations on dimensions of baggage. The information is available in flight schedules and timetables, at the airline or railway information office, or through a TRAVEL AGENCY. Each piece of baggage should carry an identification label. For security, some people prefer labels that enclose the address so that it cannot be seen by onlookers. See TRAVEL SECURITY. A supply of labels, available at ticket and baggage counters, should be kept in the office. Check with the airline regarding sensitive baggage (film, cassettes, computer diskettes, and so on), how to package certain items, and how to transport them aboard so that they are not sent through X-ray machines.

Cancellation of reservation. See HOTELS, *Cancellation of reservation;* AIR TRAVEL, *Cancellation of reservation;* RAILROAD TRAVEL, *Cancellation of reservation;* AUTOMOBILE TRAVEL, *Cancellation of reservation.*

Company travel department. See TRAVEL AGENCY, *Company travel departments.*

Credit cards. See TRAVEL FUNDS, 3. *Credit cards.*

Customs. See FOREIGN TRAVEL, *Customs information.*

Expense reports. Business people who travel must document and report their travel and entertainment expenses, whether or not they receive advance funds or request reimbursement later. Some companies have their own expense-reporting forms. Otherwise, you can purchase standard forms in an office-supply store. See Chapter 11/EXPENSE ACCOUNT.

You can help your employer prepare such a form by (1) organizing cash receipts, credit card receipts, and personal notes into the categories listed on the form you are using (e.g., meals, hotels, and so on); (2) double-checking names, dates, and so on; (3) listing items for which receipts may be missing; (4) listing the expenses in each category on the report form in proper order and adding them to arrive at a total for each; and (5) typing

the rough draft approved by your employer.

IRS regulations. Since rules and regulations concerning travel and entertainment allowances vary from year to year, keep on hand a current copy of the free IRS publication 463, *Travel, Entertainment, and Gift Expenses.*

Foreign travel. When an executive plans a business or pleasure trip to a foreign country, you should make arrangements through your company travel department or an accredited travel service. (See TRAVEL AGENCY.) Agencies offer a complete service in all matters pertaining to travel throughout the world, and most have computers available to retrieve up-to-the minute schedules and fares. In addition, travel agencies have circulars and booklets describing foreign countries and each part of the country. (See also TRAVEL SECURITY.)

Travel agents who arrange a trip should be told the number in the party: names, ages, sex, and if the trip includes a foreign country; and citizenship. Also, they should be told where the party wants to go, dates of departure and return, mode and class of travel, and the approximate amount of time that can be spent. The travel agency will be able to advise about the classes of travel and rates on a particular steamship or airline and on the trains in the foreign countries and recommend hotels to conform to one's budget. See TRAVEL AGENCY, *What the travel service will do.*

When unable to decide upon a definite

itinerary. If plans are uncertain, you can give the travel agent the names of the places in which the travelers expect to need hotel reservations, approximate dates, and how much per day they will spend for hotel expenses. The agent will do the following things:

1. Provide the name of a desirable hotel in each place.

2. Give a card of introduction to the manager of each of these hotels and to the agent's foreign contact (e.g., representative from the company your employer is planning to visit).

3. Write to each of the recommended hotels asking them to give the traveler's requests their best attention.

4. Advise the agent's foreign contact in each city of the approximate date of arrival.

Passports. Application for a passport must be executed before a clerk of a federal court or a state court authorized to naturalize aliens, before an agent of the State Department, or at a post office authorized to grant passports. A travel agent will furnish information about the most expedient method of obtaining a passport in the local area.

To prove citizenship, a native United States citizen must submit with the application a birth certificate or affidavit confirming place and date of birth. The affidavit should state how knowledge of the place and date of birth was acquired. (Ask the passport office for instructions.) Two standard passport photo-graphs must be submitted with the current passport fee. Three to four weeks, sometimes longer, should be allowed for processing by the State Department.

The passport is valid for ten years and may be renewed by mail if issued within the previous eight years. Local passport agencies will supply forms and current information.

A naturalized citizen must present his or her naturalization papers and be identified in the same manner that a native-born citizen must be identified.

Some countries require health certificates and vaccinations. Check with a travel agency for current regulations and special requirements for entering and returning from particular countries.

Visas. After the traveler gets a passport, the next step is to get visas for the countries that require them. The travel agent will indicate whether a visa is required, or the traveler can inquire at the consulates of the countries in which he or she is interested. Generally, the passport must be presented at the consulate and a visa form filled out. Sometimes personal appearance of the applicant is required. As in the case of passports, the various countries have a number of special requirements for visas too, such as additional photographs, police and health certificates, vaccinations, and inoculations. Usually, there is a visa fee. The length of time required for processing a visa varies with the country.

For additional information, such as the addresses of overseas consular offices, consult the *Congressional Direc-*

tory or *Key Officers of Foreign Service Posts* (sold through the U.S. Government Printing Office in Washington, D.C.).

Customs information. Anyone going to a foreign country should know in advance what the United States customs laws and regulations are with regard to purchases made in the foreign country and brought into the United States. A travel agent will usually supply this information, as well as details about customs requirements in countries to be visited.

Whether or not a travel service is used, it is advisable to send for available customs information. If your employer is going to visit Western Hemisphere nations, send for *Know Before You Go, GSP and the Traveler, Customs Hints for Non-Residents,* and *Customs Hints for Returning U.S. Residents.* These pamphlets, available from the U.S. Treasury Department, Bureau of Customs, Washington, D.C., furnish the traveler with the general information about customs laws and regulations.

Other useful pamphlets, available from the Superintendent of Documents in Washington, D.C., are *Your Trip Abroad* and *Health Information for International Travel.*

Preparations. For travel abroad on business, the following preparation is suggested:

1. Ask the travel agent or the consulates about the special requirements imposed on commercial travelers but not on pleasure visitors. This is most important.

2. Request letters of introduction from banks, individuals, business houses, and the like to their foreign offices. Such introductions are very helpful to a commercial traveler.

3. Get a letter of authority, addressed "To Whom It May Concern," from the person authorizing the traveler to represent the firm. This is especially valuable in dealing with immigrant or customs authorities.

4. Compile a name and address list of officers and executives of firms to be visited.

5. Prepare a folder of pertinent data for each firm or person to be visited, including material on previous transactions and pending transactions.

6. Write letters (for your employer's signature) to the firms he or she will visit to provide travel, hotel, or other information.

7. Write a letter (for your employer's signature) to the Travel Officer, International Trade Services Division, Special Services and Intelligence Branch, Department of Commerce, Office of International Trade, Washington, D.C. 20230, stating the purpose of the trip and enclosing an itinerary. This office will notify all foreign offices of the upcoming visit.

8. If the company subscribes to the Dun & Bradstreet credit service, get a card from them authorizing the holder to call on their foreign offices for credit information.

9. Assemble data on the trade conditions, political aspects including security matters, geography, climate, customs, and the like of each country to be visited. Include addresses of hospitals and physicians

that the traveler can contact in case of medical emergency.

Hotels. *Reservations.* Information necessary to make a hotel reservation includes the name of the person for whom the reservation is to be made, the time of arrival and approximate time of departure, and the type of accommodations required. The reservation can be made through a company travel department or travel agent or by telephone, telegram, telex, or letter depending on how soon it is needed.

The type of accommodation desired should always be given in the request for a reservation. The usual hotel accommodations are single bedroom and bath, double bedroom and bath, and a suite consisting of a sitting-room and one or more bedrooms and baths. The location preferred may also be given in the request.

If you expect to arrive after the time a reservation is usually held, specify late arrival. A *guaranteed reservation* means that the room will be held regardless of arrival time; however, you must pay for it even if you fail to arrive as planned.

Confirmation of reservation. If time permits, request confirmation of the reservation in writing or by wire (usually sent collect). The confirmation should be attached to the copy of the ITINERARY that your employer takes along on the trip.

Cancellation of reservation. If you must cancel a hotel reservation, notify the hotel immediately (by telephone, telegram, or telex if time is short).

Sources of information. In addition to travel agencies, some credit and charge-card companies, associations, and hotel-motel chains provide a nationwide information and reservation service. Some airlines also provide information and make reservations. Detailed information about hotels is available in the latest editions of *Hotel and Travel Index* and *Official Hotel and Resort Guide,* published by Ziff-Davis Publishing Company, One Park Avenue, New York, NY 10016, and *The Hotel/Motel Red Book,* published by the American Hotel and Motel Association, 888 Seventh Avenue, New York, N.Y. 10019. Other maps, guides, and travel books are available in bookstores. The number of rooms and the price enable a person to judge the class of the hotel. Information is also available through local hotel associations or the Chamber of Commerce in the city of destination.

When the secretary travels with an employer. Some secretaries accompany their employers to process work that cannot wait and must be handled at each stopover. On such occasions, you may spend the day collecting information, typing, taking notes at meetings, making new travel plans, and so on. Rental typewriters or computers are provided by most major hotels, or you may be able to use equipment in a branch office you are visiting.

When you are with your employer, he or she will handle the tipping and payments for meals. Otherwise, keep receipts for all legitimate business-related expenses so that you can be reimbursed later. After work, your employer will probably be entertaining clients, and you will be on your own. If you attend business meetings, dress in normal business attire. For evening events, dress as you would for any other social-business event your company might hold. If you are in a foreign country, respect the customs and etiquette that apply.

Itinerary. Outline or schedule of a traveler's route or journey. The itinerary of a business trip shows (1) point of departure, (2) points of arrival, (3) name of railway or airline, (4) date and time of departure from each point, (5) date and time of arrival at each point, (6) train or flight number, (7) hotels at which the traveler is stopping, and (8) car-rental, shuttle, and similar arrangements. The itinerary should be prepared in a form similar to Figure 1. It should be typed on durable paper in triplicate: a copy for the manager, a copy for his or her family, and a copy for the secretary. Additional copies should be made if anyone else in the organization needs the information shown by the itinerary.

See also TRAVEL APPOINTMENT SCHEDULE; TRAVEL EQUIPMENT AND SUPPLIES.

Letters of credit. See TRAVEL FUNDS.

Motels. See HOTELS.

Passenger representative. Representative of a transportation company who acts as liaison between the public and the company. All large railways and airlines have a representative who solicits business for a particular line, recommends travel routes and schedules to prospective passengers, and cooperates in obtaining reservations for them.

Passport. See FOREIGN TRAVEL, *Passports.*

Plane reservation. See AIR TRAVEL.

Railroad travel. When planning a business trip by train, the traveler is interested in (1) railroads that can be used, (2) time schedules, (3) accommodations—sleeping and dining facilities, (4) cost, and (5) BAGGAGE facilities. The information can be obtained from the following sources:

1. *The Official Railway Guide.* This publication, issued monthly by the National Railway Publication Company, 424 West 33rd Street, New York, NY 10001, contains all of the schedules or timetables of Amtrak and all other passenger railroads in the United States, Canada, and Mexico, with sample fares, a description of the accommodations on each train, and other pertinent information. It can be subscribed to by the year, or single copies can be purchased. However, printed information such as this does not include up-to-the-minute changes. For the latest information, consult a travel agent or telephone the railroad.

2. *Timetables.* For both commuter and long-distance service, contact your local Amtrak or other railroad agent regarding timetables and ask to be put on their mailing lists. In this way, you will always have their latest timetables on hand. These timetables, however, will not necessarily include

ITINERARY: FIGURE 1: Travel itinerary

FROM	TO	VIA	DATE & TIME	EST ARRIVE	ACCOMMODATION	MEAL SERVICE	CAR RENTAL	HOTEL
N.Y.	Boston	Amtrak	5/6—11:30P	5/6—5:15A	Car 106 Room A Train 467	—	Hertz-Ford	Parker House
Boston	N.Y.	Eastern	5/8—3:30P	5/8—4:45P	Flight #633	Snacks	—	Home
N.Y.	Washing.	Eastern	5/13—8:30A	5/15—9:47A	Flight #431	Breakfast	Avis—Buick	Shoreham
Washing.	Atlanta	Eastern	5/15—2:50P	5/15—7:32P	Flight #565	Dinner	—	Atlanta-Baltimore
Atlanta	Cleveland	Eastern	5/19—5:50P	5/19—10:32P	Flight #732	Dinner	—	Carter Hotel
Cleveland	Chicago	United	5/22—6:10P	5/22—7:10P CST	Flight #501	Dinner	Hertz—Chevrolet	Stevens Hotel
Chicago	New York	United	5/28—12:00N	5/28—4:00P	Flight #622	Snacks	—	Home

All Standard Time one hour earlier than Daylight Time.

Checking Out Time—3:00 P.M.

the latest changes in schedules and fares. Contact a travel agent or telephone the railroad for up-to-the minute information.

3. *Travel agent.* A travel agent will handle reservations on railroads, look up all schedules, and provide you with a complete itinerary. See TRAVEL AGENCY.

Accommodations. The usual sleeping accommodations are:

1. *Bedroom.* A private room containing lower and upper berth, the lower berth serving as a sofa for daytime use; toilet facilities are in the same room in some bedrooms.

2. *Roomette.* A private room, intended primarily for single occupancy, with a bed folding into the wall and containing a sofa seat for daytime use; toilet facilities are usually in the same room.

Special cars are sometimes available for handicapped persons. Tell your travel agent about any such special needs.

Reservations. The procedure for making train reservations is similar to that for obtaining plane reservations. An intelligent idea of what you want before you phone Amtrak or another major railroad will help immeasurably.

Be sure to give complete and clear information on the point of departure and destination, time, train number or name, and the accommodations desired. For long-distance travel, trains are limited, and you might not have a choice of time. When the exact reservations that you want are not available, ask the travel agent to suggest something that is available.

The travel agent will also provide information about special services, such as taking one's car along or availability of express service between certain cities.

Although a travel agent will make all necessary reservations for you, unlike the airlines, a railway will not make reservations for the entire trip if the trip is broken by plane travel. However, Amtrak has a tour desk at its toll-free number to help you with hotels, car rentals, and bus connections.

See also TICKETS, PAYMENT FOR AND DELIVERY OF.

Cancellation of reservation. At the time reservations are made, inquire about refunds on unused tickets and cancellation procedures and requirements.

Reservations.   See AIR TRAVEL; RAILROAD TRAVEL; HOTELS.

Security.   See TRAVEL SECURITY.

Shuttle service.   See AIR TRAVEL.

Sleeping accommodations. See RAILROAD TRAVEL, *Accommodations;* HOTELS.

Supplies.   See TRAVEL EQUIPMENT AND SUPPLIES.

Tickets, payment for and delivery of.   Airlines, railroads, and travel agents make it easy to obtain and pay for tickets. Most companies whose personnel travel extensively open accounts with a travel agent or selected airlines and railroads. Individuals who make many trips can open similar accounts on the basis of their personal credit. Travelers can also use one of the popular credit or charge cards, such as Visa, Master-Card, and American Express. Each airline and railroad has its own method of making travel easy and of saving the secretary time otherwise used in picking up tickets and paying for them.

If you make reservations directly by telephone, you can request that the ticket be mailed. If you did not change the reservation, immediately upon receipt of the ticket in your office, send a check to the airline. The ticket is not valid until the airline receives your check. When you make an arrangement of this kind, you must be sure that there is ample time for receipt of the ticket by you and, in turn, receipt of the check by the airline. Railroads will mail tickets and reservations upon receipt of your check. Should your employer change plans before you mail the check, simply return the unused ticket.

Time and route schedule. Travel information prepared for someone who is planning a business trip. Usually, several possible schedules are prepared from which to make a choice. The schedule shows (1) time of departure, (2) time of arrival, (3) airline or railway, (4) flight or train number. Train and plane information should be typed on separate schedules. See AIR TRAVEL; RAILROAD TRAVEL; AUTOMOBILE TRAVEL; ITINERARY.

Timetable. A table showing the time of arrival and departure of trains or planes, the equipment and accommodations on each, and containing general travel information.

Train reservation. See RAILROAD TRAVEL, *Reservations.*

Travel agency. An agency offering complete service in all matters pertaining to travel. Many business concerns that do not have a company travel department use an agency to make all travel reservations for domestic and foreign trips. A company may open an account with an agency and be billed once a month, thus avoiding the nuisance of paying for numerous tickets throughout the month. Agents can also make reservations by personal credit card or with a company's credit or charge card.

The American Society of Travel Agents (ASTA) has members in the pricinpal cities of the United States and Canada. The members may be recognized by the ASTA emblem, which they are permitted to display if they are in good standing. The name of a nearby ASTA member may be found in the telephone directory Yellow Pages or by writing to the executive offices of the association in New York City. There are, of course, many reliable agents who are not members of ASTA, but the code of ethics of this association is high, and its members, therefore, are dependable and efficient.

Before deciding on an agency, check (1) if it is a member of a national organization with a grievance committee, (2) if fees or service charges are assessed, (3) if anyone in the agency has visited the place in question, (4) if it offers packages and other cost-cutting features, and (5) if it has a branch at the destination.

What the travel service will do. The following are some of the services that travel agents are able to provide:

1. Prepare and submit a tentative itinerary, which can be changed or adjusted.

2. Make all travel, hotel reservations, and sight-seeing arrangements for the entire trip.

3. Tell what documents are necessary, such as passport and health and police certificates, and how to get them. The travel service will get them for a client unless a personal appearance is necessary.

4. Sometimes supply, in exchange for dollars, a small amount of currency of the country to be visited, for tips, taxi fares, and the like. It will also help the traveler to get a letter of credit or traveler's checks (see TRAVEL FUNDS) and arrange for insurance.

5. Advise about all regulations, such as restrictions on currency and customs requirements.

6. Have a foreign representative meet the traveler on arrival, take care of baggage, and see the traveler through customs. (Often a business traveler is met by a member of the foreign firm he or she is visiting.)

7. Have a rental car waiting for the traveler at the destination.

8. Arrange personal and baggage insurance and even provide rain and travel insurance.

9. Suggest money-saving travel rates such as excursion or group rates.

10. Arrange for interesting side trips to points of interest or special events in the particular area where the traveler will be.

Company travel departments. Large firms often have their own travel department that functions like an outside travel agency, providing the same services for employees. Some of these departments act as a branch of an outside travel agency. Firms that have the right computer software can be linked through travel agencies directly with airline reservation services. As ticket printers become more common, company departments will be able to print tickets on demand and even provide seat selection.

Travel appointment schedule. Schedule of a traveler's appointments while on a business trip. The schedule should show the time and place of the appointment; the name, affiliation, and telephone number of the person with whom one has the appointment; and any additional useful information. (See Figure 1.)

Travel card. See TRAVEL FUNDS, 3. *Credit cards.*

Travel equipment and supplies. When business people go on a business trip, they usually take certain office supplies they will need for their work. The list may include some or all of the following items: eraser, note pad, pen and pencils, clips, stamp book, carbon paper, all kinds of

TRAVEL APPOINTMENT SCHEDULE: FIGURE 1

City & State	Date & Time	Appointment	Address	Phone	Remarks
Boston MA	5/7— 3:30P	Williams-McGregor & Co.	125 South St.	543-3485	
	5/8—10:00A	Brown & Brown	348 South St.	211-1257	
	1:00P	Norris, at Copley Plaza, Merry-Go-Round		366-2764	Luncheon
Washington DC	5/13—11:00A	Sen. Howe	Sen.Off.Bldg.	840-4884	

stationery, envelopes, scissors, rubber bands, address book, file folders, business cards, checkbook, cash, calendar, rubber stamps, stamp pad, glue, memo book, mail schedules, cellophane tape, pins, bottle opener, bandages, ruler, dictating equipment, portable computer, computer tapes or diskettes and mailing cartons, expense forms, travel guides, and pertinent files. The secretary's job is to help collect and organize these supplies, reminding the executive of any item that is missing or unavailable.

Travel funds. An executive uses one of the following plans for receiving funds while traveling.

1. *Personal checks.* A person who travels extensively usually has credit cards from the hotels where he or she stops or has a national credit or charge card such as Visa, MasterCard, or American Express or a bank-guarantee card. It is then easy to cash checks at the hotels or local banks.

2. *Traveler's checks.* These checks are available in various denominations, such as ten, twenty, fifty, or one hundred dollars. There are sev-

eral issues of traveler's checks, for example, American Express. They are available through most local banks and sometimes through machines in major airports. Your employer may have to sign the checks in the presence of the bank's representative. If the account is particularly valuable, the bank's representative may come to the office; otherwise, your employer must go to the bank.

3. *Credit cards.* Issued by credit card companies such as American Express and Diners Club, by airlines, car-rental agencies, and hotel chains. Most travelers use personal or company credit or charge cards almost exclusively for both domestic and foreign travel because they are almost universally accepted in lieu of cash. They also greatly simplify record keeping for expense-account purposes. See EXPENSE REPORTS.

4. *Letters of credit.* Travelers going to a foreign country usually buy letters of credit from their bank if they want to have funds of one thousand dollars or more. As in the case of traveler's checks, one must complete the transaction in the pres-

ence of the bank's representative. A letter of credit testifies to the holder's credit standing, serves as a letter of introduction to leading banks, and can be drawn against at banks in every part of the world until the face amount of the letter of credit has been exhausted. Many travelers find it advisable to purchase both traveler's checks and a letter of credit when planning a trip to a foreign country.

Each company has its own procedure for paying the traveling expenses of its employees. The above methods are for personal funds and for someone who uses his or her own funds for travel.

Travel security.　Travelers are especially vulnerable to theft and other illegal acts, but these potential problems can often be avoided by taking the necessary precautions. For example, you should photocopy airline tickets and other documents containing numbers before leaving and keep one copy at the office, keep another in a suitcase, and carry a third along with you, apart from the original documents.

In a hotel room, use the chain lock and dead bolt, and never open the door unless you know the caller. Keep your room key with you even when you leave the hotel. Also, have your hotel room made up during breakfast and hang a Do Not Disturb sign out the rest of the day. Then turn the television on and set the volume on low. Keep your passport with you too, in an inaccessible pocket, but do not leave it in your

hotel room or lying on a restaurant table. Before you go out, ask at the hotel desk about safe or unsafe areas to walk and avoid dark streets and parks.

Never enter a car without checking the back seat to see if someone is hiding there. Park only in well-lit places, and if you go to a garage or parking lot where you must leave the car with an attendant, take the trunk key with you. Leave items only in the locked trunk of your car. Preferably, however, use the hotel safe for jewelry and other valuables, important computer disks, and so on. In fact, do not wear expensive jewelry or something that an inexperienced thief might assume is expensive.

Avoid carrying pocketbooks and small cases. But if you do carry them, avoid walking along the curb where motorcycle thieves can snatch an object and quickly speed away. A woman should carry a shoulder bag tucked under her arm and held tightly by the strap. A man should use a money belt or, at least, only a front pocket and wrap his wallet with a heavy rubber band to prevent a pickpocket from easily sliding it out of the pocket. Also, do not leave pocketbooks, small cases, or luggage unattended while traveling, and do not use expensive designer luggage that will readily attract a thief. Use combination locks and luggage tags that conceal your name and address.

Do not carry more than two hundred dollars in cash. Use discretion in handing out money to small children appearing as beggars. In some countries, groups will prey on tourists; after you have opened your wallet, they will grab it and run. Prepay hotel and other travel costs if possible. If you use credit cards, carry as few as possible. Always destroy the carbon copy of charge forms. Your card number appears on the carbon copies, too, and can easily be retrieved from a wastebasket. Regularly check the sequence of your traveler's checks since some thieves steal only a few, hoping you won't notice.

Be certain that your personal insurance covers travel losses, and if you are robbed, call the police immediately. This is especially important in foreign countries where it is difficult or impossible to file a claim after you have left the country.

Finally, heed all government directives to travelers to avoid certain areas considered unsafe for travel because of terrorism and other threats.

Traveler's checks. See TRAVEL FUNDS.

Visas. See FOREIGN TRAVEL, *Visas.*

CHAPTER 5

OFFICE SUPPLIES AND EQUIPMENT

Addressing machines. See BUSINESS MACHINES.

Audiovisual equipment. Equipment designed to aid in teaching and in making presentations (e.g., sales and advertising presentations) by use of hearing and sight. The secretary often assists the manager in selecting and securing audiovisual aids, particularly those used at conferences and meetings. Examples of audiovisual equipment are projectors (e.g., overhead, opaque, filmstrip, slide, motion picture), screens, display boards, flip charts, and easels.

Automatic data-processing equipment. See DATA-PROCESSING EQUIPMENT.

Billing machines. See BUSINESS MACHINES.

Board basket. A desk file kept by a corporate secretary for collecting notes and material to be used at the next meeting of the corporation's board of directors.

As matters to be addressed come before the corporate secretary, he or she examines them, makes whatever notes are necessary, puts the material into shape for handling at the meeting, and then inserts it in the board basket. Shortly before the meeting, the corporate secretary or the office secretary makes up the agenda (see Chapter 3/AGENDA) for the meeting from the material in the basket, numbering the documents in the file to correspond with the numbers of the subjects listed on the agenda.

Bookkeeping and accounting machines. See BUSINESS MACHINES.

Business machines. Machines used to facilitate the office operations that occur in day-to-day business. Today, there are machines to simplify almost any office operation from writing letters to showing filed items to executives without having to send them through the interoffice mail. Often they may be leased as well as purchased, and office equipment retail stores (or manufacturers) offer maintenance contracts for regular servicing. Some of the more widely used business machines available in all price ranges are the following:

Addressing machines. These machines consist of numerous electronic or mechanical devices for addressing. They may use paper plates that can be made up on a typewriter or metal plates that are supplied by the companies manufacturing the machines. With some models, the proper plates are stacked in machines so that envelopes or checks can be fed in manually or mechanically. Mailing lists are also frequently maintained by computers, word processors, and automatic typewriters.

Billing machines. These machines are, in effect, typewriters with built-in automatic calculators. They permit the operators to post entries on ledger accounts at the same time invoices are being made up. Some of the machines accumulate totals of all postings; others make extensions automatically. (See also *Computer,* below, and Chapter 11/ACCOUNTING RECORDS.) Modern billing machines have an automatic arithmetic function, and many are but one component in a total systems concept that includes word processors, com-puter communication, and a variety of other information-processing equipment.

Bookkeeping and accounting machines. Automatic bookkeeping and accounting machines are operated from punched cards or other forms of coded instructions. They tabulate, extend, post, and total on reports, ledgers, and statements. Many offices now handle numerous bookkeeping functions with a combination of automatic and electronic equipment that not only does the computations but also holds information in storage, displays it instantly, prints it, and revises it as needed. (See also *Computer,* below and Chapter 11/ACCOUNTING RECORDS.)

Calculating machines. These machines range from simple adding machines to complicated calculating machines that perform all basic computations. Two traditional types are the printing calculator and the rotary calculator. Also common are key-driven machines and electronic calculators, including hand-held, pocket models. Many secretaries have an electronic calculator with a digital display screen on their desks at all times. The printing calculator is designed principally for businesses requiring an all-purpose machine in which every phase of figuring is required. This machine divides, multiplies, adds, and subtracts with *printed* proof of every factor used in each problem. (See also *Computer,* below, and Chapter 11/ACCOUNTING RECORDS.

Check-writing machines. Compact, inexpensive machines are available to imprint the amount of a check. It is possible to add facsimile signatures so that only two operations are necessary to write a check: (1) to type, write in, or mechanically imprint the name of the payee, and (2) to imprint the amount and signature on the check with a checkwriter. The checkwriter not only makes a better appearing check than one manually drawn, but it makes alteration impossible since it prints by partially perforating the face of the check. Check writing can also be accomplished by use of a simple imprint stamp.

Closed-circuit television. A video process allows instantaneous visual record communication among all parts of an office or plant. (see also Chapter 8/DUPLICATING PROCESSES.) Thus, closed-circuit television is widely used in all kinds of organizations for training programs, for promotional purposes (e.g., publicity films), and for problem solving (e.g., by monitoring work areas).

Computers. Basically, a sophisticated calculating machine that receives and stores data, performs some action according to a planned program, and outputs the results. The equipment varies substantially in size and performance. *Word processors* are dedicated computers; that is, they perform primarily text production, although with the right software a word processor can also do other tasks more commonly associated with a computer. See Chapter 1/WORD PROCESSING. Since small, desktop computers are commonplace even in small offices, secretaries have been relieved of many tedious, time-consuming information-processing tasks.

These highly technical machines have two major advantages over other machines: (1) the tremendous speed at which they operate, and (2) their degree of self-containment. Generally, no human intervention is necessary from the time data are fed into the machine, and corrections are made, until the computer prints out the data in report or other form through a printing device or displays them on a televisionlike screen by means of a cathode-ray tube (CRT).

An *intelligent terminal* is one that can produce material on its own without being connected to a large central computer. A *dumb terminal*, often consisting only of a keyboard and display screen, functions through the logic of the central computer. The intelligent terminal commonly consists of a keyboard (attached or detachable), a televisionlike display screen (monitor), a central processing unit (the brains of the computer), one or more disk drives (for storing and outputting information), and a printer (a device that automatically types, or prints out, what you input). Information is usually stored on removable magnetic tapes or, more commonly, diskettes or on larger capacity permanent hard disks.

Two types of software, available on removable tapes or diskettes, are the *system software*, which instructs the computer what to do, and the *special-purpose software*, which enables you to perform certain tasks such as editing or bookkeeping.

Generally, the electronic computer can sort, compute, summarize, record, communicate, and classify information. Thus it is used for many purposes in addition to word processing such as inventory control, billing, and payroll computation. In modern offices, computers are often integrated with other functions such as facsimile (see below) and electronic mail (see Chapter 2/ELECTRONIC MESSAGE SYSTEMS).

Copying machines. Any photographic equipment that makes copies on film or paper. Unlike duplicating equipment, which can produce hundreds or thousands of copies economically, copying machines are noted for economy where single copies, or a limited number of copies, are desired. Most office copying machines produce copies on paper, rather than film. Some can reduce and enlarge, copy on two sides, and copy in color. Machines vary greatly in size, cost, speed, and type of process used. For instance, copiers may be dry or wet, depending on the need for chemical solutions. Some feed paper through rollers, around drums, and some use a flat surface. Some can make only one copy at a time; others produce multiple copies at high speed. Some will accept almost any paper such as bond typing paper; others must use a specially treated paper.

Most copiers may be rented, leased, or purchased.

Dictating machines. Many mechanical devices are available to record dictation. Various machines record on plastic magnetic belts, disks, and tapes. A point to consider in choosing a dictating machine is the amount of dictation that each recording unit will take. Another point to consider if your employer dictates when he or she is away from the office is the ease with which the recording units may be transported.

Many offices today look for compatible systems, whereby components can be interchanged or used in all offices of a company. Needs vary from person to person. For example, small, pocket-size units appeal to frequent travelers; some offices look for special features, such as remote message call-in, whereby you can call in for messages from anywhere in the world, and visual display panels that show where a letter begins and ends and how much tape is left. Some accessories, such as microphones and foot-operated activating devices, are optional.

Portable machines are the smallest size units and will fit in a briefcase or pocket. Desktop units occupy a small area on a desk and may be integrated with telephone answering systems (e.g., one could telephone the office and have the machine record dictation directly). *Small work-group systems* integrate desktop and telephone-answering capabilities among a number of persons who share secretarial support. A *central dictation system* is designed to serve an entire organization. See also Chapter 1/DICTATION, TAKING AND TRANSCRIBING.

Facsimiles. One of the oldest technologies, facsimile (or fax) is a means of sending an exact duplicate of text or graphics, to a receiving terminal, over the telephone lines. Machines that both send and receive are called "transceivers." Since fax machines have no keyboard the machine must be prepared on another machine (e.g., computer) and then placed in a tray or around a cylinder, depending on the fax equipment, where it is scanned and converted into signals that will travel over the telephone lines.

Older machines, known as Group I and II, use an analog device and transmit at speeds of two to six minutes a page. Newer Group III and IV machines, using a faster digital technique, transmit a page in twenty seconds or less. See Chapter 2/ELECTRONIC MESSAGE SYSTEMS, *Facsimile.*

Facsimile machines can be purchased or leased. One can also take a document to any service establishment that offers fax service and have a duplicate copy transmitted much the same as you can have a telegram sent by Western Union.

Postal meters. Metering machines can be installed to stamp outgoing mail. If application is made to the postmaster at the mailing office, permits may be issued to persons or concerns for mailing matter without stamps affixed, the postage being paid in money, provided the mailings are presented in accordance with the regulations.

The person or concern that has obtained the permit takes the meter to the post office and buys a certain amount of postage. The postmaster then sets the meter in accordance with the amount of postage paid for and seals it. When the amount of postage paid for is used up, the meter locks and must be reset by the postmaster after additional money has been paid. It is possible, however, to buy additional postage before the meter locks. Also, remote setting systems enable users to reset their own meters and pay for postage automatically. Using a meter, which has to be set at the post office, encourages the maintenance of accurate records.

The meters can be adjusted to imprint the denomination of postage desired. The amount of postage paid must appear on each meter stamp. The indicia may be imprinted directly on the envelope, or, with the use of a meter-stamp tape attachment, the indicia may also be imprinted on a gummed strip of paper that can be affixed to bulky envelopes or packages. When used for first-class or priority mail, metered indicia must show the correct date of mailing.

Associated equipment includes electronic scales and mailing machines that automatically feed, seal, transport, stack, and imprint mail.

Tabulating machines. Some machines sort and tabulate information recorded by another machine in a total systems configuration. When information has been transcribed to punched cards (see PUNCHED-CARD EQUIPMENT), these cards can be placed in machines that will sort them according to any predetermined pattern and will tabulate the information punched on the card.

Teleprinters. Typewriterlike machines, with a keyboard whereby operators can prepare text (but not graphics) to be sent over the telephone lines to a receiving machine that will convert the signals back to text and print out the message. Teleprinters are used for sending telex messages through subscriber networks. Telex I (formerly TWX) was established by Western Union. Transmission occurs at sixty-seven words a minute. Telex II is a newer and faster form of transmission (about one hundred words a minute), but subscribers to one service can send messages to subscribers to the other without difficulty. Services are available by subscription through Western Union or any of the major international carriers such as ITT World Communications.

A similar but faster service is Teletex (about forty-five times the speed of Telex I). Whereas Telex I and Telex II are transmitted in all capitals and show inferior print quality, Teletex resembles a traditional business letter. See Chapter 2/ELECTRONIC MESSAGE SYSTEMS, *Telex.*

Typewriters. Electric and electronic typewriters are essential to the modern business office. *Electric* typewriters include the standard, proportional spacer, and Selectric (using an interchangeable type element rather than bar and carriage) models. Special features, such as a correcting key and automatic paper injector-ejector, are available on many models. The more technologically advanced *electronic* models have numerous additional features such as line, phrase, or document memory capability; a display for viewing lines of type before they are committed to paper; delete, insert, and search-and-replace features; automatic carriage return; automatic formatting (e.g., underscoring, decimal alignment, centering); spell checkers (an internal dictionary for proofreading); and many other add-on options that approach the capabilities of a word processor.

Automatic typewriters, commonly using a prerecorded master perforated roll or tape, are used for tasks such as maintaining a mailing list and producing similar, individually typed letters. They are great timesavers when the same letter is going to a large number of people. Names and addresses for each letter are typed on the same machine that automatically types the letter. Thus an original copy, with no resemblance to a form letter, is produced. The machines type much more rapidly than the fastest typist, and one operator can manage several at the same time. However, automatic typewriters have no display (such as a computer monitor) where you can see what you are typing as you work and thus fall short of the capabilities of more modern word processing equipment. See also Chapter 1/TYPING.

Word processors. See *Computers,* above.

Calculating machines. See BUSINESS MACHINES.

Calendars. *Office calendar.* A yearly calendar with notations of appointments and things to be done in the future. Either a standard desk calendar pad or a yearbook with fifteen- or thirty-minute time divisions may be used. (See also POCKET MEMO CALENDAR.) An executive's calendar should be large enough to permit notation of a caller's affiliation and the purpose of the call. Certain items, such as due dates of insurance premiums, are entered on the calendar from year to year. These items should be entered on the calendar for the forthcoming year in October or November. Entries of recurring items should be made from a list and not from the calendar for the current year, because the dates of events change. For example, if board meetings are held on the first Monday of every month, the actual dates vary from year to year.

1. *Checklist of entries to make on calendar.*

Appointments

Clients, in and out of office
Doctor and dentist
Office personnel, executives or otherwise
Social, evening and daytime

Collection Dates

Interest on notes receivable and maturity dates of notes
Coupons to be clipped
Dividends to be received

Family Dates

Anniversaries
Birthdays
Father's Day
Mother's Day

Holidays

Christmas
Easter
Election Day
Independence Day
Labor Day
Memorial Day
New Year's Day
Religious holidays
Thanksgiving
Valentine's Day

Meetings

Association meetings
Board meetings
Club meetings
Committee meetings (company and outside activities)
Stockholders' meetings

Payment Dates

Association dues
Contributions
Insurance premiums
Interest on notes payable and maturity dates
Periodic payments, such as salaries, rent, allowances to children, tuition, and the like

Renewal Dates

Automobile license and registration
Hunting and fishing licenses
Subscriptions to periodicals

Tax Dates

Federal income tax returns and payment dates for the manager's personal tax
Social security tax returns and payments
State and local taxes
Unemployment tax returns and payments
Withholding tax returns and payments

2. *Use of tickler file with calendar.* The use of a three-by-five-inch card tickler file reduces the work necessary to prepare a calendar, although it does not take the place of a calendar. (See Chapter 1/TICKLER FILE.) Recurring items can be put on one card, and the card can be moved from week to week, month to month, or year to year. Thus if a certain check is made out each Friday, one card can be made and moved each week, instead of

making fifty-two entries in the calendar. Furthermore, all necessary information can be put on the card so that anyone can make out the check and mail it without referring to any other material.

Corporation calendar. Notation of acts of a corporation that must be done at scheduled times. The acts for which a corporate secretary, and thus his or her private secretary, is usually responsible relate to (1) directors' and stockholders' meetings; (2) dividend and interest payments; (3) expiration and renewal of contracts; (4) stock exchange requirements; (5) tax matters.

A common form of corporation calendar is a card index, three by five inches, arranged chronologically behind monthly tab cards. The card contains sufficient information, in addition to the date, to give the office secretary a correct idea of what he or she is to do. The cards are made up as a transaction occurs or as the need for the card arises. Thus if the secretary is custodian of the corporate documents and is given a lease to put in the safe, he or she will note the expiration date of the lease and make up a card for that particular day.

Acts to be done at certain times but for which no definite day is specified may be entered on a monthly reminder card. For example, suppose that in a certain state the corporation is required to file a statement with the secretary of state each time a change in officers occurs. The secretary will make a note of the requirement on a card without a date and at the beginning of each month move it along to the next month. Or he or she might make a note on twelve separate cards and file one for each month.

At the beginning of each month, all items in the calendar for the succeeding two months should be examined to allow ample time for taking action on the reminders furnished by the cards. Time-consuming tasks that must be done by a certain date should be entered sufficiently in advance to permit the work to be finished on time.

If detailed schedules of meetings of parent and subsidiary companies (see Chapter 3/MEETING, Figure 1) are maintained, the calendar cards for meeting dates need not contain detailed information. Many secretaries use ordinary diary books that may be purchased at any stationery store, instead of the card system, and make up a corporation calendar in it at the beginning of each year. The advantage of the card system, however, is that it furnishes a perpetual record.

Carbon paper. The two common types of carbon papers are traditional wax carbons and solvent-coated carbons. Solvent papers usually last longer, give cleaner impressions, and produce more uniform copies. With traditional papers, select the heaviest carbon paper that will yield a sharp impression. Thin paper is required for making a large number of copies at once, whereas heavy paper, because of its durability, should be used if only one or two copies are needed.

Carbon papers are offered in different weights and in a film or plastic grade; for example, lightweight, which will yield one to ten copies; medium weight, which will yield one to five copies; heavy weight, which will yield one to two copies; film (plastic), which will yield one to ten copies. Some manufacturers identify weights numerically. For instance, No. 5 might mean one to eight copies. Carbon with a hard finish should be used unless it is for use on a noiseless typewriter. It is more durable than carbon with a soft finish and does not smear.

Carbon is made of several colors. Black is used universally; blue is the prevailing color for pencil carbon work. Carbon imprint shows up better on white, yellow, or pink second sheets than on blue, green, russet, or cherry.

To avoid curling and wrinkling, carbon should be kept carefully in the desk, with the coated side down, out of the sunlight, and away from steam pipes. Film (or plastic) paper, being more durable, can be used longer.

When quality is not important, carbon sets, with carbon paper attached to the copy paper, may be used. They are designed for speed and convenience. The carbon is used only once and discarded.

Another convenient product is the specially treated carbonless paper. Multiple copies may be attached to the top, often preprinted as a form (e.g., invoice), with no carbon paper required.

See also OFFICE PAPER; LETTER-HEAD.

Check-writing machines. See BUSI-NESS MACHINES.

Collating equipment. Machines that aid in the assembly of typed or duplicated pages. Most small jobs, which involve the assembly of only a few copies containing a few pages, are collated by hand. Sometimes mechanical aids, such as tilted racks, or revolving tables, are used. For larger assembly jobs, the secretary may have access to a mechanical collator or an automatic collator. Such equipment is often part of a total production terminal, with typesetting, printing, addressing, and mailing equipment as well. Mechanical equipment contains racks for stacking individual pages. Often a foot pedal is pressed to activate the release of one sheet from each stack. Automatic equipment, which may be complex, high-speed machines that contain up to 100 stations or bins, operates without manual intervention. Pages are released and assembled automatically by such machines. Collating devices may also be purchased to assemble on copy machines for automatic collating.

Combination envelope. See Chapter 1/ENCLOSURE.

Composing machine. See TYPESETTING EQUIPMENT; Chapter 8/COLD TYPE; HOT TYPE; LINOTYPE; LUDLOW; MONOTYPE.

Computers. See BUSINESS MACHINES, *Computers.*

Continuation sheets. Stationery used for second, third, and so on pages of a letter. Continuation sheets, also called second sheets, should be the same size and quality of paper as the letterheads. Since comparatively few letters are more than one page, continuation sheets should be ordered in considerably smaller quantities than letterheads. Depending on office policy, the name of the addressee, the number of the page, and the date may be typed across the top of each page of a letter other than the first. Some firms have the firm name, but no address, printed on the continuation sheets.

Copying machines. See BUSINESS MACHINES, *Copying machines.*

Data-processing equipment. Automated and electronic equipment that receives numeric or alphabetic information, processes (changes) it, stores it, and transmits it. Automatic equipment consists of input, storage, computing control, and output devices. Electronic circuitry in the main computing element performs arithmetic and/or logic operations automatically by means of externally programmed instructions. Electronic data processing of information by way of electronic equipment, such as an internally stored program, electronic digital computer, or other automatic data-processing machine.

See also BUSINESS MACHINES; PUNCHED-CARD EQUIPMENT; Chapter 1/AUTOMATION; DATA PROCESSING.

Diary. A daily record of what is accomplished and also of future appointments and work to be done. Diaries instead of calendars are usually kept by professional persons who keep a record of the time devoted to a specific client so the client may be charged for the time. The diary has a separate page for each day in the year. Many standard yearbooks are satisfactory. The important thing is that they should have space for work performed and the time consumed doing it, as well as space for appointments and matters to be attended to. A diary is prepared originally in the same manner as a CALENDAR. Entries of time consumed on each task are made from day to day after the work is completed.

Dictating machines. See BUSINESS MACHINES, *Dictating machines.*

Display. See BUSINESS MACHINES, *Computers.*

Duplication equipment. See Chapter 8/DUPLICATING PROCESSES.

Dvorak Keyboard. A typewriter keyboard on which the keys have been rearranged so that the left hand carries only 44 percent of the typing load and the right hand carries the other 56 percent. Also, the rearrangement reduces the distance the fingers travel from the normal typing position. The keyboard is called the Dvorak Keyboard after its inventor. It is also known as the Simplified Keyboard.

Electronic data-processing equipment. See DATA-PROCESSING EQUIPMENT; BUSINESS MACHINES, *Computers.*

Electronic computer. See BUSINESS MACHINES, *Computers.*

Envelopes. See STATIONERY.

Facsimile. See BUSINESS MACHINES, *Facsimile.*

Filing equipment. All forms of storage devices, cabinets, and containers for active and inactive files. The most common types of equipment and devices are visible files, open-shelf files, rotary and push-button files, and file cabinets. Visible files (often transparent pockets) are designed to make information available at a glance. Open-shelf files are often used to reduce space and cost of equipment. Rotary and push-button files provide for the movement or rotation of material electrically. The standard file cabinet, in legal or letter sizes, with several drawers and in a choice of colors, is basic in many offices, even when other equipment is used. Many suppliers of storage equipment provide decorating and design consulting services for offices seeking maximum benefits and efficiency in equipment layout, color coordination, and resulting employee productivity. Some types of filing devices and equipment are designed for rapid movement of material, for example, the high-speed information storage and retrieval machines and microfilming equipment. (See Chapter 1/INFORMATION STORAGE AND RETRIEVAL; MICROFILMING).

Forms. Preprinted or standard-format information blanks. The advantage of a fill-in form is that facts can be added without retyping the entire piece each time. Forms of all sizes and styles are used for applications, collection notices, standard letters, reports, and virtually any other material that can be standardized. See PRINTED LAW BLANK; Chapter 7/FORM LETTERS.

Keyboard. See BUSINESS MACHINES, *Computers.*

Law blank. See PRINTED LAW BLANK.

Legal back. A traditional backing sheet, about eight and one-half or nine inches by fifteen inches, of thick paper, used to bind legal documents. (Many offices prefer more modern procedures such as spiral or flat binding.) The covers are referred to as *backs* because they cover only the back of the papers bound in them. Certain data, referred to as the *endorsement*, are typed on the back of the cover. An endorsed back of an agreement is illustrated in Figure 1. The contents of the endorsement vary with the instrument but usually include a brief description of the instrument and the names of the parties to it. The endorsement is typed in a definite position on the backing sheet, and the sheet must be folded in a special manner so that the typing will appear in the proper position.

To type the endorsement:

1. Lay the backing sheet on the desk as though for reading.

2. Bring the bottom edge up to approximately one inch from the top and crease.

LEGAL BACK: FIGURE 1: Endorsed legal back of an agreement

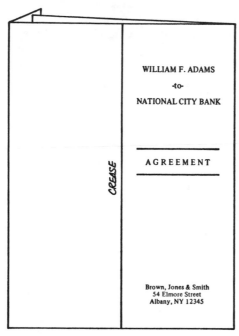

WILLIAM F. ADAMS

-to-

NATIONAL CITY BANK

CREASE

AGREEMENT

Brown, Jones & Smith
54 Elmore Street
Albany, NY 12345

3. Bring the creased end (which is now at the bottom) up to approximately one inch from the top. (You now have a fold with about one inch of the top edge of the backing sheet protruding beyond the fold.)

4. The surface of the folded sheet that is uppermost is the surface on which the endorsement is to be typed. (If the backing sheet has a printed panel or the firm's name on it, that portion of the sheet will be the uppermost surface.) Put a small pencil check in the upper *left*-hand corner of that surface.

5. Partially unfold and insert in the typewriter so that the pencil mark is on the upper *right*-hand corner of the surface when you type on it.

6. Do not type to the left of the crease. (See Figure 1.) After typing the endorsement, turn down the top edge of the backing sheet about an inch (see Step 3), crease, insert document in the crease, and staple. Fold the document and the backing sheet, creasing the document to fit the creases in the backing sheet.

Letterhead. Paper with a heading printed or engraved on it; also the heading that is printed on the paper. Common use has standardized eight and one-half by eleven inches as the most practical size for business letterheads. Envelopes, files, and business machines are all geared most efficiently to this size. It is referred to as "letterhead size," although letterheads in other sizes are used. The executive size (seven and one-fourth by ten and one-half inches) is frequently selected for the personal stationery of executives. Other variations in size are eight by eleven, seven and one-half by ten, seven by ten, and "half sheets."

Executive letterhead. Although modern letterhead designs are often innovative and colorful, the letterheads for the *personal* use of executives, particularly high officials, possess dignity to impress the reader. Their chief characteristic is simplicity, attained by a conservative color printing or engraving on white or pastel colored paper of substantial thickness and high cotton content. In addition to the company letterhead, the full name of the office is printed or engraved at the left margin, with the title of the office he or she holds directly underneath it. The size of the sheet is often smaller than standard letterhead.

Business people may use their standard business letterheads for all correspondence except answers to formal invitations, letters of condolence, or answers to letters of condolence from personal friends. For these purposes, executives should use WRITING PAPER.

For the selection of envelopes and papers for letterheads, see STATIONERY; OFFICE PAPER.

Master. See STENCILS.

Monitor. See BUSINESS MACHINES, *Computers*.

Office paper. Both LETTERHEAD stationery and plain cotton-content or bond paper are used in text preparation. Quality letterhead usually has a cotton content of 25, 75, or 100 percent. It should be twenty-pound weight or higher, in a white or conservative light color. Lightweight paper used for carbon copies is also available with a cotton content. See CARBON PAPER. Quality cotton-content paper may be used for any purpose for which appearance is important, although a high-grade bond is more common for nonstationery uses. Cotton-content is usually more expensive than bond paper, and the higher the cotton content, the more expensive the paper.

Bond paper is graded according to brightness and opacity. A No. 1 bond, the highest quality, is often used in place of a cotton-content paper for general stationery. Lower quality bond (e.g., Nos. 4 or 5) is often used for duplicating, photocopying, and drafting. The bond paper used for most typing and word processing projects is a sixteen- or twenty-pound weight. Some firms use the lighter weights (e.g., less than twenty pound) papers for drafts and certain routine work forms to cut costs. Carbon-copy paper also is available in sulfite bonds, often in a seven- or nine-pound weight.

Office supplies. Supplies used daily in an office, such as STATIONERY, CARBON PAPER, rubber bands, staples, file folders, pencils, scratch pads, and numerous other itmes. Office supplies are charged to an expense account and are deductible from income for tax purposes, whereas office equipment, such as BUSINESS MACHINES, is charged to the capital account and depreciation is written off each year. (See Chapter 11/DEPRECIATION).

Pocket memo calendar. A small pocket memorandum book in which appointments are noted. An executive usually takes the memo book to meetings, luncheons, on trips, and the like, where questions of future appointments might arise. See also CALENDARS.

Postal meter. See BUSINESS MACHINES.

Printed law blank. Printed form of a legal instrument, such as a mortgage or deed, with blank spaces to be filled in with specific information, such as the names of the parties and the description of the property being mortgaged or sold. Printed law blanks are widely used in drawing up legal instruments. Law-blank printers publish a catalog showing the numbers and titles of blanks they print. Each law blank has its title and, usually, the printer's catalog number, printed in small letters on it. The blanks are obtainable at almost any stationery store. Frequently, the secretary can fill in these blanks without any dictated instructions. When it is necessary to dictate the material to be inserted in the blanks, the usual manner of giving instructions is as follows:

The dictator numbers in pencil the spaces to be filled in, 1, 2, 3, and so on. He or she then dictates the material that should be typed in each numbered blank, thus eliminating any confusion about where each dictated insertion should be typed.

Observe the following suggestions about filling in law blanks, so the completed form will be neat and accurate:

Typing on ruled lines. Make certain that the typing is adjusted so that the bases of letters with tails that extend below the line of type (*g, p,* and *y*) just touch the ruled line.

Date of printing. Printed forms bear a printer's mark showing the number of copies printed and the date of the printing. When filling in more than one copy, use forms that were printed at the same time, because a change may have been made in the form.

Registration of printing. Before attempting to fill in more than one blank form at a time by using carbon paper, make sure that the printing on all copies registers exactly. To do this, place the edges of the forms together and hold them to the light. The printed material in one copy should be exactly over corresponding material in the other copy. After the forms and carbon paper are inserted in the typewriter, if the forms are not perfectly aligned, loosen the typewriter platen and adjust the edges of the forms. They must be exactly even, or the typing will not be properly spaced on the copies.

Fill-ins on both sides of sheet. When making carbon copies of a form that has fill-ins on both sides of the sheet, take particular care to avoid having one side the ribbon copy and the other side the carbon copy, which would render the form unfit for execution. Double-sheet forms are particularly apt to cause trouble in this respect.

Small blanks. When the blanks on the form are small, fill in each form individually; do not use carbons. Be careful not to overlook any of the small blanks. In many forms they are not indicated by underlining, but only by a small space. Many of them call only for letters identifying the person or persons signing the document. For example, a printed mortgage form might include the following: "Said mortgagee, —, —h— heirs or assigns." If there is more than one mortgagee, *s* is added to *mortgagee,* and —h— becomes *their.* If there is only one mortgagee, the first blank is not filled in, and —h— becomes *her* or *his.*

"Z" ruling. If the typed material does not fill the space provided for it on the form, make a "Z" ruling to cover the unused space, as shown here.

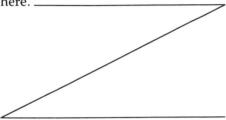

Printer. See BUSINESS MACHINES, *Computers.*

Punched-card equipment. Although punched-card equipment is considered nearly obsolete in light of more advanced electronic equipment, various models, sizes, and types of machines still use punched cards (or punched tape) for general data processing, for cost-accounting work, and for statistical and analytical research. Cards are divided into "fields," each of which has vertical columns of figures from zero to nine. The figures applicable to each field are recorded by punching out holes in the appropriate columns. The fields are arranged according to the data desired. For example, the accounts-payable card used in a retail store might have fields showing invoice date, vendor's invoice number, vendor's number, department, due date, terms, gross amount, discount, net amount, transportation, total cost, retail price, percentage markup, and posting data.

Machines used in various steps to process the punched cards are the keypunch, verifier, reproducer, sorter, collator, tabulator, communications equipment, and document writer and interpreter. Punched-card or punched-tape equipment can (1) transmit information from one machine to another mechanically (see DATA-PROCESSING EQUIPMENT; Chapter 1/DATA PROCESSING), (2) correlate data already on the cards with new information, thus eliminating the mechanical entry of standing information, (3) be mechanically controlled by means of a master wiring board in which the patterns of operation are set, (4) permit instant transmission of data between cities. Punched-card information can be transmitted over the telephone lines.

Ribbons. Ribbons for printers and typewriters are available with several types of fiber content: cotton, silk, nylon, carbon film, and polyethylene. The cotton fabric is the least expensive, but it also produces the poorest quality image. Both silk and nylon have a long life; carbon film and polyethylene are used once and discarded. Silk, nylon, and polyethylene all produce a sharp image.

Special-purpose ribbons are available: two-color (e.g., red and black), stencil (a clear, plastic ribbon), photostat (for use in ultraviolet light), offset (to type directly on offset masters), opaque (for use in conjunction with the Diazo copying machine), and correcting ribbons (for "lift-off" correction of errors).

Other features a secretary must

consider in selecting ribbons are the degree of inking desired, length of the ribbon, thickness (thin ribbons provide the sharpest image), and edge (woven-edge ribbons are more suitable for electric machines).

Improvements and new features appear on the market regularly, and the secretary should periodically study manufacturers' literature and examine new products in office-supply stores.

Second sheets. See CONTINUATION SHEETS.

Sorting device. See Chapter 1/ FILING SYSTEMS.

Stationery. Good paper enhances the effectiveness of a LETTERHEAD. The features to be considered in selecting paper for a business letterhead are (1) taction, (2) workability, (3) permanence, and (4) cost. *Taction* in paper is commonly expressed as the "feel." It is one of the standards by which letterhead papers are evaluated. High-grade papers have good bulk, crispness, and crackle like a new bank note. *Workability* determines the ease of use, economy of operation and quality of work in the office and in the pressroom. In the office, the workability of a paper is judged by its ability to reproduce clearly defined characters, to withstand erasures, and to permit a smooth flowing signature. In the pressroom, workability means the adaptability of paper to the various printing processes. *Permanence* or *strength* and *durability* are prime requisites of good letterheads and envelopes.

The quality of paper is judged by weight and content.

Weight. The term *basis weight* refers to the weight of paper measured by the ream, which consists of five hundred sheets in the standard size for the grade in question (offset, reprographic, and so on). The basis weight of bond paper in a typical grade might be designated as "Substance 20," meaning that five hundred sheets in a standard seventeen-by-twenty-two-inch size weighs twenty pounds. A good quality of paper weighs more than a poor quality. See OFFICE PAPER.

Content. Most business letterheads are made from wood pulp, from cotton fiber, or from a combination of the two. (Recycled stock is available for many business purposes.) Letterhead paper made from wood pulp is sulfite bond, manufactured in different grades of quality. The most durable, the best-looking, and the most expensive paper is that with a 100 percent cotton content, that is, made entirely from cotton fiber. See OFFICE PAPER. Formerly, the watermark *rag content* was used by all fine paper mills to describe their better grades of paper containing cotton fibers. The watermark *cotton content* is being used today to describe more adequately the basic fiber contained in fine papers.

Grain. All paper has a "grain," or chief fiber direction. It comes from the process by which the paper is made. In letterheads the grain should be parallel to the direction of the writing, that is, the eight-and-one-half-inch way. (Letterheads used with one of the duplicating processes are an exception.) The sheets hug the typewriter platen better and provide a smoother, firmer surface for the type impression. Erasing is easier with the grain parallel to the platen, and paper always folds easier *with*, rather than *against*, the grain. Every sheet of paper has a "felt" side and a "wire" side. The letterhead should be printed on the felt side.

How to order stationery. Get a written quotation that specifies the weight and content of paper and the kind of engraving or printing that will be on it.

In placing the order, specify: (1) the quantity in reams or sheets, (2) the weight, (3) the content, (4) the grain, (5) that the letterhead should be printed on the "felt" side of the paper, (6) the size, (7) the color, (8) the previous order number if a repeat number, (9) the supplier's reference number if an initial order. Include a sample with the order if possible.

Envelopes for letterheads. Envelopes should be of the same quallity as the letterhead. The most popular sizes for business are:

Monarch	3⅞" by 7½"
No. 6¾	3⅝" by 6½"
No. 9	3⅞" by 8⅞"
No. 10	4⅛" by 9½"

No. 6¾, No. 9, and No. 10 fit eight-and-one-half-by-eleven-inch letterheads. The Monarch size is used with a letterhead size seven and one-fourth by ten and one-half inches, the executive stationery. No. 5, four and one-fourth by five and one-eighth inches, Baronial is also used by business executives for their personal stationery. (See WINDOW ENVELOPE.)

Continuation sheets. CONTINUATION SHEETS should be of the same size and quality as the letterhead. They should be ordered when the letterhead is ordered, although fewer sheets may be needed. After you have placed two or three orders for stationery, you will be able to judge fairly accurately the proportion of continuation sheets to letterheads.

Letterheads for foreign mail. Lightweight business letterheads are used for foreign correspondence. The order should specify *cotton content onionskin.* Lightweight paper made from clean, strong cotton fibers produces crisp letterheads that are outstanding in appearance and have the stamina to withstand frequent handling.

Stencils. Each duplicating process—fluid, stencil, offset, photocopy—uses its own stencil or master copy. The traditional *stencil* is a thin cellulose paper coated with wax, attached to a backing sheet, often supplied with a pilofilm cover. Cushion sheets may also be provided to reduce the impact of the typewriter keys on the stencil sheet. Stencils are prepared by typing or writing directly on the waxed sheet. A special fluid is used to make corrections. A common size stencil is eight and one-half by fourteen inches, with areas marked off for letter-size and postcard dimensions. The stencil process is popular for duplicating needs where the quality of copies is not critical. Stencils are used on duplicators commonly known as mimeograph machines.

A *fluid master* has a master sheet of paper and a sheet of carbon paper fastened at one end, with a tissue between that must be removed before typing.

An *offset master* may be either paper or metal. Paper masters are made of a specially treated master that has guide marks for typing similar to those on a stencil. Unlike the fluid master, there is no carbon, and unlike the stencil, there are extra sheets. All stencils and master, however, are alike in that they must be handled with care to avoid smudging or tearing.

Supplies. 1. *Office.* See OFFICE SUPPLIES.

2. *Travel.* See Chapter 4/TRAVEL EQUIPMENT AND SUPPLIES.

Tabulating machines. See BUSINESS MACHINES, *Tabulating machines.*

Teleprinter. See BUSINESS MACHINES, *Teleprinters.*

Television. See BUSINESS MACHINES, *Closed-circuit television.*

Typesetting equipment. Also called composition equipment. Machines that will set type in various sizes and type faces, with justified right and left margins (lines of predetermined, equal width). Type is frequently classified as "hot" (set with metal) or "cold" (set by typewriter or photographic methods). Equipment used for cold-type composition might vary from a typewriter to a computer (now popular for desktop publishing) to electronically controlled photocomposition equipment.

Economy is sometimes a principal factor in selecting cold type, although the typewriter method (depending on the equipment used) may produce a lower quality product. Hot-type equipment most often refers to the linotype and monotype machines. Linotype machines produce solid lines of type by dropping letters into place; monotpye works in a simliar way but produces single type characters. See Chapter 8/COLD TYPE; HOT TYPE; TYPE FACE.

Typewriters. See BUSINESS MACHINES, *Typewriters.*

Typewriter-correction supplies. See Chapter 1/ERASURES AND CORRECTIONS.

Visible filing equipment. See FILING EQUIPMENT.

Window envelope. A special type of envelope made with a rectangular hole at the point where the address is usually typed. The hole is covered with transparent paper. The inside address shows through this transparent "window." The inside address must be typed at a certain point on every letter, and the letter must be folded in the prescribed manner so the address will show through the window. Window envelopes are a great timesaver, but their usage is generally restricted to invoices, statements, circulars, and the like. Probably the reason this type of envelope is less popular for general correspondence is that, with a fixed position for the inside address, the layout of the letter will not present a good appearance. (See Chapter 7/INSIDE ADDRESS; LAYOUT.)

Word processors. See BUSINESS MACHINES, *Computers.*

Writing paper. Paper used for writing social communications. Writing paper should not be referred to as *stationery.* An executive's writing paper should be engraved or printed only with his or her residence address or initials. Initials are preferable to a monogram for a man's writing paper. The paper should be white, cream, gray blue, oxford blue, or another pastel color, with black or other dark color engraving. It should be heavy or medium weight, six by seven inches, with envelopes six by three and one-half inches. An executive may use his or her *business* letterheads for all correspondence except handwritten invitations, answers to formal invitations, letters of condolence, and answers to letters of condolence from personal friends.

See also LETTERHEAD; OFFICE PAPER; STATIONERY.

PART II

WRITTEN COMMUNICATION

CHAPTER 6

GRAMMAR AND VOCABULARY

Abbreviations. Short versions of words and phrases. In correspondence and general text copy, abbreviations of common, nontechnical words (e.g., *mgr*, for manager) should be avoided. However, abbreviations of specialized or technical terminology (e.g., *dBu* for decibel unit) are often used, especially in technical writing, in tables and footnotes, and in forms such as purchase orders. Since authorities disagree in matters of capitalization and punctuation, (e.g., *AC* or *ac* for alternating current), the important thing is to be consistent in usage. However, there is a strong trend toward wide use of small letters without periods, as the following list of general abbreviations illustrates. (See Chapter 2/POSTAL SERVICE, Figure 1, for a list of postal abbreviations.)

GENERAL ABBREVIATIONS

A	answer
aa	author's alteration(s)
aar, AAR	against all risks
abbr.	abbreviated; abbreviation
abr.	abridged; abridgement
a/c	account
A/C	account current
a/d	after date
a.d.	before the day
A.D.	in the year of our Lord (*Anno Domini*)
ad fin.	to or at the end (*ad finem*)
ad inf.	without limit (*ad infinitum*)
ad init.	at the beginning (*ad initium*)
ad int.	in the meantime (*ad interim*)
ad lib., ad libit.	at one's pleasure; freely to the quantity or

	amount desired (*ad libitum*)	©, copr.	copyright
ad loc.	to or at the place (*ad locum*)	c	carat; chapter(s); about (*circa*)
ad val., a/v	according to value (*ad valorem*)	c. and s.c.	capital letters and small capitals (caps and small caps)
aka	also known as	ca	about (*circa*); capital account; credit account; current account; chartered accountant; commercial agent; close annealed
a.m.	before noon (*ante meridiem*)		
anon.	anonymous		
a/o	account of		
a to oc	attached to other correspondence		
		cal.	calendar; caliber
app.	appendix	can.	canceled; cancellation
as.	at sight	caps	capital letters
a/s	after sight	CBX	computerized branch exchange (telephone)
AST	Atlantic standard time		
att.	attached	cc	carbon copy
attn., atten.	attention	cert., ctf.	certified; certificate; certification
au.	author	cf.	compare (*confer*)
AV	authorized version	ch.	chapter; chart
		chap., chaps.	chapter(s)
b	born; brother		
bal.	balance	chg.	change; charge
bc	blind carbon copy	cir/	circular; circulation; circumference
B.C.	before Christ		
bd	bank draft	cl	center line; carload lots
BE	bill of exchange	CLT	code language telegram
B/E	bill of entry	co.	company; county
bf	boldface; brief (legal)	c/o	in care of; cash order; carried over (bookkeeping)
bibl.	library (*bibliotheca*)		
bibliog.	bibliography		
biog.	biography	COD	cash, or collect, on delivery
bkt.	bracket	col.	column
B/L	bill of lading	colloq.	colloquial
bo	branch office; back order	comp.	compiler; compiled by
b/p	blueprint	con.	against (*contra*)
Bros.	Brothers	conj	conjunction
bs	backspace	cont.	continued
b/s	bill of sale; bill of store (commerce)	corp.	corporatinon; corporal; to the body (*corpori*)
bw	please turn page (*bitte werden*)	CST	central standard time
		CT	central time

ctn.	carton	eng.	engraved; engineer; engineering; engine
ctr.	center; counter	Eng.	English
cum	with; cumulative	eo	by authority of his office (*ex officio*)
cur.	current		
d	died; daughter	eod	every other day (advertising)
D/A	deposit account; documents against acceptance; discharge afloat	e&oe	errors and omissions excepted
dba	doing business as (co. name)	eohp	except as otherwise herein provided
dec.	decision; decimal	esp.	especially
def.	definition	Esq.	esquire
deg.	degree(s)	est.	estimated; estate
dept.	department	EST	eastern standard time
dia., diam	diameter	eta	estimated time of arrival
diag.	diagram; diagonal	et al.	and others (*et alii*)
dict.	dictionary	etc.	and the others; and so forth (*et cetera*)
div.	division		
dl	demand loan	et seq.	and the following (*et sequens*)
DL	day letter (telegraph)	ex	out of or from; without or not including
dld	delivered		
DLO	dead letter office	ex.	example
do.	ditto (the same)	exp.	express; expenses
d/s	days after sight		
D.V.	God willing (*Deo volente*)	f.	following (after a numeral; *pl.* ff.); feminine
dy	delivery		
ea.	each	fac.	facsimile; fast as can
eaon	except as otherwise noted	FD	free delivery; free dispatch
ed.	editor; edition(s); edited by; education	Fed. Reg.	*Federal Register*
Ed. Note	editorial note	ff	following (after a numeral); folios
EDP	electronic data processing	fig(s).	figure(s)
EDT	eastern daylight time	fl.	flourished (*floruit*)
EE	errors excepted; Early English	fn.	footnote
		fo	firm offer
e.g.	for example (*exempli gratia*)	fob	free on board
		foc	free of charge
enc.	enclosure	fod	free of damage
ency., encyc.	encyclopedia	fol.	folio; following
		fr.	from
end.	endorse; endorsement	Fr.	French

frt.	freight
fv.	on the back of the page (*folio verso*)
fwd	forward
fx	foreign exchange
FYI	for your information (interoffice use)
gen	genus
GI	government issue; general issue
Gk.	Greek
GNP	gross national product
gr.	gross; grain
hdqs., hq., HQ	headquarters
hon.	honorable
HR	House bill (federal); House of Representatives
hyp.	hypothesis
ibid.	in the same place (*ibidem*)
id	the same (*idem*)
i.e.	that is (*id est*)
in pr.	in the beginning (*in principio*)
in re	in regard to
Inc.	Incorporated
incl.	inclusive
inf.	infinity; below (*infra*)
int.	interest
introd.	introduction
IQ	intelligence quotient
ital.	italics
l (*pl.* ll)	line (s)
L.	Latin
L. Ed.	Lawyers Edition
L/A	letter of authority
lat.	latitude
lc	lowercase
LC	deferreds (cable message)
lf	lightface; ledger folio

lmsc	let me see correspondence
loc. cit.	in the place cited (*loco citato*)
log.	logarithm
long.	longitude
loq.	he/she speaks (*loquitur*)
ls	place of the seal (*locus sigilli*)
LT	letter message (cables)
Ltd.	limited (British)
lv.	leave
m	married; masculine
M	thousand; monsieur (*pl.* MM); noon (*meridies*)
max.	maximum
mc	marked capacity (freight cars)
MC	master of ceremonies; member of Congress
med.	medium; medicine; medical
Messrs.	Misters (Messieurs)
mfg.	manufacturing
min.	minimum; minute(s)
misc.	miscellaneous
Mlle.	Mademoiselle
mm	necessary changes being made (*mutatis mutandis*)
MM	Messieurs
Mme.	Madame
Mmes.	Mesdames
mo	money order
mo.	month(s)
MP	member of Parliament; military police
ms(s)., MS(S)	manuscript(s)
Msgr.	Monsignor; Monseigneur
mst.	measurement
MST	mountain standard time
mt	empty

n	note (*pl.* nn); number; net; born	o/o	order of
		op	out of print
NA, N/A	not available	op. cit.	in the work cited (*opere citato*)
natl., nat'l	national		
n.b., N.B.	note well (*nota bene*)	os, o.s.	old series
NCO	noncommissioned officer	o/s	out of stock
		OS, O.S.	one side; Old Style
nd, n.d.	no date	ow	one way (fare)
ne	not exceeding	p.	page (*pl.* pp.)
nes	not elsewhere specified	pa	by the year (*per annum*); power of attorney
NG	no good		
NL	night letter (telegraph)	PABX	private automatic branch exchange (telephone)
NLT	night letter cable		
NM	night message	pam.	pamphlet
N/m	no mark	par.	paragraph
no.	number	pass.	throughout (*passim*)
noe	not otherwise enumerated	pat.	patent
		PBX	private brands exchange (telephone)
nohp	not otherwise herein provided		
		pc	photocopy
nom.	nominative; nominal	pct., %	percent
nom. std.	nominal standard	pd	per diem
non obs.	notwithstanding (*non obstante*)	pd.	passed; paid
		pkg.	package
non pros.	does not prosecute (*non prosequitur*)	pl.	plural; plate
		p&l	profit and loss
non seq.	does not follow (*non sequitur*)	p.m.	afternoon (*post meridiem*)
		PM	postmaster
nop	not otherwise provided for	p/n	please note
		PO	post office; payable on receipt
nos	not otherwise specified		
np, n.p.	no place; no publisher	pp	parcel post
NP	notary public	pp.	pages
ns	new series	ppd.	prepaid; postpaid
NS, N.S.	New Style (dates)	ppi	parcel post insured
nspf	not specially provided for	pr.	pair
		pref.	preface; preferred
ntp	no title page	princ.	principle; principal
ob.	died (*obiit*)	pro tem.	for the time being (*pro tempore*)
obs.	obsolete		
oc	office copy	prox.	proximate; of the next month (*proximo*)
oe	omissions excepted		
OE	Old English	P.S.	postscript
oo	on order	PST	Pacific standard time

PT	Pacific time
pub.	publication; publisher; published by
PX	please exchange; post exchange; private exchange (telephone)
q	question; query
Q.E.D., q.e.d.	which was to be proved or demonstrated (*quod erat demonstrandum*)
qq	questions; queries
qr.	quarter
q.v.	which see (*quod vide*)
r	recto; reigned
R/A	return to author
R/C	recovered; reconsigned
rcd., recd., rec'd	received
re	in regard to
ref.	reference; referred; referee
reg.	registered; regulation(s)
rep.	report
repr.	reprint; reprinted
res.	research; residue; reserve; residence; resigned; resolution
rev.	review; revised; revision
rm.	ream (paper); room(s)
rom.	roman (type)
rop	run of paper
rotn. no.	rotation number
rp	reply paid (cable); return premium
RSVP	please reply (*répondez, s'il vous plaît*)
s	substantive; son
/s/	signed
sa	without year (*sine anno*); under the year (*sub anno*); subject to approval
sc	small capital letters (small caps); namely, to wit (*scilicet*); scene

sd	without a day being named (*sine die*)
sec(s).	section(s)
seq.	the following; in sequence
ser.	series
sg., sing.	singular
sgd.	signed
shpt.	shipment
sic	so; thus (to confirm a word that might be questioned)
sl	without place (*sine loco*)
sol.	solution
SOP	standard operating procedure
sp.	supra protest
ss	namely (*scilicet*)
st.	stanza; street
St.	saint; street
sta.	station
stat.	statute(s)
std.	standard
stg.	sterling; storage
sup.	above (*supra*)
supp., suppl.	supplement
s.v. (*pl.* s.vv.)	same year; under the word (*sub verbo*)
svp	if you please (*s'il vous plaît*)
syn.	synonymous
taw	twice a week (advertising)
tb	time base
tel.	telegram; telegraph; telephone
tf	till forbidden (advertising)
tl	time loan
tm	trademark; true mean
tr.	transpose
trans.	transitive; translated; transportation; transaction

ts	typescript	at. wt.	atomic weight
twp.	township	au	astronomical unit
U, univ.	university	Au	gold
uc	uppercase	av., avdp.	avoirdupois
ud	as directed	a/w	actual weight
ugt.	urgent (cable)	bbl	barrel
ui	as below (*ut infra*)	bbl/d, b/d	barrel per day
ult	of the last month (*ultimo*)	bdl	bundle
		bhp	brake horsepower
up	under proof	bl	bale(s)
u.s., ut sup.	as above (*ut supra*)	bm	board measure
		bp	boiling point
usw.	and so forth (*und so weiter*)	Btu, BTU	British thermal unit
		bu.	bushel
ut	universal time	c	cycle (radio)
v	value; versus	C	Celsius; Centigrade; centi (prefix: one-hundredth)
v.	verse (*pl.* vv.); verb; versus; verso		
v.i.	see below (*vide infra*)	C/	case(s)
vid.	see (*vide*)	cal.	small calories
viz.	namely (*videlicet*)	cd.	cord
vol.	volume	cd. ft.	cord foot
vs., v.	versus	cg	centigram
vv	vice versa	ch, c-h	candle-hour(s)
wa	will advise	cl	centiliter
wd.	word; warranted	cm	centimeter
wf	wrong font (typesetting)	c/m	cycles per minute
wp, WP	word processing; without prejudice	cm²	square centimeter
		cp	candlepower
wpp	waterproof paper packing	cwt	hundred weight
xp	express paid	d	deci (prefix: one-tenth)
		da	deka (prefix: ten)
z.	zone; zero	dag	dekagram
		dal	dekaliter
		dam	dekameter
TECHNICAL ABBREVIATIONS		dam²	square dekameter
a, amp.	ampere	dB	decibel
ac	alternating current	dBu	decibel unit
af	audiofrequency	dc	direct current
a-h	ampere-hour	dg	decigram
AM	amplitude modulation	dl	deciliter
at.	atmosphere	dm	decimeter
at. no.	atomic number	dm²	square decimeter
at. vol.	atomic volume		

174

dr.	dram	kl	kiloliter
dw	dead weight	km	kilometer
dwc	dead weight capacity	km²	square kilometer
dwt	deadweight ton(s); pennyweight(s)	kn	knot (speed)
		kt	kiloton; carat
dyn	dyne	kV	kilovolt
EHF	extremely high frequency	kVa	kilovoltampere
EMF	electromotive force	kW	kilowatt
esu	electrostatic unit	kWh	kilowatt-hour
eV	electron volt	l	liter
F	Fahrenheit; farad	lf	low frequency
fbm	board foot; board foot measure	lin. ft.	linear foot
		l/m	lines per minute
FM	frequency modulation	l/s	lines per second
ft. H₂0	conventional foot of water	m	meter; milli (prefix: one-thousandth)
g	gram; gravity	m²	square meter
G	gauss; giga (prefix: one million)	M	mega (prefix: one million); thousand
gal.	gallon	ma	milliampere
GeV	gigaelectronvolt	mbar	millibar
GHz	gigahertz	mc	millicycle
h	hecto (prefix: one hundred)	Mc	megacycle
		MeV	megaelectronvolts
H	henry	mF	millifarad
ha	hectare	mg	milligram
hf	high frequency	mG	milligauss
hg	hectogram	mH	millihenry
hl	hectoliter	mHz	millihertz
hm	hectometer	MHz	megahertz
hm²	square hectometer	mi./hr., mi/h	mile(s) per hour
hp	horsepower	ml	milliliter
Hz	hertz	mm	millimeter
ihp	indicated horsepower	mm²	square millimeter
		mol. wt.	molecular weight
J	joule	ms	millisecond
k	kilo (prefix: one thousand); knot; carat	mt	metric ton
		Mt	megaton
kc	kilocycle	mV	millivolt
keV	kiloelectronvolt	mW	milliwatt
kg	kilogram	MW	megawatt
kG	kilogauss	μ	micro (prefix: one-millionth)
kgf	kilogram-force		
kHz	kilohertz	μF	microfarad

µg	microgram		u	atomic mass unit
µH	microhenry		uhf	ultrahigh frequency
µin.	microinch			
µm	micrometer		v	velocity; volt
µs	microsecond		V	volt
µV	microvolt		Va	volt ampere
µW	microwatt		vf	video frequency
			vhf	very high frequency
n	nano (prefix: one-billionth)		V/m	volt per meter
na	nanoampere		W	watt
nhp	nominal horsepower		Wh	watt-hour
nm	nanometer			
nmi.	nautical mile		z	zero hour
npt	nominal pressure and temperature		zf	zero frequency
ns	nanosecond			

<table>
<tr><td>oz.</td><td>ounce (avoirdupois)</td></tr>
</table>

nt	net ton

COMPUTER ACRONYMS AND ABBREVIATIONS

oz.	ounce (avoirdupois)		ABM	automated batch mixing
p	pico (prefix: one-trillionth)		abort	abandon activity
			ABP	actual block processor
pct., %	percent		abs	absolute
pk.	peck		AC	automatic/analog computer
p/m	parts per million		ACC	accumulator
ps	picosecond		ACF	advanced communication function
pt.	pint			
pW	picowatt		ACM	area composition machine
ql	quintal		ADC	analog-to-digital converter
qt.	quart		ADIS	automatic data interchange system
R	rankine; roentgen		ADP	automatic/advanced data processing
rf	radio frequency			
rhp	rated horsepower		ADR	address; adder; analog-to-digital recorder
r/min.	revolutions per minute			
rms	root mean square		ADV	advance
r/s	revolutions per second		AFR	automatic field/format recognition
rva	reactive volt ampere			
s	second (time)		ALCOM	algebraic computer/compiler
sh. tn.	short ton			
shp	shaft horsepower		ALGOL	Algorithmic Language
sw	shipper's weights		ALP	automated language processing
t	metric ton		ALU	arithmetic and logic unit
T	tera (prefix: one trillion); tesla		ANACOM	analog computer
			AOC	automatic output control
tMW	thermal megawatt		APL	A Programming Language

APT	Automatic Programmed Tools (language)
AQL	acceptable quality level
ARQ	automatic repeat request; automatic request for correction
ARU	audio response unit
ASC	automatic sequence control
ASCII	American Standard Code for Information Interchange
ASM	auxiliary storage management
ASP	attached support processor
ASR	answer, send, and receive
AUTODIN	automated digital network
B	bit; magnetic flux density
BA	binary add
BAM	basic access method
BASIC	Beginner's All-Purpose Symbolic Instruction
BC	binary code
BCD	binary-coded decimal
BDU	basic device/display unit
BIM	beginning of information marker
bit	binary digit
BIU	basic information unit
BN	binary number system
BOF	beginning of file
BOS	basic operating system
BOT	beginning of tape
bpi	bits per inch
bps	bits per second
BPS	basic programming support
BS	backspace character
BTU	basic transmission unit
C	computer; compute; control
CA	channel adapter
CAD	computer-aided design
CAD/CAM	computer-aided design/ computer-aided manufacturing

CAI	computer-aided instruction
CAI/OP	computer analog input/ output
CAL	computer-aided learning
CAM	computer-aided manufacturing
CAN	cancel character
CAR	computer-assisted retrieval
CAT	computer-assisted training/ teaching
CDC	call directing code
CHAR	character
CIOCS	communications input/ output control system
CIU	computer interface unit
CLAT	communication line adapter
CLK	clock
CLT	communication line terminal
CMC	code for magnetic characters
CMND	command; instruction
CMS	conversation monitor system
CNC	computer numerical control
COBOL	Common Business-Oriented Language
CP	central processor
cph	characters per hour
cpm	characters per minute; cards per minute; critical path method
CP/M	controlled program monitor; control program/ microcomputers
CPS	conversational programming system; central processing system
CPU	central processing unit
cr	carriage return
CR	call request; control relay
CRAM	card random access method
CROM	control read-only memory
CRT	cathode ray tube

177

CTR	computer tape reader		GPC	general-purpose computer
CTU	central terminal unit		GPR	general-purpose register
CU	control unit		HSM	high-speed memory
CWP	communicating word processor		HSP	high-speed printer
			HSR	high-speed reader
DAA	direct-access arrangement		IC	integrated circuit; input circuit
DAC	data acquisition and control; digital/analog converter		ID	identification
DASD	direct-access storage device		I/O	input/output
DBAM	database access method		IOB	input-output buffer
DBMS	database management system		IOC	input-output controller
			ipm	impulses per minute
DD	digital data		ISR	information storage and retrieval
DDS	digital-display scope			
DE	display element		k	about a thousand (in storage capacity)
DIP	dual in-line package			
DLC	data-link control		KB	keyboard
DMA	direct memory access		kb	kilobytes
DNC	direct numerical control		KSR	keyboard send and receive
DOS	disk operating system		LCD	liquid crystal display
DOV	data over voice		LIFO	last in, first out
DP	data processing		LILO	last in, last out
DRO	destructive readout		LP	linear programming
DTR	data terminal ready		lpm	lines per minute
DUV	data under voice		lsc	least significant character
EDP	electronic data processing		lsd	least significant digit
EOF	end of file		M	mega
EOJ	end of job		mag.	magnetic
EOP	end of paragraph		Mb	megabyte
EOR	end of record/run		MC	master control
ESI	externally specified index		MCP	master control program
ETB	end of transmission block		MIS	management information system
F	feedback			
FDOS	floppy-disk operating system		MPS	microprocessor system
			msc	most significant character
FF	flip-flop		msd	most significant digit
FIRST	fast interactive retrieval system		MSU	modem-sharing unit
			MT	machine translation
FORTRAN	Formula Translation (language)		MUX	multiplexer
			n	nano-
GDT	graphic display terminal		NAM	network access machine
GP	general program		NAU	network addressable unit

178

NC	numerical control
NCP	network control program
NL	new-line character
NO-OP	no-operation instruction
ns	nanosecond
OCR	optical character recognition
ODB	output to display buffer
OEM	original equipment manufacturer
OLRT	on-line real time
OP	operations
opm	operations per minute
OR	operations research
OS	operating system
OSI	open-system interconnection
P	pico-
PA	paper advance
PC	program counter
PCI	process control interface
PCM	punch-card machine
PCS	punched-card system
PDN	public data network
PERT	program evaluation and review technique
PIU	path information unit
PRT	production-run tape
RAM	random-access memory
RAX	remote access
READ	real-time electronic access and display
REM	recognition memory
ROM	read-only memory
RT	real time
RTU	remote terminal unit
R/W	read/write
RWM	read-write memory
RZ	return to zero
SAM	sequential-access method; serial-access memory
S/F	store and forward
SLT	solid-logic technology

SOP	standard operating procedure
STX	start of text
TLU	table lookup
TOS	tape operating system
UCS	user control storage
USASCII	USA Standard Code for Information Interchange
VDI	video display input
VDT	video display terminal
WC	write and compute
WFL	work-flow language
WIP	work in progress
WO	write out
wp, WP	word processor
WS	working storage/space
XMT	transmit

ABBREVIATIONS OF ACADEMIC DEGREES

A.B.	Bachelor of Arts
A.M.	Master of Arts
B.A.	Bachelor of Arts
B.B.A.	Bachelor of Business Administration
B.C.	Bachelor of Chemistry
B.C.E.	Bachelor of Chemical Engineering
B.E.	Bachelor of Education; Bachelor of Engineering
B.E.E.	Bachelor of Electrical Engineering
B.S.	Bachelor of Science
B.S.Ed.	Bachelor of Science in Education
Ch.D.	Doctor of Chemistry
Ch.E.	Chemical Engineer
D.C.L.	Doctor of Canon Law; Doctor of Civil Law
D.D.	Doctor of Divinity
D.D.S.	Doctor of Dental Surgery
D.S. *or* D.Sc.	Doctor of Science

D.Th. *or* D.Theol.	Doctor of Theology	AIB	American Institute of Banking
D.V.M.	Doctor of Veterinary Medicine	AID	Agency for International Development
Ed.B.	Bachelor of Education	AMA	American Medical Association
Ed.D.	Doctor of Education		
Ed.M.	Master of Education	AP	Associated Press
E.E.	Electrical Engineer	ARC	American (National) Red Cross
J.D.	Doctor of Laws; Juris Doctor; Doctor of Jurisprudence	ARS	Agricultural Research Service
LL.B.	Bachelor of Laws	ASA	American Standards Association; American Statistical Association
LL.D.	Doctor of Laws		
LL.M.	Master of Laws	ASTA	American Society of Travel Agents
M.A.	Master of Arts		
M.B.A.	Master in, *or* of, Business Administration	BLS	Bureau of Labor Statistics
M.Ed.	Master of Education	BTA	Board of Tax Appeals
Ph.B.	Bachelor of Philosophy	CAB	Civil Aeronautics Board
Ph.D.	Doctor of Philosophy	CAP	Civil Air Patrol
S.B. *or* Sc.B.	Bachelor of Science	CBS	Columbia Broadcasting System
S.D. *or* S.D.	Doctor of Science	CCC	Commodity Credit Corporation
Sc.M. *or* S.M.	Master of Science	CEA	Commodity Exchange Administration
Th.D.	Doctor of Theology	CEC	Commodity Exchange Commission
V.M.D.	Doctor of Veterinary Medicine	CED	Committee for Economic Development
		CIA	Central Intelligence Agency
		CID	Criminal Investigation Department

ABBREVIATIONS OF ORGANIZATIONS

AA	Alcoholics Anonymous	CORE	Congress of Racial Equality
AAA	American Automobile Association	CPSC	Consumer Product Safety Commission
ABA	American Booksellers Association; American Bankers Association; American Bar Association	CSC	Civil Service Commission
		EEC	European Economic Community
		EEOC	Equal Employment Opportunity Commission
ABC	American Broadcasting Company	EPA	Environmental Protection Agency
AEC	Atomic Energy Commission		
AFL-CIO	American Federation of Labor-Congress of Industrial Organizations	FAA	Federal Aviation Agency
		FBI	Federal Bureau of Investigation

FCA	Farm Credit Administration		KC	Knights of Columbus
FCC	Federal Communications Commission		KKK	Ku Klux Klan
FDA	Food and Drug Administration		LC	Library of Congress
FDIC	Federal Deposit Insurance Corporation		NAACP	National Association for the Advancement of Colored People
FHA	Federal Housing Administration		NALS	National Association of Legal Secretaries
FMC	Federal Maritime Commission		NAM	National Association of Manufacturers
FPC	Federal Power Commission		NAS	National Academy of Sciences
FRB	Federal Reserve Board; Federal Reserve Bank		NASA	National Aeronautics and Space Administration
FRS	Federal Reserve System		NATO	North Atlantic Treaty Organization
FSA	Federal Security Agency		NBC	National Broadcasting Company
FTC	Federal Trade Commission			
GAO	General Accounting Office		NBS	National Broadcasting Service
GHQ	General Headquarters (Army)		NEA	National Education Association; National Editorial Association
GPO	Government Printing Office			
GSA	General Services Administration		NIH	National Institutes of Health
HHFA	Housing and Home Finance Agency		NLRB	National Labor Relations Board
HUD	Housing and Urban Development (Department of)		NMB	National Mediation Board
			NOW	National Organization for Women
ICC	Interstate Commerce Commission		NPS	National Park Service
IFC	International Finance Corporation		NRC	Nuclear Regulatory Commission
IFTU	International Federation of Trade Unions		NSC	National Security Council
ILO	International Labor Organization		NSF	National Science Foundation
IMF	International Monetary Fund		OAS	Organization of American States
INP	International News Photos		OECD	Organization for Economic Cooperation and Development
INS	International News Service			
IRO	International Refugee Organization		OEO	Office of Economic Opportunity
IRS	Internal Revenue Service		OMB	Office of Management and Budget
ITO	International Trade Organization			
IWW	Industrial Workers of the World		PBS	Public Broadcasting Service
			PHA	Public Housing Administration

PHS	Public Health Service
PSI	Professional Secretaries International
REA	Rural Electrification Administration
ROTC	Reserve Officers' Training Corp
RRB	Railroad Retirement Board
SBA	Small Business Administration
SEATO	Southeast Asia Treaty Organization
SEC	Securities and Exchange Commission
SSA	Social Security Administration
SSS	Selective Service System
TC	Tax Court of the United States
TVA	Tennessee Valley Authority
UN	United Nations
UNESCO	United Nations Educational, Scientific, and Cultural Organization
USIA	United States Information Agency
UNICEF	United Nations Children's Fund
UNRRA	United Nations Relief and Rehabilitation Administration
UPI	United Press International
UPS	United Parcel Service
USDA	United States Department of Agriculture
USIA	United States Information Agency
VA	Veterans Administration
VFW	Veterans of Foreign Wars
VISTA	Volunteers in Service to America
WHO	World Health Organization

Adjective. Adjectives modify nouns and pronouns.

An adjective usually adds *-er* or *-*

est to mean more or most or may be preceded by *more* or *most*.

Comparison to indicate less or least of a quality is accomplished by using the words *less* and *least* before the adjective.

Some adjectives are compared irregularly, such as: *good, well, better, best,* or *bad, worse, worst.*

Do not use double comparisons, such as *more slower* and *more faster.* Be sure to use the comparative when you have just two to compare and the superlative for three or more: "Jack is the *better* (not *best*) editor of the two."

Compound adjectives are two or more words used together as an adjective. Usually, hyphenate the two words when they precede a noun (*well-known* speaker) but not when they follow a noun (the speaker is *well known*). However, some adjectives that precede a noun are not hyphenated when usage over many years has established a common understanding of the term (the *social security* program).

Adverb. Often, but not always, recognized by *-ly* ending. Like adjectives, adverbs can add *-er* or *-est* or may be preceded by *more* or *most, less* or *least.*

Adverbs modify verbs, adjectives, and other adverbs.

1. A common error is the misuse of an adjective to modify another adjective.

He submitted a *really* [not *real*] good report to the president. (*Good* is an adjective and must be modified by the adverb *really*, not by the adjective *real*.)

2. Frequently a verb is used not primarily for its own meaning but to link the subject to a word following the verb that specifies a quality or condition of the subject. In such a case, this word should be an adjective, not an adverb.

The report sounded *strange* [not *strangely*] to me in view of the circumstances. (*Strange* modifies report, not *sounded*.)

When the word following the verb does *not* qualify the subject, but qualifies the action of the verb, it should be an adverb. The same verb can take both constructions. See also PREDICATE NOMINATIVE.

His laugh sounded *hollowly* through the room.

Agreement of verb with subject. A verb should always agree with its subject in number and person. The rule is simple, but the number of subjects is not always clear. Mistakes sometimes occur when two or more subjects are joined by *and* (see COMPOUND SUBJECT); when two or more subjects are joined by *or, nor,* and the like (see ALTERNATE SUBJECT); when a noun intervenes between the subject and the verb (see INTERVENING NOUN); and when a verb is followed by a PREDICATE NOMINATIVE.

Alternate subject. 1. Two or more singular subjects in the third person joined by *or, nor, and not, but, either . . . or,* or *neither . . . nor* take singular verbs in the third person.

2. If two or more subjects differing in number or person are joined

by *or, nor, and not, but, either . . . or, neither . . . nor,* the verb agrees with the subject nearest to it. If it often wise to recast the sentence to avoid awkwardness.

Apostrophe ('). A mark of punctuation used for the following purposes:

1. To denote a contraction or omission of letters, for example, *it's* for *it is.* (The apostrophe is omitted in contractions formed by dropping the first letters of a word if the contraction is in common usage, e.g., *phone*).

2. To form the plural of letters, figures, and symbols, for example, *q's, 5's,* except when the figure does not require an apostrophe for clarity, for example, *1980s.*

3. To indicate the possessive case of nouns but not of pronouns.

4. To indicate the plural of a word referred to as a word without regard to its meaning, for example, "There are three *and's* in the sentence."

5. To denote the plural or some other form of an abbreviation, for example, *ABC's,* except when the abbreviation does not require an apostrophe for clarity, for example, YWCAs.

Appositive. An explanatory modifier; a word or phrase inserted in a sentence to explain or identify another word or phrase in the same sentence. If an appositive identifies the preceding word or phrase, it is *restrictive* and is not set off by commas, for example, *the witness Jones.* If the appositive gives additional information that is not essential to the meaning of the sentence, it is *nonrestrictive* and is set off from the rest of the sentence by commas.

> Mr. Brown, *the president of our company*, is in Europe. (nonrestrictive)

The rule for children and spouses is that spouses are always set off with commas. Children should *not* be set off with commas since a child's name is essential (restrictive) to indicate *which* child.

> Her husband, *Bill*, is here.
> *My son Bill* is married, but *my son Adam* is single.

Brackets [ ]. See PARENTHESES.

Capitalization. Although authorities differ widely on the rules and principles of capitalization, the trend is toward more general use of lowercase letters.

1. Abbreviations of degrees and titles (*Ph.D.*), initials (*J. D. Brown*), and single-letter abbreviations (*F* for Fahrenheit) are normally capitalized. The letters *a.m.* and *p.m.* and common abbreviations such as *fob* may be lowercase. See ABBREVIATIONS for examples.

2. Official titles of specific acts, bills, codes, and laws are capitalized (*Securities Exchange Act*) but not general terms (*the securities act*).

3. Amounts of money are usually written with each word capitalized (*Four Hundred Sixty-Five Dollars*—$465) in financial and legal copy but are lowercased in general text (for five dollars).

4. Capitalize names of military services (*United States Army*) but lowercase words (*army*) that are not the official title.

5. Capitalize titles of great distinction that refer to a specific person and might be confused with a similar title but lowercase all other titles (*the judge*) unless followed by a proper name (*Judge Baker*).

> The *General of the Army* was seated next to another *general*.

6. Capitalize geographical regions or divisions (*East*) but lowercase directions (*toward the south*).

7. Capitalize words such as *government, federal, state, city, county, district*, and *national* only when part of a title (*Her Majesty's Government*); otherwise use lowercase (*the federal government*).

8. Important events (*Superbowl*), holidays (*Thanksgiving*), and historical terms (*World War II*) are capitalized.

9. Capitalize each part of a hyphenated word that would be capitalized if not hyphenated (*Anglo-Saxon*) but lowercase the second word if both are considered as one word (*Twenty-three*).

10. Capitalize the title of an organization (*Iowa State University*) but lowercase references to it that are not the official title (*the university*).

11. Capitalize all personal titles that precede a name (*Governor Jones*) but lowercase titles following a name or used in place of it (*the governor*).

12. Capitalize names of political parties but not the word party (*Democratic party*) and capitalize political party *-ist* designations (*Communists*) but lowercase *-ism* derivates (*communism*).

13. Capitalize references to the U.S. Supreme Court (the *Court*) and the U.S. Constitution (the *Constitution*) but lowercase other general references (the *trial court*; the *state constitution*).

14. Capitalize the first word of an exact quotation if it is a complete sentence; if it is not, lowercase the first word.

"Robert," she asked, "don't you want to attend the seminar?"
He denied that he was "a golf fanatic."

15. Capitalize names of ethnic groups (*Jewish*), planets (*Mars*), trade names (*Teletype*), and the principal words in music, drama, and art (*Beethoven's Fifth Symphony*).

Collective noun. A collective noun is singular if the writer is referring to the group as such, plural if referring to the individual persons or things of which the group is composed. The number of the verb and pronoun depends upon whether the collective noun is used in the singular or plural.

The council (as a unit) *is* acting in accordance with *its* policies.
The council (members) *are* acting in accordance with *their* policies.

In some cases, it is a matter of discretion whether the singular or plural sense should be used, but after the choice is made, the verbs and pronouns must all agree. It is incorrect to use a singular verb in one sentence and begin the next sentence with a plural pronoun, or vice versa.

Colon (:). A colon is most often used after a word, phrase, or sentence that introduces a list, a series, tabulations, extracts, texts, and explanations that are in apposition to the introductory words. (The following is an extract from the report: . . .). A colon should not be used to introduce items that are the direct objects of a preposition or verb or that follow a form of the verb *to be* (*wrong*: The requirements of a good secretary *are*: ability to . . .). Other uses of the colon are to indicate time (9:30 A.M.), following the city and state in footnotes (Englewood Cliffs, N.J.: Prentice-Hall), and in biblical references (Matthew 10:4). Do not use a dash with a colon (*not* the following book:—).

Comma (,). Mark of punctuation indicating a slight break in thought. The comma is used for the following purposes:

1. To set off a nonrestrictive AP-POSITIVE.

Our president, *Mrs. Clark*, is out of town.

2. To separate the name of a city from the name of a state (*Princeton, N.J.*).

3. To separate the independent clauses of a compound sentence.

He had to work late, but it was important to finish the report.

4. To separate the day of the month from the year (*January 14, 1988*).

5. To set off a nonrestrictive clause, that is, one that adds an additional thought to the sentence but is not essential to its meaning.

The answer, *which most of us realize*, is to increase productivity.

6. To indicate that one or more easily understood words have been omitted.

He arrived late; the others, early.

7. To separate an introductory word from the rest of the sentence.

8. Between the name and *Inc.*, *Esquire*, and the like.

9. To set off parenthetical words or phrases, such as *I believe, for example*, and *however*.

10. To separate words and phrases in a series. A comma also precedes the conjunction connecting the last two members of the series (*coat, hat, and gloves*).

A comma should never separate a verb from its subject, object, or predicate nominative. A comma should *not* be used in the following constructions:

1. Between two nouns, one of which identifies the other.

The *witness Jones* testified about the capitalization of the company.

2. To set off a restrictive clause, that is, a clause that is not merely descriptive but is essential to the meaning of the sentence.

The car *with the flat tire* is still parked along the street.

3. Between a name and *of* indicating place or position (*Mr. Edwards of Brown & Co.*).

4. In street, room, post office box, and telephone numbers (*142 West Hyland Drive*).

5. To separate a participle from the noun it modifies when the noun is not the subject of the sentence.

The operators [no comma] having agreed to arbitrate, the union called off the strike.

Compound personal pronoun. Also called "reflexive pronoun." It is formed by adding *-self* (sing.) or *-selves* (pl.) to *him, her, my*, and *your* and can be used only when the sentence includes the word to which they refer.

1. It is used to call attention to the subject and to emphasize a noun or pronoun.

RIGHT: *He* hurt *himself* more than anyone else by his attitude.
RIGHT: The *president himself* made a report to the employees.

2. A common error is the use of a compound personal noun in place of the objective case of the pronoun.

WRONG: Best regards from George and *myself*.
RIGHT: Best regards from George and *me*.

3. Another common error is the ommission of a possessive pronoun

when a word is joined to a compound personal pronoun. Test the sentence by omitting the compound personal pronoun.

WRONG: He hurt *himself and family* by his attitude. (The absurdity of "He hurt family" is obvious.)
RIGHT: He hurt *himself and his* family by his attitude.

Compound subject. Two or more subjects joined by *and*. Usually, a compound subject takes a plural verb.

If the compound subject consists of two nouns referring to the same person or thing, the verb is singular.

The vice-president and treasurer of the company *is* out of the city. (When both offices are filled by the same person.)
The vice-president and the treasurer of the company *are* out of the city. (When separate individuals fill the two offices.)
When *each, every, many, a,* and the like modify the complete subject, the verb is singular.

Each (or *Every*) officer and member was [not *were*] present.

Compound term. Two or more short words written together, joined by a hyphen, or written separately but expressing a single idea. Thus *editor-in-chief, businessperson,* and *attorney general* are all compounds. The authorities differ about whether certain compounds should be written separately, hyphenated, or written as one word. The following rules are a guide to writing compounds.

1. *Consistency.* Be consistent. When there is a choice, decide whether you want to hyphenate two or more words, to write them as one word, or to write them as separate words. Follow the form you choose consistently.

2. *Usage.* Do not hyphenate or join words together for the sole reason that they are frequently used together. Wait until the authorities accept them in compounded form.

3. *Adjectives.* Usually, hyphenate two or more words used as an adjective when they precede a noun (*short-term* loan, *no-par* stock, *above-mentioned* law). Do not hyphenate well-known compounds that for many years have had a commonly accepted meaning (*public relations* consultant). Do not hyphenate compound adjectives that follow a noun (He is *well informed*). Do not hyphenate color variations used as an adjective (*navy blue* dress, *light gray* paint).

4. *Fractions.* Hyphenate fractions when the numerator and the denominator are both one-word forms (*one-third, three-fourths, one-hundredth*).

5. *Nationalities.* Hyphenate two or more words to indicate that the person or thing shares in the qualities of both (*Anglo-American, Sino-Japanese, Latin-American* [but *Latin America*], *Scotch-Irish*).

6. *Coined phrases.* Hyphenate all coined phrases (*middle-of-the-road course, pay-as-you-go, drive-it-yourself, ready-to-wear*).

7. *Adverbs.* Do not use a hyphen to connect an adverb and an adjective. Adverbs properly modify adjectives. Do not use a hyphen to connect

an adverb ending in -ly and a past participle (*closely held stock*).

8. *Titles.* Do not hyphenate most titles (*rear admiral, chief of staff*), but do hyphenate *secretary-treasurer* and other coined compounds. Also hyphenate *ex-president, president-elect*, and *vice-president-elect*.

9. *Prefixes.* Compounds formed with the prefixes *inter-, non-, semi-*, and *sub-* are not hyphenated (*nonstandard*) unless used with a proper noun (*non-American*). Nearly all compounds formed with the prefix *self-* are hyphenated (*self-educated*).

Plurals of compound terms. In the plural of compound terms, the most important word takes the plural form (*attorneys* general, *judge* advocates). When both words are of equal importance, both take the plural form (*men employees*). When no word is of importance in itself, the last word takes the plural form (pick-me-*ups*).

1. When a noun is compounded with a preposition, the noun takes the plural form (*lookers*-on).

2. When neither word in the compound term is a noun, the last word takes the plural form (go-*betweens*).

3. Compound nouns written as one word form their plurals regularly. Words ending in -*ful* are the only ones that cause any trouble (bucket*fuls*).

If it is necessary to convey the meaning that more than one container was used, write the compound as two words and add *s* to the noun (four *buckets* full).

For the possessive form of compound terms, see POSSESSIVES.

Dash (—). Used to show sudden interruption or to set off and emphasize words and clauses of explanation. Do not use a dash with other punctuation marks in succession (not *Yes,—*) and do not space before or after a dash.

We have paper, pens, and erasers—everything you need.
His new car—actually, last year's model—is parked by the door.

Diacritical marks. Accents that indicate a change in phonetic value from the same element if unmarked.

´	Acute accent
`	Grave accent
˘	Breve
ˇ	Haček
¨	Diaresis
^ or ˆ or ˜	Circumflex
˜	Tilde
¯	Macron
¸	Cedilla

Division of words. To avoid a ragged right-hand margin, it is sometimes essential to divide a word at the end of a line. It is preferable not to have two successive lines with a divided word at the end; there should never be more than two. The last word in a paragraph should not be divided, nor should the last word on a page, except in some legal documents where the last word is divided to show continuity.

The correct division of a word depends first of all on the breakdown of the word into syllables. American dictionaries syllabicate according to pronunciation and not according to derivation. A few simple rules in addition to the rule of syllables, as shown in the dictionary, govern the division of a word: (1) Never divide words pronounced as one syllable (*through*). (2) Never divide a four-letter word (*into*). (3) Never separate one-letter syllables at the beginning of a word (*alone*), from the rest of the word. (4) Divide a word with a one-letter syllable within the word *after* the one-letter syllable (*prolifera-tion*), except in the case of the suffixes -*able* or -*ible*. (There are many words, such as *ca-pa-ble*, that end in -*able* or -*ible* in which the *a* or *i* does not form a syllable by itself. These words are divided after the *a* or *i*.) (5) Do not carry over a two-letter syllable (call*er*), at the end of a word). (6) Avoid separating two-letter syllables at the beginning of a word (*re*deemed) from the rest of the word. (7) When the final consonant in a word is doubled before a suffix or verb ending, the second consonant belongs with the letters following it (*occur-ring*). (8) Do not carry over to the next line single or double consonants in the root word (*divid-ing*). (9) When two consonants occur within a word, divide the word between the consonants (*expres-sive*). (1) Avoid dividing a compound, hyphenated word (*vice-president*) except where the hyphen naturally falls. (1) Do not divide abbreviations, contractions, or acronyms (*NAACP*). (12) Avoid dividing numbers. If it is necessary to divide them, divide on a comma and retain the comma (*2,302,-700,000*). (13) Divide dates between the day and the year (*May 2, / 1983*), not between the month and the days. (14) Do not separate the initials of a name (*E. R./ Taylor*) and avoid separating initials, titles, or degrees (*James Thompson, Ph.D.*) from the name; also avoid dividing proper names (*Robert Mason*).

Double negatives.   The use of two negatives to express a negative thought is wrong. Some double negatives (*don't want no*) are obviously wrong. The insidious double negatives occur with words that convey a negative idea (*hardly, barely, scarcely, but, but that*), rather than with words that are definitely negative (*no, none, never*).

Ellipsis points (. . .).   Three or four consecutive periods are used to indicate the omission of part of a quoted sentence. Three periods are used if the omission occurs at the beginning or in the middle of a sentence.

". . . the show is contemporary . . . and well presented."

Four periods are used if the last part of the sentence is omitted or if whole sentences or paragraphs are omitted.

The policy manual has been revised. . . . it now includes detailed procedural guidelines. . . .

Exclamation point (!).   Used at the end of an exclamatory sentence, phrase, or even a single word expressing emphasis or strong emotion.

What a wonderful show! Let's go! Help!

To be effective, this mark should be used sparingly.

Future tense. The *future tense* expresses action that will take place in the future. A common error is the use of the future tense, instead of the *future perfect tense*, to express action *completed* before a time in the future.

RIGHT: She *will finish* the book next month. (simple future)
RIGHT: She *will have finished* the book *before* the end of the month. (future perfect expressing completed action)
WRONG: She *will finish* the book *before* the end of the month. (future incorrectly expressing completed action)
RIGHT: Next month, I *will have been* his secretary ten years. (future perfect)
WRONG: Next month I *will be* his secretary ten years. (future incorrectly expressing completed action)
RIGHT: I *will write* the letter tomorrow. (simple future)
RIGHT: I *will have written* the letter by that time. (future perfect)

Gerund. A verbal form ending in *-ing* and used as a noun.

1. Possessive nouns, pronouns, or prepositions, not objects, precede gerunds.

I had not heard of the *company's* [not *company*] buying the building.

2. A gerund may take an object or be completed in meaning by a predicate noun or adjective.

Recording test data required concentration.
Recording is simple.
Recording is the first step.

3. The gerund is identical in form with the present participle and is often confused with it. The use of the gerund with a possessive may give the sentence a meaning entirely different from that given by the use of a participle.

I do not approve of the *girl's reading* the book. (gerund)
I do not approve of the *girl reading* the book. (participle)

4. If a verb has a noun form, use the noun form instead of the gerund.

POOR: *Accepting* the position was an ill-advised move.
BETTER: *Acceptance of* the position was an ill-advised move.

Grammar and vocabulary. See ADJECTIVE; ADVERB; AGREEMENT OF VERB WITH SUBJECT; ALTERNATE SUBJECT; APPOSITIVE; COLLECTIVE NOUN; COMPOUND PERSONAL PRONOUN; COMPOUND SUBJECT; COMPOUND TERM; DOUBLE NEGATIVE; FUTURE TENSE; GERUND; INDEFINITE PRONOUNS; INFINITIVE; INTERVENING NOUN; OMISSION OF WORDS; PARTICIPLE; PAST TENSE; PERFECT TENSE; POSSESSIVES; PREDICATE NOMINATIVE; PREPOSITION AT THE END; PRESENT TENSE; PRONOUN; SEQUENCE OF TENSES; SUBJUNCTIVE MOOD; VERB.

Hyphen (-). Mark of punctuation. A hyphen is used (1) as a connecting link in some COMPOUND TERM (*fast-moving train*); (2) at the end of a line to show that part of a word has been carried over to another line; (3) to indicate a span of time (*1945-60*). In a series of hyphenated words having a common base, a hyphen is placed after the first element of each word, and the base is written after the last word only (*fourth-, fifth-, sixth-grade pupils*) A suspended hyphen is sometimes used in numerical descriptions (*3- by 5-inch cards, one- to two-year project*).

Indefinite pronoun. A pronoun that does not indicate a particular person or thing (*anyone, everybody, some*). Most indefinite pronouns take a singular verb.

Everyone *is* welcome to attend.

Some take a plural verb, and a few may take either a singular or plural verb, depending on meaning.

Several *are* fresh out of school.
Most of the work *is* easy.

Infinitive. A verbal noun usually preceded by *to*. 1. *Tense.* Use the present infinitive, not the perfect, after past conditions, such as *should have liked, would have been possible*.

It would have been possible *to reduce* [not *to have reduced*] the cost at that time.

2. *Split infinitives.* The infinitive sign *to* and the verb naturally go together; it is best not to split the infinitive by placing a word or words between *to* and the verb.

To *compete successfully* [not *to successfully compete*], we must improve our skills.

Split infinitives are preferable to awkwardness.

AWKWARD: Efforts *to unite firmly* bolters from the party were a failure.
IMPROVED: Efforts *to firmly unite* bolters from the party were a failure.

Intervening noun. A noun that comes between the subject and the verb. The intervention of a noun will sometimes cause trouble if the intervening noun is different in number from the subject. The verb agrees with its subject, not with the intervening noun.

Celluloid used as handles on umbrellas and canes *is* [not *are*] of high quality.

Intransitive verbs. See VERB.

Language. The language of a modern business communication should be natural, simple, and *vital*. Progressive writers no longer use the stilted and verbose style of the last century. Some suggestions to improve the language of a business communication follow:

1. Avoid stilted or trite words and phrases, such as those in the list under TRITE EXPRESSIONS.

2. Avoid unnecessary words or phrases (*final* completion for completion; *month* of January for January).

3. Do not use two words with the same meaning for emphasis (not *first* and *foremost; we refuse* and *decline*).

4. Simple, short words do a better job than big words. *Rich people* is preferable to *propertied interests; go beyond* to *transcend*.

5. Use different words to express various shades of meaning. Thus a cigar has an *aroma*; a flower, a *fragrance*; gas, an *odor*.

6. Use short sentences.

7. Avoid words that antagonize (your *failure*, your *complaint*, you *claim*).

8. Use the positive approach.

NEGATIVE: We cannot ship these goods before August 8.
POSITIVE: We will ship the goods on or shortly after August 8.

9. Use active sentences (*they decided*) instead of passive sentences (*it was decided*).

10. Avoid vogue words (*viable*) and gobbledygook (*the report will impact on our procedural practices before we can interface with . . .*).

Simplicity of language is not a license for the use of incorrect or sloppy grammar.

Mood. See SUBJUNCTIVE MOOD.

Noun. The name of any person, place, or thing. It may be preceded by *a* or *the*. Most nouns can be made plural (e.g., *letters*), and most can show possession (e.g., the *boy's* letters). Nouns occur as subjects of a sentence, as objects of verbs or prepositions, and as predicate nouns after certain verbs.

Omission of words. Words may be omitted from a sentence if they can be supplied *clearly* and *exactly* from a parallel portion of the sentence. A common error, however, is the omission of a word that cannot be clearly and exactly supplied. (See also Chapter 8/QUOTED MATERIAL.)

1. In two clauses, if one subject is singular and the other plural, the verb should not be omitted.

2. Part of a verb phrase should not be omitted if it is different in form from the corresponding part of the parallel verb phrase.

WRONG: The company always *has* and always *will give* recognition when it is due.
RIGHT: The company always *has given* and always *will give* recognition when it is due.

3. An article, a personal or relative pronoun, or a preposition that is necessary to the grammatical completeness or to the clear understanding of a sentence should not be omitted.

WRONG: I have great sympathy but no confidence in that class of people.
RIGHT: I have great sympathy for that class of people but no confidence in them.

Parentheses ( ). Used to enclose comments, explanations, and quoted material when a separation stronger than commas or dashes is desired.

1. Enclose parenthetical or explanatory expressions in parentheses.

The shipment will arrive on time (*we hope*).

2. Enclose figures in parentheses when they follow the amount in words (One Hundred (*$100*) Dollars).

3. Enclose enumerations that run into the text.

You have a choice of (1) monarch stationery or (2) standard eight-and-one-half-by-eleven-inch letterhead.

4. Use single parentheses, such as a) or 1), in outlines, although double

parentheses are more common, for example (a) or (1).

5. Enclose punctuation within the parentheses only if it belongs to the parenthetical clause.

The battle occurred in World War II. (This is documented in Dr. Jones's recent text.)

6. To enclose parenthetical material within other parenthetical material, use a combination of brackets and parentheses.

(This is documented in Dr. Jones's recent [1983] text).

Participle. A verbal adjective; word derived from a verb and modifying a noun or pronoun.

Dangling participles. A participle or participial phrase used as an adjective must modify a definite noun or pronoun within the sentence.

WRONG: When *writing* this book, an attempt was made to organize the material to best advantage. (What does *writing* modify?)
RIGHT: When *writing* this book, the *author* attempted to organize the material to best advantage.

EXCEPTIONS: Certain participles may indicate a general rather than a specific action—an action in which no particular actor is implied. They do not then need a noun or pronoun to modify and are not dangling. Some participles that may be used in this manner are *allowing, coming, granting, considering, speaking, talking, learning, owing.*

Misplaced participles. The misplacement of a participial modifier can result in a meaningless sentence.

WRONG: I saw the *file cabinet walking* up the stairs.
RIGHT: *Walking* upstairs, *I* saw the file cabinet.

Past tense. 1. Use the simple past tense to express action that was completed at some definite time before the time of the statement.

The report concerns events that *occurred* many years ago.
He *had* [not *has had*] practical ideas on every phase of the problem.

2. Avoid substitution of the past tense for the present perfect or past perfect tenses.

WRONG: I *was filing* when he returned, but I *was typing* the report before that time.
RIGHT: I *was filing* when he returned, but I *had been typing* the report before that time. (Past perfect.)

3. In dependent clauses, a *permanently true* fact is usually put in the present tense, even when the main verb is in the past tense.

We *were taught* in school that Hamlet *is* Shakespeare's greatest tragedy.

This rule does not apply to independent clauses or sentences with one verb.

Hamlet *was* Shakespeare's greatest tragedy.
San Francisco *was* the birthplace of the United Nations.

Perfect tense. The perfect tenses are formed by adding the auxiliaries *has, have, had* to the past participle.

Only the illiterate use the past participle without an auxiliary.

PRESENT PERFECT TENSE:

> I (he) *have (has) looked* for the keys.
> I (he) *have (has) taken* the keys.

PAST PERFECT TENSE:

> He *had looked* for the keys.
> He *had taken* the keys.

FUTURE PERFECT TENSE:

> We *shall (will) have looked* for the keys by then.
> We *shall (will) have taken* the keys by then.

Period (.). Mark of punctuation indicating a complete break in thought. A period follows a declarative or an imperative sentence. It is also used after initials and abbreviations (*Ph.D.*) and numbers used in lists (*1.*). A period should be omitted after contractions (*sec'y*), roman numerals (*II*) except in outlines (*II.*), sums of money without cents (*$50*), short forms of words in common use (*memo*), federal agencies (*FAA*), and radio or television stations (*NBC*).

The period is always placed inside QUOTATION MARKS even if only one or two words are quoted. When an expression in parentheses comes at the end of a sentence and is part of the sentence, the period is placed outside the parentheses; if the expression is independent of the sentence and a period is necessary, it is placed within the parentheses.

Plurals of compound terms. See COMPOUND TERM.

Possessives. 1. *Compound nouns and proper names.* The possessive is formed by adding *'s* to the word nearest the object possessed (attorney *general's* argument; John Brown, *Jr.'s* office; John Brown *II's* office; Mr. Mason of *Consolidated's* staff; notary *public's* seal). Use the *of* phrase to form the plural possessives of a compound noun (arguments *of* the attorneys general; seals *of* notaries public).

2. *Awkward or sibilant sounds.* Drop the *s* and add only an apostrophe to form the possessive when the use of *'s* would cause a hissing or an awkward sound (the *executrix'* signature; for *consciences'* sake; for *goodness'* sake).

3. *Words ending in s.* The singular possessive of words ending in *s* is formed by adding *'s;* the plural possessive by adding only the apostrophe (Mr. *Jones's* car; the *Joneses'* car; Misses *Smiths'* reception; *bus's* motor). The apostrophe without the *s* is used in poetic or biblical expressions (*Jesus'* life; *Achilles'* heel; *Mars'* Hill).

4. *Words ending in ss.* If a word ends in *ss,* in most cases form the possessive by adding an apostrophe and *s* if a new syllable is formed in the pronunciation of the possessive (the *witness's* testimony; my *boss's* office).

5. *Of phrase.* An *of* phrase may be used to show possession. When the thing possessed is a *specific* number or group belonging to the possessor, the *'s* also is used, thus forming a double possessive.

That remark *of the commentator's* aroused interest. (a specific remark)

When the thing possessed is not restricted or limited to a specific number or group, the *'s* is not used.

The remarks *of the commentator* aroused interest. (generally speaking)

6. *Appositives and explanatory words.* Whenever possible, the use of appositives or explanatory words with the possessive case should be avoided. If the object possessed is named, the word nearest the object takes the possessive. If the object is not named and the appositive or explanatory words end the sentence, the first noun takes the possessive form. When in doubt, change the construction of the sentence and use of the *of* phrase.

RIGHT: His guardian, *Mr. Nelson's,* control of the money is mandatory.
BETTER: Control of the money *by his guardian, Mr. Nelson,* is mandatory.

When the APPOSITIVE is restrictive and therefore not set off by commas, the awkward construction does not arise.

The defendant *Adams's* defense changed my mind.

When the explanatory words are parenthetical, and especially when they are enclosed in parentheses, the construction *must* be changed to avoid the possessive.

AWKWARD: Mrs. Stone's (formerly Miss Dix) house is being remodeled.

BETTER: The house of Mrs. Stone, formerly Miss Dix, is being remodeled.

7. *Inanimate objects.* An inanimate object cannot actually possess anything. It is usually better to show relation by the use of the *of* phrase. However, usage has attributed possession to some inanimate objects, especially those expressing time or measure (*one day's* vacation; *two weeks'* pay; *five dollars'* worth; *six pounds'* weight). Many of these expressions form compound adjectives and can be hyphenated instead of written as possessives (a *one-day* vacation; a *six-pound* weight).

Predicate nominative. A noun or pronoun following an intransitive verb (one that does not take an object), thereby completing, or helping to complete, the predicate. As its name implies, a predicate nominative is always in the nominative case.

1. Forms of the verb *to be* (*is, are, was, were*) do not take an object but are followed by a predicate nominative. A common error is the use of the objective case of a pronoun (*me, us, her, him, them*) as a predicate nominative. The phrase "It wasn't me" is a colloquialism that is technically incorrect and should be avoided in writing.

2. A verb agrees with its subject and not with the predicate nominative. Difficulty is caused by the use of a singular subject and plural predicate nominative, or vice versa.

A valuable *by-product* of training conferences *is* the numerous *opportunities* afforded for management to observe the trainees' reactions. (*By-product* is the subject of *is*; *opportunities* is the predicate nominative.)

Progressive *interviews are* a useful *form* for training personnel. (*Interviews* is the subject of *are*; *form* is the predicate nominative.)

Prefix. That portion of a word that is placed before the root (*predetermines*). As a rule (1) do not double the last letter of the prefix when it is different from the first letter of the root (*disappear*); (2) keep the last letter of the prefix when the root begins with the same letter (*misstatement*); (3) do not use a hyphen to divide the prefix from the root (*anticlimax*; *postscript*).

To prevent misreading, however, use a hyphen (1) when the prefix begins with an *i* or an *a* and the root begins with the same letter (*ultra-active*; *anti-intellectual*); (2) for those few words using the prefix *re* to distinguish them from words of the same spelling but different meaning (to *re-collect* the tickets; to *recollect* the error; to *re-form* the group; to *reform* behavior); (3) with prefixes added to capitalized word (*pro-American*; *mid-February*); (4) for family terms using the prefix *great* (my *great-grandfather*; her *great-aunt*); (5) when the word *self* is used as a prefix (*self-addressed*; *self-evident*).

Preposition at the end. It is not grammatically incorrect to place a preposition at the end of a sentence; it is better to end a sentence with a preposition than to use an awkward construction. It is incorrect to place an *unnecessary* preposition at the end of the sentence.

WRONG: Where is the file *at*?

Present tense. 1. Use the present tense to indicate acton that is taking place at the present time.

He told me that the company's home office *is* [not *was*] located in New York. (The office is still located in New York.)

2. The present tense is used idiomatically to express future action.

Congress *adjourns* [for *will adjourn*] next week.
My vacation *starts* [for *will start*] next Friday.

3. Use the progressive form, not the simple present, to express action in progress.

WRONG: When I write in the morning, as I *write* now, I compose with more facility than in the evening.
RIGHT: When I write in the morning, as I *am writing* now, I compose with more facility than in the evening.

Pronoun. 1. *Antecedents*. A pronoun stands for a noun, and the noun for which it stands is the antecedent. The sentence structure should not leave even a momentary doubt about which noun is the antecedent.

2. *Agreement in number*. A pronoun must agree with its antecedent in number.

WRONG: The firm *has* demonstrated that *they are* qualified to look after the interests of *their* clients.
RIGHT: The firm *has* demonstrated that *it is* qualified to look after the interests of *its* clients.

3. *As objects.* When a pronoun is used as an object, it is always in the objective case. A common error is the use of the nominative case of the first and third person pronouns (*I, we, he, she, they*) instead of the objective case (*me, us, him, her, them*), especially when the pronoun is joined to another object. (The second-person pronoun, *you*, causes no trouble because the nominative and objective cases, singular and plural, have the same form.) The sentence can be tested by omitting the first object. The omission will show the absurdity of the use of the nominative instead of the objective.

WRONG: I know you and *he* to be my friends. (I know . . . he to be?)
RIGHT: I know you and *him* to be my friends.

Punctuation. The purpose of punctuation is to make the structure and meaning of the written word clear to the reader. Punctuation in moderation adds emphasis and stress to the writer's words, but it is not a panacea for a poorly constructed sentence. Sentences that are difficult to punctuate or that require the use of a great many commas are usually weak and should be expressed differently. See APOSTROPHE; COLON; COMMA; DASH; ELLIPSIS POINTS; EXCLAMATION POINT; HYPHEN; PARENTHESES; PERIOD; QUESTION MARK; QUOTATION MARKS; SEMICOLON; VIRGULE.

Question mark (?). Mark of punctuation used after interrogatory sentences. The interrogation point is placed after a direct question but not after an indirect question. The question mark is not used after a question that is a request to which no answer is expected.

Will you please return the signed copy as soon as possible.

In a series of questions included within one sentence, a question mark is usually placed after each question, and each question usually begins with a capital. When used with quoted material, the question mark comes before or after the quotation marks, depending on whether or not the entire question is quoted.

'How much can we improve the quality of life?"
How much can we improve the "quality of life"?

Quotation marks. Marks of punctuation enclosing one or more words. Quotation marks are used to enclose the exact words of a speaker or writer but not words that are not quoted exactly.

He said, "We can begin now."
He said that we can begin now.

They are used to enclose an unusual word or phrase or one used with a special trade meaning (the "missile mania" atmosphere) but not after *so-called* (the so-called truce). Quotes are also used around the titles of articles, chapters or parts of books, pamphlets and unpublished material, television shows, sketches, short poems, and songs ("Five Steps to Easy Living"; "Dallas"; "Star Spangled Banner"). *Single quotation marks* are used to enclose a quotation within a quotation.

"It is classified as 'lost territory.' "

Placement of quotation marks and other punctuation. Periods and commas are always placed inside quotation marks, even if only one word is enclosed in quotation marks. ("yes."). Colons and semicolons are always placed outside quotation marks ("yes":). Question marks (interrogation points) and exclamation points are placed outside the quotation marks if the entire sentence is interrogatory or exclamatory; inside the quotation marks if only the quoted material is a question or exclamation. (See the examples under QUESTION MARK.) When quoted material is more than one paragraph in length, quotation marks are placed at the beginning of each paragraph but only at the close of the last paragraph.

See also Chapter 8/QUOTED MATERIAL; EXTRACT.

Section sign (§). A mark used to signal the beginning of a new section or subdivision in a piece of writing, sometimes followed by the number of the section (§ 3.027).

Semicolon (;). Mark of punctuation indicating a break in thought more pronounced than the comma indicates and less pronounced than the period indicates. A semicolon is used to separate the parts of a compound sentence when the conjunction is omitted.

The invoice is past due; action will be taken shortly.

A semicolon is also used to separate clauses that are punctuated by commas.

She completed the typing, filing, and billing; processed the outgoing mail; and picked up the stationery, copy paper, and type cleaner.

It is used to separate items in enumerations unless they are short.

The following action was taken: (a) amendment of the charter, bylaws, and preamble; (b) adoption of new resolutions; and (c) removal of directors.

Sequence of tenses. When two or more verbs are used in the same sentence, the relation of the tenses or *sequence of tenses* is important and sometimes troublesome.

1. The purpose of changing the tense in a sentence is to indicate a change in time.

I *remember* I *owe* him a debt of gratitude. (The whole situation is in the present.)
I *remembered* I *owed* him a debt of gratitude. (The whole situation is in the past.)
I *remember* I *owe* him a debt of gratitude. (Implication: The debt is no longer owed.)

2. The past perfect tense is used with the past tense to refer to a preceding event.

He pledged the bonds he *had bought* [not *bought*] last week.

3. After a future tense in a main clause, the present tense is used in a dependent clause.

198

The chairperson *will open* the meeting as soon as the speaker *arrives.*

4. A fact that is *permanently true* is usually put in the present tense, even when the main verb is in the past tense.

5. The perfect participle expresses an action that has been completed *at the time* indicated by the main verb. A common error is the use of the present participle instead of the perfect.

He completed the report on schedule, *having worked* [not *working*] unusually long hours.

See also FUTURE TENSE; PAST TENSE; PERFECT TENSE; PRESENT TENSE.

Split infinitive. See INFINITIVE.

Subjunctive mood. Although the trend is away from the subjunctive mood, correct usage still requires the subjunctive in some cases.

1. The subjunctive mood is used to express a condition contrary to fact. Contrary-to-fact statements are generally introduced by *wish* or *if.*

If the company *were* [not the indicative *was*] in a sound financial position, a merger would not be necessary. (The company is not in a sound financial position.)

Many clauses introduced by *if* do not express impossible or contrary-to-fact conditions, but merely a condition or a doubt. In those clauses, the subjunctive is not generally used.

If he *was* [not *were*] at the meeting, we did not see him. (But it is possible he was there.)

2. The *past* subjunctive is used to express a *supposition* or *condition* in clauses introduced by *as if* or *as though.*

She acted *as though* the file *were* [not *was*] missing.

3. The subjunctive is used in *that* clauses when the main verb expresses importance, necessity, demand, recommendation, order, and the like.

He gave instructions that the office *be* closed early.

4. Use the subjunctive in formal writing to express a motion, resolution, or ruling.

Resolved: That the bylaws *be* amended.

Suffix. An affix at the end of a word, base, or phrase. Some of the common forms of usage follow:

1. *Suffixes -able, -ous.* Words ending in *e* preceded by *c* or *g* do not drop the final *e* before the suffixes *-able* and *-ous* (*serviceable; advantageous*) but do drop the final *e* before the suffix *-ible* (*deducible*).

2. Suffixes *-sede, -ceed, -cede.* Only one word in our language ends in *-sede: supersede.* Only three end in *-ceed: proceed, exceed, succeed.* All others end in *-cede.*

3. *Suffix -ance, -ence.* When the suffix is preceded by a *c* having the

sound of *k*, or *g* having a hard sound, use *-ance, ancy,* or *-ant* (*extravagant; significant*); when *c* has the sound of *s*, or *g* the sound of *j*, use *-ence, -ency,* or *-ent* (*negligence; convalescent*).

4. *Suffixes -ise, -ize.* There is no rule governing the use of *-ise* or *-ize*. Words such as *compromise* use *-ise*. Otherwise, the preferred American usage is *-ize* (*unionize*).

Tense. See SEQUENCE OF TENSES.

Troublesome words. See WORDS, COMMONLY MISUSED.

Trite expressions. Expressions worn out by usage, trite, or old-fashioned. These words and phrases add little to the meaning of a business communication. Here are examples of expressions that should be avoided:

advise. Used with too little discrimination and best reserved to indicate actual advice. Often *say* or *tell* is better.

as per; per. Correctly used with Latin word: *per annum* and *per diem* but best avoided otherwise.

at all times. Often used with little meaning. Better to use *always.*

at this time. Also unnecessary in most cases. Try *at present* or *now.*

at your convenience; at an early date. Trite, vague, and unnecessary in most cases. Be specific.

beg. Avoid expressions such as *beg to state, beg to advise, beg to acknowledge.*

contents carefully noted. Contributes little to a letter.

duly. Unnecessary.

enclosed please find. Needless and faulty phraseology. The word *please* has little meaning in this instance. The word *find* is improperly used.

esteemed. Too flowery and effusive.

favor. Do not use the word favor in the sense of letter, order, or check.

handing you. Out of place in correspondence today.

have before me. A worn-out expression.

hereto. Trite.

herewith. Often redundant.

in re. Avoid except in subject line. Use *regarding* or *concerning.*

inst. Avoid the abbreviation of the word *instant* and the word *instant* itself.

our Mr. Becker. Say *our associate Mr. Becker* or just *Mr. Becker.*

proximo. A Latin word meaning "on the next." Better to give the exact name of the month.

recent date. Vague and unbusinesslike. Better to give the exact date.

same. A poor substitute for one of the pronouns, *it, they,* or *them.*

State. Often too formal. Better to use *say* or *tell.*

take pleasure. A trite expression. Better to say *are pleased, are happy,* or *are glad.*

thanking you in advance. Discourteous and implies that your request will be granted.

ultimo. A Latin word meaning the preceding month. No longer used in modern correspondence.

under separate cover. Meaningless. Better to be specific and give the method of shipping (*first-class mail*).

valued. Too effusive and suggestive of flattery. Better to omit.

wish to say; wish to state; would say. All are examples of needless, wordy phraseology. Simply omit.

Verb. A verb shows action or state of being. It must always agree with its subject in number and person. A verb is indispensable and is the only part of speech that can stand alone to express meaning (*Come*).

According to their relationship to objects, verbs are classified as transitive or intransitive. The action of a *transitive verb* goes from the doer to the receiver, from a subject to an object. The action of an *intransitive verb* either does not include an object, is limited to the subject, or the verb shows no action at all.

She opened the window. (transitive)
He is a skilled machinist. (intransitive, no action)

Verbs may be classified as principal or auxiliary according to their use. A verb phrase uses the principal verb together with auxiliary verbs. The principal verb may be used alone to express an act or state. When used with an auxiliary, the principal verb carries the leading thought.

I *know.* (principal)
You *may* come. (auxiliary)

Frequently used auxiliaries include *be, can, do, have, may, must, shall, will, ought.* Sometimes more than one occur together in combination.

You *should have* seen the show.

Although almost all verbs form the past and perfect tenses by adding *-ed* to the present (*look, looked, looked; ship, shipped, shipped*), many are irregular, and there is no rule for the formation of the past and perfect tenses.

Form the PERFECT TENSE by adding the auxiliaries *has, have,* or *had* to the past participle. Thus, I *do,* I *did,* I *have done.*

It is incorrect to use that form of the verb *without* an auxiliary. It is also incorrect to use an auxiliary with the past tense of the verb.

I did. (never *I have did*)
I have done. (never *I done*)

Virgule (/).   Also called slash, diagonal, and solidus. The virgule is used in fractions (*1/2*), identification numbers (*21967/5R*), abbreviations (*B/E*), for *per* (*rev./sec.*), in dates (instead of a hyphen) to show a span of periods or calendar years (*1988/89*), and between lines of poetry run into the text ("The winter comes / The seasons change"). Do not space before or after a slash, except put equal space on either side between lines of poetry.

Vocabulary.   See entries listed under GRAMMAR AND VOCABULARY.

Voice.   The quality of a transitive verb that shows when the subject is acting (active voice) or being acted upon (passive voice). Voice is ordinarily not troublesome.

1. Do not mix the voices by shifting from active to passive.

WRONG: The jurors *deliberated* for forty-eight hours before they *were discharged.*
RIGHT: The jurors *deliberated* for forty-eight hours before the judge *discharged* them.

2. The passive voice is less emphatic than the active.

WEAK: The manuscript *was rejected* by the publisher.
BETTER: The publisher *rejected* the manuscript.

Word division.   See DIVISION OF WORDS.

Words, commonly misused. Certain words are especially troublesome, and many are commonly misused both in conversation and in correspondence. The following are examples of such words.

A while, awhile. *A while* is a noun phrase referring to a period or interval.

Please wait *a while* longer.

Awhile is an adverb that means for a short period.

Let's work *awhile* before going to lunch.

Ability, capacity. *Ability* is the mental or physical power to do something; *capacity* is a physical measure of content (*two gallons*) or the power to learn (*a capacity* for math).

Adapt, adopt (vbs.). *Adapt* means to make fit or suitable, to adjust (*adapt* the pipe to fit); *adopt* means to take as one's own, to accept formally (*adopt* the proposal).

Addicted to, subject to (vbs.). *Addicted to* means devoted to persistently, as to a bad habit or indulgence; *subject to* means liable to or conditional upon (*subject to* approval).

Adverse, averse (adjs.). *Adverse* means in opposition, unfavorable (*adverse* opinion); *averse* means having a dislike for (*averse* to loud parties). *Adverse* refers chiefly to opinion or intention; *averse* to feeling or inclination.

Advise, inform (vbs.). Use *advise* in the sense of counsel, to warn (*advise* against); use *inform* in the sense of to acquaint, to tell, to communicate knowledge to (*inform* the participants).

Affect, effect. 1. The word *affect* is not used as a noun, except as a technical psychological term; *effect*, used as a noun, means result (the *effect* of the new policies).

2. These two verbs are totally different in meaning. *Affect* means to influence, to concern; *effect* means to cause, produce, result in, bring about.

Passage of this bill will *affect* [influence, concern] the entire country.
Passage of this bill can be *effected* [brought about] by cooperation of all parties.

3. *Affect* is also used in the sense of assuming or pretending.

He *affects* a blustery manner to hide his shyness.

Alike (adj.). Similar; having resemblance. *Alike* should not be preceded by *both*.

All. 1. When used as a noun, *all* is either singular or plural, depending on the meaning.

2. When used with a pronoun, *all* is a noun and is followed by *of*. When used with a noun, *all* is, properly, an adjective; *of* is not needed.

Count *all of* them.
Count *all* circulars and brochures.

Already, all ready (adv.). *Already* means *beforehand* or *by this time*. *All ready* means *completely ready* or *prepared*; the *all* adds emphasis.

It's *already* moving.
The report is *all ready* for mailing.

Altogether, all together (adv.). *Altogether* is frequently misused for *all together*. *Altogether* is correct only in the sense of *entirely, on the whole*.

It's *altogether* possible.
We were *all together* for Christmas.

Anyone, any one (pron.). Frequently incorrectly used one for the other. Of the two forms, *anyone* is correct when *anybody* can be substituted in the sentence with no change in meaning. In all other uses, *any one* is the correct form.

If we send *anyone,* it should be Mr. Jones.
If we send *any one* of the salespeople, it should be Mr. Jones.

Both *anyone* and *any one* are singular and take a singular verb and singular pronoun.

As. Frequently used incorrectly.

1. Use *as . . . as* in affirmative statements; *so . . . as* in negative statements and in questions implying a negative answer.

This window display is *as* attractive *as* the last one.
This window display is *not so* attractive *as* the last one.
Could any ambitious young man be *so* foolish *as* to turn down the offer? (implying a negative answer)

2. Use *as* as a conjunction; use *like* as a preposition to express comparison. *As*, or *as if*, introduces a clause containing a verb; *like* takes an object.

Copy the report exactly *as* it is written.
Their product is not *like* ours in quality.

3. *As if* and *as though* are used interchangeably to express a supposition. These expressions are always followed by a past subjunctive verb. The mistake of putting the verb into the present indicative tense is especially common after *it looks* or *it seems*.

Some employees act *as though* they *had* [not *have*] nothing to do.

4. Avoid using *as to* in lieu of a simple preposition, such as *of, about, among, upon*.

Barely, hardly, scarcely. *Barely* means narrowly; *hardly* means with difficulty; *scarcely* means by a narrow margin.

The key *barely* fits.
He could *hardly* stay awake.
They could *scarcely* believe the score.

Between (prep.). **1.** Use the objective case after *between*.

2. Use *between* when reference is made to only two persons or things (*between* you and me); use *among* when reference is made to more than two (*among* the guests).

3. Do not use *each* or *every* after *between* or *among* when *each* or *every* has a plural sense.

WRONG: Some of the visitors left *between* each speech.
RIGHT: Some of the visitors left *between* speeches.

Both (adj., pron., conj.). Frequently used incorrectly. *Both* is unnecessary with the words *between, alike, at once,* and equal(*ly*) and should be omitted unless the omission of the other words is preferable. *Both* is always used with a *plural* verb and pronoun or noun.

WRONG: *Both* the president and the treasurer are *equally* eager to pass the bill.
RIGHT: The president and the treasurer are *equally* eager to pass the bill.

Can, could (vbs.). Frequently used incorrectly.

1. *Could* is the past tense of *can.* Remember this when using *can* or *could* in sentences with other verbs. See SEQUENCE OF TENSES. Use *can* with verbs in the present, perfect, and future tenses; use *could* with verbs in the past and past perfect tenses.

I give/ I have given/ I shall give/ what I *can.*
I gave/I was giving/ I had given/ what I *could.*

2. Use *could,* not *can,,* when *would* is used in the main clause.

Even if the company *could* ship the order by Monday, the material *would* not reach the factory soon enough.

3. A common error is the misuse of *could* for *might* in conditional sentences. *Could* expresses ability; *might* expresses permission or possibility.

If the certificate fails to make provision for the issuance of stock in series, it *might* [*not could*] subsequently be amended to include that provision. (The thought is that the certificate *would perhaps* be amended; there is no question that it *can* be amended).

Can, may (vbs.). *Can* denotes ability or power; *may* denotes permission.

We *can* ship the goods next week.
May we ship the goods next week?

Canvass (vb.). To scrutinize, discuss, solicit (*canvass* the neighborhood). Not to be confused with *canvas.*

Capital, capitol (n.). *Capital* is a city that is the seat of a government; *Capitol* is the building in which Congress meets or a building in which a state legislature meets. State capitols may be spelled with either uppercase or lowercase *c*, but the United States Capitol is spelled with an uppercase *C. Capital* has several other meanings but they do not cause confusion.

Compare, contrast. To *compare to* is to indicate general similarity between objects; to *compare with* is to indicate specific similarity between objects.

We had a voter attendance of 75 percent *compared with* 60 percent last year. (specific percentages compared)
Our winter was mild compared to yours. (general comparison)

Contrast is used to show difference or unlikeness. The noun is followed by *to,* but the verb is usually followed by *with.*

There are more advanced features in electronic typewriters in *contrast to* the electric machines.
Today's fashions *contrast* markedly *with* those of the 1950s.

Complacent (adj.), *-ency* (n.); *complaisant* (adj.), *-ance* (n.). *Complacent* people are pleased with themselves or with things that affect them personally (*complacent* about work). *Complaisant* people are eager to please by compliance or indulgence (a *complaisant* mood).

Complement, compliment (n. or vb.). *Complement* is that which is required to complete or make whole (a part that *complements* another); *compliment* is an expression of admiration (a nice *compliment*).

Compose, comprise. *Compose* means to make up by combining; *comprise* means to include.

The company is *composed* of three divisions.
The company *comprises* three hundred employees.

Consensus (n.). Agreement in opinion. An erroneous expression frequently used is *consensus of opinion.* The words *of opinion* are redundant.

Continual, continuous (adjs.). *Continual* means occurring in close succession, frequently repeated (*continual* advertising); *continuous* means without stopping, without interruption (*continuous* operation). The same distinction applies to the adverbs continually and *continuously*.

Credible, credulous, creditable (adjs.). *Credible* means believable; *credulous* means easily imposed upon, believing too easily; *creditable* means praiseworthy.

He is not a *credible* witness.
The readers are indeed *credulous* if they believe the editorial completely.

His summation of the case was *creditable.*

Data. (n). Frequently incorrectly used as a singular noun. This word is plural; the singular form, *datum,* is now seldom used.

We have proved that *these* [not *this*] *data are* [not *is*] reliable.

Defer, delay, postpone. *Defer* means to put off until later (*defer* the decision until next week); *delay* means to stop something and set it aside (*delay* work); *postpone* means to put off until a later, specific time (*postpone* the meeting until Tuesday).

Depositary, depository (n.). *Depositary* applies to the person or authority entrusted with something for safekeeping. It may also be used to apply to the place where something is deposited or stored. *Depository* applies only to the place where something is deposited or stored.

Doubt that, doubt whether. Questions and negative statements usually call for the use of *doubt that. Doubt whether* is used in situations of strong uncertainty.

I *doubt that* we can meet the deadline.
I *doubt whether* anything will come of it.

Due to. Often misused for *owing to. Due* is an adjective and must be attached to a noun or pronoun, whereas *owing to* is now considered a compound preposition. *Due to* means *caused by.* The sentence can be tested by substituting *caused by* for *due to.*

WRONG: The labor movement is losing ground *due to* the methods of some of its leaders. (There is no noun for *due* to modify. The ground was not caused by the methods.)

RIGHT: The labor movement suffered a severe setback *due to* [caused by] the methods of some of its leaders. (The setback was caused by the methods).

Each. 1. When used as a subject, *each* invariably takes a singular verb (*each is*) and pronoun (*each* department filed *its* report).

2. When *each* immediately *follows* a plural noun or pronoun, the verb is plural (officers *each give*).

3. When *each* refers to a preceding plural noun or pronoun, the number of a subsequent noun or pronoun depends on whether *each* comes before or after the verb. Use the plural when *each* precedes the verb, the singular when *each* follows the verb.

The employees *each have their* own assignments. (precedes the verb)

The employees *are* responsible *each* for *his or her* own assignment. (follows the verb)

Each other, one another. *Each other* should be used when only two things are referred to and *one another* when more than two are referred to.

James and I meet *each other* regularly for lunch.

James, Helen, and I meet *one another* regularly for lunch.

Either. 1. Singular, followed by singular verb. The use of a plural verb after *either* is a common error.

Either of the pictures *is* acceptable.

2. Use *either* to designate one of two persons or things; *any one* to designate one of three or more.

You may choose *either* of the two new typewriters or *any one* of the three old machines.

The authorities do not agree about this distinction. Some writers use *either* in relation to more than two.

Either . . . or. Correlative conjunctions. The construction after correlatives should be the same; for example, if *either* is followed by a verb, *or* must be followed by a verb. The misplacement of *either*, a common error, frequently results in unbalanced construction after the correlatives.

WRONG: You *either are required* to register by the 15th *or to drop* the course. (*Either* is followed by a verb and *or* an infinitive phrase.)

RIGHT: You are required *either to register* by the 15th *or to drop* the course.

Eminent, imminent (adjs.). *Eminent* means prominent, distinguished, and is applied to persons (*eminent* senator from Ohio). *Imminent* means impending, threatening, close at hand, and is applied to events (storm is *imminent*).

Every (adj.). Always singular. Followed by singular verb and singular pronoun.

Every one, everyone. Write as one word only when *everybody* is meant (something for *everyone*). Thus *every one* is always written to refer to objects; also if *of* is used, the expression must be written in two words (*every one* of us).

Example, instance, sample. *Example* refers to a particular item that represents a group (an *orange* is an *example* of fruits); *instance* is a situation that illustrates something (in this *instance* [situation]); and *sample* is a part or specimen (the *sample* blade).

Farther, further. Both words refer to distance. In reference to actual distance traveled, the correct word is *farther*. The word *further* is used to express distance in a figurative sense.

The drive from the airport to the city center was *farther* than we expected.
We must examine the problem *further.* (to a greater extent)

Former (adj.). Correct when used to designate the first of two persons or things; incorrect when used to designate the first of three or more.

WRONG: He called on Bill, Edna, and Carl. The *former* was absent.
RIGHT: He called on Bill, Edna, and Carl. *Bill* was absent.

Good, well. *Good* is an adjective. *Well* may be an adverb or an adjective.

John got *good* grades in school. (adjective)
John does not feel *well* today. (adverb)
John looks *well.* (adjective)

Guarantee, guaranty. For the verb, always use *guarantee.* Business convention has established a specialized use of *guaranty* as a noun. However, *guarantee* is never wrong, even in these expressions. A safe rule to follow is: when in doubt, use *guarantee* (*guarantee* delivery).

Identical (adj.). When followed by a preposition, *with,* not *to,* is correct (*identical with* his).

Kind (n). Pl., *kinds* The explanation here applies also to *class, sort, type, size, breed, brand, quality, variety, species,* and similar words.

1. The singular form is modified by *this* and *that,* not *these* and *those.*

2. The expression *kind of* is followed by a singular noun unless the plural idea is particularly strong. The common error is inconsistency.

The *kind of position* [not *positions*] that appeals to me doesn't interest her.
The company has numerous positions open. What *kind of positions* are they?

3. It is incorrect to follow *kind of* by *a* (*not* kind of *a* position).

4. After the plural form *kinds of,* a singular or plural noun may be used (kinds of *investment;* kinds of *investments*).

Incidentally, incidently. *Incidentally* means by chance; *incidently* is a misspelling of *incidentally.*

Incidentally, is the storeroom open?

Latter (adj.). Of two objects, the one mentioned second. 1. The word *latter* may be used to designate the second of two persons or things previously mentioned but should not be used when more than two have been mentioned.

WRONG: Here are the keys, cleaning tools, and shoppping list. You can throw the *latter* away when you are finished.
RIGHT: Here are the keys, cleaning tools, and shopping list. You can throw *the list* away when you're finished.

RIGHT: Here are the keys and the shopping list. You can throw the *latter* away when you're finished.

2. The expression *the latter part of* is incorrect. The correct expressions are *toward the end of, the last part of.*

Lay, lie (vbs.). *Lay* means to put or set down, place, deposit; *lie* means to recline, to be in a certain position or location. *Lay* must have an object; *lie* does not. The principal parts of *lay* are *lay, laid, laid, laying.* The principal parts of *lie* are *lie, lay, lain, laying.* The common error is the use of *lay* or one of its principal parts for *lie* or one of its principal parts. Thus *lay* is used incorrectly in place of *lie.*

LAY, LAID, LAID, LAYING:
You *lay* the *book* on the table, and it *lies* there.
You *laid* the *book* on the table yesterday, and it *lay* there until Mary picked it up.
I *lay* the *letters* in the same place on his desk each morning.
I *laid* the *letters* on his desk before I left the room.
The brickmason *has laid* the *stones* in an irregular pattern.
The brickmason *is laying* the *stones* in an irregular pattern.

LIE, LAY, LAIN, LYING:
I *lie* in the sun for an hour every day.
I *lay* in the sun for an hour yesterday. (past tense)
The book *has lain* there for a month.
The book *is lying* here where you laid it.

Libel and slander (ns. or vbs.). That which tends to injure the reputation of a living person or the memory of a deceased person; to expose the person to public hatred, disgrace, ridicule, or contempt; or to exclude the person from society is known as *defamation. Slander* is *oral* defamation of one person by another in the presence of a third person or persons; *libel* is *written* or *printed* defamation of one person by another, published before a third person or persons. A corporation is a person in this sense. For a slanderous statement to be actionable, it must be false and must cause injury to the person to whom the statement refers. In libel actions, no injury need be proved, although, of course, proved injury will affect the amount of damages awarded.

Omission, oversight. *Omission* refers to something left out or neglected (the *omission* in the bylaws). *Oversight* is a failure to notice or an error due to carelessness (error was an *oversight*).

Practical, practicable (adjs.). *Practicable* means feasible, capable of being put into practice; *practical* means useful or successful in actual practice. *Practical* may be used with reference to either persons or things, but *practicable* can be used only with reference to things.

My boss is a *practical* woman (a doer).
The plan is *practicable.* (can be carried out)

Principal, principle. The word *principle* is a noun only and cannot be used as an adjective. *Principle* means a fundamental or general truth, a rule (*principle of sovereignty*). *Principal* is used in all other cases. As a noun *principal* has a variety of meanings (the *principal* in the company); as an adjective, it means *chief, main, most important* (*principal* factor).

Reaction, reply, response. *Reaction* is any response to stimulli (*reaction* to injection); *reply* is a verbal or oral response (a *reply* sent by messenger); *response* is a reply or answer (a negative *response* to the idea).

Shall (should); will (would) (vbs.). *Should* is the past tense of the auxiliary verb *shall; would,* of the auxiliary *will.*

1. In a simple future or conditional statement *shall* or *should* is used in the first person (I, we); *will* or *would* in the second or third persons (you, he, she, it, they, the company). In practice, *will* is now used in the first person as well. To express determination, intention, willingness, command, *will* or *would* is used in the first person; *shall* or *should* in the second and third persons. These sentences are simple future or conditional statements.

If we support the farm block *we shall* be going against the interests of our own section of the country.

If they support the farm block *they will* be going against them.

I *should* like your permission to use the copy room.

ABC Company would [not *should*] like your permission to send a proposal. (When the name of the company or The Company is the subject, it is third person, even though the writing is in the name of the company.)

These sentences express determination, willingness, command, and the like.

I *will see* that shipment is made on the first. (a promise)

All *manuscripts shall be* submitted to the executive editor. (command)

2. In *that* clauses after *intend, desire, demand, be anxious,* and the like, *shall* and *should* are used in all persons. (But see 3.)

3. In questions, the use of *shall* (*should*) or will (*would*) is determined by the answer expected.

The following testimony from a famous trial illustrates the use of *should* and *would* in questions.

COUNSEL: *Would* you be willing to perjure yourself in this trial? (if occasion presented itself)
WITNESS: I *should not.* (if occasion presented itself)
COUNSEL: I know that you *should* not, but would you?
WITNESS: I *would* not.

In the strictest sense, the witness was right the first time (see 1.). Counsel's question should have been, "*Should* you be willing to perjure yourself (if occasion presented itself)?"

4. In indirect discourse, the auxiliary that would properly be used if the quotation were direct is used.

I said that *she would* understand the report if she studied it. (*You will* understand the report of you study it.)

5. *Should* is used in all three persons to express a sense of obligation or duty, in the sense of *ought to. Should* does not imply as strong an obligation as *ought to.*

6. *Would* is used to express past habitual action.

He *would* take the same train every morning.

That, which. Used in reference to persons, animals, and objects. *That* is used to introduce essential clauses without which the meaning would not be clear. *Which* is used to introduce nonessential clauses. The nonessential clause should be set off with commas; the essential clause should not be set off.

Michael's account of the accident, *which* I sent yesterday, should explain the damage.

He has the kinds of skill *that* invoke admiration.

Verbal. Relates to either written or spoken words (*verbal* contract). *Verbal* is used carelessly in place of *oral* with reference to spoken words (*oral* instructions).

Very, very much. 1. These words are overworked. Although they are good modifiers, excessive use of them has destroyed their force. *I am delighted* is as emphatic as *I am very much delighted*.

2. Those who insist on using *very* and *very much* should observe correct usage. These terms are not interchangeable. The problem is whether to use *very* or *very much* before a passive participle. Use *very* when the passive participle has the force of an adjective.

A *very delighted* crowd heard the news.

Use *very much* (or *much*) when the passive participle is used in the predicate with verbal force.

I was *very much* [or *much*] delighted at the result of the game.
I shall be *very much* [or *much*] inconvenienced by the delay.

EXCEPTION: A passive participle that, although used as a verb, has lost its verbal force by common usage is preceded by *very*.

I am *very* [not *very much*] tired of hearing about the matter.

Viable, workable. *Viable* means capable of existing (a *viable* firm); *workable* means practicable or feasible of working (a *workable* plan).

We. The editorial *we* instead of *I* in a letter written on behalf of a company should be avoided. Use *I* when referring to the writer individually and *we* when referring to the company. *I* and *we* may be used in the same letter.

I [the writer] will look after this order. You can be sure *we* [the company] will ship it tomorrow.

While, although. When used as a conjunction, *while* means "during the time that" or "as long as." It should be used in this sense only and not as a substitute for *although, whereas,* or *but. Although* means "regardless" or "even though."

He waited *while* she completed the letter.
Although [not *while*] some persons complained, the motion passed easily.

Who, whom. *Who* is used in the subjective case; *whom* is used in the objective case.

The woman *who* spoke at the meeting had just returned from Europe. (*Who* is the subject of *had returned*.)
The woman whom we just met is in charge of research. (*Whom* is the subject of *met*.)

CHAPTER 7

CORRESPONDENCE

Acceptance, letters of. 1. *Letters of acceptance.* See SOCIAL-BUSINESS LETTERS.

2. *Formal invitation.* See INVITATIONS.

Acknowledgment letters. *Business correspondence.* Acknowledgment of a business letter received during the absence of the addressee is a business courtesy. The acknowledgment letter may (1) simply acknowledge the incoming letter or (2) acknowledge and answer the letter.

1. *Simple acknowledgment letter.* The letter should respond promptly and express appreciation if something is received, state that the addressee is out of the city or away from the office (but should not say that he or she is ill), give the expected date of return, and assure the writer that his or her message will receive attention when the addressee returns. If the delay may cause inconvenience to the writer, add a note of apology.

Mr. Roberts is in England now and plans to return to Washington the second week of June. I'll bring your letter about the AMA conference to his attention at that time, and I'm certain that he will contact you promptly.

Please accept my apologies for this unavoidable delay.

2. *Acknowledgment letter that also answers incoming letters.* The important factor in answering a letter in the absence of the addressee is *knowledge of the facts*. The letter should respond promptly and express appreciation if something is received, identify the incoming letter, state that the addressee is away, state the facts that answer the letter, and if appropriate or desirable, state that the addressee will write upon return.

Your letter asking Ms. Nelson to speak before the Rotary Club of your city on

April 10 arrived a few days after she had left town on a business trip.

Checking Ms. Nelson's schedule for April 10, I find that she is to make a special report to the Board of Directors on that day. It therefore will be impossible for her to address the members of your club.

I know that Ms. Nelson will nevertheless appreciate your kind invitation and will write to you when she returns to Memphis.

Expressions of sympathy. In case of the death of a member of your employer's family, descriptions of floral pieces should be written on the back of each accompanying card. There should be separate files of mass cards and letters, all arranged in alphabetical order according to the name of the sender. There should also be a separate list of people who have sent both flowers and mass cards and of those who have written and also sent flowers or mass card. Lists similar to those illustrated in Figure 1 should be prepared for convenience in acknowledging the expression of sympathy.

A list of the names and addresses of those who performed special services, such as doctors, nurses, priest or minister, and editorial writers, should be compiled. Your employer may want to send letters of appreciation to them.

There is a difference of opinion about whether good taste permits a

ACKNOWLEDGMENT LETTERS: FIGURE 1: Lists for acknowledgment of flowers and cards

List No. 1

FLOWERS

Name and address (Alphabetical)	Kind of flowers	Remarks
Brown, Mr. and Mrs. R. S. (Catherine and Bob) 275 E. 86th St. New York, NY 10028	Spray, calla lilies	See Mass list
Jones, Mrs. A. (Mary) 79 W. Adams St. Boston, MA 02144	Iris, white stock	Also wire from Mr. Jones (Tom)

List No. 2

MASSES

Name and Address (Alphabetical)	Particular form of card; how many masses	Remarks
Brown, Mr. and Mrs. R. S. (Catherine and Bob)	Society for the Propagation of the Faith	See Flowers list
Murphy, Thomas E. (Tom) 44 5th Ave. New York, NY 10003	6 masses	

typed acknowledgment or an engraved acknowledgment card. If there are comparatively few acknowledgments to write, undoubtedly your employer should write them in longhand. However, in the case of a prominent person, when hundreds of people send flowers, mass cards, and letters, the task of acknowledging each by a handwritten letter is too formidable. Engraved acknowledgment cards may be used to acknowledge letters of sympathy, flowers, and mass cards from people who are unknown to the bereaved, but they should not be sent to acquaintances.

From the lists prepared by the secretary, it is simple to handle the acknowledgments. The first column gives the proper salutation ("Dear Mary," or the like); from the information in the second column, a special comment on the type of flowers or mass card can be made in the acknowledgment. The column headed *Remarks* gives any other pertinent information. A thank you letter should also be sent to those who sent memorial contributions to organizations. The notices from the organizations tell who made the contributions.

Your employer will select from the lists the friends to whom he or she wishes to write in longhand and will dictate acknowledgments to others. You will draft and type acknowledgments, for your employer's signature, to the remainder of the names on the lists.

Orders. Prompt processing of orders results in many cases in the delivery of goods as quickly as an acknowledgment of the order could be made. Many firms, therefore, have discontinued the practice of acknowledging orders. However, some firms believe a personal letter acknowledging a large order promotes good customer relations. Many others welcome new customers by acknowledging a first order.

The tone should be cordial. The letter should thank the customer, restate the order if it is involved, tell the customer when and how the order is being shipped, and express pleasure in serving the customer. The letter might also include a brief sales talk to make the customer more enthusiastic about the product.

See also APPOINTMENT LETTERS; INVITATIONS; SOCIAL-BUSINESS LETTERS.

Address on letters. See INSIDE ADDRESS; ENVELOPES.

Addressing officials (chart). This chart (pages 215–240) gives the correct form of written address, salutation, and complimentary close in letters to persons holding official or honorary titles, whether of high or low rank. It also gives the correct form for referring to those persons in a letter and the correct form to use in speaking or to informally introducing them.

The form of address shown throughout is for a man, except where applicable. For a woman, substitute *Madam* for *Sir*, and *Mrs.*, *Miss*, or *Ms.* for *Mr.*

The informal salutation is generally preferable unless the communication is strictly official.

If only the title of the official is known, he or she should be addressed by the title prefaced by *The*

(*The Lieutenant Governor of California*). The salutation would be *Sir.* But it is preferable to use his or her name.

When a person is acting as an official, the word *Acting* precedes the title in the address but not in the salutation or spoken address (*Acting Mayor of Memphis, Dear Mayor Blank*).

Women in official or honorary positions are addressed just as men in similar positions, except that *Madam, Mrs., Miss,* or *Ms.* replaces *Sir,* or *Mr.* For example, the formal salutation *Sir* becomes *Madam.* The *Mr.* preceding a title becomes *Madam* (*Madam Secretary*). The *Mr.* preceding the name of the official becomes *Mrs., Miss,* or *Ms.* (if her marital status is unknown or if she has stipulated that she prefers *Ms.*).

The wife of an American official does not share her husband's title. She is always addressed as *Mrs. Blank.* Nor does an untitled man share his wife's title. Together they would be addressed as *Ambassador* Jane Blank and *Mr.* Robert Blank or *Ambassador* Jane and *Mr.* Robert Blank.

A person who has held a position entitling him or her to be addressed as *The Honorable* is addressed as *The Honorable* after retirement. The title itself, such as *senator* or *governor,* is not used in the address or salutation. Even a former president is called *Mr.* An exception to this practice is the title of *judge.* A person who has once been a judge customarily retains his or her title even when addressed formally. Retired officers of the armed forces retain their titles, but their retirement is indicated (*Lieutenant General John D. Blank, U.S.A., Retired*).

Authorities disagree in matters of address, salutation, and complimentary close. Some, for instance, prefer more formal salutations (*My dear*) in all situations; others believe less formality (*Dear*) is the preferred modern approach. The examples in the address chart are traditionally acceptable forms of usage.

Adjustment in account, letters making. These letters fall into four classes: (1) when the amount of an item is incorrect; (2) when the total is incorrect; (3) when an item not purchased is charged to the account; (4) when returned merchandise has not been credited. The tone of adjustment letters should be firm but reasonable. Little is ever accomplished by a brash, irrational attitude.

1. *When the amount of an item is incorrect.* The letter should give the name and number of the account; describe the incorrect item and tell how it is incorrect; state your version of what the item should be, giving any documentary information you may have; and ask for a corrected statement *or* enclose a check for the correct amount and ask that the error be rectified on the account.

The September statement of Donald Northrup's account shows a charge of $35.00 for dinner for two on the evening of August 15. Evidently this amount should have been charged to someone else's account since Mr. Northrup was out of town that evening.

I have deducted $35.00 from the total amount of the statement and am enclosing Mr. Northrup's check for $50.80.

CORRECT FORMS OF ADDRESS

United States Government Officials

Personage	Envelope and Inside Address (Add City, State, Zip)	Formal Salutation	Informal Salutation	Formal Close	Informal Close	1. Spoken Address 2. Informal Introduction or Reference
The President	The President The White House	Mr. President	Dear Mr. President:	Respectfully yours,	Very respectfully yours, *or* Sincerely yours,	1. Mr. President 2. Not introduced (The President)
Former President of the United States[1]	The Honorable William R. Blank (local address)	Sir:	Dear Mr. Blank:	Respectfully yours,	Sincerely yours,	1. Mr. Blank 2. Former President Blank *or* Mr. Blank
The Vice-President of the United States	The Vice-President of the United States The White House	Mr. Vice-President:	Dear Mr. Vice-President	Very truly yours,	Sincerely yours,	1. Mr. Vice-President *or* Mr. Blank The Vice-President
The Chief Justice of the United States Supreme Court	The Chief Justice of the United States The Supreme Court of the United States	Sir:	Dear Mr. Chief Justice:	Very truly yours,	Sincerely yours,	1. Mr. Chief Justice 2. The Chief Justice
Associate Justice of the United States Supreme Court	Mr. Justice Blank The Supreme Court of the United States	Sir:	Dear Mr. Justice: *or* Dear Justice Blank:	Very truly yours,	Sincerely yours,	1. Mr. Justice Blank *or* Justice Blank 2. Mr. Justice Blank

Note: In this chart the form of address for a man is used throughout except where not applicable. To use the form of address for a woman in any of these positions, use the substitution *Madam* for *Sir* and *Mrs., Miss,* or *Ms.* for *Mr.* Thus *Dear Madam; Mrs. Blank,* Respresentative from New York; The Lieutenant Governor of Iowa, *Miss Blank*; The American Minister, *Ms. Blank.* The *Mr.* preceding a title becomes *Madam.* Thus *Madam Secretary; Madam Ambassador.* Use *Esquire* or *Esq.* in addressing a man or woman where appropriate.

1. If a former president has a title, such as *General of the Army,* address him by it.

United States Government Officials *continued*

Personage	Envelope and Inside Address (Add City, State, Zip)	Formal Salutation	Informal Salutation	Formal Close	Informal Close	1. Spoken Address 2. Informal Introduction or Reference
Retired Justice of the United States Supreme Court	The Honorable William R. Blank (local address)	Sir:	Dear Justice Blank:	Very truly yours,	Sincerely yours,	1. Mr. Justice Blank *or* Justice Blank 2. Mr. Justice Blank
The Speaker of the House of Representatives	The Honorable William R. Blank Speaker of the House of Representatives	Sir:	Dear Mr. Speaker: *or* Dear Mr. Blank:	Very truly yours,	Sincerely yours,	1. Mr. Speaker *or* Mr. Blank 2. The Speaker, Mr. Blank (The Speaker *or* Mr. Blank)
Former Speaker of the House of Representatives	The Honorable William R. Blank (local address)	Sir:	Dear Mr. Blank:	Very truly yours,	Sincerely yours,	1. Mr. Blank 2. Mr. Blank
Cabinet Officers addressed as "Secretary"[2]	The Honorable William R. Blank Secretary of State The Honorable William R. Blank Secretary of State of the United States of America (if written from abroad)	Sir:	Dear Mr. Secretary:	Very truly yours,	Sincerely yours,	1. Mr. Secretary *or* Secretary Blank *or* Mr. Blank 2. The Secretary of State Mr. Blank (Mr. Blank or The Secretary)
Former Cabinet Officer	The Honorable William R. Blank (local address)	Dear Sir:	Dear Mr. Blank:	Very truly yours,	Sincerely yours,	1. Mr. Blank 2. Mr. Blank

2. Titles for cabinet secretaries are Secretary of State; Secretary of Defense; Secretary of Education; Secretary of Energy; Secretary of the Interior; Secretary of Agriculture; Secretary of Commerce; Secretary of Labor; Secretary of Health and Human Services; Secretary of Housing and Urban Development; Secretary of Transportation.

United States Government Officials *continued*

Personage	Envelope and Inside Address (Add City, State, Zip)	Formal Salutation	Informal Salutation	Formal Close	Informal Close	1. Spoken Address 2. Informal Introduction or Reference
Postmaster General	The Honorable William R. Blank Postmaster General,	Sir:	Dear Mr. Postmaster General:	Very truly yours,	Sincerely yours,	1. Mr. Postmaster General *or* Postmaster General Blank or Mr. Blank 2. The Postmaster General, Mr. Blank (Mr. Blank or The Postmaster General)
The Attorney General	The Honorable William R. Blank Attorney General of the United States	Sir:	Dear Mr. Attorney General:	Very truly yours,	Sincerely yours,	1. Mr. Attorney General *or* Attorney General Blank 2. The Attorney General, Mr. Blank (Mr. Blank or The Attorney General)
Under Secretary of a Department	The Honorable William R. Blank Under Secretary of Labor	Sir:	Dear Mr. Under Secretary: *or* Dear Mr. Blank:	Very truly yours,	Sincerely yours,	1. Mr. Blank 2. Mr. Blank
United States Senator	The Honorable William R. Blank United States Senate	Sir:	Dear Senator Blank:	Very truly yours,	Sincerely yours,	1. Senator Blank *or* Senator 2. Senator Blank
Former Senator	The Honorable William R. Blank (local address)	Dear Sir:	Dear Mr. Blank:	Very truly yours,	Sincerely yours,	1. Mr. Blank 2. Mr. Blank

United States Government Officials *continued*

Personage	Envelope and Inside Address (Add City, State, Zip)	Formal Salutation	Informal Salutation	Formal Close	Informal Close	1. Spoken Address 2. Informal Introduction or Reference
Senator-elect	The Honorable William R. Blank Senator-elect United States Senate	Dear Sir:	Dear Mr. Blank:	Very truly yours,	Sincerely yours,	1. Mr. Blank 2. Senator-elect Blank *or* Mr. Blank
Committee Chairman— United States Senate	The Honorable William R. Blank, Chairman Committee on Foreign Affairs United States Senate	Dear Mr. Chairman:	Dear Mr. Chairman: *or* Dear Senator Blank:	Very truly yours,	Sincerely yours,	1. Mr. Chairman *or* Senator Blank *or* Senator 2. The Chairman *or* Senator Blank
Subcommittee Chairman— United States Senate	The Honorable William R. Blank, Chairman, Subcommittee on Forgeign Affairs United States Senate	Dear Senator Blank:	Dear Senator Blank:	Very truly yours,	Sincerely yours,	1. Senator Blank *or* Senator 2. Senator Blank
United States Representative or Congressman[3]	The Honorable William R. Blank House of Representatives The Honorable William R. Blank Representative in Congress (local address) (when away from Washington, DC)	Sir:	Dear Mr. Blank:	Very truly yours,	Sincerely yours,	1. Mr. Blank 2. Mr. Blank, Representative (Congressman) from New York *or* Mr. Blank

3. The official title of a "congressman" or "congresswoman" is *Representative*. Senators are also congressmen or congresswomen.

United States Government Officials *continued*

Personage	Envelope and Inside Address (Add City, State, Zip)	Formal Salutation	Informal Salutation	Formal Close	Informal Close	1. Spoken Address 2. Informal Introduction or Reference
Former Representative	The Honorable William R. Blank (local address)	Dear Sir: *or* Dear Mr. Blank:	Dear Mr. Blank:	Very truly yours,	Sincerely yours,	1. Mr. Blank 2. Mr. Blank
Territorial Delegate	The Honorable William R. Blank Delegate of Puerto Rico House of Representatives	Dear Sir: *or* Dear Mr. Blank:	Dear Mr. Blank:	Very truly yours,	Sincerely yours,	1. Mr. Blank 2. Mr. Blank
Resident Commissioner	The Honorable William R. Blank Resident Commissioner of (Territory) House of Representatives	Dear Sir: *or* Dear Mr. Blank:	Dear Mr. Blank:	Very truly yours,	Sincerely yours,	1. Mr. Blank 2. Mr. Blank
Directors or Heads of Independent Federal Offices, Agencies, Commissions, Organizations, etc.	The Honorable William R. Blank Director Mutual Security Agency	Dear Mr. Director (Commissioner, etc.):	Dear Mr. Blank:	Very truly yours,	Sincerely yours,	1. Mr. Blank 2. Mr. Blank
Other High Officials of the United States, in general: Public Printer, Comptroller General	The Honorable William R. Blank Public Printer The Honorable William R. Blank Comptroller General of the United States	Dear Sir: *or* Dear Mr. Blank:	Dear Mr. Blank:	Very truly yours,	Sincerely yours,	1. Mr. Blank 2. Mr. Blank

United States Government Officials *continued*

Personage	Envelope and Inside Address (Add City, State, Zip)	Formal Salutation	Informal Salutation	Formal Close	Informal Close	1. Spoken Address 2. Informal Introduction or Reference
Secretary to the President	The Honorable William R. Blank Secretary to the President The White House	Dear Sir: *or* Dear Mr. Blank:	Dear Mr. Blank:	Very truly yours,	Sincerely yours,	1. Mr. Blank 2. Mr. Blank
Assistant Secretary to the President	The Honorable William R. Blank Assistant Secretary to the President The White House	Dear Sir: *or* Dear Mr. Blank:	Dear Mr. Blank:	Very truly yours,	Sincerely yours,	1. Mr. Blank 2. Mr. Blank
Press Secretary to the President	Mr. William R. Blank Press Secretary to the President The White House	Dear Sir: *or* Dear Mr. Blank:	Dear Mr. Blank:	Very truly yours,	Sincerely yours,	1. Mr. Blank 2. Mr. Blank

State and Local Government Officials

	Envelope and Inside Address (Add City, State, Zip)	Formal Salutation	Informal Salutation	Formal Close	Informal Close	1. Spoken Address 2. Informal Introduction or Reference
Governor of a State or Territory[1]	The Honorable William R. Blank Governor of New York	Sir:	Dear Governor Blank:	Very truly yours,	Sincerely yours,	1. Governor Blank *or* Governor 2. a) Governor Blank b) The Governor c) The Governor of New York (used only outside his or her own state)

1. The form of addressing governors varies in the different states. The form given here is the one used in most states. In Massachusetts by law and in some other states by courtesy, the form is *His (Her) Excellency, the Governor of Massachusetts.*

State and Local Government Officials *continued*

Personage	Envelope and Inside Address (Add City, State, Zip)	Formal Salutation	Informal Salutation	Formal Close	Informal Close	1. Spoken Address 2. Informal Introduction or Reference
Acting Governor of a State or Territory	The Honorable William R. Blank Acting Governor of Connecticut	Sir:	Dear Mr. Blank:	Very truly yours,	Sincerely yours,	1. Mr. Blank 2. Mr. Blank
Lieutenant Governor	The Honorable William R. Blank Lieutenant Governor of Iowa	Sir:	Dear Mr. Blank:	Very truly yours,	Sincerely yours,	1. Mr. Blank 2. The Lieutenant Governor of Iowa, Mr. Blank *or* The Lieutenant Governor
Secretary of State	The Honorable William R. Blank Secretary of State of New York	Sir:	Dear Mr. Secretary:	Very truly yours,	Sincerely yours,	1. Mr. Blank 2. Mr. Blank
Attorney General	The Honorable William R. Blank Attorney General of Massachusetts	Sir:	Dear Mr. Attorney General:	Very truly yours,	Sincerely yours,	1. Mr. Blank 2. Mr. Blank
President of the Senate of a State	The Honorable William R. Blank President of the Senate of the State of Virginia	Sir:	Dear Mr. Blank:	Very truly yours,	Sincerely yours,	1. Mr. Blank 2. Mr. Blank
Speaker of the Assembly or The House of Representatives.[2]	The Honorable William R. Blank Speaker of the Assembly of the State of New York	Sir:	Dear Mr. Blank:	Very truly yours,	Sincerely yours,	1. Mr. Blank 2. Mr. Blank

2. In most states the lower branch of the legislature is the House of Representatives. The exceptions to this are: New York, California, Wisconsin, and Nevada, where it is known as the Assembly; Maryland, Virginia, and West Virginia—the House of Delegates; New Jersey—the House of General Assembly.

State and Local Government Officials *continued*

Personage	Envelope and Inside Address (Add City, State, Zip)	Formal Salutation	Informal Salutation	Formal Close	Informal Close	1. Spoken Address 2. Informal Introduction or Reference
Treasurer, Auditor, or Comptroller of a State	The Honorable William R. Blank Treasurer of the State of Tennessee	Dear Sir:	Dear Mr. Blank:	Very truly yours,	Sincerely yours,	1. Mr. Blank 2. Mr. Blank
State Senator	The Honorable William R. Blank The State Senate	Dear Sir:	Dear Senator Blank:	Very truly yours,	Sincerely yours,	1. Senator Blank *or* Senator 2. Senator Blank
State Representative, Assemblyman, or Delegate	The Honorable William R. Blank House of Delegates	Dear Sir:	Dear Mr. Blank:	Very truly yours,	Sincerely yours,	1. Mr. Blank 2. Mr. Blank *or* Delegate Blank
District Attorney	The Honorable William R. Blank District Attorney, Albany county Country Courthouse	Dear Sir:	Dear Mr. Blank:	Very truly yours,	Sincerely yours,	1. Mr. Blank 2. Mr. Blank
Mayor of a city	The Honorable William R. Blank Mayor of Detroit	Dear Sir:	Dear Mr. Mayor: *or* Dear Mayor Blank:	Very truly yours,	Sincerely yours,	1. Mayor Blank *or* Mr. Mayor 2. Mayor Blank
President of a Board of Commissioners	The Honorable William R. Blank, President Board of commissioners of the City of Buffalo	Dear Sir:	Dear Mr. Blank:	Very truly yours,	Sincerely yours,	1. Mr. Blank 2. Mr. Blank

State and Local Government Officials *continued*

Personage	Envelope and Inside Address (Add City, State, Zip)	Formal Salutation	Informal Salutation	Formal Close	Informal Close	1. Spoken Address 2. Informal Introduction or Reference
City Attorney, City Counsel, Corporation Counsel	The Honorable William R. Blank, City Attorney (City Counsel, Corporation Counsel)	Dear Sir:	Dear Mr. Blank:	Very truly yours,	Sincerely yours,	1. Mr. Blank 2. Mr. Blank
Alderman	Alderman William R. Blank City Hall	Dear Sir:	Dear Mr. Blank:	Very truly yours,	Sincerely yours,	1. Mr. Blank 2. Mr. Blank

Court Officials

Personage	Envelope and Inside Address (Add City, State, Zip)	Formal Salutation	Informal Salutation	Formal Close	Informal Close	1. Spoken Address 2. Informal Introduction or Reference
Chief Justice[1] of a State Supreme Court	The Honorable William R. Blank Chief Justice of the Supreme Court of Minnesota[2]	Sir:	Dear Mr. Chief Justice:	Very truly yours,	Sincerely yours,	1. Mr. Chief Justice *or* Judge Blank 2. Mr. Chief Justice Blank *or* Judge Blank
Associate Justice of a Supreme Court of a State	The Honorable William R. Blank Associate Justice of the Supreme Court of Minnesota	Sir:	Dear Justice: *or* Dear Justice Blank:	Very truly yours,	Sincerely yours,	1. Mr. Justice Blank 2. Mr. Justice Blank
Presiding Justice	The Honorable William R. Blank Presiding Justice, Appellate Division Supreme Court of New York	Sir:	Dear Justice: *or* Dear Justice Blank:	Very truly yours,	Sincerely yours,	1. Mr. Justice (or Judge) Blank 2. Mr. Justice (or Judge) Blank

1. If his or her official title is *Chief Judge* substitute *Chief Judge* for *Chief Justice*, but never use *Mr.*, *Mrs.*, *Miss*, or *Ms.* with *Chief Judge* or *Judge*.
2. Substitute here the appropriate name of the court. For example, the highest court in New York State is called the Court of Appeals.

Court Officials *continued*

Personage	Envelope and Inside Address (Add City, State, Zip)	Formal Salutation	Informal Salutation	Formal Close	Informal Close	1. Spoken Address 2. Informal Introduction or Reference
Judge of a Court[3]	The Honorable William R. Blank Judge of the United States District Court for the Southern District of California	Sir:	Dear Judge Blank:	Very truly yours,	Sincerely yours,	1. Judge Blank 2. Judge Blank
Clerk of a Court	William R. Blank, Esq. Clerk of the Superior Court of Massachusetts	Dear Sir:	Dear Mr. Blank:	Very truly yours,	Sincerely yours,	1. Mr. Blank 2. Mr. Blank

3. Not applicable to judges of the United States Supreme Court.

United States Diplomatic Representatives

Personage	Envelope and Inside Address (Add City, State, Zip)	Formal Salutation	Informal Salutation	Formal Close	Informal Close	1. Spoken Address 2. Informal Introduction or Reference
American Ambassador	The Honorable William R. Blank American Ambassador[1]	Sir:	Dear Mr. Ambassador: *or* Dear Ambassador Blank:	Very truly yours,	Sincerely yours,	1. Mr. Ambassador *or* Mr. Blank 2. The American Ambassador[2] (The Ambassador or Mr. Blank)
American Minister	The Honorable William R. Blank American Minister to Rumania	Sir:	Dear Mr. Minister: *or* Dear Minister Blank:	Very truly yours,	Sincerely yours,	1. Mr. Minister or Mr. Blank 2. The American Minister, Mr. Blank (The Minister or Mr. Blank)

1. When an ambassador or minister is not at his or her post, the name of the country to which he or she is accredited must be added to the address. For example: *The American Ambassador to Great Britain.* If he or she holds military rank, the diplomatic complimentary title *The Honorable* should be omitted, thus *General William R. Blank, American Ambassador (or Minister).*

2. With reference to ambassadors and ministers to Central or South American countries, substitute *The Ambassador of the United States* for *American Ambassador* or *American Minister.*

United States Diplomatic Representatives *continued*

Personage	Envelope and Inside Address (Add City, State, Zip)	Formal Salutation	Informal Salutation	Formal Close	Informal Close	1. Spoken Address 2. Informal Introduction or Reference
American Chargé d' Affaires, Consul General, Consul, or Vice Consul	William R. Blank, Esq. American Chargé d'Affaires ad interim (Consul General, Consul, Vice Consul)	Sir:	Dear Mr. Blank:	Very truly yours,	Sincerely yours,	1. Mr. Blank 2. Mr. Blank
High Commissioner	The Honorable William R. Blank United States High Commissioner to Argentina	Sir:	Dear Mr. Blank:	Very truly yours,	Sincerely yours,	1. Commissioner Blank *or* Mr. Blank 2. Commissioner Blank *or* Mr. Blank

Foreign Officials and Representatives

Foreign Ambassador[1] in the United States	His Excellency,[2] Erik Rolf Blankson Ambassador of Norway	Excellency:	Dear Mr. Ambassador:	Very truly yours,	Sincerely yours,	1. Mr. Ambassador *or* Mr. Blankson 2. The Ambassador of Norway (The Ambassador or Mr. Blankson)

1. The correct title of all ambassadors and ministers of foreign countries is *Ambassador (Minister of* _____ *(name of country),* with the exception of Great Britain. The adjective form is used with reference to representatives from Great Britain—*British Ambassador, British Minister.*

2. When the representative is British or a member of the British Commonwealth, it is customary to use *The Right Honorable* and *The Honorable* in addition to *His (Her) Excellency,* whenever appropriate.

Foreign Officials and Representatives *continued*

Personage	Envelope and Inside Address (Add City, State, Zip)	Formal Salutation	Informal Salutation	Formal Close	Informal Close	1. Spoken Address 2. Informal Introduction or Reference
Foreign Minister[3] *in the United States*	The Honorable George Macovescu Minister of Rumania	Sir:	Dear Mr. Minister:	Very truly yours,	Sincerely yours,	1. Mr. Minister *or* Mr. Macovescu 2. The Minister of Rumania (The Minister or Mr. Macovescu)
Foreign Diplomatic Representative with a Personal Title[4]	His Excellency,[5] Count Allesandro de Bianco Ambassador of Italy	Excellency:	Dear Mr. Ambassador:	Very truly yours,	Sincerely yours,	1. Mr. Ambassador *or* Count Bianco 2. The Ambassador of Italy (The Ambassador or Count Bianco)
Prime Minister	His Excellency, Christian Jawaharal Blank Prime Minister of India	Excellency:	Dear Mr. Prime Minister:	Respectfully yours,	Sincerely yours,	1. Mr. Blank 2. Mr. Blank *or* The Prime Minister
British Prime Minister	The Right Honorable Godfrey Blanc, K.G., M.C., M.P. Prime Minister	Sir:	Dear Mr. Prime Minister: *or* Dear Mr. Blanc:	Respectfully yours,	Sincerely yours,	1. Mr. Blanc 2. Mr. Blanc *or* The Prime Minister
Canadian Prime Minister	The Right Honorable Claude Louis St. Blanc, C.M.G. Prime Minister of Canda	Sir:	Dear Mr. Prime Minister: *or* Dear Mr. St. Blanc:	Respectfully yours,	Sincerely yours,	1. Mr. St. Blanc 2. Mr. St. Blanc *or* The Prime Minister

3. The correct title of all ambassadors and ministers of foreign countries is Ambassador (Minister) of _____ (name of country), with the exception of Great Britain. The adjective form is used with reference to representatives from Great Britain— *British Ambassador, British Minister.*
4. If the personal title is a royal title, such as *His (Her) Highness* or *Prince,* the diplomatic title *His (Her) Excellency* or *The Honorable* is omitted.
5. *Dr., Señor, Don,* and other titles of special courtesy in Spanish-speaking countries may be used with the diplomatic title *His (Her) Excellency* or *The Honorable.*

Foreign Officials and Representatives *continued*

Personage	Envelope and Inside Address (Add City, State, Zip)	Formal Salutation	Informal Salutation	Formal Close	Informal Close	1. Spoken Address 2. Informal Introduction or Reference
President of a Republic	His Excellency, Juan Cuidad Blanco President of the Dominican Republic	Excellency:	Dear Mr. President:	Respectfully yours,	Sincerely yours,	1. Your Excellency 2. Not introduced (President Blanco *or* the President)
Premier	His Excellency, Charles Yves de Blanc Premier of the French Republic	Excellency:	Dear Mr. Premier:	Respectfully yours,	Sincerely yours,	1. Mr. de Blanc 2. Mr. de Blanc *or* The Premier
Foreign Chargé d'Affaires (de missi)[6] in the United States	Mr. Jan Gustaf Blanc Chargé d'Affaires of Sweden	Sir:	Dear Mr. Blanc:	Very truly yours,	Sincerely yours,	1. Mr. Blanc 2. Mr. Blanc
Foreign Chargé d'Affaires ad interim in the United States	Mr. Edmund Blank Chargé d'Affaires ad interim[7] of Ireland	Sir:	Dear Mr. Blank:	Very truly yours,	Sincerely yours,	1. Mr. Blank 2. Mr. Blank

6. The full title is usually shortened to *Chargé d'Affaires*.
7. The words *ad interim* should not be omitted in the address.

The Armed Forces/Army

Personage	Envelope and Inside Address (Add City, State, Zip)	Formal Salutation	Informal Salutation	Formal Close	Informal Close	1. Spoken Address 2. Informal Introduction or Reference
General of the Army	General of the Army William R. Blank, USA Department of the Army	Sir:	Dear General Blank:	Very truly yours,	Sincerely yours,	1. General Blank 2. General Blank
General, Lieutenant General, Major General, Brigadier General	General (Lieutenant General, Major General, or Brigadier General) William R. Blank, USA[1]	Sir:	Dear General (Lieutenant General, Major General, Brigadier General) Blank:	Very truly yours,	Sincerely yours,	1. General Blank 2. General Blank
Colonel, Lieutenant Colonel	Colonel (Lieutenant Colonel) William R. Blank, USA	Dear Colonel (Lieutenant Colonel) Blank:	Dear Colonel (Lieutenant Colonel) Blank:	Very truly yours,	Sincerely yours,	1. Colonel Blank 2. Colonel Blank
Major	Major William R. Blank, USA	Dear Major Blank:	Dear Major Blank:	Very truly yours,	Sincerely yours,	1. Major Blank 2. Major Blank
Captain	Captain William R. Blank, USA	Dear Captain Blank:	Dear Captain Blank:	Very truly yours,	Sincerely yours,	1. Captain Blank 2. Captain Blank
First Lieutenant, Second Lieutenant[2]	Lieutenant William R. Blank, USA	Dear Lieutenant Blank:	Dear Lieutenant Blank:	Very truly yours,	Sincerely yours,	1. Lieutenant Blank 2. Lieutenant Blank
Chief Warrant Officer, Warrant Officer	Chief Warrant Officer (Warrant Officer) William R. Blank, USA	Dear Mr. Blank:	Dear Mr. Blank:	Very truly yours,	Sincerely yours,	1. Mr. Blank 2. Mr. Blank
Chaplain in the U.S. Army[3]	Chaplain William R. Blank, Captain, USA	Dear Chaplain Blank:	Dear Chaplain Blank:	Very truly yours,	Sincerely yours,	1. Chaplain Blank 2. Chaplain Blank (Chaplain Blank)

Note: Although civilian writers traditionally spell out the rank for all branches of the service, military writers use abbreviations such as *CPT* for *Captain* and *1LT* for *First Lieutenant*.
1. *USA* indicates regular service, *USAR* signifies the reserve.
2. In all *official* correspondence, the full rank should be included in both the envelope and the inside address, but not in the salutation.
3. Roman Catholic chaplains and certain Anglican priests are introduced as *Chaplain Blank* but are spoken to and referred to as *Father Blank*.

The Armed Forces/Navy

Personage	Envelope and Inside Address (Add City, State, Zip)	Formal Salutation	Informal Salutation	Formal Close	Informal Close	1. Spoken Address 2. Informal Introduction or Reference
Fleet Admiral	Admiral William R. Blank, USN Chief of Naval Operations, Department of the Navy	Sir:	Dear Admiral Blank:	Very truly yours,	Sincerely yours,	1. Admiral Blank 2. Admiral Blank
Admiral, Vice Admiral, Rear Admiral	Admiral (Vice Admiral or Rear Admiral) William R. Blank, USN United States Naval Academy[1]	Sir:	Dear Admiral (Vice Admiral, Rear Admiral) Blank:	Very truly yours,	Sincerely yours,	1. Admiral Blank 2. Admiral Blank
Commodore, Captain, Commander, Lieutenant Commander	Commodore (Captain, Commander, Lieutenant Commander) William R. Blank, USN USS Mississippi	Dear Commodore (Captain, Commander) Blank:	Dear Commodore (Captain, Commander, Lieutenant Commander) Blank:	Very truly yours,	Sincerely yours,	1. Commodore (etc.) Blank 2. Commodore (etc.) Blank
Junior Officers: Lieutenant, Lieutenant Junior Grade, Ensign	Lieutenant (Lieutenant Junior Grade, Ensign) William R. Blank, USN USS Wyoming	Dear Mr. Blank:	Dear Mr. Blank:	Very truly yours,	Sincerely yours,	1. Mr. Blank[2] 2. Lieutenant (etc.) Blank (Mr. Blank)

1. *USN* signifies regular service; *USNR* indicates the reserve.
2. Junior officers in the medical or dental corps are spoken to and referred to as *Dr.* but are introduced by their rank.

The Armed Forces/Navy *continued*

Personage	Envelope and Inside Address (Add City, State, Zip)	Formal Salutation	Informal Salutation	Formal Close	Informal Close	1. Spoken Address 2. Informal Introduction or Reference
Chief Warrant Officer, Warrant Officer	Chief Warrant Officer (Warrant Officer) William R. Blank, USN USS Texas	Dear Mr. Blank:	Dear Mr. Blank:	Very truly yours,	Sincerely yours,	1. Mr. Blank 2. Mr. Blank
Chaplain	Chaplain William R. Blank, Captain, USN Department of the Navy	Dear Chaplain Blank:	Dear Chaplain Blank:	Very truly yours,	Sincerely yours,	1. Chaplain Blank 2. Captain Blank (Chaplain Blank)

The Armed Forces—Air Force

Air force titles are the same as those in the army *USAF* is used instead of *USA,* and *USAFR* is used to indicate the reserve.

The Armed Forces—Marine Corps

Marine Corps titles are the same as those in the army, except that the top rank is *Commandant of the Marine Corps. USMC* indicates regular service, *USMCR* indicates the reserve.

The Armed Forces—Coast Guard

Coast Guard titles are the same as those in the navy, except that the top rank is *Admiral, USCG* indicates regular service; *USCGR* indicates the reserve.

Church Dignitaries/Catholic Faith

Personage	Envelope and Inside Address (Add City, State, Zip)	Formal Salutation	Informal Salutation	Formal Close	Informal Close	1. Spoken Address 2. Informal Introduction or Reference
The Pope	His Holiness, The Pope *or* His Holiness, Pope ___ Vatican City	Your Holiness: Most Holy Father:	*Always Formal*	Respectfully yours,	*Always Formal*	1. Your Holiness 2. Not introduced (His Holiness or The Pope)
Apostolic Pro-Nuncio	His Excellency, The Most Reverend William R. Blank Titular Archbishop of ___ The Apostolic Pro-Nuncio	Your Excellency:	Dear Archbishop Blank:	Respectfully yours,	Sincerely yours,	1. Your Excellency 2. Not introduced (The Apostolic Delegate)
Cardinal in the United States	His Eminence, William Cardinal Blank Archbishop of New York	Your Eminence:	Dear Cardinal Blank:	Respectfully yours,	Sincerely yours,	1. Your Eminence *or less formally* Cardinal Blank 2. Not introduced (His Eminence or Cardinal Blank)
Bishop and Archbishop in the United States	The Most Reverend William R. Blank, D.D. Bishop (Archbishop) of Baltimore	Your Excellency:	Dear Bishop (Archbishop) Blank:	Respectfully yours,	Sincerely yours,	1. Bishop (Archbishop) Blank 2. Bishop (Archbishop) Blank
Bishop in England	The Right Reverend William R. Blank Bishop of Sussex (local address)	Right Reverend Sir:	Dear Bishop:	Respectfully yours,	Sincerely yours,	1. Bishop Blank 2. Bishop Blank
Abbot	The Right Reverend William R. Blank Abbot of Westmoreland Abbey	Dear Father Abbot:	Dear Father Blank:	Respectfully yours,	Sincerely yours,	1. Father Abbot 2. Father Blank

Church Dignitaries/Catholic Faith *continued*

Personage	Envelope and Inside Address (Add City, State, Zip)	Formal Salutation	Informal Salutation	Formal Close	Informal Close	1. Spoken Address 2. Informal Introduction or Reference
Monsignor	Reverend Msgr. William R. Blank	Reverend Monsignor:	Dear Monsignor Blank:	Respectfully yours,	Sincerely yours,	1. Monsignor Blank 2. Monsignor Blank
Superior of a Brotherhood and Priest[1]	The Very Reverend William R. Blank, M.M. Director	Dear Father Superior:	Dear Father Superior:	Respectfully yours,	Sincerely yours,	1. Father Blank 2. Father Blank
Priest	*With scholastic degree:* The Reverend William R. Blank, Ph.D. Georgetown University	Dear Dr. Blank:	Dear Dr. Blank:	Very truly yours,	Sincerely yours,	1. Doctor (Father) Blank 2. Doctor (Father) Blank
	Without scholastic degree (but member of religious order) The Reverend William R. Blank, S.J.[2] St. Vincent's Church	Dear Father Blank:	Dear Father Blank:	Very truly yours,	Sincerely yours,	1. Father Blank 2. Father Blank
Brother	Brother John Blank 932 Maple Avenue	Dear Brother:	Dear Brother John:	Very truly yours,	Sincerely yours,	1. Brother John 2. Brother John

1. The address for the superior of a Brotherhood depends on whether or not he is a priest or has a title other than superior. Consult the *Official Catholic Directory.*
2. When the order is known, the initials immediately follow the person's name, preceded by a comma.

Church Dignitaries/Catholic Faith continued

Personage	Envelope and Inside Address (Add City, State, Zip)	Formal Salutation	Informal Salutation	Formal Close	Informal Close	1. Spoken Address 2. Informal Introduction or Reference
Mother Superior of a Sisterhood (Catholic or protestant)[3]	The Reverend Mother Superior, O.C.A. Convent of the Sacred Heart	Dear Reverend Mother: or Dear Mother Superior:	Dear Reverend Mother: or Dear Mother Superior:	Respectfully yours,	Sincerely yours,	1. Reverend Mother 2. Reverend Mother
Sister Superior:	The Reverend Sister Superior (order, if used)[4] Convent of the Sacred Heart	Dear Sister Superior:	Dear Sister Superior:	Respectfully yours,	Sincerely yours,	1. Sister Blank or Sister St. Teresa 2. The Sister Superior or Sister Blank (Sister St. Teresa)
Sister[5]	Sister Mary Blank St. John's High School	Dear Sister: or Dear Sister Blank:	Dear Sister Mary:	Very truly yours,	Sincerely yours,	1. Sister Mary 2. Sister Mary

3. Many religious congregations no longer use the title *Superior*. The head of a congregation is known instead by another title such as *President*.
4. The address of the superior of a Sisterhood depends on the order to which she belongs. The abbreviation of the order is not always used. Consult the *Official Catholic Directory*.
5. Use the form of address preferred by the person if you know it. Some women religious prefer to be addressed as "Sister Blank" rather than "Sister Mary" in business situations, but others object to the use of the last name.

Church Dignitaries/Jewish Faith

Personage	Envelope and Inside Address (Add City, State, Zip)	Formal Salutation	Informal Salutation	Formal Close	Informal Close	1. Spoken Address 2. Informal Introduction or Reference
Rabbi	*With scholastic degree:* Rabbi William R. Blank, Ph.D.	Sir:	Dear Dr. Blank: *or* Dear Rabbi Blank:	Very truly yours,	Sincerely yours,	1. Rabbi Blank *or* Dr. Blank *or* 2. Rabbi Blank *or* Dr. Blank
	Without scholastic degree: Rabbi William R. Blank	Sir:	Dear Rabbi Blank:	Very truly yours,	Sincerely yours,	1. Rabbi Blank 2. Rabbi Blank

Church Dignitaries/Protestant Faith

Personage	Envelope and Inside Address (Add City, State, Zip)	Formal Salutation	Informal Salutation	Formal Close	Informal Close	1. Spoken Address 2. Informal Introduction or Reference
Archbishop (Anglican)	The Most Reverend Archbishop of Canterbury *or* The Most Reverend John Blank Archbishop of Canterbury	Your Grace:	Dear Archbishop Blank:	Respectfully yours,	Sincerely yours,	1. Your Grace 2. Not introduced (His Grace or The Archbishop)
Presiding Bishop of the Protestant Episcopal Church in America	The Right Reverend William R. Blank, D.D., L.L.D. Presiding Bishop of the Protestant Episcopal Church in America Northwick House	Right Reverend Sir:	Dear Bishop Blank:	Respectfully yours,	Sincerely yours,	1. Bishop Blank 2. Bishop Blank

Church Dignitaries/Protestant Faith continued

Personage	Envelope and Inside Address (Add City, State, Zip)	Formal Salutation	Informal Salutation	Formal Close	Informal Close	1. Spoken Address 2. Informal Introduction or Reference
Anglican Bishop	The Right Reverend The Lord Bishop of London	Right Reverend Sir:	Dear Bishop Blank:	Respectfully yours,	Sincerely yours,	1. Bishop Blank 2. Bishop Blank
Methodist Bishop	The Reverend William R. Blank Methodist Bishop	Reverend Sir:	Dear Bishop Blank:	Respectfully yours,	Sincerely yours,	1. Bishop Blank 2. Bishop Blank
Protestant Episcopal Bishop	The Right Reverend William R. Blank, D.D., L.L.D. Bishop of Denver	Right Reverend Sir:	Dear Bishop Blank:	Respectfully yours,	Sincerely yours,	1. Bishop Blank 2. Bishop Blank
Archdeacon	The Venerable William R. Blank Archdeacon of Baltimore	Venerable Sir:	Dear Archdeacon Blank:	Respectfully yours,	Sincerely yours,	1. Archdeacon Blank 2. Archdeacon Blank
Dean[1]	The Very Reverend William R. Blank, D.D. Dean of St. John's	Very Reverend Sir:	Dear Dean Blank:	Respectfully yours,	Sincerely yours,	1. Dean Blank or Dr. Blank 2. Dean Blank or Dr. Blank
Canon	The Reverend William R. Blank, D.D. Canon of St. Andrew's Cathedral	Reverend Sir:	Dear Canon Blank:	Respectfully yours,	Sincerely yours,	1. Canon Blank 2. Canon Blank
Protestant Minister	*With scholastic degree:* The Reverend William R. Blank, D.D., Litt.D. *or* The Reverend Dr. William R. Blank	Dear Dr. Blank:	Dear Dr. Blank:	Very truly yours,	Sincerely yours,	1. Dr. Blank 2. Dr. Blank
	Without scholastic degree: The Reverend William R. Blank	Dear Mr. Blank:	Dear Mr. Blank:	Very truly yours,	Sincerely yours,	1. Mr. Blank 2. Mr. Blank

1. Applies only to the head of a cathedral or of a theological seminary.

Church Dignitaries/Protestant Faith *continued*

Personage	Envelope and Inside Address (Add City, State, Zip)	Formal Salutation	Informal Salutation	Formal Close	Informal Close	1. Spoken Address 2. Informal Introduction or Reference
Episcopal Priest (High Church)	*With scholastic degree:* The Reverend William R. Blank, D.D., Litt.D. All Saint's Cathedral *or* The Reverend Dr. Wiliam R. Blank	Dear Dr. Blank:	Dear Dr. Blank:	Very truly yours,	Sincerely yours,	1. Dr. Blank 2. Dr. Blank
	Without scholastic degree: The Reverend William R. Blank St. Paul's Church	Dear Father Blank: *or* Dear Mr. Blank	Dear Father Blank: *or* Dear Mr. Blank:	Very truly yours,	Sincerely yours,	1. Father Blank *or* Mr. Blank 2. Father Blank *or* Mr. Blank

College and University Officials

Personage	Envelope and Inside Address (Add City, State, Zip)	Formal Salutation	Informal Salutation	Formal Close	Informal Close	1. Spoken Address 2. Informal Introduction or Reference
President of a College or University	*With a doctorate:* Dr. William R. Blank *or* William R. Blank, L.L.D., Ph.D. President Amherst College	Sir:	Dear Dr. Blank:	Very truly yours,	Sincerely yours,	1. Dr. Blank 2. Dr. Blank

College and University Officials *continued*

Personage	Envelope and Inside Address (Add City, State, Zip)	Formal Salutation	Informal Salutation	Formal Close	Informal Close	1. Spoken Address 2. Informal Introduction or Reference
President of a College or University	*Without a doctorate:* Mr. William R. Blank President Columbia University	Sir:	Dear President Blank:	Very truly yours,	Sincerely yours,	1. Mr. Blank 2. Mr. Blank *or* Mr. Blank, President of the College
	Catholic priest: The Reverend William R. Blank, S.J., D.D., Ph.D. President Fordham University	Sir:	Dear Dr. Blank:	Very truly yours,	Sincerely yours,	1. Doctor (Father) Blank 2. Doctor (Father) Blank
University Chancellor	Dr. William R. Blank Chancellor University of Alabama	Sir:	Dear Dr. Blank:	Very truly yours,	Sincerely yours,	1. Dr. Blank 2. Dr. Blank
Dean or Assistant Dean of a College or Graduate School	Dean (Assistant Dean) William R. Blank School of Law	Dear Sir: *or* Dear Dean Blank:	Dear Dean Blank:	Very truly yours,	Sincerely yours,	1. Dean (Assistant Dean) Blank 2. Dean (Assistant Dean)
	(If he holds a doctorate) Dr. William R. Blank Dean (Assistant Dean), School of Law University of Virginia	Dear Sir: *or* Dear Dean Blank:	Dear Dean Blank:			*or* Dr. Blank, the Dean (Assistant Dean) of the School of Law
Professor	Professor William R. Blank	Dear Sir: *or* Dear Professor Blank:	Dear Professor Blank:	Very truly yours,	Sincerely yours,	1. Professor (Dr.) Blank
	(If he holds a doctorate) Dr. William R. Blank *or* William R. Blank, Ph.D. Yale University	Dear Sir: *or* Dear Dr. (or Professor) Blank:	Dear Dr. (or Professor) Blank:			2. Professor (Dr.) Blank

College and University Officials *continued*

Personage	Envelope and Inside Address (Add City, State, Zip)	Formal Salutation	Informal Salutation	Formal Close	Informal Close	1. Spoken Address 2. Informal Introduction or Reference
Associate or Assistant Professor	Mr. William R. Blank *or* *(If he holds a doctorate)* Dr. William R. Blank *or* William R. Blank, Ph.D. Associate (Assistant) Professor Department of Romance Languages Williams College	Dear Sir: *or* Dear Professor Blank: Dear Sir: *or* Dear Dr. (or Professor) Blank:	Dear Professor Blank: Dear Dr. (or Professor) Blank:	Very truly yours,	Sincerely yours,	1. Professor (Dr.) Blank 2. Professor (Dr.) Blank
Instructor	Mr. William R. Blank *or* *(If he holds a doctorate)* Dr. William R. Blank *or* William R. Blank, Ph.D. Department of Economics University of California	Dear Sir: Dear Sir: *or* Dear Dr. Blank:	Dear Mr. Blank: Dear Dr. Blank:	Very truly yours,	Sincerely yours,	1. Mr. (Dr.) Blank 2. Mr. (Dr.) Blank

College and University Officials *continued*

Personage	Envelope and Inside Address (Add City, State, Zip)	Formal Salutation	Informal Salutation	Formal Close	Informal Close	1. Spoken Address 2. Informal Introduction or Reference
Chaplain of a College or University	Chaplain William R. Blank Trinity College *or* (If he holds a doctorate) The Reverend William R. Blank, D.D. Chaplain Trinity College	Dear Chaplain Blank: *or* Dear Dr. Blank:	Dear Chaplain (Dr.) Blank:	Very truly yours,	Sincerely yours,	1. Chaplain Blank 2. Chaplain Blank *or* Dr. Blank

United Nations Officials[1]

Personage	Envelope and Inside Address (Add City, State, Zip)	Formal Salutation	Informal Salutation	Formal Close	Informal Close	1. Spoken Address 2. Informal Introduction or Reference
Secretary General	His Excellency, William R. Blank Secretary General of the United Nations	Excellency:[2]	Dear Mr. Secretary General:	Very truly yours,	Sincerely yours,	1. Mr. Blank *or* Sir 2. The Secretary General of the United Nations *or* Mr. Blank
Under Secretary	The Honorable William R. Blank Under Secretary of the United Nations The Secretariat United Nations	Sir:	Dear Mr. Under Secretary: *or* Dear Mr. Blank:	Very truly yours,	Sincerely yours,	1. Mr. Blank 2. Mr. Blank

1. The six principal branches through which the United Nations functions are The General Assembly, The Security Council, The Economic and Social Council, The Trusteeship Council, The International Court of Justice, and The Secretariat.
2. An American citizen should never be addressed as "Excellency."

United Nations Officials *continued*

Personage	Envelope and Inside Address (Add City, State, Zip)	Formal Salutation	Informal Salutation	Formal Close	Informal Close	1. Spoken Address 2. Informal Introduction or Reference
Foreign Representative (with ambassadorial rank)	His Excellency, William R. Blank Representative of Spain to the United Nations	Excellency:	Dear Mr. Ambassador:	Very truly yours,	Sincerely yours,	1. Mr. Ambassador *or* Mr. Blank 2. Mr. Ambassador *or* The Representative of Spain to the United Nations (The Ambassador or Mr. Blank)
United States Representative (with ambassadorial rank)	The Honorable William R. Blank United States Representative to the United Nations	Sir: *or* Dear Mr. Ambassador:	Dear Mr. Ambassador:	Very truly yours,	Sincerely yours,	1. Mr. Ambassador *or* Mr. Blank 2. Mr. Ambassador *or* The United States Representative to the United Nations (The Ambassador or Mr. Blank)

2. When an item not purchased is charged to the account. The letter should give the name and number of the account; describe the item charged in error, including the price and the date charged; give any additional pertinent information that you have; request that the charge be investigated; and request a corrected statement.

The June statement of Mrs. Robert Walker's account, no. 14825, shows a charge of $68.95 on May 15 for two boxes of copy paper. Mrs. Walker charged two boxes of copy paper for $68.95 on May 10 and again on May 20, but she did not charge any copy paper on May 15. The four boxes she bought were properly charged to her account.

Naturally, Mrs. Walker is concerned that someone might have used her account without her permission. Would you please investigate and let her know what happened?

3. *When returned merchandise has not been credited.* Follow the same pattern as when the amount of an item is incorrect.

On May 4 Ms. Karin Carter, whose account number is 15836, returned for credit a desk organizer that she purchased from you on May 2. The price was $11.98, including tax.

Ms. Carter's June statement does not show this credit. A credit slip was given to her, but unfortunately, it has been misplaced. She would appreciate it if you would verify the credit and send her a corrected statement.

In the meantime, I am enclosing Ms. Carter's check for $146.25, which is the amount of the statement less the price of the returned merchandise.

Appointment letters. Letters concerning appointments fall into two broad groups: (1) letters asking for an appointment and (2) replies to letters asking for an appointment. The letter should refer to the purpose of the appointment; be definite about place, time, and date; and ask for a confirmation.

1. *Letters asking for appointment.*

Letter 1

Mr. Brown will be in Memphis for a few hours on Tuesday, March 22, and would like to discuss with you the recent Supreme Court decision in the McNally case.

Will it be convenient for Mr. Brown to call at your office at three o'clock on March 22?

Letter 2

Ms. Jones is returning from Chicago the end of this week and would like to discuss with you the result of her conference with the president of Electromatic Corporation.

Will you please ask your secretary to telephone me at 254-9200 and let me know when it will be convenient for you to see Ms. Jones?

Thank you.

Letter 3

The papers in connection with the trust you are creating for your daughter are now complete, except for your signature. Mr. Nelson would like to know if you could come to his office early next week to sign them. Please telephone me (631-9000) to arrange a convenient time for you to do this.

Thank you.

2. *Replies to letters asking for appointment.*

Letter 4

Ms. Smith has asked me to let you know that she will be glad to see you on Monday, December 27, at two o'clock in her office, Room 1000, to discuss the program for the annual convention.

Letter 5

Thank you for your letter asking for an appointment with Mr. Davis.

Unfortunately, he is away from the office now and is not expected back until the end of the month. However, I will write to you just as soon as I know when he will be able to see you.

Letter 6

Ms. Adams has considered very carefully all that you said in your letter of December 21. If there were any possibility that a meeting with you would be helpful, she would be glad to see you. However, she does not believe that would be the case and has asked me to let you know and to thank you for writing.

Attention line. Designation of a specific person or department in letters addressed to a business firm. This practice marks the letter as a business rather than a personal letter and insures that it will be opened in the absence of the individual to whom it is directed.

On the letter, the attention line is typed two spaces below the address. The Postal Service asks that it be typed left of the address block on the envelope on any line above the second line from the bottom of the address.

The word *of* is not necessary. The attention line has no punctuation and is not underscored. When a letter addressed to a firm has an attention line, the salutation is *Gentlemen*, because the salutation is to the firm, not the individual. It is permissible to direct the letter to the attention of an individual without including his or her given name or initials, if they are unknown.

PREFERABLE:
    Attention Mr. Walter R. Richardson
PERMISSIBLE:
    Attention Mr. Richardson

Blind-copy notation. See COPY-DISTRIBUTION NOTATION.

Body of letter. Part of the letter that carries the message. The body begins two lines below the SALUTATION or SUBJECT LINE, if any. The body should be single spaced, unless it is extremely short, with a double space between paragraphs. When block style or full-block style of LAYOUT is used, each line begins flush with the left margin. When semiblock style of LAYOUT is used, the first line of every paragraph is indented five to ten spaces. The body should be approximately centered on the letterhead.

Business cards. All executives who call on clients or customers or who make business calls for any reason carry business cards.

The business card is usually three and one-half by two inches (which is larger than a social visiting card). On the executive level, a business card often has the executive's name in the middle of the card and his or her title and the firm name in the lower left-hand corner, either one above the other. The address is then in the lower right-hand corner. If the business is in a large city, the street address and the city are used, but the state may be left out. If the company offices are in a small town, the name of the state is written on the same line as the town, no street address being necessary. Some very prominent executives omit their title from the card; only the executive's name and the name of the company appear on it.

High-level executives may prefer a conservative style of type, such as block or roman, engraved in black on quality parchment or white card stock. But some executives today prefer a more informal, modern look. Initials and abbreviations, although not correct on social calling cards, may be used on business cards. However, the word *Company* should be written out unless the abbreviation *Co.* is part of the registered name of the firm. A title such as *Mr.* or *Ms.* does not precede the executive's name on a business card, as it does on a social card. The title *Miss* or *Mrs.* may, but usually does not, precede a woman's name. A woman with a professional title may use either her maiden name or her married name combined with her first name and her title. Some women also hyphenate their maiden and married names (*Janet Nelson-Roberts, M.D.*). Generally, women follow the same forms of address for women used in other business situations when having cards printed.

On business cards of company representatives below the executive level, the firm name is usually imprinted or engraved in the center of the card and the individual's name, title, and department in the lower left corner. The address and the telephone number may be in the lower right corner. Sometimes the person's name and title will be centered and the name will be in the left-hand corner and the address in the right-hand corner.

Cards used by salespersons or other representatives to advertise a company or a product frequently carry a trademark or emblem or an eye-catching design. The printing or engraving may be done in color. A calendar or advertising matter may appear on the back of the card. The telephone number is always on a card of this type. Doctors and dentists frequently put their office hours on their cards.

Office-supply stores and printers have a wide selection of card stock and type faces, if you are ordering for the first time. Rules concerning business-card style have relaxed in recent years. Raised offset printing, for instance, is popular and acceptable as a substitute for engraving, which is much more costly. Also, the traditional arrangement of copy is no longer strictly adhered to.

Carbon-copy notation. See COPY-DISTRIBUTION NOTATION.

Christmas card lists. See HOLIDAY CARD LISTS.

Complaint, letters of. See ADJUSTMENT IN ACCOUNT, LETTERS MAKING.

Complimentary close. Closing phrase in a letter expressing the regard of the writer for the addressee. The complimentary close varies with the tone of the letter and the degree of acquaintance between the writer and the addressee. The degree of formality should correspond with the SALUTATION. The close is typed two lines below the last line of the letter. It begins slightly to the right of the center of the page, except in the full-block or simplified style of LAYOUT, where it begins flush with the left margin. It should never extend beyond the right margin of the letter. Common forms of complimentary close are *Sincerely yours, Very sincerely yours, Cordially yours, Sincerely, Cordially, Best regards, Regards,* and *Best wishes.*

For complimentary closes to persons holding honorary or official positions (*Respectfully, Yours very truly*), see ADDRESSING OFFICIALS (CHART).

Condolence, letters of. See SOCIAL BUSINESS LETTERS; ACKNOWLEDGMENT LETTERS; Chapter 1/SYMPATHY, EXPRESSIONS OF.

Confidential notation. See PERSONAL NOTATION.

Congratulations, letters of. See SOCIAL-BUSINESS LETTERS.

Copy-distribution notation. Notation on letter indicating that a copy is to be sent to one or more persons.

The distribution notation should be typed flush with the left-hand margin, below all other notations. If space permits, it should be separated from the other notations by two spaces in the following way:

fc
Enclosure
cc: S. A. Williams
    R. L. Nelson

The words *Copy to* or *pc* instead of *cc* are used to indicate that the copies are photocopies instead of carbon copies. The notation *rc* means reprographic copy, and *bc* means blind copy. A *blind-copy notation* indicates that the addressee of the letter does not know that a copy was sent to anyone. The notation should be typed in the upper left-hand corner *only* on the office file copy and the copy sent to the blind-copy recipient, *not* on the original of the letter.

Continuation page. If the letter runs over the first page, use a plain sheet for the additional page, without a letterhead but of the same size and quality of paper as the letterhead. (However, your company may have special stationery for the continuation pages.) Do not use the word *continued* at the bottom of the first page; the fact that no signature appears at the end of the page indicates that another page follows.

The heading should contain the name of the addressee, the number of the page, and the date; the margins should be the same as those used on the first page. Leave two or more lines between the continuation heading and the body of the letter.

Henry Smith   2   July 7, 19——

or

Henry Smith
July 7, 19——
page two

Carry at least two lines of the body of the letter, exclusive of complimentary close, signature, and so forth, over to the top of the continuation page.

Credit and collection letters.   Matters involving money always require the utmost skill and accuracy. Although these letters are frequently prepared by specialists, the secretary needs to be familiar with the tone and pattern.

1. *Credit letters.*   Any letter that concerns the reputation of a person or a company must present the facts accurately, honestly, and fairly. Some letters provide credit information; others request credit or credit information. Asking for credit can be a delicate task. Indicate what type of credit you want, what terms you want, and items in your credit history that are applicable. Offer to supply additional information if needed.

Our training department regularly includes binders and pocket folders as part of the package supplied to our enrollees. The educational materials you offer for this purpose would be well suited to our needs, and we would like to place some orders with you in the future.

Our department currently spends from $300 to $500 a month on binders and pocket folders. Would you be able to extend your usual credit terms to our department for amounts within this range? I'm enclosing the name of our bank and other suppliers who are presently extending credit to us.

Please let me know if you need additional information for us to establish an account with you. Thank you very much.

2. *Collection letters.* Most collection letters are developed as a series of letters, from the first casual reminder to the final demand for payment preceding legal action. Know the facts before preparing your letter, and always give the customer a chance to pay before threatening other action. Although specialists usually compose the final demands for payment, secretaries frequently must send casual reminders to clients and customers. (Sometimes preprinted forms or form letters are used for first and even second or third notices.)

Just a friendly reminder that we would very much appreciate your payment of $17.50 for the copy of our conference proceedings that you purchased on October 9.

If your check is already in the mail, please disregard this notice and accept our thanks. If it is not, won't you take a moment to mail it today?

Dateline.   The part of a letter showing the date it is written. The standard position of the dateline is two to four lines below the last line of the letterhead, flush with the right margin. The dateline is written flush with the left margin of a full-block or simplified style of letter (see LAYOUT, Figure 1 and Figure 4). A comma separates the day of the month from the year; no period follows the date. In most organizations, the dateline should be typed conventionally (*January 15, 19——*).

Declination, letters of. See SOCIAL-BUSINESS LETTERS.

Enclosure notation. Notation on a letter indicating that the letter contains one or more enclosures. The notation *Enclosure* or the abbreviation *Enc.* is typed flush with the left-hand margin, one or two spaces beneath the IDENTIFICATION LINE. The number of enclosures should be indicated (*Enclosures* 2). Especially important enclosures should be identified (*Enc. Mtge.—Nelson to Jones*). If an enclosure is to be returned, the notation should so indicated (*Enc. Policy 36 4698-M, to be returned*).

Envelopes. The items in the address on the envelope are the same as those in the inside address. (See INSIDE ADDRESS.) Follow the requirements of the U.S. Postal Service and use the official two-letter state abbreviations, followed by the zip code. When mailing reports or other material in large envelopes that do not fit easily into the typewriter, type the address on a mailing label.

In order for the Postal Service to process your envelopes using an optical-character reader (OCR), you must write the envelope address in block style. Leave at least one inch from the left edge and five-eighths inch of space on the bottom. With window envelopes, the insert should show at least one-fourth-inch space

at the left, right, and bottom edges of the window. Type the address in all capitals without punctuation as shown here:

WEST INDUSTRIES
ATTN MR JV DAVIS
22 E 62 ST RM 1400
MILWAUKEE WI 12345

Put suite numbers and other unit numbers on the same line as the street and put box numbers *before* station names. Type personal notations in all capitals to the left and two lines above the address block; type the attention line left of the block on any line above the second line from the bottom of the address; and type mail instructions such as *Special Delivery* in all capitals two to four lines beneath the postage. Many post offices have supplies of a free brochure, *Secretarial Addressing*, that describes precise OCR requirements.

How to fold and insert letters in envelopes. See Chapter 1/OUTGOING MAIL, *Folding letters.*

Chain feeding envelopes. See Chapter 1/CHAIN FEEDING.

See also Chapter 5/WINDOW ENVELOPES.

Follow-up letters. A letter requesting a reply to a previous letter. If correspondence in a follow-up file is not answered by the follow-up date, a follow-up letter should be written to the addressee. (See Chapter 1/FOLLOW-UP SYSTEM.) It should identify the original letter, enclose a copy of the original letter unless it was very short, and request a prompt reply.

1. *Copy of original letter not enclosed.*

On February 2 we ordered from you 200 copies of your latest bulletin "Successful Selling Techniques," but we have not yet had an acknowledgment of the order. Since our first order evidently went astray, please consider this a duplicate.

Please let us know by return mail when we may expect delivery of the bulletins. Thank you.

2. *Copy of original letter enclosed.* Since this is a follow-up of a letter requesting a favor, it is written for your employer's signature.

In the rush of work, you probably have not had time to answer my letter of October 25 about using some of your selling ideas in our Real Estate Guide with credit to you. On the chance that this letter did not reach you, I am enclosing a carbon copy of it.

I would like to include your selling ideas in the next supplement of the guide. This will be possible if I have your reply by December 15.

Thanks very much.

Form letters. A timesaving and money-saving method of correspondence, used in recurring situations in which there is no necessity to direct the letter to a particular reader or no necessity to make personal and individual remarks to the reader. *Model form letters* are simply MODEL LETTERS that are retyped as personal letters each time a situation arises that requires that particular letter as an answer. *Model form paragraphs* are used in letters, with the remainder of the letter changed to meet the particular situation. *Processed form letters* are form letters that have been reproduced by a mechanical process, such as offset printing, computer or automatic typewriter, or copier.

Situations that can be covered by mechanically processed form letters vary with the business. The factors that determine which letters might be mechanically processed are (1) frequency of use, (2) purpose of the letter, and (3) the probable response of the recipient.

Difference of opinion exists about the effectiveness of form letters, but if they are properly handled and personalized, there can be no logical objection to them. When the letter is purely routine, or when the recipient is interested only in the information it contains, a mechanically processed letter can be used to advantage. For example, such letters are used in acknowledging orders and requesting overdue payments.

The appearance and LAYOUT of processed form letters can be personalized by (1) using good quality paper; (2) typing in the dateline, the inside address, and the salutation; (3) carefully matching the ribbon used for the fill-ins with the type density in the printed letter; (4) signing the letter with pen and ink; (5) sealing the envelope; and (6) sending the letter first-class mail.

Many secretaries keep a forms folder (or notebook) in which they collect copies of letters or paragraphs that might be repeated. Such models could also be kept on a computer disk or diskette file. One could then view the model on the screen, edit in the changes, and print out the desired copies. (For mailing instructions, see

Chapter 2/POSTAL SERVICE, 2. *Mailable items and how to dispatch them.*)

Holiday card lists. You should keep an alphabetical list of the names and addresses of people to whom your employer sends holiday cards. If your employer alone sends cards to some people and sends cards jointly with his or her spouse to others, separate lists should be kept. A separate list of business associates who receive cards should be kept if different types of cards are sent to business associates and personal friends. Check addresses on envelopes as cards are received and note changes of address.

Each year add new names (persons who send cards, new contacts made by your employer). He or she will indicate which, if any, to retain. See Chapter 1/PRESENTS.

Identification line. NOTATION on letter showing who dictated the letter and who typed it. The only purpose of the identification line is for reference by the business organization *writing* the letter. Therefore, some companies put the identification line only on file copies. It is typed two lines below the typed signature, flush with the left margin of the letter.

Forms. In the following illustrations SRD is the dictator and *rt* the typist. Lowercase letters are used instead of capitals for the typist's initials.

SRD:rt	Usual form
HRL:SRD:rt	When the name signed to the letter is not that of the dictator
rt	When the letter is composed by the typist
SRDJr:rt	When the father and son with the same name are in the organization
SRDavis:rt	When the dictator's name is not included in the typed signature

Unless company policy requires it, the dictator's initials are not included in the identification line when his or her name is typed in the SIGNATURE.

Indention. A line(s) set in from the margin. In typing, the indention is usually five to ten spaces from the left margin and five to ten spaces from the right. Sometimes, to save space, there is no indention from the right. Indentions are used for emphasis, for the sake of appearance, in quoted material, and in tabulating and itemizing. See LAYOUT; CHAPTER 8/EXTRACT; Chapter 1/TABULATED MATERIAL.

Information, letters that process. Letters that concern information received or requested include those that (1) supply information about things such as products and services, (2) acknowledge the receipt of information, and (3) answer inquiries about things such as delivery dates and prices. These letters should identify the incoming letter and acknowledge any information received; state that the addressee is away, if that is the case, and advise the writer that the person will contact him upon his or her return; provide the information requested, if possible; and indicate any action the recipient should take.

1. *Request for information.*

Thank you for your letter of January 25, addressed to Ms. Smith, concerning the proposed plant expansion.

Ms. Smith will be out of town until February 3, but I know that she will give your request her immediate attention as soon as she returns.

2. *Information received.*

Thank you for sending information about your July sales presentation to Mr. Harris. He will be away from his office until June 24, but I will see that this is called to his attention as soon as he returns.

3. *Supply information.*

In Ms. Cole's absence, I'm replying to your request for information about our Model ABC office copier. This copier is in stock and available at $1,560. A brochure describing its many new features is enclosed.

I hope this will be of some help to you until Ms. Cole returns next Monday, September 20. She will be happy to call you then to answer any further questions you have.

4. *Omission of enclosures.*

Mr. Symonds is out of town this week, but I noticed that in your letter of April 12 to him you mentioned that you were including the proposed plans for the new tennis courts; however, they were not enclosed.

I believe Mr. Symonds will need the plans in order to discuss this matter with the Board of Trustees. Since they are meeting early next week, would you please send them by the next mail? Thank you.

Inside address.   The address on the letter itself as distinguished from the address on the envelope. Traditionally, the inside address and the address on the envelope were written in exactly the same form. The U.S. Postal Service, however, recommends that envelope addresses be typed in all capitals to facilitate sorting by use of Optical Character Readers. See ENVELOPES.

Questions often arise concerning the use of titles in connection with the name of the person addressed.

1. Precede the name of the person addressed with a title such as *Mr., Mrs., Miss, Ms., The Most Reverend, Mesdames* or *Mmes., Dr.,* or *Messrs.* (But see 3 below.)

2. Place any business title or position after the name of the person addressed; it does not take the place of the usual title that precedes the name (*Mr. A. B. Smith, President*). However, omit the business title if it causes the address to run over four lines.

3. Abbreviations indicating scholastic degrees are sometimes placed after the name of the person addressed, in lieu of the title that usually precedes the name. Use only the abbreviations of the highest degree; more than one degree may be used, however, if the degrees are in different fields. A scholastic title is not used in combination with abbreviations indicating that degree, but another title may be used in combination with abbreviations indicating scholastic degrees (*Ralph Jones, D.D., LL.D.: The Most Reverend Ralph Jones,*

D.D., LL.D.). Usually, one lists the degree pertaining to the person's profession first (*Nancy Jones, LL.D., Ph.D.,* if she is a practicing attorney by profession).

4. *Messrs.* may be used in addressing a firm of men when the names denote specific individuals.

5. *Esq.* (for *Esquire*) may be used after the name of a prominent attorney or other high-ranking professional person who does not have another title. A title such as *Mr.* or *Ms.* does not precede the name when *Esq.* follows it.

6. *Mesdames* or *Mmes.* is used in addressing a firm composed of women, either married or unmarried. Use *Ms.* in preference to *Mrs.,* or *Miss* in addressing a woman whose marital status is unknown.

7. Address a woman with a professional title by her title, followed by her first and last names.

For addressing letters to persons holding official or honorary titles, see ADDRESSING OFFICIALS (CHART).

Introduction, letters of. See SOCIAL-BUSINESS LETTERS.

Invitations. *Letters of invitation.* See SOCIAL-BUSINESS LETTERS.

Formal invitations. All formal invitations are written in the third person. They are of three basic types: (1) engraved for the occasion, (2) partially engraved, and (3) handwritten. Companies also send printed invitations for social-business functions, such as an open house.

1. *Engraved invitations.* Engraved invitations should be engraved in

black on heavy white or light cream paper. There should be no address, monogram, or initial on the paper. If a coat-of-arms is used, it should be embossed on the paper without colors. The invitation of traditional size requires folding before it is inserted in the envelope, but modern style invitations are inserted without folding.

2. *Partially engraved invitations.* Many people who entertain frequently use partially engraved invitations when the number of guests is too small to justify engraving invitations especially for the occasion. (See Figure 1.) The wording is the same as a fully engraved invitation, but spaces are left for the name of the guest, the nature of the entertainment, the time, and the date. People who entertain

INVITATIONS: FIGURE 1: Partially engraved invitation

Mr. and Mrs. John Nelson
request the pleasure of

Miss Pellman's
company at dinner

on *Friday, the twentieth of June*
at *half-past seven o'clock*
Eleven Arlington Boulevard

R.S.V.P.   *Black Tie*

frequently with small dinners of twenty or more guests also engrave the fourth line, leaving only the name of the guest, the date, and time to be filled in. If the entertainment is in honor of someone, the phrase "in honor of _____" may inserted after the nature of the entertainment, if space permits. If there is not sufficient space for the additional wording, as is usually the case, then "to meet _____" may be written across the top of the invitation above the host's name.

A stiff white or ivory card, about three and one-half by five inches, is usually used for partially engraved invitations. However, the invitation may be engraved on the same kind of paper that is used for fully engraved invitations.

3. *Handwritten formal invitations.* Handwritten invitations are used when the number of guests to be invited does not justify engraved invitations. (See Figure 2.) Heavy white or cream personal writing paper, which may have an engraved address or initials for men, or a monogram for women, should be used. If the address is engraved at the top of the stationery, it is not repeated in the invitation. If initialed stationery is used, the address is written below the date and hour. The invitations should be written in script. The wording and spacing are the same as on a partially engraved invitation. When there is a guest of honor, the words "to meet _____" are added after the nature of the entertainment. The words "in honor of" are used only on engraved invitations.

INVITATIONS: FIGURE 2: Invitation to a formal dinner.

4. *What to include.* (a) *Names.* Those who send formal invitations identify themselves fully on the assumption that there might be others by the same name. Only the last name of the guest is used, on the assumption that further identification is unnecessary although the full name is always used on the envelope.

(b) *Date.* The year is not given.

(c) *Hour.* The correct form for noting the hour is "half-past eight o'clock" or "half after eight clock"—never "eight-thirty." If the invitation is for a quarter hour, which is unusual, the correct form is "at quarter-past-eight" or "at quarter before eight."

(d) *Abbreviations.* The only abbreviations used in a formal invitation are *Mr., Mrs.,* and *Dr.,* and *RSVP.* The words *senior* and *junior* are written out and begin with a small letter.

(e) *Titles.* Courtesy titles, such as *Excellency* and *Honorable,* are never used by the holder in issuing invitations. Senators and judges refer to themselves as *Mr.*, *Mrs.*, or *Miss.*

5. *Informal invitations.* Standard fill-in cards are available in stationery stores for more informal events. The host or hostess writes in the appropriate information in pen and ink and usually adds a number for replies by telephone (instead of expecting replies in writing). See Figure 3.

Answering Invitations. Invitations should be answered promptly, in the same form in which they are issued. A formal invitation in the third person is answered in the third person. (See Figure 4.) If a person particularly regrets having to decline an invitation, he or she may also write a letter, but this is in addition to the formal regret. (See Figure 5.) Formal answers are written by hand, in script, on personal writing paper. Writing paper with a business

INVITATIONS; FIGURE 3: Informal invitation to dinner

Lynda Stromburg

requests the pleasure of your company

at   *Dinner*

on   *Saturday, August 5, at 8 o'clock*

at   *The Newtown Arms*

     22 East Boulevard

     Concord

RSVP

445-6100

INVITATIONS FIGURE 4: Acceptance to formal invitation

INVITATIONS: FIGURE 5: Regret to formal invitation

Mr. and Mrs. Mark Roberts
accept with pleasure
the kind invitation of
Mr. and Mrs. Nelson
to be present at dinner
on Friday, the twentieth of June
at half-past seven o'clock
Eleven Arlington Boulevard

Miss Jane Pellman
regrets that she will be unable
to accept the kind invitation of
Mr. and Mrs. Nelson
to be present at dinner
on Friday, the twentieth of June

letterhead may be used to answer invitations to business luncheons, dinners, or receptions when they have been sent to the office. (See Chapter 5/WRITING PAPER.)

1. *What to include.* (a) *Names.* The person answering an invitation writes his or her own name in full, on the assumption that there might be others with the same name, but omits the first name of the person sending the invitation. If the invitation is issued in the name of more than one person, each name is mentioned in the answer.

(b) *Wording.* In a regret the expression "very kind invitation" may be used instead of "kind invitation."

(c) *Date and hour.* Specify the date and hour in an acceptance but only the date in a regret. The year is not included in the date.

(d) *Abbreviations.* The only abbreviations used are *Mr., Mrs.,* and *Dr.* The words *senior* and *junior* are written out and begin with a small letter.

(e) *Excuses.* It is unnecessary to state the reason for regretting a formal invitation unless it is issued by the White House or royalty.

(f) *Titles.* Courtesy titles, such as *Excellency* and *Honorable,* are never used by the holder in answering invitations. Senators and judges refer to themselves as *Mr., Mrs.,* or *Miss.*

Record of invitations received. Frequently, an executive takes an invitation home to consult with his or her spouse before accepting it and sometimes forgets to bring it back. It is advisable, therefore, for the secretary to make a copy of all incoming invitations. Then when the executive asks the secretary to reply to the invitation, or when the date of the occasion arrives, the secretary has available all necessary data concerning host, time, place, and the like.

Layout. *Of letter.* Physical arrangement of parts of the letter. The relative position of one part to another is determined by modern practice, although the letter writer has a choice of several styles or forms of layout. The standard styles of layout are full block (Figure 1), block (Figure 2), semiblock (Figure 3), and simplified (Figure 4). The official style of layout (Figure 5) is popular for SOCIAL-BUSINESS LETTERS. The distinguishing features of each style are indicated in the text of the illustration. The precise placement on the page is determined by the length of the BODY OF LETTER, which should be approximately centered on the letterhead. The secretary acquires skill in placement as he or she gains experience in gauging the length of the letter from his or her notes. If a letter is transcribed from a dictaphone, the dictaphone mark pad indicates the length of the letter.

Letters. The aim of almost every letter is to make personal contact in the simplest way. The language, therefore, should be natural, as though the writer were talking to the reader. (See Chapter 6/LANGUAGE.) The LAYOUT of the parts of the letter,

together with the quality of stationery and neatness of typing, determine the appearance of the letter and, consequently, whether or not it will make a favorable first impression. The essential parts of a letter are the DATELINE; INSIDE ADDRESS; SALUTATION; BODY OF LETTER; COMPLIMENTARY CLOSE, and SIGNATURE. A letter might also contain one or more of the following: ATTENTION LINE; REFERENCE LINE; SUBJECT LINE; ENCLOSURE NOTATION; MAILING NOTATION; PERSONAL NOTATION; COPY-DISTRIBUTION NOTATION; POSTSCRIPT.

Personal letters, many of which the secretary composes, now play an essential part in maintaining goodwill in business relations. See SOCIAL-BUSINESS LETTERS for models of letters of appreciation, condolence and sympathy, congratulations, seasonal good wishes, introduction, invitation, and declination.

Models of letters the secretary frequently writes over his or her own signature are shown in ACKNOWLEDGMENT LETTERS; APPOINTMENT LETTERS; FOLLOW-UP LETTERS; INFORMATION, LETTERS THAT PROCESS; ADJUSTMENT IN ACCOUNT, LETTERS MAKING; CREDIT AND COLLECTION LETTERS; Chapter 3/ NOTICE OF MEETING.

See also FORM LETTERS; LAYOUT; MODEL LETTERS.

Mailing notation. Notation placed on envelope and letter when the letter is sent by any method other than regular mail. The method of mail, such as special delivery (see Chapter 2/POSTAL SERVICE), is typed four spaces above the INSIDE ADDRESS, or it may be typed flush with

LAYOUT: FIGURE 1: Full-block style

[LETTERHEAD]

July 16, 19——

Ms. Sheila Jones
The Modern School for Secretaries
12 Harrington Place
Greenpoint, NJ 07201

Dear Ms. Jones:

You asked me to send you examples of letter styles being used in offices throught the country. This letter is an example of the full-block style of letter, which has been adopted as a standard at The Communications Company. We have reproduced it in our Employee Manual so that everyone will be familiar with the form and the instructions for its use.

Since The Communications Company is a leading exponent of modern business methods, we naturally use the most efficient letter form. This style saves time and energy.

As you see, there are no indentations. Everything, including the date and the complimentary close, begins at the extreme left. This uniformity eliminates several mechanical operations in typing letters.

Our dictaphone typists always use this form unless the dictator instructs otherwise. The dictator is at liberty to alter the form if a change is desirable for business reasons.

Since the dictator's name is typed in the signature, it is not considered necessary to include his or her initials in the identification line.

Sincerely,

Martha Scott
Correspondence Chief

hc

LAYOUT: FIGURE 2: Block style

[LETTERHEAD]

July 16, 19———

Your reference 12:3:1

Mrs. Jane Carter
The Modern School for Secretaries
12 Harrington Place
Greenpoint NJ 07201

Dear Mrs. Carter:

You asked me about the advantages of the block letter style. Many business concerns use the block style, because its marginal uniformity saves time for the typist. This letter is an example of the block style.

As you can see, the inside address is blocked and paragraph beginnings are aligned with the left margin, as they are in the full-block form. Open punctuation is used in the address.

The date and reference lines are flush with the right margin. The dateline is two to four spaces below the letterhead, and the reference line is two spaces below the dateline. The complimentary close begins slightly to the right of the center of the page. Both lines of the signature are aligned with the complimentary close.

I do not advocate including the dictator's initials in the identification line, because his or her name is typed in the signature.

Sincerely yours,

Mary A. De Vries
Managing Editor

cf

LAYOUT: FIGURE 3: Semiblock style

[LETTERHEAD]

July 16, 19——

Ms. Paula Anderson
The Modern School for Secretaries
12 Harrington Place
Greenpoint NJ 07201

Dear Ms. Anderson:

      Thank you for your letter requesting a semiblock style letter to add to your correspondence manual. Most companies have a definite preference of letter style. Some leading business corporations prefer that all letters be typed in semiblock style, which combines an attractive style with utility.

      This style differs from the block form in only one respect— the first line of each paragraph is indented five to ten spaces. In this example the paragraphs are indented ten spaces. As in all letters, there is a double space between paragraphs.

      The dateline is flush with the right margin, two to four spaces below the letterhead. The complimentary close begins slightly to the right of the center of the page. All lines of the signature are aligned with the complimentary close. Open punctuation is used in the address.

      No identification line is used in this example. Because the dictator's name is typed in the signature, his or her initials are not necessary.

Very sincerely yours,

Nancy Davis
Chairperson, Business
Education Department

LAYOUT: FIGURE 4: Simplified style

[LETTERHEAD]

July 16, 19——

Mr. William Warner
The Modern School for Secretaries
12 Harrington Place
Greenpoint NJ 07201

SIMPLIFIED LETTER FORMAT

You asked for an example of the simplified letter style, Mr.
Warner. This letter is an example of the modern, easy-to-prepare
simplified format.

Unlike the semiblock, block, and full-block styles, the simplified
format omits the salutation and complimentary close. Like the
full-block style, however, all structural parts are typed flush left.
The subject line is typed in all capitals without the word SUB-
JECT. The signature also is typed in all capitals, flush left, in one
line.

Businesses that use the simplified style, Mr. Warner, make it a
point to mention the reader's name in the opening and closing
paragraphs.

JENNIFER T. PENNINGTON—OFFICE MANAGER

rm

LAYOUT: FIGURE 5: Official style

[LETTERHEAD]

July 16, 19——

Dear Miss Kennedy:

Every correspondence manual should include a sample of the official style. It is used in many personal letters written by executives and professional persons and looks unusually well on the executive-size letterhead.

The structural parts of the letter differ from the standard arrangement only in the position of the inside address. The salutation is placed two to five spaces below the dateline, depending upon the length of the letter. It establishes the left margin of the letter. The inside address is written block form, flush with the left margin, from two to five spaces <u>below</u> the final line of the signature. Open punctuation is used in the address.

The identification line, if used, should be placed two spaces below the last line of the address and the enclosure mark two spaces below that. Because the dictator's name is typed in the signature, it is not necessary for the letter to carry an identification line. The typist's initials may be on the carbon of the letter, but not on the original.

Sincerely yours,

Leslie Thomas
Correspondence Secretary

Miss Janice Kennedy
12 Harrington Place
Greenpoint NJ 07201

the left margin two spaces below the IDENTIFICATION LINE. It is also typed on the envelope in the space below the stamps and above the address.

Memo. An informal, written communication. Memos are sometimes written on a special size paper, such as six by nine inches. They have no salutation or complimentary close and no address, except perhaps a room number of the branch location. Some organizations have special forms for memos with space for the name of the addressee, the writer, and the subject. Figure 1 illustrates a common style.

An interoffice memo that is not confidential is sent in an open envelope, often with a routing slip attached or the names of the persons to whom it should be circulated written on the envelope:

1. Mr. J. Brown
2. Mrs. R. Smith
3. Ms. L. Jones

A person receiving a memo to be sent on to another person crosses off his or her name. Memos are not signed manually unless the subject matter needs an official signature.

Some companies place the name of the sender before the body of the memo, thus:

TO: I. R. Brown
FROM: L. E. Jones

The person receiving the memo can then simply strike out his or her name and return the memo to the sender with the reply written on it.

The letters FYI (For Your Informa-tion) after the name of a person to whom a copy of the memo is being sent indicate that the copy is intended merely to keep him or her informed.

Model letters. Carefully planned letters designed to meet certain situations that may be used every time a similar situation arises. They differ from form letters in that they serve merely as a model and might require some adaptation to meet the exact circumstances about which a letter is being written. For model letters appropriate for certain situations see ACKNOWLEDGMENT LETTERS; APPOINTMENT LETTERS; FOLLOW-UP LETTERS; INFORMATION, LETTERS THAT PROCESS; ADJUSTMENT IN ACCOUNT, LETTERS MAKING; CREDIT AND COLLECTION LETTERS; SALES PROMOTION LETTERS; Chapter 3/NOTICE OF MEETING. For model personal business letters, see SOCIAL-BUSINESS LETTERS.

Notation. Note, instructions, or comment on letter not directly relating to the contents of the letter. Notations frequently used in business communications are ENCLOSURE NOTATION; MAILING NOTATION; PERSONAL NOTATION; COPY-DISTRIBUTION NOTATION; IDENTIFICATION LINE; REFERENCE LINE; POSTSCRIPT.

OCR addressing. See ENVELOPES.

Personal letters. See SOCIAL-BUSINESS LETTERS.

Personal notation. Notation placed on a letter and envelope when no one but the addressee is supposed to see

MEMO: FIGURE 1: Sample memo format

[LETTERHEAD]

To: Bernard Steinberg   From: Marilyn Forrestor

Subject: Memo Format   Date   November 11, 19——

Memo formats vary widely, from specially designed company memo letterheads to standard multiple-copy forms sold in office supply stores. However, most memo stationery contains the guide words To, From, and Date at the top of the page, as shown in this illustration. Some memos also include the word Subject at the top and the word Signature with a line at the bottom.

Paragraphs are commonly typed flush left. The writer's initials may be typed two to four spaces below the last paragraph if the memo does not include a signature line at the bottom of the page. Other notations such as the enclosure notation and the typists initials are positioned the same as they would be in a traditional letter format.

Memo formats permit fast and easy typing. The efficiency of this type of correspondence has encouraged many organizations to use memos for external as well as internal correspondence in numerous situations where a formal letter format is unnecessary.

MF

---

the letter. The word *Personal* or *Confidential* is typed four spaces above the ADDRESS at the top of the letter, and on the ENVELOPE two spaces above the address, slightly to the left.

Photocopy notation. See COPY-DISTRIBUTION NOTATION.

Postscript. When it is necessary to add a postscript to a letter, type it two spaces below the identification line or the last notation on the letter. Indent the left margin of the postscript the same as you indent paragraphs in the body of the letter. You may include or omit the abbreviation *P.S.* (or *PS.*). Use *P.P.S.* (or *PPS*) with a second postscript (although a second postscript should be avoided if possible). Type the dictator's initials after the postscript.

Reference line. Notation showing file reference. If a file reference is given in an incoming letter, it should be included in the reply. File reference of an outgoing letter is placed beneath the incoming reference.

When letterheads include a printed reference notation, such as *In reply please refer to*, the reference line is typed after it. Otherwise, the reference line is usually typed at the right of the letter about two to four spaces beneath the date.

January 5, 1983

Your file 3476
Our File 275a

Some companies type the reference line above the dateline:

19F027-11XL

November 16, 1983

Refunds, letters requesting. 1. *When a ticket is returned for a refund.* Enclose and describe the ticket, giving all pertinent facts (airline and flight number or train, class of travel and/or accommodation, departure and arrival times, travel points, dates, charges for the ticket). Give the date of cancellation. Request a full refund, stating the amount if known. State to whom the refund should be made and, if a check is desired, where it should be mailed. If the reservation was made by charge account, give full data on the account—name and number—and request that the amount of the refund be credited to that account.

I am enclosing unused ticket No. 7632, for Mr. A. H. Smith, on Flight 577 out of Chicago on Monday, June 20, leaving at 9:45 a.m., CST, for Los Angeles, arriving at 2:45 p.m., PST.

Mr. Smith cancelled this reservation by telephone this morning, June 6. The reservation, originally confirmed by telephone on April 28, was made on Smith and Associates' air travel card No. 66511. The full amount of this refund should be credited to this account.

Please send us confirmation by return mail.

2. *When a cancelled order has not been credited.* The letter should give the name, the company, and the account number; state the date; tell how and when it was cancelled; state the amount that has been incorrectly charged; and ask for a

corrected statement. Or you may enclose a check for the correct amount and ask that the error be rectified on the next statement.

Account 711-298-067-A

Alfred R. Ace

Winston Motors, Inc.

Your statement of September 1 to Mr. Ace includes a charge of $56 for rental of your conference suite F-101 on August 22. We originally reserved this room by telephone and received your letter of confirmation on July 28.

However, on Mr. Ace's instructions I cancelled our reservation by telephone on the morning of July 29 and confirmed this cancellation in my letter of that date.

Enclosed is Mr. Ace's check for the amount of your September 1 statement, minus the charge for this room rental. Please credit Mr. Ace's account in full.

Regret to formal invitation. See INVITATIONS.

Reprographic-copy notation. See COPY-DISTRIBUTION NOTATION.

Reminders. See FOLLOW-UP LETTERS.

Sales promotion letters. Although most sales promotion letters are prepared by specialists, secretaries in some offices assist in the preparation of such messages. Frequently, these letters are intended for reproduction as FORM LETTERS or MODEL LETTERS.

A sales message should arouse interest and prompt the recipient to take the action you desire. Describe what you are offering and tell the reader why he or she needs it. Leave the door open to further contact.

We're happy to send you the new Office Aids catalog you requested. The peel-and-stick labels you asked about are described on page 11.

These self-adhesive labels are still available in a continuous strip for fast typewriter feeding, but something completely new has been added! Now you can have the name and address of your company imprinted on the labels in a choice of bold black, brilliant blue, or bright red. If you like, we will even add your company logo to ensure quick recognition by your customers. What better way to cash in on your good name?

For a limited time, label imprinting is being offered to special customers like you for half price! That's right—for any order you place within the next 30 days, you may deduct a full 50 percent from the cost of imprinting.

Just follow the easy instructions on the enclosed order blank and send us your order within 30 days or call us toll-free at 800-616-7702.

We look forward to hearing from you!

Salutation. Expression of courtesy to the addressee of a letter. Approved forms are: (1) to a man—*Dear Mr. Blank* or *My dear Mr. Blank* (formal). (2) To a woman—*Dear Ms. (Miss or Mrs.) Blank* or *My dear Ms. (Miss or Mrs.) Blank* (formal). (3) To a company or group composed entirely of men—*Gentlemen.* (4) To a company or group composed of men and women—*Ladies and Gentlemen.* (5) To a man and a woman—*Dear Mrs. Blank and Mr. Smith.* (6) To a married couple—*Dear Mr. and Mrs. Blank.* (7) To a group composed entirely of women—*Mesdames* or *Ladies.* (8) In a letter that is not addressed to any particular person or firm, such as a general letter of recommendation—*To Whom It May Concern.*

See ADDRESSING OFFICIALS (Chart) for correct salutations to use in letters to people in official or honorary positions.

Other rules of form to observe are: (1) *Mr., Mrs., Ms.,* and *Dr.* are the only titles that are abbreviated. (2) A business title or designation of position is never used in a salutation. (3) A title in the salutation should be followed by the surname, for example, *Dear Professor Blank,* not *Dear Professor.* (4) When in doubt about whether the addressee is a man or woman, use the person's first and last names (*Dear Leslie Rogers*). When in doubt whether the addressee is a married or single woman, use the salutation *Ms.*

The salutation is typed two lines below the address, flush with the left margin, unless the letter has an ATTENTION LINE; then it is typed two spaces below that line. A colon follows the salutation. If *My dear* is used in a formal letter, *dear* does not begin with a capital.

Seasonal good wishes, letters of.
See SOCIAL-BUSINESS LETTERS.

Signature.   The signature part of a letter usually consists of the typed name of the writer, his or her business title, and the manually written signature. The writer's name is typed because manually written signatures are usually illegible; therefore, if the name is printed on the letterhead there is no need to type it. The inclusion in the signature of the writer's business title or position indicates that he or she is writing the letter in an official capacity. Thus if an officer of a company writes a letter

on firm stationery about a purely personal matter, his or her position is not included in the signature.

Sometimes the name of the company is also typed in the signature, but the trend is to omit it, except in a signature to formal documents. When the firm name is included in the signature, it should be typed two lines below the complimentary close, the writer's name four lines below the firm name, and the writer's position either on the same line or on the next line. When the firm name is not included, the writer's name and position should be typed four lines below the complimentary close. The signature is aligned with the first letter in the complimentary close.

Forms of signature for women.   1. An *unmarried woman* may precede her typed signature with *Miss* (but not *Ms.*) in parentheses or omit it.

Eleanor Davis

Eleanor Davis

Eleanor Davis

(Miss) Eleanor Davis

2. A *married woman* should indicate in her signature the title to be used in addressing her. She may precede her typed signature with *Mrs.* in parentheses, or she may type her married name in parentheses beneath the written signature. The latter form is compulsory for social usage. If she wants to be addressed as *Ms.,* she would omit any title before her name. Some women use both married and maiden names combined. Others use their maiden names professionally.

264

Cleanor Davis

(Mrs.) Eleanor Davis

Cleanor Davis

(Mrs. John R. Davis)

Cleanor Holt-Davis

Eleanor Holt-Davis

Cleanor Holt

Eleanor Holt

3. A *widow* signs her name as she did before her husband's death.

4. Assuming that a *divorcee* does not use her maiden name, she may sign her first name, with or without the initial of her maiden name, and her former husband's surname. The typed signature is the same as the written signature preceded by *Mrs.* in parentheses. Or the typed signature may combine her maiden name with her former husband's surname; or her first name with maiden name and her former husband's surname preceded by *Mrs.* or *Miss.*

RIGHT

Cleanor M. Davis

(Mrs.) Eleanor M. Davis

Cleanor M. Davis

(Mrs. Montgomery Davis)

Cleanor Montgomery Davis

(Miss) Eleanor Montgomery Davis

WRONG

Cleanor M. Davis

(Mrs. John R. Davis)

Secretary's signature. When you sign your employer's name to a letter, place your initials immediately below it.

Miriam R. Jones M.G.

Miriam R. Jones
President

When you sign a letter in your own name as secretary, do not include your employer's initials unless another person in the organization has the same name. Always precede his or her name by a title.

RIGHT

Elizabeth Mason

Secretary to Mr. Nelson

WRONG

Secretary to Mr. R.S. Nelson
Secretary to R.S. Nelson

Social-business letters. In every business and profession there are many occasions when personal letters should be written to business acquaintances. To be effective, these letters must be opportunely timed, personal in tone, cordial and friendly but not gushy, and written with a sincerity that lends conviction to the message. The SALUTATION and COMPLIMENTARY CLOSE should be appropriate for the friendly tone of the letter. The types of personal letters generally written to business acquaintances, and the pattern each follows, are discussed here.

In social-business letters, you should write naturally and sincerely. Indicate the reason for your letter; offer to reciprocate for a kindness, if appropriate; encourage further contributions, in appropriate situations; focus upon the occasion and do not detract from it with other discussion; and, in most instances, be brief.

1. *Letters of appreciation.* These letters are written in appreciation of a personal favor or service; assistance to firm, club, or association; hospitality; message of congratulation; message of sympathy; and favorable mention in a speech, article, or book. They reflect genuine sincerity and honest gratitude, not merely the writer's desire to conform with the rules of etiquette. The tone is one of friendly informality, the degree of which is determined by the extent to which the favor, service, or courtesy performed is personal, the degree of friendship existing between the writer and the recipient, and the age and temperament of the recipient.

For Assistance

Looking back on last week's convention, I feel its success was a direct result of the consistent excellence, as well as the variety, of the program.

I want to tell you how much I appreciate your tireless efforts in developing this outstanding program. Your splendid work vastly simplified my job as general convention chairperson and I owe you a real vote of thanks for your cooperation and support. You also deserve the gratitude of members of the association for contributing so much of interest and value to them.

It was good to see you, and I hope we'll have another opportunity to visit soon again.

2. *Letters of condolence or sympathy.* These letters are written upon death, personal injury or illness, and material loss or damage. Sincerity and tact are the most important qualities. Such letters should not contain words or sentiments that might distress the reader or quotations from scripture or poetry. They should not be long and involved. The length is based upon the degree of friendship between writer and reader, the situation that prompts the letter, and the tastes and temperament of the reader.

To Business Friends

Upon my return to the city this morning, I was deeply saddened to learn of the sudden death of Mrs. Williams.

You have my deepest sympathy. I only wish there were some small way in which I could lighten your burden of sorrow.

3. *Letters of congratulations.* These letters are written to a business acquaintance who receives a professional or civic honor or a promotion, makes a speech, writes an article or book, retires from business, renders an outstanding community service, or celebrates a business anniversary. They are brief, expressed naturally, and enthusiastic.

For Honor

I just read in today's paper about your election as mayor of Albany, and I want to congratulate both you and the community you represent. I'm sure you will bring to your job the same ability that has made your business such a success.

My very best to you now and in the days ahead.

4. *Letters of seasonal good wishes.* These letters are written in mid-

December. They express appreciation for the addressee's friendship, confidence, and cooperation and offer good wishes for the holiday season and the coming year. The tone and content are influenced by the relationship involved, but they all have the essential qualities of informality, friendliness, sincerity, and brevity.

Holiday Wishes

As we approach the end of 1987, I realize that the enjoyable association with you has contributed much toward making it a very pleasant year for me.

In sending you these words of thanks for your kindness on several occasions, I wish for you the happiest of holiday seasons. May the New Year bring you continued health, happiness, and success!

5. *Letters of introduction.* These letters are mailed directly to the addressee or delivered in person by the one introduced. In the latter case, the envelope should be left unsealed. The preferable practice is to send the note directly to the addressee if there is sufficient time for the letter to reach its recipient before the arrival of the person introduced. These letters are written in the spirit of asking a favor. They include the name of the person being introduced; the purpose or reason for the introduction; all relevant and appropriate details; personal or business; and a statement to the effect that any courtesy shown will be appreciated by the writer. A letter introducing the writer's friend on a basis both social and business is informal in tone; an introduction for purely business reasons is more conservative.

Introducing Associate

This letter will be handed to you by my friend and associate Horace Bowes, a well-known writer of articles on business.

Horace is preparing a book in which he hopes to outline the development of the textile industry during the last half-century. He believes that through a talk with you he can obtain both information and inspiration that will be valuable to him in his work.

Since you are the authority on your particular phase of the industry, he has asked for an introduction to you. I would appreciate any courtesies you can show him, and I know he will be most grateful to you for taking time to talk with him.

6. *Letters of invitation.* These letters are usually invitations to attend a banquet, luncheon, or entertainment or to give an address or informal talk. They are cordial and gracious, entirely free of stilted formality. They should be complete in detail, telling *when* and *where*, and, if the occasion is essentially business, *why*.

To Give Informal Talk

The subject of "How to Write Good Business Letters" is interesting to every business and professional person. For a long time I have intended, when it came my turn to arrange a program for the Business Club, to invite a real authority in the field to talk to the club on that subject.

My turn came today, when I was asked to arrange the program for Tuesday noon, November 17. I know of no other person as well qualified as you to speak on the technique of writing business letters, and I am hoping very much that you will find it possible to accept my invitation.

Our luncheon meetings are held in the Banquet Room of Hotel Cleveland. They begin at 12:15 p.m. and are usually over about 1:30 p.m. The talks range from thirty to forty minutes.

If you can be our guest on the 17th, I know you will receive a most enthusiastic welcome. I'd appreciate it if you could give me your answer next week.

7. *Letters of acceptance.* These letters accept invitations to banquets, luncheons, entertainments, or of hospitality for an overnight visit; speaking invitations; membership in professional or civic organization; and invitations to serve on civic or professional committees or boards. They convey appreciation and enthusiasm. A brief note is sufficient.

To Serve on Committee

I was both pleased and complimented to receive your letter yesterday.

It will be a pleasure to serve on the Planning Committee for the "Better Burlington" campaign, and I am looking forward to a pleasant association with you and Mr. Norton in his work.

8. *Letters of declination.* These letters decline invitations to banquets, luncheons, or entertainments; for an overnight visit; for speaking invitations (or cancel speaking engagements previously accepted); for membership in professional or civic organization; to serve on civic or professional committee or board; to support charitable or other organization; and requests for information or material.

Offer of Hospitality

Your gracious invitation for me to spend next weekend in your home is keenly appreciated. I only wish my travel program were such that I could accept.

Immediately after my talk in your city, I have to catch a night train to St. Louis and make connections for Topeka, Kansas, where I'm scheduled for a talk Monday afternoon.

I'm disappointed that my travel schedule is going to prevent me from spending a pleasant weekend with you. However, I want to thank you most sincerely for the invitation.

9. *Letters of apology.* When there is an adequate and convincing explanation of a situation that requires an apology, a few words can be devoted to the explanation. If no justification exists, a frank admission of that fact usually has a disarming effect upon the reader. Regardless of the circumstances, any situation that requires a letter of apology requires a tone of warmth and friendliness.

Failure To Attend Meeting

I hope you will accept a sincere apology for my absence from the Credit Association meeting yesterday afternoon.

When I told you earlier in the week that I planned to be there, I fully intended to be. But a meeting of our own credit department staff yesterday afternoon lasted much longer than I expected, and it was impossible for me to get away.

When I see Jim Davis at lunch tomorrow, I will ask him to bring me up to date on yesterday's developments.

10. *Letters expressing thanks.* A thank you letter for some special favor or kindness is usually brief. Any thank you message must sound sincere and reflect genuine gratitude. If the letter must refuse some offer, use a positive tone and, if practical, suggest other alternatives to the writer.

For Special Favor

Many thanks for all of your help while I was out of the country last month. Without your capable assistance at the office, I could never have managed to be away that long.

I know the extra work must have put an extra strain on your own work load, and I truly appreciate the special effort you put forth on my behalf. I just hope some day I can be of as much help to you.

Sincerest thanks,

Stationery. See Chapter 5/STATIONERY.

Subject line. Designation of subject matter of a letter. Subject lines are a convenience to both the writer and the reader. They make it unnecessary for the writer to devote the first paragraph of a letter to a routine explanation of the subject of the letter they facilitate the distribution of mail to various departments; they also expedite subject filing.

Center the subject line two spaces beneath the salutation. If the full-block or simplified style of letter (see LAYOUT) is used, type the subject line flush with the left-hand margin. Never place the subject line before the salutation. It is part of the body of the letter, not of the heading.

Sometimes the subject line is preceded by *Re* or *Subject*. The modern practice is to omit these words, except in letters about legal matters. In these letters *In re* is customarily used. No punctuation follows *In re;* a colon follows *Subject*. The important words in a subject line are capitalized. The last line may be underlined, but the modern trend is to omit the underlining.

Thank you letters. See SOCIAL-BUSINESS LETTERS.

Transmittal letter. A letter transmitting a formal enclosure or attachment. A letter of transmittal is written in the same style and has the same LAYOUT as any kind of letter. It describes the enclosure or attachment and serves as a record. It may also explain or comment on various aspects of the transmitted document.

Visiting cards. Visiting cards should be of medium to heavy white card stock. The appropriate size is three by one and one-half inches. The engraving should be in black; Roman lettering is in good taste. When ordering for an executive, be sure to order some matching envelopes so they may be sent with flowers or gifts.

Initials should be avoided as much as possible, and, in any case, one first name must be written in full. It is better to write out the entire name. *Mr., Mrs.,* and *Dr.* are the only abbreviations that should be used before the name. If the name is very long, *senior* and *junior* may be abbreviated and capitalized, but it is preferable to write the words out with a small letter. It is a matter of choice whether an address is engraved on the personal visiting card. If used, the house address appears in the lower right-hand corner. Stationery stores and printing firms have samples of different card stocks and styles of type.

CHAPTER 8

WRITING, EDITING, AND PUBLISHING

Advertising. The means by which sales messages are brought to the attention of the general public. The principal media available for advertising include newspapers, magazines, radio and television, and direct mail. Other media are outdoor advertising, car cards, premiums, specialties, and trade and business papers.

Advertisers are concerned with the distribution or circulation of their messages—how many people they reach and the types of audiences reached. Advertising messages may be sent directly to the various media or through an advertising agency, which in turn prepares and places the advertisement with the appropriate media. Current rate guides can be secured directly from the media. Circulation and rate data can also be found in directories such as *Ayer's*

Directory of Newspapers and Periodicals (N. W. Ayer & Son, Philadelphia) and various rate guides published by Standard Rate and Data Service (Skokie, Illinois). You can find the major directories and guides in the reference room of a library.

Agate line. Measurement of space by which most newspaper and some magazine advertising is sold. There are always fourteen agate lines to a column-inch regardless of the width of the column.

Appendix. (pl. *appendixes*). Material added at the end of a book, article, or report that is not essential but adds information or interest. Appendixes may be lettered or numbered in sequence (A, B, C, and so on) and also may have subject titles.

Associated Press (AP). One of two wire services in the United States that provides most of the newspapers' international and nonlocal news. AP is an association of member newspapers, each of which supplies news of its own locality. News items are automatically transmitted from one member newspaper to the others. News releases sent to any AP newspaper are automatically considered a potential AP story for all of them. See also UNITED PRESS INTERNATIONAL (UPI).

Backbone (of book). The outside back edge of the cover on which the title, author's name, and publisher's imprint appear. Frequently called the "spine" of the book.

Back matter. The portion of a book where concluding materials are gathered, such as (1) appendixes, (2) notes, (3) glossary, (4) bibliography, and (5) indexes. Back-matter pages are numbered in Arabic numerals, continuing in sequence after the last chapter.

Ben Day process. Frequently written as *benday*. A process invented by Benjamin Day that permits the reproduction of a wide variety of shadings or tintings. The shading tints, which give the realism of a photograph, consist of a pattern of tiny dots or lines that create a gray effect.

Bibliography. A descriptive list of publications that gives the reader a source of additional information on a given subject; the bibliography also may be limited to the sources used by the author in the preparation of published material. A bibliography that includes selected sources but not all of the sources used by the author in footnotes is called *Selected Bibliography*. Bibliographical references are arranged alphabetically according to author. The order of items in a book reference is as follows: (1) name of the author, with last name first (when there are two or more authors, it is permissible to reverse only the first author's name); (2) title of the book (and edition when given); (3) the volume, chapter, or page references if given; (4) city where the publisher is located; (5) name of publisher; (6) year of publication. A bibliographical reference to a periodical may contain the name of the author, article, periodical in which it is published, volume and issue number, year, and inclusive pages. Figure 1 illustrates a common style to follow in arranging and typing the list of publications. Items that are underlined on the typewriter appear in italics in a published bibliography.

Blueprinting. An economical method of duplicating material in the same size. Prepared on sensitized paper, the printed material appears blue after processing. The blueprint process is one of the oldest means of preparing proofs for customers in the printing industry.

Secretaries who check blueprints (or any other proof) for errors should verify that (1) no pages are missing or out of order, (2) facing pages are the same length, (3) illustrations appear

BIBLIOGRAPHY: FIGURE 1: Sample bibliography references

Anonymous, <u>American Standard Abbreviations for Use on Drawings</u> (ASA Z32.13-1046). New York: American Standards Association, 1946.

Crane, E. J., "Words and Sentences in Science and Industry," <u>Science</u> 86, no. 50 (1987): 549–53.

Douglas, P. F., <u>Communication Through Reports</u>. Englewood Cliffs, N.J.: Prentice-Hall, 1957.

Gould, J. R., "What Is Technical Writing?" <u>Writer</u> 70 (July 1977): 16–18.

Hawkins, R. R., "Technical Books," <u>Library Journal</u> 82 (May 1, 1986): 1157–64.

Jordan, Richard C., and Marion J. Edwards, <u>Aids to Technical Writing</u>, Bulletin no. 21, vol. 47, no. 24. Minneapolis: University of Minnesota Experiment Station, 1985.

Wall, Florence E., "The Future of Desktop Publishing," Master's thesis, University of Alabama, 1988.

---

in the proper position on the proper page, (4) errors appearing in the page proofs have been corrected on the blueprint, and (5) any other problems have been resolved.

Boldface (bf). A heavy-face type, used principally for side and center headings, emphasis, short quotations, display lines and display headings. **This is boldface type.** A wavy line drawn under the word or words in a manuscript instructs the typesetter to set the words in boldface type.

Cold type. A term used to distinguish composition—primarily typewriter and photographic methods of composition—that does not use "hot" metal. Typewriter and computer composition are examples of cold type. Cold type can be photographed directly and an offset printing plate prepared from the negatives. Cold type is sometimes selected when speed and economy are important considerations, although quality may be inferior depending on the equipment used. See HOT TYPE; TYPE FACE; Chapter 5/TYPESETTING EQUIPMENT.

Contents. See TABLE OF CONTENTS.

Copy. Manuscript to be sent to the typesetter or printer and set in type. The MANUSCRIPT becomes "copy" after the copy editor has prepared the manuscript by marking it for type and attending to other numerous details necessary for its production. See MANUSCRIPT.

Copy editing. Rewriting, revising, styling, and polishing copy. Generally, preparing material for typesetting by verifying facts, accuracy of grammar, consistency of style, corrections of spelling and punctuation, and by marking type specifications. (See TYPEMARKING.) Copy editors should use standard PROOFREADERS' MARKS and mark directly on the manuscript. Secretaries often find it helpful to follow a checklist in checking an edited manuscript for errors and omissions. See also MANUSCRIPT; PROOFREADING; PROOFREADERS' MARKS.

Copyfitting. See WORD COUNT.

Copy preparation. See MANUSCRIPT; Chapter 1/TYPING, *Typing manuscript.*

Copyright. Published and unpublished works that are fixed in a copy or phonorecord have been subject to a single system of statutory protection since January 1, 1978. Registration of a work in the Library of Congress Copyright Office is not necessary to have a valid copyright but it is necessary for bringing a court action in regard to infringement.

The maximum total term of copyright protection for works already protected by federal statute before 1978 is seventy-five years, including a first term of twenty-eight years from the date of the original copyright plus a renewal term of forty-seven years. Renewals must be applied for within one year before the first twenty-eight-year term expires. Copyrights already renewed that were in their second term between December 31, 1976, and December 31, 1977, have been automatically extended to last the full seventy-five years. (Write to the Copyright Office for free copies of Circular R15 and renewal Form RE.) Under the new law there is a single copyright term with no renewal requirements. Works existing on January 1, 1978, but not copyrighted and not in the public domain are subject to automatic federal copyright protection.

The term of protection under the new law is a life-plus-fifty-years system. Thus protection applies for the life of the author(s) plus fifty years after the death of the last surviving author. Protection for works made for hire and anonymous or pseudonymous works applies for seventy-five years from publication or one hundred years from creation, whichever is shorter. Copyright terms run through the end (December 31) of the calendar year in which they would otherwise expire. The renewal period for works copyrighted between 1950 and 1977 runs from December 31 of the twenty-seventh year of the copyright until December 31 of the following year. Works in the public domain are not protected under the new law, and copyright that has been lost on a work cannot be restored.

Fair use. Four criteria are used to determine whether copying material from a copyrighted source without permission or payment is fair: (1) the purpose and character of the use, including whether such use is of a commercial nature or is for nonprofit educational purposes; (2) the nature of the copyrighted work; (3) the amount and substantiality of the portion used in relation to the copyrighted work as a whole; and (4) the effect of the use upon the potential market for, or value of, the copyrighted work. Section 107 of the 1976 law states that "the fair use of a copyrighted work, including such use by reproduction in copies or phonorecords or by any other means specified by that section, for purposes such as criticism, comment, news reporting, teaching (including multiple copies for classroom use), scholarship, or research, is not an infringement of copyright." Although the law does not include guidelines for classroom copying, systematic reproduction and distribution of single or multiple copies of books and periodicals by libraries (instead of their purchase) is forbidden, and spontaneous copying for classroom use must not exceed the number of students in a course. Also, each copy must bear a copyright notice, and the amount copied must be brief.

Registration. A proper notice in a printed work must include (1) the letter *c* in a circle (and may also include the word *copyright* or the abbreviation *copr.*), (2) the year of first publication of the work, and (3) the name of the copyright owner (*Copyright © 1988 by Prentice-Hall, Inc.*). A U.S. citizen whose work includes a proper copyright notice also receives protection in all other countries that are members of the Universal Copyright Convention. For free instructions and registration forms, write to the Copyright Office, Library of Congress, Washington, D.C. 20559. Specify the kind of work—book, magazine, artwork, and so on—that you want to register.

Cropping. Also called *scaling*. Cropping is a process of indicating the portion of a piece of art or a photograph that is to be reproduced. Using a grease pencil if the surface is glossy, an editor or artist usually places small crop marks in the margins or borders of the photograph or illustration, or on an acetate overlay, to show the area to be retained. (If you use an overlay, do not press down with a pen or pencil on top of the photograph surface or you will leave creases that may show up in reproduction.)

Dimensions of width and depth must be proportional. For instance, if a photograph must be reduced to a square size of three by three inches, the original glossy must be cropped proportionally, marking off a square area of seven by seven or six by six (but not seven by four or eight by six) inches and so on. Cropping also requires an understanding of balance and composition in deciding what detail to keep and what to crop out.

Cut. An engraving, line cut, or halftone, used by printers to reproduce artwork. For example, the artwork might be sent to an engraver to have a woodcut made. The cut, in turn, would then be sent to the printer and would become part of a PLATE used in letterpress (relief) printing. See LINE CUTS AND HALFTONES.

Dummy. A page-by-page layout of copy and illustrations for a booklet, magazine, or book. Usually blank sheets are cut and assembled to look like the proposed book or booklet. Layouts are generally drawn, and copy is stripped into the dummy to give the general appearance of the finished product. A *cut dummy* consists of plain sheets of paper on which engraver's proofs of cuts have been pasted, one cut to a page. Beneath each proof the corresponding label and credit line are typed. A *page dummy* is made by cutting GALLEY PROOFS to size and pasting them on the blank sheets, allowing spaces at the appropriate places for illustrations, tables, and the like.

How to make a page dummy. Get a pad of layout paper from an art or stationery supply store large enough to mark off two facing pages. For an eight-and-one-half-by-eleven-inch publication you will be marking off an eleven-by-seventeen-inch area. Next mark off the margins, column areas, and so on. Then cut and paste onto the guide sheets a duplicate set of galleys, at the same time placing the cuts and captions in the proper position on each page. Try to allow proper spacing before and following cuts. It is a good plan to experiment with the placing of cuts and type on a page before actually pasting them down. It is always a good idea to consult your printer if you have any questions about this procedure or about what the printer requires from you to produce your material accurately and without unnecessary expense.

A page dummy should contain no type corrections, additions, or deletions. All such changes, even those necessary to lengthen or shorten pages to make them come out right,

should be made on the master set of galleys.

Long or short pages must be remedied. In the case of a long page, one can generally find a line at the end of a paragraph on that page that is very short. By shortening the sentence of which that line is a part, one is able to save a line. If the page is short, one might look for a full line at the end of a paragraph, and by adding a word or two to the sentence, one could make an additional line. If the page is long or short by several lines and one is unable to remedy the situation, ask the author to delete or add a few lines. If both facing pages (that is, an even and an odd page) are one line long or short, they are allowed to stay that way.

There should be at least three lines of type between a center heading and the bottom of a page and two lines between a side heading and the bottom of a page. A page must not begin with a WIDOW line.

See also MECHANICAL.

Duplicating processes. Processes by which duplicate copies of office communications and records are made. Processes whereby one to ten copies can be made economically are usually called *photocopying*. Those processes whereby economies usually begin with a greater number of copies, often hundreds or even thousands, are called *duplicating*. In general, duplicating first requires making a master, such as a stencil.

Dry copiers are widely used because of their convenience in requiring no time-consuming preparation, in contrast with other methods. Some copiers do not require special paper; others require a special sensitized paper.

Fluid duplicators, mimeograph machines, and offset presses make duplicates from stencils or masters that can be cut by hand or in a typewriter. Fluid masters are often intended for ten to five hundred copies; mimeograph stencils, one hundred to three thousand copies; and offset duplicators, eleven to ten thousand copies.

Ozaliding makes same-sized prints by passing light through the item to be copied onto sensitized paper.

Multilithing is done on a small offset printing press and is useful for reproducing material in quantity.

Photostating is a photographic process that uses a sensitized paper. It employs the same principles as photography. It can reduce or enlarge, and it produces a negative from which innumerable positive prints can be made.

Quality varies by the process and machine. Offset copies, for instance, are considered superior to either the fluid or the mimeograph process. Some photocopiers produce low-quality facsimile material, but others are capable of making "art" quality copies. See also Chapter 1/LETTERPRESS; OFFSET; MICROFILMING; Chapter 5/BUSINESS MACHINES.

Editing. See COPY EDITING; MANUSCRIPT.

Ellipsis points. See QUOTED MATERIAL.

Extract. A printer's term for QUOTED MATERIAL or an excerpt that is usually indented and set in a smaller size of type or different type face from the rest of the text. Quotation marks are omitted. Lists, examples, problems, and quotations of over eight lines may be set as extracts. See QUOTED MATERIAL, Figure 1.

Footnotes. A note referring to a statement in the main text of written material. The footnote may be the source of a statement in the text, an explanation of a statement in the text, or an acknowledgment of credit.

The order of items in a footnote is usually the same as in a BIBLIOGRAPHY, with two exceptions: (1) The name of the author is not reversed, the first name being given first. (2) Book volume, or chapter or page references, if given, come at the end of the reference.

The following examples illustrate appropriate styles of citation. The items in italics should be underlined in a manuscript.

Citation of book: Pierce C. Kelly and Norris B. Brisco, *Retailing*, 3d ed. (Englewood Cliffs, N.J.: Prentice-Hall, 1957), pp. 311–15.

Citation of an article: Earl J. Hamilton, "Prices and Wages at Paris under John Law's System," *Quarterly Journal of Economics* 1, no. 51 (November 1948): 42.

Citation of unpublished material: John King, Jr., "The Middle East Crisis" (Ph.D. diss., New York University, 1975), p. 121.

Citation of chapter in book: David McKenzie, "Monetary Skill," in *High Finance*, ed. J. William Crawley (Chicago: University of Chicago Press, 1981), pp. 64–81.

Acknowledgment: Acknowledgment is made to Charles B. Hicks and Irene Place, *Office Management* (Boston: Allyn and Bacon, 1956), p. 98.

Typing footnotes. Each footnote must have a corresponding reference in the text. The footnote reference figure (called a SUPERIOR FIGURE) follows the word or statement in the text to which the footnote applies. Avoid note numbers in the middle of a sentence. Place them after a period, semicolon, or colon. Never use multiple numbers (*not* 11, 12, 13) together at the same place. In a double-spaced paragraph (if the typed material is to be printed, it must be double-spaced) the superior figure is written thus:

Only one solution is offered:[1]

In a single-spaced paragraph, the superior figure is written thus:

One solution is offered /2/:

On the printed page, a footnote (except a footnote to a table) may appear at the bottom of the page on which the superior figure appears, or all footnotes in a chapter may be collected in a "Notes" section at the end of the chapter, or all notes in all chapters may be collected in a "Notes" section at the end of the publication (before the bibliography). Most footnotes, regardless of where they appear on a page or in a chapter, are typed and later typeset in paragraph style:

1. Donald Parker, *Computer Technology for the Modern Business Office* (New York: Office Publishers, 1982).

In drafts, the footnotes may be typed (a) in a separate line immediately following the text where the reference appears, separating the footnote from the preceding and following text by lines typed across the page; (b) at the bottom of the page on which they occur, separating the footnote from the preceding text by a line typed across the page; (c) on a separate sheet immediately following the page on which the superior figures appear, or (d) on a separate sheet(s) at the end of the chapter or at the end of the manuscript. On the final draft, typesetters and printers prefer to have footnotes typed on separate pages at the end of the chapter or at the end of the manuscript (before the bibliography). The printer is then able to have the footnotes set in type while the text is being set.

Front matter. Also called preliminaries.

This section of a book often includes:

1. Half-title page (book title only)
2. Title page (title plus author and publisher)
3. Copyright notice
4. Dedication
5. Table of contents
6. List of illustrations (figures and tables)
7. Foreword
8. Preface
9. Acknowledgments (if not part of preface)
10. Introduction (if not part of main text)

Front-matter pages, beginning with the table of contents, should have lowercase Roman numerals (i, ii, etc.) typed on them. If the book contains a half-title page, title page, copyright page, and dedication page preceding the table of contents, Roman numeral v would be typed on the contents page.

Full measure. Printer's term for setting a line of type the full width of the column or page, flush with both margins. This instruction on the Copy is not necessary unless the printer might assume that some kind of indentation or centering was intended.

Galley proof. In the Hot type process, a galley is a shallow metal tray into which each line of type is deposited as it comes from the typesetting machine. When a galley is filled (it may hold enough lines to make about two pages in an average book), it is removed and another put in its place until the entire book is set. Proof of each hot type galley is made on a small proof press. This proof contains no illustrations, is not broken up into pages, and contains no Running head. Each footnote often appears directly beneath the reference to it in the text or at the bottom of the galley proof, and chapter titles are not necessarily set in the type in which they will finally appear. The paper on which the galley proofs are made is no indication of the paper that will actually be used in the book. A galley proof is also called a *galley.* Compositors and printers commonly use the term *galley* to refer to any proof of typeset material that has not yet been divided into individual pages.

Cold-composition galley proofs appear similar to those from hot type, but they are made by photocopying the original typeset sheet produced in the cold-composition process. See Cold type. Printers and typesetters often supply three sets to customers, one on which to mark corrections (the master set) and return, another to cut apart and use in making a pasteup Dummy, and the third for the customer's files. Secretaries who proofread galleys should mark corrections in the margins as shown in Proofreaders' marks, Figure 2. See also Proofreading.

Gravure. A printing process in which the type or design is cut into the printing plate below the general level. Short runs of up to one hundred thousand are best handled by a sheet-fed gravure press. Runs over one hundred thousand are suitable for a web-fed rotogravure press. Rotogravure is also referred to as an *intaglio* process. Reproduction of type tends to be of lower quality than reproduction of photographs.

Halftone. See Line cuts and halftones.

Hot type. A term used to distinguish composition by metal, such as Linotype or Monotype. Hot type machines have keyboards by which operators drop letters or lines of metal type characters into trays to make up a page. The quality of hot type may be superior to some cold type, depending on the equipment. See also COLD TYPE; Chapter 5/ TYPESETTING EQUIPMENT.

Index and indexing. A detailed list of the contents of a book, report, or any written material, arranged alphabetically and indicating the page numbers where the item can be found. There are four steps in making an index:

1. *Selecting key words and phrases.* Read through the page proofs and typeset material and, using a colored pencil, underline key terms on each page. References to some terms appear over and over on succeeding pages. Continue underlining them no matter how many times they appear on new pages, since each new occurrence will represent a page number on the completed index entry, for example:

Statistics
      capitalization of 93
      sources of 166, 184–85
      typing 175, 177, 180–86
      in word division 76

To help you visualize what type of words and phrases to underline, study the index in a published book.

2. *Entering the items on cards.* The most convenient cards to use are three by five inches. *Use a separate card for each item.* This is a fundamental rule in indexing. See Figure 1 for one method of entering the item on the cards. In the example, the word *Securities* is repeated on all six cards

to indicate that each of the items written on the six cards belongs under the main heading, or key word *Securities*. The dots preceding the subitems indicate the degree of subordination. *Securities* is the main heading. One dot indicates that an item is to be placed immediately under *Securities*. Two dots indicate that an item belongs in a subgroup. For example, the two-dot item *by bank* belongs under the one-dot item *delivery of,* which in turn belongs under *Securities*. Repeating the main heading for each subitem, and repeating both the main heading and subheading for each sub-subitem, keeps errors to a

INDEX AND INDEXING: FIGURE 1: Index cards before they have been edited or alphabetized

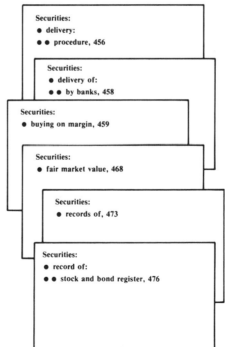

Securities:
  ● delivery:
  ● ● procedure, 456

Securities:
  ● delivery of:
  ● ● by banks, 458

Securities:
  ● buying on margin, 459

Securities:
  ● fair market value, 468

Securities:
  ● records of, 473

Securities:
  ● record of:
  ● ● stock and bond register, 476

minimum and simplifies the second step in indexing.

3. *Arranging the cards in alphabetical order.* First sort the cards into twenty-six piles—all the A's in one pile, all the B's in another, and so on—according to the first letter of the main entry. Then arrange each pile in alphabetical order according to the main heading. Finally, alphabetize the subitems under each main entry and the sub-subitems under each subentry.

4. *Editing the cards.* When the cards have been arranged in alphabetical order, go through them and cross out the headings that were repeated only as guidelines, as shown in Figure 2. Then edit the remaining items, paying special attention to the following points:

(a) Make certain the correct number of dots appears for each item—one dot for subitems, two dots for sub-subitems.

(b) Capitalize the first word of each main entry; all remaining words should be LOWERCASE unless they require capitalization for other reasons.

(c) Check to see that no entry consists of an adjective standing alone. For example, the entries *Stockbroker* and *Stock certificate* cannot be combined as:

> Stock
>   broker
>   certficate

In this case, *Stock* must be repeated in both items.

INDEX AND INDEXING: FIGURE 2: Index cards after they have been edited and alphabetized

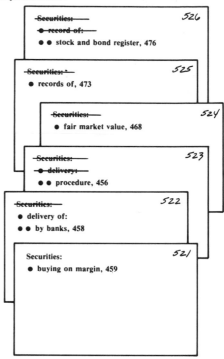

Inferior figure. See SUPERIOR FIGURE.

Information sources. Secretaries are often called upon to collect information for reports and other material issued from their office or organization. Sources vary, depending on the type of information needed, from in-house personnel and company libraries to outside organizations and libraries, consultants, and clubs and associations. Local sources are listed in the Yellow Pages. Other sources are often listed in directories, guides, and out-of-town telephone books. The following books, publications, services, and so on, listed alphabetically, are among the well-known sources that a secretary may need to consult. See also RESEARCH.

Abstracting service. A service that prepares condensed versions of original reports, articles, and other material. Often such organizations offer their abstracts on a subscription basis. Some periodicals also publish abstracts of selected subject matter, and computer-search organizations may provide abstracts as well as bibliographies of selected topics. See RESEARCH.

Almanacs. Books containing descriptive and statistical data on a wide range of subjects from population data to sporting events, for example, *The World Almanac and Book of Facts* (New York: Doubleday), published annually, and the *Information Please Almanac* (New York: Simon and Schuster), published annually.

Annual reports. See Chapter 10/ ANNUAL REPORT.

Appendix. See APPENDIX.

Atlas. Books containing a collection of detailed maps and related information on subjects such as climate, mineral resources, and manufacturing. Examples are the *Rand McNally Sales & Marketing Atlas* (Chicago: Rand McNally), published annually; the *National Geographic Atlas of the World* (Washington, D.C.: National Geographic Society); and the *Rand McNally Road Atlas* (Chicago: Rand McNally), published annually. Other useful atlases are the *Ambassador World Atlas* and the *International World Atlas* (Maplewood, N.J.: Ham-

mond); *Goode's World Atlas* (Chicago: Rand McNally); and *Encyclopaedia Britannica World Atlas* (Chicago: Encyclopaedia Britannica). In addition, motor clubs, such as the American Automobile Association, often provide an atlas as part of their membership benefits.

Bibliography. See BIBLIOGRAPHY.

Businesses, list of. See *Directories*.

Card catalog. Libraries list all books by author, title, and subject on index cards filed in alphabetical drawers called the "card catalog." The cards are prepared by the Library of Congress and distributed to libraries. Other information on the cards includes coauthors, publication date and place, Dewey decimal classification number, and Library of Congress call number.

Clipping Service. A service that will clip articles from journals, newspapers, and other sources on subjects you specify. Most services mail these clippings to subscribers frequently, for example, on a weekly basis.

Computer research. See RESEARCH.

Dictionaries. Every secretary should have an up-to-date dictionary of definitions on his or her desk. An example of a good general desk dictionary is the *Webster's Ninth New Collegiate Dictionary* (Springfield, Mass.: Merriam-Webster). However, offices frequently want a larger dictionary as well, for example, the *American Heritage Dictionary of the English Language* (Boston: Houghton Mifflin) or *Webster's Third New International Dictionary* (unabridged) (Springfield, Mass.: Merriam-Webster).

Other dictionaries are specialized, such as *The Dictionary of Mathematics* (New York: Facts on File), *The Bantam Medical Dictionary* (New York: Bantam), and *Blacks Law Dictionary* (St. Paul: West). Books that simply list thousands of words, spelled, divided, and accented, without definitions, are known as spelling dictionaries or word books. Such guides frequently include spelling rules and related style and grammatical information. One example is *The Word Book II* (Boston: Houghton Mifflin).

Directories. Numerous directories of names and addresses have been published for different fields of business and for the professions. For example, there are directories of manufacturers, banks, hotels, exporters and importers, newspapers, warehouses, shipping firms, lawyers, accountants, doctors, clergymen, and many others. Usually, the directories give descriptive and factual information about the company or person in addition to the name and address.

Libraries have numerous directories of *individuals in business* in the reference room. Some of the directories in various fields are the *National Directory of Addresses & Telephone Numbers* (Tinton Falls, N.J.: Concord Reference Books); *Poor's Register of Corporations, Directors and Executives* (New York: Standard and Poor's Corporation); *World Who's Who in Commerce and Industry, Who's Who in Labor, Who's Who in Finance and Industry* (throughout the world), *Who's Who in Banking,* and numerous other *Who's Who* directories (Chicago: Marquis).

The best-known directories for locating names and addresses of *manufacturers* are *Thomas' Register of American Manufacturers* (New York: Thomas Publishing Co.), published annually; *MacRae's Bluebook* (Chicago: MacRae's Bluebook Co.), published annually; and *Kelly's Manufacturers & Merchants Directory* (Surrey, Eng.: Kelly's Directories), published annually, 2 vols.

The best-known *law directory* is the *Martindale-Hubbell Law Directory* (Summit, N.J.: Martindale-Hubbell), published annually, in seven volumes;

Among the directories that list corporations are the *Middle Market Directory* (New York: Dun & Bradstreet), published annually, updated monthly, for corporations with a net worth of five hundred thousand dollars to one million dollars; the *Million Dollar Directory* (New York: Dun & Bradstreet), published annually, updated monthly, for corporations with a net worth exceeding one million dollars; and *Jane's Major Companies of Europe* (New York: Franklin Watts), published annually.

Note: Not all "directories" include that word in their titles. Gale's *Encyclopedia of Associations,* for example, has content similar to that of other directories. Biographical dictionaries of the *Who's Who* type give data about living individuals such as date of birth, marital status and children, education, positions held, publications authored, club affiliations, and directorships. They have been published in numerous fields, for foreign countries and for various regions of the United States. Their titles may be located through *Books in Print* (See *Indexes*). Examples are *Who's Who*

(New York: Macmillan), published annually; *Who's Who in America* (Chicago: Marquis), published biennially, with monthly supplements; *Who's Who in American Art* (New York: Bowker); *Leaders in Education* (New York: Bowker), published irregularly; *Who's Who in Finance and Industry* (Chicago: Marquis), published annually. For biographical material of historical figures, see *Webster's Biographical Dictionary* (Springfield, Mass.: Merriam-Webster), published annually, for details about a person's life, education, profession, and artistic accomplishments.

A *social register* is a directory of socially prominent persons. One is published for each city in the United States. Registers give the names and addresses of the persons, members of their families, club affiliations, colleges attended, and dates of graduation.

Encyclopedias. Timesaving sources of a wide variety of descriptive and factual information. Examples of general (i.e., a wide range of topics) encyclopedias are *Encyclopaedia Britannica* (Chicago: Encyclopaedia Britannica) and *Encyclopedia Americana* (New York: Americana Corporation). There are also specialized encyclopedias in numerous fields. They can be located by consulting the *Subject Guide to Books in Print.* (See *Indexes.*) Library reference rooms also have specialized encyclopedias such as *Van Nostrand's Scientific Encyclopedia, McGraw-Hill Encyclopedia of Science and Technology, International Encyclopedia of the Social Sciences,* and *Encyclopedia of Associations* (Detroit: Gale).

Financial information. Secretaries may have occasion to look for the following three types of information about securities owned by their employers:

1. *Current information,* such as quotations of security prices, dividend action, securities called for redemption, new issues, announcements on stock rights, financial and business news affecting the securities market, trends of security prices, stock and bond yields.

2. *Compiled information* about companies and their securities, such as the history of the company; its business and products; the address of the general office; the name and address of the transfer agent, registrar, and dividend-paying agent; statistical records of dividends, price range, income statements, and balance sheets; complete descriptions of each class of stock outstanding and of bond issues.

3. *Tax information,* such as taxation of capital gains and losses, taxation of stock dividends, stock rights, exchanges of stock, dividends received in stock of another company. See TAX INFORMATION.

In addition to newspapers and financial periodicals, there are *securities services* that are sources of information for each of the above-mentioned groups.

Three leading security services are Bernhard, Moody, and Standard and Poor's. They attempt to give as complete a picture on all phases of investment as possible. The heart of each service is the data assembled on individual companies. These publications are kept current through looseleaf services with periodic cumulations. Some of the publications of these companies are listed below:

1. Arnold Bernhard and Co., 5 East 44th Street, New York, NY 10017: (a) *Value Line Investment Survey*, looseleaf service.

2. Moody's Investors Service, 65 Broadway, New York, NY 10006: (a) *Moody's Dividend Record*, semiweekly, cumulative record; (b) *Moody's Bond Record*, pocket guide; (c) *Moody's Manual of Investments, American and Foreign*, annual volumes; (d) *Moody's Industrial Manual*, annual with weekly supplements. Examples of other volumes in this series are the *Bank and Finance Manual, Transportation Manual*, and *Public Utilities Manual*; (e) *Moody's Handbook of Common Stocks*, quarterly.

3. Standard and Poor's Corporation, 25 Broadway, New York, NY 10014: (a) *Standard Corporation Records*, six looseleaf volumes, issued daily; (b) *Bond Guide*, monthly; (c) *Industry Surveys*, quarterly; (d) Standard and Poor's periodials also include its *Daily Stock Price Record, Dividend Record, Earnings Forecaster, Outlook, Statistical Service*, and *Stock Guide*.

Other financial information can be found in publications such as the *Kiplinger Washington Letter* and Fitch's *Rating Register, Commerical Reports, Municipal Reports*, and *Institutional Reports*.

Government publications. The U.S. government publishes a massive amount of material, covering an almost unlimited range of subjects in the form of books, periodicals, releases, and statistical statements. All material published by the federal government on a specific topic can be located through the following indexes, regardless of the department issuing the publication:

1. *The Monthly Catalog of United States Government Publications* (Washington, D.C.: U.S. Government Printing Office), published monthly, annual cumulations, and author, title, and subject indexes.

2. *U.S. Government Books*, published quarterly.

3. Other government material available through the U.S. Government Printing Office includes the *Congressional Directory, Federal Register, Domestic Mail Manual, International Mail Manual, U.S. Government Printing Office Publications Reference File*, and *United States Government Manual*. The various departments of the government have indexes to their own publications. International data can be found in the *U.N. Monthly Chronicle*.

Indexes. References are usually given under subjects, titles of articles and publications, and authors. They are found in any large library, and small libraries will have some of them. Examples are *The Reader's Guide to Periodical Literature* (New York: Wilson), published monthly, with quarterly and annual cumulations; *Applied Science and Technology Index* (New York: Wilson), published monthly, with annual cumulations; *Business Periodicals Index* (New York: Wilson), published monthly, with quarterly and annual cumulations; *Public Affairs Information Service: Cumulative Author Index* (New York: Public Affairs Information Service), forty-four issues a year, with annual cumulations; *New York Times Index* (New York: New York Times Company), published twice a month, with annual cumulations; *Books in Print* (New York: Bowker), published annually; *Subject Guide to Books in Print* (New York: Bowker), annual subject index; *Business Books in Print* (New York: Bowker), published annually; *Wall Street Journal Index* (New York: Dow, Jones and Company), monthly index with annual cumulations; *Monthly Catalog of U.S. Government Publications* (Washington, D.C.: U.S. Government Printing Office), mostly pamphlets and leaflets; *Government Periodicals and Subscription Services: Price List 36* (Washington, D.C.: U.S. Government Printing Office.

Letter books. Books devoted to the composition of written communication, primarily letters and memos, with heavy emphasis on models. Examples are *The Prentice-Hall Complete Secretarial Letter Book* and the *Handbook of Business Letters* (both Englewood Cliffs, N.J.: Prentice-Hall). Other books, such as the *Complete Secretary's Handbook* (Englewood Cliffs, N.J.: Prentice-Hall), also have sections devoted to letters and related correspondence.

Market research. The compilation by questionnaire or study of facts and figures that describe the market in which a product or service can be sold. Market research concerns itself with determining the general social and national income status of the community. It inquires into standards of living, consumption habits, available purchasing power, and saving patterns. It also attempts to solve specific sales problems: Where can products be sold most easily? How do they compare in customers' minds with competitors' products?

Research consultants and advertising agencies both perform market research surveys. The fundamentals are the same regardless of who does the research work. They comprise planning the market research, collecting the information, and digesting and organizing the information.

Quotation sources. The best-known book of quotations from literature is *Bartlett's Familiar Quotations* (Boston: Little, Brown).

Secretarial books. Books like *Private Secretary's Encyclopedic Dictionary* (Englewood Cliffs, N.J.: Prentice-Hall) that provide practical and informative material to help secretaries and other office personnel at work. Write to publishers for a list of available books.

Statistical data. Statistical data on business subjects such as prices, production, cost of living, income, are usually needed for either (1) a series of years from which trends can be determined or (2) the current situation. For that reason, the statistical references are given in two groups—cumulative statistics and current statistics.

All of the sources mentioned here contain figures on many subjects, presented in well-organized tables and sometimes with charts and graphs. For any statistical source, it is necessary to understand whether the figures given are actual figures (e.g., the number of cars produced) or an index, such as the index of the cost of living. An index number furnishes a basis for measuring changes from year to year or month to month. A normal period is selected as a base, which is represented by one hundred, and the figures for the various periods are reported in relation to the base figure. Statistical tables always indicate whether the figures are actual or index numbers.

1. *Statistical Abstract of the United States*, U.S. Bureau of Census (Washington, D.C.: U.S. Government Printing Office), published annually.

2. *Survey of Current Business* (Washington, D.C.: U.S. Bureau of Commerce), monthly. Indexes of production and general business activity are kept current by the leaflet *Survey of Current Business, Weekly Supplement*.

3. *Federal Reserve Bulletin* (Washington, D.C.: U.S. Board of Governors of the Federal Reserve System), published monthly.

4. *The Conference Board Business Record* (New York: National Industrial Conference Board), published monthly.

5. *Economic Indicators* (Washington, D.C.: U.S. Government Printing Office), published monthly.

6. *Current Industrial Reports* (Washington, D.C.: Department of Commerce), monthly, quarterly, semiannual, and annual reports, available by subscription.

Style books. Some books are written as guides to book making, style (capitalization, footnotes, and so on), production of printed material, typesetting, and printing. Examples are *The Chicago Manual of Style* (Chicago: University of Chicago Press) and the *United States Government Printing Office Style Manual* (Washington, D.C.: U.S. Government Printing Office).

Tax information. Numerous books, pamphlets, and digests, as well as several complete and abridged loose-leaf tax services, are published on federal taxes. Many of the publications are available in bookstores as well as libraries. Two well-known publishers of tax publications and services are Prentice-Hall (Englewood Cliffs, N.J.) and Commerce Clearing House (Chicago). Write to the publisher asking for a list of current materials.

Thesaurus. A word book that enables the user to find a word to fit an idea. Instead of starting with a word and finding its meaning, as in a dictionary, the user starts with an idea and finds a word to fit. The basic purpose of the thesaurus is to classify words by ideas—the invention of Peter Mark Roget, more than one hundred years ago. A thesaurus gives not only the synonyms of a word but all related words, phrases, expressions, and opposites in one place, graded according to shades of meaning, and all placed near the words expressing the same or similar ideas and concepts. Examples are *Roget's International Thesaurus* (New York: Harper & Row) and *New World Thesaurus* (Springfield, Mass.: Merriam-Webster).

Travel information. Bookstores, libraries, travel agencies, automobile clubs, and other organizations carry numerous travel guides and other literature (see also *Atlases*). Examples are the *Hotel and Motel Red Book* (New York: American Hotel Association Directory Corporation); the *Official Airline Guide* (Chicago: Donnelley), bimonthly service; and *The Official Guide of the Railways* (New York: National Railway Publications Company), annual subscription or purchase of single copies.

Vertical file service. Libraries usually file monographs, pamphlets, and similar material in cabinets or in boxes on shelves. To locate a specific document, consult the vertical-file-service catalog.

Yearbooks. These publications provide a variety of informational and statistical data on countries of the world. Examples are *The Statesman's Year-Book* (London: Macmillan), published annually; and the *Statistical Yearbook* (New York: International Documents Service, Columbia University Press), published annually.

Italic. A style of type characterized by oblique letters, *as in these words.* Italic type is used principally for emphasis and side headings. In typing, material that is to be set in italic type should be underlined. Although *italic* is derived from a proper name, it is usually written with a LOWER-CASE *i*.

lc. The abbreviation for LOWERCASE (small) letters. this sentence is set entirely in lowercase letters.

Layout. *Of material to be printed.* A design of the job to be printed, showing, page by page, margins, blocks or columns of type, illustrations, heading, captions, and the like, each drawn to exact size. Every item, even page numbers and credit lines, is carefully identified for size. See DUMMY.

Letterpress. A printing process in which the printing surface (the actual design or letter) is raised *above* the base level of the type or plate, just as lettering on a rubber stamp is raised above the rubber plate. This process is also known as the *relief* process. Letterpress, the oldest printing process, is a versatile method that can produce either very high-quality or very low-quality printed material.
See also OFFSET printing.

Libel. See Chapter 6 WORDS, COMMONLY MISUSED, *Libel and slander.*

Lightface (lf). Any type face with lines fine enough to give a light impression when printed, in contrast to BOLDFACE (bf).

Line drawing. See LINECUTS AND HALFTONES.

Linecuts and halftones. Types of cuts from which illustrations are reproduced. Linecuts are made of those illustrations (drawings, charts, graphs, pictographs) that consist only of lines and areas of black and white. Linecuts required only for letterpress (relief) printing are also referred to as *zinc etchings, line etch-*

ings, *line engravings, line blocks*, and *line plates*. Offset and other processes produce line drawings and halftones by other means. A halftone must always be used to reproduce gradations or shadings of tone between black and white found in photographs, paints, and wash drawings.

Line drawings may be prepared in a variety of ways: with pen and ink, brush and ink, crayon and ink, ink combined with the BEN DAY PROCESS, and so on. Line drawings usually print well on all types of paper, although very fine lines may look best on a smooth paper. When there is any doubt, one should consult a printer before proceeding.

Linotype. A method of typesetting in which an entire line of type is set and cast in metal in one continuous machine operation. The result is known as a *slug*. If a mistake is made in setting the line, the slug cannot be corrected without resetting and recasting a complete new line. Also called HOT TYPE. See also MONOTYPE; COLD TYPE.

Lithographic. See OFFSET.

Logo. Also *logotype*. A special design of type or of type in combination with artwork that is used by an organization to distinguish its name or product(s). The logo of a company may be imprinted on its letterhead and other stationery items, on packaging materials, on promotional literature, and on its product labels.

Lowercase. Pertaining to small letters of the alphabet, as opposed to capital (uppercase) letters. To *lower-case* a letter is to change it from a capital to a small letter. The abbreviation used in marking instructions for a typesetter is *lc*.

Ludlow. A method of composition in which the type is set by hand and then cast by machine. Ludlow is used principally for headings and display lines.

Manuscript. Written material to be sent to the printer for setting in type and publication. The manuscript is also called COPY.

Checking manuscript. Examining a manuscript carefully for errors before it is sent to the typesetter or printer. Checking saves time and money and contributes to a better finished product. *Read the manuscript over several times,* looking for errors. Each error corrected on the typed manuscript will save the expense of resetting a line or even a whole paragraph. Here are some of the guides to follow when checking the copy:

1. *Be consistent.* If a word can be spelled, abbreviated, or capitalized in more than one correct form, choose the one you prefer and use it consistently. On the first reading, make a list of your selections of optional spellings to guide you towards consistency.

2. Make *short corrections* in double-spaced copy by crossing out the incorrect word and writing the correction over it, *not* in the margin. The margin is used for instructions to the printer. To make *lengthy corrections,* cross out the incorrect matter and type the correct matter

on a separate sheet of paper. Mark the correction as an insert and show clearly where it is to be inserted.

3. *Circle* notations on the page that you do not want the typesetter to set in type. Thus any instructions to the typesetter or printer should be circled.

4. In checking the manuscript, do not indicate *type corrections* to be made in the margins; *make all such changes directly on the manuscript.*

5. To start a *new paragraph,* insert a ¶ sign; to run in material typed as a new paragraph, draw a line from the word starting the new paragraph to the last word of the preceding paragraph.

6. To *separate two words* typed as one, draw a vertical line between them.

7. To make *deletions,* use a heavy pencil and neatly and heavily cross out what you do not want.

8. To *retain material already crossed out,* insert a row of dots beneath it and circle the word *stet* in the margin beside it. Be sure, however, that the crossed-out material you want to retain is legible; if there is any doubt, retype it as an insert.

9. *Number the pages* of the manuscript consecutively after all corrections and insertions have been made.

10. Select the *style of type and size* from a book supplied by the typesetter and mark all heads and body copy on each page. The typesetter can be helpful in *copyfitting*—estimating the space the copy will occupy after it has been set.

Some secretaries keep a checklist in front of them while reading the manuscript as a reminder to check for accuracy, consistency, completeness, and readability of front matter and end matter; the opening and ending; sections and subdivision headings; paragraph transition; sentence structure; footnotes; illustrations; grammar; spelling; punctuation; capitalization style; word choice; voice (active vs. passive); conciseness; cliches; irrelevancies; clarity; preciseness; pomposity; vogue words; jargon; gobbledygook; euphemisms; prefixes and suffixes; trite expressions; and discriminatory expressions.

See also TYPEMARKING; COPY EDITING; PROOFREADERS' MARKS; PROOFREADING; Chapter 1/TYPING, *Typing manuscript.*

Mat. Common name for matrix. A matrix or mat is a lightweight paper containing an impression of type or pictures used to make duplicate metal printing plates, a process called *stereotyping.* Because mats are light, they are easy to ship. Advertisers and syndicates frequently send mats to newspapers, and some printers are equipped to cast metal from mats. Since many newspapers and printers use offset and prepare plates photographically, it is wise to find out if a mat can be used before preparing and mailing it.

Mechanical. Sometimes called a *pasteup.* A mechanical is a finished layout prepared for photographing and then reproduction by a printer. Proofs of typeset copy are prepared on slick paper and pasted down, often on heavy paper or "boards," *precisely* as they are to appear in the printed material. Guidelines (e.g., boxes) are drawn to show *exactly* where a halftone or other artwork is to be stripped in later. Mechanicals are usually prepared in black and white, with overlays showing any portions to be printed in color.

Media, advertising. See ADVERTISING.

Mimeograph. See DUPLICATING PROCESSES.

Monotype. A method of composition in which each character of the copy is separately cast in metal. An individual character in an assembled line can be corrected without resetting any of the other characters. This method is used chiefly for technical or mathematical works, for setting up charts and complicated tabular material, and for heavily illustrated work in which the type has to be fitted around illustrations. See also LINOTYPE; HOT TYPE; COLD TYPE.

Negative proof. See BLUEPRINTING; DUPLICATING PROCESSES, *Ozaliding*.

News release. Information submitted to a paper or papers for publication; also called "press release." *Release forms* are sheets bearing the name, address, and phone number of the organization issuing the release. If prepared release forms are not available, type a heading as shown in Figure 1.

A news release should be typed on news release stationery, standard business letterhead, or plain white paper of the standard eight-and-one-half-by-eleven-inch size. Text should be double-spaced. Paragraphs should be indented at least five spaces. Only one side of the paper should be used. If the text runs to more than one sheet, type *-more-* at the bottom of each sheet except the last one, and pages should be numbered. Type *-30-* at the end of the last page.

The form should specify near the top of the page the date the information is offered for release, for example: *For Immediate Release*. The first paragraph of copy should open with the city, state, and date of the announcement, for example: *San Francisco, Calif.; October 5, 1988*. The text must be very factual and straightforward. Adjectives such as *tremendous* and *fantastic* are out of place in a news release, which should convey only facts, as objectively and unemotionally as possible. The first paragraph should answer the questions *who, what, where, when, why,* and *how*.

If the information is to be released to several papers, it should be mimeographed or reproduced by some other inexpensive mechanical process. Editors of the publication prepare the headlines and edit the release.

Radio releases are designed to be read aloud within a limited time frame, such as 30 seconds or 1 minute. The time should be noted at the top of the release form, for example: *One-Minute Radio Spot*. Television releases, also time controlled, must be typed in two columns, with camera and actor directions typed in caps at the left, for example: *JOHN*

NEWS RELEASE: FIGURE 1: Format for news release heading

[LETTERHEAD]

For further information:

David Winters
617-777-7000

FOR IMMEDIATE RELEASE

Boston, Mass. (June 24, 1983). _____

_____

_____

_____

_____

LOOKS UP; CAMERA ZOOMS IN. An understanding of the special language used in television is required to prepare a TV script properly. See also PUBLICITY.

Offset. A printing process in which the printing is done from a very thin zinc plate on which the letters are not raised above the surface of the plate. This plate is prepared by a photographic process. The matter to be reproduced is photographed and transferred to the plate. The impression on the plate never comes in direct contact with the paper, but it is inked and the inked impression is trans- ferred to a "rubber blanket," which in turn comes in contact with the paper on which the book is printed. Offset printing is also known as *planographic* or *lithographic* printing.

Offset is often used to print from typewritten copy without incurring the expense of setting type; to reprint a book when the type for it has been destroyed and no electrotypes have been made; and to print heavily illustrated books with a great many photographs and drawings, although the reproduction of photographs may be inferior to LETTERPRESS reproduction, depending on the offset-press capability.

291

Ozalid. See DUPLICATING PRO-CESSES.

Page proof. When the GALLEY PROOF is returned to the compositor, with corrections indicated by the publisher and the author, and with the positions of all illustrations indicated, the compositor makes the corrections, places the illustrations in the proper places, and breaks the type up into pages, just as it will appear in the final book. The compositor then pulls a proof of these pages, and that proof is known as *page proof.* As with galley proofs, more than one set may be provided so you can mark final corrections on one set and return it and keep another for your files.

In reading page proofs, check that facing pages are of equal length; that illustrations, footnotes, and so on are positioned properly; that page numbers and RUNNING HEADS appear on each page; and that all errors marked on the GALLEY PROOFS have been corrected on the page proofs. Finally, examine each page for errors you may have missed in an earlier reading or new errors the typesetter or printer may have introduced. But avoid new, unnecessary revisions, which are costly once material has reached the page proof stage.

Pasteup. See MECHANICAL.

Patent. See Chapter 9/PATENT.

Photocopying. See DUPLICATING PROCESSES.

Photographs. See LINECUTS AND HALFTONES; CROPPING.

Photostat. See DUPLICATING PRO-CESSES.

Pica. 1. A printer's measure. There are six picas to an inch and twelve POINTS to a pica.

2. A size of type used on typewriters, slightly larger than elite type. Measured horizontally, ten spaces of pica type measure one inch, whereas twelve spaces of elite type measure one inch.

Planographic. See OFFSET.

Plate. A flat or curved sheet of metal or plastic used in printing; also the impression made from such a plate. All printing is done from a master surface of some sort. The type is etched on the surface, and a printed impression is made from that master surface or plate. A plate may consist entirely of text or of text and a CUT. It is inaccurate to refer to a cut as a plate.

Point. A type measurement. A point is one-twelfth of a PICA. Type size and the space between lines (leading) are measured in points.

Preface to a book. An introduction to a book, which usually includes a statement of the purposes of the book. Any remarks the author wants to make to the reader are placed in the preface. Acknowledgments of assistance are generally included in the preface, but they may be placed under a separate heading, especially if they are numerous. If someone other than the author writes the preface, the writer should sign his or her full name. If the author writes the preface, his or her name is usually omitted.

Press release.   See NEWS RELEASE.

Printing.   See BEN DAY PROCESS; BLUEPRINTING; CUT; DUMMY; DUPLICATING PROCESS; GRAVURE; LAYOUT; LETTERPRESS; LINECUTS AND HALFTONES; MAT; MECHANICAL; OFFSET; PLATE; REPRO PROOF.

Proofreaders' marks.   Standard symbols and abbreviations used for marking errors on printer's proof. They save time and are clearly understood by the printer. Figure 1 illustrates standard proofreaders' marks; Figure 2, a page of corrected proof. Here are some guides to follow when correcting proof: (1) Place all marks in the margin of the proof, left or right, whichever is nearer, on the same line as the error. (2) Separate corrections on the same line (e.g., lc/tr) and arrange them in order so they read consecutively from left to right. (3) If the same correction is to be made in two places in the line, with no intervening correction, write the correction only once and follow it with two slant lines. (4) When material is to be added to the line, place a caret (∧) in the text at the point of insertion and write the addition in the margin. (5) When material is to be deleted and none added in its place, cross out the unwanted characters and place a delete sign in the margin. (6) When material is to be substituted for a deletion, do not use the delete sign; just cross out the unwanted material and write the substitution for it in the

margin. (7) Use ink or pencil of a color different from any of the markings already on the proof.

Proofreading.   Reading proof for errors. It is not enough to read for sense and accuracy of facts, dates, and statistics. Each word and each mark of punctuation should be examined. The proof should be read word for word against COPY, preferably by having one person read aloud from the copy each word and mark of punctuation as another person follows the proof. Certainly, all tables, equations, statistics, and the like should be read against copy. (See PROOFREADERS' MARKS for standard proofreaders' marks and a piece of corrected proof.)

Proofs.   See GALLEY PROOF; PAGE PROOF; BLUEPRINTING; DUPLICATING PROCESSES, *Ozaliding.*

Public domain.   A work is in the public domain if (1) it was published in the United States without notice of COPYRIGHT; (2) it was published in the United States with copyright notice but the copyright was not renewed upon expiration; (3) it was *first* published in a government publication. No permission is needed to quote from a work that is in the public domain. See COPYRIGHT.

Publicity.   Information with news value disseminated to gain public attention or support. Although the terms are sometimes used interchangeably, one usually associates *advertising* with a paid announcement, *public relations* with an intro-

PROOFREADERS' MARKS: FIGURE 1

∧	Make correction indicated in margin.
Stet	Retain crossed-out word or letter; let it stand.
Stet (with dots)	Retain words under which dots appear; write "Stet" in margin.
X	Appears battered; examine.
=	Straighten lines.
✓✓✓	Unevenly spaced; correct spacing.
‖	Line up; i.e., make lines even with other matter.
run in	Make no break in the reading; no paragraph.
no ¶	No paragraph; sometimes written "run in."
out-see copy	Here is an omission; see copy.
¶	Make a paragraph here.
tr	Transpose words or letters as indicated.
d	Take out matter indicated; delete.
ʒ	Take out character indicated and close up.
ø	Line drawn through a cap means lower case.
⦶	Upside down; reverse.
◡	Close up; no space.
#	Insert a space here.
⊥	Push down this space.
⊡	Indent line one em.
[	Move this to the left.
]	Move this to the right.
⌐	Raise to proper position.
⌊	Lower to proper position.

////	Hair space letters.
wf.	Wrong font; change to proper font.
Qu?	Is this right?
lc.	Set in lowercase (small letters).
s.c.	Set in small capitals.
Caps	Set in capitals.
c+sc	Set in caps and small caps.
rom.	Change to roman.
ital.	Change to italic.
≡	Under letter or word means caps.
=	Under letter or word means small caps.
—	Under letter or word means italic.
∼∼∼	Under letter or word means boldface.
⋏	Insert comma.
⅂	Insert semicolon.
⁚⅂	Insert colon.
⊙	Insert period.
/?/	Insert interrogation mark.
/!/	Insert exclamation mark.
⅃	Insert hyphen.
⩘	Insert apostrophe.
⩖⩖	Insert quotation marks.
⩛	Insert superior letter or figure.
⩜	Insert inferior letter or figure.
[/]	Insert brackets.
(/)	Insert parentheses.
⊣⊢	One-em dash.
⩵	Two-em parallel dash.
⊚	Spell out.

PROOFREADERS' MARKS: FIGURE 2: A page of corrected proof

HOW TO CORRECT PROOF

It does not appear that the earliest printers had any method of
correcting errors before the form was on the press. The learned
learned correctors of the first two centuries of printing were not
proofreaders in our sense, they were rather what we should term
office editors. Their labors were chiefly to see that the proof corre-
sponded to the copy, but that the printed page was correct in its
Latinity / that the words were there, and that the sense was right.
They cared but little about orthography, bad letters or purely printers'
errors, and when the text seemed to them wrong they consulted fresh
authorities or altered it on their own responsibility. Good proofs, in
the modern sense, were impossible until professional readers were employed,
men who had first a printer's education, and then spent many years
in the correction of proof. The orthography of English, which for
the past century has undergone little change, was very fluctuating
until after the publication of Johnson's Dictionary, and capitals, which
have been used with considerable regularity for the past 80 years,
were previously used on the miss or hit plan. The approach to regularity,
so far as we have, may be attributed to the growth of a class of professional
proof readers, and it is to them that we owe the correctness of modern
printing. More errors have been found in the Bible than in any other
one work. For many generations it was frequently the case that Bibles
were brought out stealthily, from fear of governmental interference.
They were frequently printed from imperfect texts, and were often
modified to meet the views of those who published them. The story is
related that a certain woman in Germany, who was the wife of a printer,
and had become disgusted with the continual assertion of the superiority
of man over woman which she had heard, hurried into the composing room
while her husband was at supper and altered a sentence in the Bible, which
he was printing, so that it read Narr instead of Herr, thus making
the verse read "And he shall be thy fool" instead of "And he shall be thy
lord." The word not was omitted by Barker, the King's printer in
England in 1632, in printing the seventh commandment. He was fined
£3,000 on this account.

duction of someone or something to the public, and *publicity* with efforts to attract public attention by disseminating information or promotional material.

Businesses regularly publicize activities such as the development of a new product, the opening of a new store, or a change in service. Other events also can be reported that will make the public aware of an organization by keeping its name in the news, for example, job promotions, retirements, a business-sponsored event, charitable activities, or some form of community service. The nature of an organization's product or service and various newsworthy events can be reported to the outside world through articles, press releases (see NEWS RELEASE), letters, brochures, print and broadcast advertisements, public service announcements, and any other form of message transmission.

Specialists are often retained to prepare ADVERTISING and publicity material such as newspaper and magazine ads or broadcast spots. Large firms often have their own advertising and public relations departments. Many outside agencies specialize in either advertising or public relations or both.

Query. An interrogation point (?) used as the sign of a question or indicating doubt. A query on a MANUSCRIPT, GALLEY PROOF, or PAGE PROOF indicates doubt about a detail and is a request to the editor or author to clarify or supply the detail. For example, when a page number is missing, the proofreader places a query on the proof where the page number should be. The query is carried on the proof through each stage of printing until the editor or author is able to supply the missing detail.

Quoted material. Quoted material of more than eight to ten typed lines is usually indented (see EXTRACT; Chapter 7/INDENTION) from each margin, at least five spaces, with an additional five-space indention for the beginning of a paragraph. If the quoted material does not have paragraph indentions, type each paragraph block style with a line space between paragraphs. Also, if the quoted material begins in the middle of a paragraph, the paragraph indention is omitted. (See Figure 1.) Quoted material is double-spaced in manuscript copy and single-spaced in printed material with an extra space between paragraphs. An additional space also precedes and follows the quoted material.

Quotation marks. If the quoted material is typed the same as the general text copy, and not set off or indented as a separate block of copy, double quotation marks are placed at the beginning and end of the quoted material and at the beginning of each new paragraph within the quoted material. Quotations within quotations should be enclosed in single quotations marks when the material is *not* set off or indented but is typed the same as the rest of the text. If the quoted material is typed as a separate, indented block of copy, beginning and ending quotation marks are not used, and any quoted remarks *within* the indented block of copy are enclosed in *double* quotation marks.

QUOTED MATERIAL: FIGURE 1: Exact (Chinese) copy of quoted material

---

The pertinent part of the opinion rendered by the Copyright Office at our request reads as follows:

The Copyright Office does not undertake to pass upon his (the author's) rights, leaving the question to the courts in case of dispute. . . . it simply <u>records</u> [italics theirs] his claims, and by this recording gives him certain rights <u>provided his claims can be substantiated</u>. . . .

This (copyright) is taken out in the name of the publisher rather than of the author, as the contract itself is really a license to sell from the publisher to the authro [sic]. It is also the duty of the publisher to take all necessary steps to effect renewals. . . .

An author should be "guided" by his publisher in all questions of copyright. [Emphasis ours.]

We contend that this opinion strongly supports the contention of the petitioner.

Refer to Figure 1 for a an example of quoted words within an extract.

Errors. Quoted material is usually quoted exactly, even with obvious errors. Errors are indicated as they are in an exact copy of any material. (See Chapter 1/CHINESE COPY.).

Italics. If words in the original are in italics, they are underscored in your manuscript copy. If words that are not in italics in the original are underscored at the direction of the dictator, the words *Italics ours* in parentheses are added at the *end* of the quotation. It frequently happens that part of a quoted passage is already italicized and that the dictator wants to emphasize another part of it. In that case, *Italics theirs* in brackets is placed immediately following the italicized matter, and the words *Italics ours* or *Emphasis ours* in brackets are added at the end of the quotation. In Figure 1, the word *records* was already italicized in the original. The rest of the underscoring was added by the dictator for emphasis.

Omissions. Omissions of part of a quotation are indicated by the use of ellipsis points. They may be dots (periods), which are preferred in most offices, or asterisks, and are in groups of three if the omitted copy falls in the middle of a sentence. If the omitted words fall at the end of a sentence, there would be a period plus the usual three points or asterisks. Space before and between the three points or the last three of four points. There is no space before the first of four points representing a normal period at the end of a sentence.

Whether points or asterisks are used, they take the place of words and are placed accordingly. Thus if a quotation begins in the middle of a sentence, there is no space between the quotation mark and the first ellipsis point, but there is a space between each ellipsis point and before the first word quoted. If an entire sentence is omitted, place a period as usual after the last sentence followed by three ellipsis points.

Omission of one or more entire paragraphs may be indicated by a separate line of three to five centered ellipsis points, five spaces apart or, preferably, by a period plus three ellipsis points at the end of the sentence preceding the missing paragraph(s).

Figure 1 illustrates a quotation with points showing omissions. The word *sic* in brackets also shows errors that were in the material being copied. (See Chapter 1/CHINESE COPY.) The first sentence begins in the middle of a paragraph, so it is flush left. The second and third paragraphs start with no sentences missing at the beginning, so they are indented normally. Several paragraphs are missing between the second and the final paragraph, and four dots are used to show the omission; the last paragraph is quoted in full.

Relief printing. See LETTERPRESS.

Report. A written presentation of information necessary for the understanding of a given problem. The report may state the writer's conclusions or recommendation or may be merely factual. A report may be periodical, referred to as a *routine* or *progress* report, or it may be special, prepared to cover a nonrecurring situation. Reports serve many useful purposes in business. Management keeps abreast of company activities through internal reports, both periodical and special. (See Chapter 10/

INTERNAL REPORTS). The board of directors of a corporation submits an annual report to stockholders and others. (See Chapter 10/ANNUAL REPORT.) A certified public accountant prepares financial reports for clients.

A report may be informal, set up as a letter or memo (see Chapter 7/ LETTERS; MEMO), or it may be formal. All but short memo reports usually include the following parts, in the order listed: (1) cover or title page; (2) TABLE OF CONTENTS; (3) body, consisting of introduction, development, conclusions or recommendations; and (4) supplementary material, such as tables, charts, BIBLIOGRAPHY, and APPENDIX. A formal report may also include (1) a letter of transmittal addressed to the person receiving the report, which follows the title page; (2) a list of illustrations, which follows a table of contents; (3) a foreword or abstract (a one-page summary), which follows the list of illustrations; (4) an appendix, which follows the body; (5) a list of references or "Notes" section and a BIBLIOGRAPHY, which follow the appendix; and (6) an index, which follows the bibliography. Some reports have various other parts, as needed, such as a copyright page if the report is being published, and a glossary.

Title page. All formal reports have a title page. Short (e.g., memo), informal reports do not. Usually, the title page is the front cover, but if a report is enclosed in a binder, the title page is the first page beneath the cover. The items of information on the title page are (1) the title of the report, (2) to whom submitted, (3) by whom submittcd, and (4) the date. When an item is written on more than one line, the material should be divided at a logical point. Adjectives and articles are not separated from the words they modify; a preposition is not separated from its object; and a line does not end in a conjunction. Thus the title "The Participation of the White-Collar Worker in Modern Labor Unrest" should not be divided between *collar* and *worker* but between *worker* and *in*. The items are centered horizontally on the available space, exclusive of the part taken up by binding or fastening. Items (e.g., by whom submitted and to whom submitted) should be separated by at least four line spaces to give the page a balanced appearance. Titles and other material on the title page may be single- or double-spaced.

Headings. The body of a report is usually divided into topics and subtopics with headings. Topics of equal importance should be given equal emphasis. Emphasis is shown in typed material by centering and by the use of caps, spacing, underlining, or a combination of these techniques. Headings of the same relative importance should be identical in form.

In typing a long report, one should prepare a pattern of the style of headings to be used throughout the report, for example:

FIRST TOPIC HEADING
SUBDIVISION HEADING
Minor subdivision heading

If the report requires more breakdowns, the following pattern could be used:

FIRST TOPIC HEADING
SUBDIVISION HEADING
S u b o r d i n a t e   H e a d i n g
M i n o r   H e a d i n g

Least important subdivision heading.

Or you could indent the lowest level subheading the same as each paragraph, for example, the way the subhead *Typing* is indented below.

When words are letter-spaced, there is a double space between words. There should be a triple space between a center heading and the text that precedes it, a double space between the heading and the text that follows.

Report writing. The preparation of a report involves several steps: (1) organization—developing the theme, checklist of things to do and supplies needed, and so on; (2) research—making a list of sources of information, scheduling appointments, developing an outline of topics to be researched, taking notes and preparing a bibliography, getting releases for photographs and other material, and so on; (3) drafting—converting each item on the topic outline into a sentence, each sentence into a paragraph, and so on; positioning footnotes, appendixes, illustrations, and other material; and preparing front and back matter such as the table of contents and glossary; (4) revision—verifying facts and figures; rechecking the placement of illustrations and other items; polishing the flow of copy; rearranging copy as needed; checking grammar, spelling, language, and style consistency; and generally making the draft as perfect as possible.

Typing. Reports are usually prepared by computer or typewriter on plain white, twenty-pound paper, eight and one-half by eleven inches. Memo reports are prepared on memo paper. Short, informal reports may be single-spaced, but the manuscript for a formal report is usually double-spaced (although the typeset version is likely to be single-spaced). The pages of the TABLE OF CONTENTS and any other pages that precede the report proper are numbered with small Roman numerals (i, ii, iii, iv). Pages of the report proper, the appendixes, and the index are numbered with Arabic numerals, starting with 1. The appendixes may be numbered or lettered in sequence. (A, B, C). Each appendix also has a subject or title.

For instructions on typing tables, see Chapter 1/TABULATED MATERIAL; STATISTICAL TYPING. For information on typing footnotes and bibliographies, see FOOTNOTES; BIBLIOGRAPHY, Figure 1.

Repro proof. Pages of type prepared with the intent of photographing them for reproduction. Usually, the type is on white, coated paper that has been carefully prepared (corrected and "pasted" on boards) to avoid any flaws. Corrections and changes made at this late stage in the reproduction process are costly and should be avoided. See also GALLEY PROOF; PAGE PROOF; BLUE-PRINTING; DUPLICATING PROCESSES, *Ozaliding.*

Research. The process of fact finding. Depending on the type of information you need, you may consult one or more sources (in-house files, outside libraries, consultants, schools, and so on). The type of information you need will also influence your choice of fact-finding methods (review of published material, interviews, and so forth) and tools (pencil and paper, tape recorder, camera, questionnaire, and so on).

1. *Library research.* Company, public, and specialized libraries have a wealth of published material. The card catalog and various indexes will indicate what books and other material are available. See INFORMATION SOURCES. Ask the reference librarian for help in locating unfamiliar reference works.

2. *Computer research.* If you have a telephone, a computer, and a modem (modulator/demodulator), you can reach electronic libraries, or databases, from your own office. The modem converts data into signals that travel over the telephone lines. Some databases will respond with a list of citations for the topic you want to research; others will give both citations and abstracts (summaries) of the published works. Such services are available by subscription and/or hourly rate charges. Ask the reference librarian for a list of current database names and addresses. Computer-search services and libraries that have a computer will provide research for a fee and/or hourly rate. The library or organization will need a list of key words from you; these

words are coded for the computer, which prints out a list of related reference sources.

3. *Interviewing.* After securing an appointment with an interviewee, and before you arrive, collect all the material you need. Study the subject in advance and review your proposed questions. Sometimes it is helpful to prepare a questionnaire to help guide the discussion. Take along pen, pencils, paper, and any other note-taking material you may need. If you want to tape-record the session, ask for permission and be certain the recorder and cassettes are working properly. Request permission to take required pictures and be certain your camera and film are ready. Get a written release from the subject for any photograph or direct quote you intend to use. Follow up later with a visit or telephone call to clarify any confusing points.

Roman.   A basic design of type characterized by upright letters. Originally, roman referred to type of the Italian school of design as distinguished from the typical black-letter German style of type. Today, the term is also used to refer to type faces that are not ITALIC. Unless it is otherwise marked, a printer will set typed material in roman. Usually, *roman* (in reference to type) is written with a LOWERCASE *r*.

Running head.   The line that runs across the top of every page of a book, magazine, pamphlet, and the like, often giving the book title or chapter title, or in the case of a

magazine, the name of the magazine or date of issue.

Sources of information.   See INFORMATION SOURCES.

Spine.   See BACKBONE (OF BOOK).

Stet.   A proofreader's mark meaning to retain material already crossed out. Dots are placed beneath the crossed-out material that is to be retained, and the word *stet* is written in the margin. The material to be retained must be legible.

Superior figure.   A figure raised above the line of type, for example, R^2. Superior figures are used principally to indicate footnotes. (See Figure 1 under PROOFREADERS' MARKS for the correct way to tell a printer to use a superior figure.) An *inferior* figure is just the opposite of a superior figure. Inferior figures are used principally in symbols, such as H_2O.

Table of contents.   List of titles and numbers, if any, of the chapters or topics of a printed work and the number of the page on which each begins. The items are listed numerically according to the page on which each begins.

Typing.   Whether you prepare the contents by computer or typewriter, center the items horizontally and vertically on the sheet. Double-space a short table; single-space a long table. Type the chapter or topic number, if any, at the left; space about three times and follow with the title. List the page numbers at the right-hand margin. Period leaders

TABLE OF CONTENTS: FIGURE 1: Table of contents with subtopics material

---

CONTENTS

---

may be used to guide the reader's eye across the page between title and page number. (See Figure 1.)

Title page. See REPORT, *Title page.*

Type face. The design of a style of type letter. Type faces are usually known by the name of the person who designed them, as, for example, Baskerville and Granjon. This text is set in 10-point Palatino.

Following are sample type faces:

This type is TIMES ROMAN BOLD

This type is TIMES ROMAN BOLD ITALIC

This type is HELVETICA

This type is HELVETICA ITALIC

This type is HELVETICA BOLD CONDENSED

This type is UNIVERS

This type is UNIVERS BOLD

Type measurements. The following information will be helpful in planning the arrangement of a table:

1. Six line spaces equal one inch, measured vertically.

2. Ten spaces of pica type equal one inch, measured horizontally.

3. Twelve spaces of elite type equal one inch, measured horizontally.

4. A sheet of paper eight and one-half by eleven inches has eighty-five spaces of pica type on a horizontal line.

5. A sheet of paper in eight and one-half by eleven inches has 102 spaces of elite type on a horizontal line.

6. A sheet of paper eight and one-half by eleven inches has sixty-six vertical line spaces.

Typemarking. Marking on a manuscript the type specifications, position of spacing around subheads, paragraph indentations, page dimensions, and so on—all instructions a typesetter needs to prepare your copy for reproduction. Instructions of this nature are usually written beside the material in question and circled. For instance, *10/12 Times Roman* written and circled beside a block of copy means you want the typesetter to set that copy in a Times Roman type face and a ten-POINT type size. The "12" refers to spacing between the lines (called *leading*) and is also expressed in points. This text is set in 10/12 Palatino.

See also MANUSCRIPT; TYPE FACE; COPY EDITING; TYPE MEASUREMENTS.

Typesetting. See COLD TYPE; HOT TYPE; LINOTYPE; LUDLOW; MONOTYPE; GALLEY PROOF; PAGE PROOF; PICA; POINT; PROOFREADERS' MARKS; TYPE FACE; TYPE MEASUREMENTS; TYPE-MARKING; WORD COUNT.

Typing manuscript. See Chapter 1/ TYPING, *Typing manuscript*.

United Press International (UPI). One of two wire services in the United States that provide most of the newspaper's international and nonlocal news. UPI is an independent company with its own staff that offers subscriber service to newspaper. News releases should be directed to the nearest division headquarters unless there is a "stringer" in your area. See also ASSOCIATED PRESS (AP).

Uppercase. Pertaining to capital letters of the alphabet, as opposed to small (lowercase) letters. To uppercase a letter is to change it from a small letter to a capital. The abbreviation used in marking instructions to the typesetter is *uc*.

Whiteprint. See DUPLICATING PROCESSES, *Ozaliding*.

Widow. *Printing*. A short last line of a paragraph carried over from the previous page or column to the top of a page or column. The text should be adjusted to avoid a widow.

Word count. Method of estimating length of copy by counting the words in it. Whereas some computer/word processor software programs specify the number of words or characters in a document, typewriters usually do not have this capability. To make a manual count: (1) Find the average number of words to a line by counting the number of words in several lines and dividing this total by the number of lines counted. (2) Multiply the average number of words to a line (Step 1) by the number of lines to a page to get the average number of words per page. (3) Multiply the average number of words to a page (step 2) by the number of pages.

Printers and typesetters usually have guides available for their customers that show the number of characters per line for different type faces and sizes set at various line widths.

PART III

BUSINESS LAW AND ORGANIZATION

CHAPTER 9

BUSINESS LAW

AFL-CIO. A united labor federation resulting from the merger, in 1955, of the American Federation of Labor and the Congress of Industrial Organization.

Acceleration clause. A CONTRACT, promissory note, or mortgage clause that permits the lender to demand the full and unpaid balance owed in the event of default.

Accounting. The rendering or delivering of a formal statement by a person who is under a legal duty to account for property or money of another. Thus accountings are made by executors and administrators, agents, assignees in bankruptcy, guardians, and surviving partners.

Acknowledgment. The act by which a person who has signed a legal instrument goes before an authorized officer, such as a NOTARY PUBLIC, and declares that he or she executed the instrument. The authorized officer signs the *certificate of acknowledgment*, which entitles the instrument to be recorded or filed and authorizes it to be given in evidence without further proof of its execution. See also CONTRACTS.

The six essential parts of a typed acknowledgment are the venue (place), date, name of person making the acknowledgment, signature of person taking it, date of officer's commission expiration, and the notarial seal. (See Figure 1.) In some jurisdictions officers who are not notaries may attest acknowledgments, and the seal and expiration date may not be required.

Affidavit. A written statement signed and sworn to before some person authorized to take an oath, frequently accepted as proof when no other evidence of a fact is avail-

ACKNOWLEDGMENT: FIGURE 1

Certificate of Acknowledgment of Individual

STATE OF
COUNTY OF
} ss.

On this the _____ day of ____, 19 ____, before me, _____, the undersigned officer, personally appeared ALBERT JONES, known to me or sufficiently proven to be the person whose name is subscribed to the within instrument and acknowledged that he executed the same for the purpose therein contained.

IN WITNESS WHEREOF, I have hereunto set my hand and official seal.

_____
Notary Public
My Commission expires _____

able. The person making the affidavit is the *affiant* or *deponent*. An affidavit is a complete instrument within itself and is an affirmation that the statements made are true. By contrast, an ACKNOWLEDGMENT is appended to another document. An affidavit is sworn to, but an acknowledgment is not. Both the person making the affidavit and the officer administering the oath sign an affidavit; only the officer taking an acknowledgment signs it. An affidavit has a JURAT, but an acknowledgment does not (see JURAT). Affidavits are frequently attached to a legal pleading (or a court document) to support that document, for example, Motion for Summary Judgment.

The seven essential parts of an affidavit are the venue (place), name of affiant, averment of oath, statement of facts, affiant's signature, jurat, and NOTARY PUBLIC's signature. (See Figure 1.)

Agent. Someone authorized by another person to act for that person. An agent is therefore entrusted with another person's business.

American Digest System. A series of digests covering all reported legal cases in America since 1658. The topics are arranged alphabetically in numerous volumes, and an extensive index makes up several volumes in itself.

American Jurisprudence. Usually cited as *Am. Jur.*, this is a legal encyclopedia that is cross-referenced with AMERICAN LAW REPORTS.

American Law Reports. Usually cited as *A.L.R.*, or *ALR*, this is a large series of books that report selected cases in full along with a related annotation, or commentary.

Amicus curiae. Latin for "friend of the court." *Amicus curiae* refers to an individual or, more commonly, an organization that is allowed to appear in a lawsuit by furnishing his or her or its opinion, or filing a brief, presenting a point of view not otherwise represented, although that person or organization has no right, or standing, to appear otherwise.

Answer. A defendant's formal written statement of defense, prepared and signed by his or her attorney. An answer is supplied in response to a COMPLAINT and may deny some or all of the complaint's allegations. The eight essential parts are the caption, or heading; introduction; denials; counterclaims, if any; "wherefore"

AFFIDAVIT: FIGURE 1

STATE OF
COUNTY OF
} ss.

AFFIDAVIT

JOHN DOE, being duly sworn, deposes and says:

He is the Secretary of ARC Corporation, and that no stockholder of said Corporation has filed with the Secretary thereof a written request (other than such written request or requests as may have heretofore expired or been withdrawn) that notices intended for him shall be mailed to some address other than his address as it appears on the stock book of the said Corporation.

_____

Secretary

Sworn to before me this

_____ day of _____, 19 _____

_____

Notary Public

clause, or a demand for dismissal of the complaint; "prayer," in stating any counterclaims; signature of the defendant's attorney; and verification, if the complaint is verified.

Antitrust laws. *Federal antitrust laws.* Federal legislation designed to prevent restraint of trade, MONOPOLY, and unfair practices in interstate commerce (see INTERSTATE COMMERCE, INTRASTATE COMMERCE). The statutes described briefly below constitute a great patchwork of loophole plugging and exempting enactments. (See below for state legislation.)

1. *Sherman Act (Antitrust Act of 1890).* "An act to protect trade and commerce against unlawful restraints and monopolies," this act prevents not only the means by which mo-

nopoly is sought, but also the ends achieved.

2. *Clayton Act.* The Clayton Act was passed in 1914 to bring within the coverage of the antitrust laws abuses that experience had shown were inadequately provided against in the Sherman Act. The Clayton Act seeks to nip anticompetitive transactions *before* they are put into practice. It upholds the use of the "rule of reason" and defines certain unreasonable acts, including some unfair trade practices.

3. *Robinson-Patman Act.* The Robinson-Patman Act was passed in 1936 to plug loopholes in the Clayton Act, which it amended. Generally, the act prohibits not only price concessions not justified by cost differences but also price discriminations that result from brokerage, advertising, and service allowances.

4. *Miller-Tydings Act.* This act, which amended the Sherman Act in 1937, legalized contracts or agreements in interstate commerce that prescribe prices for resale of branded commodities when such contracts or agreements are lawful as applied to intrastate transactions under state resale price maintenance (fair trade) laws.

State antitrust laws. The states passed legislation to codify, clarify, and amend the COMMON LAW rules regarding restraint of trade and MONOPOLY before the federal government. A few states incorporated in their constitutions declarations of policy regarding monopolies. A larger number of states adopted constitu-

tions with broader provisions to prevent combinations that suppress competition, and some enacted statutes for the purpose. In general, these statutes were merely declaratory of the common law. But there was this difference: restraints that were unenforceable under common law were expressly made illegal. Furthermore, the parties to such actions were made indictable, and injured parties were granted recovery rights against those who injured them. In practice, these state laws were comparatively useless. With few exceptions, enforcement was neglected and, if undertaken, was done so haphazardly. Moreover, many combinations were beyond the reach of the state laws because they were engaged in interstate commerce, which fell within the province of the national government. Today, enforcement of federal antitrust legislation has, as a practical matter, made prosecution under state antitrust laws unusual. See FAIR-TRADE ACTS.

Appeal. A review procedure started in a higher court to examine the determination of a lower court or of some government official or agency. The higher court then examines the record and decides whether the decision was in accordance with law.

Arbitration. A method whereby differences may be settled without litigation by a single arbitrator or a panel of arbitrators whose decision is binding on the parties if they have so agreed. It is frequently used to settle labor disputes. *Compulsory arbitration* is that required by a governmental agency. *Voluntary arbitration* arises by consent of the disputing parties, usually as part of an underlying contract.

Assessment. 1. The amount of damages that the successful party in a lawsuit is entitled to. **2.** In real estate, *assessment* refers to the value placed on real property for purposes of property taxation.

Assignment. An act whereby a party (the assignor) transfers property or some right or interest in property to another party (the assignee).

An assignment may be oral or written unless it involves a CONTRACT required to be written according to the STATUTE OF FRAUDS. It may be a formal document or an endorsement on a contract and it must effect an immediate transfer to a specific assignee.

Like any CONTRACT, to be valid, an assignment must be executed by a party having legal capacity. Every assignment is a transfer, but not every transfer is an assignment.

Attachment. The process of seizing or taking into custody. Attachment is a legal proceeding used by a creditor to have the property of a debtor seized under court order, pending a determination of the creditor's claim. An attachment is recorded in the appropriate public records as notice that a claim has been made, which, if found valid, would affect the value of the property attached. An attachment creates or perfects a LIEN on property.

Attestation. The act of signing a written instrument as witness to the signature of a party, at the party's request. See Figure 1. For example, witnessing signatures to a CONTRACT or will. The witness is called a *subscribing witness,* because he or she signs the instrument as a witness. A legend or clause that recites the circumstances surrounding the signing of an instrument often precedes the signature of the attesting witnesses and is called the *attestation clause.* The wording of the attestation clause varies from a simple "In the presence of" to the rather lengthy clause used in wills. It is typed at the left of the signature. When the secretary of a corporation attests to an instrument, he or she impresses the corporate seal upon it. (See Chapter 10/CORPORATE SEAL.) Attestation is the act of the witness, and EXECUTION is the act of the party to the instrument.

Bailment. A delivery of PERSONAL PROPERTY for some particular purpose, upon a contract, express or implied, that the property will be returned to the person delivering it after the accomplishment of the purpose for which it was delivered. An essential of a bailment is that return of the property or an accounting in accordance with the terms of agreement is contemplated. A bailment may be created by express agreement, implied by the conduct of the parties or by implication of law. The person delivering the property is a *bailor;* the person receiving it is a *bailee.*

If under the terms of the contract

ATTESTATION: FIGURE 1: Legend and signature lines for two groups of witnesses

IN WITNESS WHEREOF, we, the lessors and the lessee, have hereunto set our hands to the foregoing lease, consisting of twenty-two pages (22), on this _____ day of April 19—.

Signed and delivered by lessors in)
the presence of:)
)
)
)
_____)
)
)
_____)

_____
Lessors

Signed and delivered by lessee in the)
presence of:)
)
)
)
_____)
)
)
_____)

_____
Lessee

Source: Besse May Miller, revised by Mary A. De Vries, *Legal Secretary's Complete Handbook* (Englewood Cliffs, N.J.: Prentice-Hall, Inc., 1953, 1970, 1980).

the bailee is obligated to pay a sum of money instead of returning the goods, the obligation is a debt and not a bailment. Thus a conditional sale is distinguished from a bailment (see Chapter 13/CONDITIONAL SALE) by the fact that the purchaser has an obligation to pay the purchase price, at which time he or she acquires title to the property. This is so even though the contract states that it is a bailment.

Bankruptcy. A state of insolvency in which the property of a debtor is taken over by a receiver or trustee in bankruptcy for the benefit of the creditors. (See Chapter 13/INSOLVENCY.) This action is performed under the jurisdiction of the courts as prescribed by the federal Bankruptcy Act.

Voluntary bankruptcy. Voluntary bankruptcy is brought about by the filing of a petition in bankruptcy by the debtor. The form of the petition is prescribed by the act. By filing a voluntary petition, debtors seek, first, to have their assets equally distributed among all creditors but on the basis of established priorities; and second, to free themselves of their debts. They are thus able to begin business life anew, free of those debts discharged in bankruptcy.

Voluntary bankruptcy is open to all individuals, firms, partnerships, and corporations, except banking, building and loan associations, insurance, railroad, and municipal corporations. No minimum debt is required. A person owing one dollar or several million dollars may file a petition in voluntary bankruptcy.

Involuntary bankruptcy. Involuntary bankruptcy is brought about by the filing of a petition by the creditors against an insolvent debtor. Before creditors can throw a debtor into bankruptcy, the debtor must owe the creditors filing the petition a specified amount more than the value of the liens the creditors hold on the debtor's property, and the debtor must have committed an act of bankruptcy (such as admitting an inability to pay debts) preceding the filing of the petition.

Involuntary bankruptcy proceedings cannot be brought against a wage earner, farmer, building and loan association, or banking, insurance, railroad, or municipal corporation.

The Bankruptcy Act provides for the relief and rehabilitation of debtors, and the intent is to restore the debtor to a viable entity by reconstituting the debtor's financial and business operations.

Bill of sale. A legal document that conveys from seller to buyer the title to, or interest in, personal property.

Binder. See Chapter 15/BINDER.

Blue law. A state law that forbids the selling of goods or services or other activities on Sunday.

Blue sky law. A law that regulates and supervises the sales of stock and other activities of investment companies. It is intended to protect the public from fraudulent stock deals.

Books and records (corporate). State corporation laws sometimes prescribe that certain books be kept by a corporation and indicate who shall have charge of them and whether or not they must be kept at the corporation's principal office. (See also Chapter 10/CORPORATION.) These statutes must be strictly followed. Provision for the maintenance of corporate books is also generally included in the bylaws, which follow the requirements of the statute. (See Chapter 10/BYLAWS.) Generally, the rights of stockholders to inspect the books are also covered in the bylaw provisions relating to books and records.

The books and records usually directed by statute or the bylaws to be kept are the minutes book (see Chapter 3/MINUTES); stock certificate book; stock book and transfer books (sometimes described as stock ledgers. See also Chapter 10/STOCK LEDGER). It is well established that the original books and records of a private corporation, when properly authenticated, are the best evidence of the corporation's act and proceedings.

Control of the corporate books. The books and records are the property of the corporation and not of the officers or employees; however, custody of the books normally resides with the corporate secretary (or clerk). In the absence of a statutory provision, the stockholders and directors are free to entrust any person with custody of such books and records. When the term of office of the officer having custody of the books expires, it is his or her duty to deliver them to a successor. If the officer refuses to deliver the books, he or she may be compelled to do so by judicial process.

Under COMMON LAW and under most statutes, the stockholders have a right to inspect the corporation's books and records at proper and reasonable time.

Bona fide. Latin for honest, in good faith, or real.

Boycott. An attempt by many persons to injure another by refusing to do business with the object of the boycott. A *secondary boycott*, which is an attempt to injure someone by applying economic pressure to a third party, is illegal.

Breach of contract. The failure or refusal by one of the parties to a contract to perform some act the contract calls for without legal excuse. A contract may also be breached by preventing or obstructing performance by the other party or by "anticipatory" breach, as the unqualified announcement by a seller, before delivery date, that he or she will not deliver the goods. A right of action occurs or is complete upon the other party's failure to do the particular thing he or she agreed to do. Damages may be obtained only for losses that can be shown to have resulted directly from the breach.

Breach of warranty. Providing a false WARRANTY to a buyer. The buyer may accept the goods for a reduced price, keep them and seek damages, refuse them and bring action for damages, rescind the CONTRACT before delivery, or return the goods after delivery and recover what has been paid.

Brief. A written summary or condensed statement; often, a written statement filed in court by one side in a lawsuit to explain its case. A brief usually contains a fact and law summary and an argument about how the law applies to the facts. A brief is also a summary of a published opinion in a case.

Bulk sales law. A law intended to protect creditors from being defrauded when a seller liquidates all or most assets to a single buyer. Bulk transfers are controlled under Article 6 of the UNIFORM COMMERCIAL CODE adopted in most states.

Capital. As applied to corporations, in the strict legal sense, that portion of the consideration received by the corporation upon the issuance of stock that has been set up on its books as capital in accordance with the laws of the state in which the corporation is organized. It cannot be impaired through the payment of dividends or the acquisition of the corporation's own stock. In a broader sense, it may refer to the entire assets of a corporation or simply to the corporate assets employed in the conduct of the corporate business for the creation of profits.

Capital stock. See Chapter 11/ CAPITAL STOCK.

Caveat emptor. Latin for "let the buyer beware." This COMMON LAW doctrine or maxim imposes on the buyer the duty of examining what he or she buys. The purchaser must examine, judge, and test the property, whether realty or personalty. It is applied when the seller makes no express warranty and is not guilty of fraud.

Exceptions to the *caveat emptor* doctrine are made under the following circumstances: (1) A fiduciary relation exists between the parties, as between principal and agent, attorney and client, trustee and beneficiary. (2) The defects are not obvious, and the buyer has not had an opportunity for thorough inspection. (3) The sale was made by sample or by description. (4) The sale was for a specific purpose.

The scope of the doctrine of *caveat emptor* has been narrowed in recent years. Both case law and statutory law have tended to enlarge the responsibilities of the seller as warranties are being inferred from the facts and circumstances of the transaction. It is not necessary that the seller state that he or she warrants a product since the intent to warrant may be implied from the language and acts. The UNIFORM COMMERCIAL CODE has greatly expanded the scope and application of implied warranties to the sale of goods.

Certiorari. Latin for "to make sure." A request for *certiorari* is filed with an appellate court asking the court to review the trial court decision. It is not an APPEAL of right, and the appellate court may refuse to accept the case for consideration.

Chattel. See PERSONAL PROPERTY.

Chose in action. A phrase used to describe a "right" to PERSONAL PROPERTY that is not reduced to physical possession and that requires some form of legal action to acquire or recover possession. Some of the most important choses in action are contracts, promissory notes, checks, trade acceptance, stocks, bonds, bank accounts, and the right of legal action to recover money or property.

Citations to legal authorities. Most citations occur in legal briefs, memorandums of law, and a lawyer's opinion letters. References are usually made to constitutions, statutes, and codes; to law reports; and to texts and periodicals. Some common forms of legal citations are given below. For details on style in specific cases, consult *A Uniform System of Citation* (Harvard Law Review, Cambridge, Mass.). A citation is broken down to indicate the volume, name of the book, page number, and year.

Constitution: U.S. Const. art IV, §2.

Statutes and codes: Act of April 17, 1937, c. 761, 38 Stat. 648, 40 U.S.C. 176b.

Cases in official reports and reporters: United States v. Adams Co., 240 U.S. 340, 81 S.Ct. 432 (1961).

Unpublished Case: Roe v. Doe, No. 252 U.S. Sup. Ct., Feb. 10, 1962.

Slip decision: Jonesbury v. Hendricks, No. 67, U.S. Sup. Ct., No. 122, 1971 (30 U.S. Law Week).

Treatise: 4 Pomery, *Equity Jurisprudence* §428 (5th ed., Symonds, 1941).

Law Reviews: 43 *Yale L.J.* 418 (1932).

Civil Rights Act. See FAIR EMPLOYMENT PRACTICES.

Clayton Act. See ANTITRUST LAWS.

Class action. A lawsuit brought by one or more plaintiffs on behalf of other persons who are similarly situated or have suffered a similar wrong. For example, a group of stockholders in a corporation may bring a class action on behalf of all other stockholders who have a similar grievance.

Codicil. A supplement or addition to a will that alters, modifies, or explains but does not replace the original document.

Collection agency. An organization that specializes in the collection of past-due accounts. Agencies frequently press for collection more forcefully than the creditor might be willing to do. Charges for this service often amount to a percentage of monies collected. When the agency's routine collection measures fail, its attorney or the creditor's attorney commonly proceed to legal action against the debtor.

Commerce clause. The clause in Art. I, Sec. 8, of the Constitution that gives the federal government power to regulate "commerce among the several states"; it is the basis for all federal regulation of business. The purpose of the clause was to facilitate free trade among the states and to insure the uniform regulation of commerce free from local pressure and discrimination. See INTERSTATE COMMERCE, INTRASTATE COMMERCE; REGULATION OF BUSINESS.

Commodity Exchange Act. An act established to regulate commodity exchanges and dealers trading in commodity futures. It created a commission of five members appointed by the president with the approval of the Senate and known as the Commodity Futures Trading Commission, whose duty is to enforce the act. The commission regulates the commodity exchanges and dealers who trade in commodity futures (See Chapter 13/COMMODITY EXCHANGES.

Common law. A system of law, or body of legal rules, developed in England and carried over into the American legal system, which is derived from decisions of judges based upon accepted customs and traditions. It is known as the *common law* because it is believed that these rules were generally recognized and were in full force throughout England.

Common law is now the basis of the laws in nearly every state.

Statutes have been enacted to supplement and supersede the common law in many fields; the common law, however, still governs where there is no statute dealing with a specific subject and is continually expanding and changing. Although the common law is written, it is called the *unwritten law* in contradistinction to STATUTORY LAW enacted by the legislatures.

Complaint. The statement a plaintiff makes that sets forth the grounds upon which the plaintiff is suing a defendant and asks for damages or other relief. (See ANSWER.) The essential parts of a complaint are the caption, or heading; the introduction; body; the "prayer" or "wherefore" clause demanding judgment; signature of plaintiff or plaintiff's attorney; and verification, if required in the particular state. The complaint is usually the initial document filed in a court action.

Consent decree. A decree arrived at by agreement of the parties. Provided the agreement is approved by the court, it is entered into the record and is enforceable as a judgment. For example, in antitrust cases, a consent decree ends a controversy between the government and a private firm in a manner agreeable to both sides. The defendant agrees to changes in operating procedure that will bring him or her in agreement with antitrust laws. Once a federal court of appeals has reviewed the decree, the case is considered settled without the right of appeal to the Supreme Court. In a consent decree the defendant neither admits nor denies the allegations made by the plaintiff or the prosecution. See ANTITRUST LAWS; FAIR-TRADE ACTS; REGULATION OF BUSINESS; PRICING PRACTICES.

Consideration. See CONTRACTS, 4. *Consideration.*

Constructive receipt. The term *constructive* generally applies to that which amounts in the eyes of the law to an act, although the act itself is not necessarily performed. The law presumes an act to have been performed and applies the term to many situations. Constructive receipt of income usually constitutes taxable income. For example, any time during the year, commissions may be credited on a firm's books to a salesperson who may draw upon the firm to the amount of the credit. The commission is said to be constructively received. Whatever amount is credited to the salesperson would have to be reported by him or her as income in the year the amount was credited on the books, even if the money was not drawn until the following year.

Contracts. An agreement, enforceable at law, by which two parties mutually promise to give some particular thing or to do or abstain from doing a particular act. A contract may be formal or informal; it may be oral or written, sealed or unsealed, except that state statutes, usually designated as the STATUTE OF FRAUDS, require certain agreements to be in writing. A contract may be *executed*—one that has been fully carried out by both parties—or *executory*—one that is yet to be performed. It may be executed on the part of one party and executory on the part of the other. For example, the purchase of merchandise on credit, followed by delivery, is executed on the part of the seller and executory on the part of the buyer. Under the UNIFORM COMMERCIAL CODE (UCC), adopted by most states, a contract may be *express*—all terms definitely expressed in the oral or written agreement—or *implied*—the terms not expressed but implied by the law from the actions of the parties. For example, when a person gets on a bus, his or her action implies a contract with the transit company.

To be enforceable at law, a contract must have the following four elements:

1. *Offer and acceptance.* Before a contract can be formed, there must be an offer by one party, called the *offeror*, to do or to refrain from doing a certain thing and an acceptance of the proposal by another party, called the *offeree*. During the negotiation of a contract (particularly in real estate), there is often a counteroffer by the offeree. This requires the acceptance of new terms and/or price by the offeror.

An offer is considered open until it is revoked, rejected, or accepted or until after the lapse of a reasonable time. The only case in which an offeror cannot withdraw an offer before acceptance is the case in which he or she has entered into an OPTION contract, which is an agreement supported by the payment of a sum of money, or for some other consideration, to hold an offer open for a definite period. As a general rule, an offer, once accepted, cannot be withdrawn or revoked.

An acceptance is an indication by the offeree of willingness to be bound by the terms of the offer. The acceptance may take the form of an act, the signing and delivery of a written instrument, or a promise communicated to the offeror. Silence on the part of the offeree is not an acceptance, unless the previous dealings between the parties create a duty upon the part of the offeree affirmatively to reject the offer.

The acceptance must be unequivocal and must show an intention to accept all the terms of the offer. In the language frequently used by the courts, there must be a "meeting of the minds" of the offeror and the offeree.

2. *Competent parties.* All persons are presumed to have unlimited power to contract—except infants, insane persons or persons with impaired mental faculties, intoxicated persons, and corporations.

Under common law, a person is in infancy until the age of twenty-one, although many states provide that people become of age at eighteen, and other states provide that marriage removes the infancy status. Contracts by infants are not void, but generally, they may be disaffirmed by the infant. An infant is not bound by an executory contract unless he or she affirms the contract after coming of age. Contracts for necessities, such as food, clothing, shelter, medical care, and education, may be binding upon an infant.

Like infants, insane persons are not absolutely incapable of making contracts; their contracts are voidable, not void, and they may be held liable for necessities. A person who is so intoxicated that he or she is deprived of reason and does not understand the nature of some act is in the same position as a mental incompetent.

A corporation's ability to contract is limited by its charter and by various statutes.

3. *Legality of subject matter.* A contract is illegal if it calls for the performance of an act forbidden by law or against public policy. Usurious contracts (see USURY), for example, are generally held to be illegal. Federal and state laws make illegal those contracts that restrain trade, fix prices, or result in unfair practices.

4. *Consideration.* Something of benefit to the person making a promise must be given or some detriment must be suffered by the person to whom a promise is made to make a contract binding. *Consideration* is the price, motive, or matter inducing the contract; it may consist of (a) doing some act that one is not obligated to perform; (b) refraining from doing something that one would otherwise be free to do; (c) giving some money or property; (d) giving a promise.

Contracts under seal. The placing of a SEAL on a contract has lost the significance formerly attached to it, but it is still required in some states on contracts of major importance. Deeds, mortgages, and other conveyances of real estate are among the contracts requiring a seal in some states.

The UCC. In states that have adopted the Uniform Commercial Code, its provisions govern all contracts dealing with the sale of goods. The UCC defines a *contract* as the total legal obligation that results from the parties' agreements as affected by the code and any other applicable rules of law. An *agreement* is the bargain of the parties in fact as found in their language or by implication from other circumstances, including course of dealing or usage of trade or course of performance as provided in the code. A *bargain* is defined as an agreement of two or more persons to exchange promises or to exchange a promise for a performance.

Recision of contract. To *rescind* a contract means to abrogate, annul, void, or cancel it. The term is frequently used to refer to the action of one party to a contract.

Types of contracts. A *unilateral contract* is one in which one party promises to do something without receiving any promise, acceptance, or consideration from the other party. A *bilateral contract* is one in which *each* party has rights and duties. An *oral contract* is one not in writing and not signed by the parties. A *cost-plus contract*, often used in government contracts, is one in which a contractor is paid the cost of producing the goods or service plus a stated percentage, the percentage being the contractor's profit. An *output contract* is one in which one party promises to deliver an entire production and the other party promises to purchase it. See also ACKNOWLEDGMENT; ATTESTATION; TESTIMONIUM CLAUSE.

Cooling-off period. A period (usually thirty to ninety days) during which a union is barred from striking or an employer is barred from locking out its employees. Provided for under certain state labor laws and the Taft-Hartley Act, it is part of a policy covering management-labor disputes and designed to encourage peaceful settlements of such disputes.

Corporate law. See REGULATION OF BUSINESS; Chapter 10/CORPORATION.

Corpus Juris Secundum. *Corpus Juris* is a legal encyclopedia that represents a complete statement of the body of American law. The most recent update is *Corpus Juris Secundum* (usually cited as *C.J.S.* or *CJS*). A descriptive word index helps locate discussions and supporting authorities in the various volumes.

Courts. *Court* may refer to the law, the persons assembled under authority of the law, or a specific court of law. Proceedings are conducted for and on behalf of the parties to an action (e.g., a lawsuit) by attorneys at law. The written statements that are part of a court action are called *pleadings*. Court proceedings may consist of a simple, informal hearing in a judge's chambers or a complete, formal trial before a judge or judge and jury.

The American court system consists of the U.S. Supreme Court, other federal courts such as courts of appeal and district courts, and various systems in the states such as appellate courts and circuit courts. A case is brought and tried before a lower court and may proceed until it reaches the state's highest appellate court. A limited number of cases go on to be heard before the U.S. Supreme Court.

Court pleadings consist of a series of written statements of the claims and defenses of the parties to a court action. In most states, in a civil legal proceeding the plaintiff makes a written statement of the facts that caused him or her to bring the suit. The designation of this first pleading might be called a *complaint*, a *declaration*, a *libel*, or a *petition*. In some states, the first pleading in an equity action is designated as a *bill in equity* or a *bill of complaint*. A summons, or its equivalent, is issued and served upon the person against whom the action is brought. The defendant answers the summons and complaint, defending himself or herself by raising legal arguments or by denying the facts stated by the plaintiff. When the case is submitted to the court for a decision, the judge decides controversies about legal points; a jury, or a judge acting in place of a jury, decides questions of fact.

Covenants. Written agreements between two or more persons promising to do or not to do something. *Covenants in deeds* are promises made between parties in the sale of real property. Some deed covenants impose restrictions on the use of real property in a development and apply to all parcels or units in the project. *Covenants of title* are assurances that a deed conveys good and unencumbered title to real property.

Default. A failure to perform what is required by law or duty, for example, the failure of a borrower to repay a loan according to terms of the transaction. When someone is sued and fails to appear in response to a summons, he or she is in default.

De facto corporation. See Chapter 10/DE FACTO CORPORATION.

De jure corporation. See Chapter 10/DE JURE CORPORATION.

Department of Labor. A department of the federal government whose aim is "to foster, promote, and develop the welfare of the wage earners of the United States, to improve their working conditions, and to advance their opportunities for profitable employment." The Department of Labor plays an essential part in the interpretation and administration of a number of federal labor statutes. Other major jobs are to collect facts and statistics, to promote and develop a nationwide system of public employment offices and cooperate with the states in administering a federal-state unemployment insurance program, to handle problems of reemployment of veterans, to safeguard the welfare of apprentices; to promote industrial safety, to promote the welfare of wage-earning

women, to take part in international labor affairs.

States also have a department of labor or an equivalent agency whose authority is defined by statute.

Derivative action. A lawsuit by a stockholder of a corporation, often against an officer of the corporation, to compel management to act properly to protect the corporation's rights. Before a suit can be brought, the complaining stockholder must ask the board of directors to take the desired action, and it must refuse to do so.

DIALOG. A computerized information service accessible through WESTLAW and other systems. It includes business databases such as *Standard and Poor's Register, Thomas' Register, Dun & Bradstreet,* and *Chase Econometrics.* See WESTLAW; LEXIS.

Disability benefit laws. Certain states have enacted laws providing for cash benefits to workers who lose wages because of nonoccupational illness or accident. These laws are the counterpart of workmen's compensation insurance laws (see Chapter 16/WORKER'S COMPENSATION INSURANCE), which provide benefits for occupational injuries or illness.

An employer may be insured under a state plan or under a voluntary plan approved by the state agency administering the program. Benefits payable under such insurance usually are geared to the average weekly wage of the claimant, with the claimant being paid a fixed percentage thereof. As in the case of unemployment compensation, the benefits are paid for a certain period up to a maximum number of weeks. There is usually a waiting period before a claimant is eligible for benefits, which is designed to prevent claims for brief illnesses. Eligibility depends on whether the claimant is within the labor market and specifically within that portion of the labor market intended to be protected.

Disaffirm.   To repudiate or take back consent once it is given; to refuse to stick by former acts.

Discharge of contract.   To end the obligation specified by an agreement; to release the parties from their obligations under the contract. Discharge of contract may occur by performance or the carrying out of the contract terms; by mutual agreement to end the contract; by impossibility of performance because certain assumed factors no longer exist; by operation of law, such as a change in the law; or by breach, or failure of one party, thereby discharging the other of obligations.

Discrimination.   See FAIR EMPLOYMENT PRACTICES.

Docket.   In legal practice, a brief formal record of the proceedings of a court of law or the book or file containing such record. It is sometimes used to describe the list or calendar of cases scheduled to be heard at a specific term, prepared by the clerk of court.

Doing business.   See INTERSTATE COMMERCE, INTRASTATE COMMERCE.

Eminent domain.   The power of federal, state, and local governments to appropriate property for public use or the public welfare. When such property is taken, the owner is reimbursed according to a fair appraisal and has the right to sue for a greater amount. Public service corporations (public utility corporations) are also given the power of eminent domain. See also Chapter 10/PUBLIC UTILITY CORPORATION.

Endorsement.   *On back of legal documents.*   See Chapter 5/LEGAL BACK; Chapter 14/CHECK, *Endorsement.*

Estoppel.   A bar raised by law preventing a person from taking a position, denying a fact, or asserting a fact, in court, inconsistent with the truth as established by judicial or legislative officers or by his or her own deed or acts, either express or implied. For example, *A* sells *B* a house that he (*A*) does not own, giving *B* a covenant and warranty deed, in which he warrants that he has title to the house. Later, *A* obtains title from the actual owner and attempts to eject *B* on the ground that *A* is now the true owner and *B* is not. *A* would be estopped from disputing what he formerly warranted, namely, that he was the true owner when he sold the house.

Execution.   **1.** *Of judgment.* A legal writ directing an officer of the law to carry out a judgment is an execution of judgment.
   2. *Of instrument.* The signature and delivery of a written instrument

constitutes execution of the instrument.

Fair employment practices. Government regulations aimed at the prevention of discrimination in employment are embodied in state "fair employment practices acts" and in the federal Civil Rights Act. The purpose of these acts is to guard against discrimination because of an employee's race, creed, color, sex, or national origin. The law prohibits asking questions on employment blanks that would indicate the race, creed, color, or national origin of the applicant.

The federal government has moved to prevent discrimination in employment by enactment of the Civil Rights Act of 1964. Under the act, it is unlawful for an employer engaged in an industry affecting commerce and having fifteen or more employees to fail or refuse to hire or to discharge any individual or otherwise to discriminate against any individual with respect to employment because of race, color, religion, sex, or national origin. It is also unlawful to limit, classify, or segregate an employee in a way that would adversely affect his or her status as an employee on the basis of race, color, religion, sex, or national origin. Discrimination is also prohibited by laws governing contracts covering federal projects or federally funded projects.

Fair Labor Standards Act. See Wage-hour law.

Fair-trade acts. All but a few states have passed laws dealing with resale-price maintenance, known as "fair-trade" acts. The typical state fair-trade law does two things: (1) It permits a manufacturer of branded merchandise to make a contract with a distributor whereby the distributor agrees to sell the product at a fixed price. (2) It provides for the enforcement of prices fixed in this way against those who sign price-fixing agreements.

Later a law was passed providing that minimum resale-price agreements can be enforced against nonsigners as well as signers, if the state law applies to nonsigners. Courts in several states, however, have held "nonsigner" provisions to be unconstitutional.

Some of the advocates of fair trade have since given up requiring their distributors to contract to sell their products at fixed prices.

Featherbedding. See Chapter 10/ Featherbedding.

Federal Trade Commission Act. This act, passed in 1914, declares that unfair methods of competition (e.g., misrepresenting the terms under which a product is sold) in interstate commerce are unlawful. It was an innovation in regulatory laws in that it is in the nature of preventive legislation. It seeks to preserve competition as far as possible by supervisory action of the commission. Its specific purpose is to stop "unfair methods of competition" and "unfair or deceptive acts or practices." The statute does not define these terms, and the courts have generally allowed great flexibility of interpretation and application. The scope of these terms is determined on a case-by-case approach.

Fiduciary.   Someone or some organization that manages money or property or both for another party and who acts in the capacity of trust and confidence and therefore has special ethical responsibilities and duties.

Franchise.   A right to sell or rent a company's products or services or methods of operation and use its name to do business. Also, a right conferred by the government such as the right to vote or to form a corporation. See also Chapter 12/FRANCHISE TAX.

Fraud.   False representation of some fact that causes deception. Fraud consists of (1) a false and material representation by someone who knows it is false or is ignorant of the truth, (2) intent that the false representation be relied on by someone else in a manner reasonably contemplated, (3) someone's ignorance of the false representation, (4) someone's rightful reliance, and (5) injury to someone caused by the misrepresentation.

Legal, or *constructive*, *fraud* is an act or omission that causes damage to another. *Positive fraud*, or *fraud in fact*, is an act or omission with intent to defraud. *Extrinsic fraud* is an intentional act whereby one party prevents a losing party from having a fair trial of all issues in a controversy. *Intrinsic fraud* is fraudulent representation that influences a judgment about something. *Fraud in the factum* arises when there is a difference between

an instrument actually executed and the one intended to be executed. *Fraud in the inducement* occurs when something false intends to and does persuade someone to execute an instrument or make an agreement.

Garnishment.   The right of a creditor to compel a third party owing money to, or holding money for, a debtor to pay the money to the creditor instead of to the debtor. The third party against whom the proceedings are brought is called the *garnishee*. Not only wages and salaries but trust funds, insurance disability payments, and the like may be garnisheed. The laws that govern the right of garnishment differ considerably in the various states, and in some states it is referred to as a *factoring process* or *trustee process*.

Guaranty.   The term is used interchangeably with *suretyship* by courts and lawyers as well as laypersons, although a distinction may be drawn about the degree of liability wherein the surety is primarily liable upon the engagement and the guarantor is secondarily liable and not chargeable with nonperformance until notice is given. A contract of guaranty or of suretyship is a contract whereby one person agrees to be responsible to another for the payment of a debt or the performance of a duty by a third person. It must be in writing and is not enforceable if made orally.

The term *guaranty* (or *guarantee*) is often loosely used in the sense of WARRANTY. In a strict legal and commercial sense, it is the essence of a contract of guaranty that there should be a principal, liable directly to perform some act or duty. An agreement by a third party guaranteeing the honest and faithful performance of a contract of sale is a *contract of guaranty;* an agreement in a sales contract "guaranteeing" the efficient performance of a product for a certain number of years is a *contract of warranty.*

Holder in due course. The transferee of a NEGOTIABLE INSTRUMENT who acquires the instrument under conditions defined in the UNIFORM COMMERCIAL CODE (Article IX as adopted by state legislatures).

ICC. See INTERSTATE COMMERCE COMMISSION.

Indemnification of directors and officers. Reimbursement of corporate directors and officers for litigation expenses and/or damages they may be required to pay under a court decision. In suits brought by stockholders against directors and officers for alleged misconduct in office, the accused directors or officers are often put to great expense to defend themselves. Often they cannot recoup these expenses as costs even if they are vindicated. Therefore, some states have laws permitting corporations to reimburse directors and officers for such litigation expenses under specified circumstances. Indemnify means to protect and hold harmless.

Indemnity. An express or implied contract to compensate someone for loss, damage, expense, or trouble. The indemnity may be payable to the indemnitee or someone else authorized to accept payment.

Indenture. A term used formerly to refer to a formal paper; identical copies were provided for all signers of the document.

Independent contractor. Someone hired to perform a service who is responsible for the end results of the effort. The hirer has no control over the contractor's methods of performance or other details of work such as one would have over an employee's labor. Usually, the independent contractor has no employee benefits. See Figure 1 for a sample agreement

INDEPENDENT CONTRACTOR: FIGURE 1: Agreement form

INDEPENDENT CONTRACTOR AGREEMENT FORM

Agreement dated _____, 19 ____, between

_____, hereinafter called (Company)

(Corporation) (Last Name) and _____, hereinafter

called (Contractor) (Last Name).

WHEREAS, THE (Corporation) desires to enter into this agreement with (Contractor) to the extent and upon the terms and conditions hereinafter set forth, and

WHEREAS, (Contractor) is willing to enter into this agreement with respect to his/her time, services, and workmanship upon the terms and conditions hereinafter set forth,

NOW, THEREFORE, in consideration of the premises and the mutual agreements hereinafter set forth, the parties hereto agree as follows:

1. Relationship Between Parties. The (Contractor) shall perform and contract as an independent contractor and nothing herein contained shall be construed to be inconsistent with this relationship or status.

2. Duties/Services. (as required)

3. Time Requirements. (as required)

4. Compensation. (as required)

5. Workmanship. (as required)

6. Working Supervision by (Contractor). The (Contractor) agrees to be responsible for and will supervise the execution of all works covered by this agreement.

7. (Contractor) to Furnish Labor and Materials. The (Contractor) shall furnish at his/her own expense all labor, materials, equipment, and other items necessary to carry out the terms of this contract.

IN WITNESS WHEREOF, (Corporation) has caused this agreement to be executed in its corporate name by its corporate officers, and (Contractor) has set his/her hand and seal, as of the date and year first above written.

(CORPORATION):   (CONTRACTOR):

By _____   _____

Attest _____
           Secretary

CORPORATE SEAL

a hirer may use to confirm the status of someone retained for a job.

Injunction. A writ issued by a court of equity restraining a person or corporation from doing or continuing to do something that threatens or causes injury or requiring the defendant to do a particular act. Injunctions may be classified as prohibitory and mandatory. A *prohibitory injunction* restrains the commission or continuance of an act. Thus a prohibitory injunction may restrain a board of elections from placing a certain candidate's name on the ballot. A *mandatory injunction* commands acts to be done or undone. For example, a mandatory injunction may compel a property owner to open a road he or she had closed by constructing a fence across it, thus depriving another property owner of the use of the road.

Injunctions may also be classified as (1) restraining orders, (2) temporary injunctions, and (3) permanent injunctions. A *restraining order* may be granted without notice to the opposite party, for the purpose of restraining the defendant until the court has heard an application for a temporary injunction. A *temporary restraining order* (commonly abbreviated TRO) is used frequently in domestic relations problems. A *temporary injunction* is granted on the basis of the application, before the court has heard the case on its merits. It restrains the defendant during the litigation of a case and may be either dissolved or made permanent when the rights of the parties are determined. Tempo-

rary injunctions are also called preliminary, interlocutory, or injunction *pendente lite. Permanent injunctions* are granted on the merits of the case. They are often called final or permanent injunctions.

Installment contract. See Chapter 13/INSTALLMENT SALE.

Interstate Commerce Commission. An independent, presidentially appointed commission that was created to regulate water or land transportation—railroads, water carriers, freight forwarders, and motor carriers—engaged in interstate commerce. (See INTERSTATE COMMERCE, INTRASTATE COMMERCE.) It is an administrative board invested with powers of supervision and investigation.

Interstate commerce, intrastate commerce. The Constitution gives the federal government power to regulate "commerce among the several states" (Art. I, Sec. 8). (See REGULATION OF BUSINESS.) But it does not define either commerce or interstate commerce. The courts decided originally that *commerce* meant buying and selling. Hence if the buying and selling is part of an interchange of commodities or intangibles between states, it is *interstate commerce.* Today, the courts avoid giving the term *interstate commerce* a comprehensive definition; however, it includes transportation of persons and property, transmission of power, and communication—radio, television, telephone, and telegraph.

Interstate commerce also comprises general movements of commodities. For example, on different occasions the courts have upheld the regulation of both buying and selling of livestock at the stockyards and buying and selling of grain futures. (See Chapter 13/COMMODITY EXCHANGES.)

Under the broad interpretation given the commerce clause, Congress has power to regulate interstate commerce and to regulate local (i.e., intrastate) incidents thereof.

A company is engaged in *intrastate commerce* as distinguished from interstate commerce if most of its business (isolated cases of interstate commerce do not count) takes place entirely within a state and is not part of an interchange or movement of tangible or intangible commodities.

As a general rule, a state cannot prohibit foreign corporations (corporations chartered in other states) from doing interstate business within its borders; however, it can prohibit them from doing intrastate business unless they meet certain qualifying conditions.

If a corporation "does business" in a state without "qualifying" (i.e., meeting the state's requirements), it may become subject to certain fines or it may lose the right to sue in state courts on contracts made within the state.

It is important to differentiate between intrastate and interstate commerce under most of the federal regulatory laws as well. For example, the Fair Labor Standards Act (WAGE-HOUR LAW) regulates labor conditions in industries not only "engaged in commerce" but also in the "production of goods for commerce" or "in

any process or occupation necessary to the production." The Supreme Court held that the act covered an owner who employed personnel to service his or her building in which tenants produced goods for interstate commerce.

The regulatory laws are not consistent in their definition of what is interstate commerce, although the tendency is toward uniformity. Thus businesspeople cannot take for granted that because they are in "intrastate commerce" under one law and exempt from federal regulation, they have a similar exemption under other laws.

Joint Tenancy.   See Chapter 15/ JOINT TENANCY.

Judgment.   An adjudication by a court, after a trial or hearing, of the rights of the parties. Broadly, an adjudication by a court of law or of equity is considered a *judgment*, but technically, an adjudication by a court of equity is a *decree*. See COURTS. The sentence in a criminal case is the judgment. If, following judgment, the debtor fails or refuses to pay the award of the court, the judgment or debtor may direct that a writ of execution be issued by the clerk of court. Pursuant to the terms of the writ, the sheriff may seize and sell any property of the debtor not exempt by law in satisfaction of the judgment. If no property is available for seizure to satisfy the judgment, the court may order that the debtor's wages be garnished.

If a party fails to obey the order of a court, he or she may be found in contempt. If the party against whom a judgment is rendered appeals to a higher court, execution of the judgment is stayed pending the higher court's decision.

Jurat. A clause in an official certificate attesting that the affidavit or deposition was sworn to at a stated time before an authorized officer, such as a NOTARY PUBLIC. It is often referred to as the "sworn to" clause. The term *jurat* is not commonly used; *acknowledgment* is used more frequently. The form of jurat varies slightly in the different states. In a few states, the jurat recites the title of the officer and the state, or state and county, in which he or she is authorized to act. In a few other states, the name of the affiant is repeated in the jurat. The most common form of jurat is:

Subscribed and sworn to before me this _____ day of _____ 19 ___.

_____

Notary Public

Signature of notary. The notary signs immediately beneath the jurat and affixes the notarial seal and the expiration date of his or her commission. In some states, the expiration date precedes the signature.

Labor Department. See DEPARTMENT OF LABOR.

Laches. Unreasonable delay in bringing suit or seeking remedy in an equity court. To plead laches as a defense to a suit, a defendant must show that he or she suffered from the plaintiff's delay in bringing suit.

Legal tender. Coin, money, or other medium that, according to law, must be accepted in payment for all transactions expressed in money terms.

LEXIS. A legal database, or reference library, regularly updated, offered by Mead Data in New York City that can be accessed by certain data terminals. Users receive a printout of selected legal information that is used primarily for legal research to locate cases previously decided or for legal precedent. For current rates and access instructions, contact Mead Data Central, 200 Park Avenue, New York, NY 10016. See also WESTLAW; DIALOG.

Libel and Slander. Both libel and slander tend to damage a person's character or reputation by false and malicious statements (*defamation*). *Slander* is oral, or spoken, defamation of one person by another in the presence of a third party. *Libel* is written or printed defamation of one person by another published before a third party. A libelous statement, for example, might be made in a letter or newspaper.

Lien. An encumbrance imposed on property by which the property is made security for the discharge of an obligation. Some liens, particularly those on personal property, must be accompanied by actual possession of the property: a *lienor* (the holder of a lien) who parts with possession loses the lien. Other liens, particularly those on real estate, need not be accompanied by possession: the lienor gives notice of the lien he or she claims by a public record of it. Some of the common liens are vendor's lien, mechanic's lien, mortgage lien, and tax lien.

Liquidated damages. The amount specified in a contract to be paid for a loss resulting from *Breach of contract*. The amount must be in proportion to the actual loss or the agreement cannot be enforced.

Lockout. The refusal of an employer to permit employees to work, a tactic used in labor (employer-union) disputes.

Miller-Tydings Act. See ANTITRUST LAWS.

Monopoly. Under COMMON LAW, an abuse of free commerce whereby one company or group endeavors to get exclusive control over strategic sources of materials, means of production or distribution within a given area for a product or service. Possessing such sole rights, the monopolist is in a position to dictate prices and terms and to stifle potential competition until it is exterminated or reduced to insignificance. The common law consistently condemned complete and partial monopolies in any recognizable guise.

The common-law principles have been clarified and extended through statutory enactments by the federal government and by the states. See ANTITRUST LAWS; REGULATION OF BUSINESS.

Monopoly price. A price charged by a monopoly or, generally, the prices set in markets that are subject to some degree of monopoly control or restraint of trade. See ANTITRUST LAWS; FAIR-TRADE ACTS; REGULATION OF BUSINESS; PRICING PRACTICES.

National Labor Relations Act. (Wagner Act, 1935.) The Wagner Act of 1935, which sought to reduce labor disputes, defined five labor practices as unfair to employees:

1. To interfere with, restrain, or coerce employees in the exercise of their rights to collective bargaining and self-organization

2. To prevent or dominate the formation of any labor organizations

3. To discriminate in hiring and other employment practices (e.g., against union members)

4. To discriminate against employees who filed charges or testified under the act

5. To refuse to bargain collectively with the employees' representative

In 1947 the act was amended by enacting the Labor-Management Relations Act—the Taft-Hartley Act. This act outlawed the closed shop, defined unfair union practices, and established a "cooling-off" period and right-to-work laws.

National Labor Relations Board. A federal agency that administers the National Labor Relations Act. Its chief responsibilities are to arrange elections among workers to select the labor organization that will be the bargaining agent of the workers and to investigate and render decisions on unfair labor practices.

National Reporter System. The published opinions of all federal and state supreme courts. These opinions are first published in weekly pamphlets called *advance sheets.* Thereafter they are published in the bound volumes of the National Reporter System. In addition to cases from state supreme courts and federal courts, a digest for each region is given. See also CITATIONS TO LEGAL AUTHORITIES.

Negotiable instrument. A written instrument, signed by a maker or drawer, containing an unconditional promise or order to pay a certain sum of money, which can be passed freely from one person to another without a formal assignment in a manner that constitutes the transferee the holder. If payable to bearer, the instrument may be negotiated simply by delivery; if payable to order, it is negotiated by endorsement of the holder, completed by delivery.

The UNIFORM COMMERCIAL CODE (Article 9) governs negotiable instruments in all states and territories except those few states that still retain the older Uniform Negotiable Instruments Law. The code states the manner in which a negotiable instrument shall be transferred, and it fixes the rights and duties of the maker, the payee, the holder, and the endorser. For example, under the law an endorser of a negotiable instrument vouches for its genuineness. If it is a forgery, the endorser is liable to the holder in due course of the instrument after delivery. See HOLDER IN DUE COURSE.

Strictly speaking, documents of title (such as order bills of lading and warehouse receipts) are not negotiable instruments because they do not contain an order to pay a sum of money. However, various statutes have given certain documents of title the quality of negotiability. They are known as *quasi-negotiable instruments.*

Nonnegotiable instrument. A written instrument, title to which cannot be transferred from one holder to another without formal assignment. A valid contract may be nonnegotiable because of its express terms or because it contains or fails to contain matters affecting negotiability. See NEGOTIABLE INSTRUMENT.

Notarize. To acknowledge or attest a document as a NOTARY PUBLIC. A notary public should observe the following details when notarizing a document:

1. If the document recites that it is "under seal," the notary should be sure that the signature to the instrument is followed by "L.S." or "Seal." However, this convention is obsolete in most jurisdictions.

2. When a corporation is a party to an instrument, the notary should be sure the corporate seal is impressed on the instrument if required (see also Chapter 10/CORPORATE SEAL); seals are usually required on corporate instruments.

3. The notary should fill in all blanks on the certificate of ACKNOWL-EDGMENT or the JURAT and should make sure the instrument is fully signed and properly witnessed, if required.

4. The notary should show the date of the expiration of his or her commission, when required.

5. The notary should be sure to impress his or her notarial seal on the certificate when required. Some states do not require a notary's seal on papers acknowledged within the state.

6. The notary should be sure that rubber stamps make legible imprints. A black stamp pad is preferable because black ink photocopies more distinctly than other inks.

7. If the notary does not personally know the party executing the instrument, he or she should require proper identification and should be satisfied that the party has executed the instrument willingly and without duress.

Although not required, it is a good idea for the notary to keep a record of the documents notarized, indicating the person signing the document, date of the signature, county, and title of the document or a description. Books may be purchased from office-supply stores for this purpose. If any questions come up, this record will substantiate whether a notary notarized a particular document.

Notary public (pl. notaries public). A commissioned officer of a state, whose powers and duties con-sist, among others, in administering oaths, certifying to the genuineness of documents, and taking acknowl-edgments. In some states, a notary is authorized to act only in the county in which he or she is com-missioned; in others, he or she is qualified to act throughout the state. Frequently, the secretary is a notary public. His or her principal duty as such is taking acknowledgments. (See ACKNOWLEDGMENT.)

A commission as a notary public is a trust; it confers certain powers upon the notary as well as requiring that he or she perform certain duties. In exercising those powers and du-ties, a notary should observe punctil-iously the "letter of the law."

A notary public should never take an acknowledgment without the ac-tual appearance of the individual making the acknowledgment. To do so is illegal. Nor should a notary ever antedate or postdate a certifi-cate of acknowledgment. To do so constitutes fraud and deceit in the exercise of one's powers. See also NOTARIZE.

Novation. The substitution of a new contract, or debtor or obligor, for an existing one. The substitution must be agreed to by all of the parties, for example: *A* sells a car to *B*, who makes a small down payment and agrees to pay the balance in installments. Unable to make the payments, *B* sells the car to *C*, who agrees to make the payments to *A*. If *A* agrees to release *B* from the con-tract and to look to *C* for payment, a novation is created.

Offer and acceptance. See CONTRACTS, 1. *Offer and acceptance.*

Official reports. Court opinions prepared by an appointed reporter for publication by authority of statute. The best known group of unofficial reports is the NATIONAL REPORTER SYSTEM.

Open shop. A business in which an employer may hire nonunion personnel, although in some cases all employees must join the union within a specified period.

Option. An agreement, usually in consideration for the payment of a certain sum of money by the offeree, to hold an offer open for a definite period. The offer ceases to be an offer and becomes a contract of option; it cannot be withdrawn until the option period expires. Although an option is generally based upon a consideration, a few states require no consideration if the contract is in writing. Others recognize an option under seal as binding, because a seal, at COMMON LAW, indicates consideration. The consideration for an option is not returnable to the optionee if he or she fails to take up the option; it is, however, usually applied to the purchase price if the offer is accepted.

Patent. An exclusive right granted by the federal government for a fixed period to make, use, and sell an invention. A person who perfects a new machine, process, or material, or any new and useful improvement of them, or who invents or discovers and reproduces a distinct and new variety of plant may make application to the government for a patent for it. The person to whom a patent is granted is called the *patentee.* Patent rights are issued in the form of *letters* and run to the patentee, heirs and assigns, generally for a period of seventeen years. A *design patent,* which is an ornamental design to be placed on an article of manufacture, runs for three and one-half, seven, or fourteen years, according to the application made by the patentee. A patent is not renewable. Anyone producing a patented product without the owner's consent may be compelled to pay damages.

A patent application is usually prepared by an attorney. A covering letter should accompany the application and enclosed material:

The Commissioner of Patents
United States Patent Office
Washington, D.C. 20013

Dear Madam or Sir:

We are enclosing for filing the application of (inventor) for Letters Patent (name or title), Case _____. We are also enclosing our check for $ ____ to cover the first government fee.

Sincerely,

Personal property. A right or interest, protected by law, in something that is not land or anything permanently attached to land and is capable of ownership. (See Chapter 15/REAL PROPERTY.) Generally, personal property is movable. It may be tangibles (also called *chattels*), such as money, gold, merchandise, or any movable

object susceptible to physical possession, or intangibles, such as contracts
or stocks. (See CHOSE IN ACTION.)
Personal property may be an interest
in land: a ninety-nine-year lease may
be personal property. Products of the
soil become personal property when
severed from the land: trees and
crops that are sold while attached to
the land constitute real property, but
when severed from the land, they
constitute personal property.

Piercing the corporate veil. An
expression used by the courts that
means they will disregard the corporate entity, because it is being used
for purposes contrary to public policy
(see Chapter 10/CORPORATE ENTITY),
or for fraud, or in a situation in which
the owner uses the corporation to
conduct his or her personal affairs.
The result of piercing the corporate
veil is that stockholders, directors, or
officers may be held personally liable
for the acts of the corporation.

Pledge. Turning over personal property to a lender as security until a debt
is paid. Stocks, bonds, and certain
pawned articles are commonly used
as collateral for a loan in this manner.
See also Chapter 13/PLEDGE.

Power of attorney. A written instrument in which the principal (the
person giving the power of attorney)
authorizes another to act for him or
her. The instrument may be a blanket
authorization, but more commonly it
authorizes the agent to represent the
principal in one specific transaction,
as the closing of a real estate deal, or
to do a certain act continuously, as

the signing of checks. The person
appointed is commonly called an
attorney-in-fact. A power of attorney
may be revoked at the will of the
principal, unless it was given to the
agent for a consideration. The death
of the principal constitutes an instantaneous revocation, but, again, there
is no revocation when consideration
was given for the power.

Preemptive rights. In corporations,
the right of a stockholder to have
first chance at buying new stock
issues, before the shares are offered
to outsiders. Stockholders may determine whether they have preemptive
rights by examining the Articles of
Incorporation.

Price discrimination. See PRICING
PRACTICES.

Price fixing. See FAIR-TRADE ACTS;
PRICING PRACTICES.

Pricing practices. The federal government and most states have laws
that regulate pricing policies and
practices. On the whole, they cover
the following fields:

1. *Resale-price maintenance.* The
Miller-Tydings Act (see ANTITRUST
LAWS) and corresponding fair-trade
acts in most of the states permit
individual sellers to establish minimum prices that subsequent sellers
may not undercut. See FAIR-TRADE
ACTS.

2. *Discounts and price discrimination.* The Robinson-Patman Act prohibits sellers from charging different
prices for the same product if the

effect is to injure competition. See ANTITRUST LAWS; FAIR-TRADE ACTS.

3. *Advertising allowance.* Advertising allowances must be granted to all customers on proportionately equal terms.

4. *Brokerage payments.* The Robinson-Patman Act prohibits an individual seller from making brokerage payments to buyers, under the theory that brokerage payments should be paid only to agents for services rendered. Such payments must not be used to conceal discriminatory discounts.

5. *Basing-point and zone pricing.* Prices that include delivery costs must accurately reflect actual shipping costs. Any pricing that includes delivery costs and tends to injure competition may be prohibited under the Sherman Act or the FEDERAL TRADE COMMISSION ACT. (See ANTITRUST LAWS; Chapter 13/BASING-POINT SYSTEM.)

6. *Sales below cost.* There is *no* federal legislation that forbids sales below cost. Such sales are liable to attack, however, under the Sherman Act and the Federal Trade Commission Act if they are part of a systematic combination to drive competitors out of business.

7. *Price advertising.* The Federal Trade Commission will take action if the public interest is threatened by advertising that deludes buyers about prices.

8. *Price fixing.* The Sherman Act and the Federal Trade Commission Act expressly outlaw price fixing of any kind that is not allowed under the Miller-Tydings Act. (See FAIR-TRADE ACTS.)

Principal. A person who authorizes another person (an AGENT) to do things for him or her; a person directly involved with committing a crime; a person primarily or ultimately responsible or liable in a legal obligation.

Protest. A formal certificate attesting the dishonor of a negotiable instrument after negotiation. (See Chapter 13/DISHONOR.) A protest is usually made by a notary public but may be made by a responsible citizen, in the presence of two witnesses. The certificate must state (1) the time and place of presentment, (2) the fact that presentment was made and the manner thereof, (3) the cause or reason for protesting the bill, and (4) the demand made and the answer given or the fact that the drawee or acceptor could not be found. The protest is attached to the dishonored instrument or a copy of it. Notice of protest is then sent to the parties who are secondarily liable (drawer and endorser). Protest is required only when a bill of exchange or check drawn in one state (or country) and payable in another is dishonored, but as a matter of business practice, domestic instruments are often "protested." The word *protest* is loosely applied to the process of presenting an instrument for payment, demanding payment, and giving notice to the drawer or endorser.

Quasi. (Latin). A term in legal phraseology to indicate that one subject resembles another, with which it is compared, in certain characteristics, but that there are intrinsic and material differences between them. Thus a *quasi-contract* is an obligation similar to that of a contract, which does not arise from an agreement between parties but from some relation between them or from a voluntary act by one of them.

Ratification. The approval of an act that had not been binding previously; ratification, or affirmance, reverts and becomes effective as of the date the act was performed. An infant (see CONTRACTS, 2. *Competent parties*) may ratify, or affirm, contracts after he or she reaches majority; a principal may ratify, or affirm, the unauthorized acts of an agent; a corporation may ratify, or affirm, the unauthorized acts of its officers. A corporation cannot ratify or affirm the acts of its incorporators before the corporation was formed because it was not in existence and could not possibly have entered into a contract at that date. (See also Chapter 13/CORPORATION; INCORPORATORS.) It may, however, *adopt* the acts of the incorporators.

Regulation of business. All business is subject to some degree of state and federal regulation. Regulatory bodies created by law act in diverse fields such as communications (Federal Communications Commission), public utilities (state Public Service Commissions), finance (Securities and Exchange Commission), railroads (Interstate Commerce Commission), banking (Federal Reserve Board and State Banking Commissions), and general trade (Federal Trade Commission).

The laws aim to prevent (1) specific abuses arising from the action of individuals or groups against the "public interest" (pure food and drug laws); (2) abuses caused by firms or individuals acting against each other or in combination against the public (antitrust laws, including fair-trade and unfair-practice acts); (3) abuses caused by employer-employee differences (wages and hours laws, and collective bargaining laws).

Regulation is achieved in many ways. Independent regulatory bodies, such as the Federal Trade Commission, head the list in importance. Such bodies are part executive in their administration of the law, part judicial in their enforcement, and part legislative in their establishment of rules. In some instances, the laws are administered by the executive branch of the government, for example, the Interior Department's Bureau of Mines and Commerce Department's Pure Food and Drug Administration. Punitive taxes, such as the state chain-store tax, are imposed to regulate certain businesses. They are aimed to encourage one activity and discourage another. Licenses, such as those required to sell liquor or practice a profession, regulate numerous fields. Franchises or certificates of convenience and necessity are used principally in public utility regulation—the franchise as permission to operate in a specified area and the certificate as a permit for expansion or alteration to satisfy the public necessity. (See ANTI-TRUST LAWS; BLUE SKY LAWS; FAIR-TRADE ACTS; PRICING PRACTICES; INTERSTATE COMMERCE, INTRASTATE COMMERCE.)

Representative action. A lawsuit brought by one stockholder to redress injury to many or all stockholders in a corporation.

Resale price maintenance. See FAIR-TRADE ACTS; PRICING PRACTICES.

Rescind. To undo or unmake a contract.

Right-to-work laws. Laws that prohibit an employer from denying employment to someone because of membership or nonmembership in a union.

Robinson-Patman Act. See ANTI-TRUST LAWS.

Sale. An agreement whereby the seller transfers property to the buyer for a consideration, called the price. To be enforceable, a sale must have all of the elements necessary to the validity of a CONTRACT, namely: (1) offer and acceptance, (2) competency of parties, (3) legality of subject matter, (4) consideration. The sale of "goods" is governed by the UNIFORM COMMERCIAL CODE in those states adopting the code. Under the code, a *sale* is defined as the passing of title from the seller to the buyer for a price.

Seal. An impression upon an instrument. Material affixed to an instrument and intended as a seal, or the writing of the word *Seal* or *L.S.* (*locus sigilli,* Latin for "place of the seal") after the signature is considered a seal. The process of affixing the seal is referred to as *sealing* the instrument, and the instrument then becomes a *sealed* instrument. If an instrument is to be sealed, the testimonium will so indicate. (See TESTIMONIUM CLAUSE; Chapter 10/ CORPORATE SEAL.) In most jurisdictions, the COMMON LAW rule regarding seals has been modified in judicial decision or statutory enactment. The UNIFORM COMMERCIAL CODE provides that the affixing of a seal to a contract for the sale of goods does not constitute such writing of a sealed instrument. In many states, the requirement of a seal being affixed to contracts or other instruments has been abolished, and others require a seal only on certain instruments, such as deeds.

Securities Act of 1933. A federal statute that regulates the offering of securities for sale to the public by use of the mails or the channels of Interstate Commerce. It is administered by the Securities and Exchange Commission. (See Chapter 13/SECURITIES AND EXCHANGE COMMISSION.) The function of the act is to require that full and accurate information concerning the security be made available to purchasers and the public and that no fraud be practiced in connection with the sale of securities.

This act is designed to control initial issues of securities; however, not all securities are subject to its terms. For example, if the security issue is offered solely to residents within one state where the issuer is also resident and doing business, it is exempt.

Securities Exchange Act of 1934. A federal statute enacted to insure maintenance of fair and orderly securities markets and to prevent excessive use of credit for securities transactions. It was enacted for the purpose of controlling dealings in securities subsequent to the initial issuance. It is administered by the Securities and Exchange Commission. (See Chapter 13/SECURITIES AND EXCHANGE COMMISSION.) The act purports to provide, in the public interest, means to prevent abuses and unsocial practices and to insure free competitive markets. Exchanges are required either to register with the commission or to secure exemption on the ground that registration is impractical because of the small volume of business done.

In addition to providing for the registration of exchanges, and control over exchange rules, and the registration and regulation of securities, the act provides for regulation of credit, short selling, and options, and prohibits wash sales and matched orders and the dissemination of misleading information. (Refer to Chapter 13/ SHORT SALE; WASH SALE.) The act requires corporate officers to disclose holdings in their own corporation to prevent misuse of information by insiders.

Service of process. The law requires giving notice of a suit to a defendant, which makes him or her a party to the suit and compels the defendant to appear in court or suffer judgment by default. The means of compelling a defendant to appear in court is called *process;* giving the notice is known as *service of process.* (See SUMMONS.) Although service is generally personal or upon the agent of the defendant, under some circumstances service is made by publication, that is, by publishing a notice in a newspaper a required number of times.

In some jurisdictions, service may also be accomplished by attachment of some property of the defendant found within the jurisdiction. Many states have adopted *long-arm statutes,* which designate a method for service of process on out-of-state defendants. Usually, service is affected by service upon some state official such as the secretary of state who is deemed to be the agent of the defendant.

Sherman Antitrust Act. See ANTITRUST LAWS.

Signatures. See ATTESTATION, Figure 1; CONTRACTS.

Slander. See LIBEL AND SLANDER.

Social Security Act. A federal act designed primarily to safeguard individuals against some of the major hazards of life arising out of old age, unemployment, disability, and poverty. In the case of the death of a person receiving social security benefits, the survivors may be eligible for benefits. Originally, the act included taxing provisions for the payment of social security benefits, and these taxes were, and still are, commonly known as "social security taxes." The taxing provisions of the act have been superseded by the Federal Insurance Contributions Act (FICA), the Self-Employment Contributions Act, and the Federal Unemployment Tax Act. (See Chapter 12/SOCIAL SECURITY TAXES; STATE UNEMPLOYMENT INSURANCE TAX.)

State fair employment practice acts. See FAIR EMPLOYMENT PRACTICES.

Statute of frauds. A common law concept enacted by statute, with variations in all the states, providing that certain contracts cannot be enforced unless they are in writing, signed by the party against whom the contract is sought to be enforced. (Consult the statutes in your state for a list of pertinent contracts.) The writing need not be a formal document signed by both parties—a written note or memorandum of the transaction signed by the party to be bound by the agreement is sufficient.

Statute of limitations. A state statute that limits the time within which legal action may be brought. There are usually different statutes of limitations for particular kinds of civil action (e.g., personal injury or breach of contract) or criminal prosecution. State and federal statutes also limit the time within which certain crimes can be prosecuted. The purpose of the time limitation is to make it impossible to bring suit many years after a cause of action originates, during which time witnesses may have died or important evidence may have been lost. When a debt is involved, it is possible to interrupt (or "toll") the running of the statute—that is, to lengthen the period in which action may be brought—by obtaining a payment on the debt or a promise to pay. A promise to pay a debt that has been barred by the statute of limitations does not require new consideration (see CONTRACTS, 4. *Consideration*), but many states require such a promise to be in writing. The statutes often differentiate between oral and written contracts.

Statutory law. Rules formulated into law by legislative action. The Constitution of the United States and the constitutions of the various states are the fundamental written law. All other law must be in harmony with the constitutions, which define and limit the powers of government.

Congress, cities and towns, and other governmental units find in the constitutions their authority, either express or implied, to enact certain laws. These legislative enactments are called *statutes* and constitute the greater part of the written or statutory law. Statutory law supplements and supersedes COMMON LAW. Statutes are often implemented by regulations.

Statutory redemption. See Chapter 13/REDEMPTION, 2.

Stipulation. A formal agreement between lawyers or parties on opposite sides of a lawsuit. It is usually in writing and may concern court procedure, for example, an agreement to extend the time in which a pleading is due. An agreement to settle a lawsuit is also called a stipulation. Or the parties may agree to or "stipulate" to certain facts.

Subpoena. A writ or order commanding the person named in it to appear and testify in a legal proceeding. Anyone who fails to obey a subpoena without reasonable cause may be subject to contempt of court and liable for damages sustained by the aggrieved party. A *subpoena duces tecum* is a writ commanding a person to appear in court with particular objects or documents.

Summons. A legal notice requiring a person to answer a complaint within a specified time. The act of serving the summons is commonly referred to as SERVICE OF PROCESS. A copy of the summons must be left personally with (served upon) the person against whom it is directed. A corporation is served with process when a copy of the summons is left with an agent of the corporation as indicated in the records of the secretary of state. In a few jurisdictions, the summons may be left with an adult member of the defendant's household or with some person at the defendant's place of business. An attorney-at-law is often authorized to accept service of a summons for a client. When the summons is served, the process server endorses the summons when, where, and upon whom served, with an affidavit to that effect. This procedure is called the "return of the summons" or "return of service." After return of the summons, the court has jurisdiction over the defendant.

In most states, a summons consists of three principal parts: (1) the caption, or heading; (2) the body, wherein the defendant is commanded to appear; and (3) the signature and seal of the clerk of the court.

Suretyship. See GUARANTY.

Taft-Hartley Act. See NATIONAL LABOR RELATIONS ACT.

Tenancy in common. See Chapter 15/TENANCY IN COMMON.

Testimonium clause. Clause with which a written instrument or document, such as CONTRACTS, deeds, and wills, closes. It immediately precedes the signature. It is a declaration by the parties to the instrument that their signatures are attached in testimony of the preceding part of the instrument. The testimonium clause is not to be confused with the *witness* or *attestation* clause. (See ATTESTATION.) The testimonium clause relates to those who sign the paper as witnesses, not as parties to the instrument.

Often, the testimonium clause will guide the secretary in setting up the signature lines. It will indicate (1) what parties are to sign the instrument, (2) what officer of a corporation is to sign, (3) whether the instrument is to be sealed, and (4) whether a corporate seal is to be attested. For example, from the following clause, which is a form commonly used, the secretary knows that the president of the corporation is to sign, that the seal is to be affixed, and that the secretary of the corporation is to attest the seal:

IN WITNESS WHEREOF, Alvin Corporation has caused its corporate seal to be hereto affixed, and attested by its secretary, and these presents to be signed by its president, this 26th day of October, 1983.

On the other hand, from the following clause, also commonly used, the secretary knows that the instrument is not to be sealed:

IN TESTIMONY WHEREOF, the parties hereto have hereunto set their hands the day and year first above written.

Typing the testimonium clause. The introductory words to the testimonium clause, *in witness whereof, in testimony whereof,* and the like, are usually typed in solid caps. The word following begins with a lowercase letter, unless it is a proper name. A comma usually follows the introductory words.

Tort. A civil wrong or injury inflicted otherwise than by a *breach of contract.* Elements of tort are (1) a wrongful act or a wrongful failure to act and (2) an injury to some person. Tort gives the injured party the right to sue for any damages resulting from the defendant's breach of some duty. Persons (including minors) and corporations are liable for torts. For example, a visitor to a department store (even one having no expressed intention to make a purchase but intending merely to examine the merchandise) can recover damages from the proprietor for injuries caused by the negli-

gent maintenance of the store premises. Action arises not from breach of contract but from breach of duty.

Trademark. A mark, symbol, or design that is used to distinguish a particular make of merchandise or an individual service. The purpose of the trademark is to point out the source of the article so it may be readily identified as a product of a certain quality. In this sense, the trademark is a symbol of goodwill. Registration of a trademark with the U.S. Government Patent and Trademark Office is not obligatory, for a trademark rightfully belongs to the first person who has used it. Furthermore, federal registration applies only to the use of trademarks in interstate and foreign commerce. Although federal law now offers wider protection, state registration may still be sought in certain states for protection in intrastate commerce.

Registration does not automatically protect the owner from litigation. Once the trademark has been registered, the Patent and Trademark Office is empowered to refuse the registration of infringing ideas, but the owner has to bring suit actually to restrain the use by another who has unlawfully appropriated his or her trademark.

Certificates of registration for trademarks are in force for twenty years, subject to cancellation at the end of six years unless the registrant files an affidavit within the year preceding the expiration of a six-year period. The affidavit is intended to show continued use of the trademark or nonuse under special circumstances without any intent to abandon the mark.

Trespass. The common meaning of *trespass* is unauthorized entry on the land of another. It also means an unlawful and violent interference with the person or property of another. In the practice of law, an *action in trespass* is brought to recover damages sustained by the plaintiff as the immediate result of trespass.

The COMMON LAW recognizes a distinction between *trespass*, which is a direct injury, and *trespass on the case*, which is an indirect or consequential injury; however, in modern practice, the distinction has lost much of its importance since an action of TORT comprehends all cases in which a remedy is afforded.

Trust. A holding of property subject to the duty of applying the property, the income from it, or the proceeds for the benefit of another, as directed by the person creating the trust. A trust is created when *A* transfers property to *X*, the trustee; and *X* undertakes to apply the property and income from it for the purposes and in the manner directed by *A*. The elements of an ordinary trust are (1) the *trustor* (also called *settlor*, *donor*, or *grantor*), who furnishes the property to be put in trust; (2) the *subject matter* or *property* that is put in trust (called the *trust principal*, *corpus*, or *res*); (3) the *trustee*, who holds the property and administers the trust; and (4) the *beneficiaries*, for whose benefit the trust exists. A trust may be created by oral declaration, by writing, or by operation of law. The trust may be established by will (*testamentary trust*) or by deed (*inter vivos* or *living trust*). A trust may be created for any purpose not in contravention of law or public policy. It is frequently used as a vehicle for transacting business or as part of an estate plan. A person might put property in trust to pay the income to a spouse for life and then to pay the principal to the children. In these situations, the receiving spouse would be an *income beneficiary* (or *equitable life tenant*) and the children would be *remaindermen*. See Chapter 15/LIFE ESTATE.

Trust deed. Also called a *deed of trust*, *trust agreement*, and *trust indenture*. A document whereby one person transfers legal ownership of land and what is on it to another person. See Chapter 15/TRUST DEED OR DEED OF TRUST; MORTGAGE. An agreement between a corporation and a trustee who serves as guardian of bondholders' interest would set forth the terms and conditions of a bond issue and the rights, duties, and powers of the parties involved.

Unemployment insurance. A form of unemployment protection that pays a weekly income to unemployed persons for a specified period. Funds are derived by means of a payroll tax. The amount of funds paid to the unemployed person is based on the amount of money paid into that person's account by his or her employer according to the employee's income.

Unfair competition. See ANTITRUST LAWS; MONOPOLY; PRICING PRACTICES.

Unfair employment practice. Action by an employer or union that violates a FAIR EMPLOYMENT PRACTICES law or executive order prohibiting discrimination in employment because of race, creed, color, sex, or national origin.

Unfair practices. See ANTITRUST LAWS; FAIR-TRADE LAWS; REGULATION OF BUSINESS; PRICING PRACTICES.

Uniform Commercial Code. A comprehensive body of laws and principles covering the field of commercial transactions. The Uniform Commercial Code (UCC), which has replaced the older Uniform Negotiable Instruments Law in most states, was first published in 1952 and has been revised several times since. It consists of nine articles intended to "simplify, clarify, and modernize the law governing commercial transactions; to permit the continued expansion of commercial practices through custom, usage, and agreement of the parties; and to make uniform the law among the various jurisdictions" (Article 1).

Usury. Contracting for or receiving something in excess of the amount of interest allowed by law for the loan or forbearance of money, as in the sale of goods on credit or under the installment plan. In some states, a lender who charges a usurious rate of interest loses the right to collect any interest, although a few states permit this party to collect the legal rate. In some states, both principal and interest are forfeited. Service charges, investigation fees, and commissions charged by an agent are not usually considered interest and may be added to the legal rate without usury. In some states, the parties to a contract may agree upon a rate of interest higher than the legal rate but within a statutory limit; in a few states, they may agree on any rate. In some states, loans to corporations, but not to individuals, may be made at more than the legal rate. Certain types of loans, such as small personal loans, are not covered by the usury law but are subject to special laws.

Void, voidable. That which is *void* is of no legal force or effect; that which is *voidable* may be rendered void. For example, a gambling or wagering contract is void (see CONTRACTS, 3. *Legality of subject matter*), whereas an infant's contracts are merely voidable at his or her election (see CONTRACTS, 2. *Competent parties*).

Voting trust. See Chapter 10/ VOTING TRUST.

Wage-Hour Law. A federal law that establishes minimum wage and overtime requirements and restricts child labor in companies engaged in interstate commerce (see INTERSTATE COMMERCE, INTRASTATE COMMERCE); also known as Fair Labor Standards Act. A 1963 amendment, known as the Equal Pay Act, seeks to eliminate wage differentials based on sex in companies covered by the Fair Labor

Standards Act. Despite its length and numerous provisions, the act deals essentially with three fields: wages, hours of work, and child labor. The law sets up a minimum hourly wage that varies according to the type of employment and a maximum of forty hours per week at the "regular rate" of pay. The employee must be paid time and one-half the regular rate for hours over forty. "Regular rate" means the hourly rate actually paid for the normal nonovertime work week. It is defined so as to exclude gifts, bonuses, certain premium payments, payments for vacations and illness, profit sharing and pension payments, and the like.

The Wage-Hour law is the major federal statute regulating wages and hours. Although it applies only to interstate commerce, the act has a very wide coverage, because the courts have broadly interpreted interstate commerce. There are state statutes dealing with wages and hours, but they are not generally as comprehensive as the Fair Labor Standards Act.

Waiver. The surrender, either expressed or implied, of a right to which one is entitled by law.

Waiver of notice is a voluntary and intentional surrender of the right to be notified of an event or fact, such as a meeting. The writing setting forth such surrender is also called a waiver.

The directors of a corporation may waive notice of a meeting before it is held, but in the absence of a permissible statute, directors who are absent from a meeting, the time and place of which were not fixed, cannot waive the required notice after it has been held.

Waiver by All Directors of Notice of Meeting (Annual, Regular, or Special)

We, the undersigned, being all of the directors of _____ Corporation, a corporation organized and existing under the laws of the State of _____, do hereby waive any and all notice as provided by the laws of the State of _____, or by the Articles of Incorporation or Bylaws of the said Corporation, of the time, place, and purpose of a _____ (*insert annual, regular* or *special*) meeting of the Board of Directors of said Corporation, and do hereby fix the _____ day of _____, 19___, at _____ o'clock in the _____ noon, as the time, and the office of the Corporation, _____ (*Street*), _____ (*City*), _____ (*State*), as the place, and the following as the purposes of the said meeting:

(Insert purposes of meeting.)

We hereby consent to the transaction of any business, in addition to the business herein noticed to be transacted, that may come before the meeting. Dated _____, 19___.

_____
_____
_____

(To be signed by all directors)

Notice of a meeting of stockholders, whether required by statute, charter, or bylaws, may be waived by the stockholders. Waivers may be either in writing or by action.

Waiver of Notice of Special Meeting Signed by Individual Stockholders

I, the undersigned, being a stockholder of the _____ Corporation, a corporation organized under the laws of the State of _____, holding _____ (____) shares of stock of the said Corporation, do hereby waive any and all notice required by the laws of the State of _____, or by the Articles of Incorporation or Bylaws of said Corporation, and do hereby consent to the holding of a special meeting of stockholders of said Corporation, on the _____ day of _____, 19 ____, at _____ o'clock ____ M., or any adjournment or adjournments thereof, at the office of the Corporation __ (Street), _____ (City), _____ (State), for the following purposes:

(Insert purposes.)

I do further consent to the transaction of any business, in addition to the business noticed to be transacted, that may come before the meeting.

Dated at the City of _____, State of _____, this _____ day of _____, 19 ____.

_____
(Signature of stockholder)

Warranty.   Affirmation of a material fact or promise by the seller, which acts as an inducement for the buyer to make a purchase. A warranty may be *express* (a direct statement made by the seller) or *implied* (one that is indicated by the nature of the contract). The UNIFORM COMMERCIAL CODE has adopted this distinction and has added a class of warranties that are stated neither as express nor as implied. This additional class of warranties consists of warranties of title and against infringement. Warranties relate to many things: fitness of the goods sold for a special purpose; merchantability of the goods; title to real or personal property; and quiet enjoyment of premises. All representations made by an applicant for insurance, whether material or not, are deemed warranties. The term *guaranty* is loosely used in the sense of warranty. The common guaranty of a product is, strictly, a warranty and not a guaranty. (See GUARANTY.) Any warranty made by a seller that proves to be false gives the buyer a right of legal action.

WESTLAW.   A computerized legal reference library, or database (similar to LEXIS), offered by West Publishing Company. Users with an appropriate data terminal can access the library and receive a printout of selected legal information that is used primarily for legal research to locate cases previously decided or for legal precedent. For current rates and access instructions, contact West Publishing Company, Box 3526, St. Paul, MN 55165. See DIALOG; LEXIS.

Without recourse.   A phrase used in an endorsement that relieves the endorser from assuming liability in the event the maker fails to pay the instrument when due. See Chapter 14/CHECK, *Endorsement.*

Witness to signature. See ATTESTA-TION.

Workers' compensation laws. Laws, passed in most states, that provide for compensation to workers injured during employment. Employers are liable even though they take appropriate precautions and even though the employee is negligent. The injury does not have to take place on the employer's property but must be within the scope of employment. Companies pay into a fund to cover such liabilities. See also Chapter 16/WORKER'S COMPENSATION INSURANCE.

Writ. An order issued by a court, or judge, in the name of the state, for the purpose of compelling the defendant to do something mentioned in the order.

A *writ of error* is a court order commanding judges that the record be examined to correct some alleged error in proceedings. A *writ of execution* is a court order directing a sheriff to seize and sell a debtor's property to pay a creditor out of the proceeds.

CHAPTER 10

BUSINESS ORGANIZATION
AND MANAGEMENT

Abstract company. A business organization that searches land records and summarizes all recorded instruments that affect title to a particular tract of land. See also Chapter 15/ABSTRACT OF TITLE; LAND DESCRIPTION.

Advertising agency. A business firm that primarily plans and creates advertising on order from its clients, the advertisers. Many advertising agencies also perform market research and provide other related services.

Affiliated companies. Companies that are related through ownership of their stock by a common PARENT CORPORATION or through a community of interest. The community of interest may arise through the same person or persons serving as directors or merely through the influential ownership of stock of one person or a closely associated group.

Affirmative action. A term used in the National Labor Relations Act in regard to the employment of minority groups and women. Affirmative action requires remedial action by employers for wrongdoing; such action includes reimbursement of lost wages and reinstatement. Under various federal laws that prohibit discrimination, affirmative action may be required to remedy the effect of past discrimination, usually on the grounds of race, sex, or national origin, and to insure that discrimination will not take place in the future.

Agency. The relationship that exists when one person authorizes another to act for him or her. The one granting the authority is the *principal;* the one authorized to act is the *agent.* For an agent to act, a *third party,* with whom the agent contracts, is necessary. An agency relationship is created when a person gives a power of attorney or a proxy and in other situations. (See Chapter 9/POWER OF ATTORNEY; Chapter 3/PROXY.) An agency may be *general*—the agent has broad powers to represent the principal; or the agency may be *special*—the agent represents the principal for a specific purpose or for a series of routine tasks. The principal is liable for the acts of his or her agent within the scope of the agency.

Agribusiness. A combination of agricultural and business operations, for example, crop and livestock production, the manufacture and distribution of agricultural equipment and supplies, and the processing, storage, and distribution of farm products; large corporate agricultural operations as opposed to small family owned farms; business closely related to or combined with agriculture.

Alien corporation. A business organization incorporated outside the United States and its territories. The state statutes make no distinction between an alien and a FOREIGN CORPORATION, except in those few states that do not recognize alien corporations.

Annual report. A report containing the audited financial statements for the period sent by a corporation at the close of its fiscal year to its stockholders and others. (See Chapter 11/ BALANCE SHEET; INCOME STATEMENT; FISCAL PERIOD.) Usually, it contains a letter from the president or chairperson of the board of directors of the corporation with his or her comments on the year's operations and plans for the future. The trend is toward attractive and readable reports, which give full information about the progress of the company, as well as frank and understandable accounts of its financial condition. The reports attract attention by means of the style and quality of their artwork, layout, paper, typography, printing, and reporting. (See various terms defined in Chapter 8, "Writing, Editing, and Publishing," for more about the production aspects.) The principal reason the annual report has been humanized is that top executives have learned the report can serve several purposes and not be merely an obligatory report to stockholders. The report can (1) build stockholder interest in the company, (2) create better understanding between the company and its employees, and (3) improve industrial and public relations.

Arbitration. See Chapter 9/ARBITRATION.

Articles of incorporation. See CORPORATION.

B/L. See BILL OF LADING.

Backlog. The accumulation of unfinished or incomplete work, materials, or orders.

Bankruptcy. See Chapter 9/BANKRUPTCY.

Bill of exchange. See Chapter 13/ BILL OF EXCHANGE.

Bill of lading. A contract for transportation between the shipper and the organization furnishing the transportation that defines the terms under which the carrier agrees to transport the goods. It is also a receipt for the goods and a document of title to the goods. A negotiable bill of lading, or an *order*, states that the goods are to be delivered to the order of a specific person.

Bill of sale. See Chapter 9/BILL OF SALE.

Board of directors. A group of individuals elected by stockholders, who, *as a body,* manage a corporation.
Who is qualified to act as director. Any person who is legally competent to contract can be a director, unless the statute, charter, or BYLAWS provide otherwise. Ownership of stock is generally, but not always, a statutory charter or bylaw requirement. Some statutes require residence in the state of incorporation by one or more directors; a few require United States citizenship.
Number of directors. The minimum number, usually three, is generally fixed by statute; the maximum is also sometimes fixed by statute. The actual number within statutory limits is fixed by charter or bylaws of the corporation and may be revised by amendment.
Election. The charter, or Certificate of Incorporation, usually names the first board of directors; statutes give stockholders the right to elect directors annually thereafter.
Term of office. The term is usually fixed by the bylaws. Directors continue to hold office and must discharge their duties until their successors are elected.
Resignation. A director may resign at any time unless prevented by the corporation's charter or bylaws or by statute of the state of incorporation. A director who has made a contract with a corporation to serve a definite period is liable for damages caused by his or her resignation before the expiration of that period.
Powers. The directors have power to conduct the ordinary business activities of the corporation. They are free to exercise their independent judgment upon all matters before them, without interference by the stockholders, except in matters requiring stockholders' consent.
Liabilities. Directors must act in good faith and with reasonable care and must handle the affairs of the corporation with prudence. They are not personally liable for losses resulting from accident or mistakes of judgment. Their relation to the corporation is fiduciary, and they are not to use their positions of trust and confidence to further their private interests. Directors also incur liabilities under certain federal and state statutes.
Meetings. Generally, directors can bind the corporation by their acts only when they are assembled in a meeting. Bylaws usually provide for the place of the meeting and the method of calling it. A majority of the members of the board is neces-

sary to constitute a quorum. A director cannot vote by proxy and is forbidden to vote on any matter in which he or she is personally interested. (See Chapter 3/QUORUM; PROXY; DIRECTORS' MEETINGS.)

Compensation. Directors are not legally entitled to compensation for performing their duties as directors or for attending meetings (see DIRECTORS' FEES) in the absence of charter or bylaw provision. State corporation laws rarely regulate compensation of directors. Directors who perform duties beyond the scope of a director's duties are entitled to compensation for their services. See INTERLOCKING DIRECTORATES.

Budget. A financial plan, prepared by a person or organization, that estimates income and expenses for a specified period such as a year; an appropriation for a designated purpose.

Business corporation. A CORPORATION organized for the purpose of doing business and making profits, as distinguished from a CHARITABLE CORPORATION or NONPROFIT CORPORATION. Thus a manufacturing or railroad corporation ordinarily is a business corporation, and a corporation created for the opening and maintenance of an orphan asylum ordinarily is a nonprofit corporation. Both are established in accordance with state statutes.

Business organization, forms of. The legal form of a business organization determines (1) the manner of distributing profits; (2) who controls the business; (3) the risk, or liability, to creditors of those who have contributed ownership capital to the business. An individual entering business, either as an active owner or as an investor, is interested, therefore, in the relative advantages and disadvantages of each form of organization. Factors that influence his or her decision are (1) the ease with which capital can be raised; (2) the extent of risk—whether liability of the owners to creditors is limited or unlimited; (3) stability of existence—whether the organization is disrupted by death, insanity, or bankruptcy of an owner; (4) method by which ownership can be transferred; (5) taxation; (6) flexibility of management and control; (7) clarity of the legal status of the form of organization; (8) ease of organization; (9) power to do business in any state.

The chief forms of business organization in the United States are (1) the sole or individual proprietorship (see PROPRIETORSHIP, SOLE), (2) the PARTNERSHIP, and (3) the CORPORATION. Other less common forms are (1) the JOINT STOCK COMPANY, (2) the LIMITED PARTNERSHIP, and (3) the MASSACHUSETTS TRUST. See the particular form of organization for an explanation of how the above-mentioned factors apply to each of them.

Bylaws. Rules adopted by a corporation to regulate its conduct as a corporate entity and to define and determine the rights and duties of its stockholders and the rights, powers, and duties of the directors and officers. Bylaws are permanent, except insofar as they may be amended.

The power to adopt and amend bylaws rests with the stockholders. The board of directors, however, may be authorized to adopt and amend bylaws by the statute under which the corporation is organized, by the corporation's articles of incorporation (see CORPORATION), or by resolution of the stockholders. The bylaws may limit but not extend the powers granted to a corporation in its charter. To insure the protection of the stockholders and directors, legal counsel generally drafts the bylaws.

Bylaws usually relate to the following topics: BOARD OF DIRECTORS; OFFICERS OF A CORPORATION; CORPORATE SEAL; Chapter 3/STOCKHOLDERS' MEETINGS; Chapter 13/DIVIDENDS; STOCK; Chapter 9/BOOKS AND RECORDS (CORPORATE).

Preparation of bylaws. Most bylaws of a corporation include the following:

1. Location of stockholders' meeting
2. Date and hour of such meeting
3. When notice of annual meeting must be given
4. Who may call special stockholders' meetings
5. When notice of such special meetings must be given
6. Percentage of stock constituting a quorum
7. Location of directors' meetings
8. When regular directors' meetings are to be held
9. When notice of such regular meetings must be given
10. Who may call special directors' meetings
11. When notice of such special meetings must be given
12. Number of directors constituting a quorum
13. Officers who are to sign/countersign checks
14. Officers who are to sign/countersign stock certificates
15. Specification of end of fiscal year

Capital. In business, the actual wealth or total assets of the business in money, tangible property (such as a factory), or intangible property (such as goodwill). A distinction is ordinarily made between working capital and fixed capital. See Chapter 11/WORKING CAPITAL; FIXED ASSETS; Chapter 9/CAPITAL.

Capital stock. See Chapter 11/CAPITAL STOCK; Chapter 13/STOCK.

Capital structure. This term refers to the kinds of securities that make up the capitalization of a corporation, that is, whether capitalization consists of a single class of stock, several classes of stock with different characteristics, various issues of bonds, a large or small surplus, and the like. (See Chapter 11/CAPITALIZATION.) *Capital structure* is used interchangeably with *capitalization*, although it carries a connotation of the various components of the structure, whereas *capitalization* generally refers to the structure as a whole. The term is also used interchangeably with *financial structure*. Equity securities (corporate stock) and long-term debt securities (bonds) are usually the principal parts of a company's capital structure. To enable the corporation to raise permanent capital with a minimum of effort and cost, these elements must be kept flexible. Since flexibility is affected by the terms of the securities that are outstanding, upon the creation of any class of stock or bond issues (see Chapter 13/STOCK; BOND), considerable attention is given to the characteristics of the securities issued by the corporation.

Cartel. An association of producers that enters into an agreement to regulate output, divide markets, and establish prices at which it will sell its products. Although American corporations have entered into cartel arrangements with foreign corporations, there are no purely American cartels, since they violate the antitrust laws by fostering monopolistic practices.

Certificate of incorporation. Sometimes called *charter, articles of incorporation,* and *articles of association.* It tells what a CORPORATION is authorized to do. Each state's laws provide what must and may be included in the certificate. Most certificates must include:

1. Corporate name
2. Purpose or nature of business
3. Place of business

4. Amount of capital stock and number of shares (see Chapter 13/STOCK; Chapter 9/CAPITAL)
5. Maximum allowable indebtedness
6. Duration of corporate existence
7. Incorporators' names and residences
8. What officers are to conduct corporate affairs (or statement that this is specified in BY-LAWS)
9. Number of directors and names and addresses of first-year directors
10. Statement that indicates compliance with requirements regarding subscription to, and payment for, capital stock, plus amount that must be paid in before commencing business
11. Name and address of registered agent (person to receive summons in case of suit)

Preparation of certificate. Most attorneys provide clients with at least three additional copies, one for the headquarters office, one for the minute book, and another file copy. The certificate should be typed double spaced on good quality eight-and-one-half-by-eleven-inch bond paper. Words such as *Board of Directors, Bylaws,* and *Certificate of Incorporation* should be capitalized. Numbers must be written out and followed by figures in parentheses. Numbered or lettered items and similar material should be indented at least five spaces. Since a charter, or certificate, is usually a sealed document, (*SEAL*) or (*L.S.*) should be typed after each signature line.

Filing the certificate. After the copies have been signed (some states require that an original copy be filed with each public official), the required number of copies must be sent to the proper state official with a letter of transmittal, for example:

We are enclosing an original and two conformed copies of the Certificate of Incorporation of Johnson Development, Inc. Please record the original of the Certificate in your offices and certify and return to us the conformed copies.

We are also enclosing our check for $70 to cover the organization tax, $10; the filing and indexing fee, $25; the recording fee, $15; the fee for certification of copy for recording, $10; and the fee for certification of one extra copy, $10.

If the certificate is acceptable, you will receive a certificate of approval and receipt for tax and fees. Conform the office copy and file the certified copy with the proper local official, if required. Affix the tax receipt in the minute book.

Chairperson of the board. The presiding officer of a corporation's board of directors. Frequently, he or she is the senior person in the corporate leadership and acts as a spokesperson for the corporation in its public relations. The chair is sometimes given specific powers, such as the power to call a director's meeting.

Charitable corporation. A corporation organized and operated for charitable or nonprofit purposes, such as a public charity, hospital, or school, as distinguished from a BUSINESS CORPORATION, which exists for business and profit purposes.

Charter. See CORPORATION.

Close corporation. A corporation whose capital stock is held by a limited group, in contrast to one whose stock is sold to the public generally. Usually, a close corporation is comparatively small, but there are some large closely held companies; for example, until 1956 Ford Motor Company was a close corporation.

Closed shop. A business in which employees holding certain jobs must be members of a particular union.

Collection agency. See COLLECTIONS.

Collections. All organizations must have some means of collecting past-due accounts. Many offices send their own routine follow-up notices. Organizational systems and sample letters of such activity are described in Chapter 1/FOLLOW-UP SYSTEM; Chapter 7/ FOLLOW-UP LETTERS; CREDIT AND COLLECTION LETTERS. Some organizations also rely on attorneys and collection agencies to handle collections. The attorney or agent will send a planned series of follow-up notices and letters, culminating in a suit if payment is not received after other suitable measures have been taken. Most collections are handled on a contingent-fee basis at standard Commercial Law League rates.

Committee. A group of individuals, usually small in number, or even consisting of one person, to whom an organization or authority delegates the study, consideration, management, or decision of a particular matter or problem or a category of matters or problems. In corporate affairs, details of study and recommendation for decision of many matters are entrusted to committees such as the EXECUTIVE COMMITTEE and the FINANCE COMMITTEE. These committees are appointed by RESOLUTION of the BOARD OF DIRECTORS in accordance with the provisions of the BYLAWS. As a general rule only members of the board are eligible for membership on the committees of the board.

Common carrier. An organization that offers communication services such as telex transmission.

Common stock. See Chapter 13/ STOCK.

Conditional sale. See Chapter 13/ CONDITIONAL SALE.

Committee. See TASK FORCE.

Conglomerate. A diversified corporation formed by acquiring and consolidating companies in different industries. See also CONSOLIDATION.

Consignment. A shipment of merchandise from the owner (*consignor*) to another party (*consignee*), who becomes a selling agent of the owner. A consignment is not a sale, since the title to consigned goods remains with the consignor. A consignment contract must follow closely certain legal requirements: (1) The consigned goods must be kept apart from the other merchandise or must be marked clearly and distinctly as the property of the consignor. (2) The proceeds from the sale of the consigned goods must be kept separate from the consignee's general funds.

Consolidation. A combination of two or more corporations into a new CORPORATION in a manner prescribed by the laws under which the existing corporations are organized. When the plan goes into effect, the constituent corporations go out of existence and only the new corporation, with the combined rights, privileges, franchises, properties, and liabilities of the constituents, remains. See MERGER.

Consortium. A group of persons or companies that combine their resources to undertake some enterprise. See also SYNDICATE.

Controller (comptroller). Chief accounting officer of a CORPORATION. Unlike the office of TREASURER, the office of controller is not compulsory under state statutes, and many small and medium-sized corporations do not have a controller. He or she is usually the head of the accounting division, prepares analyses, and interprets business results. The controller is responsible for tax matters and is in charge of preparing the annual budget covering all activities of the business.

Corporate entity. The concept of the CORPORATION as a fictitious person or entity, separate and distinct from its stockholder-owners. The corporate entity, not individual stockholders, directors, or officers, contracts, sues, and transacts corporate business in general. The separate entity of the corporation is disregarded, and the individual owners are held liable for the acts of the corporation when it is used for improper purposes. (See Chapter 9/ PIERCING THE CORPORATE VEIL.)

Corporate seal. An engraved device used by a CORPORATION to make an impression upon its business papers. The seal usually bears the name of the corporation and the year and state of incorporation. A corporation's BYLAWS usually provide that any instrument signed on behalf of the corporation shall be impressed with the corporate seal. An officer of the corporation impresses the seal on the instrument when it is signed. In many cases, the corporate secretary must bear witness, or "attest," to the fact that the imprint on the paper is the seal of the corporation. When the document states that the seal is to be attested, the following is typed on the left-hand side of the page, opposite the signature lines:

ATTEST

_____
    Secretary

Corporation. An organization formed under a state statute for the purpose of carrying on an enterprise in such a way as to make the enterprise distinct and separate from the persons who are interested in it and who control it; "an artificial being, invisible, intangible, and existing only in contemplation of law" (*The Trustees of Dartmouth College* v. *Woodward*, 17 U.S. 518, 636 [1819]).

A corporation must be organized strictly in compliance with the laws of the state in which it is incorporated. Legal advice is essential. The laws vary, but all of them provide that a certain number of persons, generally three or more, may form a corporation (1) by filing in the office of a designated state official a statement giving certain specified information, (2) by paying initial taxes and filing fees, and (3) by holding certain organization meetings at which specified details or organization must be completed. The required statement is known as the *Articles of Incorporation,* the *Certificate of Incorporation,* or the corporate *Charter.* A corporation is referred to as a *domestic corporation* in the state in which it is incorporated, as a *foreign corporation* in any other state, as an *alien corporation* if incorporated in a country outside the United States and its territories.

A corporation has certain fundamental characteristics that have made it the most popular form of business organization. They are (1) easy transferability of ownership, (2) continuity of existence, and (3) limited liability of stockholders.

The ownership of the corporation is represented by its capital stock, which is divided into identical units or groups of identical units called shares. (See Chapter 11/CAPITAL STOCK; Chapter 13/STOCK.) These shares are represented by written instruments called certificates of stock. The owners of the shares are called stockholders. Every stockholder has the right to transfer his or her shares—a right based on the inherent power of a person to dispose of property. Since the shares of stock of a corporation can be transferred by sale or otherwise from one owner to another without affecting the corporate existence, the corporation enjoys continuous succession. The existence of the corporation is not disturbed by death, insanity, or bankruptcy of individual stockholders or by change of ownership. The liability of the stockholders is limited as follows: the owner of fully paid stock ordinarily has no liability to creditors; the owner of stock that has not been fully paid is liable, in case of insolvency of the corporation, to pay, as far as is necessary to satisfy creditors, the amount required to make his or her stock fully paid. A share of stock is considered fully paid when the corporation has received the full par value or, if the stock is without par value, when it has received the price fixed for it on original issuance.

In a large corporation with many stockholders, those who have contributed to the capital of the business do not ordinarily conduct its affairs. Management is concentrated in the hands of a BOARD OF DIRECTORS elected by the stockholders. The directors may own only a small portion of the stock. Stockholders cannot bind the corporation by the acts merely because they are stockholders. (See STOCKHOLDER.)

The corporation is generally in a better position to raise large sums of capital than any other form of organization because it can sell stock and other securities to the public. Since purchases of stock can be made in any number of shares, large numbers of widely scattered investors may become stockholders.

Since a corporation owes its existence to the state in which it is organized, no other state need recognize its existence. However, all of the states permit foreign corporations to do business in the state by complying with special state requirements. (See FOREIGN CORPORATION.)

Public corporations are subdivisions of the state, such as cities and tax districts, as well as government-owned corporations. *Publicly held corporations* are corporations whose stock is sold to the public. Sale of stock is regulated by the Securities and Exchange Commission, which administers the Securities Act of 1933 and related subsequent statutes. *Corporations not for profit*, such as religious groups, do not have capital stock and do not pay dividends. *Corporations for profit*, which do have stock and do pay dividends, include moneyed corporations, such as banks, public service corporations (e.g., utility companies), and private business corporations (e.g., a machine tool company). See also CHARITABLE CORPORATION.

Incorporating procedure. Secretaries may assist in a number of the organization steps: reserving a corporate name, preparing the incorporating papers, executing and filing the papers, and arranging for the first incorporators' meeting and the first directors' meeting. See RESERVATION OF CORPORATE NAME.

Corporation service company. A company that performs for corporations certain services the corporations themselves would find prohibitively expensive or inconvenient to perform, such as incorporating them in states other than those in which the actual INCORPORATORS reside, and obtaining, establishing, and maintaining RESIDENT AGENTS and REGISTERED OFFICES.

Cumulative preferred stock. See Chapter 13/STOCK.

Cumulative voting. A system of voting for directors of a corporation under which each stockholder is entitled to a number of votes equal to the number of shares he or she owns multiplied by the number of directors to be elected. The stockholder may cast all votes for one candidate—cumulate them—or distribute the votes among the candidates in any way. This system enables the minority stockholders to elect one or more of the directors. The right to cumulative voting cannot be claimed unless provided for (1) by statute, (2) by the corporation's charter or bylaws, or (3) by contract among all stockholders, provided the agreement is not otherwise illegal.

To determine how many shares one should hold or control to insure the election of a certain number of directors:

1. Multiply the total number of shares entitled to vote by the number of directors one wants to elect.

2. Divide the figure found in (1) by one more than the total number of directors to be elected.

3. Add one to the figure obtained in (2); the result will be the least number of shares it will be necessary to hold or control to elect the desired number of directors.

Thus if a company has outstanding 1,000 voting shares, if five directors are to be elected, and if it is desired to elect two out of the five, the least number of shares it will be necessary to hold or control to accomplish this result will be found as follows:

$$\frac{1,000 \times 2}{5 + 1} + 1 = 334\frac{1}{3}$$

The desired result, therefore, can be accomplished only if 335 shares are held or controlled (where there is a fraction, it is to be counted as an extra share).

De facto corporation. A corporation that has not met some of the state's requirements of a legal corporation but continues to function as one "in good faith." Thus it exists in fact but not in law as does a DE JURE CORPORATION.

De jure corporation. A corporation that has met all legal requirements governing incorporating procedure.

Thus a de jure corporation exists in law as well as in fact, unlike a DE FACTO CORPORATION.

Directors. See BOARD OF DIRECTORS.

Directors' fees. Compensation paid to its directors by a corporation for their attendance at board meetings. In many cases when directors are members of the working organization of the corporation and are under salary, no directors' fees are paid. Some corporations adopt the policy of paying no directors' fees even in those cases where all or a number of the directors are not receiving salaries from the corporation as officers or executives. Sometimes fees are paid only to those directors who do not receive a salary as officers of the corporation.

Many corporations pay directors' fees in bank notes. In some companies, the practice prevails of issuing checks for directors' fees, although this custom appears to be the least favored one.

Generally, if directors' fees are paid, each director receives a stipulated amount for each meeting. In some companies, however, a definite sum is appropriated by resolution for each directors' meeting and is distributed among those present at the meeting. Thus the greater the number of absentees, the larger will be the share of each attending director.

The corporate secretary usually distributes directors' fees, but in some cases, the treasurer is charged with this duty. If the corporate secretary distributes the fees, he or she usually draws from the treasurer before the meeting a sum equivalent to the fees payable to the directors whose attendance is expected. He or she returns any amount on hand because of nonattendance of any director, unless the *members present take all* rule exists.

As a rule, fees are given to the directors after meetings without being enclosed in envelopes, although many companies prefer to use envelopes. When checks are used, the practice of many companies is to send the check by mail after the meeting.

Directors' meeting. See Chapter 3/ DIRECTORS' MEETINGS.

Docket. In corporation terminology, the agenda or list of matters to be taken up at a meeting. The term is seldom used today. (See Chapter 3/ AGENDA; Chapter 9/DOCKET.)

Domestic corporation. A corporation organized under the laws of a particular state is a domestic corporation in that state, as distinguished from a FOREIGN CORPORATION, which is organized under the laws of a different state.

Dummy incorporators. Individuals to whom shares of stock in a new CORPORATION are issued for the purpose of nominally qualifying them as INCORPORATORS of a corporation in which they have no real interest. Dummy incorporators are used to meet the requirements of state statutes that incorporators be residents of the state or to avoid immediate public revelation of the names of the persons actually forming the new corporation.

Dun & Bradstreet.   An agency that collects and distributes capital and credit information about persons and organizations in all trades. Dun & Bradstreet ratings show a firm's credit standing and its estimated financial strength.

Economy of scale.   The decrease in the new item cost of production of a commodity or service as output is increased.

Eleemosynary corporation.   See CHARITABLE CORPORATION.

Equal-opportunity employer.   An employer that does not discriminate in hiring and other employment practices because of race, color, sex, religion, or nationality. See also Chapter 9/FAIR EMPLOYMENT PRACTICES.

Ergonomics.   An applied science that studies the relationship or interaction between people and their work environment in order to improve performance and increase productivity.

Executive committee.   A COMMITTEE appointed by the BOARD OF DIRECTORS of a corporation to exercise many of the board's powers between board meetings. The committee meets more often than the board. In many large corporations, the members of the executive committee are at the offices of the corporation all of the time and are paid a regular salary. See FINANCE COMMITTEE.

Featherbedding.   Unproductive labor practices in which unnecessary personnel are hired or workers are paid for work they have not done.

Finance committee.   A COMMITTEE appointed by the BOARD OF DIRECTORS of a CORPORATION to exercise the power of the board relating to corporate finance between board meetings. *Finance committee* is the name given by some corporations to their EXECUTIVE COMMITTEE, but many corporations have both committees.

First-in, first-out (FIFO).   A method of valuing the inventory of merchandise. This method assumes that the goods first acquired are the goods first sold, in typical grocery store style. It is the method in most common use, largely because it conforms most nearly to the physical flow of the goods. By pricing inventory at the cost of the most recent acquisitions equal to the quantity on hand, this method puts the oldest costs into the cost of sales of the period. When goods are continually turned over and replaced, as in usual business, this method tends to increase inventory values in periods of rising prices, even though there may be no material change in the relative composition or quantity of the entire inventory. See also LAST-IN, FIRST-OUT (LIFO).

Foreign corporation.   A corporation doing business in a state of the United States other than the state in which it was created or incorporated. A foreign corporation must comply with certain terms and conditions imposed by the state. The state statutes make no distinction between a foreign corporation and an ALIEN CORPORATION; both are regarded as foreign, except in those few states that do not recognize alien corporations.

Foreign trade. The exporting and importing of goods and services to countries outside the United States. Foreign trade is a commercial field with its own practices and regulations.

Franchise. See Chapter 9/FRANCHISE.

General contractor. A person or organization that assumes responsibility for an entire project, often hiring other contractors (subcontractors) to perform specific tasks.

Goodwill. An intangible asset that in business is computed as the difference between a firm's book value and a greater purchase or sale price. See Chapter 11/GOODWILL.

Holding company. Any company that holds the stock of other corporations may be called a holding company. However, the term is usually restricted to two types of organizations: pure holding companies and mixed holding companies. A *pure holding company* is a nonoperating company organized for the purpose of investing its capital in the stocks of other companies, the affairs of which it undertakes to direct or administer. A holding company that is itself an operating company is called a *mixed holding company*. It is also called a

holding-operating company. Any company owned or controlled by another to the extent that it is a mere instrument to carry out the orders of the owning company is called a SUBSIDIARY. The owning company itself is usually called the PARENT CORPORATION. Holding companies may be vulnerable to antitrust prosecution when used as a device to suppress competition or to create a monopoly.

Incorporated partnership. There is no such thing as an *incorporated partnership*. The term is merely a synonym for CLOSE CORPORATION, expressing the idea that stockholders in a close corporation want the advantages of doing business in both the partnership and the corporate form. Professionals such as doctors and lawyers who often form partnerships are now permitted to incorporate in most states.

Incorporators. Persons who agree among themselves to organize themselves into a corporate body or CORPORATION and who perform the acts and execute and file the documents required for the incorporation of a corporation.

Many states require three or more incorporators, with one or more being a state resident. Some states also require that the organization meeting be held in the state. To meet this requirement, corporations may have DUMMY INCORPORATORS, who act for the principals until the organization meeting.

Individual proprietorship. See PROPRIETORSHIP, SOLE.

Interested director. A director who has a personal, usually pecuniary, interest in a matter that may be profitable for his or her corporation. This may cause the director's voting on the matter to be personally biased. An interested director therefore is usually disqualified from voting on the matter in which he or she is interested. If the director does vote and his or her vote is necessary to carry the matter, the directors' action thereon may be voidable or void.

Interlocking directorates. Boards of directors of two or more corporations having one or more directors in common. Through this method of control, the will of the dominant stockholders is carried out. The law does not look with favor upon interlocking directorates and closely scrutinizes dealings between corporations with interlocking directorates.

Internal reports. Reports of business activities and affairs, intended primarily for use by and within the business organization only. (See Chapter 8/REPORT.) Management may call for an investigation and special report covering a nonrecurring situation, but the majority of internal reports are periodical. They are submitted by every department in an organization and cover every phase of the business.

Interstate commerce, intrastate commerce. See Chapter 9/INTERSTATE COMMERCE, INTRASTATE COMMERCE.

Inventory. The aggregate of goods awaiting sale in the ordinary course of business (merchandise of a trading concern and the finished goods of a manufacturer), goods in the process of manufacture (work in process), and goods to be consumed directly or indirectly in production (raw materials and supplies). This aggregate is found by taking a *physical inventory*, which involves counting, listing, and valuing all of the items that make up the raw materials and supplies, work in process, and finished goods. Included in the inventory are items in transit (material that has left a supplier's place of business just before an inventory "cut-off" date but that has not arrived at destination before inventory taking), goods in warehouses, and goods transferred to a consignee, agent, or other factor for sale.

Investment company. An organization that invests in securities of other companies and sells its own shares to the investing public, thus making diversification and professional management possible for the small investor. (See Chapter 13/MUTUAL FUND.)

Job lot. An odd or miscellaneous assortment of goods for sale; a quantity less than the usual amount sold such as a partial case of some item.

Joint venture. An association of two or more persons or business entities for a given, limited purpose, without the usual powers, duties, and responsibilities that go with a PARTNERSHIP. Thus if two people buy a specific piece of real estate for resale at a profit, they become parties to a joint venture; but if they enter into an agreement whereby each contributes money and services in establishing and carrying on a real estate busi ness, they become members of a partnership.

Joint stock company. A form of business organization created by an agreeement of the parties. This agreement is commonly called *articles of association.* This type of company is similar to the CORPORATION in the following respects: (1) the ownership is represented by transferable certificates; (2) management is in the hands of a board of governors or directors elected by the members (shareholders); (3) the business continues for its fixed term notwithstanding the death or disability of one or more of the members. It is unlike the corporation and like the PARTNERSHIP in that each shareholder is personally liable for the company's debts.

In many states, the laws affecting taxation and regulation of corporations make the definition of a corporation broad enough to include joint stock companies. These states regard a joint stock company organized in another state as a FOREIGN CORPORATION. In other states, a joint stock company may conduct business in the state without being subject to restrictions imposed upon corporations.

Junior board of directors. A board of junior executives that mirrors the stockholder-elected board of directors. It is used to introduce junior executives to top management procedures and to give them a sense of participating in the running of the business. In most cases, the junior board, after a unanimous vote, is empowered to make suggestions to the senior board of directors or to senior executives. As the personnel of the board changes, usually from year to year, management is progressively better able to judge junior executives, and the junior executives become more familiar with management.

LCL. Less than carload. The term refers to less than the amount necessary to apply the carload rate charged by the railroads for freight transportation.

LIFO. See LAST-IN, FIRST-OUT (LIFO).

LTL. Less than truckload. This term refers to less than the quantity of freight required to apply the truckload (TL) rate charged by motor carriers for transportation.

Last-in, first-out (LIFO). A method of valuing an inventory of merchandise. This method is the opposite of the FIRST-IN, FIRST-OUT method and assumes that the units sold are those most recently acquired and that the units on hand are those first acquired. In most cases in actual practice, this is a fiction that attempts to accomplish a measurement of economic income by assuming that, especially in a period of changing prices, the real income to the business is measured by the difference between current cost (or most recent cost) and selling price. LIFO produces less profit than the first-in, first-out method in periods of rising prices and more profit in periods of declining prices.

Limited partnership. A partnership in which the liability of one or more limited partners for debts of the firm is limited to the amount of his or her investment in the business. Limited partners have no voice in the management of the partnership. They merely invest money and receive a certain share of the profits. There must be one or more general partners who manage the business and remain liable for all of its debts.

As in a general partnership, the death, insanity, or partnership of only one of the general partners dissolves the limited partnership. See PARTNERSHIP.

To organize a limited partnership, one usually files a certificate in a public office and publishes a notice in the newspaper. Many state statutes pertaining to limited partnerships are codified as the Uniform Limited Partnership Law and must be strictly observed.

Liquidation. The process of distributing the assets of a dissolved corporation or other business (whether voluntarily or involuntarily dissolved) to its stockholders after corporate debts have been paid.

Management guide. An organization manual that delineates the functions, responsibilities, authority, and principal relationships of a particular position or a series of positions in an organization. Thus a management guide for the office of treasurer might have principal headings such as (1) function, (2) responsibilities and authority, and (3) relationships. Under responsibilities and authority, items such as the following would be spelled out: activities, organization of department, personnel of department, and finances of department. Under the relationships heading, relations with the following insiders and outsiders would be clarified: the president, other department managers, federal and state agencies, banks, financial institutions, insurance companies, registrars and trustees, and the public.

Management by objectives. A method of managing whereby goals are established and employees are encouraged to work toward those goals, with periodic meetings to review their progress.

Markdown. A reduction that lowers the price of an article below the original retail price. A restoration of a markdown that does not increase the selling price above the original retail is a "markdown cancellation." See MARKUP.

Markup. 1. The difference between the selling price of an article of merchandise and the cost price.

2. Additions that raise the selling price above the original retail price. Deductions that do not decrease the selling price below the original retail are called *markup cancellations*. (See MARKDOWN.)

Markup may be expressed in dollars and cents figures or as a percentage. The markup percentage may be stated as a percentage of cost price, which is called *markup on cost*, or as a percentge of the sales price, which is called *markup on retail*. In retailing, markup is generally figured as a percentage of the selling price.

Massachusetts trust. A business association formed under a deed of trust, which is really a contract between the trustees and beneficiaries. It is also known as a *business trust* or a *common-law trust*. Its structure closely resembles that of a CORPORATION. The interests of the beneficiaries are represented by certificates, frequently called certificates of stock, which may be divided into several classes of common and preferred stock and may be listed on stock exchanges. The trustees correspond to the directors and the certificateholders to the stockholders. The trustees manage the property and pay dividends out of the profits. They usually appoint and remove the officers. Unlike a corporation, the management is permanent. The trustees are personally liable in dealing with outsiders unless they clearly indicate that the creditors shall look only to the trust property for payment.

Massachusetts trusts are regarded as corporations under many taxing statutes and federal acts.

The liability of the certificateholders depends upon their control over the trustees and property of the association. If they have the power to remove and elect trustees or to manage the property, the association is considered a partnership instead of a trust, and the certificateholders are personally liable as partners; otherwise, they have no personal liability.

The duration is limited by statute in most states, but the parties inter-

ested at the time the trust expires can agree to another trust.

Merchandising, retail. The buying, selling, and control of mechandise. The essence of merchandising is the adjustment of stocks to consumer demand; it requires a thorough and continual study of consumer market trends and fashions. Advertising and publicity are aids to merchandising; they help move the products that are stocked in response to demand. Sales promotion creates demand; it may be used to introduce a new item or to increase sales of existing items above the "norm."

Merger. The joining of two or more corporations to form a new entity or the absorption of one or more corporations by another existing corporation, which may retain its identity and take over all the rights, privileges, franchises, properties, and liabilities of the absorbed companies. (See CONSOLIDATION.)

Merit rating. Periodic review of an employee's performance for purposes of salary increase, promotion, firing, layoff, or training.

Moneyed corporation. Stock corporations are classified as (1) moneyed, (2) railroad, (3) transportation, (4) business, and (5) cooperative. A moneyed corporation is organized under the Banking Law or Insurance Law. Generally, a corporation dealing in money or lending money.

No-par stock. See Chapter 13/PAR VALUE STOCK AND NO-PAR STOCK.

Noncumulative preferred stock.
See Chapter 13/STOCK

Nonprofit corporation. A corporation organized for purposes (e.g., religious, educational, scientific) other than the making of profits for its members; in some cases, a CHARITABLE CORPORATION, as distinguished from a BUSINESS CORPORATION. See also NONSTOCK CORPORATION.

Nonstock corporation. Any corporation other than a STOCK CORPORATION. Nonstock corporations include membership corporations, religious, educational, and charitable institutions, and some public corporations. Usually, special laws are passed to regulate the management of these various nonstock corporations. See CHARITABLE CORPORATION; NONPROFIT CORPORATION.

Officers of a corporation. Statutes in most states specifically require a corporation to have a president, secretary, treasurer, and a resident agent for service of process upon the corporation. Generally, the charter or bylaws specify the qualifications of the officers. In some states, the statutes prescribe certain qualifications, as, for example, that the president must be a director. One person may hold two offices in the same corporation, unless the statute prohibits certain combinations of office. The board of directors in most states has the power to appoint officers.

Term of office. The term of office is usually fixed by the statute of the state in which the corporation is organized or by the corporation's charter or bylaws. If the term of office is not fixed, an officer holds office at the pleasure of the corporation or until he or she resigns and a successor is elected. An officer's term of office does not expire merely because the term of the directors who appointed the officer has expired.

Resignation. An officer may resign at any time, although elected for a fixed period, unless he or she is restricted by the corporation's charter or bylaws, by the laws of the state in which the corporation is organized, or by the terms of his or her contract with the corporation. The resignation may be written or oral, and no particular form is required.

Powers and duties. An officer derives his or her power from the state corporation laws, the corporation's charter and bylaws, and resolutions of the board of directors and committees appointed by that board. An officer's power exists merely by virtue of his or her holding a particular office. The officer's duties vary widely from one corporation to another.

Liabilities. An officer is a fiduciary, bound to exercise the utmost good faith in transactions touching his or her duties. The officer is not chargeable for loss caused by mistakes or errors of judgment. He or she is bound by the restrictions in the bylaws and is liable for loss resulting from failure to observe those restrictions. A corporate officer also incurs liabilities under certain federal and state statutes.

Compensation. An officer is not legally entitled to compensation for services rendered as incident to his or her office unless authorized by charter, bylaw, resolution of the board of directors, or express or implied agreement between the officer and the corporation. As a practical matter, however, most officers perform ministerial duties for which they are entitled to compensation unless they agree to serve gratuitously.

See PRESIDENT; VICE-PRESIDENT; SECRETARY (CORPORATE); TREASURER; CONTROLLER (COMPTROLLER).

Open shop. See Chapter 9/OPEN SHOP.

Outstanding stock. See Chapter 13/ STOCK.

Par value stock. See Chapter 13/ PAR VALUE STOCK AND NO-PAR STOCK.

Parent corporation. A corporation that owns the majority of the stock of another corporation, which is called its SUBSIDIARY.

Partnership. "An association of two or more persons to carry on as coowners a business for profit" (Uniform Partnership Law). A partnership is organized by oral or written agreement among the parties. Agreement may also be implied from the acts and representations of the parties. Partnerships are governed by fairly uniform laws, which are codified in many states by the Uniform Partnership Law. A partnership may carry on business in any state without paying greater taxes than residents of the state pay.

Each partner of a general partnership is fully liable personally for all partnership debts regardless of the amount of his or her investment. (See LIMITED PARTNERSHIP.) All types of capital produced or acquired by the partnership become partnership property. Real estate is generally acquired in the individual names of the partners or in the name of one partner who holds the property in trust for the partnership.

In the absence of a specific contract, partners share profits and losses equally. It is customary, however, to provide in the partnership agreement that profits and losses shall be distributed pro rata according to the amount of capital contributed by each or in any other ratio to which they agree. Partners have no right to salaries unless they are agreed upon, even though one partner may devote all of his or her time to the business and the other may devote little or none. The agreement may provide for the division of profits after allowing each of the partners an agreed-upon salary.

Partnerships are dissolved without violation of the partnership agreement by (1) withdrawal of one of the members under some circumstances; (2) operation of law through death or bankruptcy of one of the partners or a change in the law that makes the partnership's business illegal; (3) court decree granted because of incapacity or insanity of one of the partners, gross misconduct, or neglect or breach of duty.

On the books of a partnership, the net worth (see Chapter 11/NET WORTH) is represented by a capital account for each of the partners (in an amount equal to the interest of each).

Profits and losses of the partnership are reflected in the capital accounts in the proportion in which profits are shared and losses borne. Withdrawals by any partner are shown as charges to his or her capital account; further investments of any partner are shown as credits to his or her capital account.

Preemptive right. See RIGHTS.

Preferred stock. See Chapter 13/ STOCK.

President. The principal executive officer of a corporation. (See OFFICERS OF A CORPORATION.)

In companies using the office of chairperson of the board of directors, the president is ordinarily subordinate to the chairperson but is still considered, subject to the control of the chairperson, the principal officer in general charge and control of the business. For this reason, all other officers are considered as subordinate to the president.

Promoters. Persons who undertake to form a new corporation, to procure for it the rights and capital by which it is to carry out the purposes set forth in its certificate of incorporation or charter, and to establish for it the prosecution of its business. Frequently, the promoters become affiliated with the corporation in some official capacity.

Proprietorship, sole. One of the three most common forms of business organization. Ownership of the business is vested in one proprietor.

The other two common forms of organization are PARTNERSHIP and CORPORATION.

Individual proprietorship is the earliest and simplest form of business organization. No formalities are necessary to establish it. All that the individual need do is to ascertain whether a license is required to conduct the particular business, and whether a license fee or tax must be paid to state or local authorities. A sole, or individual, proprietorship is not limited in its duration by law. It is not, however, a stable form of organization, for illness of the owner may interrupt it, and his or her death may terminate it.

The individual owner is personally liable for all the debts of the business to the full extent of his or her property. The owner cannot limit liability to creditors to the amount put into the business. All profits are his or hers to reinvest in the business or to dispose of as the owner chooses.

The proprietor may raise additional capital needed for the business by borrowing from banks and from others, by purchasing goods on credit, and by personally investing additional amounts in the enterprise. He or she may carry on business in any state without paying greater taxes than the residents of that state pay.

Proxy. See Chapter 3/PROXY.

Public corporation. A CORPORATION organized by the federal government or a state government to serve as an administrative agency of that government. This includes municipal corporations, which are creatures of state government.

Public service corporation. See PUBLIC UTILITY CORPORATION.

Public utility corporation. A corporation engaged in supplying services usually regarded as public necessities, such as railroad, electric, gas, power, telephone, or water services. It usually is specially franchised by a federal, state, or municipal authority and is subject to supervision and regulation by a public service commission. It is also known as a *public service company*.

Pyramiding. The technique by which a few individuals who control a top HOLDING COMPANY gain control over vast properties with an investment of relatively small sums in each of a number of interrelated companies. The pyramided structure is made up of a holding company at the apex and various levels of intermediate holding and operating companies. Pyramiding is generally done for speculative profit and not to serve as an improvement in the operations of the individual companies involved.

Quasi-public corporations. Corporations that are not PUBLIC CORPORATIONS organized as instruments of government administration, but that contribute to the safety, comfort, or convenience of a community, such as a telephone company. See also PUBLIC UTILITY CORPORATION.

Registered office. An office of corporation in a state in which the corporation is only nominally incorporated, or in which it does business, maintained merely to satisfy that state's statutory requirements that the corporation maintain a registered office and RESIDENT AGENT there for service of process, holding of stockholders' meetings, and the like.

Reorganization. In the financial sense, an overall revision of the entire capital structure of a corporation. Reorganization is accomplished under the jurisdiction of a court. It is usually forced on management by creditors. Often a new corporation is formed to take over the assets of the old corporation, and the old management is supplanted by a new management.

The term is common in connection with bankruptcy proceedings. For example, reorganization under Chapter 11 of the Bankruptcy Law allows corporations to restructure their obligations. See Chapter 9/BANKRUPTCY.

Reservation of corporate name. A corporate name must use the word *company, association, incorporated,* or some other word or abbreviation to indicate that the firm is a corporation. Usually, only a banking institution may use the word *bank* or *trust*.

The appropriate state official, such as the secretary of state, can tell you if your chosen name is already in use or if another name too closely resembles it. If time is short, you might ask for a reply by wire, for example:

Please let us know if the name Walter Morris, Inc., is available for a domestic corporation we want to organize under the laws of your state.

If the name is available, please reserve it for us for the statutory period. Our check of $ _____ is enclosed in payment of the reservation fee.

Please reply by telegram, collect. Thank you.

For a foreign corporation, change the first sentence to ". . . a foreign corporation we are about to qualify to transact business in your state."

Resident agent. Sometimes called registered agent. An employee or agent of a corporation, or one obtained through a CORPORATION SERVICE COMPANY, who resides in a state that is only nominally the residence of a corporation incorporated therein and who performs for the corporation the services required by that state's statutes to be performed there by the corporation.

Resolution. A formal expression, usually in writing, of the decision, or will, or opinion of an official group or body, such as the stockholders or directors of a corporation, adopted by vote in accordance with established procedure. Usually, the idea or decision thus to be formally established as the will of the group is introduced by a motion, voted upon, and adopted. (See Chapter 3/MOTION.)

A resolution applies to a single act or decision, as distinguished from a BYLAW, which is a permanent and continuing rule adopted for the government of the corporation, its officers, directors, and stockholders. A resolution may be passed at any properly called meeting of the directors or stockholders.

A resolution may change a previous resolution if it does not interfere with the rights of persons who claim protection under the previous resolution.

Resolutions book. A book or looseleaf binder in which are kept copies of every RESOLUTION adopted by a corporation or other organization. In many companies, this book is carefully indexed. This procedure avoids the inconvenience of having to leaf through pages of minutes of unrelated matter when reference is made to a particular action authorized by resolution.

Retailing. See MERCHANDISING, RETAIL.

Rights. Certificates distributed by a corporation to existing stockholders, entitling them to subscribe to additional shares of the same issue at a stipulated price and before a fixed date. Stockholders have *preemptive rights*, upon the issue of additional shares by the corporation, to purchase their proportion of the new stock to maintain their relative interest in the corporation. Usually, the rights give shareholders the privilege of purchasing the new stock at less than market price; thus the rights have a market value.

When stock-carrying rights are sold, the rights usually go with the stock until the day of closing of the company's books for such rights.

After that time, quotations of the stock on the stock exchange are made *ex-rights*. This means that the stock is bought and sold without the rights and that the rights are bought and sold separately also.

Seal. See CORPORATE SEAL; Chapter 9/SEAL.

Secretary (corporate). An officer of a CORPORATION. As the title indicates, the corporate secretary is charged with the keeping of the minutes of meetings, including those of the directors, the stockholders, and the committees. (See Chapter 3/ MINUTES; MEETING.) He or she has charge of the records and is generally authorized to sign, with the PRESIDENT, all contracts, leases, mortgages, bonds, stock certificates, and other such documents and to affix the CORPORATE SEAL. He or she has charge of the stock certificate book, transfer book, and stock ledger.

Seniority. Job status based upon length of service that commonly implies preference in job security, promotions, and other rewards.

Shares. See Chapter 13/STOCK.

Silent partner. A partner who has no voice in the management of the business. Except for special partners (see LIMITED PARTNERSHIP), a silent partner is equally responsible with other partners for debts of the business.

Sole practitioner. One who practices a profession on his or her own such as a lawyer or doctor who is not associated with others for the purpose of practicing the particular profession.

Sole proprietorship. See PROPRIETORSHIP, SOLE.

State of incorporation. The state in which a corporation is organized. A corporation in the state of incorporation is a DOMESTIC CORPORATION and in all other states a FOREIGN CORPORATION. Outside the United States, it is an ALIEN CORPORATION.

Stock. The term *stock* refers to the aggregate ownership interest in a business corporation; hence it refers to ownership of the *corporation,* not of the corporation's *assets,* which are in turn owned by the corporation. See Chapter 13/STOCK.

Stockbook. See STOCK LEDGER.

Stock certificate. Written evidence of ownership in a CORPORATION. The certificate is issued, and registered on the records of the corporation, in the name of the owner of the shares of stock represented by the certificate. A certificate may represent one share or numerous shares. When ownership of the share is transferred, the certificate held by the original owner is canceled, another certificate is issued to the new owner, and appropriate changes are made on the records of the corporation. The procedure for issuing a stock certificate to the original owner of the stock varies slightly from the procedure for issuing a certificate upon the transfer of ownership. Usually, a TRANSFER AGENT handles these details for the corporation, but in a small corporation it is frequently the secretary's duty to help issue the certificates.

Issuance of stock certificate to original owner of stock. Here are the steps the secretary should take when it is his or her duty to help issue a stock certificate to the original owner:

1. Enter the name and address of the person to whom the certificate is issued, and the number of shares for which it is issued, on the stub.

2. Tear the certificate out of the stock book.

3. Type on the face of the certificate the name of the person to whom it is issued, the number of shares it represents, and the date.

4. Have the certificate signed by the officers whose signatures are required.

5. Impress the corporate seal in the space provided.

6. If possible, have the receipt on the stub of the certificate signed. If the person in whose name the certificate is issued is not present to sign the stub, type the receipt on a slip of paper the size and shape of the receipt printed on the stub. Be certain that the information on the receipt corresponds with the stub. Enclose the receipt with the certificate and request the person in whose name the certificate is issued to sign and return it. When it is received, paste it over the receipt portion of the stub.

7. Affix it to the stub and cancel documentary stamps for stamp tax. (See Chapter 12/STAMP TAX.)

8. Send certificates to owner by registered mail.

Issuance of stock certificate upon transfer of stock. The back of the certificate has a form for an assignment or transfer of stock from one holder to another. When shares of stock are transferred, the corporation issues a new certificate to the new owner and cancels the old certificate. The holder of a one-hundred-share certificate might want to transfer fifty shares and keep the other fifty. In that case, two new certificates of fifty shares each are issued—one to the transferee and one to the original owner.

When a certificate is transferred, the secretary should take the following steps *in addition* to the procedure for the original issuance of a certificate:

1. Write "Canceled" in ink across the face of the certificate.

2. Date and initial the canceled certificate.

3. Affix documentary stamps (see Chapter 12/STAMP TAX) to the canceled certificate and cancel the stamps.

4. Paste the canceled certificate to its stub in the bound stock certificate book as nearly as possible in the certificate's original position in the book.

The above procedures are to be followed when the secretary is acting *for the corporation issuing the stock.* When the executive sells securities, the procedure is entirely different. See Chapter 13/STOCK; TRANSFER OF SECURITIES; DELIVERY OF SECURITIES.

Stock corporation. A CORPORATION that has capital stock (see Chapter 11/ CAPITAL STOCK) divided into shares of STOCK and that is authorized by law to distribute to the holders of these shares proportional amounts of its profits in the form of dividends when it has a surplus. See Chapter 13/DIVIDENDS; STOCK.

Stock insurance company. A corporation that operates under the principles of private enterprise. Its net earnings are distributed to stockholders. It usually does business through agents and brokers. See Chapter 16/INSURANCE COMPANIES.

Stock ledger. A permanent corporate record of each stockholder's interest in the corporation and of all transfers of any part of any stockholder's interest. The record is kept in terms of shares issued, not in money values. Every canceled certificate and every new certificate issued is recorded in the particular stockholder's record. A separate page or record card is maintained for each stockholder. Appropriate forms may be obtained at local stationers. A separate ledger is maintained for each class of stock. From the stock ledger the corporation determines the number of votes each stockholder may cast at election, the amount of dividends to which the stockholders may be entitled, who is entitled to proxies (see Chapter 13/PROXY) and notices of meetings, who is entitled to RIGHTS upon an increase in stock, and the like.

In a small corporation, it is frequently the secretary's duty to keep the stock ledger.

Stockholder. Owner of one or more shares of stock. Stockholders do not participate *directly* in the control of the ordinary affairs of a corporation; they elect the directors at a stockholders' meeting and, in that manner, exercise *indirect* control. (See Chapter 13/STOCK; Chapter 3/STOCKHOLDERS' MEETING.) State statutes or the articles of incorporation generally require the consent of all or a portion of the stockholders before the following actions are taken:

1. Acceptance of the corporate charter

2. Amendment of the corporate charter

3. Adoption of bylaws, unless the power is expressly given to the board of directors by the state laws or by the articles of incorporation

4. Amendment of the bylaws, if the power to amend is not expressly given to the board of directors

5. Removal of directors

6. Merger of consolidation of the corporation with another company

7. Transfer of all of the assets of the corporation by sale or lease

8. Voluntary dissolution and liquidation of the corporation

9. Assessment on fully paid stock

10. Increase or decrease in the amount of stock the corporation is authorized to issue

Laws of the state in which a corporation is organized, the charter, and the bylaws give the stockholders certain rights and powers that must be exercised at a meeting. Sometimes these powers can be exercised in writing, and a meeting may not be necessary; however, as a matter of expediency, it is wise to hold a meeting. The validity of the action taken at a meeting does not always depend on whether the meeting was held in a formal way. Before an objecting stockholder can succeed in nullifying action taken at a meeting, he or she must show that, by an irregularity, his or her rights have been affected.

Subchapter S corporation. A small corporation that earns limited money and chooses to be taxed as an ordinary partnership. Its stockholders thus have limited personal liability and are taxed individually.

Subsidiary. A company that is controlled by another corporation, known as a holding or parent corporation, which owns all or a majority of its stock. See HOLDING COMPANY.

Syndicate. An association of persons formed to conduct some business transaction, usually financial. Most syndicates are formed temporarily for a specific objective and terminate when the objective is realized. See also CONSORTIUM.

Task force. A COMMITTEE or working group formed temporarily to accomplish a specific objective.

Trademark. See Chapter 9/TRADEMARK.

Transfer agent. An individual, bank, or trust company that keeps the STOCK LEDGER of a corporation and records all transfers of stock. (See Chapter 13/STOCK.) It is the transfer agent's duty to make certain that the act of transfer is executed properly.

Treasurer. The financial officer of a corporation. The treasurer is the custodian of the corporation's assets and is primarily responsible for financial planning, including the procurement, use, and investment of funds. He or she has the right to sign checks for payment of obligations and also to endorse checks, notes, and other obligations payable to the corporation. The treasurer has custody of the securities owned by the corporation and is usually in charge of the credit and collections department. There is a lack of uniformity in the division of administrative duties between treasurers and controllers among the various corporations, but in all cases the treasurer is primarily in charge of finance, and the controller is primarily in charge of accounting. See CONTROLLER (COMPTROLLER).

Treasury stock. See Chapter 13/STOCK.

Vetoing stock. See VOTING AT STOCKHOLDERS' MEETINGS.

Vice-president. An officer of the corporation who performs all of the usual duties of the president in his or her absence or disability. There are no basic functions for a vice-president such as those for TREASURER, SECRETARY, and CONTROLLER (COMPTROLLER). In large corporations, the vice-president is usually a department head. There may therefore be as many vice-presidents as there are departments, designated as the first vice-president, second vice-president, and so on or as vice-president in charge of sales, vice-president in charge of production, and the like. They perform duties prescribed for them by the board of directors or the president.

Voting at stockholders' meetings. Every owner of capital stock (see Chapter 11/CAPITAL STOCK; Chapter 13/STOCK) has the right to vote the stock at all meetings of stockholders unless the right is denied by statutory or charter provision or by an agreement under which the owner holds his or her shares. The bylaws usually provide that the person who is the registered owner on the books of the corporation on a certain day fixed by the directors has the right to vote the stock. The general rule is that each stockholder is entitled to one vote for each share of stock owned. Absent stockholders may vote by proxy. (See CUMULATIVE VOTING; VOTING TRUST; Chapter 3/PROXY.)

Frequently, a certificate of incorporation (see CORPORATION) will provide that a certain class of stock shall not have the right to vote at all. Sometimes the voting stock represents a much smaller ownership than the nonvoting stock. Generally, it is the preferred stock of industrial and public utility companies that is de-

prived of voting power. Absolute deprivation of voting power is not as usual, however, as limitation of voting power. Thus in many corporations, a class of stock that has no right to elect directors will have voting power on questions that affect the relation of the group to the corporation. Such stock may be called *vetoing stock*. Frequently, this power to vote on certain questions is included to meet the requirements of the law under which the corporation is organized. (See STOCKHOLDER.)

Sometimes nonvoting stock is given the right to elect or assist in electing directors under certain circumstances, such as failure to pay dividends for a certain period. This stock may be called stock with *contingent voting power*.

Voting trust. A method devised for concentrating the control of a company in the hands of a few people. A voting trust is usually organized and operated under a *voting-trust agreement*. This is a contract between the stockholders and those who manage the corporation, called the *voting trustees*. The stockholders transfer their stock to the trustees, giving them the right to vote the stock during the life of the agreement. The trustees, in turn, issue certificates of beneficial interest, called *voting-trust certificates*, to the stockholders, who are entitled to the dividends. All stockholders may become parties to the agreement, which is generally subject to statutory regulation. The trust is usually for a definite period. When it is terminated, the certificateholders are notified to exchange their trust certificates for certificates of stock.

This centralization of control of the affairs of a corporation may be found necessary or desirable upon organization, upon REORGANIZATION, upon MERGER or CONSOLIDATION, in raising capital, or in carrying out any other corporate plan. Its most common use is in connection with reorganization.

Voting trusts cannot be used by competing corporations to form a monopoly.

Voting-trust certificate. See VOTING TRUST.

Watered stock. See Chapter 13/ WATERED STOCK.

PART IV

ACCOUNTING AND FINANCE

CHAPTER 11

ACCOUNTING AND BOOKKEEPING

Accounting. The process of recording, classifying, summarizing, and reporting transactions in the financial records to show the financial status of a business and the results of operations.

All accounting procedures from (1) the records made in BOOKS OF ORIGINAL ENTRY to (2) POSTING to LEDGER accounts to (3) making CLOSING ENTRIES and ADJUSTING ENTRIES to (4) taking a TRIAL BALANCE are directed toward (5) the preparation of an income statement (profit and loss statement) and a BALANCE SHEET at the close of the accounting period. These five steps are usually called the "accounting cycle." They are the essence of accounting.

Modern businesses use the computer to simplify the accounting process. Computer software such as spreadsheet analysis, general ledger and accounting packages, database-management systems, and tax packages reduce repetitive work and enable operators to perform complex, error-free calculations. Journals and ledgers can be maintained by computer (provided they meet Internal Revenue Service requirements), and financial statements can be prepared quickly and accurately by computer. See ACCOUNTING RECORDS.

Accounting period. See FISCAL PERIOD.

Accounting records. Business accounting records may be kept manually in columnar books or by computer, with data stored and printed out as needed. According to the Internal Revenue Service, if you keep records in an automatic data-processing (ADP) system, the system must include a method of producing legible records that will provide proof of your tax liability.

An ADP system is acceptable under Internal Revenue Service standards if it complies with the following guidelines;

1. It must print out your general ledger and its source references for the same period as your tax year. It must also periodically print out any subsidiary ledgers.

2. It must provide an audit trail so that details (invoices and vouchers) of the summary accounting data may be identified and made available upon request.

3. It must provide a way to trace any transaction back to the original source or forward to a final total. If printouts of transactions are not made when they are processed, your system must be able to make a record of these transactions.

4. It must have adequate storage facilities for machine-sensible data media, printouts, and all supporting documents. These records must be kept in the same way as records under a manual accounting system. You need not keep punched cards if the information is on magnetic tapes or disks or is recorded in some other way.

5. It should have available a full description of the ADP part of the accounting system and the controls you use to insure accurate and reliable processing.

Executives with large estates and diversified investments usually have an accountant set up a complete bookkeeping system, which a secretary may help maintain. Three broad classes of records are usually kept:

1. Records of what the executive owns, such as stocks, bonds, and real estate

2. Records that must be kept for income and other tax purposes

3. Records of living expenses that are not deductible under the income tax law, in addition to records for other purposes

For supporting records, see the forms under Chapter 12/REAL ESTATE RECORDS; CAPITAL GAIN AND LOSS; Chapter 13/SECURITIES RECORD.

Separate columns should be allotted to income and to expenditures. There should be a separate column for each source of recurring income and a miscellaneous column for nonrecurring items. Because of the special tax treatment accorded stock dividends, it is important that dividends be kept separate from other income.

A separate column should be allotted to each class of deductible expenses (see Chapter 12/DEDUCTIONS) that recur frequently. Deductible items that occur only occasionally may be entered in an "Other Deductions" column and analyzed at the end of the year for the executive's federal income tax return. Nondeductible expenditures may be kept in a "Nondeductible Expenses" column. In addition to keeping accounting records, the executive may want a record of one or more of the following expenses:

1. House expenses.
2. Wages paid to domestic employees. (See Chapter 12/ SOCIAL SECURITY TAXES).
3. Life insurance and other premiums. (See Chapter 16/INSURANCE RECORDS.)
4. Education of children.
5. Clothes.
6. Recreation.
7. Money spent in support of a dependent.
8. Travel. (See EXPENSE ACCOUNT.)
9. Automobile expenses.
10. Membership dues, other than those that are deductible.
11. Hobbies, such as expenditures on greenhouses.
12. Gifts.
13. Contributions to individual retirement accounts on behalf of the executive or spouse.

Accounts. An item in bookkeeping listed as an asset, a liability, or owner's equity, revenue, or expense. For descriptions of specific accounts, see ACCOUNTS PAYABLE; CASH ACCOUNT; CONTROL ACCOUNT; NOTES PAYABLE; NOTES RECEIVABLE; PROFIT AND LOSS.

Accounts payable. 1. An account in the general ledger representing the amount owed by the business to its general creditors on open purchases of merchandise. It is a CONTROL ACCOUNT equaling the total of the individual account balances in the accounts payable ledger. (See LEDGER.)

It first appears on the books of account through the purchase JOURNAL when a charge purchase is recorded.

Debit Purchases
    Credit Accounts Payable

When the creditor is paid, the entry is made in the CASH DISBURSEMENTS JOURNAL:

Debit Accounts Payable
    Credit Cash

This assumes that the amount of cash paid equals the amount owed. When deductions are made for items such as cash discounts, returned merchandise, and inferior merchandise not returned but for which allowances are made, the entry recording payment in full of the account becomes:

Debit Accounts Payable
    Credit Purchase Returns
    Credit Purchase Allowances
    Credit Purchase Discounts
    Credit Cash

Accounts Payable is a current liability (see CURRENT LIABILITIES) and is included under that heading in the BALANCE SHEET.

2. (*Sing.*) An individual account in the accounts payable ledger.

ACCOUNTING RECORDS for an executive usually do not include an accounts payable account.

Accounts receivable. 1. An account in the general ledger representing the amount due the business from its customers. It is a CONTROL AC- COUNT equaling the total of the individual account balances in the accounts receivable ledger. (See LEDGER.)

It first appears on the books of account through the sales JOURNAL when a charge sale is recorded:

Debit Accounts Receivable
　　　　Credit Sales

When the customer pays his or her account, the entry is made in the CASH RECEIPTS JOURNAL.

Debit Cash
　　　　Credit Accounts Receivable

This assumes that the amount of cash received equals the amount due. When deductions are made by the customer for items such as cash discounts, returned merchandise, and inferior merchandise not returned but for which allowances are made, the entry recording the receipt of payment in full of a customer's account becomes:

Debit Cash
Debit Sales Returns
Debit Sales Allowances
Debit Sales Discounts
　　　　Credit Accounts Receivable

Accounts Receivable is a CURRENT ASSET and is included under that heading in the BALANCE SHEET.

2. (*Sing.*) An individual account in the accounts receivable ledger.

ACCOUNTING RECORDS for an executive usually do not include an accounts receivable account.

Accrual accounting.　A method of keeping the books of account by which expenses and income are allo- cated to periods to which they are applicable, regardless of when payment for such expenses and income is made. Revenue is thereby recognized when earned and expenses when incurred. The books are said to be kept on an accrual basis, as distinguished from a cash basis. (See CASH ACCOUNTING.)

ADJUSTING ENTRIES are made in the JOURNAL to record accrued income, expenses, and other allocations.

ACCOUNTING RECORDS for an executive usually are on a cash accounting basis.

Accrued assets.　The amount of income earned through commissions, interest on notes receivable, and the like but not yet received. The accrued assets are set up on the books at the close of a fiscal period through ADJUSTING ENTRIES when the ACCRUED INCOME is credited to profit and loss for the period. Accrued assets usually appear in the BALANCE SHEETS as ACCOUNTS RECEIVABLE.

Accrued expenses.　Expenses such as wages, interest on notes payable, taxes, and interest on bonds payable, incurred on or before the close of a fiscal period but not to be paid until some time in the future. The accrued expenses get into the books of account through ADJUSTING ENTRIES, which charge the current profit and loss properly for expenses applicable to the period and set up the accrued liability as an account payable. See ACCRUED LIABILITIES.

Accrued income. Income earned, such as commissions and interest on notes receivable, but not collected. At the close of the fiscal period, the accrued income gets into the books of account through Adjusting entries, which credit the current profit and loss properly for income applicable to the period and set up the Accrued asset as an account receivable.

Accrued liabilities. The amount of wages, interest on notes payable, interest on bonds payable, taxes, and the like incurred but not paid. The accrued liabilities are set up on the books at the close of a fiscal period through Adjusting entries when the Accrued expenses are charged to profit and loss for the period. Accrued liabilities appear in the balance sheet as Current liabilities.

Acid-test ratio. See Chapter 13/ Acid-test ratio.

Adjusting entries. An accounting term for Journal entries made at the close of a Fiscal period to take up income and expense in the proper period and make the profit and loss statement show the net income from operations during a stated period and to insure that balance sheet accounts reflect the proper amounts. Adjusting entries are also made to correct errors discovered when the books of account are audited at the close of the fiscal period preliminary to preparing a profit and loss statement (Income statement) and Balance sheet.

Assets. Items of value owned by a business or an individual. In a Balance sheet, assets are usually grouped as Current assets, long-term investments, Fixed assets, Intangible assets, and other assets. The relation of an asset to the business determines its classification. For example, in a business engaged in buying and selling trucks, the trucks are classified as a current asset (inventory account); but if the trucks are used by the business for delivery purposes, they are classified as a fixed asset.

Audit. A verification of the Assets, Liabilities, and Capital of a business enterprise as of a given date and the verification of financial transactions during a Fiscal period then ended. An *internal audit* is performed by a business's own personnel whereas an *external audit* is performed by an independent accountant hired from outside the business. Lending institutions generally require audited financial statements before making a major lending decision.

During an audit an Auditor examines the records and supporting documents of a firm. The secretary can be of assistance in locating the necessary materials and seeing, in advance, that records and files are up to date and in their proper place for immediate access.

Auditor. An accounting officer of a corporation who goes over the accounts to see if the funds have been properly handled and to report to the directors on the financial position of the company. Not all large corporations and few small companies provide for the office of auditor. The auditor's functions are performed in many instances by the controller or by outside accountants. (See Chapter 10/CONTROLLER [COMPTROLLER]). Corporations that have internal auditors also employ outside accountants to make independent audit reports.

Bad debt losses. 1. Losses on ACCOUNTS RECEIVABLE and NOTES RECEIVABLE caused by the failure of customers to pay. Under ordinary circumstances they should be charged to the PROFIT AND LOSS of the year in which they are known to be bad. However, in most businesses, this practice would result in unpredictable and uneven charges to profits, because bad debts vary from year to year, and large losses may occur only once in several years. A device is therefore used to apportion the losses evenly over the years. This device consists of making an annual Allowance for Doubtful Accounts by setting aside from Profit each year an amount for expected bad-debt losses. This amount may be determined based on an aging of accounts receivable or as a percentage of credit sales. Debts written off as bad are charged to the Allowance for Doubtful Accounts rather than to the current Profit and Loss account.

The amount of the Allowance for Doubtful Accounts is shown in the BALANCE SHEET as a deduction from the current asset Accounts Receivable.

2. If a manager makes a business-related loan that is not repaid, he or she may deduct the amount from income for tax purposes. See Chapter 12/DEDUCTIONS.

Balance sheet. A systematic statement of the ASSETS, LIABILITIES, and CAPITAL of a business organization at a specified date. This financial statement is included in every annual report. (See Chapter 10/ANNUAL REPORT.)

The traditional form of balance sheet is the *account form*. The assets are listed on the left side of a double sheet, the liabilities and owners' equities (capital) on the right side. The arrangement of the accounts follows a fundamental accounting equation. Assets equal Liabilities plus Capital ($A = L + C$). The assets and liabilities shown on a balance sheet follow a definite order. On the assets side, the usual order is:

Current assets
Investments
Fixed assets
Deferred charges and other assets

On the liabilities side, the usual order is:

Current liabilities
Long-term liabilities
Capital accounts

In the *report form* of balance sheet, current assets are listed first in a single column followed by current liabilities, the total of which is deducted from total current assets to arrive at "working capital." Other assets are then added to the working capital and other liabilities are deducted from this total to arrive at "net assets."

Preparing the balance sheet. Some businesses regularly enter data by computer, using a standard format in which figures are arranged electronically. A balance sheet can then be printed out automatically at a moment's notice, without setting up and typing the statement from scratch each time. When using a typewriter to prepare an account-form balance sheet on a double page, type the longest side first. Count the number of lines used and then approximate the number of lines the other side will take. Space the items on the shorter side so that the balance sheet will not look one-sided. Both sides should end on the same line of the typed page. Figure 1 illustrates a typical account-form comparative balance sheet.

When there are only a few accounts, some accountants prefer that all accounts be placed on the same page, *Assets* at the top of the page, *Liabilities* and *Capital* at the bottom. Even in a single-page arrangement, the balance sheet is still in account form, in that it is still "in balance" (Total Assets equal Total Liabilities and Capital).

Basis for gain or loss. See Chapter 12/CAPITAL GAIN AND LOSS.

BALANCE SHEET: FIGURE 1: Account-form comparative balance sheet on double page

WASHINGTON CO. AND SUBSIDIARY COMPANIES

COMPARATIVE BALANCE SHEET   SEPTEMBER 30, 19— AND 19—

ASSETS	19—	19—	LIABILITIES	19—	19—
CURRENT ASSETS:			**CURRENT LIABILITIES**		
Cash	$ 5,767,825	$ 5,113,776	Trade accounts payable	$ 5,645,278	$ 5,730,155
United States Government securities	741,524	1,465,703	Accrued expenses and other		
Accounts receivable, less allowance for			liabilities	4,477,096	4,537,961
doubtful accounts	2,249,583	1,956,227	Federal and state income taxes	1,885,747	3,602,040
Inventories of merchandise, priced at			Notes payable	1,350,000	350,000
the lower of cost or market	22,516,940	23,440,729	TOTAL CURRENT		
			LIABILITIES	13,358,121	14,220,156
TOTAL CURRENT ASSETS	31,275,872	31,976,435			
PREPAID RENT, INSURANCE, TAXES,					
ETC.	2,014,423	1,225,080			
INVESTMENTS AND OTHER ASSETS:					
Investments in affiliated and			10½ % NOTE, due August 15, 1980:		
other companies, at cost	1,604,413	2,042,394	accounts ranging from $350,000 to		
Estimated net recovery of prior			$500,000 due annually (current		
years' Federal income taxes	440,000	440,000	maturity included above)	2,950,000	3,300,000
TOTAL INVESTMENTS AND					
OTHER ASSETS	2,044,413	2,482,394			
FIXED ASSETS, at cost:					
Land	22,000	37,000			
Buildings (on owned and leased land)	1,554,101	1,596,100			
Equipment	18,591,051	17,699,910	**CAPITAL STOCK AND SURPLUS:**		
	20,167,152	19,333,010	Common stock, $10 par value—		
Less accumulated depreciation.	8,575,604	8,270,736	Authorized 1,955,522 shares;		
			issued and outstanding 1,292,485		
TOTAL FIXED ASSETS	11,591,548	11,062,274	shares	12,924,850	12,924,850
			Retained earnings, per		
			accompanying		
			statement	16,693,286	16,301,178
GOODWILL, LEASEHOLDS,					
LEASEHOLD IMPROVE-			TOTAL CAPITAL STOCK		
MENT, ETC., at nominal amount	1	1	AND SURPLUS	29,618,136	29,226,028
	$45,926,257	$46,746,184		$45,926,257	$46,746,184

Book value. 1. The net amount at which an asset is carried on the books of a company as distinguished from its market or intrinsic value. The book value of fixed assets is usually cost plus additions and improvements, less accumulated depreciation.

2. *As applied to capital stock:* The book value of common stock is determined by dividing the NET WORTH of a corporation—the excess of ASSETS over LIABILITIES as they appear on the BALANCE SHEET—by the number of shares of common stock outstanding. The book value of the shares of a company that has a net worth of one million dollars and ten thousand shares of stock outstanding would be one hundred dollars per share. If the corporation has an issue of preferred stock outstanding, in addition to the common stock, the book value of common stock is determined only after deducting from the "net worth" the liquidation value of the preferred stock and after subtracting cumulative preferred dividends in arrears. Treasury stock should be eliminated from the calculation of net worth before determining the book value of common stock. Book value of preferred stock may also be calculated although not dealt with here.

It is generally not advisable to judge the quality of a common stock on the basis of its book value. That value represents only the amount stockholders theoretically would obtain per share on liquidation of the company. There have been instances when substantial book values have been shown for common stocks of companies on the verge of bankruptcy. A better criterion for the value of common stock is the earning power of the company. The computation of book value is useful, however, in analyzing the value of a preferred stock.

Books of final entry. The LEDGERS to which accounting entries are transferred from JOURNALS or BOOKS OF ORIGINAL ENTRY. The most common book of final entry is the general ledger.

Books of original entry. The JOURNALS in which financial transactions of a business are originally recorded. Books of original entry are contrasted with books of final or secondary entry, known as LEDGERS. See BOOKS OF FINAL ENTRY.

Calendar-year basis. See FISCAL PERIOD.

Capital. 1. In the economic sense, one of the three factors of production. The other two are land and labor.

2. In the accounting sense, the NET WORTH of a business as shown in the capital account of a sole proprietor; the sum of the capital accounts of the partners in a partnership business; the sum of the CAPITAL STOCK; PAID-IN CAPITAL, and RETAINED EARNINGS Less Treasury Stock accounts in a corporation. See Chapter 13/STOCK.

Capital asset. An ASSET such as equipment that is acquired for long-term use. See CURRENT ASSETS and FIXED ASSETS.

Capital expenditure. Any expenditure for FIXED ASSETS such as equipment, land, and buildings. Capital disbursements are charged to the ASSET accounts, unlike other expenses that are charged to the profits of a company.

Capital gain and loss. See Chapter 12/CAPITAL GAIN AND LOSS.

Capital stock. The aggregate ownership interest of a corporation. In accounting, it is the account set up to reflect the amount received from the sale of stock regarded as legal capital. It appears on the credit side of a BALANCE SHEET and is recorded at the par value of the shares issued. See Chapter 13/PAR VALUE STOCK AND NO-PAR STOCK; STOCK.

Capitalization. The total amount of a corporation's securities outstanding in the form of CAPITAL STOCK and long-term bonds. In an accounting sense, the term represents the total accounting value of the capital stock, PAID-IN CAPITAL, and borrowed capital, which consists of bonds or similar evidence of long-term debt. The term is used interchangeably with capital structure. See Chapter 10/CAPITAL STRUCTURE.

Cash. In an accounting sense, cash represents the total individual CASH ACCOUNTS belonging to the company.

Cash account. An account in the general LEDGER used for each bank account owned by the company.

Debits to the account, entered through the CASH RECEIPTS JOURNAL, represent deposits made to the bank account. Credits to the account, entered through the CASH DISBURSEMENTS JOURNAL, represent checks drawn on the bank account. A separate cash account is kept for each bank account. See Chapter 14/BANK ACCOUNTS.

This account differs from one commonly called "Cash on Hand" or "Petty Cash." The latter represents cash in the company's drawer or till. Debits and credits to this account have no direct effect upon the bank account as such. See PETTY CASH.

Certain items are often erroneously considered to be cash, notably postdated checks, dishonored checks, IOUs, and postage stamps. For accounting purposes, nothing should be included under the cash classification that is not money or an instrument that calls for the payment of money from definite funds on deposit with a bank.

Cash accounting. A method of keeping books of account in which consideration is given to cash receipts and cash disbursements only. Income is not considered unless received; expenses are not chargeable to profit and loss unless paid. The books are said to be kept on a cash basis as distinguished from an accrual basis. Generally, individuals account for income and expenses on a cash basis. In addition, for tax purposes, most service businesses (doctors, lawyers, and other professionals) or businesses that do not deal in inventories maintain their

CASH DISBURSEMENTS JOURNAL: FIGURE 1

Page 2

Date	Account Debited	Ck. No.	PR	General Dr.	Accts. Pay. Dr.	Cash Cr.
198— May	Rent Expense	1234	34	700.00		700.00

accounting records on a cash basis. See ACCRUAL ACCOUNTING. The AcCOUNTING RECORDS for an executive usually are on the cash basis.

Cash disbursements journal. A multicolumn account book; one of the BOOKS OF ORIGINAL ENTRY in which disbursements of cash represented by checks drawn on a bank are recorded. Books may be maintained manually or by computer (as described in ACCOUNTING RECORDS). Frequent entries involve payments for rent, salaries, and merchandise. Figure 1, for example, shows a sample entry in a cash disbursements journal for rent expense. (*PR* stands for "Posting Reference," where the corresponding ledger-account page is listed.)

Since deductions from salaries are usually made for social security, federal income tax withheld, state taxes, and items such as payments on employees' bond accounts, columns may be provided for these accounts. Other disbursements are for general and sundry reasons, and a "sundries" column may be provided for them. If all of the transactions can be handled by one bookkeeper, a combination cash disbursements and CASH RECEIPTS JOURNAL can be used.

Cash journal. A multicolumnar account book; one of the BOOKS OF ORIGINAL ENTRY, in which all transactions are entered, whether or not cash is involved. Books may be maintained manually or by computer (as described in ACCOUNTING RECORDS).

The number and headings of the columns vary with the need. Thus if the accounting records include a cash journal, and they frequently do, the cash journal would have a separate column for each of the items that is deductible for income-tax purposes and also a column for wages paid to domestic employees, because that record is necessary for social security tax purposes. There might be one column for all nondeductible items, or there might be a separate column for each of several frequently recurring expenses, such as children's education and clothes. Income can be carried in one column if it is received from only a few sources, and the entries can be analyzed when POSTING to the general ledger.

Cash receipts journal. A multicolumnar account book; one of the BOOKS OF ORIGINAL ENTRY, in which receipts of cash (deposits in bank account) are recorded. The most frequent entry involves a receipt of

CASH RECEIPTS JOURNAL: FIGURE 1

Page 3

Date	Account Credited	PR	General Cr.	Accts. Rec. Cr.	Cash Dr.
198— *June 31*	*B. M. Lighting Co.*	*17*		*165.00*	*165.00*

payment from a customer. Figure 1, for example, shows an entry for income received from B. M. Lighting Co. (PR stands for "Posting Reference," where the corresponding ledger-account page is listed.)

Since this type of entry often involves deductions made by a customer for returns, allowances, and discounts, columns may be provided in the cash receipts journal for these items as well as for accounts receivable. Other receipts are for general and sundry reasons, and a "sundries" column may be provided for them. Special columns may be provided for frequently recurring items not taken care of by the columns mentioned. If all transactions can be handled by one bookkeeper, a combination cash receipts journal and CASH DISBURSEMENTS JOURNAL can be used.

Check. See Chapter 14/CHECK.

Circulating capital. See WORKING CAPITAL.

Closing entries. 1. Entries made in the general journal at the end of an accounting period to transfer all of the balances of the income and expense accounts to balance sheet accounts. This has the effect of clearing all balances in the revenue and expense accounts so that the revenue and expense accounts all begin a new accounting year with zero balances, and profit for that year may be determined. The closing entries first transfer the balances to the profit and loss account, which in turn is closed by closing entries into the capital account of a chief proprietorship or partnership or into the RETAINED EARNINGS account of a corporation. Balance sheet amounts are not closed; they are carried forward.

2. Entries having the effect of balancing an account, a set of accounts, or a LEDGER.

Comparative balance sheet. A type of BALANCE SHEET covering one accounting period with adjacent columns in which corresponding amounts for previous periods are shown. Annual reports of corporations commonly include a comparative form of balance sheet. One major purpose of comparative balance sheets is to reveal trends in accounts over the years indicating directions of growth.

Comparative income statement. A type of INCOME STATEMENT covering one accounting period with adjacent columns in which corresponding amounts for previous periods are shown. Annual reports of corporations commonly include a comparative form of income statement.

Constructive receipt. See Chapter 9/CONSTRUCTIVE RECEIPT.

Control account. An account in the general LEDGER that shows in summary form what appears in detail in the corresponding subsidiary ledger. There is a separate control account for each subsidiary ledger. Thus the accounts receivable control account shows in summary form the totals of all DEBITS AND CREDITS appearing in the customers' accounts in the accounts receivable ledger. The balance of the control account equals the aggregate of the account balances in the subsidiary ledger.

Controller (comptroller). See Chapter 10/CONTROLLER (COMPTROLLER).

Cost accounting. An accounting system that uses general accounting principles to examine the cost of operating a particular business activity. Management uses cost accounting to insure efficient and profitable operations by providing data essential to evaluate costs and performance and to examine the effects of new policies, pricing changes, expansion, and the like. Cost accounting is most frequently used in businesses involving manufacturing and is mainly directed at the preparation of reports for internal management decision making. (An example of such a report is a budget.)

Credit. An accounting term meaning an entry on the right side of a LEDGER account in DOUBLE-ENTRY BOOKKEEPING. See DEBITS AND CREDITS. Credit memos are evidence that the issuing company has credited the account of the recipient.

Cross-footing. See FOOTING.

Current assets. ASSETS that, in the course of business, will be realized or converted within the accounting cycle, generally one year. For example, ACCOUNTS RECEIVABLE is a current asset. The ordinary accounts receivable are due in ten, thirty, or sixty days. In that specified time they will be paid in cash, or if not paid they may be replaced by notes receivable. Inventory, in the course of business, will be sold within one year (converted into accounts receivable or cash). Hence it, too, is a current asset. Thus we see that the ordinary operations of a business involve the circulation of capital within the group of current assets—from Cash to Inventory to Accounts Receivable to Cash again. When the inventory generally takes more than one year to sell (such as a crop that must age several years) the item is still considered a current asset, hence the term *accounting cycle,* or *operating cycle,* rather than *one year* in the general definition.

Included under the current asset heading in the BALANCE SHEET are

Cash (in banks), Cash on Hand, Accounts Receivable (due within one year), Notes Receivable (due within one year), Marketable Securities (that represent the investment of cash available for current operations), Inventory of Merchandise, Accrued Income, and other items. In some cases, PREPAID EXPENSES are also included.

Current capital. Gross working capital or circulating capital. See WORKING CAPITAL.

Current liabilities. Debts or obligations that must be satisfied from CURRENT ASSETS or by incurring additional LIABILITIES. Current liabilities are liquidated within the accounting cycle, generally one year. For example, ACCOUNTS PAYABLE is a current liability. The ordinary accounts payable are due in ten, thirty, or sixty days. In that specified time they will be paid in cash, or they may be replaced by notes payable. Expenses arising currently, such as salaries and rent, are also considered current liabilities.

Included under the current liability heading in the BALANCE SHEET are ACCOUNTS PAYABLE (due within one year), NOTES PAYABLE (due within one year), ACCRUED EXPENSES, Taxes Payable, and other items. Unearned Income may also be included.

Current ratio. The ratio of CURRENT ASSETS to CURRENT LIABILITIES; also called "working-capital" ratio. It shows the number of dollars of current assets for each dollar of current liabilities, thereby revealing a

company's *liquidity* ((the ability of an entity to meet current liabilities out of current assets). The sufficiency of a company's WORKING CAPITAL is tested by finding the current ratio by use of the following formula:

$$\frac{\text{Current Assets}}{\text{Current Liabilities}} = \begin{array}{l}\text{Current Ratio}\\ \text{or Working}\\ \text{Capital Ratio}\end{array}$$

Companies may use their own current ratio to compare their position with a competitor's and as a forecasting aid for financial planning. Lenders may also use this ratio to determine the ability of the borrower to repay loans.

Debit and credit. Entries in DOUBLE-ENTRY BOOKKEEPING that record additions to or reductions in an account. An entry on the left side of the account is a debit, abbreviated *Dr.;* an entry on the right side is a credit, abbreviated *Cr.* A few simple principles apply to debits and credits:

DEBIT

Increases asset accounts (cash, accounts receivable, furniture and fixtures, and other property owned)
Increases expense accounts (salaries, office supplies, taxes, and the like)
Decreases capital accounts
Decreases liability accounts (notes payable, accounts payable, accrued expenses, and the like)

CREDIT

Decreases asset accounts
Increases the capital accounts
Increases income accounts
Increases liability accounts

As a verb, *debit* means to record a debit by a bookkeeping entry; *credit* means to record a credit.

Deficit. The amount by which LIABILITIES and CAPITAL accounts (other than retained earnings) exceed ASSETS. A deficit results in a debit balance in the retained earnings account.

Depletion. The expiration of the cost of natural resources, such as mineral deposits and timber tracts, caused by their conversion into a salable product. During the course of coal mining, for example, the value of the coal properties will decrease through the depletion of the resources. When the coal properties are completely exhausted, they will have to be written off. Instead of taking the loss at the beginning (charging the coal properties to profit and loss upon acquisition) or when the coal properties are completely exhausted, the original cost is allocated over the fruitful life of the properties. The process of allocation is known as depletion.

Depreciation. The periodic writing down of the cost of buildings, equipment, and other limited-life assets because of wear and tear from use or disuse, obsolescence, accidents, or inadequacy. *Depreciation* is loss of value; *deterioration* is loss of substance. The term *depreciation* is not applied to the exhaustion of wasting assets, such as mineral deposits and timberlands. (See DEPLETION.) Depreciation is not applied to small tools or items of supplies such as stationery. (See PREPAID EXPENSES.) In general, depreciation assigns to a fiscal period a portion of the original cost of the FIXED ASSETS.

The federal income tax law allows a deduction (see Chapter 12/DEDUCTIONS) from GROSS INCOME for exhaustion, wear and tear of property used in a trade or business, or property held for the production of income. The simplest and most widely used method of computing depreciation is to spread the cost of the property evenly over the years of its estimated life (*straight-line method*). Another method is to assign a greater portion of the cost of the property to the early years of its useful life (*accelerated depreciation*). Since land does not wear out, its value is excluded from the cost of real property in computing depreciation.

Under the *sum-of-the-years'-digits method*, a changing fraction is applied to the cost of the asset reduced by the estimated salvage value. The fraction numerator equals the remaining life of the asset in years, and the denominator equals the sum of the numbers representing the years of an asset's life.

The *production method* uses hours of operation or units produced to allocate depreciation for assets that have a limited useful life.

Beginning in 1981, the IRS required the use of a depreciation method referred to as *ACRS* (accelerated cost recovery system). Tables are published reflecting the annual percentage rate that must be applied to the asset's original cost to arrive at the year's depreciation. Taxpayers may elect to use the straight-line method under certain circumstances.

Double-entry bookkeeping. The method of recording business financial transactions by equal DEBITS AND CREDITS. In recording financial transactions in the JOURNAL, two phases of the transaction (debit and credit) are recorded in each individual entry. For instance, the purchase of machinery for cash is recorded by:

Debit Machinery	$5,000
Credit Cash	$5,000

The entries signify the two phases of the transaction.

Since the debits and credits in journal entries must always equal each other, and these balanced entries, in turn, are posted to a LEDGER, it follows that the aggregate of the debits in all of the ledger accounts must be equal to the aggregate of the credits in these accounts. This is the basic concept of double-entry bookkeeping.

Equity capital. The portion of a business' CAPITAL that is furnished by stockholders rather than creditors.

Expense account. A statement of an individual's expenses, usually covering a limited time and purpose. A business concern pays the expenses incurred by an employee on its behalf. The company advances money to the employee, who returns the unused portion, or the employee uses his or her own funds, and the company reimburses the employee.

If employees account to the company for expenses incurred on its behalf, they need not report on their income tax return those expenses charged to the company or those for which they were reimbursed. The expenses and reimbursements balance, thus having no effect on income.

If employees do *not* account to their company for expenses, they must report them on their returns. They must also attach a statement showing the total of all amounts received from the employer, including the amounts charged to the employer.

Secretaries should keep a record of expenses incurred by their employers on behalf of the company. The record should show the company the amount spent for each item and also serve as a record for income tax purposes. Any form of record that shows the date, description, and amount of the expenditure is satisfactory. In addition, the IRS requires that one have receipts for all business expenses in excess of twenty-five dollars. All business expenses, regardless of amount, should be recorded in a log book with information similar to that illustrated in Figure 1. As a result of rules effective after December 31, 1986, regarding the deductibility of meals and entertainment expenses, separate accounts should be maintained for these items.

EXPENSE ACCOUNT: FIGURE 1: Record of expenses of business trip

Mo. Day	Description	Fares	Meals	Lodging	Tips	Automobile Expenses	Misc.

Financial statement. A written presentation of financial data prepared from the accounting records. The usual financial statements include a BALANCE SHEET, INCOME STATEMENT, Statement of RETAINED EARNINGS, Statement of Changes in Financial Condition, and Notes to Financial Statements.

Fiscal period. The period covered during one cycle of business operations, generally one year—also known as the accounting period or fiscal year. It may coincide with the calendar year, in which case the firm is said to be on a "calendar-year basis," or it may include twelve successive calendar months terminating at the end of the same month each year. The fiscal year may consist of thirteen four-week periods. In that case, the extra day (two days in leap year) is added to the last week.

Fiscal periods may be semiannual, quarterly, or monthly, when the gain and loss figures are desired for any of these periods. Fiscal periods shorter than one month and longer than one year are infrequent. See NATURAL BUSINESS YEAR.

Fiscal year. See FISCAL PERIOD.

Fixed assets. Those ASSETS of a permanent nature with a life in excess of one year that the business or individual does not intend to dispose of or that could not be disposed of without interfering with the operation of the business. These assets usually include land, buildings, equipment, furniture, and fix-tures. They are included in the fixed asset group in a BALANCE SHEET.

Fixed costs. Those expenses that are not affected by routine variations in the volume of business, for example, rent and salaries. Fixed costs, however, may be changed by management decision or by changes in operational capacity.

Fixed expenses (charges). See FIXED COSTS.

Footing. The total of a column in books of account, FINANCIAL STATEMENTS, financial schedules, WORKING PAPERS, and the like. The footings are obtained by adding, or *footing*, the entries in the columns.

Cross-footing. The total of the debit footings and the total of the credit footings—the footings *across* the JOURNAL or any financial account or schedule. A balanced set of books is a basic requirement in accounting. The debit and credit in each entry must be equal; the total debits must equal the total credits. Each of the columns in a financial account or schedule that contains debits and credits should be *footed* (totaled); then the sum of the columns standing for debits should be checked against the sum of the columns standing for credits. This procedure is known as "cross-footing." If the two sums are not equal, the columns should be footed again. If the mistake is not found by refooting, each entry should be reviewed to see whether its DEBITS AND CREDITS are equal to each other. If each debit entry has an equal credit entry, as it should, the cross-footing will produce equal debits and equal credits.

Funded debt. A debt acquired to purchase an ASSET or pay off a number of short-term debts. Funded debts are usually long-term debts, for which a specified schedule of repayments has been made.

Gain or loss. See Chapter 12/ CAPITAL GAIN AND LOSS.

General ledger. See LEDGER.

Goodwill. An INTANGIBLE ASSET arising when the amount paid to acquire a business is greater than the book value of the underlying assets. Generally, goodwill relates to the value of the acquired company's name, reputation, customer lists, and so on.

Gross income. INCOME before deducting any expenses; an expression used in accounting for individuals, financial institutions, and the like. Gross income, generally, includes gains (see Chapter 12/CAPITAL GAIN AND LOSS); income received as salary; fees; profits from business; interest, dividends, and rents (see Chapter 13/ INTEREST; DIVIDENDS; Chapter 15/ RENT). Certain deductions are subtracted from gross income to arrive at adjusted gross income in the computation of a taxpayer's income tax. See Chapter 12/DEDUCTIONS; ADJUSTED GROSS INCOME.

Gross profit. See PROFIT.

Gross revenue. A term used to emphasize the fact that no deduction for cost has been made from REVENUE.

Holding period for securities. See Chapter 12/CAPITAL GAIN AND LOSS, *The period the investment was held.*

Imprest fund. See PETTY CASH.

Income. In accounting terminology, *income* is money or money's worth earned or accrued during an accounting period, increasing the total of previously existing assets and arising from sales and rentals of any type of goods or services and from the receipt of gifts and windfalls from outside sources. Income is any element, other than additional investment, that increases the owners' equity. Thus the money invested by stockholders in additional stock is not income. Income may be the gain from capital (for example, dividends on securities held by a corporation), or from labor (the manufacture of a product for sale at a profit), or through a combination of both. Income also includes gain from the sale or conversion of capital assets (the sale of a plant at a profit produces income). Thus income includes not only operating profits (or operating income) but also extraneous profits.

As used by some accountants, the terms *income, revenue,* and *profit* are synonymous; as used by others, they have different meanings. When the words *gross* and *net* are prefixed to income, revenue, or profits, the terms again have different meanings because of the differences in the meanings of the basic terms. More-over, the different usage sanctioned by various regulating commissions and tax laws prevents standardization of meanings.

See also GROSS INCOME; NET INCOME; REVENUE.

Income and expense statement. See INCOME STATEMENT.

Income statement. A summary of the INCOME and expenses of a business, in classified form, showing the net income or loss for a specified period. In nonprofit organizations, the income statement is called the STATEMENT OF REVENUE AND EXPENDITURES. An income statement is synonymous with a profit and loss statement. Two forms of income statement are in general use: the *multistep,* or *report, form* and the *single-step,* or *short,*

form. The names are indicative of the arrangement of the contents of the statement. See Figure 1 as a guide to typing a short form of statement. Firms that use computers in preparing financial statements would enter the desired format specifications and current data. A current statement could then be printed out at any time according to the format specified.

Intangible assets. Those ASSETS of a business that have value but are neither tangible property nor a direct right to tangible property. They include items such as patents, trademarks, copyrights, franchises, licenses, goodwill, and leaseholds. Most intangible assets have a limited life, for example, seventeen years for patents. In accounting, the cost expended for such items is written off over the period of years representing

INCOME STATEMENT: FIGURE 1: Short form

XYZ Corporation
Statements of Income
Years Ended December 31, 1988, and 1987

	1988	1987
Sales, net of returns and allowances	$132,532	$108,560
Cost of sales	68,305	56,295
Gross Profit	64,227	52,265
Selling expenses	26,211	23,582
General and administrative expense	18,560	16,893
Income from operations	19,456	11,790
Interest expense	12,082	8,563
Income before income taxes	7,374	3,227
Income tax expense	3,687	1,613
	$ 3,687	$ 1,614

the life of the asset, the writeoff being accomplished during a period of forty years or less by charges to income and credits to accumulated amortization.

Interest. See Chapter 13/INTEREST.

Journal. Any BOOK OF ORIGINAL ENTRY in which transactions are recorded chronologically in a specific manner. Journals are either specialized or general. Specialized journals, also known as subsidiary journals, are used to record transactions of a like kind that occur frequently. The most common are the Sales Journal, Purchase Journal, Purchase Returns Journal, Sales Return Journal, Cash Receipts Journal, Cash Disbursements Journal, and Petty Cash Journal. (See definitions of these terms.) Transactions not provided for in the specialized journals are recorded in the *general journal*. In any journal, the entry shows the date of the transaction, account debited, account credited, amount so debited and credited, and an explanation of the item.

Subsidiary journals save time, space, and labor. The use of separate columns for accounts that are frequently debited or credited eliminates entering the name of the accounts to be debited and credited.

Also, the time and amount of POSTING are reduced. Postings from the subsidiary journals are made periodically instead of after each entry as is done with the general journal. The column totals are posted in a single amount to the proper CONTROL ACCOUNT in the general LEDGER. See also CASH JOURNAL.

Ledger. A book in which the financial transactions of a business are classified by separate accounts, each bearing its own name. Entries in the ledger are made by POSTING from BOOKS OF ORIGINAL ENTRY. They are therefore called BOOKS OF FINAL ENTRY. The ledger may be a bound book, looseleaf book, unbound looseleaf sheets, or a card record. Entries may be made manually or by computer (as described in ACCOUNTING RECORDS).

The following are the usual kinds of ledgers:

General ledger. The ledger that contains all of the accounts of the business except those that are maintained in a subsidiary or private ledger. The general ledger contains the CONTROL ACCOUNTS for each of the subsidiary and private ledgers. The balances in the general ledger for asset, liability, and capital accounts become the basis for data set forth in the BALANCE SHEET. The balances in the income and expense accounts become the basis for data set forth in the INCOME STATEMENT. Figure 1 shows a ledger entry that was posted from the cash receipts journal transaction illustrated in CASH RECEIPTS JOURNAL, Figure 1.)

Subsidiary ledger. A ledger maintained for subsidiary accounts of a homogeneous nature. The balances of the accounts in the subsidiary ledger equal the total of the balance shown in the control account for the particular subsidiary ledger maintained in the general ledger. The usual subsidiary ledgers are the customers' ledger, creditors' ledger, factory ledger, expense ledger, plant

GENERAL LEDGER: FIGURE 1

Accounts Receivable   *Page 17*

Date		PR	Dr.	Cr.	Balance Dr.	Cr.
198— Jun. 1	*Balance*	✓			200.00	
		CR 3		165.00	165.00	

and equipment ledger, stores ledger, and others.

Private ledger. A separate ledger in which accounts containing data of a confidential nature are maintained. Examples are management salaries, withdrawals, loans, capital investment, and items that show profit or, like inventories, are required in the computation of net income. All of the accounts in a subsidiary ledger are similar (for example, all accounts in the customers' ledger are accounts receivable), whereas each account in the private ledger is different, the only similarity between them being their confidential nature. The treasurer usually keeps the private ledger. A control account called *private ledger* is maintained in the general ledger. This control account does not reveal the details of the entries in the private ledger.

Liabilities. Debts or obligations of a business, the satisfaction of which will require the use of the ASSETS of the business for the benefit of creditors. Liabilities also include future services required for which advance payment has already been received (e.g., a legal retainer fee). Normally, the liabilities appear on the credit side of a BALANCE SHEET and are segregated into current (e.g., due within one year) and long-term (e.g., bonds, mortgages payable) liabilities to facilitate the determination of WORKING CAPITAL. Contingent liabilities such as a lawsuit may be included in financial statement disclosures as a footnote.

Natural business year. An accounting period or FISCAL PERIOD that ends with the close of the month in which the activities of a business are at or near their lowest point. Since natural business years end at various times, the accountant is able to spread his or her work more evenly throughout the year if clients operate under a natural business year. To change from a natural year to a calendar year, a business must apply for permission from the Internal Revenue Service.

Net assets. The excess of the BOOK VALUE OF ASSETS over LIABILITIES. Also called "net worth" or "stockholders' equity."

Net income. Difference between INCOME derived from performing services and the expenses attached to performing those services.

Net profit. See PROFIT.

Net working capital. The excess of CURRENT ASSETS over CURRENT LIABILITIES. See WORKING CAPITAL.

Net worth. The value of the proprietary interests in a business. Basically, BOOK VALUE OF ASSETS minus LIABILITIES gives net worth. In the case of a sole proprietorship, it is reflected in the proprietor's capital account; in the case of a partnership, in the total of the partner's capital accounts; in the case of a corporation, in the total of the PAID-IN CAPITAL and the RETAINED EARNINGS less any treasury stock.

Notes payable. (See Chapter 13/ NOTE.) An account in a general LEDGER showing the amount of promissory notes given by the business. Notes payable usually require the payment of interest. The item is on the LIABILITIES side of the BALANCE SHEET. It may include (1) the amount owing on notes to merchandise creditors for supplies or merchandise purchased; (2) notes payable to banks, representing money borrowed from the banks by discounting the debtor's own notes; (3) notes payable for paper sold through note brokers; (4) notes payable to others, representing notes given when a loan is obtained or other obligations are incurred from sources other than the first two mentioned.

Notes receivable. An account in the general LEDGER showing the amount of negotiable promissory notes received from customers in payment for goods sold and delivered and from other debtors. Notes receivable usually involve the receipt of interest. The item is on the ASSETS side of the BALANCE SHEET. See Chapter 13/ NOTE.

Obsolescence. The end of an ASSET's normal useful life due to some factor such as economic changes or new developments.

Operating expenses. Those expenses incurred in the conduct of ordinary business activity, for example, administrative costs and selling expenses.

Operating statement. See INCOME STATEMENT.

Overhead. A synonym for expenses of a business, such as indirect labor, fuel, and depreciation on machinery. *Factory overhead* is the factory cost to manufacture an item other than direct material and direct labor costs. Overhead may be classified as either fixed or variable. See VARIABLE COSTS.

Owner's equity. The value of one's net worth, capital, or proprietorship; the assets remaining after all debts are paid.

Paid-in capital. The amount received by a corporation from its stockholders whether in cash, property, or services. A minimum amount of paid-in capital may be required by statute before a corporation can commence business. Paid-in capital is a major BALANCE SHEET item. It is reflected in the CAPITAL STOCK.

Paid-up capital. The aggregate of par value stock and the stated value of no-par stock for which full consideration has been received by the corporation. See Chapter 13/PAR VALUE STOCK AND NO-PAR STOCK.

Payroll. A record showing gross salary or wages of each employee, deductions for taxes withheld from wages, employee's contributions to his or her own bond or savings account, other deductions, and net amount of pay for a definite payroll period. This period is usually weekly, semimonthly, or monthly.

Statutory requirements. The payroll department must comply with and understand its obligations under the following federal, state, and local laws:

1. Federal income tax withholding at the source. (See Chapter 12/WITHHOLDING.)

2. State and local income tax withholding at the source. (See Chapter 12/WITHHOLDING.)

3. Federal old age, survivors, and disability insurance tax law. (See Chapter 12/SOCIAL SECURITY TAXES.)

4. Federal unemployment tax act.

5. State unemployment insurance and disability benefit tax laws. (See Chapter 12/STATE UNEMPLOYMENT INSURANCE TAX.)

6. Federal wage and hour law.

7. Other federal laws and orders affecting wages and hours. The most important one is the Fair Labor Standards Act.

8. Other state laws affecting wages and hours. They include state minimum wage laws, state labor relations laws, state antidiscrimination laws, state arbitration laws, state laws regarding payment of wages, and state child labor laws. These laws vary from state to state and, therefore, should be checked in the state in which a particular organization is doing business to insure compliance with them.

Payroll records. All federal "payroll" laws require employers to keep records of certain information concerning their employees. Severe penalties may be imposed for failure to comply.

The records used in the preparation of the payroll at each period fall into the following categories: (1) authorization records, which include notices of new employees added, changes in rate of pay, transfer, leaves of absence, terminations, and overtime authorization; (2) timekeeping records, which are the original entries from which the payroll department can determine employee gross pay for the pay period; and (3) payroll preparation records. The latter are used in the actual making up of the payroll. They include (a) the PAYROLL JOURNAL, (b) individual earning records (see Figure 1), (c) pay-

PAYROLL: FIGURE 1: Employee's individual earnings record

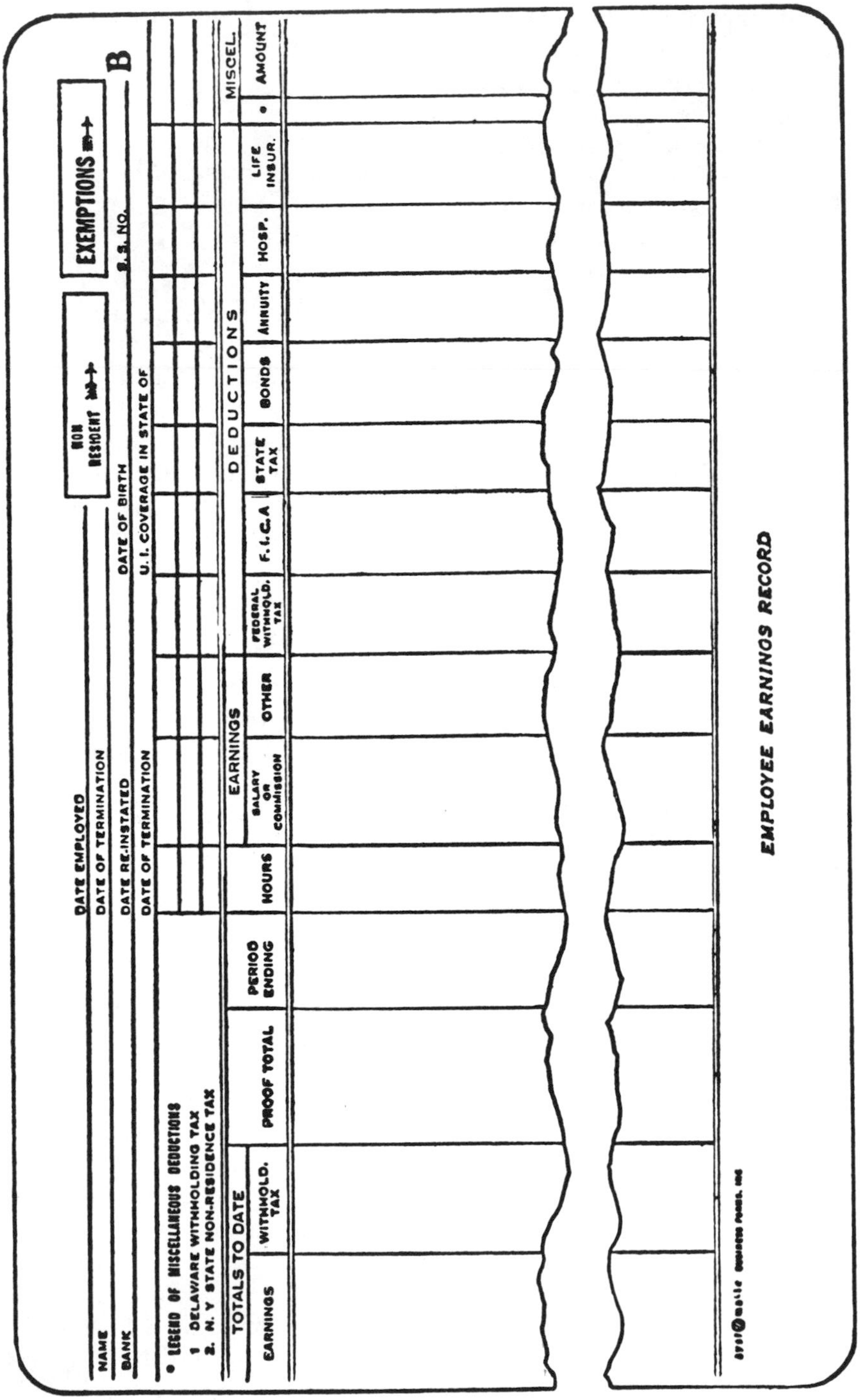

check or employer's receipt, and (d) a statement of earnings and deductions for the employee's use. Many companies find that payroll records can be maintained more effectively at less cost by using their own computers or the computer payroll services of banks and outside computer-based companies.

Payroll journal. A payroll system usually provides for maintaining a record for each payroll period, showing the amount of compensation paid to each employee. This record is called a "payroll journal," "payroll sheet," "payroll record," "payroll summary," or the like. The heading of each payroll journal should show the ending date of the paychecks. Each sheet of the payroll journal should be numbered.

The payroll journal is usually a columnar form that provides for listing the following information under appropriately entitled column headings—employee name and number, gross pay, tax withholdings, deductions (individually listed), total deductions, net pay, period ending, and check number. The payroll sheet used by most companies also has columns for the regular overtime hours worked and the hourly rate.

It is good practice to number each payroll and to have all papers pertaining to a particular payroll identified by the same number.

Large firms use computers to record payroll data and compute earnings, tax withholdings, deductions, and other items. Supporting records may include carbon copies of paychecks or other remittance forms.

Records and forms may vary depending on the size of the company, but complete and accurate data are necessary to compute and file federal, state, and local payroll tax reporting forms such as federal Form 941 (Employer's Quarterly Federal Tax Return) and Form 940 (Employer's Annual Federal Unemployment [FUTA] Tax Return).

Petty cash. An amount of cash on hand used for disbursements that are too small to justify the use of checks.

Petty cash is usually maintained on the imprest system, which operates as follows: Assume that a firm's experience shows that it needs approximately one hundred dollars a week for petty disbursements. It starts the fund by drawing a check to the Petty Cash account and cashes it at the bank. it places this one hundred dollars in a cash drawer. Disbursements are made from the cash only upon receipt of a properly approved petty-cash voucher describing the exact purpose for which the cash has been withdrawn, by whom, and the amount. The total of the cash remaining in the drawer and the amount on the vouchers equals the amount of the fund (one hundred dollars in this case). At the end of the week, the vouchers are collected from the drawer, itemized, and canceled. A check is then drawn in the amount of the canceled vouchers, thereby bringing the fund back to its original amount (one hundred dollars in this case). Although this replacing check is made out to Petty Cash, it is entered in the CASH DISBURSEMENTS JOURNAL with charges to the proper expense accounts as shown by the canceled petty-cash vouchers.

The fund is known as an "imprest fund" because it is forced periodically at the designated level. Most treasurers find that funds of a size requiring not more than two or three reimbursements during a month are most practical.

If petty-cash transactions are numerous and involved, a petty-cash journal is employed to itemize the various charges of petty-cash disbursements. If there is a petty-cash journal, checks drawn to Petty Cash for reimbursement purposes are not itemized in the Cash Disbursements book.

Posting. The bookkeeping procedure of transferring Debit and credit entries from the Books of original entry to the proper accounts in the Ledger.

Procedure for posting from Cash journal *to accounts in the general ledger:*

1. Foot (see Footing) each column in the journal. Then cross-foot the debit columns and the credit columns. Enter the totals in pencil. The totals of debit and credit columns must equal each other. If they do not, there is an error in the entries or in addition. When the accuracy of the totals has been proved, enter them in ink.

2. Post the totals from all columns in the journal except General Ledger to the corresponding accounts in the general ledger to the debit or credit side of the account, as indicated by the journal. Also enter the date of the posting and the page number of the journal.

3. As each column is posted, draw a double red line beneath it to show that it has been posted. Also place beneath the column the page number of the ledger where the item is posted.

4. Since the items in the General Ledger column of the journal are miscellaneous, they cannot be posted as a whole. Post the individual items to the respective accounts in the general ledger, showing the date the entry was made and the page number of the journal. In the journal, show the page number of the ledger to which each item was posted.

Prepaid expenses. Expenses paid for but not applicable to the current period. For example, fire insurance premiums are frequently paid three years in advance. One-third of the three-year premium is chargeable to the first year's Profit and loss. The other two-thirds is considered as prepaid expenses. Other common prepaid expenses are rent, taxes, commissions, and interest. Prepaid expenses usually appear separately on the Balance sheet as a Current asset.

Profit. Excess of income over the cost of merchandise sold and the expenses of doing business. Accountants distinguish between *profits*, which are derived from the sale of merchandise, and *income*, derived from rendering services or from any other source. The difference between the selling price and the cost of merchandise sold is *gross profit*. The difference between gross profit and the general and administrative expenses of conducting a business, such as rent, office salaries, and telephone service, is net profit before income taxes. Income taxes are then deducted to arrive at net profit.

Profit and loss. A temporary account in the general ledger to which the balances of all accounts reflecting revenues, income, profits, expenses, and losses are transferred periodically. The balance of the Profit and Loss account shows the net income or loss for the period. It is transferred, or "closed out," to the RETAINED EARNINGS account in the case of a corporation and to the CAPITAL account in the case of a sole proprietorship or partnership. See CLOSING ENTRIES.

Profit and loss statement. See INCOME STATEMENT.

Quick assets. Those CURRENT ASSETS that are quickly convertible into cash. They usually include cash, receivables, and temporary investments in marketable securities. Inventories are generally omitted because it takes time to convert them into receivables. However, commodities immediately salable at a quoted price on the open market would be "quick." See Chapter 13/ACID-TEST RATIO.

Replacements. Also called "renewals." A FIXED ASSET acquired to re-

place a similar, existing asset possessing the approximate capacity.

Retained earnings. The accumulated earnings of a corporation remaining in business from the date of incorporation. Reductions in retained earnings occur through distributions of dividends. Additions occur through closing out the PROFIT AND LOSS account at the close of the FISCAL PERIOD, when that account shows a profit or credit balance.

Retained earnings are part of the stockholders' equity and are added to CAPITAL STOCK to get the NET WORTH of the business. Appropriations from retained earnings for specific purposes are considered subdivisions of retained earnings because the directors can at any time return them to retained earnings.

Revenue. 1. Gross sales of products and gross income from services. Accountants commonly apply the term to the principal classes of gross operating income of various business entities. For example, the first item on the profit and loss statement of a railroad is *operating revenue*, whereas a real estate agent would use the term *commission income*.

Semivariable cost. Expenses that are generally fixed but at some level of production or activity may become variable. For example, rent is generally a fixed cost, but if production should triple, more facilities may be required, making rent a semivariable cost.

2. The GROSS INCOME of a govern-

mental unit derived from taxes, customs, and other sources.

Selling expenses. The cost of selling or distributing a service or product, for example, sales staff salaries, commissions, travel costs, shipping costs, advertising, and depreciation of showroom furniture and fixtures.

Single-entry bookkeeping. When no attempt is made to maintain the primary equation of DOUBLE-ENTRY BOOKKEEPING (Assets = Liabilities + Capital), the system of bookkeeping is known as single entry. In its simplest form, single-entry bookkeeping consists merely of keeping accounts with debtors and creditors, although in actual practice an account with "cash" is also kept. Single-entry books, of themselves, do not show either the financial condition of the business or the cause of the changes in the condition. The financial condition of the business can be found only by taking an actual inventory of all physical assets, such as merchandise, furniture, and fixtures, and using these figures in conjunction with the ASSETS and LIABILITIES shown on the books to set up a statement of assets and liabilities. Such a statement shows the NET WORTH of the business at a particular time. The defect of the single-entry system is that it does not show the *causes* of changes in the financial condition of the business. The system has been supplanted by double-entry bookkeeping.

Statement of changes in financial position. Also commonly referred to as the "funds statement," the statement of changes in financial position is a report of how a business has financed its activities and how the various financial resources have been used. It is a statement that traces the flow of resources related to major financial events during a specific reporting period.

The statement of changes evolves from the same data used in preparation of the BALANCE SHEET and INCOME STATEMENT, but it provides unique business insights not gained from examination of these two statements. For example, one can determine from reading the statement of changes where the profits went, how equipment acquisition was financed, how dividends were able to be paid, or what the proceeds were from new stock issuances.

The statement of changes can be prepared on either the working-capital or cash basis. The *working-capital basis* defines balance sheet changes in terms of the effect each change has on the working capital of a business (*working capital* is current assets minus current liabilities). The *cash-basis statement* traces all balance sheet charges in terms of their effects on the movement of cash through a business. The cash basis requires a reconciliation of the beginning and ending cash balances for a particular accounting period.

Generally, the statement of changes in financial position offers valuable information concerning a business's potential ability to meet liabilities or to handle an increased debt load due to expansion.

Statement of financial position. See BALANCE SHEET.

Statement of revenue and expenditures. The name given to the INCOME STATEMENT of a nonprofit organization. The statement emphasizes the content of INCOME and expenditures as opposed to measurement of NET PROFIT for profit-oriented entities.

Subsidiary journal. See JOURNAL.

Subsidiary ledger. See LEDGER.

T-account. A simple visual device used by accountants to analyze debit and credit entries for a transaction. In a T-account, the left side of the T is the debit side, and the right side represents credits. Figure 1 shows a debit of $2,340 in the Cash account.

Tax accounting. Accounting performed to arrive at tax-related financial information for use in preparing annual tax returns.

Tax records. See ACCOUNTING RECORDS.

T-ACCOUNT: FIGURE 1

Cash

23 40

Trial balance. A listing of the DEBIT AND CREDIT balances of accounts in a LEDGER (usually the general ledger) for the purpose of proving that the total debit balances equal the total credit balances. The trial balance is one of the WORKING PAPERS and is used as a basis for preparing FINANCIAL STATEMENTS.

Variable costs. Expenses that fluctuate indirectly with the level of production or in concert with the activities of a business. Examples are direct materials and direct labor.

Wasting asset. A natural resource that is subject to depletion, included as an organization's ASSET.

Work sheet. Any columnar sheet used to analyze a TRIAL BALANCE and to organize figures for use in preparing financial statements. The BALANCE SHEET accounts are listed first followed by the INCOME STATEMENT accounts. Opening balances are written in the first two columns, transactions for the specific accounting period in the next two columns, adjusting entries in the next two columns, and the final corrected balances in the last two columns.

Working capital. ASSETS available for use in the everyday operations of a business. Accountants use the term to mean CURRENT ASSETS less CURRENT LIABILITIES. Those current assets that are changed in the ordinary course of business from one form to another, for example, from cash to inventories, from inventories to receivables, and from receivables back to cash, are sometimes called "circulating capital." Companies without sufficient working capital are forced to borrow to meet their day-to-day needs.

Working papers. The schedules, analyses, records, and memos developed in connection with the preparation of a FINANCIAL STATEMENT or in connection with an AUDIT.

Write-off. A charge against profits of the ACCOUNTS RECEIVABLE and the NOTES RECEIVABLE that have been deemed uncollectable by management. Worthless assets of many kinds (fixed assets, intangible assets) may be written off to a loss account.

CHAPTER 12

TAXES

Accrual Accounting. See Chapter 11/ACCRUAL ACCOUNTING.

Ad valorem taxes. Taxes or duties assessed as a percentage of the value of goods or property.

Adjusted gross income. For federal income tax purposes, gross income after deductions in connection with the expense of producing income (see Chapter 11/GROSS INCOME)—for example, unreimbursed travel expenses directly related to a business; certain losses on sales, exchanges, or other dispositions of property; and payments to retirement plans.

Alternative minimum tax. A special tax enacted to insure that taxpayers who benefit from special treatment to some kinds of income and/or special deductions from some kinds of expenses will pay at least a mini-mum amount of tax. This tax exists for both corporate and individual taxpayers. The alternative minimum tax is figured on certain tax benefits known as "tax preference items." In 1987 the minimum tax rate for noncorporate taxpayers was 21 percent and for corporate taxpayers, 20 percent.

Assessed valuation. See ASSESSMENT.

Assessment. 1. The valuation of property to establish a basis for a PROPERTY TAXES.

2. The levying of a tax

3. The additional amount that a taxpayer is required to pay because of a DEFICIENCY

Under the CAPITAL GAIN AND LOSS provisions of the federal income tax law, a capital asset is any property held by the taxpayer, except:

1. Stock in trade or other property included in inventory or held for sale to customers

2. Accounts or notes receivable you received for services in the ordinary course of your trade or business or from the sale of any property described in Item 1 or for services you performed as an employee

3. Generally, depreciable property used in trade or business

4. Copyrights; literary, musical, or artistic compositions and similar property (a) created by your personal efforts or (b) prepared or produced for you (in the case of a letter, memo, or similar property) or (c) that you received from a taxpayer mentioned in (a) or (b) in a way (e.g., by gift) that entitled you to the basis of the previous owner

5. Federal, state, and municipal obligations issued on or after March 1, 1941, on a discount basis and payable without interest at a fixed maturity date not exceeding one year from the date of issue

6. U.S. government publications that you received from the government other than by purchase at the normal sales price, or that you got from another taxpayer who had received them in a similar way if your basis is determined by reference to the previous owner

The term *capital asset* includes tangibles such as shares of stocks and bonds, unless they fall under one of the exceptions mentioned. See CAPITAL GAIN AND LOSS.

Basis. A way of measuring an investment in property for tax purposes. Basis is used to figure depreciation, amortization, depletion, casualty losses, or whether you have a gain or loss on its sale or exchange. Property you buy usually has an original basis that is equal to its cost. Property received some other way, such as by gift or inheritance, requires a basis other than cost.

Various events may take place to change the original basis, and these events increase or decrease the original basis. The result is called the "adjusted basis." Basis must be *increased* by the cost of permanent improvements, legal fees, other charges you choose to capitalize, and any other capital expenditure, including amounts spent after a casualty to restore the damaged property. Basis must be *decreased* by amounts you receive that are a return of capital and by all other amounts that should be charged to a capital account.

When you cannot use cost as a basis, *fair market value* may be important. The Internal Revenue Service defines this as the price at which the property would change hands between a buyer and a seller, neither being required to buy or sell and both having reasonable knowledge of all necessary facts. Sales of similar property, on or about the same date, may be helpful in figuring the fair market value of the property.

See also CAPITAL GAIN AND LOSS,

Basis for gain or loss on security transactions.

Capital gain and loss. For tax years beginning after 1986, new capital gains tax regulations are in effect for both individual and corporate taxpayers. In 1987 individuals' capital gains were taxed as ordinary income at rates up to 28 percent. Corporations were also taxed at their regular rates for all capital gains. Although preferential tax treatment for capital gain was eliminated under the Tax Reform Act of 1986, the provisions concerning characterization of income as ordinary or capital and gains as long or short term still exist and merit some discussion.

Gain or loss on security transactions. The disposition of securities for money (a sale) or for other property (an exchange) or for a combination of both almost always results in a gain or loss, because there is usually a difference between what was paid for the security given up and what was received for it. Before the taxable gain or loss, if any, on a security transaction can be determined, the taxpayer must know these principal factors:

1. The cost or other basis of the securities disposed of

2. The amount realized upon the disposal of the security

3. The period the investment was held before it was disposed of

Basis for gain or loss on security transactions. Basis is the term used in the tax law to indicate the amount to be compared with the sales proceeds to determine what the gain or loss is. The basis depends on the manner in which the securities were acquired. It may be the actual cost, the fair market value, or a substituted basis.

The amount realized. The amount realized includes both money and fair market value of any property received on the sale or other disposition of the securities. Fair market value is a question of fact to be determined from evidence.

The period the investment was held. Gains or losses from the sale or exchange of a security held for more than one year are long-term capital gains or losses for securities acquired before June 23, 1984, or acquired after December 3, 1987. The long-term capital gain holding period is more than six months for securities acquired after June 22, 1984, and before January 1, 1988.

In computing the period held, the day on which the property was acquired is *excluded;* the day on which it was disposed of is *included.*

In certain security transactions, particular rules must be followed for determining when the security was acquired. These rules give the *date basis.*

Date basis. In the case of securities bought or sold through stock exchange transactions, the dates of the trade rather than the settlement dates constitute the dates of acquisition or disposition.

Computation of gain or loss on a sale of securities acquired by purchase. On a sale of securities that were acquired by purchase, the basis is the cost of the securities. This includes the commission paid the broker. The amount realized is the selling price of the securities less the commission paid the broker for the sale, less the Securities Exchange Commission tax. The following example shows the computation of a loss on a sale of securities.

Sold 100 shares at 24	$2,400.00
Less commission	22.00
	$2,378.00
Less SEC tax	40
Selling price for tax purpose	$2,377.60
Cost	$3,345.81
Loss	$968.21

Computation of gain or loss on sales of securities acquired other than by purchase. As indicated above, the basis for determining gain or loss depends on the manner in which the owner acquired the securities sold. Also, the date basis depends on the particular security transaction. Space does not permit us to show the rules that would apply if the securities sold were acquired other than by purchase. Generally, however, the secretary can help by taking these steps:

1. If stocks or bonds are sold, determine how the security was acquired, that is, whether it was acquired by inheritance, gift, as a nontaxable stock dividend, as a taxable stock dividend, through conversion, in a split, or through some other change in the corporation's capital structure.

2. Find out, through a tax service or from someone who knows the tax rule (a) what the basis is for determining gain, (b) what the basis is for determining loss, (c) what the date basis is.

Other security transactions that may involve gain or loss. The receipt, exercise, or sale of stock rights may have tax consequences (see also Chapter 10/RIGHTS), as may certain exchanges of one type of security for another or the receipt of cash or other assets when a corporation liquidates or redeems stock outstanding. The secretary is again advised to consult a tax service or someone acquainted with the tax rules to determine how the change in the securities must be treated for tax purposes.

In 1987 a net capital loss was deductible from ordinary income up to three thousand dollars. Any excess could be carried over indefinitely.

Record of capital gains and losses. For income tax purposes, a list must be kept of all security transactions involving gains and losses, for they are capital gains and losses and must be so reported. The form shown in Figure 1 has been devised for this purpose. A new form must be started each year.

As soon as a sale has been made, the transaction is entered on Figure 1. The final schedule of capital gains and losses realized during the year, which must accompany a final income tax return, is made up from the records maintained in this form.

Carry-back, carry-over. A tax law provision that allows individuals or corporations to use an operating or capital loss in one year to reduce taxes for preceding years (carry-back) or succeeding years (carry-over). A net operating loss can be carried back three years and then forward for fifteen years. See CAPITAL GAIN AND LOSS.

CAPITAL GAIN AND LOSS: FIGURE 1: Capital gain and loss record

SECURITIES SOLD												
CAPITAL ASSETS		PURCHASE DATA		SALES DATA		RECOGNIZED GAINS OR LOSSES		CAPITAL GAINS AND LOSSES				TRANSFER TAXES	
								SHORT-TERM (HELD 4 MONTHS OR LESS) 100% OF ACTUAL GAIN OR LOSS		LONG-TERM (HELD MORE THAN 4 MONTHS) 80% OF ACTUAL GAIN OR LOSS			
NUMBER OF SHARES OR AMOUNT OF BONDS	NAME OF STOCKS OR BONDS SOLD DURING YEAR	DATE ACQUIRED	COST OR OTHER BASIS	DATE SOLD	PROCEEDS (EXCL STATE TRANSFER TAXES AND ACCRUED INTEREST)	NET GAINS	NET LOSSES	SHORT-TERM CAPITAL GAINS	SHORT-TERM CAPITAL LOSSES	LONG-TERM CAPITAL GAINS	LONG-TERM CAPITAL LOSSES	FEDERAL & SEC	STATE

Cash accounting. See Chapter 11/ CASH ACCOUNTING.

Casualty loss. Loss resulting from the destruction of property in a fire, storm, automobile accident, shipwreck, or other loss caused by sudden, unexpected, or unusual forces. For federal income tax purposes, the loss is deductible from ADJUSTED GROSS INCOME in itemized DEDUCTIONS. In 1987 the amount of the loss to be deducted was measured by the fair market value of the property just before the casualty, less its fair market value immediately after the casualty, reduced by any insurance or compensation received and one hundred dollars. The resulting loss was deductible only to the extent that the total loss amount for the year exceeded 10 percent of adjusted gross income.

Charitable contributions. See CONTRIBUTIONS.

Child- and dependent-care credit. A taxpayer is allowed a credit against federal income taxes equal to 20 percent of qualifying child- or dependent-care expenses, provided the expenses are incurred to enable the taxpayer to be employed gainfully. In 1987 the maximum amount of employment-related expenses to which the credit could be applied was $2,400 for one qualifying DEPENDENT and $4,800 for two or more. The child or dependent must be under fifteen and eligible to be claimed as a dependent or any other individual, including the taxpayer's spouse, who is mentally or physically incapacitated and for whom the taxpayer has furnished more than half of the individual's support. Certain limitations apply based on the taxpayer's amount of adjusted gross income and filing status.

Computation of gain and loss for tax purposes. See CAPITAL GAIN AND LOSS.

Constructive receipt. See Chapter 9/CONSTRUCTIVE RECEIPT.

Contributions. Donations to schools, churches, synagogues, hospitals, and charitable and other nonprofit organizations.

At certain times of the year, numerous organizations make drives for contributions. It is usually advisable to accumulate the requests in a folder and give a batch of them to one's employer at an opportune time. An executive gets a better perspective of the demands being made than if he or she receives the requests singly. The secretary should never destroy a request for a contribution unless instructed to do so. Some people, particularly those in public positions, make a practice of responding, at least in a small way, to nearly every request.

The secretary's record of donations. Someone who is considering whether to make a certain donation is interested in knowing (1) the amount he or she gave to a specific organization the preceding year and (2) the total amount of donations for the current year. The amount donated the previous year should be noted on each request before the request is given to the manager. A running record of donations for the current year should also be given to one's employer with each request. Figure 1 illustrates an appropriate running record for the current year. If someone customarily makes a contribution to each organization in a lump sum, simply type the date, name of the organization, and the amount on a looseleaf sheet as each donation is made. There should also be another sheet on which the organizations are listed alphabetically. At the end of each year, the contributions to each organization are entered in a column headed with the particular year. If kept from year to year, this record will enable the secretary to give a quick answer to questions such as, "What did I give the Red Cross last year and the year

CONTRIBUTIONS: FIGURE 1: Record of contributions

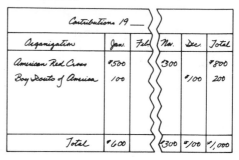

before?" "How much have I given the Boy Scouts in the past five years?"

As deduction for tax purposes. In 1987 one could give up to 50 percent (30 percent in the case of gifts of certain appreciated property) of AD-JUSTED GROSS INCOME to charity and deduct the entire amount for income tax purposes. The deduction applied to contributions by individuals to religious organizations, regular educational institutions, and hospitals and other public charities. For gifts to other charitable groups, the limitation was 20 percent. Such deductions are generally measured by the value of the gift rather than its cost.

EXCEPTION: If the appreciated property given would have produced ordinary income or short-term capital gain on sale, the deduction is the fair market value minus the amount that would be ordinary income or short-term capital gain upon sale of the property. Special rules apply to gifts of art works. The running record illustrated in Figure 1 will facilitate preparation of the income tax return.

Corporations are also entitled to a deduction for charitable contributions, but the limitations differ from those applied to contributions by individuals.

Credits, tax. The IRS allows certain expenditures to be applied directly against the taxpayer's income tax. The types of credit include credit for the elderly; child- and dependent-care expenses; federal tax on gas, special fuels and lubricating oil; federal tax on gasoline, diesel fuel, and special fuels used in qualified taxicabs; taxes paid by a regulated investment company; alcohol used as fuel; increasing research; foreign taxes: jobs; WIN; overpaid windfall profits tax; and individual retirement deposits.

Care must be taken to distinguish between deductions and credits. Deductions reduce ADJUSTED GROSS INCOME, which is then used to compute the tax. Credits are applied to the tax itself to arrive at the taxpayer's actual liability.

Date basis. See CAPITAL GAIN AND LOSS, *Date basis.*

Deductions. For purposes of income tax, (1) those items that may be subtracted from gross income (see Chapter 11/GROSS INCOME) to arrive at ADJUSTED GROSS INCOME, for example, mortgage interest on income producing property; and (2) those items that may be subtracted from adjusted gross income to arrive at TAXABLE INCOME, for example, mortgage interest on a personal residence. These deductible items materially reduce one's income tax. It is, therefore most important to keep meticulous records of the various items, not only to substantiate the deductions but also to facilitate preparation of the income tax return.

Deductions for adjusted gross income. The items in the first classification are referred to as deductions *for* adjusted gross income. The following list shows allowable deductions in the group to which an executive will most likely be entitled. However, since Internal Revenue Service regulations change from year to year, consult current taxpayer instructions.

1. Expenses that are ordinary and necessary to the executive's trade or business
2. Ordinary and necessary expenses and certain other deductions on property held for producing rents and royalties
3. Outside salesperson's expenses in earning a salary, commission, or other compensation
4. Certain other employee business expenses
5. Certain losses on sales, exchanges, or other dispositions of property
6. Payments by employees and self-employed persons to their own retirement plans
7. Allowable depreciation and depletion by a life tenant or a beneficiary of a trust or estate if the depreciation of depletion is not deductible by the trust or estate
8. Alimony paid
9. Disability income exclusion

411

10. Excess foreign living expenses
11. Amortization of the costs of forestation or reforestation when you do not have to file Schedule C or Schedule F
12. Certain required repayments of supplemental unemployment benefits

Deductions from adjusted gross income. The items in the second classification are referred to as deductions *from* adjusted gross income. They include the deduction for personal EXEMPTIONS and "other itemized deductions" and are subtracted from adjusted gross income to arrive at TAXABLE INCOME. Deductible items include (1) TAXES OTHER THAN FEDERAL INCOME TAX; (2) INTEREST; (3) CONTRIBUTIONS; (4) MEDICAL AND DENTAL EXPENSES; (5) CASUALTY LOSS and thefts; (6) Moving expenses; and (7) certain employee business expenses. See the entries of items (1) through (5) for restrictions on the deductions and for appropriate forms of records. Consult current Internal Revenue Service regulations for any recent changes.

See also STANDARD DEDUCTION, which the taxpayer may take instead of itemizing deductions.

Deferred-compensation agreement. Contracts for payments to be made in the future in consideration of services chiefly rendered in the past. Deferred-compensation plans today constitute an important method of compensating executives. Under this plan one is currently paid compensation less than one might otherwise have received, payment of additional compensation being spread over a future period. Deferred-compensation agreements are made as a means of obtaining substantial tax savings. Many people want to postpone receipt of income in the hope that lower tax rates will prevail or until retirement or other causes will reduce gross income and the applicable tax rates. (See Chapter 11/GROSS INCOME.) However, deferred-compensation plans are adopted for purposes other than tax reduction: to provide a savings plan or to postpone part of one's compensation as a guaranty of continued performance or as a stimulus for greater future effort.

Deficiency. Generally, the amount by which taxes, as determined by federal, state, and local authorities, exceed the taxes shown on the RETURN filed by the taxpayer, plus additional previous ASSESSMENTS and minus previous rebates (refund). (See Chapter 13/REBATE [REFUND].) Deficiencies can arise under any law that compels the taxpayer to calculate the amount of tax due and file a return. Each law contains its own definition of deficiency. When a taxpayer fails to file a return, the deficiency is the entire amount calculated by the tax authorities plus assessments and minus rebates.

When an audit of a taxpayer's return indicates a deficiency, the federal government sends that person a deficiency (90-day) letter giving him or her 90 days in which to appeal. The taxpayer may also receive an earlier, less formal notice. A similar procedure is followed by the states.

The procedure for settling or protesting a deficiency is usually involved and technical, and it is advisable to consult an accountant or lawyer.

Dental expense. See MEDICAL AND DENTAL EXPENSES.

Dependent. For federal income tax purposes, you can take an exemption not only for yourself—and your spouse if you file a joint return—but for each dependent who meets five dependency tests: (1) you provided more than half of total support; (2) the dependent's gross income was less than $1,000; (3) an unrelated dependent lives with you as a member of your household for the entire year; (4) the dependent is a United States citizen, a resident, or a national or a resident of Canada or Mexico for some part of the year; and (5) you are not allowed an exemption for your dependent if he or she files a joint return. Special rules apply to students, children of divorced or separated parents, dependents supported by two or more taxpayers, and in cases of birth or death during the tax year. The total number of exemptions multiplied by the amount of the exemptions is subtracted from AD-JUSTED GROSS INCOME to arrive at TAXABLE INCOME.

Depreciation. According to the Internal Revenue Service, if you buy property to use in a trade or business or to earn rent or royalty income and the property has a useful life of more than a year, you cannot deduct its entire cost in one year but must spread the cost over more than one year and deduct a part of it each year. For most types of property, this is called "depreciation." (Two other methods, amortization and depletion, permit deductions similar to those allowed by depreciation.)

Property is depreciable if it meets all of these tests:

1. It must be used in business or held for the production of income (e.g., to earn rent or royalty income).

2. It must have a useful life that can be determined and its useful life must be longer than one year. The useful life of a piece of property is an estimate of how long you can expect to use it in your business or to earn rent or royalty income.

3. It must be something that wears out, decays, gets used up, becomes obsolete, or loses value from natural causes.

Partial business use. If you use property in part for business and in part for personal purposes, you can only depreciate the business part. If your employer requires you to use your own car on the job, you may be able to depreciate the car for the percentage of time you use it at work. If you use part of your home for business, you may be able to take a depreciation deduction for this use.

Declaration not claimed in an earlier year. If in an earlier year you did not claim depreciation that you were entitled to deduct, you must still reduce your BASIS in the property by the amount of the depreciation that you did not deduct. You may not deduct the unclaimed depreciation in the current year or in any later tax year. However, you may claim the depreciation on an amended return (Form 1040X) for the earlier year.

Figuring depreciation. To figure depreciation deductions, you must know what your basis in the property is, when the property was placed in service, and which method of depreciation you are permitted to use.

Nonbusiness property changed to business use. If you change property that was not used for business to a business use, you must determine your basis in the property for figuring depreciation. This amount is determined as of the date of the change. It is the fair market value of the property on that date or your adjusted basis in the property on that date, whichever is less.

Placed in service. Property is considered placed in service when it is in a condition or state of readiness and availability.

Direct tax. 1. A tax that is collected from someone who is expected to bear the entire tax cost; opposed to "indirect" or "hidden" taxes, which are usually concealed in the price of goods and hence borne by others. For example, SALES AND USE TAXES and admissions taxes are direct taxes. State gasoline taxes are sometimes hidden taxes, depending on how they are levied. Manufacturers' Excise TAXES, however, are usually indirect taxes since in most cases they are included as costs in establishing selling prices.

2. A type of tax that is limited according to the Constitution, which states that "direct taxes shall be apportioned among the several states" (Art.I, Sec.2) and that "No capitation, or other direct, tax shall be laid, unless in proportion to the census" (Art.I, Sec.9). Hence a federal property tax is outlawed barring an amendment to the Constitution. The Sixteenth Amendment to the Constitution was needed to enable Congress to pass an INCOME TAX law.

Disability income exclusion. See SICK PAY.

Documents tax. See EXCISE TAXES; STAMP TAX.

Donations. See CONTRIBUTIONS.

Entertainment expense. See MEALS AND ENTERTAINMENT EXPENSES.

Estate tax. A federal or state EXCISE TAX usually levied on a graduated basis on the right to transfer property from the dead to the living. It includes transfers taking effect at death and certain other transfers that are defined by the laws as having been made in "contemplation of death." Estates of $600,000 or less are exempt from this tax.

Estate taxes should not be confused with "inheritance" taxes, which are excise taxes levied by all states except Nevada on the right of the living to receive property from the dead. Inheritance taxes are payable by the heirs and not by the estate of the deceased.

See also CHAPTER 15/ESTATE PLANNING.

Estimated tax. A federal tax return showing income and tax as estimated for the current year. The tax withheld by an employer (see WITHHOLDING) does not always pay the tax bill in full. To keep income tax payments on a pay-as-you-go basis, the government, in some cases, requires the taxpayer to estimate his or her tax for the current year and to pay it in four installments, in addition to the tax withheld by an employer. A taxpayer who files a regular income tax return (Form 1040) for the preceding year should also file a Declaration of Estimated Tax (Form 1040 ES) if his or her estimated tax is five hundred dollars or more and the total amount of income tax that will be withheld from a person's income will be less than the lesser of (1) 90 percent of expected tax liability for the coming year or (2) 100 percent of the tax shown on the preceding year's income tax return. See Chapter 11/ GROSS INCOME.

Excise taxes. Federal, state, and local taxes that are imposed on acts rather than as a DIRECT TAX on property. They are usually a levy on the right to follow a particular occupation or trade, carry on a business, or transfer and receive property. ESTATE TAXES are excise taxes on the right to transfer property from the dead to the living, whereas inheritance taxes are excise taxes on the right to receive such property. Federal manufacturer's excise taxes are usually determined as a percentage of the manufacturer's selling price as, for example, the excise tax on automobiles, cameras, and watches. Other federal excise taxes, such as admissions taxes, taxes on safe deposit boxes, and communication and transportation taxes, are borne directly by the consumer. Most of the consumer-borne taxes are collected by the person who receives payment for the goods or services; they are remitted by that person to the government at legally stated intervals.

State excise taxes include franchise, stock transfer, document recording, death and gift, motor fuel, admissions and amusements, chain store, tobacco, and "severance" taxes (taxes on the use of natural resources such as timber and minerals). Most state and local excise taxes that are paid directly by the consumer are deductible from ADJUSTED GROSS INCOME to arrive at Taxable income, but federal excise taxes are not deductible. See Chapter 11/ACCOUNTING RECORDS for appropriate records of excise taxes.

Exclusions. A federal income tax term denoting items of income that are exempt from tax by the federal government, for example, interest on state and municipal bonds. In filing a return, the taxpayer generally is allowed to exclude such items from gross income. (See Chapter 11/GROSS INCOME.) Some items that are excludable in a limited amount, for example, SICK PAY, are reported in full on the RETURN, and the excludable portion is then subtracted from the total before DEDUCTIONS for ADJUSTED GROSS IN-

COME. Exclusions should not be confused with deductions.

Exemptions. See DEPENDENT.

Experience rating. See MERIT RATING.

Federal Insurance Contributions Act (FICA). See SOCIAL SECURITY TAXES.

Federal unemployment tax. See STATE UNEMPLOYMENT INSURANCE TAX.

Franchise tax. A capital stock tax imposed on corporations by most of the states. Such taxes may be called *qualification taxes, corporation fees, license fees,* and *privilege taxes.* They are all taxes on the privilege of operating as a corporation and apply to a domestic corporation and a foreign corporation alike. (See also Chapter 10/DOMESTIC CORPORATION; FOREIGN CORPORATION.) Franchise taxes are usually levied on either (1) issued capital stock, (2) authorized capital stock, or (3) capital used in the state levying the tax. Franchise taxes must be paid before a corporation can do business within the state. See Chapter 9/INTERSTATE COMMERCE, INTRASTATE COMMERCE.

Gift tax. A federal or state EXCISE TAX that is levied on the transfer of money or property from one person to another without an adequate consideration (see Chapter 9/CONTRACTS, *Consideration*) in money or money's worth. Essentially, the federal law imposes a GRADUATED (PROGRESSIVE) TAX that approaches the ESTATE TAX

that would have been payable on the donor's death if the gift had not been made.

The law allows certain exemptions toward determining the net taxable amount, and the federal law contains specific provisions for gifts made between husband and wife or by both to a third party.

Federal gift taxes are reported and paid on an annual basis. Both the donor and the donee must file a gift tax return by April 15 of the year following the gift if gifts to any one person exceed ten thousand dollars. The return is filed with the director of the district in which the donor resides. The donor pays the tax. A secretary should keep a record of gifts made by his or her employer so that the executive will be able to furnish the information necessary to complete the gift tax form. The record should show the date of the gift, to whom it is made, and the money or property given as a gift. If securities are given, the names of the securities and the fair market value of each at the date of the gift should be listed.

Graduated (progressive) tax. Any tax rate that increases as the "value" that is being taxed increases. For example, a state income tax law might specify a tax of 1 percent on the first $1,000 of net income, 2 percent on the next $1,500, and so on. Hence on a net income of $1,500, *A* would pay the following tax:

$$\begin{array}{rcl} \$1,000 \times 1\% & = & \$10.00 \\ 500 \times 2\% & = & \underline{10.00} \\ \text{Total tax} & & \$20.00 \\ & & \$20.00/\$1,500 = 1\tfrac{1}{3}\%, \\ & & \text{effective tax rate.} \end{array}$$

On a net income of $2,000, *B* would pay the following tax:

$1,000 × 1%   = $10.00
$1,000 × 2%   =   20.00
  Total tax $30.00
                $30.00/$2,000 = 1½%,
                  effective tax rate.

Head of household. For federal income tax purposes, an unmarried taxpayer who furnishes over half the cost of maintaining a home and has living with him or her throughout the year (1) an unmarried child, grand-child, stepchild, adopted child, or foster child, whether dependent on the taxpayer or not; (2) a married child, grandchild, stepchild, adopted child, or foster child claimed as a dependent; (3) a mother or father claimed as a dependent (who need not live with the head of household), or (4) any other relative claimed as a DEPENDENT. Multiple-support dependents (see MULTIPLE-SUPPORT AGREE-MENT) do not qualify the taxpayer as a head of household. A special favor-able tax rate applies to a head of household.

Holding period. See CAPITAL GAIN AND LOSS.

Income. In a broad sense, all wealth that flows in to the taxpayer other than as a mere return of capital. It includes gains and profits from any source, including gains from the sale or other disposition of capital assets. (See CAPITAL GAIN AND LOSS.) It is not a gain *accruing* to capital, not a growth or an increase in the value of an investment, but a gain or profit, something of exchangeable value, proceeding from the capital.

EXAMPLE 1

Margaret Walsh purchased 100 shares of *X* stock on August 2 for $20 per share, or a total of $2,000. On December 31, the stock she held was listed at $25 per share on the stock exchange. This $500 increase in the value of the 100 shares of stock (from $2,000 to $2,500) is *not* income but a growth or increment in the value of the stock. This growth or increment will not become income until its realization through the sale or exchange of the stock.

EXAMPLE 2

On January 2, Thomas Clemons bor-rowed $300 from the Fourth National Bank. He was required to repay the loan, plus 12 percent interest, by the end of the year. This he did. Of the $336 received by the bank during the year, $300 (return of capital) is not income to the bank. The $36 interest is income since it constitutes a realized gain.

Income tax. A federal, state, or local tax levied on the income of individuals and corporations, estates, and some trusts.

Under the federal pay-as-you-go income tax collection system (see WITHHOLDING), most individuals pay all or a substantial part of their income tax during the year in which they receive their income. The tax is with-held from their wages or is paid in quarterly installments based on a declaration of estimated tax or both. But the amount paid rarely equals the tax liability. It is necessary, therefore, for each taxpayer to file an income tax return after the close of the year showing his or her actual tax liability. Any additional amount due is payable then or, in some cases, in installments. Any overpayment is refunded or credited to the taxpayer.

Under most of the laws, taxpayers may report on an accrual basis or a cash basis, and the accounting period may be a calendar or a fiscal year.

Most income taxes are GRADUATED (PROGRESSIVE) TAXES. The rates increase as the amount of income reported increases. The rates are usually based on *taxable income,* which is ADJUSTED GROSS INCOME less certain DEDUCTIONS allowed by tax laws and the deduction for your exemptions.

Income tax deductions. See DEDUCTIONS and items referred to.

Income tax files. The income tax files consist of all previous years' records relating to income taxes and a current income tax folder. The previous years' records may be kept in large expansion portfolios, labeled "Federal Income Tax, 19—(*name of taxpayer*)." These records are kept perpetually and are never destroyed, unless one's employer decides to discard them *after all possible statutes of limitation have run out.*

At the beginning of each year, a folder should be set up labeled "Federal Income Tax, 19—(*Name of taxpayer*)." This is a general folder for income tax material that does not get into the separate folders or records. See Chapter 11/ACCOUNTING RECORDS.

Separate files should be maintained for one's employer, for his or her spouse, and for each member of the family whose tax records are the secretary's responsibility.

Income tax return. See RETURN.

Individual retirement programs. Tax-deductible contributions to an individual retirement savings program may be made through:

1. *Individual retirement accounts* (IRAs) at a participating bank, federally insured credit union, savings and loan association, or other institution that may act as a trustee or custodian

2. *Individual retirement annuity* or endowment contract of a life insurance company

3. *Individual retirement bonds* purchased from the United States government

4. *Trust account* established by an employer or an employee association

A contribution to an individual retirement savings program is an adjustment to income and thus may be claimed as a deduction even if you use the standard deduction. The deduction is claimed for the year in which the contribution was made. For the tax years after 1986, certain restrictions on the deductibility of individual retirement contributions exist if ADJUSTED GROSS INCOME exceeds set amounts. However, even if a contribution to an individual retirement account is deemed to be nondeductible, a contribution may still be made up to $2,000 if one has sufficient earned income, and the interest earned on the contribution remains tax free.

After retirement, funds derived from the program are taxed as ordinary income. Early withdrawals from individual retirement accounts are subject to a severe penalty tax.

Information return. Information required under the Internal Revenue Code to be furnished by persons or organizations who pay certain classes of taxable income to others. The principal types of income to be reported on Form 1099 relate to wages of six hundred dollars or more, if not shown on Form W-2, dividends in excess of ten dollars, and payments to noncorporate recipients of interest, rents, and royalties of six hundred dollars or more. Estates, trusts, and partnerships must also file information returns, the data supplied including details of revenues and expense, and distributable shares of net income, if any. The returns are used by the government to insure that the person receiving the income includes it in his or her tax return.

Inheritance tax. See ESTATE TAX.

Interest. Amounts paid on indebtedness. Interest paid on personal indebtedness is listed in the "Itemized Deductions" section of the taxpayer's individual income tax return, and the total of the itemized deductions is subtracted *from* adjusted gross income. (See RETURN; ADJUSTED GROSS INCOME.) On the other hand, interest paid in connection with income-producing property is deductible from gross income to arrive at adjusted gross income (see DEDUCTIONS) and is entered as an expense in a special schedule of the tax return.

The 1986 tax-reform law disallows any deduction for personal interest (e.g., interest on personal credit-card debt). However, mortgage interest on a taxpayer's principal residence and one other home is deductible to the extent that the mortgage does not exceed the lesser of fair market value or the cost of the home plus improvements. Interest on mortgage debt incurred before August 17, 1986, is not subject to the limitation concerning purchase price plus improvements. Interest on additional mortgage indebtedness up to fair market value that is incurred for qualified educational or medical expenses can also be deducted. The 1986 law specified that the disallowance of personal interest would be phased in over five years. In 1987, 65 percent of such interest would be deductible; in 1988, 40 percent; in 1989, 20 percent; in 1990, 10 percent, with no deduction allowed in later years.

Invalid-care expense. See CHILD-AND DEPENDENT-CARE CREDIT.

Joint return. Income tax return filed jointly by husband and wife. A special federal income tax schedule applies to a joint return. The return produces a tax equivalent to splitting the combined TAXABLE INCOME in half and multiplying the tax on one-half the taxable income by two. It is usually advantageous to file a joint return because the higher the taxable income, the higher the tax rate. For purposes of the tax law, persons are considered married for the entire tax year if (1) they were married as of December 31, or (2) one of the spouses died during the tax year. They are not considered married if they were separated during the tax year under a final decree of divorce or separate maintenance. See also SURVIVING WIDOW OR WIDOWER.

Keogh retirement plans. See Chapter 13/RETIREMENT PLANS.

Losses. See CAPITAL GAIN AND LOSS.

Meals and entertainment expenses. The law provides for a deduction for meals and entertainment expenses if the taxpayer can demonstrate a clear business purpose for the expense, although only 80 percent of such expenses was deductible in 1987. It is important that a secretary or office manager maintain accounting records for meals and entertainment expenses separate from other business or travel expenses.

Medical and dental expenses. For income tax purposes, amount paid for medical or dental care by the taxpayer for himself or herself, a spouse, or any dependent who received over half of his or her support from the taxpayer.

Normally, a taxpayer may deduct from ADJUSTED GROSS INCOME medical and dental expenses in excess of 7.5 percent (1987) of that figure. Expenses compensated by health insurance are not included in the total amount.

Someone with a large income may not consider it worthwhile to keep records of medical and dental expenses if he or she feels that the expenses will not exceed 7.5 percent (1987) of adjusted gross income. However, in the majority of cases, it is necessary to keep careful records of these expenses so that the taxpayer may take the deduction when entitled to it and when his or her state allows the deduction in full.

Figure 1 illustrates a form of record of medical and dental expenses that will facilitate preparation of the tax return, because the medicine and drug items are separated from the other expenses. Receipted bills for these expenses should be kept together and filed with the papers pertaining to the particular year's income tax return. See also Chapter 11/ACCOUNTING RECORDS.

Medical expense. See MEDICAL AND DENTAL EXPENSES.

Merit rating. One of the purposes of the state unemployment compensation laws is to encourage employers to stabilize employment. To achieve this purpose, most of the unemployment compensation laws make some provision for a reduction in the STATE UNEMPLOYMENT INSURANCE TAX or contribution rate for those employers who have stabilized their employment. Under some of the laws, higher rates are imposed on employers who have heavy labor turnovers. The change in contribution rates on the basis of stabilization is popularly known as *merit rating* or *experience rating*.

Miscellaneous deductions. A federal income tax term denoting miscellaneous expenses a taxpayer can

MEDICAL AND DENTAL EXPENSES: FIGURE 1: Record of medical expenses

		Medical Expenses 19___			
Date	*Whose Illness*	*Nature of Expense*	*Name + address of Payee*	*Amount*	
1/10	Son, James	Eyeglasses	Charles Johnson Optometrist 21 Main St.	$200	—
2/3	Wife	X-ray	Dr. Robert Smith Lakeville, N.Y.	150	—
2/7 2/8	Daughter, Florence "	Hospital bill	Memorial, N.Y.	1,800	—
3/1	Family	Hospitalization insurance	Quarterly deduction from salary	480	68
3/8	Daughter, Florence	Trip to Florida on Dr. Smith's recommendation	Various	1,500	—

deduct from ADJUSTED GROSS INCOME to arrive at TAXABLE INCOME. They include (1) union dues, (2) tax-return preparation fee, and (3) other. The "other" includes employee expenses such as subscriptions to professional journals, expenses of producing income, such as accounting fees, and other deductible expenses, such as appraisal fees. In 1987 these miscellaneous expenses were deductible only to the extent that they exceeded 2 percent of ADJUSTED GROSS INCOME. A record should be kept of all expenditures for these miscellaneous items for tax purposes.

Multiple-support agreement. A federal income tax term applied to an agreement designating one of several taxpayers to claim as an exemption an individual to whose support they all contributed. If two or more taxpayers provide over half the support of an individual, the federal income tax law permits one of them to claim that individual as an exemption provided that (a) the taxpayer claiming the exemption contributed over 10 percent of the support; (b) each of the taxpayers who would have contributed over half the support would have been entitled to claim the individual as a DEPENDENT; and (c) each of the taxpayers, other than the one claiming the exemption, makes a declaration on Form 2120 (Multiple Support Declaration) that he or she will not claim the individual as a dependent for that tax year.

Old age, survivors, and disability insurance (OASDI). See SOCIAL SECURITY TAXES.

Other deductions. See MISCELLANEOUS DEDUCTIONS.

Payroll taxes. Taxes based on payroll. The term applies to taxes the employer must pay and also to the taxes the employer must withhold from the employee's pay. The employer must pay (1) SOCIAL SECURITY TAXES; (2) Federal Unemployment Tax; (3) STATE UNEMPLOYMENT INSURANCE TAX in some states; and (4) disability contribution or tax (see Chapter 9/DISABILITY BENEFIT LAWS) in some states. The employer must withhold from the employee's pay (1) federal INCOME TAX (see WITHHOLDING); (2) SOCIAL SECURITY TAXES; (3) STATE UNEMPLOYMENT INSURANCE TAX in some states; (4) disability contribution or tax (see Chapter 9/ DISABILITY BENEFIT LAWS) in some states; and (5) state or city income tax in some states.

Penalties. If you do not file your return and pay your tax by the due date, you may have to pay a penalty. You may also have to pay a penalty if you substantially understate your tax, if you file a frivolous return, or if you fail to supply your social security

number. Consult Internal Revenue Service instructions for current penalty and interest rates.

Personal exemption. See DEPENDENT.

Personal property taxes. See PROPERTY TAXES.

Property taxes. State and local taxes levied on personal property (tangible, intangible, or both), such as automobiles and jewelry, and real property, such as land and improvements. (See Chapter 9/PERSONAL PROPERTY; Chapter 15/REAL PROPERTY.) Most of the taxes on personal property have been difficult to administer. They are not rigorously enforced, particularly with respect to compelling taxpayers to disclose the exact value and makeup of their personal property. Personal property taxes are allowed as a deduction from ADJUSTED GROSS INCOME on the federal income tax return.

Real estate records. *For tax purposes.* Rent from real property is taxable income. Reporting it for tax purposes involves records showing depreciation, repairs and maintenance, and other expenses. If an executive owns real estate that he or she rents, it is essential that the secretary keep a record similar to that shown in Figure 1. The following checklist shows the more common items usually considered DEDUCTIONS in computing the net rent. All except depreciation and repairs would appear in the expense column in Figure 1.

REAL ESTATE RECORDS: FIGURE 1

REAL ESTATE

LOCATION

DESCRIPTION

PURCHASED FROM	DATE PURCHASED	PURCHASE PRICE	AGENT EMPLOYED	ASSESSED VALUE
RECORDED IN	COUNTY OF	STATE OF	DEED BOOK NO.	PAGE NO.	WHERE DEED KEPT

MORTGAGE DATA

REMARKS

SO_D TO	DATE SOLD	SALE PRICE	AMOUNT CASH RECEIVED	HOW BALANCE PAYABLE
AGENT EMPLOYED		AGENT'S FEE		PROFIT OR LOSS

MORTGAGE DATA

REMARKS

DATE	DESCRIPTION	EXPENSE	DEPRECIATION AND REPAIRS	FIXED IMPROVEMENTS	NET INVESTMENT	RETURNS RECEIVED			
						4	5		
	TOTALS BROUGHT FORWARD		10						
	MAKE AS FIRST ENTRY UNDER "NET INVESTMENT" THE ORIGINAL PURCHASE PRICE								
	TOTALS CARRIED FORWARD								

423

Building maintenance expenses

Carpentry expenses

Casualty loss

Commission for obtaining lease (amortized, which means applying the commission over the life of the lease and taking as a deduction each year's portion of the commission)

Damage-claim payments

Decorating expenses

Depreciation, building and equipment

Fire loss

Interest on mortgage

Liability insurance

Management fees

Old-age benefit taxes

Other interest

Painting

Plumbing repairs

Property insurance

Real estate taxes

Repairs

Salaries and wages

Storm-damage loss

Theft

Travel expenses

Taxes paid on real estate that is not held for production of income, such as a private residence, are deductible as an itemized deduction. See Chapter 11/ACCOUNTING RECORDS.

For insurance purposes. See Chapter 16/INSURANCE RECORDS, *Insurance other than life.*

Real estate taxes. State and local taxes levied on real property. (See Chapter 15/REAL PROPERTY.) Owning property involves payment of taxes. Usually, there are several taxes, such as a county tax, a village tax, and a school district tax. Tax bills are re-

ceived from the taxing authority. They show clearly what they are for, the assessed value of the property, when the tax must be paid, to whom it must be paid, the penalties that will be imposed if the tax is not paid when due, and the discount that will be allowed if the bill is paid in full by a certain date. Usually, payment can be made in halves. If only one-half is paid, there is no discount; no bill is rendered for the second half. Failure to receive a tax bill is no excuse for delay in payment or for nonpayment. The secretary must note tax payments dates on his or her calendar. (See Chapter 5/CALENDARS.)

For purposes of the federal income tax, real estate taxes fall into two categories: (1) taxes on real property held for production of income and (2) taxes on real property held for personal use, such as a residence. Taxes in the first category are included in the group of DEDUCTIONS that are subtracted from gross income (see Chapter 11/GROSS INCOME) to arrive at ADJUSTED GROSS INCOME. (See REAL ESTATE RECORDS for appropriate record of these taxes.) Taxes in the second category are classed as "itemized deduction" and are subtracted from adjusted gross income to arrive at TAXABLE INCOME. See Chapter 11/ACCOUNTING RECORDS.

Retirement income credit. See CREDITS, TAX.

Return. Forms used to file tax information with the government. Each tax law requires its particular return, states the rules for "preparation" and filing of the return, and usually stipulates penalties for failure to file.

Below is a partial list of important federal tax forms:

Form Number	Explanation
W-2	*Wage and Tax Statement:* Copy A (filed by employer with the District Director of Internal Revenue), Copy B (filed by employee), and Copy C (for employee's records)
W-4	*Employee's Withholding Allowance Certificate:* Form given by employee to employer indicating the number of dependency exemptions that the employee is entitled to
1040	*U.S. Individual Income Tax Return*
1040ES	*Declaration of Estimated Tax for Individuals*
4868	*Application for Automatic Extension of Time to File U.S. Individual Income Tax Return*
1040X	*Amended U.S. Individual Income Tax Return:* Used to claim a refund or report balance due after filing original return
1099 series	*Statements:* Used to report income from dividends, interest, rents, royalties, and other payments (see INFORMATION RETURN)
1120	*U.S. Corporation Income Tax Return*
1120S	*U.S. Small Business Corporation Income Tax Return*
1065	*U.S. Partnership Return*
940	*Employer's Annual Federal Unemployment Tax Return*
941	*Employer's Quarterly Federal Tax Return:* Combines federal withholding and old-age returns

Royalties.   Payments or rentals made to the owner of a patent for the privilege of manufacturing or renting the patented article. The term is also applied to payments made to authors and composers for the sale of copyrighted material and to payments under gas, oil, mining, or mineral leases. Royalties constitute income for tax purposes and are usually reported by the taxpayer as "Income from Rents and Royalties" on Form 1040. But if the taxpayer holds an operating oil, gas, or mineral interest or is in business as a self-employed writer, inventor, artist, and so on, gross income and expenses should be reported on Schedule C of Form 1040.

Sales and use taxes.   State and local taxes imposed as a flat rate on sales. Generally, sales taxes take the form of (1) retail sales taxes; (2) taxes on gross sales or "turnover" of retailers, wholesalers, and manufacturers; and (3) taxes on the gross incomes from sales of commodities and services.

The "use" tax was devised to counteract avoidance of the sales tax by those who bought in neighboring, nonsales jurisdictions, for example, residents of a state that has a sales and use tax who purchase cars in another state that does not or whose tax rate is lower. They avoid their state's *sales* tax but not its *use* tax. *Reason:* When they register the cars in their home state, they will be billed for the use tax.

Those sales and use taxes paid by the retailer, wholesaler, or manufacturer usually allow certain exemptions from gross sales or turnover before the tax is applied. Sales taxes paid by the retail customer usually start on all sales over a minimum amount, which may be as small as ten cents.

For tax years beginning January 1, 1987, no deduction for sales tax is allowed against individual income tax.

Self-employment tax.   A federal tax levied on the income of self-employed persons for social security benefits. (See SOCIAL SECURITY TAXES.) The tax rate on self-employed individuals was 13.02 percent for 1988.

Sick pay.   Sick pay received from an employer is taxable, except for disability income exclusion. However, benefits received under an accident or health insurance policy for which you paid premiums are not taxable, and payments for sickness or accident disability under a plan set up by an employer are not subject to social security tax withholdings.

Social security taxes.   Taxes levied under the Federal Insurance Contributions Act (FICA) on employers and employees in amounts based on wages paid in performance of employment, commonly referred to as social security taxes because the Social Security Act originally levied the tax. The taxes levied on employees are withheld by the employers from wage payments. These tax withholdings, as well as the taxes levied on the employers, are remitted via periodic deposits in an authorized Commercial or Federal Reserve Bank by the employers to the Director of Internal Revenue. Depending on the amounts involved, deposits may have to be made as often as every week. The taxes provide for payments to retired people age sixty-five or older (younger in certain cases), to their dependents and survivors, and to totally and permanently disabled workers between ages fifty and sixty-five. The benefits are technically known as "old age, survivors, and disability insurance."

If an individual works for two or more employers during a calendar year, each employer is required to pay the tax on his or her wage payments to the employee up to the current limit and to make similar deductions from the employee's wages. The employee can obtain a refund from the government in the form of a credit against tax for any excess deducted taxes; the employers cannot obtain a refund.

The amount of taxes deducted from the employee's wages must be reported to the employee, but there is no prescribed method. The usual practice is to show the deduction on either (1) the pay envelope if wages are paid in cash, or (2) a perforated check stub if wages are paid by check. A record of the deductions must be kept on the payroll records. (See Chapter 11/PAYROLL, Figure 1.) The employee cannot deduct his or her share of the social security tax from ADJUSTED GROSS INCOME.

When the social security taxes are deducted from the employee's wages, they are liabilities on the books of the employer. Such liabilities are liquidated when these taxes are deposited. The employer's share of the tax is treated as an expense of the business.

Wages paid to domestic employees. An employer is required to pay social security taxes on the wages of domestic employees and, also, to withhold the employees' share of the tax and to file a tax report at the end of each quarter. (An employer may pay the employees' share of the tax if desired.) The form of report used is furnished by the federal government, but it is different from that used in business organizations. It is a special envelope addressed to the Internal Revenue Service, with spaces for the employee's name, social security account number, wages paid, and taxes due. Since wages paid to domestic employees are personal expenses, neither the employer nor the employee can deduct the tax from AD-JUSTED GROSS INCOME. It is, therefore, unnecessary to keep a record for tax purposes, but a running record should be kept to facilitate preparation of the quarterly report referred to above. See also STATE UNEMPLOY-MENT INSURANCE TAX.

Stamp tax. A tax collected by the states through the sale of stamps that must be affixed to certain documents and securities before they are bought, sold, or transferred; also known as a *transfer tax.*

Most state laws make any of the parties to a taxable transaction liable for the tax. Although those concerned may agree among themselves about who shall pay the tax, the agreement does not relieve the others from liability. State stamps are issued by the various state tax commissions, which usually designate certain commercial banks as sales agents for stamps. Records must be available at all times for inspection by the tax authorities.

Effect on federal income tax. State stamp taxes placed on the transfer of securities are treated as itemized DE-DUCTIONS. Therefore, one should keep separate records of state stamp tax payments. (See CAPITAL GAIN AND LOSS, Figure 1.) The amount of state taxes is indicated on the sale confirmation.

Standard deduction. A flat amount allowed each taxpayer as a deduction. The amount varies depending on filing status and is built into the tax tables. See also DEPENDENT for a discussion of exemptions.

State and local taxes. See TAXES OTHER THAN FEDERAL INCOME; STATE INCOME TAXES.

State income taxes. A secretary will be concerned with state income taxes payable by his or her employer if (1) the executive lives in a state that has a personal income tax or (2) is employed in a state that taxes him or her as a nonresident. In almost all instances, the records maintained for, and used in, filing the federal income tax will be adequate for taking care of the state income tax. One *caution* must be noted. There may be deductions permissible in a particular state that are not allowed under the federal income tax law.

Specifically, the secretary should do the following or assist the executive with the following in regard to state income taxes:

1. Include on a calendar the dates when reports must be filed and taxes paid. (See Chapter 5/CALENDARS.)

2. Obtain the required forms from the state tax commission or other taxing authority. Get at least three copies of the form, one for filing with the tax official, one to be retained by the employer, and one to be used as a work sheet.

3. Keep any necessary records of deductions beyond those required for federal income tax purposes.

4. Prepare reminders of reports to be filed and taxes to be paid.

5. Have available, when needed, a copy of the latest federal income tax return filed and the return for the previous year; also, a copy of the previous year's state income tax return. These materials are invariably needed in preparing the current year's return.

6. File reports and pay taxes.

7. File all of the state income tax papers for the particular year in an envelope folder labeled "State Income Tax, 19—."

See INCOME TAX; TAXES OTHER THAN FEDERAL INCOME.

State unemployment insurance tax. A payroll tax imposed by state unemployment insurance laws to pay benefits to unemployed persons who meet certain requirements. The state laws are more or less alike because they all conform to standards specified in the federal Social Security Act. Conformance is necessary so that employers can be allowed a credit for the state tax against the federal unemployment tax. But the laws vary in many important respects. For example, each state law specifies the minimum number of employees an employer must have to be subject to the law, the types of employment that are exempted, and so forth. The amount of benefits payable also varies from state to state. All state laws provide for some form of MERIT RATING under which a reduction in the state contribution rate is allowed to employers who have given steady employment.

Unemployment insurance taxes usually concern only the secretary to a professional person who employs enough people to be subject to the unemployment insurance taxes of the state in which he or she carries on a profession. In other cases, the responsibility for these taxes usually rests with the person who handles the firm's payroll.

Stock transfer tax. See STAMP TAX.

Surtax. An extra tax on something already taxed.

Surviving spouse. See SURVIVING WIDOW OR WIDOWER.

Surviving widow or widower. A federal income tax term applied to a taxpayer whose spouse died during either of the two preceding taxable years. Under certain conditions a surviving widow or widower may compute her or his income tax by including only her or his income, exemptions, and deductions, but otherwise computing the tax as if a JOINT RETURN had been filed. The conditions are that the taxpayer (a) must not have remarried, (b) must have a child or stepchild for whom the taxpayer is entitled to claim a deduction as an EXEMPTION, (c) must have been entitled to file a joint return in the year of the spouse's death, and (d) must have paid more than half the cost of keeping up the home, which is the principal home of the dependent child for the whole year.

Tax files. See INCOME TAX FILES.

Tax lien. A lien against real or personal property by a taxing authority. If the taxpayer's obligation to the taxing authority is not paid when due, the property can be disposed of through a tax sale.

Tax return. See RETURN.

Tax sale. The sale of a taxpayer's property by a taxing authority as a means of satisfying the nonpayment of taxes when due.

Taxable income. Income subject to tax by any governmental authority; the amount of income upon which the income tax is computed. To arrive at the amount of income subject to federal INCOME TAX, certain deductions are subtracted from gross income (see Chapter 11/GROSS INCOME) to arrive at ADJUSTED GROSS INCOME. Additional deductions are subtracted from adjusted gross income to arrive at taxable income. (See DEDUCTIONS and items referred to.)

Taxes other than federal income. Besides the federal INCOME TAX, the following taxes may require the atten-

tion of the secretary: (1) STATE INCOME TAXES; (2) state and local personal property taxes (see PROPERTY TAXES); (3) REAL ESTATE TAXES; (4) SOCIAL SECURITY TAXES; (5) STATE UNEMPLOYMENT INSURANCE TAX (see also Chapter 9/DISABILITY BENEFIT LAWS); (6) GIFT TAX.

Taxes, the secretary's duties. The secretary's duties involving an employer's federal INCOME TAX matters include the following: (1) keeping the INCOME TAX FILES; (2) keeping records of all income received by the executive (see Chapter 11/INCOME); (3) keeping records of all expenditures that may be taken as DEDUCTIONS when the executive computes his or her income tax; (4) keeping a calendar of dates on which returns are to be filed and payments made (see Chapter 5/CALENDARS).

See TAXES OTHER THAN FEDERAL INCOME and the items therein referred to for the secretary's duties involving other taxes. See also Chapter 11/ACCOUNTING RECORDS.

Transfer tax. See STAMP TAX.

Unearned income. See DEFERRED-COMPENSATION AGREEMENT.

Withholding. Making a deduction at the source of income for part of the recipient's income tax liability, as required by federal, state, or local laws. The withholding agent must pay the amount withheld to the proper taxing authority.

Federal withholding of income taxes. The federal withholding-tax law requires employers (with one or more employees) to withhold from each payment of wages made to their employees an amount representing a proportionate part of the employee's approximate income tax liability for the year (assuming employee's entire income is from wages). Generally, the law applies to all employees who are paid wages. The specific records you must keep for income tax withholding are:

1. Each employee's name, address, and social security number

2. The total amount and date of each wage payment and the period the payment covers

3. For each wage payment, the amount subject to withholding

4. The amount of withholding tax collected on each payment and the date it was collected

5. If the taxable amount is less than the total payment, the reason why it is

6. Copies of any statements furnished by employees relating to nonresident alien status, residence in Puerto Rico or the Virgin Islands, or residence or physical presence in a foreign country

7. The fair market value and date of each payment of noncash compensation made to a retail commission salesperson, if no income tax was withheld

8. For wage continuation plans, information about the amount of each payment

9. The withholding exemption certificates (Form W-4) filed by each employee

10. Any agreement between you and the employee for the voluntary withholding of additional amounts of tax

11. The dates in each calendar quarter on which the employee worked for you, but not in the course of your trade or business, and the amount paid for that work

12. Copies of statements given you by employees reporting tips received in their work, unless the information shown on the statements appears in another item on this list

13. Requests by employees to have the tax withheld figured on the basis of their individual cumulative wages

An employee's earnings ledger, which you can purchase at most office supply stores, usually has space for the information required in Items 1 to 4.

The amount to be withheld can be computed by a "percentage" method or may be determined from specially prepared tables. Tables for different pay periods (weekly, biweekly, etc.) are obtainable from the District Director of Internal Revenue. Reference to the amount of wages and number of withholding exemptions gives the amount to be withheld.

Withholding deposits.   Social security taxes and withheld income tax must be deposited periodically. These deposits must be made in an authorized commercial bank or in a Federal Reserve Bank on or before due date for payment. Special rules have been established for these tax deposits.

Each employer is provided with tax-depositary coupons used to deposit withheld income taxes and social security taxes reported quarterly on Form 941. These taxes include income taxes and social security taxes withheld from employees plus the employer's share of the social security taxes it must pay for its employees. They must be deposited with an authorized commercial bank depositary or a Federal Reserve Bank.

When to make deposits. Generally, the deposit requirements are as follows: For FICA and withheld income tax, each month of the return period is divided into eight deposit periods. These periods end on the third, seventh, eleventh, fifteenth, nineteenth, twenty-second, twenty-fifth, and last day of every month. At the end of a deposit period, a deposit will be required if the tax you owe—the amount that has not yet triggered another deposit requirement—reaches a threshhold level:

1. If the tax you owe is three thousand dollars or more at the end of any of the eight deposit periods during the month, you must deposit at least 95 percent of what you owe within three banking days. (You must then make up the difference in another deposit—no later than the first deposit after the fifteenth of the next month. Details are given on Forms 941, 941E, and 943.)

2. If the tax you owe is five hundred dollars or more at the end of the month, you must deposit all of it by the fifteenth of the next month. However, this rule does not apply if the three thousand-dollar rule applied during the same month.

At the end of the return period, if your undeposited tax is less than five hundred dollars, you must deposit it by the end of the next month or pay it when you file your return.

State and local withholding of income taxes. Some states that have income tax laws require employers to withhold income taxes from nonresidents. The laws vary from state to state concerning the amount to be withheld, exemptions from withholding, and time for withholding.

Some cities require employers to deduct and withhold income tax on salary and wages.

CHAPTER 13

BUSINESS MATHEMATICS, INVESTMENTS, AND FINANCE

Acid-test ratio. A test often applied in extending credit to determine the immediate ability of a business to meet current liabilities. The ratio of liquid or quick assets to current liabilities is found. (See Chapter 11/ CURRENT LIABILITIES; QUICK ASSETS.) Liquid current assets include cash, accounts receivable, notes receivable, and marketable securities. They do not include merchandise inventory and prepaid expenses. The ratio shows the number of dollars of liquid current assets for each dollar of liquid current liabilities and is considered a more stringent test of liquidity than the current ratio. A ratio of 100 percent, or 1 to 1, is the generally accepted standard. A ratio that does not come up to this level is not necessarily considered poor without further analysis, since the rate varies depending on the industry.

Addition, shortcuts. Time can be saved in adding columns of figures by using the following method: Add each column separately, setting the sums one place to the left each time. After the last column has been added, add the individual sums in regular order, that is, from right to left, for example:

$$
\begin{array}{r}
4572 \\
3986 \\
2173 \\
5911 \\
2765 \\
\underline{4937} \\
24 \\
32 \\
40 \\
\underline{20} \\
24344
\end{array}
$$

Proving. A common method of verifying arithmetic computations is by casting out the 9's. This is the simplest of all methods of verification and may be used to good advantage in many cases, for example:

4572	0
3986	8
2173	4
5911	7
2765	2
4937	5
24344 − 8	26 − 8

EXPLANATION

The sum of the digits of 4572 is 18 (4 + 5 + 7 + 2). Cast out the 9's and set down 0 (18 = 9 + 9). If a number contains a 9, skip it in adding the digits; thus in 3986, 3 + 8 + 6 = 17. Cast out the 9 from 17 (17 − 9) and set down 8. Find the check number of each line in the same way. Add the check numbers and cast the 9's out of their sum [26 − (9 + 9) = 8]. Find the check number of the sum of the column being verified. In both cases, it is 8. See MULTIPLICATION, SHORTCUTS; DIVISION, SHORTCUT.

Aliquot part. Any number contained in another number an exact number of times (an *aliquant* part is also contained in another number but with a remainder). An aliquot part provides a means for shortcut multiplication and division. Thus 5, 10, $16\frac{2}{3}$, 20, 50, are aliquot parts of 100; 5 = $\frac{1}{20}$ of 100, 10 = $\frac{1}{10}$ of 100; $16\frac{2}{3}$ = $\frac{1}{6}$ of 100, and so on. Time is saved in multiplication and division by using the decimal equivalent of a common fraction.

EXAMPLE 1 (MULTIPLICATION)

You purchased 256 units at $12\frac{1}{2}$ cents each and want to find the cost quickly.

Solution: 256 × $\frac{1}{8}$ × 1.00 − $32.00

Explanation: $0.12\frac{1}{2} = \frac{1}{8}$; therefore, divide 256 by 8.

EXAMPLE 2 (DIVISION)

Divide 4,875 by $16\frac{2}{3}$.

Solution:
$$\begin{array}{r} 48.75 \\ \underline{6} \\ 292.50 \end{array}$$

Explanation: Since $16\frac{2}{3}$ is $\frac{1}{6}$ of 100, divide 4,875 by $\frac{1}{6}$ of 100, or $\frac{100}{6}$. This is the same as multiplying by $\frac{6}{100}$. Therefore, divide by 100 by pointing off two decimal places from the right and multiply the result by 6. The answer is 292.50 or $292\frac{1}{2}$.

American Stock Exchange. See STOCK EXCHANGES.

Amortization. 1. The process of gradually extinguishing a debt by a series of periodic payments to the creditor. The most frequently used method of amortization calls for equal periodic payments made at equal intervals of time. In such an amortization, each payment includes interest on the outstanding debt and a repayment of part of the principal. It is used principally in the liquidation of bonded indebtedness and mortgages.

2. The gradual reduction in the book value of fixed or intangible assets having a limited life by allocating the original cost over the life of the asset. (See Chapter 11/FIXED AS-SETS; INTANGIBLE ASSETS; DEPRECIA-TION.)

3. The process of writing off BOND DISCOUNT AND BOND PREMIUM.

4. As defined by the U.S. Trea-sury Department, the rapid writeoff or accelerated depreciation of certain facilities for income tax purposes.

5. The process of writing off prepaid expenses (see PREPAID EXPENSES) and deferred charges.

Amortization schedule. A schedule, usually run and printed out by computer, showing principal and interest after each monthly payment and balance due on a note and mortgage.

Amortized loan. A long-term loan on real estate under which the borrower makes definite periodical repayments of principal, together with INTEREST payments. Payments of either principal or interest, or both, may be made at any interval agreed upon between borrower and lender. The most popular plan today is the declining-balance or *direct-deduction* monthly payment plan, which requires the borrower to make regular simultaneous payments to principal and interest. See STRAIGHT LOAN.

Annuity. A stipulated payment made to a named person(s) at stated intervals, either for life or for a certain number of years. The contract under which the payments are made is also called an annuity. The person receiving the payments is an *annuitant*. The contract may provide for annual, semiannual, quarterly, or monthly payments; the more frequent the payments, the higher the cost of the annuity. An *immediate annuity* may be purchased for a single premium, the payments to begin six months or a year later. A *deferred annuity* may be purchased by paying a single premium or an annual premium payable over a period of years, the annuity payments to begin at the end of a term of years. In recent years, premium rates on annuities have increased considerably, principally because of the increasing length of the life span. Some companies have discontinued the issuance of single-premium life annuities, both immediate and deferred. Others have discontinued issuance to individuals, but will sell single-premium deferred annuities for pension trust purposes.

If a series of payments are to be made to the annuitant or his or her beneficiary at periodic intervals for a definite number of years only, regardless of any life contingency, the annuity is an *annuity certain*. If payments are to be made for the life of the annuitant with payment to continue to the beneficiary if he or she should die before a specified number of years, the annuity is technically an *annuity certain and life*, commonly referred to as a *years certain annuity*. Most annuities are based on the duration of a life or lives. The most common form is the *life annuity*, variously known as an *ordinary-life*, *straight-life*, *regular-life*, *single-life*, or *maximum-income life annuity*. A life annuity is for the duration of one life, purchased by a single premium or installment premiums. The payments continue during the lifetime of the annuitant and terminate with his or her death. A great variety of immediate and deferred annuity contracts are offered by life insurance companies.

See also VARIABLE ANNUITY.

Annuity certain. See ANNUITY.

Arabic numerals.

Trillions	Billions	Millions	Thousands	Hundreds
7,	256,	423,	896,	384

(7,256,423,896,384)

NOTE: In the United States and France a billion is a thousand millions (1,000,000, 000). In Britain and Germany a billion is a million millions (1,000,000,000,000).

Arithmetic. See BUSINESS ARITHMETIC.

Asked. See BID AND ASKED PRICES.

Assessment. The additional amount that equity holders may be required to pay. This is a common practice in some tax-shelter programs, especially oil and gas drilling. If more funds are required to complete a well, each participant will be assessed additional monies to complete on a pro-rata basis, up to a previously stated maximum. Assessment also relates to values assigned by taxing authorities and to taxable holdings such as real estate and inventories. (See Chapter 10/STOCKHOLDER; CORPORATION.)

Assignment. 1. *Of rights.* Assignments are made (a) by the act of the parties, as in the case of a tenant assigning his or her lease to another; or (b) by operation of law, as in the case of death or bankruptcy. The party transferring the right is the *assignor;* the party to whom the rights are transferred is the *assignee.*

An assignment need not be in any particular form; it may be oral or written. It may be a formal document or an endorsement on the contract signed by the assignor. An assignment does not require any consideration (see Chapter 9/CONTRACTS, 4. *Consideration*), but it must effect an immediate transfer to a specific assignee.

2. *Of securities.* See TRANSFER OF SECURITIES.

Assumed bonds. Bonds that a corporation other than the issuing corporation has agreed to take over as its obligation. This may result from a merger or from one corporation's assumption of another corporation's debts. They differ from GUARANTEED BONDS in which the obligation continues to be that of the issuing corporation and the guarantor merely pays the interest and principal when the issuing corporation fails to do so.

At the market. See LIMIT ORDER.

At the opening. An expression used in securities trading meaning an order given to a stockbroker to buy or sell securities at the beginning of trading in the security. See GTC ORDER; LIMIT ORDER; MARKET ORDER; STOP-LOSS ORDER.

Authorized capital stock. See Stock.

Averages. *Arithmetic mean* is a general average obtained by dividing the total value of items by the number of items. For example, the mean of 2, 4, and 6 is 4. *Median* is the middle number or value in a series of numbers (or the arithmetic average of the two middle numbers if there is no single middle number). The median of 1, 2, and 3 is 2. *Mode* is the most frequent value in a series of numbers. The mode of the series 1, 2, 2, 2, 3, 3, and 4 is 2. See also Dow JONES AVERAGES.

Baby bond. Any BOND issued in denominations smaller than the standard $1,000 bond. See TREASURY NOTES AND BONDS.

Bankers' shares. See STOCK, *Other stock.*

Basing-point system. A device for computing delivered price. Manufacturers or producers of a given product (generally, a standard product) add to the price set for the product at the basing point the freight or other transportation cost from the basing point—not the point of production—to the point of delivery. Freight charges included in the delivered prices rarely are the actual freight charges; sometimes they are more, sometimes less. When they are more than the actual charges from the point of shipment to the destination, the seller is charging "phantom freight." When they are less, the seller is "absorbing" freight.

Sometimes more than one basing point is used. Then base and non-base mills alike include in their delivered price at a purchaser's destination transportation charges from the basing point nearest the purchaser to the destination. A system that includes more than a single

basing point is called a "multiple basing-point system."

Basis point. An expression of variations in yield changes of fixed-income securities, especially bonds. One gradation on a one hundred-point scale represents 1 percent. Thus the difference between 9.76 percent and 9.79 percent is three basis points.

Bearer bonds. See COUPON BONDS.

Bearer instrument. A negotiable instrument payable on demand to anyone who is in possession of the instrument.

Bearish. A stock market term for a pessimistic attitude toward the trend of future security prices, as opposed to a BULLISH, or optimistic, outlook.

Bears. A stock market term for investors or operators who believe that security prices are about to decline, as opposed to BULLS, who are optimistic about the trend of security prices.

Bid and asked prices. Stock market expression referring to the amount buyers of a stock were offering to pay (Bid) and the amount sellers were asking (Asked) after the last transaction, and before the close, of the stock trading day. The figures (bid and asked) are the "current quotes," which result from the trades taking place. The combined bid and asked prices are known as "quotations." The difference between the bid and asked price represents the dealer's "spread."

Big board. A popular expression for the New York Stock Exchange.

Bill of exchange. A written order, signed by the issuer, that requires the addressee to pay a specified sum of money to a third party. See also Chapter 14/BANK DRAFT; CHAPTER 10/ BILL OF LADING.

Bill of sale. A formal document issued by a seller to a buyer, as evidence for transfer of title to the goods described in the instrument. A bill of sale may be used in the case of any sale of personal property. See Chapter 9/PERSONAL PROPERTY.

Black market. The illegal purchase and sale of goods, often scarce or restricted and usually above other competitive or allowable market prices.

Blue-chip stocks. Common stock in a corporation recognized widely and regarded favorably for its stability and earning power.

Blue-sky laws. See Chapter 9/BLUE-SKY LAWS.

Board of trade. See COMMODITY EXCHANGES.

Bond. The written promise of a corporation or government, under seal, to pay a specified sum of money at a fixed date in the future, usually more than ten years after the promise is made, with interest at a fixed rate payable at specified dates. A corporate bond is usually one of a number of similar bonds, all of which are covered by a deed of trust, or indenture, that sets forth the terms under which the loan is made and the bonds issued. The bondholder does not ordinarily bother to get a copy of the indenture, but it is available if he or she wants it. See TREASURY NOTES AND BONDS.

Distinction between stocks and bonds. A *bond* is evidence of a debt; *stock* is evidence of ownership. STOCKS and bonds differ from each other on the following principal points: (1) *Rights to income.* A bond pays interest; stock pays dividends. A corporation promises to pay the interest on a bond in the amount and at the dates specified in the bond. The interest on the bond is a fixed charge for the corporation; it must be met before the directors can pay dividends even to the preferred stockholders. (2) *Rights to a voice in management.* Bondholders ordinarily do not have voting rights and therefore have no voice in the management of the corporation. Stockholders have voting rights and therefore have a voice in management. (3) *Rights to a return of principal.* The amount of the bond indicated on its face is the principal of the bond, which is payable at the maturity of the bond. The obligation of the corporation to repay the principal constitutes a basic distinction between bonds and stocks. The bond obligation is a liability to creditors; stock is part of the net worth and represents ownership, not a debt. Even the redemption clause in a preferred stock does not make the stock a liability.

Corporate bond issues may be secured or unsecured. A bond is "secured" by a pledge of assets (plant or equipment), title of which would be transferred to the bondholder in the event of foreclosure. A secured bond does not necessarily have greater investment merit than an unsecured bond because the grade of the bond depends more upon the earnings of the issuer than upon the security pledged to protect it. Generally, if earnings are adequate, interest is paid and the question of security never arises. Security is merely a device for giving the bondholder a somewhat stronger position in case of financial failure, and it becomes important only in case the issuer is unable to meet its interest and other obligations under the bond.

All bonds—secured or unsecured—may have the following features:

1. *Redemption provisions.* Most indentures created in recent years give the company the right to call in bonds issued under them before maturity. The call feature, also known as the redemption feature, enables the corporation to pay off the bonds before maturity, if the company can afford to do so, or to refund the bonds by issuing other securities, less costly to the corporation, in their place. Bonds with the redemption feature are known as "redeemable" and "callable bonds."

The owner of a callable bearer bond has the burden of watching announcements in the financial pages of daily newspapers or other publications to see whether the bond has been redeemed. This is necessary because a bearer bond is payable to the holder and not registered in an individual's name. Notification is thereby impossible other than by public announcement. If one misses the notice, one may not discover that one's bond has been called until the next interest-paying date. Then one finds that for six months the money invested in those bonds has not earned interest. The premium on the bonds (see BOND DISCOUNT AND BOND PREMIUM) does not make up for such a loss.

2. *Conversion provisions.* A *convertible bond* is one that gives the security holder the right to exchange his or her bonds for some other security, usually preferred stock or common stock of the corporation, at a fixed price described in the indenture. The conversion privilege adds a speculative interest to bonds and is given to make them more attractive and salable. For example, a $1,000 bond may be convertible into common stock at $110. If the common stock is perhaps selling at $115, the conversion privilege has a real value.

3. *Sinking-fund provisions.* A *sinking-fund bond* is one that imposes upon the corporation the obligation to set aside a certain sum from earnings periodically for the purpose of reducing or retiring the bonded indebtedness. Since the fund is usually turned over to the trustee to be invested in the "same issue," it is not actually a fund but a partial extinction of the debt.

See BOND TRANSACTION; COUPON BONDS; REGISTERED BOND; FIDELITY

BOND; SURETY BOND; TREASURY NOTES
AND BONDS.

Bond discount and bond premium.

The difference between the par value
of a bond and the price for which it is
sold by the issuer. If the price is less
than par value, the difference is
called "bond discount"; if it is more,
the difference is called "bond premium." The bond discount and bond
premium are written off over the life
of the bond by a process called
AMORTIZATION of bond discount and
bond premium.

The terms *discount* and *premium*
also apply to the purchase of bonds in
the open market. They are purchased
at a discount (for less than the par
value) and at a premium (for more
than the par value). For example, a
bond paying 5 percent when current
interest rates are 10 percent would
trade at a discount, so the purchaser
would get 5 percent interest plus the
difference in par to equal a return on
investment of 10 percent. The process
of amortization is also applied to
bonds purchased at discount or premium.

The amortization of bond discount
on a bond purchased at 95 with ten
years to run would be the amount of
the discount ($50) divided by the
number of years to maturity (10), or
$5 per year. The amortization of bond
premium on a bond purchased at 108
with ten years to run would be the
amount of the premium ($80) divided
by the number of years to maturity
(10), or $8 per year. (See BOND
TRANSACTION.)

When bonds are purchased as an
investment, it is permissible to
charge the bond account with the
price of the bond, instead of charging
the account with the par value and
setting up an account for discount or
premium. This practice should not be
followed by the corporation issuing
the bonds because liability is par
regardless of the price received.

Bond power. See STOCK (OR BOND) POWER.

Bond quotation. See BOND TRANS-ACTION.

Bond transaction. Corporate bonds
are quoted (priced) at a percentage of
their FACE VALUE, usually in eighths
of a point. A smaller fluctuation, such
as $\frac{1}{32}$ of a point, is sometimes permitted by a securities exchange. The
trading unit in bonds is one bond of a
par value of $1,000. (A few corporate
bonds are issued in smaller denominations.) Thus a quotation of $97\frac{1}{4}$
means a price of $976.25 ($0.97\frac{1}{4}$ ×
$1,000). Government bonds fluctuate
in thirty-seconds of a point. Thus a
quotation of 100.4 means $100\frac{4}{32}$, or
$1,001.25.

Interest on bonds is ordinarily
paid semiannually; between interest
dates the interest accrues to the
owner. For that reason bonds are
sold at a price plus interest. For
example, suppose a 10 percent
$1,000 bond, with interest-payment
dates of January 1 and July 1, is sold
on October 1 at 99. The buyer must
pay the seller $25 of interest for the
three months (July, August, and
September) during which the interest accrued. The bond is sold, however, for $1,005. But at the next

interest-payment date, the purchaser gets back the interest he or she had paid the former owner. Defaulted bonds are traded *flat,* that is, without interest.

Figure 1 is an example of bond quotations from the *Wall Street Journal.* Such listings always include the abbreviation for the company, such as ATT, and the identification of the bond by its interest rate and maturity date ($8\frac{3}{8}90$ would mean an interest rate of $8\frac{3}{8}$ and a maturity date in 1990). High and low prices at which the bond sold during the particular trading day are given along with a plus or minus indication of whether there was a price increase or decrease from the preceding stock trading day.

Broad market. A situation in which a large number and numerous types of securities or commodities may be bought or sold.

Broker. An intermediary who brings parties together and assists them in negotiating a contract. He or she usually performs this service for a commission or fee. An agency relationship is established between brokers and the principals who employ them. There are basically two kinds

of brokers. A *full-service broker* will develop a portfolio for an investor based on the individual's level of risk comfort. This broker will have a research department to call on for assistance as well as a tax department and other aids. A *discount broker* makes no recommendations regarding investments but rather takes only buy or sell requests. Because these services are limited, the fees paid a discount broker are considerably less than those paid a full-service broker. See Chapter 10/AGENCY.

Securities broker. A person who executes orders to buy or sell securities for a commission. This may be through an established exchange or OVER-THE COUNTER MARKET. See STOCK EXCHANGES.

Broker's monthly statement. At the end of the month, the broker sends the customer a statement of account. It shows all *completed* transactions on which deliveries have been made by the broker. Thus if there have been purchase transactions toward the end of the month and the securities bought have not been received by the broker, they will not appear on the statement until the following month. Figure 1 illustrates a broker's state-

BOND TRANSACTION: FIGURE 1

NEW YORK STOCK EXCHANGE BONDS

Monday, March 23, 19—

Bond	Current Yield	Volume	High	Low	Close	Net Change
ATT $8\frac{3}{4}00$	8.6	93	$102\frac{1}{8}$	$102\frac{1}{8}$	$102\frac{1}{8}$	. . .
Exxon $6\frac{1}{2}98$	7.1	123	$91\frac{1}{4}$	$91\frac{1}{8}$	$91\frac{1}{8}$	$-\frac{1}{4}$
GMA $7\frac{1}{4}90$	7.2	25	$100\frac{1}{2}$	$100\frac{1}{4}$	$100\frac{1}{2}$	$+\frac{1}{4}$

BROKER'S MONTHLY STATEMENT: FIGURE 1: Broker's statement of cash account

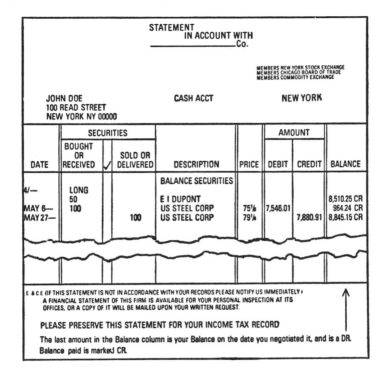

ment of a cash account. A broker's statement for a margin account is somewhat different.

The items under "Long" at the head of the statement refer to securities held by the broker at the beginning of the month. Below this list are the itemized transactions in chronological order. The purchases are entered in the debit column, the sales in the credit column. Any dividends collected on securities held in the account will be entered in the credit column. The daily balance appears in the balance column.

Attached to the statement is a list of securities held in the account at the end of the month. They may be securities bought and paid for but not yet delivered to the customer or securities delivered by the customer to the broker for sale and not yet sold.

Broker's purchase and sale confirmation. As soon as an order for a securities transaction is executed by a broker, a confirmation of the purchase or sale is sent to the customer. Figure 1 illustrates a purchase confirmation and Figure 2, a sale confirmation.

Quantity. This item is the number of shares or bonds bought or sold. It is recorded in Figures 1 and 2 in the spaces provided for "You Bought" and "You sold."

Description. The name of the security is given.

441

BROKER'S PURCHASE AND SALE CONFIRMATION: FIGURE 1: Broker's purchase confirmation

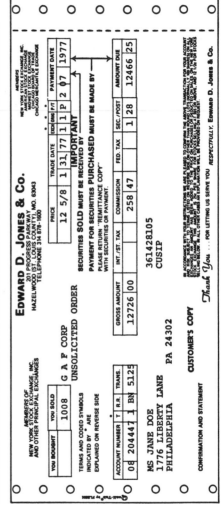

BROKER'S PURCHASE AND SALE CONFIRMATION: FIGURE 2: Broker's sale confirmation

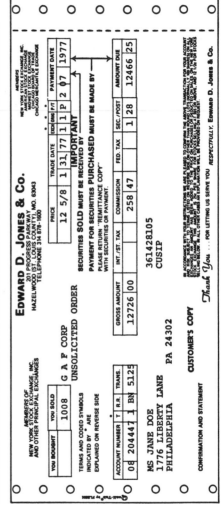

Price. This item is the price per share or per bond at which the trade was made.

Trade and Payment Dates. The "trade date" is the date the security is traded, and the "payment date" is the date upon which payment is required.

Symbols. Various symbols are explained on the reverse side of the confirmation slip. For example, on Figure 2, EXCH, number 1, is described on the back of the purchase confirmation slip as "New York Stock Exchange."

Gross Amount. This figure is the product of multiplying the price by the number of shares or bonds.

Interest. This item appears only on a bond transaction. The buyer pays the interest that has accrued up to the date of delivery. Thus the purchase slip on a bond purchase will show the amount of interest charged to the purchaser; the sales slip will show the amount of interest credited to the seller.

Commission. The brokerage commission charged for a transaction.

Federal and state taxes on sales. Taxes, if any, consist of (1) a federal tax in a bond transaction or on a federal security and (2) state transfer taxes on stocks.

SEC Fees and Postage. Fees are imposed by the Securities and Exchange Commission on all stock transactions. On Figure 2, they are combined with a postage charge.

Amount Due. The net amount that must be paid to the broker in the case of a purchase or the amount that will be received from the broker in the case of a sale.

Account. The name of the account for which the transaction was effected often appears at the bottom of the form. Other account data consists of the account number, the registered representative's code or number, the transaction number, and a computer identification number.

Bullish. A stock market term for an optimistic attitude toward the trend of future security prices, as opposed to a BEARISH, or pessimistic, outlook.

Bulls. A stock market term for the investors or operators who hold the opinion that security prices are about to advance, as opposed to BEARS, who are pessimistic about the trend of security prices.

Business arithmetic. The use of fundamental principles of arithmetic in solving mathematical problems that occur in day-to-day business activities. For some of the more common methods of computation, see the words that usually suggest the particular problems. For example, see ADDITION, SHORTCUTS; ALIQUOT PART; DIVISION, SHORTCUT; CASH DISCOUNT; INTEREST; MULTIPLICATION, SHORTCUTS; PERCENTAGE; YIELD; Chapter 14/BANK DISCOUNT. The explanations include shortcuts as well as explanations of the usual mathematical processes.

Call. See PUTS AND CALLS.

Callable bonds. See BOND.

Callable preferred stock. See STOCK, PREFERRED STOCK.

Carrying charge. In securities, the charge made by a broker for carrying a customer's transactions on MARGIN. In retailing, a service charge on installment sales.

Cash discount. A deduction ordinarily ranging from 1 to 10 percent allowed to customers to induce them to pay their bills within a definite time. Cash discount terms are stated in the invoice in the following manner: 2/10 net 30, or 2/10/30. This means that 2 percent may be deducted from the invoice amount if paid in ten days; otherwise, the bill must be paid net within thirty days.

A buyer who takes advantage of cash discounts saves considerable money on purchases, as shown by the following example:

Assume that merchandise is sold on 30 days' credit and 2 percent discount is given for cash if payment is made in ten days. Under these terms, one who buys goods amounting to $1,000 on March 1 may deduct $20 if one pays the bill on or before March 11. If one does not pay on March 11, one may not deduct the discount; one pays $20 for the use of $1,000 for twenty days (the interim between March 11 and March 31, the day the bill is due). In this case, one pays for the use of money at the rate of 36 percent per year ($2\% \times \frac{360}{20} = 18 \times 2\% = 36\%$) by not paying within ten days and taking advantage of the discount.

The following table shows the rate of savings under various discount terms.

$\frac{1}{2}\%$ 10 days net 30 days =	9% per annum
1% " " " " " =	18% " "
$1\frac{1}{2}\%$ " " " " " =	27% " "
2% " " " " " =	36% " "
2% " " " 60 " =	14% " "
2% 30 " " " " =	24% " "

2% " " " 4 mos. =	8% " "
2% 40 " " 60 days =	36% " "
2% 70 " " 90 " =	36% " "
3% 10 " " 30 " =	54% " "
3% " " " 4 mos. =	10% " "
3% 30 " " 60 days =	36% " "
4% 10 " " " " =	29% " "
4% " " " 4 mos. =	13% " "
5% " " " 30 days =	90% " "
5% " " " 60 " =	36% " "
5% " " " 4 mos. =	16% " "
6% " " " 60 days =	43% " "
6% " " " 4 mos. =	20% " "
7% " " " " " =	23% " "
8% " " " " " =	26% " "
9% " " " 60 days =	65% " "
10% " " " 90 days =	45% " "

Charge-account credit. A type of consumer credit offered by credit-card companies, banks, and other institutions that, depending upon the issuer, may allow consumers to withdraw cash up to a specified limit or pay for purchases in a series of installments, usually monthly. Finance or service charges may range from 1 to 25 percent per annum and are normally computed based upon the unpaid balance each month or upon the average daily balance each month.

Bank cards sometimes enable holders to write checks exceeding the amount of cash in their regular checking accounts up to the amount of cash available in their preapproved credit reserve. Other bank-issued cards, such as Visa, may be used for both cash advances and consumer purchases. Retail-store credit cards such as Sears, Roebuck and Company normally provide for consumer purchases on credit but not cash advances.

Closing price. The price at which the last sale of a particular stock, bond, or commodity was effected before the closing of the exchange. The daily newspapers generally report the following prices for securities traded on the New York Stock Exchange: first (the opening transaction), high, low, last (closing price), and net change (the difference between the closing price on the day reported and the preceding stock trading day). Some publications include closing BID AND ASKED PRICES. This means that after the last transaction for the day, and before the close of the trading day, buyers of the stock were offering to pay the amount shown as "Bid" and sellers were asking the amount shown as "Asked."

Collateral. Something of value deposited as a PLEDGE with a lender to secure the repayment of a loan. If the borrower is unable to meet the loan when due, the lender is free to sell the collateral and collect the debt from the proceeds of the sale. A problem may develop if the collateral value drops below the balance of the loan, and additional collateral may be required.

Collateral trust bonds. Bonds secured entirely by a pledge of other securities. Sometimes leaseholds, rents, franchises, and patents are offered as additional collateral. The primary purpose of the pledge of the securities and other collateral is to enable the trustee to reimburse the bondholders should the corporation fail to pay the bond obligation when it becomes due.

Commission. The amount a fiduciary (see Chapter 9/FIDUCIARY) receives as compensation for services. Commissions are normally a percentage of the principal or income or both. In securities and commodities, a commission is the fee charged by brokers. The rate is set by the COMMODITY EXCHANGES.

Commodity exchanges. Organized markets in which staple commodities (wheat, cotton, hides) are traded on a "cash" basis or a "futures" basis.

The difference between the two types of trading is principally in the form of the sales contract. "Cash" or "spot" trading calls for immediate delivery. *Futures* are standard contracts prescribed by the exchanges for future delivery. They specify grade, amount, price, and delivery date by month and allow the seller to deliver any time during the specified month.

The futures market performs an important function in the process of distribution. It helps to reduce the cost of products to the consumer. Trading in futures through *hedging* provides an insurance against violent price fluctuations. To illustrate: A cotton merchant buys cotton to have an ample stock on hand to fill orders for his or her cotton mill customers. The merchant may buy several thousand bales without having an immediate outlet for them. The operations of the cotton markets enable a farmer to sell cotton when desired. But a merchant who buys several thousand bales without an immediate outlet for them at the mills runs the risk that the market may decline sharply before the merchant can resell the cotton. Consequently, the merchant sells on the Exchanges cotton for future delivery in a quantity approximating the amount bought. When the merchant sells the actual cotton on hand, he or she disposes of the future "hedges" (sales). If the price has advanced, the merchant makes up on the spot (cash) cotton what the merchant loses on future sales. Conversely, if the price declines, the merchant's loss in the sale of spot cotton is compensated by a similar profit on futures contracts because spot and futures markets almost always move up and down together. This procedure, known as "hedging," is the standard method used by various industries for protection against price fluctuations.

Commodity Exchange Commission. A federal commission, established by the Commodity Exchange Act of 1936, consisting of the secretaries of agriculture and commerce and the attorney general. The commission regulates commodities trading, prevents fraud, and sets trading limits to prevent excessive speculation. The enforcement agency of the commission is called the Commodity Exchange Authority.

Common stock. See STOCK.

Compound interest. See INTEREST.

Conditional sale. An installment sale. The buyer usually gives the seller a promissory note secured by a conditional sale contract or a chattel mortgage. (See Chapter 15/MORTGAGE.) A *conditional sale contract* is a contract for the sale of goods under which the goods are delivered to the buyer but in which the title remains in the seller's name until the goods are paid for in full or until the conditions of the contract are fulfilled. When a chattel mortgage is used, the seller transfers the goods to the buyer, who in turn executes a chattel mortgage in favor of the seller. This instrument gives the seller a lien on the goods.

The seller's choice of a security depends upon the laws in his or her state. The seller studies the laws and selects the type of instrument that provides the most protection with the least inconvenience. The instrument usually includes a provision that if an installment is not paid when due the entire debt becomes payable at once. This clause, called the acceleration clause, is essential in any installment contract. (See Chapter 9/ACCELERATION CLAUSE.) Otherwise, the seller would have to sue for the amount of each installment as it became due or would have to wait until the entire debt matured.

Contingent interest. A future interest in real estate or personal property that depends on some stated condition being met.

Contingent rent. Rental based on other than the passage of time (e.g., percentage of sales).

Convertible bonds. See BOND.

Convertible preferred stock. See STOCK, *Preferred stock.*

Cost-plus pricing. A charge that includes the cost of providing goods or services plus a fee that represents the seller's profit. Such contracts are common when costs are unknown in advance.

Coupon bonds. Bearer bonds that have certificates (coupons) attached to them representing the amount of interest due on the bond during its entire term. Each individual coupon is an obligation of the issuer of the bond to pay interest for a stipulated period, usually six months.

For example, a ten-year, 10 percent bond that provided for semiannual interest payment would have twenty coupons attached to it, one of each six-month period. For a one thousand dollars bond, each coupon would be (1) worth fifty dollars when due, (2) dated consecutively so interest could not be collected before it was due, (3) numbered to correspond with the bond from which it was detached.

When the interest is due, the bondholder clips the coupon and may either sell it, deposit it in a bank account, or present it for payment to the issuer's agent.

An interest coupon is a negotiable instrument and does not need to be endorsed. See Chapter 9/NEGOTIABLE INSTRUMENT.

Credit cards. See CHARGE-ACCOUNT CREDIT.

Cumulative dividends. When DIVIDENDS on cumulative preferred STOCK have not been paid in one or more years, the dividends accumulate and must be paid before any dividends may be paid on the common stock. If dividends are noncumulative, dividends omitted in any year do not have to be made up in later years. If the preferred stock certificate does not state whether it is entitled to cumulative or noncumulative dividends, the stock is generally cumulative.

Cumulative preferred stock. See STOCK, *Preferred stock.*

Current Statistics. See Chapter 8/ INFORMATION SOURCES: *Statistical data.*

Day order. In the securities and commodities trade, an order to a broker to buy or sell a security or commodity that is good only for the day on which it is given. If the order is not executed on that day, it is automatically canceled.

Debentures. Bonds issued without security and therefore not protected by any specific LIEN upon property. (See Chapter 9/LIEN.) They are simply the promise of the borrower to pay a certain sum of money at a stipulated time and place, with interest at a fixed rate.

Deferred stock. See STOCK, *Other stock.*

Del credere. (Italian.) A term applied to agents who, for a higher commission, guarantee their principals that they will pay for goods sold on credit if the buyers do not. *Del credere* agencies are common in businesses that employ commission merchants or agents whose relatively independent financial status enables them to guarantee their customers' accounts.

Delivery of securities. When securities are sold, delivery must be made by the fifth business day following the sale. Delivery may be made by taking the securities to the broker's office or sending them there by messenger or by mail. A nonnegotiable security must be properly assigned before it is ready for delivery. See TRANSFER OF SECURITIES.

Delivery of securities by mail. Negotiable securities, such as COUPON BONDS, *must* be sent by registered mail and insured. Certificates of stock (see Chapter 10/STOCK CERTIFICATE) and REGISTERED BONDS are nonnegotiable unless they are assigned in blank. When they are sent by mail, the assignment on the back of the security should not be signed. Instead, a separate stock or bond power is sent to the broker, who endorses the securities for transfer when he or she receives them. The seller should insert the broker's name in the power if it is sent with the securities. If the power is signed in blank, it should be sent to the broker separately from the securities. Although the securities are nonnegotiable, if they are lost, the owner must post an indemnity bond with the issuing corporation to obtain duplicates. This bond may cost several hundred dollars, depending on the market value of the lost securities. If the securities are sent by registered mail, the indemnity from the post office reimburses the owner of the lost securities for the costs involved in obtaining the duplicates. Brokers, therefore, generally recommend that their clients send securities to them by registered mail. (Brokers are covered by commercial insurance.) However, some sellers prefer to take the risk of sending securities to their brokers by regular first-class mail because the securities must be registered at their full value, and the fee is high. There is little advantage in sending securities by certified mail. (See Chapter 2/POSTAL SERVICE.) The post office pays no indemnity for lost certified mail; it is handled in the same manner as first-class mail except that a return receipt may be requested after mailing.

Depreciation. See Chapter 11/DEPRECIATION.

Discount. The difference between the price of a product or security and its sale or redemption value. For example, a $195 chair that is available at $145 is discounted $50. A bond with a face value of $5,000 and a current market value of $4,500 is selling at a $500 discount.

Dishonor. Refusal to pay a negotiable instrument when due. (See Chapter 9/NEGOTIABLE INSTRUMENT.) Notice of dishonor is usually given to endorsers and drawers, who, in addition to the maker, are liable on the instrument. Notice of dishonor may be given orally or in writing. If it is not given, endorsers and drawers are discharged from liability.

Dividends. *On stock.* A distribution of current or accumulated profits of a corporation to stockholders in the form of cash, stock, scrip, or in kind.

Usually, dividends are declared by a formal resolution of the board of directors that fixes (1) the rate or amount of the dividend per share, (2) the class of stockholders to whom the dividend is payable, (3) the date set for determination of who is entitled to the dividend (see Ex-DIVIDEND), (4) the date of payment, and (5) the medium in which the dividend is to be paid. Dividends are usually declared and paid quarterly, semiannually, or annually; they are paid either as a percentage of par value per share or in dollars and cents per share. The amount of the dividend declared is usually charged to earned surplus. For example, assume a $1 dividend per share of outstanding common stock to be paid quarterly is declared. You, as a common-stock stockholder, own 1,000 shares of stock. Your quarterly dividend will be $250.

Cash dividends are paid in cash, usually by check. It is inaccurate to refer to a cash dividend *on* stock as a stock dividend.

Stock dividends are distributions of additional stock to the stockholders, pro rata according to their stockholdings. For example, a 10 percent stock dividend means that ten additional shares will be distributed to owners for each one hundred shares held. They rank next to cash dividends in frequency and amount. A stockholder may refuse to accept the shares offered as a stock dividend, but one cannot demand cash in lieu of the shares, unless an optional dividend is declared. (See below.) In most circumstances, stock dividends are not subject to federal income tax. For that reason, during periods of high earnings and high income tax rates, corporations, especially close corporations, often declare an extra dividend in the form of a stock dividend. (See Chapter 10/CLOSE CORPORATION.) Another reason for issuing a stock dividend is that the corporation is able to conserve its cash and at the same time make a distribution to stockholders, who can sell their stock dividends if they want cash.

Stock dividends are sometimes confused with STOCK SPLITS because stockholders also receive additional shares of a stock through a "split" of the shares they hold into a larger number. The chief difference is that when a stock dividend is declared, the amount of the stock dividend is transferred from surplus to capital stock and the par or stated value of each share remains the same. (See Chapter 11/CAPITAL STOCK.) On the other hand, in a split, an increased number of shares is issued without changing the value of the corporation's capital stock, thus making it necessary to reduce the par value of each share. (See PAR VALUE AND NO-PAR STOCK.)

Optional dividends are paid in either cash or stock, as the stockholder prefers. An optional dividend differs from a stock dividend in that the stockholder may take cash or may apply the dividend to the purchase of additional shares of stock. One is usually given a certain number of days in which to make a choice. Optional dividends, even if the stockholder chooses stocks, are treated the same as cash dividends for tax purposes.

Property dividends are paid in physically divisble surplus property of the corporation, other than cash. Thus if a corporation with a surplus holds stock in another corporation, that stock is legally distributable to the extent of the surplus precisely the same as if it were cash. A stockholder cannot be compelled to accept a property dividend, but one does not have the option to receive an equivalent amount of cash in lieu of a property dividend.

Bond dividends are paid in the form of bonds of the corporation paying the dividend. Payment in this form is unusual but is legal in the absence of statutory provisions to the contrary. The corporation may secure the bonds by a mortgage upon its property. (See CUMULATIVE DIVIDENDS.)

Accrued dividends are the proportion of a regular dividend not yet payable that has accumulated at a given time since the payment date of the preceding regular dividend.

Accumulated dividends are dividends that are unpaid as of the date they fall due.

Dividends in arrears. See DIVIDENDS, *Accrued dividends* and *Accumulated dividends*.

Division, shortcut. In some cases, the process of division can be shortened by applying the following table:

To divide by

$1\frac{1}{4}$	multiply by	8	and divide by		10
$1\frac{2}{3}$	"	6	"	"	10
$2\frac{1}{2}$	"	4	"	"	10
$3\frac{1}{3}$	"	3	"	"	10
$3\frac{3}{4}$	"	8	"	"	30
$6\frac{1}{4}$	"	16	"	"	100
$7\frac{1}{2}$	"	4	"	"	30
$8\frac{1}{3}$	"	12	"	"	100
$9\frac{1}{11}$	"	11	"	"	100
$11\frac{1}{9}$	"	9	"	"	100
$12\frac{1}{2}$	"	8	"	"	100
$14\frac{2}{7}$	"	7	"	"	100

To divide by

$1\frac{1}{4}$	multiply by	8	and divide by		10
$16\frac{2}{3}$	"	6	"	"	100
25	"	4	"	"	100
$31\frac{1}{4}$	"	16	"	"	500
$33\frac{1}{3}$	"	3	"	"	100
75	"	4	"	"	300
125	"	8	"	"	1,000
175	"	4	"	"	700
275	"	4	"	"	1,100
375	"	8	"	"	3,000
625	"	8	"	"	5,000
875	"	8	"	"	7,000

For example, to divide 5 by $6\frac{1}{4}$, multiply 5 times 16 (80) and divide by 100 (80 ÷ 100 = 0.80). Thus, $5 \div 6\frac{1}{4} = 0.80$.

Dow Jones averages. The Dow Jones Industrial Average is based on the prices of thirty selected blue-chip stocks traded on the New York Stock Exchange. It is the most popular index of the daily market trend in both volume and price. If the averages are "up," the market as a whole is considered optimistic; if the averages are "down," the market as a whole is considered to be in a slump. There are several other averages used as indicators of market trends and activities as well, most notably the New York Stock Exchange Index.

Earnest (earnest money or binder). The payment that one contracting party gives to another at the time of entering into the contract to bind the sale and that will be forfeited by the buyer if he or she fails to carry out the contract. The money is applied to the purchase price if the buyer lives up to the bargain.

Economic indicators. See Chapter 8/INFORMATION SOURCES, *Statistical data.*

Endorsement. See Chapter 14/ CHECK, *Endorsement.*

Equipment trust bonds. Bonds, notes, or certificates issued to finance the purchase of movable equipment, especially rolling stock of the railroads and new aircraft of the airlines.

Equity. *Finance and accounting.* The value of the owner's interest in property in excess of all claims and liens against it. Examples: (1) An owner's equity in his or her home is its present value less the amount of the mortgage. (See Chapter 15/MORTGAGE.) (2) The equity of the stockholders of a business is its net worth or the value of the assets of the business in excess of its liabilities.

Equity annuity. See VARIABLE ANNUITY.

Escrow. A conditional delivery of something to a third person to be held until the happening of some event or the performance of some act. To place an instrument or a fund in escrow is to deliver the instrument or fund to a person charged with its custody and disposition under the terms of a specific agreement, known as the "escrow agreement." For example, a grantor may deliver a deed in escrow to a trust company until the grantee makes certain payments on the purchase price, at which time the trust company delivers the deed to the grantee.

Ex-dividend. Stock quotation meaning that the buyer does not get a dividend that has been declared but not yet paid. Since dividends are declared payable to stockholders of record on a specific date, the stock sells "ex-dividend" usually several days before the record date, depending on the delivery rules of the securities exchange on which the stock is traded. On the "ex" date, the dividend is reserved for the seller.

Ex-rights. See Chapter 10/RIGHTS.

Face value. The nominal value of an instrument, such as a bond, note, mortgage, or other security, set forth in the document itself. (See PAR VALUE STOCK AND NO-PAR STOCK.)

Fidelity bond. A promise to pay a specified sum in case a bonded person is dishonest. If employees are "bonded," an employer is thus protected against loss for reasons such as embezzlement or larceny.

Finance charge. The additional cost for financing a purchase or the difference between the cash purchase price and the price paid by a customer who finances the purchase.

Finance and investments. The secretary's duties concerning an employer's investments in securities may include the following:

1. Maintain records of each security owned and a current list of all securities. (See SECURITIES RECORD.)

2. Keep the files relating to security transactions. (See SECURITY-TRANSACTION FILES.)

3. Prepare for delivery securities sold. (See DELIVERY OF SECURITIES.)

4. Check the BROKER'S MONTHLY STATEMENT.

5. Keep a capital gain and loss record. (See Chapter 12/CAPITAL GAIN AND LOSS.)

Founders' shares. See STOCK, *Other stock.*

Fractional share. Less than whole share of stock. A stockholder sometimes becomes entitled to less than a whole share of stock upon the declaration of a stock DIVIDEND or upon an increase of stock where rights to subscribe to additional shares are granted present stockholders. (See STOCK; Chapter 10/STOCKHOLDER; RIGHTS.) Corporations avoid issuing fractional shares. Instead, they usually pay to stockholders the cash value of any fractional shares to which they may be entitled.

Futures. See COMMODITY EXCHANGES.

GTC order. Order to buy or sell a security at a specific price limit that is "good till canceled." The order is kept on the broker's books until it is executed or canceled by the person giving the order. At the end of the month, the broker may ask the customer to confirm any GTC orders on his or her books.

General mortgage bond. A bond secured by a blanket mortgage on the property of a company.

Good till canceled. See GTC ORDER.

Growth stock. Stock that has the potential for increasing its value. Investors are attracted to such stocks for their prospective price increases rather than their dividends.

Guaranteed bonds. Bonds guaranteed as to principal or interest, or both, by a corporation other than the issuing corporation. Guaranteed bonds frequently become known in investment circles by the name of the guaranteeing company.

Guaranteed stock. See STOCK, *Other stock.*

Hedging. The financing of assets with liabilities of similar maturity. See COMMODITY EXCHANGES.

Income and adjustment bonds. A bond, the interest on which is to be paid only when the company earns it. Income bonds are rarely issued for public subscription; they result primarily from reorganizations. Hence the term *adjustment* is frequently found in combination with the word *income* or in place of it. Unpaid interest may accumulate as a claim against the issuing corporation.

Industrials. The securities of companies that produce or sell a product or service, for example, a manufacturing company or a retail store. Industrials should be distinguished from the securities of other concerns, such as financial institutions and public utility companies.

Insolvency. The state of being INSOLVENT.

Insolvent. When debtors do not have funds with which to pay their debts, they are said to be *insolvent.* The word is used in two senses: (1) Debtors whose assets exceed liabilities but who are temporarily unable to meet their obligations as they mature because their assets are not readily convertible into cash are insolvent in the *equitable* sense. (2) Debtors whose total assets are less than liabilities are insolvent in the bankruptcy sense. See Chapter 9/BANKRUPTCY.

Installment sale. A written contract of sale calling for payments in equal amounts at stated regular intervals. The terms consist of two elements: (1) the down payment required at the time of purchase and (2) the installments or unit payments to be made at regular intervals until final maturity of the debt. There is usually a service charge to meet the extra expense of carrying the deferred account. See CONDITIONAL SALE.

Interest. 1. An amount paid for the use of capital. It is usually stated as a percentage of the amount borrowed, as, for example, a BOND that pays 9 percent interest or a loan that is advanced for ninety days at 18 percent. See also BOND TRANSACTION.

2. In economics, the increment of income that capital earns as contrasted to rent, which is paid for the use of land, and wages, which are paid to labor. See Chapter 11/ CAPITAL.

Computation of interest. In interest calculations, three factors are involved: (1) principal, (2) time, (3) rate.

The *principal* is the sum of money upon which the interest is paid—the sum loaned, borrowed, or invested.

The *time* is the number of periods for which the interest is paid. One year is generally considered as the unit period.

The *rate* is the percentage per period of the principal that is paid as interest. The rate is usually expressed as a certain percentage per year.

There are two kinds of interest: (1) simple interest and (2) compound interest. If the interest is calculated on the original principal only, it is called *simple interest.* The method of computation is explained below.

Compound interest. If at the end of the first period, the interest for that period is added to the principal and the interest for the second period is calculated on this sum, and this process is continued for the given number of periods, the interest is said to be compounded, and the total interest thus realized is called *compound interest.* Tables used in computations involving compound interest may be purchased in bookstores.

State legal and contract rates of interest. The rate of interest that can be charged is governed by state laws. The legal rate of interest is charged in the absence of a contract between the parties. The contract rate is the rate upon which the parties have agreed; it cannot exceed the legal rate.

How to calculate the due date of an obligation. The date of maturity of a loan or other obligation is determined by the wording of the obligation. For example, if, in a transaction on September 5, a debtor agrees to repay a loan in *four months,* the money is due on January 5. If, on the other hand, another obligation contracted on September 5 is by agreement to run 120 days, the repayment is due on Jaunary 3. In this case, the exact number of days is counted in determining the due date because the time was stated in days.

How to calculate the time between dates. You can calculate the time between dates by the (1) ordinary method or (2) exact method.

1. *Ordinary method.* In the ordinary method (sometimes called the "bond method"), the year is considered as having 12 months of 30 days each, or 360 days. The time between dates is then calculated by subtraction, as illustrated in the following example:

EXAMPLE 1

Find the time between June 15, 1988, and August 3, 1989.

Solution:

Years	Months	Days
1988	8	3
1989	6	15
1	1	18

Since 15 cannot be subtracted from 3, 30 days, or 1 month, is "borrowed" and 15 is subtracted from 33, leaving 18. Since 1 month was borrowed, 8 becomes 7 and 6 is subtracted from 7, leaving 1.

The time between June 15, 1988, and August 3, 1989, is therefore 1 year, 1 month, 18 days, or 408 days (360 + 30 + 18 = 408).

The ordinary or bond method of calculating the time between dates is not commonly used except in interest computations involving long periods, usually a period greater than 1 year, and in the calculation of interest on bonds other than United States government and some municipal bonds. When the period is short, business people and bankers generally use the exact method.

2. *Exact method.* In the exact method of calculating the time between dates, the actual number of days in each month is counted. The first day, the day on which the obligation terminates, is included.

EXAMPLE 2

A loan made April 17 is repaid June 26. For how many days should the interest be calculated?

Solution:

Exclude the first day, April 17; include the last day, June 26. Then:

Number of days remaining in April 13
Number of days in May 31
Number of days in June
  to be counted 26

  Total number of days 70

The interest should therefore be calculated for 70 days.

When the exact number of days between dates is counted, it is the general practice of business people and bankers to exclude the first day and include the last day, as in the above example. However, in certain sections of the United States, and in some foreign countries, it is customary to include both the first and the last days. If this procedure were followed in the above example, interest would be due for 71 days instead of for 70.

Ordinary and exact simple interest.
Ordinary interest is simple interest computed on the basis of 360 days to the year. *Exact* or *accurate interest* is simple interest computed on the basis of 365 days to the year. Since calculations are much easier on the basis of 360 days to the year than 365, business houses and commercial banks generally compute simple interest on the basis of 360 days to the year, even when the exact number of days for which interest is due is counted.

Short method of finding the exact number of days between dates. Table 1 may be used as a shortcut in finding the exact number of days between dates. The exact number of days between the corresponding dates of any two months is indicated on the line of the month of the beginning date, under the month of the later date. Thus from any day in January to the same day in August, there are 212 days. In the table, this figure is found opposite January, in the column marked *Aug.*

Six percent method. Short methods of calculating ordinary interest at 6 percent:

1. *Sixty-day method.* At 6 percent per year:

Interest on $1.00 for
  360 days is $0.06
  60   "   0.01 ($\frac{1}{6}$ of $0.06)
  6   "   0.001 ($\frac{1}{10}$ of $0.01)

It is evident that interest on $1.00 for 6 days at 6 percent may be computed by moving the decimal point in the principal three places to the left. If this is true of $1.00, it is true of any principal, and a general rule may be stated as follows: Given any principal, to find the interest at 6 percent for:

6 days, point off three places to left
60   "   "   two   "   "
600 "   "   one place   "
6,000 "   the interest is the same as
           the principal

Thus interest on $1,280.00 for:

6 days at 6% is $ 1.28
60   "   "   12.80
600 "   "   128.00
6,000 "   "   1,280.00

TABLE 1
EXACT NUMBER OF DAYS BETWEEN DATES

FROM ANY DAY OF	TO THE SAME DAY OF THE NEXT											
	Jan.	Feb.	Mar.	Apr.	May	June	July	Aug.	Sept.	Oct.	Nov.	Dec.
January	365	31	59	90	120	151	181	212	243	273	304	334
February	334	365	28	59	89	120	150	181	212	242	273	303
March	306	337	365	31	61	92	122	153	184	214	245	275
April	275	306	334	365	30	61	91	122	153	183	214	244
May	245	276	304	335	365	31	61	92	123	153	184	214
June	214	245	273	304	334	365	30	61	92	122	153	183
July	184	215	243	274	304	335	365	31	62	92	123	153
August	153	184	212	243	273	304	334	365	31	61	92	122
September ...	122	153	181	212	242	273	303	334	365	30	61	91
October	92	123	151	182	212	243	273	304	335	365	31	61
November	61	92	120	151	181	212	242	273	304	334	365	30
December	31	62	90	121	151	182	212	243	274	304	335	365

In calculating the interest at 6 percent on any principal for any number of days, the time, stated in days, may be separated into parts that are multiples or fractions of 6, 60, 600, or 6,000, and the computations are greatly simplified.

EXAMPLE 1

Find the ordinary interest on $760.00 for 15 days at 6%.

Solution:
Interest for 60 days = $7.60
    "   " 15   "   = $7.60 ÷4
                   = $1.90

Explanation: Pointing off two places in the principal gives the interest for 60 days. Fifteen days is $\frac{1}{4}$ of 60 days. Hence divide the interest for 60 days by 4.

EXAMPLE 2

Find the ordinary interest on $842.60 for 124 days at 6%.

Solution:
Interest for 60 days = $ 8.4260
    "   "   60   "   =   8.4260
    "   "   4   "   =   0.5617
    "   " 124   "   = $17.4137,

                or $17.41

Explanation: Sixty days plus 60 days plus 4 days equals 124 days. The interest for the 4 days is found by pointing off three places in the principal (which gives the interest for 6 days) and then multiplying this figure by $\frac{2}{3}$, since 4 days is $\frac{2}{3}$ of 6 days.

2. *One-day or product method.* The one-day or product method is convenient when the number of days for which ordinary interest is being calculated cannot be readily divided into fractions or multiples of 6, 60, 600, or 6,000. To find the ordinary interest on any principal at 6 percent by this method:

1. Point off three decimal places in the principal; this gives the interest for 6 days.

2. Multiply the figure found in (1) by the number of days for which the interest is being calculated; this gives the interest for 6 times the number of days required.

3. Divide the result by 6.

EXAMPLE

Find the ordinary interest on $137.65 for 77 days at 6%.

Solution:

$0.13765,   interest for 6 days
      77
———
  0.96355
  9.6355
———
$10.59905,   interest for 6 × 77 days

$10.59905 ÷ 6 = $1.7665, or $1.77, interest for 77 days

Short method of calculating ordinary interest at a rate other than 6 percent. To find the ordinary interest at a rate other than 6 percent:

1. First find the interest at 6 percent by one of the methods described in the preceding pages.

2. Adjust the result by adding to or subtracting from the interest computed at 6 percent the fractional part thereof that the specified rate is greater or less than the 6 percent rate, as shown in Table 2.

EXAMPLE

Find the ordinary interest on $380.00 for 90 days at $4\frac{1}{2}$%.

Solution:

(1) First calculate the interest at 6%.

Interest for 60 days = $3.80
  "   " 30 "   = 1.90
                      ———
  "   " 90 "   = 5.70

(2) The interest at 6% is $5.70. To find the interest at $4\frac{1}{2}$%, deduct $\frac{1}{4}$ of $5.70. $5.70 ÷ 4 = $1.43, $5.70 − $1.43 = $4.27, the interest on $380.00 for 90 days at $4\frac{1}{2}$%.

Exact interest table. Table 3 gives the interest on $100 (computed on the basis of 365 days to the year) for 1 day to 100 days at various rates of interest. By reference to the table, the interest accruing for other sums and for any other number of days can be easily calculated.

EXAMPLE

Compute the interest on $920 for 22 days at 6%.

Solution:

Interest on $100 for	
20 days at 6% (from table)	0.33334
2 days at 6% (from table)	0.03333
22 days	0.367
Multiply by 9.2	
($920 is 9.2 times $100)	9.2
	734
	3303
Interest on $920 for 22 days at 4%	$2.2172, or $2.22

(Note: On sums of less than $1,000, the last three digits can be dropped—but be careful to increase the last remaining digit by 1 when the digits dropped are more than one-half. Thus 0.36667 became 0.367.)

457

TABLE 2

For	2%,	decrease the interest by	$\frac{2}{3}$	of the amount computed at 6%				
	3%,	" " "	$\frac{1}{2}$	"	"	"	"	"
	4%,	" " "	$\frac{1}{3}$	"	"	"	"	"
	5%,	" " "	$\frac{1}{6}$	"	"	"	"	"
	7%,	increase the interest by	$\frac{1}{6}$	"	"	"	"	"
	8%,	" " "	$\frac{1}{3}$	"	"	"	"	"
	9%,	" " "	$\frac{1}{2}$	"	"	"	"	"
	10%,	" " "	$\frac{2}{3}$	"	"	"	"	"
	11%,	" " "	$\frac{5}{6}$	"	"	"	"	"
	12%,	" " "	twice	"	"	"	"	"

TABLE 3
Exact Interest Table
Interest on $100 at Various Rates for Various Periods

	5%	6%	7%	8%	9%	10%	11%	12%
1	.01389	.01667	.01944	.02222	.02500	.02778	.03056	.03333
2	.02778	.03333	.03888	.04444	.05000	.05556	.06111	.06666
3	.04167	.05000	.05833	.06666	.07500	.08333	.09167	.10000
4	.05556	.06667	.07778	.08888	.10000	.11111	.12222	.13333
5	.06945	.08333	.09722	.11111	.12500	.13889	.15278	.16667
6	.08333	.10000	.11666	.13333	.15000	.16666	.18334	.20000
7	.09722	.11667	.13611	.15555	.17500	.19445	.21389	.23333
8	.11111	.13334	.15555	.17778	.20000	.22222	.24445	.26666
9	.12501	.15000	.17500	.20000	.22500	.25000	.27500	.30000
10	.13889	.16667	.19444	.22222	.25000	.27778	.30556	.33333
20	.27778	.33334	.38888	.44444	.50000	.55556	.61112	.66666
30	.41667	.50001	.58332	.66666	.75000	.83334	.91668	.99999
40	.55556	.66668	.77776	.88888	1.00000	1.11112	1.22224	1.33332
50	.69445	.83335	.97220	1.11110	1.25000	1.38890	1.52780	1.66665
60	3.8333	1.00002	1.16664	1.33332	1.50000	1.66668	1.83336	1.99998
70	.97223	1.16669	1.36108	1.55554	1.75000	1.94446	2.13892	2.33331
80	1.11112	1.33336	1.55552	1.77776	2.00000	2.22224	2.44448	2.66664
90	1.25010	1.50003	1.74996	1.99998	2.25000	2.50002	2.75004	2.99997
100	1.38890	1.66670	1.94440	2.22220	2.50000	2.77780	3.05560	3.33330

Interest coupons. See COUPON BONDS.

Interest paid. Chapter 12/INTEREST.

Issuance of stock certificate. See Chapter 10/STOCK CERTIFICATE.

Issued stock. See STOCK.

Investment. The purchase of some form of tangible or intangible property, or an interest in such property, on which one hopes to earn income and which will be held for a reasonable time. For example, someone might invest in securities, a business, and real estate.

Joint annuity. An ANNUITY in which two or more persons are interested in the proceeds under the contract. If a life annuity is payable to two or more persons while all are alive, the annuity is a *joint life annuity*. If the payments continue as long as any one of two or more designated persons lives, the annuity is a *joint and survivor annuity*. See ANNUITY.

Joint bonds. GUARANTEED BONDS backed by two or more guarantors. They arise principally in railroad financing. The corporation that has the title to a railroad terminal property, for example, issues bonds secured by a mortgage on the terminal property. The property, however, in the event of default, would be valuable only to the railroads that use it and not to any foreclosing bondholders. Therefore, the corporation owning the station issues bonds secured by a mortgage and guaranteed jointly and severally by all of the railroads that run tracks into the station.

Limit order. In *securities*, an order given to a stockholder to buy or sell securities at a specific price. In *commodities*, an order given to a commodities broker to buy or sell a contract at a specific price. Unless a specific period is stipulated, limit orders are presumed good only for the day on which they are given.

Line of credit. The amount of credit a bank will extend to a borrower over a specified period. Usually, the borrower must meet certain conditions, such as filing an acceptable financial statement and maintaining a certain checking account balance. In addition, some lenders require payment of a commitment fee on any unused portion of a line of credit.

Listed securities. Securities approved for trading by a STOCK EXCHANGE. To be listed, certain requirements and procedures of the exchange must be met by the corporation whose securities are to be listed. The New York Stock Exchange does not permit trading on its floor in securities that are not listed by it, but other exchanges sometimes permit trading in unlisted securities. Listing does not guarantee a security's worth. However, it does provide a ready market for the buying and selling of a security.

Loan on real estate. A grant of the use of money temporarily, at *interest*, repayment of which is secured by a mortgage on real property. (See INTEREST, Chapter 15/MORTGAGE; REAL PROPERTY.) Real estate loans may be classified according to their method of repayment into two general types: (1) STRAIGHT LOAN and (2) AMORTIZED LOAN. Generally, the *straight loan* is a short-term loan, whereas the *amortized loan* is a long-term loan.

Long sale. In securities and commodities markets, the sale of securities or commodities that are actually owned by the seller, as opposed to the SHORT SALE, in which the seller is not the owner.

Long-term loan. See AMORTIZED LOAN.

Management stock. See STOCK, *Other stock.*

Margin. In securities, the money or securities deposited by a purchaser of listed or otherwise approved securities with a broker to cover the difference between the amount the broker will lend against collateral (the securities) and the market price of the security. Margin is usually expressed as a percentage of the total transaction. Margin requirements are regulated by the Board of Governors of the Federal Reserve System in that they stipulate the "loan value," which is the amount a broker can loan against a transaction.

EXAMPLE

A buys 100 shares of XYZ stock at 50. With 75 percent "margin requirements," *A* need pay only $3,750; her broker supplies the balance, $1,250, using the securities that were purchased as collateral in borrowing from the bank. (Or the broker may use his own funds.) When *A* sells the stock, the loan is repaid. The broker charges *A* interest on the amount borrowed.

If the market drops and the margin becomes "too thin," the broker calls for additional margin.

EXAMPLE

Assume that the price of XYZ stock drops to $40. Then the most the broker can put up on margin is $1,000; and he will make a "margin call" for $250, the difference between the $1,250 initially put up and the current margin authorized. Conversely, should the stock price go up to $60, the broker could margin 25 percent or $1,500 at which time *A* could request this difference.

When a broker calls for additional margin and none is forthcoming, the broker sells the security. The speculator sustains the losses. Losses in excess of the margin, and which the speculator cannot repay to the broker, must be borne by the broker.

In *commodities*, margin is the percentage of the purchase price of a commodities futures contract that a broker needs to protect all parties to the agreement and to meet possible market fluctuations. The client deposits money through the broker, and the broker in turn deposits money with his or her clearinghouse as required by the Commodity Exchange. As with securities, brokers may call for additional or may remit excess margin.

Market order. An order given to a stockbroker to buy or sell securities at the market—hence at the best price obtainable when the order is received on the trading floor. See SECURITIES MARKETS; AT THE OPENING; GTC ORDER; LIMIT ORDER; STOP-LOSS ORDER.

Mathematical signs and symbols. The following is a list of mathematical signs and symbols:

$+$ Plus, the sign of addition

$-$ Minus, the sign of subtraction

$\pm$ Plus or minus

$\times$ The sign of multiplication

$\div$ The sign of division

$:$ Is to ⎫   The signs of pro-
$::$ As ⎬   portion. Thus
$:$ Is to ⎭ $3:6::4:8$

$:$ Ratio

$\because$ Because

$\therefore$ Therefore

$=$ Equals, the sign of equality

$\neq$ Not equal to

$\approx$ Nearly equal to

$>$ Greater than

< Less than

√ Square root

$\sqrt[3]{}$ Cube root, $\sqrt[4]{}$ Fourth root, $\sqrt[5]{}$ Fifth root, etc.

Σ Sum of

( ) Indicate that the figures enclosed
[ ] are to be taken together. Thus 10
{ } × (7 + 4); 8 − [9 ÷ 3]; 30 $\{\frac{7+3}{4-2}\}$

° ' "Degrees, minutes, seconds. Thus 25° 15' 10" represents 25 degrees, 15 minutes, 10 seconds.

' " Feet, inches. Thus 9' 10" = 9 feet 10 inches.

∞ Infinity

⊣ Perpendicular to

‖ Parallel to

Number; numbered

° Degree

○ Circle

∠ Angle

∟ Right angle

□ Square

▭ Rectangle

◇ Parallelogram

△ Triangle (or delta)

0 The cipher, zero

% Percent

Mathematics. See Business arithmetic for complete cross-reference to mathematical computations.

Money market. A market for short-term investment. A minimum deposit is usually required of investors, and income from the investment may be paid by the money market fund directly to the investor or reinvested in the customer's account. Interest rates change depending on many market influences, including the state of the economy.

Mortgage bond. A Bond secured by a mortgage on real property. (See Chapter 15/Mortgage; Real property.) Corporations frequently issue bonds secured by a general mortgage on the corporate assets and on assets to be acquired in the future. If interest or principal is defaulted, the securing property may be sold to satisfy the debt.

Multiplication, shortcuts. Time can be saved in multiplication by using the following shortcut methods:

Special cases. Sometimes the process can be shortened by using the following table:

Shortcuts in Multiplication

To multiply by

$1\frac{1}{4}$	add	0	and divide by	8
$1\frac{1}{3}$	"	0	" "	6
$2\frac{1}{2}$	"	0	" "	4
$3\frac{1}{3}$	add	0	and divide by	3
5	"	0	" "	2
$6\frac{1}{4}$	"	00	" "	16
$6\frac{2}{3}$	"	00	" "	15
$8\frac{1}{3}$	"	00	" "	12
$12\frac{1}{2}$	"	00	" "	8
$14\frac{2}{7}$	"	00	" "	7
$16\frac{2}{3}$	"	00	" "	6
25	"	00	" "	4
$31\frac{1}{4}$	"	000	" "	32
$33\frac{1}{3}$	"	00	" "	3
50	"	00	" "	2
$66\frac{2}{3}$	"	000	" "	15
$83\frac{1}{3}$	"	000	" "	12
125	"	000	" "	8
$166\frac{2}{3}$	"	000	" "	6
250	"	000	" "	4
$333\frac{1}{3}$	"	000	" "	3

461

For example, to multiply 5 by 2: add 0 to 2 (20) and divide by 2 (20 ÷ 2 = 10). Thus, 5 × 2 = 10.

Using factors as a shortcut in multiplication. When factors of the multiplier are used, there are only two multiplications, whereas in the ordinary method there is an addition as well.

EXAMPLE

Multiply 439 by 24.

Solution: Ordinary Method

$$
\begin{array}{r}
439 \\
24 \\
\hline
1756 \\
878 \\
\hline
10536
\end{array}
$$

Shorter Method

$$
\begin{array}{rl}
439 & 24 = 6 \times 4 \\
6 & \\
\hline
2634 & \\
4 & \\
\hline
10536 &
\end{array}
$$

Mutual fund. An open-end investment company that raises money by selling its own stock to the public and investing the capital in other securities. (See Chapter 10/INVESTMENT COMPANY.) Mutual funds redeem their shares at liquidated or net asset value and issue new shares as required, whereas closed-end investment companies do not make any provision for redemption of shares. Their stock is traded in the open market as is the stock of any other corporation. Mutual funds may be either load or no-load types. A *load fund* is typically sold by a broker and has a sales commis-sion fee attached to it. Load funds are not listed on stock exchanges. *No-load funds* are sold over the counter or by a brokerage house and typically require payment of a management fee rather than commission. No-load funds are listed on stock exchanges. See also RETIREMENT PLANS.

Negotiable instrument. See Chapter 9/NEGOTIABLE INSTRUMENT.

Negotiable securities. See TRANSFER OF SECURITIES; Chapter 9/NEGOTIABLE INSTRUMENT.

New York Stock Exchange. See STOCK EXCHANGES.

Noncumulative preferred stock. See STOCK, *Preferred stock.*

Nonnegotiable instrument. See Chapter 9/NONNEGOTIABLE INSTRUMENT.

No-par stock. See PAR VALUE STOCK AND NO-PAR STOCK.

Nonparticipating preferred stock. See STOCK, *Preferred stock.*

Note. A written promise to pay unconditionally a definite sum of money on demand or at some specified time in the future. It is signed by the *maker*—the person who promises to pay. It may be issued by corporations, individuals, or governments. The person to whom the note is payable is the *payee*. If payable to a particular person's order or to bearer, the note is negotiable; the title may be transferred by endorsement and delivery. With reference to the payee, a note is a *note receivable;* with reference to the maker, a *note payable.* Both types of notes usually require the payment of interest. To compute a note's maturity value (principal plus interest), you take the face value of the note (e.g., $5,000) times the interest rate (e.g., 10 percent) and divide by the remaining time of the note (e.g., five months). The maturity value in this example would be $5,208.33.

A note is deposited in the bank account as a collection item. (See Chapter 14/BANK ACCOUNTS.) It is not included with a regular deposit but is given to the collection teller, who gives the depositor a receipt for it. When the note is collected, the bank notifies the depositor that the amount has been placed to his or her account. See Chapter 11/NOTES RECEIVABLE; NOTES PAYABLE.

OTC. See OVER-THE COUNTER MARKET.

Odd lot. An order for less than the established unit of trading in stocks. Stocks are customarily traded in a SECURITIES MARKET in units of one hundred shares, although a few stocks are authorized for trading in units of ten shares. These are known as *round lots* or *full lots.* Odd-lot trading enables the small trader with restricted capital to make a limited investment in each of several stocks. The cost of the broker's commission, however, will be more on both the purchase and sale of odd lots than on round-lot transactions. An odd-lot transaction usually costs ⅛ of a point more than a round-lot transaction.

Options. See PUTS AND CALLS.

Outstanding stock. See STOCK.

Over-the-counter market. Unorganized securities market. The over-the-counter (OTC) market consists of a large number of dealers and brokers throughout the nation who, for their own account and as agents for customers, buy and sell securities among themselves and with the public, without the use of any exchange facilities. Quotations on the most active OTC stocks appear in newspapers. Most stock exchange member firms also operate in the over-the-counter market.

The over-the-counter market is the principal one for federal, state, and municipal bonds; for the majority of public utility, railroad, industrial, and foreign bonds; and for bank and insurance company stocks. However, most over-the-counter trading is in the securities of companies that have insufficient earnings, stockholders, or outstanding shares to meet the listing requirements of any of the organized stock exchanges. The volume of bond trading on exchanges is relatively small when compared with that of the dealers who make up the over-the-counter market. Transactions in any security that has a determinable market may be negotiated.

Paper profits. Anticipated profits, represented by an increase in value that has not been realized. The term is most commonly used in connection with securities. Today's paper profit may be tomorrow's loss.

Par value stock and no-par stock. For stock with par value, each share has been given a face value, which is indicated in the certificate of incorporation and on the face of the stock certificate. The par value may be of any amount: one, twenty, fifty, and one hundred dollars are common. The entire par value capital stock is equal to the par value of a share multiplied by the number of shares authorized to be issued. Dividends are usually expressed as a percentage of the par value. Thus 5 percent preferred stock pays 5 percent on its par value. On a twenty-dollar par share, the dividends would be one dollar a year; on a one hundred-dollar par share, five dollars a year for each share owned.

When par value stock is issued, the value of the consideration received for it must at least equal the par value of the stock. Only then can the stock be issued as fully paid and *nonassessable*, indicating that holders of such stock have no liability to creditors.

Disadvantages of par value stock. There are three principal disadvantages of par value stock: (1) It leads the uninformed owner of par value stock to think of the par value as the real value of the shares. Actually, the par value is a fictitious value or deceptive label, for the value of the stock varies with changes in the corporate earnings. (2) The requirement that the corporation must receive the full par value before the stock is "fully paid and nonassessable" sometimes makes it difficult to market the shares, particularly when the market value has declined below the par value of unissued shares. (3) When par value stock is to be issued to some of the organizers for property or services, and additional cash is to be raised by selling shares below par, a subterfuge must be used to limit the stockholder's liability on shares sold below par to the amount he or she agrees to pay for the stock. This subterfuge, or expedient, consists of issuing the shares in the first instance for the property valued at the par value of the total number of shares issued. The vendor of the property then donates to the corporation part of the stock he or she receives, and since it has been paid in full with the property, it may, as treasury stock, be sold at any price or given as a bonus. Bonus stock created in this manner has often been distributed with the sale of bonds or preferred stock. This process of "making" par value stock fully paid leads to stock "watering." (See WATERED STOCK.)

No-par stock. Although no-par stock has no face value, the price at which the shares are to be issued must nevertheless be fixed. The price at which no-par stock will be sold upon original issuance must be set in the light of legitimate considerations, such as the appraisal and sale value of assets, book values, market values of outstanding shares, present and probable earning power, market conditions, size of the issue, and reputation of the company.

Advantages of no-par stock. No-par

stock usually overcomes the disadvantages of par stock outlined above: (1) There is no fictitious figure that investors can confuse with actual value. (2) Unissued no-par stock can be sold from time to time at a price equal to its then fair value. (3) No-par stock can be given such nominal values that no legal difficulties are encountered in issuing it as bonus stock when desired.

Disadvantages of no-par stock. There are, however, certain disadvantages to no-par stock: (1) If the directors should fix the price of an increased issue of no-par stock at a figure less than the actual value of existing shares, the interest of the old stockholders in the total net assets will be less than it was before the new stock was sold, since each share after the increase has the identical value of every other share of the same issue. Such unfairness would occur, however, only if the new stock were sold to other than the existing stockholders. In such instances, stockholders' interests would be protected by the courts unless it could be shown that the transactions were fair and for the beneficial interest of the corporation. (2) Under some state laws, it is possible to designate part of the proceeds from the sale of no-par stock as paid-in surplus. (See CHAPTER 11/PAID-IN CAPITAL.) Stockholders could then be paid dividends out of the paid-in surplus that would amount to returning their capital. This might be unfair to creditors. (3) In some instances, statutes permit the corporation to list no-par stock at a nominal value such as one dollar on its balance sheet, making it extremely difficult for creditors, investors, and others to analyze the corporation's balance sheet.

Taxation of par and no-par stock. Taxation is often a factor in deciding whether to issue par and no-par stock. The taxes that may have to be considered are (1) the federal issuance tax and the state organization tax, (2) stock transfer taxes (see Chapter 12/STAMP TAX), and (3) annual state privilege taxes. It would, for example, cost less taxwise to incorporate a New York corporation with two hundred thousand shares of stock with par value of five dollars each than with two hundred thousand shares of no-par stock to be sold at five dollars each.

Partial payment of debts. A debtor who owes a large amount may by agreement make equal or unequal payments on the principal at regular or irregular intervals. There are two methods of applying these payments of principal and interest to the reduction of the debt. The method adopted by the Supreme Court of the United States is termed the *United States Rule;* the other method, which is widely used by business people, is termed the *Merchants' Rule.*

In the examples given below, the difference between the balance as computed by the United States Rule and the balance as computed by the Merchants' Rule is slight, but a much greater difference will occur when the time is long and the amount large.

It is usual to compute the balance due on obligations of one year or less by the Merchants' Rule; the balance due on obligations of more than one year is generally computed by the United States Rule.

United States Rule. The United States Rule is now a law in most states, having been made so either by statute or by court decision. The procedure under the United States Rule is as follows:

1. Payments must be applied against accrued interest before any deductions can be made from the principal.

2. Payments that do not equal the accrued interest leave the principal undiminished until other payments are made that are sufficient to cover all accrued interest.

3. Any excess remaining after the payments exceed the accrued interest is applied on the principal.

EXAMPLE

An interest-bearing note for $1,800 dated March 1, 1981 had the following endorsements:

September 27, 1981	$500.00
March 15, 1982	25.00
June 1, 1982	700.00

How much was due September 1, 1982?

Solution (United States Rule):	Yr.	Mo.	Day	Yrs.	Mos.	Days
Date of note	1981	3	1			
First payment, $500.00	1981	9	27		6	26
Second payment, $25.00	1982	3	15		5	18
Third payment, $700.00	1982	6	1		2	16
Settlement	1982	9	1		3	0
				1	6	0

Face of note, March 1, 1981	$1,800.00
Interest on $1,800 at 12% from March 1 to September 27, 6 months and 26 days	123.60
Amount due September 27, 1981	$1,923.60
Deduct payment	500.00
Balance due September 27, 1981	$1,423.60
Interest on $1,361.80 at 12% from September 27 to March 15, 5 months and 18 days, $76.26. As this interest is larger than the payment made at March 15, the interest is not added, and the payment is not deducted.	
Interest on $1,361.80 at 12% from September 27 to June 1, 1982, 8 months and 4 days	110.76
Amount due June 1, 1982	$1,534.36

Deduct sum of payments:	March 15	$ 25.00	
	June 1	700.00	725.00

Balance due June 1, 1982	$ 809.36
Interest on $692.18 at 12% from June 1 to September 1, 1982, 3 months	20.76
Balance due September 1, 1982	$ 830.12

Solution (Merchants' Rule):

Face of note, March 1, 1981		$1,800.00
Interest, 1 year at 12% to March 1, 1982		216.00
Deduct:		$2,016.00
First payment, September 27, 1981	$500.00	
Interest at 12% to March 1, 1982, 5 months and 4 days	25.66	525.66
Balance due at beginning of second year		$1,490.34
Interest on $1,395.17 at 12%, March 1 to September 1, 1982, 6 months		83.72
Deduct:		$1,574.06
Second payment, March 15, 1982	$25.00	
Interest at 12% from March 15 to September 1, 1982, 5 months and 16 days	1.38	
Third payment, June 1, 1982	700.00	
Interest at 12% from June 1 to September 1, 1982, 3 months	21.00	747.38
Balance due		$ 826.68

Merchants' Rule. The procedure under the Merchants' Rule, used in the example, is as follows:

1. The principal draws interest from the date of the loan until the date of final settlement, and such interest is added to the principal.

2. Each payment draws interest from the date of the payment until the date of final settlement.

3. The balance due is the principal plus interest minus the payments plus interest.

When the debt runs for more than one year, the principal draws interest from the date of the loan until the end of the first year (one year from the date on which the loan was made). Each payment draws interest from the date of payment until the end of the first year. The balance due at the end of the first year is the principal plus interest for one year minus the payments plus the interest from the dates on which the payments were made until the end of the

first year. The balance due at the end of the second, third, and subsequent years is calculated in a similar manner.

Participating bonds. Bonds that entitle the holders to a stipulated minimum rate of interest and more depending on the earnings of the company and the terms of the contract. This type of bond is rarely issued.

Participating preferred stock. See STOCK, *Preferred stock.*

Percentage. Division of a whole into hundredth parts, each of which is 1 percent of the whole. Hence $\frac{5}{100} = 5\% = 0.05$. If a salesperson is paid a commission of 5 percent on a $100 sale, he or she is paid a sum equal to $\frac{5}{100}$ of the total sale, or $0.05 \times \$100$, which equals $5.

The amount on which the percentage is calculated is called the "base" ($100). The number of 100th's is the percent or "rate" (5 percent). Hence

467

percentage equals base times rate. Percentage is a fundamental arithmetical principle that is used in numerous business problems. (See CASH DISCOUNT; INTEREST; PARTIAL PAYMENT OF DEBTS; YIELD; Chapter 14/BANK DISCOUNT.

Pledge. The placement of personal property by the owner with a lender as security for a debt. Pawned articles and stocks and bonds put up as collateral for a loan are the most common pledges. Essentials of a pledge are (1) a debt or obligation to be secured; (2) the thing pledged; (3) the *pledgor* (the one who gives the pledge) and the *pledgee* (the one who receives the pledge); (4) transfer of possession of the property (if actual physical possession is practically impossible, the pledgee may acquire constructive possession); (5) retention of title in the pledgor; (6) the pledgor's right to redeem the pledge; (7) a contract, express or implied, covering the transaction.

When stock is pledged as collateral, the pledgee has the right and is bound to collect the dividends and apply them to the loan, in the absence of an agreement to the contrary between the pledgor and pledgee. This is the legal theory. As a matter of practice, the stockholder makes an assignment of the stock in blank, and the stock is not transferred on the books of the corporation unless the pledgor defaults; the stockholder-pledgor therefore continues to collect the dividends.

Point. In securities, a point equals one dollar. Thus an increase of five points means a share of stock has risen five dollars.

Portfolio. In the securities trade, a list of securities and commercial paper owned by an individual, a company, a bank, or an investment house. The list is called *portfolio* because of the name of a case designed to hold the valuable papers. An investment portfolio may be designed for diversification to spread risk. A portfolio may consist of a variety of investment vehicles— stocks, bonds, precious metals, real estate, money market funds, and so on. The portfolio chosen depends on the individual's risk return preference. One of the secretary's duties may be to keep his or her employer's portfolio up to date by keeping a record of all of sales and purchases of securities. See SECURITIES RECORD.

Preferred stock. See STOCK, *Preferred stock*.

Price-earnings ratio. A ratio computed by dividing the price of a stock by its earnings per share. This ratio can be very significant to potential investors. For example, an undervalued stock may be a good buy.

Prime rate. The interest rate that commercial banks charge their best customers. Other borrowers, then, are charged a higher rate.

Prior preference stock. See STOCK, *Other stock*.

Promissory note. See NOTE.

Promoters' stock.   See STOCK, *Other stock.*

Protected preferred stock.   See STOCK, *Other stock.*

Purchase money mortgage.   A mortgage given by the buyer to the seller as part of the purchase price of real property. The mortgage is used as a means of financing the purchase of the property. See Chapter 15/MORTGAGE; REAL PROPERTY.

Puts and calls.   Options to buy or sell a certain number of securities at a stipulated price within a stipulated time, usually thirty, sixty, or ninety days, and no more than six months.

A *put* is an option giving the owner the right to sell stock at a prearranged price regardless of the current price in the market. A *call* is an option that permits the holder the right to purchase stock at a prearranged price. An option that permits the speculator to demand delivery of stock at an agreed price or to deliver stock against payment of a different agreed price is called a SPREAD. The same option, if only one price is specified, is called a STRADDLE. A market is maintained in the trading of options by the Chicago Board Options Exchange.

Puts and calls are sold for so much per hundred shares. The delivery prices stipulated in these options are either (1) the market price of the shares for which the options are contracted at the time the option is sold; or (2) for calls, a few points above the market price, and for puts, a few points below the market price.

EXAMPLE OF PUT

A speculator believes that *XYZ* stock selling currently at $35 is going to fall. He can buy a 30-day put on 100 shares at 30, which gives him the right to make the seller of the put take the 100 shares at 30. He can use a put to protect himself against a loss on a stock he already owns or as a speculative device. In the latter case, he does not own the stock. If *XYZ* stock goes below $30 to $27, he can buy in at 27 and put the stock at 30.

EXAMPLE OF CALL

A speculator believes that *XYZ* stock selling currently at $35 is bound to rise, but she is not willing to purchase the stock. Instead, for a nominal sum, she buys a 30-day call on 100 shares of *XYZ* at 40. If within 30 days the stock goes above $40 to $43, for example, she can demand delivery at $40 from the maker of the option (call) and sell the stock at $43, making a profit of $3 per share. The seller of the call thought that (1) the stock would not rise beyond $40 within 30 days, (2) the buyer would therefore not call the stock, and (3) he would earn the amount paid for the call.

Calls are also used as insurance by those making SHORT SALES. The short seller who owns a call on the stock he or she has sold short knows at what price the stock can be acquired in case it rises and hence what the maximum loss can be. The maximum possible loss of a short seller who buys a call "at the market" at the same time he or she sells short is equal to the price paid for the call. Also, an owner of a stock may write (sell) a "covered call" on his or her stock, thus fixing the price he or she will receive for the stock if the call is made. If the call is not made, the premium received by the writer is retained by him or her as well as the stock.

Pyramiding. The use of increased value of a security that was purchased on margin to purchase additional securities on margin. The original investment is thus used to pyramid profits (or losses).

Qualified stock option. An option to purchase stock of an employer corporation, given by the employer to an employee, that meets the requirements of Section 422 of the Internal Revenue Code. If the option qualifies and the employee observes certain requirements, there is no tax when the option is granted or exercised, and any profit on sale will be long-term capital gain.

If the employee sells within the proscribed three-year holding period, the difference between the option price and value of the shares on the date of exercise is ordinary income in the year the employee sells the stock. This amount is limited to the gain on the sale of the shares. The excess of the amount realized over the amount reported as ordinary income is capital gain.

Qualifying shares. The shares of stock given or sold by a corporation to prospective directors or officers to satisfy statutory or charter requirements that directors or officers be shareholders. The director or officer holds the shares only while serving in that capacity.

Quotation. See BID AND ASKED PRICES; STOCK TRANSACTION.

Ratio. The relation of one quantity or value (x) to another (y) or the comparison of one (x) to another (y). A ratio may be expressed as x or x:y (x is to y); or it may be considered as a simple fraction, decimal fraction, or percentage. Thus the ratio of 2 to 10 may also be written as 2:10 or $\frac{2}{10}$ or 0.20 to 1 or 20 percent. *Financial ratios* are those derived from comparison of balance-sheet items or of balance-sheet items with profit and loss items. A company's financial ratios should be examined by a potential investor over time to pick up trends and make a comparison with industry standards. This will give the investor an idea as to the company's current-year relative financial position. (See Chapter 11/BALANCE SHEET; PROFIT AND LOSS.) *Operating ratios* are those derived from comparison of items of income and expense.

Rebate (refund). A deduction from a fixed payment, charge, or rate. The amount is not taken out before payment but, like a refund, is *rebated* to the payer after he or she has remitted the full amount due.

Rebates (refunds) are frequently paid to taxpayers because of tax overpayments that may result from miscalculation, a change in the rates by which the original calculation was made, or excessive amounts withheld from income at the source. Each law contains its own particular provisions for rebates and stipulates the procedure that must be complied with for one to be able to obtain a rebate.

Redeemable bonds. See BOND; REDEMPTION.

Redeemable preferred stock. See STOCK.

Redemption. **1.** The exchange of securities for cash. Common stock is never *redeemed;* preferred stock may be redeemable (see STOCK, *Redeemable preferred stock*); bonds are frequently issued subject to redemption.

Purpose of redemption. The following are the more important reasons why a company might want to call its bonds before maturity: (1) *To eliminate or reduce fixed charges.* To avoid the constant burden of fixed charges, most firms will seize the first opportunity to pay off the bonds. They may even borrow at the banks at lower interest cost to reduce funded debt. (2) *To avoid burdensome terms.* Corporations may resort to redemption to eliminate restrictions on borrowing and on dividend payments. (3) *As a step in refinancing.* Redemption is frequently the first step in a refinancing plan to strengthen the financial structure of the corporation. (4) *To invest idle cash.* (5) *To strengthen a credit position.* Corporations may call their bonds before maturity to be able to say that they are "free from debt."

2. Recovery of property given as security for a debt by paying off a NOTE, BOND, or mortgage. See STOCK; Chapter 15/MORTGAGE.

Equity of redemption is the right of a mortgagor to recover (redeem) the property and obtain legal title thereto by paying the amount due in full (see Chapter 15/TITLE) with interest. Upon default, the right to redeem applies not only to the mortgagor but to any other person having an interest in the property derived directly or indirectly from the mortgagor. A clause in a mortgage waiving the EQUITY of redemption is void. The equity of re- demption is extinguished by foreclosure. (See Chapter 15/FORECLOSURE.)

Statutory redemption is the right given to the mortgagor by statute in some states to redeem his or her property within a specified time *after* foreclosure sale. The period varies in different states from two months to two years. As in the case of an equity of redemption, the statutory redemption may be made not only by the mortgagor, but by other persons interested in the property. The person making the redemption is generally required to pay the foreclosure sale price, with interest, plus expenses of foreclosure, taxes, and other items paid by the purchaser at the foreclosure sale. This may be more or less than the amount of the mortgage debt. In some states, the statutory right of redemption may be waived under the terms of the mortgage where the mortgagor is a corporation. See chapter 10/CORPORATION.

Registered bond. A bond made out, and registered on the books of the issuing company, in the name of the holder. Interest is payable by check to the registered holder. A registered bond is not a negotiable instrument unless the form of assignment on the back of the bond is signed by the registered holder. Some bonds are registered as to principal only, with negotiable coupons attached for interest payment. See COUPON BONDS; Chapter 9/NEGOTIABLE INSTRUMENT.

Restricted stock option. An option to purchase stock of an employer-corporation, given by the employer to an employee, pursuant to a plan in existence before January 1, 1964, that meets the requirements of Section 421 of the Internal Revenue Code.

Frequently, a corporation grants its employees an option to acquire its stock at reduced prices. Generally, the difference between the amount paid for the stock and its fair market value is taxable compensation to the employee at the time he or she acquires the stock. However, if the option meets the requirements of the Internal Revenue Code, the employee receives favorable tax treatment.

To get a tax benefit, the employee must not dispose of the stock within six months of the date of acquistion or within two years of the date the option was granted. If, also, the option price is at least 95 percent of the fair market value of the stock at the time it is granted, the entire gain realized when the stock is sold or exchanged is capital gain. If the shares are disposed of before meeting the holding period requirements, any difference between the option price and the price of the shares at the time the option is exercised must be reported as ordinary income.

If the above conditions are met, there is no tax on the employee at the time the stock is aquired, before selling it.

When the option price at the time a restricted stock option is granted is *at least* 85 percent and *less than 95 percent* of the fair market value of the stock, the employee receives taxable compensation (ordinary income) equal to the amount by which the option price is exceeded by the *lesser* of (a) the excess of the fair market value of the stock over the option price at the time

it was granted and (b) the excess of the fair market value of the stock over the option price at the time it was sold. The basis for your shares is increased by the amount you include in your gross income. The difference between this adjusted basis and the amount you realize from the sale or exchange of your shares is a capital gain or loss.

Retirement plans. In January 1982 employed Americans and their spouses, as well as self-employed persons, became eligible to open an individual retirement account (IRA). Such an account represents a form of savings for retirement with earnings on one's deposits being nontaxable until the money is withdrawn. The deposit itself is also tax-deferred until it is withdrawn. Banks, savings and loan institutions, insurance companies, securities firms, mutual funds, and other organizations offer such investment tax shelters. A minimum deposit is required to open an account, and thereafter, those who qualify can contribute up to $2,000 a year ($2,250 if a spouse without earned income is included).

Keogh plans are IRAs available to self-employed persons. The maximum contribution in one year is thirty thousand dollars or 25 percent of compensation if the plan is a defined-contribution plan. A self-employed person may contribute the maximum amount allowed each year to both a Keogh plan and an IRA, but different limitations on contributions apply to defined-benefit plans. Contributions cannot be withdrawn before age 59½ from either an IRA or Keogh plan without payment of a substantial penalty (except in cases of disability).

A popular type of retirement plan is the 401(k) plan. This type of plan gives participants the option of having an employer contribute amounts to the plan or receiving those amounts in cash. The employer contributions to a plan under such an arrangement will not be included in the income of a participant merely because the individual has the option of taking the contribution in cash.

Investors who prefer to make their own investment decisions may choose a *self-directed plan.* Although these plans usually are more expensive to open and maintain (most brokerage houses charge an initial fee and an annual management fee), they offer the greatest flexibility in terms of variety and charges in investments.

Reverse split. See STOCK SPLIT.

Revolving account. An account that allows a customer to reduce the balance due with equal payments. Such accounts have specified limits and allow customers to charge or draw against available credit up to the specified limit on each account.

Roman numerals. The following is a list of Roman numerals.

I	1	XXX	30
II	2	XL	40
III	3	L	50
IV	4	LX	60
V	5	LXX	70
VI	6	LXXX	80
VII	7	XC	90

VIII	8	C	100
IX	9	CC	200
X	10	CCC	300
XI	11	CD	400
XII	12	D	500
XIII	13	DC	600
XIV	14	DCC	700
XV	15	DCCC	800
XVI	16	CM	900
XVII	17	M	1000
XVIII	18	MM	2000
XIX	19		
XX	20		

GENERAL RULES IN ROMAN NUMERALS

1. Repeating a letter repeats its value: XX = 20; CCC = 300.
2. A letter placed after one of greater value adds thereto: VIII = 8; DC = 600.
3. A letter placed before one of greater value subtracts therefrom: IX = 9; CM = 900.
4. A dash line over a numeral multiplies the value by 1,000. Thus,

$\overline{X}$	=	10,000	$\overline{M}$	=	1,000,000
$\overline{L}$	=	50,000	$\overline{CLIX}$	=	159,000
$\overline{C}$	=	100,000	$\overline{DLIX}$	=	559,000
$\overline{D}$	=	500,000			

SEC. See SECURITIES AND EXCHANGE COMMISSION.

Savings bonds. United States government bonds in small denominations that have been sold to the public since 1940. They have been packaged to appeal to low- and middle-income groups. Payroll-deduction systems were established during World War II to encourage sales by making purchases a relatively "painless" procedure. Payroll-deduction systems are still being sponsored by the Treasury Department. Savings bonds are now available in Series EE and H and are available in denominations from fifty to ten thousand dollars. They all sell at a discount and are redeemed at face value. In 1987 Series EE bonds were paying interest based on a percentage of Treasury bill rates computed each six months but guaranteed not to be less than a rate as set by the government (6 percent in 1987).Savings bonds are registered, noncallable, and nontransferable and are not acceptable as collateral for loans.

Secured bonds. Bonds secured or backed by a pledge of property. See BOND; MORTGAGE BOND; COLLATERAL TRUST BONDS; EQUIPMENT TRUST BONDS.

Secured loan. A loan for which a debtor must pledge valuable property, which passes to the creditor in event of default.

Securities, delivery of. See DELIVERY OF SECURITIES.

Securities Act of 1933. See Chapter 9/SECURITIES ACT OF 1933.

Securities Exchange Act of 1934. See Chapter 9/SECURITIES EXCHANGE ACT OF 1934.

Securities and Exchange Commission. A federal agency that administers the federal laws regulating the sale of securities to the public. It was created by Congress in 1934 as an independent bipartisan agency. The various acts give the SEC certain functions that may be classified as regulatory, investigative, and quasi-judicial. It regulates largely through its authority to compel full and timely disclosure of factual information. On its own initiative, and as a matter of routine, the SEC undertakes to conduct inquiries whenever it believes any person or group subject to the acts has violated the law or its regulations. In connection with many phases of its work, the SEC has occasion to hold hearings, publicly if possible, privately if the information to be disclosed is confidential.

In addition to its quasi-judicial function, the commission often intervenes as a party to civil litigation brought by private persons. It serves at times in the role of *amicus curiae*— "friend of the court." In that event, it files briefs to aid the court in making its decision. Usually, it will act only in cases where judicial construction of one of the acts administered by the commission is involved and where novel questions of law have been raised.

The SEC has other broad powers. It may withdraw or revoke a registration of a security, procure restraining orders and injunctions to prevent violations or arrest them in process, suspend or expel members of either stock exchanges or the securities dealers association, and issue warnings and reprimands. It may also invoke criminal sanctions by referring the willful violations to the Department of Justice. In addition, the SEC publishes Accounting Series Releases that provide accounting and reporting guidelines to companies.

Securities markets. Organized or unorganized markets in which government and corporate securities are bought and sold daily through brokers and dealers.

Organized markets are represented by STOCK EXCHANGES in cities throughout the country, all of which are patterned after the New York Stock Exchange. Exchanges are essentially auction markets. Through an intricate yet smoothly functioning process, they bring together the buyers and sellers of LISTED SECURITIES to form a continuous market that publishes exact prices of all transactions immediately. One of the primary securities markets other than the New York Stock Exchange is the American Stock Exchange.

The OVER-THE-COUNTER MARKET is an unorganized market. Prices are not determined by the auction process, but by the "negotiation" and trading of dealers who buy and sell for their own account.

Securities record. An individual record of each security owned should be kept. The record may be kept in any convenient form, but it should show a description of the security; the date purchased; the price, interest, or dividends received; the date and price for which it sold; and other pertinent data. Three forms of records are described here.

Visible index record. Visible card records of securities owned are frequently used, especially by companies with large investments. The visibility of the name of the security, the interest or dividend payment dates, and maturity date in the case of a bond permit easy follow-up of amounts to be received. Interest or

dividend dates are shown by blocking out the proper months. The investment record is grouped by class of investment—government bonds (federal, state, county, municipal), railroad, public utilities, industrials— then alphabetically by investment.

Looseleaf record sheets. Many forms of looseleaf investment record sheets are available. Figure 1 is a form of looseleaf record, which may be reproduced easily in any office. This record facilitates the preparation of monthly reports on company-owned securities for the board of directors. Figure 2 is a Boorum & Pease form obtainable at local office-supply stores. The column headings are self-explanatory.

Card record. A card is illustrated in Figure 3. Since the card is usually run off in the office on a copier, it can be designed to meet specific needs. However, the card record calls for a separate card for each purchase of the same security. For this reason, a looseleaf record system or a visible index record may be more suitable

SECURITIES RECORD: FIGURE 1: Company-owned securities record

OWNED SECURITIES RECORD

Issuing Company
Character of Security
Par Value
Date of Maturity
Interest Date
Purchase Price (rates and aggregate)
Accrued Interest
Numbers of Securities
Date of Purchase
From Whom Purchased
Held by Whom (bond or trust company)

SECURITIES RECORD: FIGURE 2: Investment record sheet (stock and bond register)

STOCK AND BOND REGISTER				
NAME				
DESCRIPTION				
DATE OF ISSUE	DATE OF MATURITY	INTEREST OR DIVIDEND	% PAYABLE	SEMI-ANNUALLY
DENOMINATION				

MADE IN U S A

DATE 19__	OF WHOM PURCHASED	DATE 19__	SOLD TO	CERTIFICATE OR BOND NOS.	MATURITY	PAR VALUE	PRICE PAID	TOTAL COST	SOLD FOR	INTEREST OR DIVIDEND EARNINGS	LOSS OR GAIN

SECURITIES RECORD: FIGURE 3: Security record card showing purchase and sale of stock and dividend payments

LDM	JAN	FEB	MAR	APR	MAY	JUN	JUL	AUG	SEPT	OCT	NOV	13

100 Shares FREDERICK COMPANY

Bt. Oct. 21, 19__, through Leonard James Co. at 33 1/4 ---- $3,325.00
                                    plus Commission ----   60.30
                                                           $3,385.30

Sold Oct. 17, 19__, through Leonard James Co. at 24 ------- $2,400.00
Dividends: Mar., June, Sept, Dec.

Date	Amt.	Date	Amt.	Date	Amt.	Date	Amt.	Date	Amt.
12/25/--	50-	3/25/--	50-	3/25/--	50-	3/25/--	50-		
6/25/--	50-	6/25/--	50-	6/25/--	50-	6/25/--	60-		
6/25/--	50-	9/25/--	50-	9/25/--	75-	9/25/--	50-		
9/25/--	50-	12/25/--	50-	12/25/--	75-				

when there are numerous transactions in the same security.

See also Chapter 12/CAPITAL GAIN AND LOSS, Figure 1.

Security-transaction files. The only files that are needed in a filing system relating to security transactions are (1) the security-transactions pending file, (2) the security-transaction files, (3) the broker's statements file.

Pending-transactions folder. It takes time for a security transaction to be completed. For example, after a purchase order is placed with the broker, the purchaser must wait for the broker's purchase slip and then for delivery of the securities. Or perhaps someone has sold securities and has not yet gone to the vault to get the certificates for delivery. In the meantime, the broker's sales slips are held in the pending-transaction file. Or someone may have sent back some securities to an issuing corporation to be exchanged for new shares in a STOCK SPLIT. The transaction is not completed until the new shares are received. These are open or pending transactions.

All of the papers concerning an open transaction are kept in a pending-transactions folder, with the papers for each transaction fastened together. This is the tickler file for investments. (See Chapter 1/TICKLER-FILE.) The secretary should go through it from day to day to see what is expected and to follow up any long-delayed deliveries.

No papers are removed from the pending file, even though a transaction is complete, until the broker's monthly statement has been received and checked. After the checking, the papers relating to completed transactions are removed from the pending file and put into the security-transactions file.

Security-transactions folders. There should be a security-transactions folder for each type of security held by the manager, for example, "Stock—Preferred" and "Bonds—Municipal." If the manager handles transactions for members of his or her family in their names, the secretary should make folders for each owner of securities. All purchase slips, sales slips, receipts, delivery slips, copies of vouchers, correspondence, and other papers concerning each transaction should be placed in these folders *after* the transaction is completed. All papers relating to a particular transaction are fastened together. The file is maintained in chronological order. The papers pertaining to a particular transaction can be located easily from the date on the SECURITIES RECORD. When the contents of a folder become bulky, the dates of the first and last transactions should be written on the folder and a new file opened for that particular type of security.

Broker's statements file. A file entitled "(*Name of broker*) Monthly Statements, 19—" should be kept for each broker. Only monthly statements of the account are kept in the broker's file. The transactions shown on the broker's monthly statements and the list of securities held in the account should be checked against the purchase and sale slips in the pending-transactions file. If the statement is correct, the papers in the pending-

477

transaction file should be removed and placed in the securities-transactions file.

Serial bonds. Bonds of the same date of issue for which a certain portion of the debt becomes due each year. In serial bonds, for example, those numbered 1 to 100 will mature in one year, those numbered 101 to 200 in two years, and so on. Usually, the bonds carrying the longest term pay the highest rate of interest. See also SERIES BONDS.

Series bonds. Bonds that are issued in series under limited and open-end mortgages. These bonds are issued on different dates, unlike SERIAL BONDS, but under the same mortgage. See Chapter 15/MORTGAGE.

Shortcuts. Time- and labor-saving methods used in performing elementary arithmetical operations that occur in everyday business are explained under MULTIPLICATION, SHORTCUTS; DIVISION, SHORTCUT; ADDITION, SHORTCUTS.

Short sale. The sale of commodities or securities the seller does not own but expects to purchase after the consummation of the sale. Short sales are made by those who expect market prices to decline and who expect to profit by buying the securities or commodities for less than the price at which they are sold.

EXAMPLE

X Co. stock is selling currently around $50 a share, and John Doe believes it will drop in price in the near future. There-fore, he will sell 100 shares short at $50. Stock Exchange rules require delivery within a specified time, so his broker borrows 100 shares of X Co. and delivers them to the purchaser. If X Co. stock drops below $50 to $45, John Doe will then buy 100 shares and return them through his broker to the person from whom he borrowed to make the original delivery, thus completing the entire transaction. He pays interest on the amount borrowed. There is no time limit within which he must "cover" (return securities to the lender). Hence he has made a profit of $5 per share: he sold stock that cost him $45, for $50, less commissions and taxes. If the stock had risen to $55 instead of falling, he would have lost $5 per share, because he would have sold for $50 what cost him $55. (See PUTS AND CALLS for protection of short sales.)

The sale of securities or commodities actually owned by the seller is called a *long sale*. The SEC rules stipulate that the sales must be marked "long" or "short."

Sinking fund. A fund that consists of amounts set aside at certain periods that will eventually be used to pay off a debt. See also AMORTIZATION. Municipalities and corporations, for example, maintain sinking funds to satisfy bond issues at maturity. Sinking funds may also be used for purposes other than debt repayment such as for plant expansion.

Six percent method. See INTEREST.

Split-coupon bonds. A bond that carries a fixed rate of interest and, in addition, interest contingent on earnings. Like the income and adjustment bond, it has been issued as a result of corporate reorganization or debt adjustment, particularly in the fields of real estate and railroad finance.

Split. See STOCK SPLIT.

Spread. 1. The difference between the price paid by a securities underwriting group for an issue of securities and the price at which the securities are to be sold to the public. If the underwriting group buys an issue of bonds at $99 to be sold to the public at $101, the *spread* is two points regardless of whether or not some bonds remain unsold for a time and later have to be liquidated at $95.

2. A combination of a put and a call (see PUTS AND CALLS) at equal margins from the market price of the stock. For example, if *XYZ* stock is selling at $30, a *spread* would consist of a put at 25 (five points down) and a call at 35 (five points up).

3. The difference between the BID AND ASKED PRICES of a stock. If the bid is 36 and the asked is $37\frac{1}{2}$, the *spread* is $1\frac{1}{2}$ points.

Statistical data. Chapter 8/INFORMATION SOURCES, *Statistical data.*

Stock. The aggregate ownership interest of a business corporation. The term refers to ownership of the corporation, not of the corporation's assets, which are owned by the corporation.

Stock is divided into identical units called *shares* that are represented by written "certificates of stock." *Authorized capital stock* is the amount of stock that a corporation is empowered to issue by its certificate of incorporation. It does not change

from time to time unless the certificate of incorporation is amended. Authorized stock is divided into *issued* and *unissued stock. Outstanding stock* is issued stock in the hands of stockholders. Dividends are calculated and based on outstanding stock. Sometimes a corporation will obtain, by purchase or gift, some of its own stock. Such stock is called *treasury stock.*

There are two principal classes of stock—common and preferred.

Common stock. All corporations have common stock; some may have preferred stock in addition. The outstanding characteristic of common stock is that its holders have an unlimited interest in the corporate profits and assets. They share in dividends after the preferred stockholders' rights to dividends have been satisfied, and they participate in the distribution of assets after all prior claims have been met. They have voting rights that permit them to elect the board of directors; hence, to participate in management.

Although the New York Stock Exchange and also various government agencies have discouraged the issue of nonvoting common stock, there are still issues outstanding of Class A and Class B common stock, one with and one without voting power.) Today, corporations that issued more than one class of common stock usually do not make any voting distinction.

Preferred stock. This class of stock arose from the need to give investors an ownership security less speculative than common stock. The preferred stockholder usually has the rights of a common stockholder ex- cept that he or she is to receive a share of the profits annually before any profits are distributed to the common stockholder. Also, the holder of pre- ferred stock usually has the right to share in the distribution of assets upon dissolution before the common stock. Thus the position of preferred stock relative to earnings and assets is stronger than that of common stock, but not as strong as that of bonds. Frequently, the preferred stock is nonvoting or vetoing. (See Chapter 10/Voting at stockholders' meet- ings.) There are many variations of preferred stock, the most important of which are the following:

1. *Participating and nonparticipating preferred stock*. The most usual privi- lege attaching to preferred stock is the right to receive a fixed rate of dividend before any dividend is declared on common stock. The preferred dividend rate is commonly expressed in dollars per share or as a percentage, thus $5 preferred stock, or 7 percent preferred stock. How- ever, *participating* preferred stock gives the stockholder the right to receive dividends beyond the fixed rate.

A preferred stock that is *nonpartici- pating* is entitled only to the fixed or stated rate of dividends and to noth- ing more. A company with two kinds of preferred stock might have one class participating and the other non- participating.

2. *Cumulative and noncumulative pre- ferred stock*. Dividends upon pre- ferred stock many be cumulative or noncumulative. (See Cumulative

dividends.) When preferred stock is cumulative and dividends are not paid, the arrearages ordinarily do not bear interest. Nor do the arrearages in cumulative dividends become a liability of the corporation.

If the preferred stock is described as *noncumulative* and dividends have not been declared upon the stock, the dividends omitted in any year do not accumulate and need not be made up.

3. *Preference as to assets*. Preferred stock may be made preferred as to assets as well as to dividends. In that case, on liquidation of the com- pany, the holders of such stock will be paid back a certain amount for each share out of what is left after satisfying the creditors, before the other classes of stockholders receive anything. Chapter 10/Liquidation.

4. *Redeemable or callable preferred stock*. Frequently, preferred stock is made redeemable or callable. This means that the corporation has the right to demand that the stockholders surrender their stock and receive cash in payment for it.

The option to redeem always be- longs to the corporation because the redemption can take place only to the extent that the corporation has a surplus. Thus the original capital is not returned to the stockholders, but they are paid from a surplus repre- senting profits retained in the busi- ness or from some other surplus. The shares to be redeemed are frequently drawn by lot, although in some instances the redemption is pro rata; an equal proportion of the shares of each stockholder is called. In most cases, stock can be and often is bought in the open market at not more than the redemption price. The redemption price is usually above par and includes all dividends in arrears. (See REDEMPTION.)

5. *Convertible preferred stock.* Convertible preferred stock is stock that is convertible into some other form of security. Usually, conversion is at the option of the stockholder and permits the conversion of senior securities into junior securities of the same corporation. Thus convertible preferred stock is ordinarily convertible into common stock. Stock cannot be made convertible into bonds except at the option of the corporation (see BOND); otherwise stockholders would convert their stock into bonds when a company became insolvent and would thus gain an advantage over creditors.

The conversion provisions in the articles of incorporation express the rate at which the corporation will exchange the convertible shares in terms of the number of shares into which the security is convertible, generally called the *conversion rate,* or the price per share at which the new shares are issuable, generally called the *conversion price.*

6. *Preferred stock in series.* Some state corporation laws provide that preferred stock may be issued in series so that the board of directors, by resolution, can fix preference, restrictions, and limitations for each group at the time of issuance. Because the participation in the corporation income, preferences, and other privileges are not set forth in the certificate of incorporation, this form of stock has sometimes been called *blank stock.* At the time the directors undertake the sale of a block of such preferred stock, they give to it the attributes that will make it marketable.

Other stock. The following terms are often used to describe odd types of stock:

1. *Prior preference.* Sometimes, after a preferred stock has been issued, another stock, which, in effect, is a first preferred, may be issued with the consent of all of the stockholders. A classification of preferred stock in order of priority also gives rise to the titles *first preferred* and *second preferred.* The title of a stock does not necessarily show its rank; the choice of a name is frequently determined by popular designations at the time the issue is created.

2. *Deferred stock.* A stock on which dividends are to be deferred until a certain date or certain conditions have been met. It is usually created in connection with some form of readjustment of the capitalization.

3. *Guaranteed stock.* A term sometimes used as a synonym for preferred stock, but when so used it is a misnomer, for a company cannot guarantee dividends on its own stock. The title is correctly used when applied to a stock whose dividends are guaranteed by another corporation, usually a parent.

4. *Protected preferred stock.* Protected preferred stock provides that profits must be conserved by being placed in a "special surplus account"

to pay shortages in preferred stock dividends in the lean years when current profits are insufficient. Thus whereas the cumulative feature looks backward to clear up dividends in arrears, the protective feature looks forward to avoid nonpayment of dividends.

5. *Founders' or management shares.* Generally, this type of stock is essentially a "deferred" stock. Founders' shares are usually issued in smaller amounts than other classes of stock and generally carry dividend provisions that encourage the directors or founders who hold such shares to work toward increasing the earnings of the corporation.

6. *"Bankers' shares."* Applied to a class of stock that has sole voting power and is held by a small group, commonly the organizers of the corporation and the bankers who financed the issues. They are essentially "management shares."

7. *Promoters' stock.* This term is applied to stock given to promoters in part or full payment for services rendered. Promoters' stock is similar to management and bankers' stock. See Par value stock and no-par stock; Stock purchase warrant; Chapter 10/Stock certificate; Voting of stockholders' meetings.

Stock certificate. See Chapter 10/ Stock certificate.

Stock dividend. See *Dividends*.

Stock exchanges. Organized markets in which government and corporate securities are bought and sold daily through brokers and dealers. Stock exchanges throughout the country are patterned after the New York Stock Exchange (NYSE). All trading on stock exchanges is conducted by members. Memberships (seats) on the NYSE are limited, and hence new members must buy their seats from retiring members or the estates of deceased members, providing they can comply with the rigid qualifications for admission imposed by the exchange. Members can act as brokers or dealers but never as both in the same transaction. They buy or sell as an agent for public customers and charge a commission for their services. As dealers, they buy and sell for their own account. The New York Stock Exchange does not permit trading on its floor in securities that are not listed by it, but the American Stock Exchange (AMEX), another organized exchange located in New York City, and other stock exchanges throughout the country permit trading in unlisted securities.

The exact technicalities of executing a customer's order and the chain of events that follows up to the delivery of a new stock certificate to the buyer are extremely involved, but essentially here is what happens: Assume that someone in Dallas gives an order to a local broker to sell one hundred shares of XYZ common at (1) the market, or (2) $50 per share. The broker in Dallas transmits the order by leased wire to a commission house in New York. The New York office calls the floor of the exchange (again by direct wire), where a telephone clerk receives the order and gives it to a floor member of the commission house or to a floor broker.

If the order is to sell at the market, the last bid will be the price at which the transaction is completed. If the order is to sell at $50, the transaction will be completed when a bid is entered at 50. However, if the order reaches the floor of the exchange, the price trend is downward, and the last sale was at $49\frac{1}{2}$, the stock may not be sold that day. Since all transactions are electronically reported almost instantly throughout the country, the one who gave the order may note the trend and reenter the order at a lower price to dispose of his or her stock. If the order is not executed and remains with the broker as a GTC ORDER, the seller will have to wait until the trend reverses itself and a bid is entered at 50. A MARKET ORDER will be executed by the floor member of the commission house; an order to buy or sell at a fixed price is generally entrusted to the specialist to execute.

When the sale is executed, the notice goes back to Dallas within a matter of minutes. The Dallas broker delivers the stock to the New York commission house and credits the customer's account for the proceeds of the sale.

Stock market. See SECURITIES MARKETS; STOCK EXCHANGES.

Stock (or bond) power. A power of attorney given by the owner of securities to someone, usually his or her broker, to assign and transfer the securities on the books of the issuing corporation. A printed form of power can be obtained from any broker. When the signed power is sent to the broker by mail, it is usually sent separately from the securities that are to be assigned unless the name of the broker is filled in on the power. The reason for the precaution is that the securities, if accompanied by a signed blank power, can be assigned by anyone into whose hands they might fall. Sometimes powers are signed in blank and left with the broker to be used, for example, if the seller is out of the city and a GTC order is executed.

Stock purchase warrant. A certificate attached to preferred or senior issues of stock or bonds that entitles the holder to purchase common stock of the corporation at a certain price and within a prescribed period. This feature makes the securities to which it is attached attractive to the market at the time of original issuance.

Warrants are usually detachable instruments that may be purchased and sold apart from the security to which they were originally attached. In that case, they may be bought and sold in SECURITIES MARKETS. If the warrant is nondetachable, there can be no market in warrants alone, and the warrant can be exercised only by the presentation of the security to which it is attached. Provision is usually made to permit the holder of a nondetachable warrant to exercise a portion of the warrant.

Stock quotation. See BID AND ASKED PRICES; STOCK TRANSACTION.

Stock rights. See Chapter 10/ RIGHTS.

Stock split. Division of shares of stock into a larger number without changing the dollar amount of the capital stock or reducing the surplus. (See Chapter 11/CAPITAL STOCK.) The number of shares of stock outstanding is increased. Each stockholder receives a certain number of shares for each original share owned. In the case of par value stock, the par of each share is reduced or the stock is changed into no-par value stock. For example, a one hundred-dollar par stock may be split into four shares of twenty-five dollar par each or into four shares without par value. In either case, the certificate of incorporation must be amended. The usual purpose of a split is to lower the price per share to improve marketability. The stock split does not give the recipient anything of value from a financial viewpoint. Although the shareholder has received more shares, the total cost per share goes down. However, stock splits have a psychological value, and the reduced market price may make it easier for a small investor to buy shares in a company.

A *reverse* stock split reduces the number of shares outstanding. Each stockholder receives one share in exchange for a large number (one share for four held, for example). Devaluation and decapitalization through reverse splits were frequently employed in the early thirties to eliminate balance sheet deficits and assist in the restoration of earnings per share. It has the effect of increasing the price of a stock that is selling at a very low figure.

Stock transaction. The unit of trading in most stocks is one hundred shares; in a few it is ten shares. They are known as *round lots* or *full lots*. One can buy less than the established unit, but one pays a slightly higher price.

The price quoted for a share of stock on a STOCK EXCHANGE is the actual price of a share. Stock quotations are in eighths of a point, or multiples thereof. Thus a quotation of $78\frac{1}{8}$ means a price of $78.125 a share. Stocks are traded on a flat basis; that is, the price represents the stock and any divdend rights that go with it. When a stock is quoted Ex-DIVIDEND, it means that the buyer does not get a dividend that has been declared but not yet paid.

Figure 1 shows sample stock quotations listed in the *Wall Street Journal*. When there is no indication of *Pfd*, signifying preferred, or other designation following the name of the stock, the quotation refers to the common stock of the company. Dividends are listed in dollars and cents per share. Sales are listed in 100s, for example, 219 is 21,900 shares sold on the day in question. High, low, and close figures refer to dollars per share, for example, $32\frac{1}{2}$ is $32.50 a share. Net change refers to an increase or decrease in the closing price compared with the preceding stock trading day's closing price.

Stockholder. See Chapter 10/STOCKHOLDER.

Stop-loss order. A limit order given to a stockbroker by an owner of

STOCK TRANSACTION: FIGURE 1

TRANSACTIONS ON THE NEW YORK STOCK EXCHANGE

Friday, March 23, 19—

52 Weeks High	52 Weeks Low	Stock	Div.	Yld %	P-E Ratio	Sales 100s	High	Low	Close	Net Chg.
$33\frac{3}{8}$	26	UnLeaf	1.16	3.6	11	219	$32\frac{1}{2}$	$32\frac{1}{4}$	$32\frac{1}{2}$	...
36	$15\frac{5}{8}$	Unocal	1.00	2.7	24	6719	37	35	$36\frac{3}{4}$	$+1\frac{3}{4}$
$12\frac{3}{4}$	$10\frac{7}{8}$	UslfeF	1.08	9.6	...	35	$11\frac{1}{2}$	$11\frac{1}{4}$	$11\frac{1}{4}$	$-\frac{1}{8}$

securities who wishes to protect himself or herself against a loss. When the market price of the stock falls to the price stipulated in the order, the stock is automatically sold. "At the market," the broker will try to execute the order at the "stop" price, but there is no guarantee this can be done. The directors of a stock exchange may limit or halt the placing of stop-loss orders.

Straddle. **1.** A speculative transaction in commodity trading (see COMMODITY EXCHANGES) that consists of buying a futures contract in one month and selling a contract in another month with the expectation of making a profit on the price differential between the two contracts.

2. A combination of a put and a call, both at the same price. See PUTS AND CALLS.

Straight loan. A loan for a definite term of years, at a specific INTEREST rate, payable in full at maturity, with no payment of principal in advance of the due date. In real estate this is known as a *term* or *straight mortgage*. During the period of the loan, the borrower pays interest only on the principal. At maturity, he or she must either (1) pay the loan, (2) refinance the loan for another term, or (3) have the loan carried by the lender as an open or past due debt. The straight loan is generally made for a short term—from three to five years, and may be renewable at the end of the term. See also AMORTIZED LOAN.

Straight mortgage.   See STRAIGHT LOAN.

Surety bond.   A promise by one party to pay a debt if the obligor defaults in performance. In other words, the surety company guarantees the responsibility of the principal.

Term loan.   A bank loan set up to run for more than a year, often two to ten years. Payments are usually made in scheduled installments.

Trading in bonds.   See BOND TRANSACTION.

Trading in stocks.   See STOCK TRANSACTION.

Transfer of securities.   Every stockholder of a corporation has the right to transfer stock; every bondholder has the right to transfer bonds.

A *certificate of stock* or a REGISTERED BOND must be properly assigned by the person whose name appears on the face of it before it is ready for transfer and delivery. The assignment is made by filling in the form on the reverse side of the certificate or bond or drawing up an assignment separate from the security. A printed form of assignment may be obtained from any broker. A form of separate assignment should be used if the securities are already in the hands of the broker or dealer, or if they are to be sent by mail to the broker. The assignment should be sent separately from the securities, because it is wiser to send a nonnegotiable security through the mail; without the assignment on the back, the securities are nonnegotiable. See DELIVERY OF SECURITIES.

Usually, the seller pays the transfer tax. See Chapter 12/STAMP TAX.

A COUPON BOND does not require an assignment. It can be delivered as it is since it is negotiable, provided all unpaid coupons are attached.

If the secretary's duties involve issuance and transfer of stock certificates for a small corporation, see Chapter 10/STOCK CERTIFICATE for the procedure to follow.

Transfer of stock certificate.   See TRANSFER OF SECURITIES and DELIVERY OF SECURITIES for transfer of stock owned by an individual; see Chapter 10/STOCK CERTIFICATE for issuance and transfer of stock when the secretary is acting for the issuing corporation.

Treasury notes and bonds.   Short-term notes, bills, certificates of indebtedness, and long-term bonds that are marketed by the U.S. Treasury to meet its short- and long-term financial requirements.

Treasury bills consist usually of short-term (less than a year), low-interest obligations that are constantly being refunded. Notes and certificates of indebtedness may run as long as five years. They pay higher rates than do treasury bills.

Outstanding government bonds are (1) SAVINGS BONDS and (2) COUPON BONDS. The coupon bonds are relatively long term, maturing in from twenty to thirty years.

Although government obligations are traded in a free market (subject to SECURITIES AND EXCHANGE COMMIS-

SION regulations), the Federal Reserve Board influences the price of such obligations and attempts to stabilize the market by restricting price fluctuations within a narrow range.

Treasury stock. See STOCK.

Underwriter. A person, firm, or group in the investment banking field that assumes the responsibility of UNDERWRITING a new issue of securities.

Underwriting. *Securities trade.* A function performed by the investment banking industry in the formation of new capital for business enterprises or governments. Underwriting assures the issuer of the securities of the funds the issuer wishes to raise by the issuance of new securities. The process consists of (1) the outright purchase of the entire issue of the securities by a purchase group and the sale of the securities to the ultimate buyers, and (b) the agreement by the underwriters to purchase any of the securities not bought by stockholders to whom the issue has been offered. See Chapter 10/STOCKHOLDER.

Unlisted securities. Securities that are not listed on STOCK EXCHANGES. Unlisted securities are either traded in an OVER-THE-COUNTER MARKET or are admitted to unlisted trading privileges on some exchanges. The qualifications for "unlisted" trading on organized exchanges are far less exacting than for "listed" trading. Unlisted securities are generally more risky

(e.g., penny stocks). They may be of new companies or existing companies with financial problems.

Usury. Chapter 9/USURY.

Variable annuity. A type of ANNUITY contract under which payments are made to the beneficiary in income units rather than in fixed dollar amounts, the value of the units varying from time to time. The variance is caused by investment of the annuitant's reserve in equity securities rather than in debt securities. Because of the nature of the investment, variable annuities are also known as *equity annuities*.

Warrant. See STOCK PURCHASE WARRANT.

Wash sale. A fictitious transaction intended to stimulate trading activity and thus to induce investors to make higher bids. Such transactions, formerly common, especially on COMMODITY EXCHANGES, are now forbidden by the SECURITIES AND EXCHANGE COMMISSION.

Watered stock. Par value stock whose total value upon issuance is greater than the value of the assets received for it. (See PAR VALUE STOCK AND NO-PAR STOCK.) Watered stock is usually created in any of the following ways: (1) issuing stock against an intangible asset, like goodwill, whose actual value is less than the par value of the stock; (2) paying promoters in stock; (3) giving stock as a bonus to stockholders; (4) issuing stock against property, the value of which is less than the par value of the stock issued; a practice no longer allowable.

When-issued. Trading in securities that have not been finally approved by the Securities and Exchange Commission, or for which certificates are not ready for delivery. Contracts arising from such transactions are all contingent upon the issue of the security.

Years certain annuity. See ANNUITY.

Yield. The annual percentage rate of return on an investment in securities. If $5 is received annually in dividends on a stock that cost $100, the yield is said to be $5 ÷ $100). Yields are usually computed for (1) stocks and (2) bonds.

1. *Stocks.* The yield on a stock can be calculated by dividing the annual dividends as above by the price paid for the stock.

2. *Bonds.* Bond yield is calculated as "current yield" or "yield to maturity."

Current bond yields are the same as stock yields: the annual interest payment on the bond is divided by the price paid for the bond.

Yields to maturity are difficult to calculate accurately. They depend on the interest rate of the bond, the amount paid for the bond, the number of years to the maturity date, and the amount to be paid at maturity. For example, A purchased a bond, at 105, paying $1,050. The interest rate is 8 percent. If A holds the bond to maturity, which is ten years, and the principal is $1,000, A is going to lose $50 of capital (purchase price, $1,050—redemption price, $1,000) over the ten-year period, or an average of $5 per year. This capital loss must be considered in calculating the net average yield to maturity and would reduce A's percentage return on his average annual investment.

On the other hand, if A had purchased the bond at 95, paying $950, he would have gained $50 or $5 per year by holding to maturity, thus increasing the percentage return on his average annual investment.

Yields to maturity are usually determined by consulting specially prepared tables of yields that are available at most brokerage offices and banks.

CHAPTER 14

BANKING

Automatic teller. Automated machines, commonly located in a bank's lobby or vestibule and open twenty-four hours a day, in which customers can insert a plastic encoded card to activate the machine. Automatic tellers enable you to make immediate cash withdrawals from or payments to a checking or savings account. Often you can use the machine to transfer funds from one account to another, make deposits to checking or savings accounts, and pay certain bills such as utility or telephone bills.

Bank accounts. Most businesses maintain one or more general bank accounts and very often several special bank accounts.

General accounts. General accounts usually contain most of the organization's cash funds. They are used to receive deposits representing receipts from customers, from sale of capital stock, from proceeds of borrowing, and from other miscellaneous sources. Checks are drawn against the funds for payment of merchandise, operating expenses, repayment of prior borrowings, and the like and for transferring funds to special accounts.

Special accounts. When the work of a department requires the disbursement of cash, a special bank account may be established. Such special accounts may be subject to checks drawn over the signatures of non-officers but should be carefully controlled by maintaining them on an imprest fund (see Chapter 11/Petty cash) basis. Special accounts are generally used for payroll, dividends, bond interest, petty cash, cash refunds, and other purposes.

Some banks require that a minimum balance be kept in "regular" checking accounts. Other banks charge a fee for the number of checks drawn. Checks that are presented to the bank for payment during the month are canceled after payment. If requested by the depositor, the checks are returned to the depositor at the end of the month together with a statement that shows deposits, checks paid, and the balance in the account. (See BANK STATEMENT.) Banks keep microfilm or microfiche records of all checks drawn by their depositors.

Most banks have instituted so-called personal checking accounts to provide checking facilities for those who cannot afford to maintain the balance required for a regular checking account. Under the plan, no balance is required, but a small charge may be made for each check drawn, and/or a nominal monthly maintenance charge may be made. (See also INTEREST CHECKING.)

The banks require business firms to file a statement that specifies the members of the firm who are authorized to sign checks. The signatures of authorized signers are kept on file at the bank. For corporations, the authorization takes the form of a corporate resolution by the board of directors.

Executive's accounts. Some executives have more than one checking account. For example, people who travel frequently might maintain separate accounts on which to draw when they are out of the area if someone else signs checks drawn against their regular personal account during their absence. This arrangement makes it easier to control the accounts and avoids confusion. The second ac-count may be distinguished from the regular account by having the depositor's name and the words *Second Account*, or other descriptive words, printed on the checks under the line for signature. Or the second account may be opened at another bank; in which case identification as a second account is not necessary. The balance of the second account should be restored by a check drawn on the regular account.

Trustee's account. The term *trustee's account* is applied to funds held in trust for some beneficiary under a trust agreement. The bank usually requires a copy of the trust agreement signed by the maker of the trust and the trustees. Even if the trust is voluntary, an informal letter from the creator of the trust giving particulars is not usually deemed sufficient by the bank; it requires a formal trust agreement approved by the bank's attorney. A trust account is usually carried under a name, such as *John Jones, Trustee for the benefit of Mary Jones.* See JOINT BANK ACCOUNT.

Bank discount. The interest charge made by a bank on a loan or for converting commercial paper into cash before maturity is more commonly known as the discount or the discount rate. Bank discount is computed as simple interest on the amount due at maturity on a note or draft and is deducted in advance. (See Chapter 13/INTEREST). The amount received from the bank— amount due at maturity less the discount and collection charge—is called the "proceeds." The number of days from the date the note is discounted to the date of maturity is called the "term of discount."

How the number of days is counted in bank discount. In bank discount the time is the period from the date of discount, not including the date of discount, to and including the date of maturity of the instrument. It is the common practice of commercial banks in the United States to charge discount for the actual or exact number of days in the discount period and to compute the discount on the basis of 360 days to the year. Thus if a note due May 6 is discounted March 6, the bank counts the actual number of days between these dates, 61, and computes the discount on the basis of 360 days to the year. (See Chapter 13/ INTEREST for the method of calculating the exact number of days between dates.)

Bank discount and proceeds on noninterest-bearing paper. The procedure is as follows:

1. The amount due at maturity on noninterest-bearing paper is the amount stated on the face of the instrument.

2. Using the discount rate, compute the bank discount on the face.

3. Compute the collection charge.

4. Deduct from the face the sum of the bank discount and the collection charge; the result is the proceeds.

EXAMPLE

Compute the bank discount and proceeds on a $500 noninterest-bearing note, dated June 5, due in 60 days, and discounted June 18 at 12%; collection charge, $\frac{1}{10}$%.

Solution: Sixty days from June 5 is August 4, the due date of the note. The exact number of days from June 18, the date of discount, to August 4, the due date, is 47.

Value of note at maturity		$500.00
Bank discount: 12% on $500 for 47 days	$7.84	
Collection charge: $\frac{1}{10}$% on $500	0.50	
Total charges		8.34
Proceeds		$491.66

Bank discount and proceeds on interest-bearing paper. The procedure is as follows:

1. Compute the value of the instrument at maturity; the value of an interest-bearing statement is its face value plus the interest for the full time of the note.

2. Compute the interest on the value at maturity for the discount period, using the discount rate; the result is the bank discount.

3. Compute the collection charge on the value at maturity.

4. Deduct from the value at maturity the sum of the bank discount and the collection charge; the result is the proceeds.

EXAMPLE

Compute the bank discount and proceeds on a note for $500 dated June 5, due in 60 days, and bearing 10% interest; the note is discounted June 18 at 12%, and the collection charge is $\frac{1}{10}$%.

Solution: Sixty days from June 5 is August 4, the due date of the note. The exact number of days from June 18, the date of discount, to August 4, the due date, is 47.

Face value of note		$500.00
Interest at 10% for 60 days		8.33
Value of note at maturity		$508.33
Bank discount: 12% on $508.34 for 47 days	$7.96	
Collection charge: $\frac{1}{10}$% on $504.17	0.50	
Total charges		8.46
Proceeds		$499.87

Bank draft. A written order of one bank on another to pay money to a person named on the draft, upon demand. A *sight draft* is a commercial draft payable on demand. A *time draft* is payable at a certain time such as twenty-four hours after receipt and acceptance.

Banks keep deposits with banks in other cities so that they may draw upon them as occasion requires. In domestic trade, the bank draft may be used in a transaction such as the following: A merchant in San Francisco sells goods to someone in New York on credit. The seller asks the New York buyer to pay his account with a bank draft. The New York buyer goes to his own bank in New York and purchases a draft from that bank upon its San Francisco correspondent and forwards this draft to the merchant in San Francisco. The form of payment has an advantage over others in that the bank draft does not have to be returned to the distant drawer bank (in New York in this instance) before it is finally paid. Thus the firm that is being paid with a bank draft (the payee) has faster use of the money than if it were paid with an ordinary check that has to clear through a distant bank before it can be drawn against by the payee.

Bank by mail. A service offered by most banks that permits customers to make deposits and receive deposit receipts by mail. Deposits are usually recorded the day they are received at the bank.

Bank money order. An order drawn by a bank against itself. The order specifies on its face the name of the *remitter* (person who purchases the order). Usually, the remitter receives a copy of the order to retain as evidence of payment. Bank money orders are used in lieu of actual cash in the same way as a CASHIER'S CHECK or a postal money order.

Bank note. Federal Reserve banks issue noninterest-bearing promissory notes that are payable to bearers on demand and thus serve as money.

Bank reconciliation. See BANK STATEMENT.

Bank reserves. The funds that banks keep available to meet regular demands for cash. Such reserves include a bank's supply of cash on hand plus that available in other banks. Federal Reserve banks are legally required to keep a certain minimum available at all times.

Bank services. Banks provide a wide range of services. See the following entries in this chapter: BANK ACCOUNTS; BANK DRAFT; BANK BY MAIL; BANK MONEY ORDER; BRANCH BANKING; CASHIER'S CHECK; CERTI-

FIED CHECK; COMPUTER SERVICES; CREDIT CARDS; DIRECT DEPOSITS; INSTANT LOAN SERVICE; INTEREST CHECKING; LOANS; MONEY MANAGEMENT; MONEY MARKET CERTIFICATES; NIGHT DEPOSITORY; SAFE DEPOSIT BOX; SAVINGS ACCOUNTS; SAVINGS BONDS.

Bank statement. A monthly statement of account that a bank furnishes to a depositor. It includes amounts and dates of deposit, amounts and dates of checks paid, and the balance on hand.

The causes for differences between the bank's balance figure and one's own figure are:

1. Errors of omission and commission in bookkeeping.

2. Bank charges for various services rendered by the bank and activity in the bank account, not recorded on the books.

3. Bank credits for notes and other advices collected by the bank that have not been recorded on the books of the firm.

4. Checks outstanding at the reconciliation date (they have been deducted on the books of the firm but will not be charged to the bank account until they are paid by the bank)

5. Deposits outstanding at the reconciliation date (they have been added to the balance on the books of the firm but will not be credited to the bank account until they are received by the bank)

6. Errors on the part of the bank

The accounting department of a business prepares a bank-reconciliation statement monthly for all bank accounts. A secretary would likely prepare the reconciliation for his or her employer's personal account.

The form of the bank-reconciliation statement requires that it start with the balance shown on the books and continue with the changes applicable thereto until the bank balance is obtained. Changes to the book's balance are made with adjusting entries.

A bank reconciliation is given in Figure 1 for the following example:

EXAMPLE

Suppose the balance shown on the books on April 30 is $7,821.04. The bank statement on that date shows a balance of $7,962.08. The following errors were made: on the books, check #2045 recorded as $42.00 should have been recorded as $24.00; by bank, check reading $23.38 was charged to the account as $23.35. The bank submitted a memorandum stating that a $150.00 check deposited to the firm's account was returned with the notation "insufficient funds" and was charged to the firm's account. The following checks are determined to be outstanding at the statement date: #2043, $47.31; #2056, $35.00; #2057, $215.70. The deposit of $25.00 made April 30 was credited by the bank on May 1.

If the accounting records for an executive do not include a cash or bank account in the general ledger, the bank statement may be reconciled with the checkbook or any other record of bank deposits and withdrawals. (See Chapter 11/ ACCOUNTING RECORDS.)

Branch banking. To serve customers in a greater area, banks open

BANK STATEMENT: FIGURE 1: Reconciliation

XYZ Company
Bank reconciliations as of April 30, 19—

Balance per general ledger (cash account)			$7,821.04
Book adjustments:			
Error in recording check #2045		$18.00	
Returned check deposited		(150.00)	(132.00)
Adjusted book balance			$7,689.04
Add: Outstanding checks #2043	$47.31		
#2056	35.00		
#2057	215.70	$298.01	
Less: Outstanding deposit April 30		25.00	273.01
Correct bank balance (as should have been reported)			$7,962.05
Bank error (advise bank)			.03
Balance per bank statement (thus reconciled)			$7,962.08

branches in various locations throughout a city. The same services are generally available through each branch, although miscellaneous services, such as drive-up window hours, may differ.

Cashier's check. A check drawn by a bank against itself. Banks issue cashier's checks to pay their obligations and to transfer funds. Cashier's checks are issued to borrowers in lieu of actual cash or when the borrower's account is not credited with a deposit of the loan. They are also sold to customers for remittance purposes.

Certificates of deposit. A formal statement or certificate that indicates someone has a specified sum of money on deposit that may be withdrawn at the end of a designated period (e.g., three, six, twelve, eigh-teen, and thirty-six months) for an amount equal to the value of the deposit plus accumulated interest at a designated rate. Certificates of deposit are issued in large amounts, usually in multiples of one thousand dollars. Interest earned is at a higher rate than in a regular savings account as the bank is able to keep the money for a stated period. Most certificates are negotiable and thus may be sold by a holder in need of funds before the maturity date.

Certified check. A CHECK that has been guaranteed by the bank both as to signature and amount. Either the maker of a check or the holder can present the check for certification at the bank on which the check is drawn. The bank examines the drawer's account, charges the account immediately for the amount of the check, and marks the check *accepted or certified.* The check then ceases to be an order on the bank and becomes an obligation of the bank. Hence certification of a check makes it equivalent to cash. Certified checks are used principally in real estate and securities transactions in which cash payment is required. When drawers have a check certified, they remain liable if the bank becomes insolvent before payment. When payees have a check certified, they accept the bank as their debtor, and the drawer is not liable in case of insolvency of the bank before payment. Drawers of certified checks cannot stop payment on them. They should redeposit a check if it is still in their possession and not destroy it. If a bank certifies a check by mistake, it may withdraw the certification if it acts promptly, provided the holder has lost no right.

Check.   A written order drawn upon a bank by a depositor, requesting the bank to pay on demand a certain sum of money to the bearer or to the order of some person or corporation named on the face of the check. There are also several other kinds of checks: BANK DRAFT; BANK MONEY ORDER; CASHIER'S CHECK; CERTIFIED CHECK.

Postdated check.   A check is not invalid merely because it bears a date later than that on which it is drawn. The holder may transfer it before the date on which it is payable, but the drawer's bank will not honor it before that date. A postdated check is a promise to pay rather than an order to pay; therefore, the drawer generally cannot be prosecuted criminally if the check is refused for lack of sufficient funds.

Discrepancy in amounts.   The amount expressed in words is the sum payable when there is a discrepancy between that amount and the amount expressed in figures. Banks generally refuse to accept checks with discrepancies in amounts. The holder may endorse it, guaranteeing the correct amount, and deposit the check for collection.

Certification. See CERTIFIED CHECK.

Time within which check must be presented for payment.   A check must be presented for payment within a "reasonable time," determined by the circumstances of each particular case. Ordinarily, a check must be presented to the bank on which it is drawn during business hours of the next business day after it is received or deposited by the payee in his or her own bank for collection and presented by the collecting bank on the following day. Failure to present a check for payment within a reasonable time discharges the drawer from liability to the extent of loss caused by the delay. Thus if the bank on which a check is drawn becomes insolvent so that the drawer loses the amount he or she had on deposit to meet the check, the loss must be borne by the one who was lax in presenting the check for payment.

Checks that "bounce."   Most checks deposited will clear. Occasionally, however, a check will be returned to the depositor by the bank. When the bank does this, a statement of the reason will accompany the returned check. There are a great many possible reasons: "lack of endorsement" means that the depositor failed to endorse the check, and when this occurs, the check should be endorsed and redeposited; "no account" means that the maker of the check has no account at that bank. Unless the depositor is familiar with the appropriate steps to take when a check is returned, he or she should consult counsel within twenty-four hours. Legally prescribed steps must be followed to preserve the rights of the depositor against the maker and all endorsers.

Insufficient funds. One of the reasons why checks bounce is insufficient funds. A person who, with fraudulent intent, issues a check knowing that he or she has not sufficient funds for its payment is subject to criminal prosecution in many states.

Death of drawer. This revokes the authority of the bank to pay. If a bank pays a check without knowledge that the drawer has died, it cannot be held liable for the amount.

Given in full settlement of claim. When the amount of a claim is disputed, a check reciting that it is in full settlement, accepted or collected by the creditor without objection, discharges the debtor's obligation. A creditor cannot accept the check and then write the drawer that he or she does not consider it full settlement; nor can a creditor strike out the words *in full* and avoid acceptance as full payment. It is important to indicate clearly on the check the fact that it represents payment in full. A check should be returned at once if the amount is not acceptable.

Forged or raised check. A bank is liable to a depositor for payment of a forged or raised check. However, the depositor must notify the bank within one year after return of the paid check that it was forged or raised.

Endorsement. The endorsement appears on the reverse side of a check. When an endorsed check is received in payment of debts, there are two things to watch for: (1) The spelling of the name in the endorsement should correspond exactly with the name of the payee on the face of the check. A check made payable to J. Doe should be endorsed J. Doe and not John Doe, although it may be endorsed both J. Doe and John Doe. A check made payable to a business firm should be endorsed in the firm's name and signed by the authorized person of that firm. (2) Any additional words accompanying the signature of the endorser may have important legal significance; for example, adding "without recourse" may prevent the holder from making a valid claim against the endorser if the check proves worthless. Any wording having unfamiliar legal significance should be a warning to the recipient of the check to consult an attorney.

Knowledge of the kinds of endorsement and the uses of each kind will protect the endorser of a negotiable instrument from possible financial loss.

1. *Blank endorsement.* The writing of one's name on an instrument, or an allonge, without any additional words is a blank endorsement. Its effect is to make the paper payable to

the bearer. Thus a finder or thief might transfer a note endorsed in blank by the payee to a third party for a consideration, and the third party might then enforce payment against the maker or the endorser.

2. *Special endorsement.* The designation of a certain person to whom the instrument is payable is a special endorsement. Thus if an instrument is endorsed "Pay to Frances Jones" or "Pay to the order of Frances Jones," followed by the endorser's signature, no one but Frances Jones can receive payment for the instrument or can transfer it.

3. *Restrictive endorsement.* An endorsement that transfers possession of the instrument for a particular purpose is a restrictive endorsement. Examples: "Pay to Frances Jones only. Sam Brown." "Pay to National City Bank for collection. Sam Brown." "For deposit only. Sam Brown." A restrictive endorsement terminates the negotiability of the instrument.

4. *Qualified endorsement.* An endorsement that qualifies or limits the liability of the endorser is a qualified endorsement. If an endorser endorses an instrument "without recourse," he or she does not assume liability in the event the maker fails to pay the instrument when due.

5. *Conditional endorsement.* A special endorsement with words added that create a condition that must happen before the special endorsee is entitled to payment is a conditional endorsement. The endorser is liable only if the condition is fulfilled. For example, "Pay to Greenwood Cotton Growers Association upon delivery of warehouse receipt for twenty-five standard bales of cotton, strict to middling. Frances Jones."

6. *Irregular or accommodation endorsement.* An endorsement made for the purpose of lending the endorser's credit to a party to the instrument is an irregular or accommodation endorsement. It is also called an "anomalous endorsement." A regular endorsement transfers title to the instrument, whereas an accommodation endorsement is for additional security only. An accommodation endorser is never the maker, drawer, acceptor, payee, or holder of the instrument he or she endorses.

Check-guarantee card. See CREDIT CARDS.

Checking account. See BANK ACCOUNTS.

Checking credit. The process of reaching a decision whether to accept or deny an application for credit. Banks, other lending institutions, and business firms selling on credit terms always check credit.

Clearinghouse. A voluntary, citywide association of banks formed to facilitate the settlement of interbank debits and credits, that is, items arising from checks, postal money orders, and bond coupons.

Before checks are delivered to the clearinghouse, they are sorted by the member banks according to the banks on which they are drawn. To facilitate sorting, all checks have the bank's clearinghouse membership number printed in the upper right-hand corner.

Commercial bank. A bank chartered by the state or the controller of currency (national) that accepts demand deposits, provides short-term credit, and offers a variety of other services to customers. Most commercial banks and their branches make loans, provide checking and saving facilities, accept time deposits, discount negotiable instruments, and administer trusts. National banks are members of the Federal Reserve System, and state banks may join when qualified.

Computer services. Many banks have electronic data-processing systems that provide various fact-finding and bookkeeping services for customers. Such systems can rapidly handle tasks such as processing payroll data and computing interest and finance charges. The systems are also used for inventory controls and other related services. Some bank systems provide a data-processing service to other banks. Many banks use on-line systems that enable customers to perform banking services such as deposits or withdrawals through terminals called "automatic tellers."

Credit cards. A card bearing the holder's name and account number and identifying the issuer. Credit cards are issued by organizations such as retail stores, travel and entertainment companies, and banks. Visa and MasterCard are two well known cards issued by banks. Holders are permitted to charge purchases in certain stores or obtain cash at a sponsoring bank for amounts up to an established credit limit. A monthly statement is issued for the balance due plus a finance charge. This finance charge is usually at a high rate of interest (generally an annual percentage rate of 18 to 21 percent, although careful shoppers may find cards with lower rates). Holders may pay the amount in full within a specified time, thereby avoiding the finance charge, or pay in designated monthly installments. Banks also issue check-guarantee cards that holders may use to make payments by check in establishments that will accept checks only when accompanied by a guarantee card.

Credit checking. See CHECKING CREDIT.

Credit reserve. See INSTANT LOAN SERVICE.

Credit union. A nonprofit association that provides banking services to members. The members may deposit funds, usually by purchasing shares. A passbook may be provided, showing investments, withdrawals, and so on. Earnings of the union are distributed to members as dividends. The Federal Credit Union Act of 1970 insures depositors up to twenty thousand dollars in federally chartered unions and in state unions participating in the federal program.

Debit memo. A memorandum, or notice, of a charge made by a bank against an account, showing the reason and authority for the charge. It might be for a check that was returned by another bank, for expenses incurred by the depositor's bank in sending telegrams or cables for the depositor, or for collection expense.

Demand deposits. See DEPOSITS.

Deposits. Money balances due from banks to those who have (1) placed funds with the banks for savings and thrift accounts, or checking accounts, or (2) borrowed from the bank, which creates an account for the borrower.

The bank and the depositor are in a debtor-creditor relationship. The bank owns all deposits but owes each individual depositor an amount equal to his or her deposit balance. Banks accept "special" deposits for the purchase of securities. In this instance, the bank acts as a bailee (see Chapter 9/BAILMENT) and does not take title to the deposit or intermingle the proceeds of "special" deposits with other deposits.

Aside from special deposits, all bank deposits are either (1) time deposits or (2) demand deposits.

Time deposits. Deposits from which the customer has the right to withdraw funds at a specified date, usually thirty or more days from date of deposit. They are evidenced by passbooks or certificates of deposit. Hence all savings or thrift accounts are time deposits. Interest is usually paid on time deposits.

Demand deposits. Deposits subject to withdrawals at any time the depositor elects without notice. All checking accounts are demand deposits. Interest is paid on some checking accounts

(see INTEREST CHECKING), and many banks offer no-service-charge checking when a specified minimum balance is maintained.

Deposit items. The items deposited are cash, checks, interest coupons, money orders, postal notes, traveler's checks, drafts, and promissory notes. For the proper endorsement of checks for deposit, see CHECK ENDORSEMENT.

Depositing coupons. Interest coupons, with the exception of coupons on government bonds and well-known municipal bonds, are collection items. They should be deposited about a week before they are due. They should not be entered on the deposit slip as a cash item, but should be placed in coupon envelopes supplied by the bank. A separate envelope is required for each issue and for each maturity. The envelope should be delivered to the collection window at the bank.

The coupons on government bonds and on well-known municipal bonds, if payable in the city where the account is carried, should be deposited as cash items and not as collection items.

Depositing drafts. Bank drafts are endorsed in the same way as checks and are deposited as a cash item. Drafts drawn by a depositor or by another person are handled as a collection item and are not credited until paid.

Depositing promissory notes. Promissory notes are deposited as collection items. Therefore, they should be given to the collection teller, who gives a receipt. When the note is actually collected, the bank notifies the depositor that the amount has been placed in his or her account.

Direct deposits. Federal law permits you to authorize recurring federal payments to be deposited directly by the payer into your account. One must complete Standard Form 1199 to use this automatic deposit service.

Discount. See BANK DISCOUNT; Chapter 13/BOND DISCOUNT AND BOND PREMIUM; CASH DISCOUNT.

Draft. See BANK DRAFT.

Electronic transfer of funds. The automatic movement of funds from one source to another, such as from a checking account to a savings account or from a checking account to a utility company, without writing a traditional check or deposit slip and without taking or sending the physical document to the destination. Instead, the amount of the transaction and other details are recorded electronically, and accounts are debited and credited as required.

Endorsement. See CHECK, *Endorsement*.

FDIC. See FEDERAL DEPOSIT INSURANCE CORPORATION.

FSLIC. See FEDERAL SAVINGS AND LOAN INSURANCE CORPORATION.

Federal Deposit Insurance Corporation. A federal organization established by the Banking Act of 1933 to provide insurance for depositors in member banks. Members of the Fed-

eral Reserve System are required to join the Federal Deposit Insurance Corporation (FDIC). Insured deposits include regular commercial, checking, and savings deposits, and certain trust funds. The FDIC does not insure savings and loan deposits, which are insured by the Federal Savings and Loan Insurance Corporation.

Federal Reserve Act. This act instituted a banking system for the United States known as the Federal Reserve System. Under the system, 12 federal reserve banks have been established. Their primary purpose is to supply credit to member banks, which in turn distribute credit to their customers. They are operated under the management of local officers and boards of directors but are subject to the authority of the Board of Governors of the Federal Reserve System. All national banks are required to belong to the system; state banks may belong if they meet the requirements of the act and choose to belong.

Federal Reserve System. See FEDERAL RESERVE ACT.

Federal savings and loan associations. A corporation (also called building and loan association) that provides opportunities for saving and makes loans on real estate. Deposit accounts and investment shares are the two principal types of savings offered. Procedures are similar to those in bank savings, with passbooks showing deposits, withdrawals, and interest earned. The associations also offer investment certificates similar to bank CERTIFICATES OF DEPOSIT. Typical services include savings accounts, safe deposit boxes, investment shares, savings clubs, money orders, and redemption of government savings bonds. Some savings and loan associations now offer checking and related services as well. Deposits in some associations are insured by the Federal Savings and Loan Insurance Corporation.

Federal Savings and Loan Insurance Corporation. A federal organization created to insure depositors in federal savings and loan associations. Deposits are insured up to one hundred thousand dollars per depositor. Many associations are insured by the Federal Savings and Loan Insurance Corporation, but since some are not, prospective depositors should check this aspect before investing.

Finance companies. Companies that provide loans to borrowers, often when the business or individual cannot secure credit from another source, such as a commercial bank. Finance companies are often willing to take greater risks than banks and other such institutions. Consumer finance companies, which represent a major source of small cash loans, are controlled by state regulations. Small loans are often provided only on the signature of the borrower; interest rates for such loans are high. Businesses borrowing from commercial finance companies may be required to assign their accounts receivable and/ or pledge their inventories. Finance companies vary greatly in size and services offered, particularly the com-

mercial type as opposed to the sales finance company, which specializes in discounting installment or conditional sales to customers.

Foreign exchange. The conversion of the money of one country into its equivalent in money of another country. Dollars are converted into pounds sterling, pesos into dollars, and so forth. The rate at which the currencies are exchangeable is called the *rate of exchange.* The rate varies from time to time.

The need for foreign exchange results from the fact that each country has its own individual currency. The table under FOREIGN MONEY shows the name, abbreviation, and symbol of foreign currencies.

Foreign money. Table 1 shows the commonly recognized names and symbols of basic monetary units and their principal fractional units throughout the world.

Individual retirement accounts. See Chapter 13/RETIREMENT PLANS.

Instant loan service. A popular type of installment loan provided by commercial banks that combines personal checking with a revolving loan account. Customers who qualify are issued a credit reserve up to a specified amount. They may draw upon this reserve at any time, usually by writing a check, up to the amount specified and repay the loan in installments over a designated period. A finance charge is computed monthly on the unpaid balance, just as it is in credit-card billing, and a monthly

TABLE 1
FOREIGN MONEY

Country or area	Basic monetary unit		Principal fractional unit	
	Name	Symbol	Name	Abbreviation or symbol
Afghanistan	Afghani	Af	Pul	
Albania	Lek	L	Quintar	
Algeria	Dinar	DA	Centime	
Andorra	French franc	Fr. F	French centime	
	Spanish peseta	Sp. Ptas.[1]	Spanish centimo	
Angola	Kwanza	Kz	Lwei	
Antigua and Barbuda .	Dollar	EC$	Cent	
Argentina	Peso	M$N	Centavo	Ctvo.
Australia	Dollar	A$	Cent	
Austria	Schilling	S	Groschen	
Bahamas, The	Dollar	B$	Cent	
Bahrain	Dinar	BD	Fil	
Bangladesh	Taka	Tk	Paise	
Barbadoes	Dollar	Bds$	Cent	
Belgium	Franc	BF	Centime	
Belize	Dollar	$B	Cent	
Benin	Franc	CFAF	Centime	
Bermuda	Dollar	$B	Cent	
Bhutan	Ngultruns	N	Tikchung	
Bolivia	Peso Boliviana	$b	Centavo	Ctvo.
Botswana	Pula	P	Thebe	
Brazil	New cruzeiro	NCr$	Centavo	Ctvo.
Brunei	Dollar	B$	Cent	
Bulgaria	Lev	L	Stotinka	
Burma	Kyat	K	Pya	
Burundi	Franc	FBu	Centime	
Cameroon	Franc	CFAF	....do	
Canada	Dollar	$ or Can$	Cent	C, ct.
Cape Verde	Escudo	C.V. Esc	Centavo	
Central African Republic	Franc	CFAF	Centime	
Chad	Franc	CFAF	....do	
Chile	Peso	Ch$	Centavo	
China	Yuan	¥	Fen	
Colombia	Peso	Col$	Centavo	Ctvo.
Comoros	Franc	CFAF	Centime	
Congo	....do	CFAF	....do	
Cook Islands	New Zealand dollar .	NZ$	Cent	
Costa Rica	Colon	¢	Centimo	Ctmo.
Cuba	Peso	$	Centavo	Ctvo.
Cyprus	Pound	£ or £C	Mil	
Czechoslovakia	Koruna	Kcs	Haler	
Dahomey	Franc	CFAF	Centime	
Denmark	Krone	DKr	Øre	
Djibouti	Franc	DF	Centime	
Dominica	Dollar	EC$	Cent	
Dominican Republic ..	Peso	RD$	Centavo	Ctvo.
Ecuador	Sucre	S/	....do	Ctvo.
Egypt	Pound	£E	Piaster	
El Salvador	Colon	¢	Centavo	Ctvo.
Equatorial Guinea ...	Ekuele	EK	Centimo	
Estonia	Ruble	—	Kopek	
Ethiopia	Birr	EB	Cent	
Falkland Islands	Pound	£	Shilling	
Faroe Islands	Danish krone	DKr	Øre	
Fiji	Dollar	$F	Cent	
Finland	Finnmark	Fimr	Penni	Pia.
France	Franc	F	Centime	
French Guiana	....do	F	....do	
French Polynesia	....do	CFPF	....do	
Gabon	....do	CFAF	....do	

Country or area	Basic monetary unit		Principal fractional unit	
	Name	Symbol	Name	Abbreviation or symbol
Gambia, The	Dalasi	DD	Butut	
German Democratic Republic	Mark	DME	Pfennig	Pf.
Ghana	Cedi	₵	Pesewa	P.
Gibraltar	Pound	£	Shilling	
Greece	Drachma	Dr.	Lepton	
Greenland	Danish krone	DKr	Øre	
Grenada	Dollar	EC$	Cent	
Guadeloupe	Franc	F	Centime	
Guatamala	Quetzal	Q	Centavo	Ctvo.
Guinea	Syli	GS	Cauri	
Guyana	Dollar	G$	Cent	
Haiti	Gourde	G	Centime	
Honduras	Lempira	L	Centavo	Ctvo.
Hong Kong	Dollar	HK$	Cent	
Hungary	Forint	Ft	Filler	
Iceland	Krona	IKr	Eyrir	
Indonesia	Rupiah	Rp^2	Sen	
Iran	Rial	Rls^2	Dinar	
Iraq	Dinar	ID	Fil	
Ireland	Pound	£ or £Ir	Shilling	S., d.,
Israel	Shekel	I£	Agrirot	
Italy	Lira	Lit	Centesimo	Ctmo.
Ivory Coast	Franc	CFAF	Centime	
Jamaica	Dollar	J$	Cent	
Japan	Yen:e1	¥	Sen	
Jordan	Dinar	JD	Fil	
Kampuchea	Riel	KR	____	
Kenya	Shilling	K Sh	Cent	
Kiribati	Australian dollar	A$	...do	
Korea	Chon	W	Chun	
Kuwait	Dinar	KD	Fil	
Laos	Kip	K	At	
Latvia	Ruble	R	Kopek	
Lebanon	Pound	LL	Piaster	
Lesotho	Rand	R	Cent	
Liberia	Dollar	$	...do	
Libya	Dinar	LD	Milleme	
Liechtenstein	Swiss franc	Sw F	Centime	
Lithuania	Ruble	R	Kopek	
Luxembourg	Franc	Lux F	Centime	
Macao	Pataca	P	Avo	
Madagascar	Franc	FMG	Centime	
Malawi	Kwacha	K	Tambal	
Malaysia	Ringgits	M$	Sen	
Maldives	Rupee	Mal Re	Lari	
Mali	Franc	MF	____	
Malta	Pound	£M	Cent	
Martinique	Franc	F	Centime	
Mauritania	Ouguiya	UM	Khoum	
Mauritius	Rupee	Mau Rs^3	Cent	
Mexico	Peso	Mex$	Centavo	Ctvo.
Monaco	French franc	Fr	Centime	
Mongolia	Tugrik	Tug	Möngö	
Montserrat	Dollar	EC$	Cent	
Morocco	Dirham	DH	Centime	
Mozambique	Escudo	M. Esc.	Centavo	
Nauru	Australian dollar	$A	Cent	
Nepal	Rupee	NRs^1	Pice	
Netherlands	Guilder	f.	Cent	
Netherlands Antilles	...do	NAE	...do	
New Caledonia	Franc	CFPF	Centime	
New Zealand	Dollar	$NZ	Cent	
Nicaragua	Cordoba	C$	Centavo	Ctvo.
Niger	Franc	CFAF	Centime	
Nigeria	Naira	₦	Kobo	k.
Norway	Krone	NKr	Øre	
Oman	Riyal	ORls	Baiza	
Pakistan	Rupee	PRs	Paisa	

503

Country or area	Basic monetary unit		Principal fractional unit	
	Name	Symbol	Name	Abbreviation or symbol
Panama	Balboa	B	Centesimo	Ctmo.
Paraguay	Guarani	G	Centimo	Ctmo.
Papua New Guinea	Kina	K	Toea	
Peru	Sol	S/	Centavo	Ctvo.
Philippines	Peso	₱	....do	Ctvo.
Poland	Zloty	Zl	Grosz	
Portugal	Escudo	Esc	Centavo	
Qatar	Riyal	QRls	Dirham	
Reunion	French franc	F	Centime	
Romania	Leu	L	Ban	
Rwanda	Franc	RF	Centime	
St. Christopher-Nevis	Dollar	EC$	Cent	
St Lucia	....do	EC$	....do	
St. Pierre and Miquelon	Franc	CFAF	Centime	
St. Vincent and the Grenadines	Dollar	EC$	Cent	
San Marino	Italian lira	Lit	Centesimo	
Sao Tome e Principe	Dobra	Db	Centavo	
Saudi Arabia	Riyal	SRls[2]	Halala	
Senegal	Franc	CFAF	Centime	
Seychelles	Rupee	Sey Rs[3]	Cent	
Sierra Leone	Leone	Le	...do	
Singapore	Dollar	S$	...do	
Solomon Islands	Dollar	SI$	...do	
Somalia	Shilling	So. Sh.	...do	
South Africa	Rand	R	Cent	
Spain	Peseta	Ptas[1]	Centimo	
Sri Lanka	Rupee	Cey Rs[3]	Cent	
Sudan	Pound	£S	Piaster	
Surinam	Guilder	Sur. f.	Cent	
Swaziland	Lilangeni (emalengeni, plural)	E	...do	
Sweden	Krona	SKr	Öre	
Switzerland	Franc	SwF	Centime	
Syria	Pound	£Syr	Piaster	
Tanzania	Shilling	T Sh	Cent	
Thailand	Baht	B	Satang	
Taiwan	New Taiwan dollar	NT$	Cent	
Togo	Franc	CFAF	Centime	
Tonga	Pa'anga	T$	Seniti	
Trinidad and Tobago	Dollar	TT$	Cent	
Tunisia	Dinar	D	Millime	
Turkey	Lira	TL	Kurus	
Tuvalu	Australian dollar	A$	Cent	
Uganda	Shilling	U Sh	...do	
U.S.S.R.	Ruble	R	Kopek	
United Arab Emirates	Dirham	UD	Fil	
United Kingdom	Pound	£ or £ stg.	Shilling	S.,d.
United States	Dollar	$ or US$	Cent	
Upper Volta	Franc	CFAF	Centime	
Uruguay	Peso	N$	Centesimo	
Vanatu	Franc	FNH	Centime	
Vatican City	Italian lira	Lit	Centesimo Ctmo.	
Venezuela	Bolivar	Bs	Centimo	
Vietnam	Dông	VND	Hao	
Wallis and Futuna	Franc	CFPF	Centime	
Western Samoa	Tala	WS$	Cent	
Yemen (Aden)	Dinar	SYD	Fil	
Yemen (Sanaa)	Rial	Y Rls[2]	...do	
Yugoslavia	Dinar	Din	Para	
Zaire	Zaire	Z	Likuta	
Zambia	Kwacha	K	Ngwee	S., d.
Zimbabwe	Dollar	Z$	Cent	

[1] Singular: Pta.
[2] Singular: Rl.
[3] Singular: Re.

Source: United States Government Printing Office Style Manual (Washington, D.C.: U.S. Government Printing Office, 1984). Based on a list of currency units and abbreviations provided by the International Monetary Fund and the Department of State.

statement is provided. The service often protects checking accounts from overdrafts. If a customer accidentally exceeds the balance in his or her checking account, the bank will draw funds from the instant loan reserve to cover the overdraft. See also Chapter 13/Revolving account.

Interest checking. Sometimes known as "NOW (negotiable order of withdrawal) account." A personal checking account that also earns interest. Interest checking resembles a regular personal checking account in every way, except for the interest-bearing feature. Checkbooks are provided, and monthly statements are issued to show deposits, withdrawals, and interest or dividends earned. Usually, one must maintain a specified minimum balance for the account to draw interest.

Joint bank account. A checking, savings, or thrift account opened in the names of two or more people. The deposit agreement and the designation of the account should be specific about whether the depositors are tenants in common or joint tenants. When two depositors are tenants in common, either party can make deposits, but the signatures of both are required for withdrawal. At the death of one of them, the survivor is entitled only to his or her own interest in the account. The heirs of the deceased are entitled to the decedent's interest. When two depositors are joint tenants, either party can deposit or withdraw. At the death of one of the depositors, the survivor is entitled to the balance of

the account. The same principles apply where there are more than two depositors.

Keogh plans. See Chapter 13/ Retirement plans.

Kiting. The unethical and sometimes illegal practice of issuing checks against a bank account in which there are not sufficient collected funds to cover the check, with the expectation that, before the check drawn is presented for payment, funds will be deposited to make good the withdrawal. A bank may close the account of a depositor who is detected in this practice.

Legal tender. See Chapter 9/Legal tender.

Letters of credit. See Chapter 4/ Travel funds, *Letters of credit.*

Loans. Money or something of value borrowed for a specified period at a specified rate of interest. Commercial banks make single-payment and installment loans. A *single-payment loan* is usually a short-term loan for which collateral may be required. An installment loan is usually a longer term loan, where payments are made regularly over the period the loan covers. Collateral also may be required for installment loans. A passbook loan is a common type of single-payment loan; money is borrowed temporarily against savings to avoid disturbing the savings before an interest-credit date. Money may be borrowed only on one's signature on an *unsecured loan*, if the borrower's credit is good. On a *secured loan*, the bank requires a lien (a claim against specified property of the borrower). Car loans are secured loans—the car can be repossessed by the lender if the borrower fails to make payments as required. Commercial banks also make other types of loans. See INSTANT LOAN SERVICE; CREDIT CARDS.

Money management. Some banks, particularly the larger institutions, provide money-management services. In this capacity, a bank may give investment advice, actually invest the funds for you, monitor your financial activity, and develop and implement a financial program for you. This service is typically used by persons who have adequate financial resources to warrant a program but who do not want to be bothered personally with all of the planning, decision making, and actual detail work of managing their money. See also BANK ACCOUNTS, *Trustee's account.*

Money market certificates. Various money markets (see Chapter 13/ MONEY MARKET) offer investors certificates that represent evidence of investment. The certificates are usually issued in large amounts, often multiples of one thousand dollars. Like traditional bank CERTIFICATES OF DEPOSIT, money market certificates may be redeemed upon maturity after specified periods such as one, two, or three years.

Mutual savings banks. Banks that are operated for the benefit of deposi-

tors. Mutual savings banks are organized without capital stock and managed by a board of trustees. The net assets of the bank belong to the depositors. Maximum deposits, interest paid, and type of investments allowed are all controlled by strict state regulations. Interest is paid in the form of dividends declared by the trustees and credited to the depositor's account.

Negotiable instrument. See Chapter 9/NEGOTIABLE INSTRUMENT.

Night depository. Banks provide safeguarded depositories that may be used by customers who need to deposit receipts after banking hours. Such depositories are often found near the entrance, by a drive-in window, or in a drive-through aisle. Properly marked receipts, deposit tickets, and so on may safely be dropped into a depository, where they will be processed by a teller the following business day.

Nonnegotiable instrument. See Chapter 9/NONNEGOTIABLE INSTRUMENT.

Notes. See Chapter 9/NEGOTIABLE INSTRUMENT; NONNEGOTIABLE INSTRUMENT; Chapter 13/NOTE.

NOW account. See INTEREST CHECKING.

Postdated check. See CHECK.

Protest. See Chapter 9/PROTEST.

Rate of exchange. See FOREIGN EXCHANGE.

Rediscount rate. The discount rate charged by the federal reserve banks for discounting commercial paper presented by member banks. In this capacity particularly, the federal reserve banks are bankers' banks. Each federal reserve bank has the power to set its own rediscount rate, subject to review by the Federal Reserve Board. At times, these banks use the rediscount rate to control credit, raising the rate to limit borrowing expansion, and lowering the rate to encourage borrowing expansion.

Reserve bank. See FEDERAL RESERVE ACT.

Safe deposit box. A specially constructed box in a bank's vault available in a variety of sizes for a rental fee. Boxes are used to protect valuable papers and property against theft and destruction.

Savings account. An account or time deposit that earns interest. Commercial and savings banks and other financial institutions offer a variety of savings accounts. See CREDIT UNION; FEDERAL SAVINGS AND LOAN ASSOCIATIONS; MUTUAL SAVINGS BANKS; CERTIFICATES OF DEPOSIT; INTEREST CHECKING. Some banks require advance notice before funds over a certain amount can be withdrawn. Accounts may earn either interest or dividends. Both passbook and statement accounts are available in many banks, with both showing deposits, withdrawals, and interest or dividends earned. Interest paid by commercial and savings banks is usually less than that paid by savings and loan associations and credit unions.

Savings bonds. Bonds issued by corporations and governments that promise to pay a specified sum of money at a fixed date in the future, with interest at a fixed rate payable at specified dates. (See Chapter 13/ BOND). Government bonds in different denominations may be purchased at most commercial or savings banks. Certain bonds provide for regular interest payments; others pay interest accumulated at the time they are redeemed.

Savings and loan associations. See FEDERAL SAVINGS AND LOAN ASSOCIATIONS.

Sight draft. See BANK DRAFT.

Special account. See BANK ACCOUNTS, *Special accounts.*

Stop payment. An order to a bank, made by the drawer of a check, to refuse to honor the check when it is presented for collection by the payee. Banks will attempt to honor verbal stop payments, but they are not liable for any damages that might result from payment unless the stop payment order is in writing. A telegram is considered a written order. See CHECK.

Time deposits. See DEPOSITS.

Time draft. See BANK DRAFT.

Traveler's checks. See Chapter 4/ TRAVEL FUNDS, *Traveler's checks.*

Trust account. See BANK ACCOUNTS, *Trustee's account;* MONEY MANAGEMENT.

24-hour banking. A special service in the form of an automatic check processor and cash dispenser, often located near the bank's entrance. The machine is available to customers twenty-four hours a day. Usually, plastic identification cards are provided for customers to use in activating the machine. Transactions are recorded instantly and appear on the next statement.

Usury. See Chapter 9/Usury.

Without recourse. See Chapter 9/ Without recourse.

PART V

REAL ESTATE AND INSURANCE

CHAPTER 15

REAL ESTATE

Abstract company. See Chapter 10/ ABSTRACT COMPANY.

Abstract of title. Evidence of TITLE to REAL PROPERTY. An abstract is a condensed history of ownership of a particular tract of land. It consists of a summary of the material parts of every recorded instrument affecting the title. It begins with a description of the land covered by the abstract and then shows the original government grant and all subsequent deeds, mortgages, releases, wills, judgments, mechanics' liens, FORECLOSURE proceedings, tax sales, and other matters affecting title. Only a summary of these items is given. For example, a deed is summarized as shown in Figure 1.

The abstract concludes with the abstracter's certificate. This discloses what records the abstracter has or has not examined. For example, if the abstracter certifies that he or she has made no search for federal court proceedings affecting the property, it will be necessary to write to the clerk of the district court, who will supply the search for a small charge.

Abstract companies, lawyers, and public officials prepare abstracts. Abstracters do not guarantee clear title to the real estate in question. Because of this and other inadequacies, such as failure to disclose missing heirs, forged deeds, and transactions by incompetents, abstract of title is becoming obsolete in many places.

Usually, one gives a purchaser an abstract and title certified immediately before the closing of the sale. An original abstract is sent to the abstract company, and the company *recertifies* its accuracy and brings it down to date.

When abstracters are to be paid frequently, such as weekly or monthly, it

ABSTRACT OF TITLE: FIGURE 1

| WILLIAM JONES AND MARY JONES, HIS WIFE
to
JOHN WRIGHT | WARRANTY DEED
Dated Sept. 15, 1980
Ack. Sept. 18, 1980
Rec. Sept. 20, 1980
Bk. 21, page 23 |

Conveys a large plot of land including the premises under examination.

---

is helpful to keep a three-by-five-inch card file with columns for debit, credit, and balance. In many cases, though, payment is handled as part of closing costs.

Most states are known as either an "abstract" state or a "title insurance" state. In a title insurance state a title company researches the chain of title and prepares a title report, which outlines anything of record against the property but does not state the history of ownership. A title insurance policy is issued, which protects the purchaser from prior claims against the title. See Chapter 16/TITLE INSURANCE.

Adverse possession. The continuous occupancy and use of REAL PROPERTY by one without legal TITLE and without the consent of the owner. In order to prevail, the claimant must prove that he or she had been in actual, open and notorious, hostile, visible and distinct, and exclusive possession under a claim of right for the statutory period. It may result in the obtaining of title to the land by remaining in possession for a number of years specified by state law.

Air rights. The right to the use or control of the air space over property. Such air rights may be restrictive of surface rights. Other rights an owner may have, by state or local ordinance, zoning, or DEED restrictions could be view rights, solar rights, and so on.

Amortized loan. See Chapter 13/ AMORTIZED LOAN.

Appraisal. An estimation of the value of real estate based on factual analysis by qualified appraisers. The data on which the estimate is based is laid out in a written appraisal report. There are various approaches to appraisal. The *cost approach* adds the separately appraised parts of a property to arrive at the final value. Land value will be added to the cost of replacing a structure less depreciation. The *income approach* uses the estimated future net income from the property as the basis for the appraisal of its present value. The *market-value approach* compares the sale prices of recently sold similar properties.

Appurtenances. The incidental articles, rights, and interests that attach to and pass with the land, for example, Right-of-way, Easement, and orchards.

Assessed valuation. The value at which real or personal property is appraised for tax purposes by the appropriate governmental authority. See Real property; Chapter 9/Personal property.

Attestation. See Chapter 9/Attestation.

Bargain and sale deed. See Deed.

Beneficiary. Person for whose benefit a Trust deed or Deed of trust is given.

Binder. *Real estate.* A preliminary agreement under which a down payment for the purchase of real property is made as evidence of good faith on the part of the purchaser. The payment itself is also called a binder. See Earnest money.

Broker. *Real estate broker.* An intermediary who, for a fee, commission, or other valuable consideration, brings parties together and assists them in negotiating a contract involving Real property. (See Chapter 9/Contracts.) A broker may be a person, a firm, a partnership, an unincorporated association, or a corporation. The broker's functions are governed by state licensing requirements and thus may differ from state to state. Generally, however, a broker acts as an agent for one party in negotiating with another party for the sale, purchase, exchange, or rental or lease of real estate.

Caveat emptor. See Chapter 9/Caveat emptor.

Certificate of title. An instrument written and signed by a Title examiner stating that in his or her opinion the seller has good title to the property to be conveyed. The examiner examines the public records and issues a *certificate,* which is merely the examiner's opinion of the validity of the title based on the public records he or she has examined. It offers no protection against hidden defects. Thus the examiner does not guarantee the title but is liable for damages caused by his or her negligence. For example, if the certificate failed to show a mortgage that was recorded, the examiner would be liable to a purchaser who relied upon this certificate and purchased the property without knowledge of the mortgage. Abstract companies and lawyers issue certificates of title. A certificate of title is not to be confused with title insurance policies issued by title companies. See Chapter 16/Title insurance.

Chattel mortgage. See Mortgage; Chapter 9/Personal property.

Closing. See Real estate closing.

Cloud on the title. An encumbrance or outstanding claim on real estate, which if valid would impair or affect the owner's Title. Such might be a dower interest or a judgment. Court action or a quit-claim deed may be necessary to remove the cloud. See Deed.

Commission. *Compensation* paid to a real estate broker for services. The amount is usually a percentage of the sale price; the *tribunal* charged with the administration and enforcement of real estate license laws.

Community property. A concept of property ownership by husband and wife in force in some states. The husband and wife become equal and concurrent co-owners of all property (real and personal) acquired during marriage by their joint effort. The property is known as "community property." The main idea of the system is the same in all states where community property exists, but statutes and judicial decisions have directed the development of the system along different lines in the various states. For example, in some states only property that is acquired by the exertion or labor of either party is common, whereas in other states income from separate property is also considered community property. Generally, either husband or wife may have "separate" property, such as that belonging to either of them at the time of marriage, real estate acquired in a state that does not recognize community property, or property given to or inherited by either at any time. Property acquired in exchange for separate property is *separate property;* that acquired in exchange for community property is *community property.* In some states, the husband may dispose of or encumber the community property, but the wife may not; nor may the community property be attached for the wife's debts, except for those contracted for necessities for herself and her children.

Contract of exchange. A formal contract, entered into between two owners of separate parcels of Real property, setting forth in full the terms of the agreement between them for the transfer of their properties to one another. See Chapter 9/ Contracts.

Contract of sale. See Purchase and sale agreement.

Conveyance. The means or medium by which Title to Real property is transferred. Voluntary transfer of title during the lifetime of the owner is always accomplished by a written document known as a Deed. See also Chapter 9/Contracts; Sale; Chapter 13/Installment sale.

Deed. A formal written agreement by which Title to Real property is conveyed from one person to another. A Purchase and sale agreement is a contract to convey title, whereas a *deed* is the conveyance itself. An exception is a *trust deed* or *deed of trust,* which conveys only bare legal title. See Trust deed or deed of trust; Mortgage. The parties to a deed are the *grantor,* who conveys his or her interest in the property, and the *grantee*, to whom the conveyance is made. The grantor is the seller, and the grantee is usually the purchaser, but not necessarily. The purchaser may buy the land for the grantee. Only the grantor signs the deed, unless the grantee makes special covenants.

A *warranty deed* is the most desirable from the standpoint of the purchaser. It not only transfers title in fee simple but covenants and warrants that the grantor has the right to transfer the title to the property and that the grantee shall enjoy the premises quietly, forever. Should anyone later make a claim against the property, the grantee can sue the grantor for breach of his or her warranty.

A *bargain and sale deed* conveys title as effectively as a warranty deed, but it does not warrant the title against adverse claims or use of the property.

A *quit-claim deed* is not used to convey title but to obtain a release from a person who is believed to have some interest in or claim to the property, whether real or not. By this form of deed, the grantor "quits" any claim he or she might have, usually for a nominal consideration. These deeds do not obligate the grantor in any way, but if he or she should have full title, the quit-claim deed will operate as a full and complete conveyance of title.

A *deed of gift* is given in consideration of the "love and affection" that the grantor has for the grantee. A deed of gift passes title as completely as a deed for which there is a monetary consideration.

A *statutory deed* is a short form of deed used in some states to save space needed to record deeds. Certain covenants and warranties are made part of the deed by statute and are binding even though not set forth in the deed.

A *fiduciary deed* may have a grantor as executor, administrator, trustee, guardian, receiver, or commissioner.

A *sheriff's deed* is one prepared by a sheriff for real estate sold at public sale.

Contents of deed. Secretaries should double-check that a deed states:

1. Execution date
2. Whether grantor is individual, partnership, or corporation
3. Full name of grantor who has FEE SIMPLE and full description of grantor's office and authority when acting as a representative
4. Grantor's marital status
5. Full name of spouse if spouse must join in the conveyance
6. Grantee's full name and residence
7. Property description (see LAND DESCRIPTION)
8. Whether deed is to be a warranty, bargain and sale, quit-claim, or gift deed
9. *Consideration* (the price given for the property or the motive for giving it)
10. Recital of any MORTGAGE or other ENCUMBRANCE on the property
11. *Habendum clause* stating that the grantee is to have the property transferred to him or her

12. *Covenants* (promises made by grantor and grantee)

13. *Testimonium clause* (the closing clause immediately preceding the signature)

14. Names and official position of officers signing and acknowledging deed, if grantor is a corporation

Deed restrictions. Covenants, conditions, and restrictions are also known as "deed restrictions." These are restrictions placed on property that would exceed the limits enacted by zoning or other governmental rules or regulations. They are usually intended to maintain some uniformity in neighborhoods or general areas by the area developer or the landowner upon sale. They generally concern matters of property use and maintenance.

Deed of gift. See DEED.

Deed restrictions. See DEED, *Deed restrictions.*

Earnest money. Evidence of good faith given by a buyer in the form of a deposit of money or a down payment. See also BINDER.

Easement. The right or privilege to make some use of land belonging to another. The most common easements are RIGHT-OF-WAY, right-of-drainage, right to suspend power lines, and right to lay pipelines beneath the surface.

An easement may terminate at some future time based on some time element or the occurrence of some event. Such terminations of easements, however, would have to be established in the original granting of the easement in order to be enforceable.

An easement may be established in a number of ways: by *agreement*, which may simply be a commonly held opinion regarding the right and not necessarily a contract; by *prescription*, when adverse use of the land has been open and continuous for a period of time and a court grants the right on the presumption that a written easement was given; by *necessity*, when the right is granted by a court on the basis of the absolute necessity of the easement for the use of the land as opposed to mere convenience (e.g., on land-locked parcels).

Encumbrance. A claim or charge against property (e.g., a MORTGAGE) that lowers its value. See CLOUD ON THE TITLE. See also Chapter 9/LIEN.

Equitable title. A person's right to obtain absolute ownership of property to which another person has TITLE at law.

Equity of redemption. See Chapter 13/REDEMPTION, 2.

Escrow. Something of value, such as money or property, held by a third party until the owner completes an obligation to another party.

Estate. Technically, the estate signifies the quantity of ownership of REAL PROPERTY. Estates may be freehold or less-than-freehold estates; *freehold estates* include FEE SIMPLE, which gives complete ownership of the property without encumbrance or condition; *less-than-freehold estates* are granted for a defined and limited period. See LEASEHOLD. *Life estates* grant ownership of property for the lifetime of an individual. See LIFE ESTATE. *Conditional fee estates* have some limit or condition to the conveyance of the property such as a restriction to use for a specific purpose (e.g., a church); the property reverts to the grantor upon the cessation of such use. An *estate at will* is one that does not require any formal notice before termination; it may be terminated at will. An *estate at sufferance* exists when a person extends possession of property beyond the expiration of his or her legal term.

Estate planning. The planning of an estate during life to reduce the burdens of administering an estate after death, to provide the maximum benefits for dependents and beneficiaries, and, to as great an extent as possible within the framework of the estate plan, to reduce or eliminate income, gift, estate, and inheritance taxes.

No single plan is appropriate to all individuals since the needs and desires of each person vary immensely. In general, however, it is desirable for an estate plan to include and coordinate the following:

1. Have a well-conceived will drawn by an attorney and properly executed.

2. Secure an appropriate amount and kind of life insurance. (See Chapter 16/LIFE INSURANCE.)

3. During life, properly designate TITLE to one's own property, both real and personal. It is especially important to be careful regarding title to property when two persons, for example, husband and wife, hold title. Two people can hold title so that on death the property will go to the survivor without regard to the provisions of the decedent's will. (See TENANCY BY THE ENTIRETY and JOINT TENANCY.) The way one takes title can sometimes defeat one's testamentary desires. An attorney can guide you regarding the applicable laws of the state.

4. Take one or more persons into confidence and reveal to them the whereabouts and extent of one's property and holdings.

5. Maintain a good record of one's assets, liabilities, income, and legal rights and obligations.

6. Educate and instruct others as far as possible in the management policies of one's business and commercial affairs.

7. Consider the utility of other methods of disposal of assets, such as trusts or gifts.

Estate in real property. The right or interest in the use, enjoyment, and disposition of land and improvements attached to it. See FEE SIMPLE; JOINT TENANCY; LIFE ESTATE; TENANCY BY THE ENTIRETY; TENANCY IN COMMON.

Fee simple. The absolute ownership of real property. It gives the owner and his or her heirs the unconditional power of disposition and other rights. See REAL PROPERTY.

Fiduciary deed. See DEED.

Foreclosure. Legal process of obtaining possession of mortgaged property upon the failure of the mortgagor to meet his or her obligations under the MORTGAGE or deed of trust (see TRUST DEED OR DEED OF TRUST). In some states, the foreclosure is by advertisement and sale, held in accordance with the legal technicalities prescribed by the state statutes. In the majority of states, foreclosure is by litigation, which shuts out or bars the mortgagor's EQUITY OF REDEMPTION. However some states have laws prohibiting foreclosures on farm land for a specified period as long as interest is paid on the mortgage loan.

After an attorney has filed the required summons, complaint, and *lis pendens* (see LIS PENDENS), various steps are taken to apply for receivership, arrange for a hearing before a referee or master, and finally, arrange for sale of the foreclosed property. The specific steps depend on the case and the jurisdiction.

Grantee. See DEED.

Grantor. See DEED.

Homestead. Real estate occupied by the owner as a home at the time of filing the Declaration of Homestead (can only be filed by the head of a household). A homestead is exempt from sale or execution from the lien of every judgment and from liability in any form for the debts of the owner up to specific limits according to state statutes.

Joint tenancy. If two or more persons acquire the same estate at the same time, by the same title or source of ownership, each having the same degree of interest (including right of survivorship) as the others, and each having the same right of possession as the others, the estate is called a *joint estate* or *tenancy*. The distinguishing characteristic of a joint tenancy is that upon the death of one of the joint tenants, his or her interest automatically passes to the others by survivorship. The courts do not favor joint tenancies and in many jurisdictions permit joint tenants to defeat the right of survivorship by mortgage or conveyance. Some states have passed retroactive statutes making existing undivided interests tenancy in common, unless a contrary intent plainly appears in the instrument sufficient to negate the presumption of a tenancy in common. See also TENANCY IN COMMON.

Land description. Identification of a tract of land contained in a DEED, MORTGAGE, LEASE, or other instrument. To avoid dispute and litigation, land should always be described according to one of the following methods, known as a *record description:*

1. Metes and bounds
2. Rectangular survey system
3. The plat system

Metes and bounds. Before the government survey, the land in the area comprising the thirteen colonies (eighteen states) was held under original grants from the Crown to the colonists. In these states and in Texas, each parcel of land is different in size and shape and is described by metes and bounds.[1] A metes and bounds description is not correlated to any system of meridians and base lines, but each tract of land is described by the lines that constitute its boundaries. *Metes* are lineal measurements, and *bounds* are artificial and natural boundaries. A natural landmark, such as a tree or river, or an artificial landmark, such as a fence, stake, railroad, or street, often marks the corners and angles. These marks are known as *monuments*. A description by courses and distances constitutes part of a metes and bounds description. The direction from the starting point in which the boundary line runs is a *course*; the length of the line is a *distance*.

Rectangular survey system. In the eighteenth century, when the United States began to sell public lands, it was necessary to adopt some conventional method of describing the tracts that were sold. A rectangular system of surveys was devised by Thomas Jefferson and adopted by Congress on May 20, 1785. This system has since been adopted by thirty states. The survey divided the public lands into rectangular tracts, located with reference to base lines running east and west and *prime*, or *principal*, *meridians* running north and south. The prime meridians are numbered, as Third Prime Meridian, or named, as San Bernardino Meridian. The rectangular tracts are divided into six-mile squares, known as *townships*. A row of townships, running north and south is called a *range*, and the ranges are numbered east and west from the prime meridians. The townships are divided into thirty-six sections, each one mile square or 640 acres. (See Figure 1.) The sections are numbered from one to thirty-six, beginning with the section in the northeast corner of the township, proceeding west to boundary of the township; the next row is numbered from west to east and so on. (See Figure 2.) The sections in turn are divided into half and quarter-sections and the quarters into quarter-quarter sections, designated by their direction from the center as northwest, southwest, northeast, and southeast.

The description of a given five acres of land identified by the section and township (Government Survey) description might read:

The East Half of the Northeast Quarter of the Northeast Quarter of the Northeast Quarter of Section One, Township 39 North, Range 12 East of the Third Prime Meridian.

The shaded portion of the diagram in Figure 2 represents the parcel described above, assuming that the diagram is Township 39 North, Range 12 East.

Land identification in the twenty-nine public land states in which government survey description is used is thus precise and orderly; it is possible to designate any plot of land as small as five acres with perfect accuracy; no two parcels are de-

---

1. The United States never had original title to the land in Texas because it was annexed as an independent republic.

LAND DESCRIPTION: FIGURE 1: A section of a township

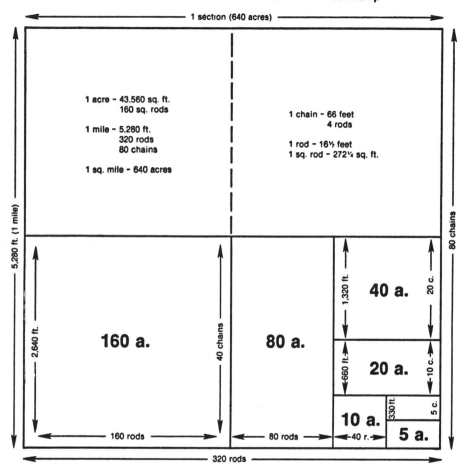

1 section (640 acres)

1 acre – 43,560 sq. ft.
160 sq. rods

1 mile – 5,280 ft.
320 rods
80 chains

1 sq. mile – 640 acres

1 chain – 66 feet
4 rods

1 rod – 16½ feet
1 sq. rod – 272¼ sq. ft.

5,280 ft. (1 mile)

2,640 ft.

160 a.

40 chains

80 a.

1,320 ft.

40 a.

20 c.

660 ft.

20 a.

10 c.

330 ft.

10 a.

5 a.

5 c.

160 rods

80 rods

40 r.

320 rods

80 chains

N

6 MILES

1 MILE

6	5	4	3	2	
7	8	9	10	11	12
18	17	16	15	14	13
19	20	21	22	23	24
30	29	28	27	26	25
31	32	33	34	35	36

W

6 MILES

E

S

LAND DESCRIPTION: FIGURE 2: Diagram of township divided into sections

519

scribed in exactly the same terms, because they are identified with reference to a specific prime meridian.

The plat system. Tracts of land described by metes and bounds or the rectangular survey may be further divided into streets, blocks, and lots. Maps or plans of these divisions are called *plats*. A *plat book* is a record maintained showing the location, size, and name of the owners of each plot of REAL PROPERTY in a given area. A plat description might read:

Lot Ten (10), Block Eight (8), Bay Shore Subdivision, as recorded in Volume 5 of Plats, Page 39, records of Blank County, State of ____.

Style in preparing descriptions. Descriptions of land to be included in an instrument are usually copied from some earlier document or from a survey or an ABSTRACT OF TITLE. They should be transcribed exactly. It is permissible, however, and sometimes desirable to write out words that have been abbreviated and to correct capitalization. The following general rules should be observed in preparing descriptions for real estate instruments:

1. Single-space, with a double space between paragraphs.

2. Do not abbreviate *Street, Avenue, Road, Boulevard,* in the text.

3. Write the words *North, Northeast, South, West, Southwest* and the like with initial capitals, but do not capitalize the words *northerly, northeasterly,* and the like.

4. Capitalize *Quarter, Township, Section, Range,* and the name or number of a *Prime Meridian.*

5. Write courses as follows: "South twenty (20) degrees, thirty-three (33) minutes, forty-five (45) seconds West."

6. Write distances as follows: "One hundred thirty-three and twenty-nine one hundredths (133.29) feet."

7. When several courses and distances are given in succession, introduced by a phrase such as " . . . the following three courses and distances. . . . " each of the courses and distances is written separately, indented, and single-spaced, separated one from the other by a double space, and each course and distance is ended with a semicolon. The sentence after the last course and distance is flush with the left-hand margin of the text preceding the itemized courses and distances.

8. It is preferable not to use figures, symbols, and abbreviations, but it is sometimes necessary to use them because of the limited space on a printed form. A description would then be written: "South 20° 33' 45" West, 50 ft." In offices with considerable real estate practice, a special key is placed on the typewriter for the symbol of the word *degrees;* otherwise, the symbol is made by turning the platen back a half space and striking the small *o.*

Checking land descriptions. An error in the description of land can cause trouble and even result in a lawsuit. The importance of checking the description cannot be overemphasized. It is easy to make an error in copying that is not always discernible merely from reading the description.

For example, the section and township description shown above contains the phrase, "of the Northeast Quarter" three times. It would be easy to omit the phrase once but difficult to realize the omission in reading over the description; yet the omission would double the amount of land conveyed by the deed. Nor is it advisable for one person to compare the description line by line. The safest method of checking the typographical accuracy of a land description is to have one person read the original copy aloud to another, slowly enough to permit him or her to follow the typed copy carefully.

Land contract.   An installment contract in which a seller agrees to convey good TITLE and a purchaser agrees to buy under certain specific terms and conditions. After offer and acceptance, the buyer (VENDEE) has an equitable title; however, legal title is withheld by the seller (VENDOR) until the contract is paid off. This contract is also referred to as an agreement for sale, a contract for deed, a conditional sales contract, a contract of sale, and a sales contract. The seller places a DEED in ESCROW or trust for future delivery, usually with payments being made into escrow for dispersal. It is an extension of credit from the seller to the buyer.

Landlord.   See LEASE.

Lease.   A contract, written or oral, under which the owner of REAL PROPERTY grants the use, possession, and occupancy of the property to another. The owner is called the landlord or *lessor*, and the party to whom the property is leased is called the *tenant* or *lessee*. The contract sets forth in detail the terms and conditions upon which the lessor grants the use and possession of the property to the lessee. The lease may be written or oral, but in most states the statutes provide that leases for periods in excess of one year must be in writing to be enforceable.

Types of leases include a *straight lease;* a *sale-and-leaseback;* a *graded lease,* also known as a *step-up lease* because it calls for prescribed increases in rent at designated intervals; and a *lease with an option to purchase,* which is self-descriptive. To be valid the lease must prescribe the price and terms of the purchase. Such an option may run for a part or for the full length of the lease. See SALE-AND-LEASE-BACK.

Office-supply stores have standard printed lease forms. Secretaries who type these forms should follow the instructions given in Chapter 1/ TYPING. *Typing on ruled lines.* Before leases are signed, they should be approved by an attorney.

Leasehold.   An ESTATE IN REAL PROPERTY granted for a definite number of years under the terms of a LEASE.

Lessee.   See LEASE.

Lessor.   See LEASE.

Lien.   See Chapter 13/LIEN; Chapter 9/LIEN.

Life estate.   An interest in property, real or personal, that lasts only for the duration of the owner's life. A life estate may also be for the duration of another's life or may terminate with the happening of a certain contingency. For example, a life estate may terminate upon the marriage of the owner. This estate may be created by an act of the parties, as by deed, will, or gift; or by operation of law, as by dower or curtesy. The owner of a life estate (called the *life tenant*) has the current use of the property and is responsible for its maintenance, including taxes and carrying charges. He or she also gets the income from the property but cannot ordinarily sell the property or do anything to impair its permanent value. However, the life tenant may be allowed to sell or consume property for self-support if the deed or will so provides. The tenant cannot dispose of the property at his or her death. The person or persons to whom the estate passes upon termination of the life estate is determined when the life estate is created. The estate that is left at the termination of the life estate is called a *remainder;* the person to whom it passes is a *remainderman* (plural, *remaindermen*).

Lis pendens. The notice filed with the clerk of court that FORECLOSURE of a MORTGAGE is pending.

Listing. Contract or agreement under which the owner of real property employs a BROKER to get a purchaser who will agree to buy the property at the price and on the terms fixed in the contract. The listing may be *exclusive*, exclusive agency, or *open*, or it may be placed with a broker who is associated with a multiple listing service. Under an *exclusive listing*, the listing broker has the exclusive right to market the property to other brokers, who must work as his or her subagents, as well as to the public. An *exclusive agency listing* is the same as an exclusive right to sell except that the owner/principal reserves the right to sell the property himself or herself without being obligated for a commission. In some states, the owner may sell the property during the exclusive period without being liable to the broker for the commission. Under an *open*, or *nonexclusive, listing*, the owner employs the broker to negotiate with respect to the property, but the contract of employment does not forbid the owner to engage other brokers for the same purpose or to dispose of the property personally.

Under the *multiple listing service*, members all receive the listings of other brokers. The broker who initially received a listing gets a percentage of the commission if another member sells the property. Any fees for the listing of a property in the multiple listing, or multilist, service are usually a set amount (not a percentage) and are usually paid by the listing broker.

Loan on real estate. See Chapter 13/ LOAN ON REAL ESTATE.

Long-term lease. LEASE of land for an extended period, generally ninety-nine years, with an obligation on the part of the tenant to improve the leased property with suitable buildings within a given period. Long-term leases are used to develop business districts in large cities. They are favored by owners of valuable land who want to create profitable estates without paying burdensome profits taxes imposed upon a sale. (See Chapter 9/SALE.) Under a long-term lease, property is merely being rented; TITLE does not pass from the owner. Long-term leases are, in effect, 100 percent loans on property, provided the tenant matches the investment with his or her own funds. The owner is spared the usual problems of management. The tenant pays taxes, looks after production and maintenance of improvements, and periodically pays RENT.

Marketable title. TITLE free from defects or flaws that may disturb the purchaser's peaceful possession and enjoyment of the property or its market value. A title is not marketable here if there is an appreciable risk of litigation regarding the validity of the title. Marketable title is also known as *merchantable title*. A seller is generally required to convey marketable title to the buyer, unless the PURCHASE AND SALE AGREEMENT provides otherwise. Whether title is unmarketable in a particular instance depends largely on the facts of each case and on the terms of the contract of sale.

Merchantable title. See MARKET-ABLE TITLE.

Metes and bounds. See LAND DESCRIPTION.

Mortgage. A conditional convey-ance. A mortgage is given by a

borrower or debtor (the *mortgagor*) to secure the payment of a debt, with a provision that the conveyance will become void on the payment of the debt by the date named. In early English times, the debtor actually turned over his or her property to the lender (the *mortgagee*), who would keep the income and profits from it. The land was "dead" to the owner and gave him or her no return, hence the word *mort-gage*, meaning "dead pledge." A mortgage may be given on real estate or on personal prop-erty, but a mortgage on tangible personal property is referred to as a *chattel mortgage*, whereas a mortgage on real estate is referred to simply as a *mortgage*. Some mortgages cover both real and personal property, for example, a mortgage on a furnished apartment building.

The word *mortgage* also refers to the instrument used to make the conveyance. The debt is evidenced by promissory notes; the mortgage is the security instrument that secures payment of the notes. In some states, the debt is evidenced by a bond instead of a promissory note. The bond takes the place of the note. Frequently, the bond and mortgage are combined in one instrument, which is referred to as a *bond and mortgage*.

Instruments other than mortgages used for securing an interest in prop-erty for the debt are promissory notes secured by TRUST DEEDS OR DEEDS OF TRUST and agreements for sale or LAND CONTRACTS. The differences in these instruments relate primarily to the methods of FORECLOSURE and redemption policies. A deed of trust does not, except by election of the lender, have a judicial procedure. The trustee may foreclose by an established procedure of notice and the holding of a trustees sale. In this procedure there is no redemption period. An agreement for sale is foreclosed by a procedure based on the percentage of the principal loan amount paid.

A *conventional mortgage* is essentially a deed stating that the mortgage will be void when the debt is paid. A *deed of trust* or a *trust mortgage,* conveys land to a third party who holds it until the debt is paid. A *second mortgage* is entitled to satisfaction after a first mortgage. A *purchase money mortgage* is one given as partial payment of the purchase price. An *open-end mortgage* allows one to reborrow up to the amount of the original loan.

A mortgage commonly (1) describes the debt, (2) indicates that it is void when paid, (*defeasance clause*), (3) states the *consideration* (either the amount of indebtedness or a nominal consideration), (4) provides an acceleration clause (see Chapter 9/ACCELERATION CLAUSE), (5) describes the property, (6) states any prepayment privilege, and (7) states whether the mortgagor may sell part of the land (*partial-release clause*).

Mortgagee. See MORTGAGE.

Mortgagor. See MORTGAGE.

Open-end mortgage. See MORTGAGE.

Open-housing law. Deals with the prohibition and eradication of discrimination in housing on the basis of race, color, national origin, sex, or religion. Grounds for rejection of buyers or renters, for reasonable cause, still exist but must apply to all persons equally. The open-housing law is also known as the Fair Housing Act, as affirmative marketing, and as equal-opportunity housing.

Opinion of title. See ABSTRACT OF TITLE.

Plat system. See LAND DESCRIPTION.

Property management, real estate. The business of operating income properties. (See REAL PROPERTY). The property manager acts as agent for the property owner and, for a fee, seeks to maximize the income obtainable from the property through keeping up the facilities, servicing tenants, and attempting to have the property 100 percent rented at all times.

Purchase money mortgage. See MORTGAGE; Chapter 13/PURCHASE MONEY MORTAGE.

Purchase and sale agreement. *Real estate.* A formal written contract (see Chapter 9/CONTRACTS) entered into between a seller (known as VENDOR) and a buyer (known as VENDEE) of real property, setting forth in full all the terms of the agreement between them for the CONVEYANCE OF TITLE within a specified time. The purchase and sale agreement, also known as "contract of sale" sets in motion the various investigations of title and encumbrances, arrangements for financing, and preparation of instruments to be signed upon closing title. (See Real estate closing). It is important that the agreement be prepared carefully to include all terms of the agreement between buyer and seller and to state them clearly, for if any dispute should arise, the courts will not admit any oral testimony in variance of the written contract.

Printed forms are available in office-supply stores. Secretaries who type on forms should follow the instructions in Chapter 1/Typing, *Typing on ruled lines.* Four copies are needed: an original and duplicate original for buyer and seller, a copy for the broker, and a copy for the files.

See Real estate closing.

Quit-claim deed. See Deed.

Real estate. See Real property.

The secretary's duties. The duties of a secretary concerning real estate owned by an employer are the following:

1. See that state and local taxes are paid promptly. (See Chapter 12/Taxes other than federal income.)

2. Keep adequate records for income tax purposes (see Chapter 12/Real estate records) if the employer receives Rent from real property.

3. Keep records of insurance. (See Chapter 16/Insurance records, *Insurance other than life.*)

Real estate closing. The transaction between seller and purchaser and their representatives in which the formalities of a sale are executed. When the purchaser agrees to buy, he or she generally pays a deposit and enters into a contract with the seller. (See Purchase and sale agreement; Chapter 9/Contracts.) The contract designates a certain day, and sometimes hour, when the deed and mortgages, if any, shall be delivered and the balance of the purchase price paid.

The initial contract sets in motion the various investigations, as well as the preparation of papers that are signed at the closing. The purchaser has the title searched and informs the seller of any encumbrances that must be removed before the closing. Arrangements for financing are made, and the lender or his or her representative is also present at the closing. Papers prepared by the seller's attorney (or escrow agent in some states) may consist of any or all of the following: (1) purchase money mortgage and bond (see Chapter 13/Purchase money mortgage), (2) Deed, (3) affidavit of title, (4) estoppel certificate (see Chapter 9/Estoppel), (5) assignment of leases, (6) indemnity agreement, (7) letter to tenants giving notice of sale. The deed is the most important closing item.

At the closing, all papers are examined to make certain they are in order, signed, and exchanged and that payments are made. Usually, a memo of the closing and a financial statement are prepared (see Figure 1). The transfer of title is complete

REAL ESTATE CLOSING: FIGURE 1: Form of closing statement

TITLE TO PREMISE NO. . . . .   closed (date) . . . .
at (place) . . . .   present (name persons attending clos-
                                                      ing)
. . . .   Title closed by delivery of following
                                                      instruments:
          DEED   Dated . . . .
. . . .   Recorded . . . . by. . . . .
           to   To be returned to . . . .
. . . .   Dated . . . .
     MORTGAGE   Recorded . . . . by. . . . .
                                 To be returned to . . . .
. . . .   Terms of mortgage . . . .
          to
. . . .

INSURANCE (insert memorandum of names and details of policies, changes to be made and by whom).

STATEMENT OF ADJUSTMENTS

	Cr.		Dr.
Purchase price			$ . . . .
Paid on signing contract	$		
Mortgage held by	$		
Interest from ____ to ____ at ____ per cent	$		
Purchase-money mortgage	$		
Insurance			$ . . . .
Rent	$	(or)	$ . . . .
Other items	$	(or)	$ . . . .
Total credits	$		$ . . . .
Total debits			$ . . . .
Total credits brought over			$ . . . .
Balance paid			$

EXPENSES (insert memorandum of fees and expenses for drawing and recording papers and by whom paid).

---

when the deed has been signed, sealed, and delivered. Also, a real estate closing in a title insurance state is not usually a formal meeting of the parties but rather the reference made regarding the recording of the transfer of time in the county recorder's office or the delivery of the deed to the purchaser.

Real estate records. See Chapter 12/ REAL ESTATE RECORDS.

Real estate taxes. See Chapter 12/ REAL ESTATE TAXES.

Real property. The land, APPURTE-NANCES, and improvements attached to it. All other property is personal property. (See Chapter 9/PERSONAL PROPERTY.) Hence in addition to the land, real property includes the buildings, natural growth, minerals, and timber that have not been separated from the land and the air space above the land. Apples on a tree constitute real property, whereas harvested apples become personal property.

An interest in real property is an *estate* and runs the entire gamut of varying rights from an estate in FEE SIMPLE (absolute ownership) to a LEASEHOLD (the right to use property during a fixed term for a specific consideration). An estate is only a designation of a particular type of interest in property; it is not a legal entity. Other forms of estates are modifications and limitations of a fee simple estate. See LIFE ESTATE; TENANCY BY THE ENTIRETY; JOINT TENANCY; TENANCY IN COMMON.

REALTOR® or REALTOR ASSOCIATE®.
These terms are registered trademarks of the National Association of Realtors® and may be used only in reference to members of that association. All real estate licensees are not, therefore, REALTORS® or REALTOR ASSOCIATES®.

Rectangular survey system. See LAND DESCRIPTION.

Rent. Regular periodic payments by a tenant to the landlord for the use of REAL PROPERTY. Rent is taxable income. See Chapter 12/REAL ESTATE TAXES; REAL ESTATE RECORDS.

Right of survivorship. This right distinguishes a JOINT TENANCY from a TENANCY IN COMMON. In a joint tenancy the deceased owner's interest in the property goes to the other owner or owners by whom the deceased is survived rather than to his or her heirs or next of kin. Joint tenancy is destroyed if the owner decides to sell his or her interest. While the other owners continue to share their joint tenancy, the new owner will hold tenancy in common with them without the right of survivorship.

Right-of-way. The right to go on or over the land of another for the benefit of one's own land. A right-of-way is an EASEMENT that may be private or public. A *private right-of-way* is generally created by a grant from or agreement with the owner of the land over which the right-of-way exists. A *public right-of-way* is the right of the public to the public streets, roads, and highways.

Sale-and-lease-back. An arrangement that companies owning land and buildings sometimes use to raise capital to finance expansion or to provide additional working capital. The property is sold to a buyer, who simultaneously enters into a LEASE agreement whereby the seller retains possession of the property and continues to use it as before. The lessee pays RENT to the buyer and assumes the obligation to maintain the property and pay insurance and taxes.

There are other variations of the device. Some alert real estate dealers provide a service whereby they find a corporation a suitable location for a plant (see Chapter 10/CORPORATION), construct the building according to specifications of the tenant-to-be, and arrange a PURCHASE AND SALE AGREEMENT to an institutional investor and a lease between the investor and the corporation. Some lease contracts even provide for repurchase of the property by the lessee under an option. (See Chapter 9/OPTION.) These contracts, however, if litigated or called into question on tax matters by the Internal Revenue Service, may be vulnerable in that they will be classified as conditional sales contracts or loan devices in substance because of the repurchase rights. If they are held to be mortgages, extensive mortgage taxes may be imposed. The income tax effect may also be costly (see Chapter 12/INCOME TAX); under a lease arrangement, the annual rent payments are deductible as operating expenses, whereas with a MORTGAGE, only the interest thereon would be deductible. See Chapter 13/INTEREST.

Sheriff's deed. See DEED.

Statutory deed. See DEED.

Straight mortgage. See Chapter 13/STRAIGHT LOAN.

Taxes. See Chapter 12/REAL ESTATE TAXES.

Tenancy in common. An estate held by two or more persons by separate and distinct title, with unity of possession only. If a DEED is made to two or more persons who are not husband and wife, and nothing is said in the deed concerning the character of the estate created by the deed, the estate created is a tenancy in common. The co-owners are tenants in common. They need not have acquired their titles at the same time or by the same instrument. Their shares need not be equal. For example, one co-owner may have an undivided one-tenth interest and the other the remaining undivided nine-tenths interest. Tenants in common are entitled to share the possession of the property according to their shares in the property. Except for their sharing of possession and income, however, the situation is almost as if each tenant in common owned a separate piece of real estate. Each tenant in common may convey or mortgage his or her interest, and the interest of each is subject to the lien of judgments against him or her. Upon death, a tenant's interest passes to his or her heirs and legatees and not to the other tenant in common.

Tenancy by the entirety. An estate held by husband and wife by virtue of title acquired by them jointly after marriage. Upon the death of either spouse, his or her interest automatically passes to the other by survivorship. A tenancy by the entirety cannot be terminated without the consent of both parties. Thus neither spouse can defeat the right of survivorship by mortgage or conveyance without the consent of the other. The courts do not look with disfavor upon a tenancy by the entirety as they do upon a JOINT TENANCY. Not all states recognize tenancy by the entirety or "tenancy by the entireties," as it is sometimes called. In many states, an absolute divorce terminates the estate by entirety, converting it into an estate in common.

Tenant. See LEASE.

Term mortgage. See Chapter 13/ STRAIGHT LOAN.

Termination of lease. Dissolving a lease as a result of its expiration or by agreement, eviction, or forfeiture.

Testimonium clause. See Chapter 9/TESTIMONIUM CLAUSE.

Title. All of the elements that prove ownership. Title to REAL PROPERTY is evidence of ownership to indicate a person's right to possess, use, and dispose of property. See ADVERSE POSSESSION; MARKETABLE TITLE; CLOUD ON THE TITLE.

Equitable title. A person's right to obtain absolute ownership of property to which another has title under the law. See MORTGAGE.

Evidence of title. Proof that a seller has apparent good title to property to be conveyed may be evidenced in any one of the following ways: (1) title insurance (see Chapter 16/TITLE INSURANCE), (2) ABSTRACT OF TITLE, (3) CERTIFICATE OF TITLE, and (4) TORRENS SYSTEM. Local custom generally determines which kind of evidence of title will be required upon a sale of REAL PROPERTY. Title insurance is customary in urban centers. An abstract of title and opinion is widely used in rural areas in the Midwest. The certificate of title is popular in the southern states. The Torrens system is used in a few localities throughout the United States.

Title closing. See REAL ESTATE CLOSING.

Title insurance. See Chapter 16/ TITLE INSURANCE.

Title search. A thorough investigation of the documented title to, or ownership of, property, along with any liens or encumbrances against it, as listed in the public records. Title searches are common before property is sold or involved in litigation. See ABSTRACT OF TITLE; CERTIFICATE OF TITLE; TORRENS SYSTEM; TITLE; Chapter 16/TITLE INSURANCE.

Torrens system. TITLE TO REAL PROPERTY registered in the Torrens system, so called because Sir Robert Torrens devised the system, which received acceptance in 1857. The basic principle of this system is the registration of a clear title instead of the recording of evidence of title under the recording system. It is less perilous than the recording system, from which purchasers must draw their own conclusions about whether the title is in fact clear, hence the necessity of a title certificate or title insurance. See Chapter 16/TITLE INSURANCE.

Under the system, a landowner who wants to register under the Torrens system first obtains a complete ABSTRACT OF TITLE to the land. He or she then files in the proper public office an application for the registration of TITLE. After certain legal procedure, the court orders the registrar of titles to register the title. The registrar makes out a certificate showing the title as found by the court. These certificates are bound in books and are public records. The registrar delivers a duplicate certificate to the owner. When land that has been registered under the Torrens system has been sold, the DEED itself does not pass title to the land. The deed must be taken to the registrar's office, and he or she issues a new certificate to the grantee. The deed is not returned to the grantee but remains in the registrar's office. Likewise, a MORTGAGE or judgment lien is not effective until a notation has been entered on the certificate of title in the registrar's office. The Torrens system is largely confined to a few metropolitan areas.

Trust deed or deed of trust. An instrument used to arrange financing of real estate (in many respects similar to a MORTGAGE). A deed of trust conveys bare legal TITLE from the grantor (TRUSTOR-debtor) to the grantee (TRUSTEE) for the benefit of the BENEFICIARY (creditor-lender) as security for a debt. (A trust deed is usually given to the beneficiary but is recorded in the name of the trustee as a grantee.) It is said to be a mortgage with a built-in power of sale.

Trustee. Individual, association, or corporation (or successor) to which bare legal TITLE is conveyed; one acting in trust for another. See TRUST DEED OR DEED OF TRUST.

Trustor. Person conveying bare legal TITLE to real estate by TRUST DEED OR DEED OF TRUST to a TRUSTEE.

Variance. Without changing the zoning regulations, an exemption may be granted by the Municipal Zoning Commission to a person wishing to build a structure that will not conform to existing zoning requirements. Such an exemption is called a variance. Variances are also issued for uses not normally allowed under existing zoning as well as for structures not normally allowed.

Vendee. One who enters into a PURCHASE AND SALE AGREEMENT and agrees to purchase the REAL PROPERTY of another (VENDOR). Every purchase and sale agreement must have a vendee (purchaser or buyer). If two or more vendees want to take TITLE as joint tenants, the contract of sale must describe them as such tenants. The buyer may be an individual or a corporation. (See Chapter 10/ CORPORATION.) If the buyer is an individual, he or she must be an adult of sound mind. If the vendee is a corporation, the purchase must have been duly authorized by the corporation's board of directors.

Vendee's lien. See Chapter 9/LIEN.

Vendor. One who enters into a PURCHASE AND SALE AGREEMENT and agrees to sell REAL PROPERTY to another (VENDEE). Every contract of sale must have a vendor, or seller. The vendor may be an individual, a partnership, a corporation, or a representative. (See Chapter 10/PARTNERSHIP; CORPORATION.) The individual may be either an adult or a minor or may enter into the contract in a representative capacity. If the vendor is a minor or an incompetent, the contract of sale should indicate that fact and give the name of the guardian, together with the date of the court order under which he or she was appointed. If the vendee is a representative, such as an agent or an executor, the contract should set forth the source of his or her authority. See Chapter 9/CONTRACTS.

Warranty deed. See DEED.

Zoning. A regulation, enforced under police powers by municipalities and states and applied to the use of both lands and buildings, whereby land use is restricted to specific purposes and building construction is controlled as to type, intensity, and volume. Most cities and large towns in the United States now have regulatory zoning laws, which exercise powerful influences upon land values.

CHAPTER 16

INSURANCE

Accident insurance. Personal insurance providing weekly indemnity for loss of time resulting from an accident. Definite sums are also paid for loss of life or certain bodily injuries resulting from accidents but not from illness. A variety of accident insurance contracts are issued to business and professional people only (commercial policies). Some cover only certain accidents, such as injuries caused by hazards of travel. Accident insurance is often issued in conjunction with a health policy. See HEALTH INSURANCE; WORKER'S COMPENSATION INSURANCE.

Actual cash value. A term used in insurance to apply to the sum of money required at the time of a loss to make restitution for the property destroyed. In general, it is replacement cost less wear and tear, depreciation, and obsolescence, but many factors may affect the actual cash value of a particular loss. *Actual cash value* is not to be confused with CASH SURRENDER VALUE of a life insurance policy.

Actuary, insurance. The official statistician of an insurance company who handles the mathematical work in connection with calculating rates charged and dividends and commissions paid. He or she performs the statistical work involved in developing new products for the insurance company to sell based on past claims and projected future loss experience.

Adjuster, insurance. The insurance company's representative who determines the amount of loss and deals with the insured or claimant in the settlement of a loss.

Sometimes insurance agents, brokers, and other representatives of the insurance company handle the adjustment function as an additional duty.

But most insurance companies do not want their agents and brokers to become involved. *Independent adjusters* have their own offices and work for insurers on a fee basis. *Public adjusters* help insured parties deal with the insurer. All adjusters typically check the validity of coverage, the value of the insured property, the insured party's share of loss, the parties to whom the loss is payable, and related matters.

Agent, insurance. An independent sales and service representative of an insurance company, who is generally paid on a commission basis. An independent insurance agent represents many insurance companies and chooses the most appropriate company for the insured. A direct writer agent represents only one insurance company. Normally, the contractual arrangement with the company is the only difference between the independent agent and the insurance broker. The vast majority of agents are also brokers. *Specializing agents* sell one or a few closely related lines of insurance. *General agents* sell all types of insurance.

Air travel insurance. See AVIATION INSURANCE.

All-risk insurance. Covers loss caused by all perils except those specifically excluded by the terms of the policy. This insurance contrasts with the ordinary policy, which names the specific peril or perils insured against.

Annuities. See Chapter 13/AN-NUITY.

Appraisal. When the insurer and insured cannot agree on the amount of a contract, a policy may provide for an appraisal of any loss. Appraisers determine the amount of loss, actual cash value of property at time of loss, and so on. If they arrive at different amounts, a neutral umpire may review the various appraisals and make a final determination. For specific value coverages under some types of policies, the appraisal must be made when the policy is written, not at the time of loss. Appraisal is not described as such under the standard fire policy but is in fact a form of arbitration confined to the examination of the value of the damaged property.

Assigned-risk plans. These plans are used mainly in the area of WORKER'S COMPENSATION INSURANCE and AUTOMOBILE INSURANCE but can also include hard-to-place FIRE INSURANCE, LIABILITY INSURANCE, and so on since some businesses need coverage that insurance companies would normally decline to provide because of undue risk situations. To deal with this, insurer associations have spread undesirable-risk applications among all insurers, who then provide, at higher rates, coverage commonly described as "assigned-risk plans." Recent state legislation has set up several plans for different liability risks such as child-care centers and municipalities.

Assignment. *Of insurance contract.* The transfer of the legal right or interest in a policy to another party. Insurance policies covering property are often assigned when the property is sold; life insurance policies are often assigned as collateral for loans. Usually, notification to the company is required.

Assured. Also *insured*. The person, partnership, or corporation in whose name an insurance policy is written.

Automobile insurance. Most policies protect the insured against the following: (1) losses resulting from legal liability for bodily injury (or death) to another person (injury sustained by the insured is not covered since this is covered by life and accident insurance and by auto medical coverage); (2) losses resulting from legal liability for damage to the property of another; (3) losses resulting by reason of damage to the insured's car through collision or upset (see COLLISION INSURANCE); (4) losses caused by theft of the car; (5) direct damage to the insured's car caused by fire, lightning, tornado, cyclone, windstorm, hail, earthquake, explosion, and other happenings (the last two types are called "comprehensive coverages," dealing with anything other than collision and including glass breakage, damage from floods or falling objects, and animal collision; see COLLISION INSURANCE); (6) legal liability of an employer for losses for which an employee is primarily responsible (called "nonowner auto coverage" if the employee is using his or her own car on the employer's business); (7) legal liability of garage keepers, service stations, and automobile mechanics for negligence resulting in losses to customers. The first

five of the above risks may be covered under separate policies or under a single contract. Generally, the assured may freely choose which risks he or she wants to insure, but it is not possible to have collision coverage without comprehensive or specified perils.

No-fault automobile insurance, adopted in many states, means that the insured's own insurance carrier pays for his or her property damage and/or bodily injury without regard to fault. *Family policies and special-package policies* are prepared for individuals and families to cover private passenger cars. The special-package policy is usually a lower-cost version of the family policy, but almost all companies are now using just the one policy form. *Garage-liability policies* are for car dealers, garages, and so on.

Automobile public liability insurance indemnifies the assured for all loss sustained by reason of legal liability for bodily injury (or death) incurred by any person other than the assured, accidentally resulting from the ownership, operation, or maintenance of the described automobile within the United States or Canada. A business firm, as the owner of an automobile, or as the employer of a person operating an automobile, is legally liable to third parties who may be injured by reason of the operation or maintenance of such automobile. The only limit to a loss of this nature is the aggregate value of all assets of the business.

The coverage granted by the liability policy is very broad. The insurance company also agrees to defend the assured in all suits for damages within the scope of the policy and to investigate all claims.

Definition of insured (omnibus clause). The standard automobile policy contains a provision, "Definition of Insured," often referred to as the *omnibus clause,* which in effect makes the insurance follow the car, with certain exceptions, rather than the named assured. Under this clause, the terms of the policy are extended to cover: (1) the legal liability of any other person using the insured automobile, with the permission of the named assured; (2) any firm or corporation legally responsible for the operation of a covered automobile. This provision extends the protection of the policy to an employer when an employee operates the automobile with the permission of the named insured.

See COLLISION INSURANCE; FLEET INSURANCE; NONOWNERSHIP LIABILITY INSURANCE; DEDUCTIBLE.

Aviation insurance. Individual airline accident policies protect against accident while the insured is traveling as a passenger on any domestic scheduled airline and on certain specifically named scheduled airlines operating outside the United States. Passengers flying on a nonscheduled trip can obtain similar policies at a higher premium. Ordinary accident policies may either exclude air hazards or permit travel only on scheduled flights of commercial airlines.

Other coverage applies to the field of property and casualty aviation insurance. Although insurance relating to the aviation industry is highly specialized, the various forms of coverage are similar to those used in the field of automobile insurance. Loss to an aircraft would be covered by hull insurance. The responsibilities of airport operators, hangar keepers, and dealers, as well as aircraft operators, to passengers and others would be covered by LIABILITY INSURANCE. WORKER'S COMPENSATION INSURANCE, written for employers, would be of the same character as it is for other activities.

Beneficiary. *Of insurance.* The person or institution to whom a life insurance policy is made payable in the event of the death of the insured. The policyholder may be the beneficiary under an endowment policy.

Binder. *Insurance.* A temporary agreement given by an insurance company or its agent to one who wants insurance coverage, *binding* the company to pay the loss if damage from the peril insured aginst should occur before the policy is written. A binder need not be in writing but should be to avoid future lawsuits regarding intent.

Blanket policy. A broad type of insurance coverage, most commonly used in fire and burglary insurance. A blanket fire insurance policy may be written to cover: (1) a building and its contents without any definite proportion of the insurance being carried on the building or its contents; (2) two or more buildings at different locations, together with the contents, without any definite proportion of the insurance being assigned to any particular location; (3) contents at several locations.

The term *blanket policy* is also used in GROUP INSURANCE.

Blue Cross Plan. A plan of group hospitalization insurance sponsored by nonprofit hospital associations throughout the United States, Canada, and Puerto Rico. The term *Blue Cross* usually appears in the names of plans, which vary from locality to locality. It signifies approval of a plan by the Blue Cross Commission of the American Hospital Association and is used colloquially to refer to the plan. All Blue Cross plans are basically similar, although benefits vary somewhat with the locality. Benefits under these plans are comparable to those under group hospitalization, surgical and medical coverage. See GROUP INSURANCE.

Blue Cross has a surgical and medical feature, known as the Blue Shield Plan, under which it pays a scheduled allowance to the surgeon or physician. Blue Cross and Blue Shield have several widely used individual plans.

Blue Shield Plan. See BLUE CROSS PLAN.

Broker. *Insurance.* A solicitor of insurance who places orders for coverage with companies designated by the insured or with companies of his or her own choosing. The broker earns a commission that he or she deducts from the premium, paying the net to the company. In most circumstances, the broker is the agent of the insured and not the insurance company. However, most of the large international brokers are increasingly using fees rather than commissions. See AGENT, INSURANCE.

Business floaters. See FLOATER POLICY.

Business insurance. See INSURANCE, BUSINESS.

Business-interruption insurance. Protects against loss of earnings resulting from interruption of business caused by damage to or destruction of property. This insurance is the sound method of meeting necessary payrolls, taxes, and other fixed expenses not provided for in the policies covering the actual physical damage to business property.

Cancellation of policy. See INSURANCE, OFFICE DUTIES.

Cash surrender value. Amount of refund to a life insurance policyholder who withdraws or cancels a contract of insurance. It is paid in accordance with the no-forfeiture value clause of the policy and is usually less than the amount paid in for premiums. The cash surrender value also indicates the amount that ordinarily can be borrowed on a life insurance policy at a particular time.

Catastrophic insurance. *Health insurance.* A form of coverage that provides benefits for high-cost (e.g., fifty thousand to one million dollars) hospital and related expenses arising from accident or sickness.

Catastrophic reinsurance. Coverage designed to protect insurers whose losses caused by some event exceed a specified amount. This allows insurers to write a maximum amount of insurance while protecting themselves from excessive loss in a single occurrence.

Claims, insurance. As soon as a loss covered by an insurance policy occurs, it should be reported to the AGENT (see AGENT, INSURANCE) or BROKER and a claim made for recovery. The agent or broker will ask for the details that the insurance company will need to settle the claim. He or she will report the claim to the insurance company, and the insurance company will usually make an investigation. The company will furnish a blank proof of claim to the agent or the broker, who sends it to the insured. When the proof of claim is completed, it is customary to return it to the agent or broker. Losses are usually adjusted with the company's ADJUSTER. Sometimes, however, losses are paid without adjustment after the proof of loss is filed. The agent or broker usually receives the company's settlement check and delivers it to the insured.

When a loss is paid under a fire insurance policy, the face amount of the policy is reduced by that amount. After the damage to the property is repaired, the insurance carried on the property should be increased to an adequate amount.

Class rating. A method of classifying insured parties by easily identifiable characteristics, such as age and sex, so all of those who are in the same category pay the same premium rate.

Coinsurance. A term used in insurance parlance to describe an agreement between the insurer and the insured whereby the insured, in consideration of the insurer's action in assuming the risk for an indicated premium, will maintain insurance in an amount equal to or greater than a specified percentage of the property's total value. Under this device, the insured is, in effect, a "coinsurer." For example, if a fire insurance policy contains an 80 percent coinsurance clause and if the property covered under the policy has a value of fifty thousand dollars, the amount of insurance to be carried is forty thousand dollars. If the amount of insurance carried is less than forty thousand dollars, the insured is considered to have assumed a proportionate part of the risk and, in the event of a loss, will have to bear a proportionate part of the loss; for example, if the insured carries thirty thousand dollars in the case given above, he or she will collect only 30,000/40,000 times the amount of the loss on a partial loss.

Coinsurance is also an important factor in CREDIT INSURANCE.

Collision insurance. AUTOMOBILE INSURANCE that protects an automobile owner from loss as the result of damage to his or her own motor vehicle. A business firm may incur a substantial loss as the result of accidental collision damage to its own motor vehicles. The collision contract protects against direct loss caused by contact of the insured with another object. The cost of full-coverage collision insurance has always been high. Consequently, policies with a DEDUCTIBLE CLAUSE are widely used. The collision policy should be examined to ascertain whether "upset" is specifically covered. Most companies agree to indemnify for loss caused "solely by accidental collision with another object or by upset."

Comprehensive theft and fire coverage. A comprehensive insurance coverage that provides a broader coverage than the specified perils of theft, fire, lightning, and transportation. It protects against loss or damage to the insured automobile from any source except collision and is subject to specific exclusions. Collision coverage may be included at the choice of the buyer. This policy form has become extremely popular.

Comprehensive theft and fire. See COLLISION INSURANCE.

Concealment. The failure to disclose material facts to an insurer. Such failure on the part of the insured or prospective insured party may cause an insurer to avoid providing coverage or to cancel coverage already provided.

Condominium association insurance. Property and liability insurance, usually excluding personal effects of residents, covering all dwellings in a condominium complex. Condominium homeowners' policies exclude building coverage but are like regular homeowners' policies in all other respects.

Contract. See INSURANCE CONTRACT.

Contributory negligence. A doctrine applied in insurance cases in some jurisdictions stating that one has personally contributed to the injury of another. Contributory negligence, when applied, can defeat someone's claim if it can be proved that the plaintiff personally contributed to the injury. Many jurisdictions now make awards based on "comparative negligence." See also LIABILITY INSURANCE.

Conversion privilege. A privilege included in group term life insurance policies, and in the certificates issued under them, giving the insured individual the right to obtain permanent insurance, without physical examination, at the rate applicable to his or her attained age when the insured ceases to be a member of the insured group. The state laws require the inclusion of this provision in the policies. Many individual-term policies provide a conversion privilege also at little or no additional cost or allow conversion, under certain circumstances, from term to a permanent type of life insurance.

Cooperative insurers. See BLUE CROSS PLAN.

Credit insurance. A contract under which the insurance company agrees to reimburse a wholesaler, manufacturer, jobber, or service organization for unusual losses occasioned by the nonpayment of accounts receivable or the insolvency of the debtor.

Credit insurance is never written for retailers. The insurance company agrees to reimburse the insured when his or her losses exceed a stated sum, known as the *normal loss deduction* or *primary loss*. The policy also requires the insured to bear a certain proportion of the bad-debt loss, from 10 to 25 percent depending on the type of policy. This feature is called Coinsurance.

Credit life insurance. This type of insurance forms a large part of the insurance industry. It is one of four categories of life insurance. Payment is provided to the creditor should the debtor die before repayment of the debt. Usually, coverage is limited to the amount of the debt and is used with installment purchases such as jewelry, furniture, and automobiles. Most of these contracts are group based (Group Creditor Life Insurance), but individual credit life insurance is also available.

Deductible. The amount of each loss that the insured agrees to assume (e.g., the first one hundred or two hundred dollars). The insurer agrees to pay the remainder up to the full amount of the policy. By use of a deductible provision, an insured may, at less premium cost, receive protection against serious losses. The deductible clause has had widespread acceptance in the case of automobile collision and upset insurance and is very common with fire and marine insurance as well. Deductibles are sometimes available on general public liability policies too, particularly property damage liability.

Types of deductibles. Level or straight deductibles may be applied to each commodity involved or to each illness or accident, or they may be applied to the total losses involved in a specified period. *Flat-amount deductibles* involve a flat amount that will decrease annually with the succession of claim-free years. *Franchise deductibles* are based on a percentage of the face amount of insurance. Loss in excess of that amount will be paid by the insurer. A deductible may also be for a specific amount or for a percentage of the loss involved. The deductible may not apply to certain forms of loss such as loss by fire under an all-risk contract. With *cumulative and participating deductibles* the insured pays 50 percent at the outset and carries the cost of losses until the total is equal to the remaining 50 percent. Further losses are paid for by the insurer. Glass insurance uses this type of deductible.

Depreciation insurance. A form of replacement insurance allowed in some jurisdictions that covers buildings and some equipment. In essence, it eliminates the deduction for depreciation usually made in computing actual cash value.

Disability insurance. Disability insurance pays benefits for income lost by an individual because of accidental injury or sickness. The insurance may be Accident insurance or Health insurance or a combination of the two. Worker's compensation insurance covers disability arising from employment.

Dividends. *On insurance policies.*
Under some life insurance policies, called *participating policies,* the insured becomes entitled to a share of the divisible surplus of the company in the form of a dividend. Such dividends are usually payable annually and are ordinarily declared at the option of the insurance company's board of directors. A few companies pay dividends at the termination of a policy contract. If death is the cause of termination, they are called *mortuary* or *postmortem dividends;* otherwise, they are called *maturity dividends* or *special-settlement dividends.* During the life of the contract, a policyholder may have his or her dividends (1) paid in cash; (2) applied as partial payment of the premium due; (3) applied to the purchase of additional insurance (*paid-up additions*); or (4) left with the company to draw interest, subject to withdrawal (*dividend accumulations*). Dividends are also returned to the insured by property and liability insurance companies (usually mutual companies) as a method of allowing the policyholder to share in profits. See MUTUAL INSURANCE COMPANY.

Double indemnity rider. Payment of double the insured amount if something specified takes place. A person carrying life insurance for fifty thousand dollars might have a double indemnity rider stating that one hundred thousand dollars will be payable to the beneficiary if death is accidental.

Employee benefit plans. See GROUP INSURANCE.

Endorsement. *On insurance policies.*
A form or clause added to an insurance policy to modify the basic policy. Basic or standard policies are not adapted to all circumstances. It is therefore necessary to alter them by means of a rider, or endorsement. Some endorsements *must* be made. For example, a description of the property insured must be added to the standard fire policy. Other endorsements *may* be made by which certain provisions are waived or additional privileges permitted. For example, an endorsement permitting an insured building to remain unoccupied more than the usual sixty days may be made on a standard fire policy. See EXTENDED COVERAGE ENDORSEMENT.

Endowment insurance. A form of life insurance that promises payment of the amount of the insurance upon death of the insured within a specified period or upon his or her survival to the end of the specified period. The premiums are considerably higher than premiums for ordinary life insurance.

Extended coverage endorsement.
An endorsement added to a fire insurance policy that extends coverage to protect against the perils of hail, tornado, cyclone, riot and civil commotion, windstorm, explosion, aircraft and motor vehicle damage, and smoke. The coverage may be extended by still other supplementary endorsements to cover other perils, such as vandalism and malicious mischief, collapse, and falling objects.

Fire insurance. A standard contract, prescribed by the law of each state, is written for this form of insurance. No other form of contract is written, but the standard form may be modified or extended by endorsement. Nearly all states have adopted the standard fire policy of New York. The courts have interpreted almost every word of this policy, and as a result, the policy has a definite and exact meaning. The standard policy insures against "direct loss by fire, lightning, and by removal from the premises endangered." Almost any type loss is covered when fire is the primary cause, whether or not it is the immediate cause. *Direct loss by fire* means only damage to the property itself. Thus a slight fire may cause a business to close down, with a resulting loss of many times the value of the property actually destroyed. Unless the policy includes an endorsement to the contrary, recovery can be had only for damage to the property actually destroyed. See BUSINESS-INTERRUPTION INSURANCE; RENT AND RENTAL-VALUE INSURANCE.

Regardless of the face value of the policy and of whether the loss is total or partial, the assured may recover only to the "extent of the actual cash value of the property at the time of loss or damage." Proper deductions are made for depreciation. Some states have a "valued policy law," which provides that, in the event of a total loss to the property, the insurance company must pay the full face amount of the insurance carried. See COINSURANCE.

Fleet insurance. Business firms owning five or more automobiles of any type may insure them under a single policy on the "fleet plan," which gives them a more flexible form of insurance than do individual specific policies. Premiums are based primarily on vehicle garaging, use, radius of operation, and size of vehicle or gross vehicle weight. Reports are made to the insurance company of suspension, disposal, and acquisition of automobiles. Automatic coverage for newly acquired cars is provided. Fleet discounts in the premium are available, depending on the number of cars.

Floater policy. An insurance policy that protects property frequently moved about from one location to another. The insurance applies no matter where the property described in the policy may be, except as to places that may be specifically excluded. See INLAND MARINE INSURANCE.

Garage liability insurance. See AUTOMOBILE INSURANCE.

General cover contract. An agreement on the part of the insurance company to furnish insurance in amounts the insured may need throughout the term although he or she pays for only the average stock value. It is also called *reporting insurance* or *reporting policy*. Thus it provides an economical method for obtaining adequate protection on fluctuating stocks of goods. Generally, a specific policy covers the maximum amount of stock to be carried. A deposit is paid up front, and a monthly report of the actual inventory is made, totalled, and divided by twelve and then multiplied by the policy rate according to the dollar value or according to the unit.

General liability insurance. See LIABILITY INSURANCE.

Government insurance programs. Social insurance is part of the govermental approach to risk treatment. Individuals and organizations are covered through state or federal government agencies. They rely on the resources of the government operating either alone or in a program of cooperation with the private sector. Such insurance is almost exclusively compulsory (e.g., social security programs of life, disability, survivors', and medical benefits; compulsory worker's compensation). Other associated programs include the Federal Deposit Insurance Corporation (FDIC), Federal Savings and Loan Insurance (FSLIC), Security Investors Protection Corporation (SIPC), the flood and crop insurance programs, and veterans' benefits.

Group insurance. Insurance of a changing group of individuals by means of a single or blanket insurance contract. This type of policy is commonly issued to an employer to cover his or her employees; it is also frequently issued to labor unions on their members. Under an employer-employee contract, the employer assumes responsibility for the collection and payment of the premium. State laws require the employer to contribute part of the premium. State laws also specify the minimum number of individuals that must be covered by the blanket policy. A general policy is issued to the group, and a certificate evidencing the insurance is issued to each individual. Coverages available on a group basis include life insurance, accidental death and dismemberment, accident and sickness, hospitalization, surgical, medical, and permanent disability.

Health insurance. Insurance protection covering sickness or injury. Policies include accident, disability, income, and hospitalization. See ACCIDENT INSURANCE; BLUE CROSS PLAN; CATASTROPHIC INSURANCE; DISABILITY INSURANCE; GROUP INSURANCE; MEDICARE; MEDICAID.

Homeowner's insurance. A property and liability contract for private single-family residences, condominiums, and so on. Policies commonly cover the dwelling and contents, although separate policies may be obtained for each. (See CONDOMINIUM ASSOCIATION INSURANCE.) A basic policy might cover property (dwelling and contents) and liability, with endorsements for theft and vandalism. Some insurers provide complete programs that also include automobile physical damage and liability as well as life and health insurance.

Income disability insurance. See ACCIDENT INSURANCE; DISABILITY INSURANCE.

Inland marine insurance. Inland marine insurance policies represent an extension of the practices of ocean marine insurance to cover risk on land. They provide coverage for inland waterway as well as rail and truck transportation losses. These losses include damage to property in transit or incidental to it such as tunnels and bridges. A broad classification of inland marine insurance coverage would divide it into business and personal, offering protection in each of these fields. Many are all-risk types of contracts, and others are named-peril contracts covering only listed causes of loss.

Insurable interest. A person has an insurable interest if he or she might be financially injured by the occurrence of the event insured against. Under American law, if an insurable interest is not present, the contract is a mere wager and is not enforceable.

In property. Insurable interest must exist at the time the loss occurs. Title to the property insured is not necessary; an owner, lessee, mortgagee, or purchaser has an insurable interest. Insured parties should tell their brokers or agents the exact nature of their interest at the time they applied for the policy so that the broker or agent may attach the proper ENDORSEMENTS to the policy. Any change in the nature of a policyholder's interest should be reported to the broker or agent immediately.

In life. Insurable interest must exist at the time the policy is written but need not exist at the time death occurs. Every person has insurable interest in his or her own life and may name anyone as beneficiary. Other examples of relations giving rise to an insurable interest are those of (1) employer and valued employee; (2) several partners of a partnership; (3) creditor and debtor; (4) corporation and its officers; (5) wife and husband; (6) dependent children.

Insurance, business. Protects business undertakings from impairment of capital by transferring the chance of loss to an insurance company. Some types are (1) *property insurance,* which protects the owner or mortgagee of the property against actual destruction by fire, windstorm, explosion and other perils; (2) *business-interruption insurance,* which protects against loss of earnings resulting from an interruption of business operations caused by damage to or destruction of property; (3) *liability insurance,* which protects against loss arising from legal liability for bodily injury and property damage to others; (4) *fidelity bonds,* which guarantee the employer against loss caused by dishonest employees, and *surety bonds,* which generally guarantee the faithful performance by others of certain duties or obligations; (5) WORKER'S COMPENSATION INSURANCE, covering working people for accidental injury and occupational disease developing from and during employment.

Various kinds or types of coverage can be had within each of these broad types. (See the list below.) No general insurance program is suitable for every business because the needs of each differ. A trained insurance AGENT (see AGENT, INSURANCE) or BROKER can analyze the perils facing a particular business and advise the business about the kinds and amounts of insurance that are needed.

See also LIFE INSURANCE as to the uses of a life insurance contract to a business undertaking.

CHECKLIST OF BUSINESS INSURANCE COVERAGE

Accident
Accounts receivable
Acid and chemical damage
Aircraft: hull and liability
Air passengers
Airport liability
Air insurance
Alternation bond
Arrest bond
Art glass
Arts: all-risk
Assumed liability
Auctioneer's bond
Automobile: car and liability
Auto trailers

Baggage
Bail bond
Bailee's customer's liability
Bank burglary and robbery
Banker's blanket bond
Banker's forgery and alteration bond
Blanket bonds, fidelity, forgery, alterations
Boiler policy
Bonds, all purposes
Breeder's policy
Bridge policy
Builder's risk
Burglary
Business interruption

Camera: all-risk
Cargo
Casualty: all types

Chain stores, multiple locations
Checks
Civil commotion
Cloudburst
Collision
Common carrier's legal liability
Compensation
Completion bond
Consequential damage
Consignee
Construction bond
Contents of buildings
Contractors:
    bonds
    compensation
    equipment floater
    liability
    protective policy
Conversion
Crash: aviation
Credit insurance
Crime: comprehensive
Crop insurance
Curios
Cyclone

Dentist's liability
Depositor's forgery bond
Destruction, money, securities, records
Dies
Drawings
Drive-other-cars

Earthquake
Electric motors and equipment
Elevator liability
Embezzlement
Employer's liability
Engines: all types
Equipment floater
Excess commercial bond
Exhibitions
Explosion
Extraordinary alterations

Farm equipment and liability
Fidelity bonds
Fiduciary bonds
Fine arts floater
Fire
Fleet coverage
Flood
Flywheel
Forgery bonds
Fraud bonds
Freezing
Freight policy
Fur floater
Furrier's customer's floater

Garage liability
Garage-keeper's legal liability
Glass
Goods-in-process
Guarantee bonds

Hail
Hangar-keeper's liability

Inland marine floater policies
Inland transit policy
Insurrection

Landlord's liability
Larceny
Laundry policy
Leakage
Leasehold insurance
Legal liability
Liability: all types
Lightning
Livestock

Machinery
Malicious mischief
Malpractice
Manufacturer's liability
Manuscripts
Marine insurance
Mercantile burglary
Merchant's protective bond

Messenger robbery
Money and securities
Motor truck carrier's form
Musical instruments floater

Negligence liability

Occupancy insurance
Office burglary and robbery
Officer's and director's liability
Owner's liability

Parcel post insurance
Patterns
Paymaster robbery
Performance bond
Personal effects floater
Personal liability
Personal property floater
Physician's liability policy
Plate glass insurance
Power interruption
Products liability
Professional liability
Property: all types
Property damage liability

Rain
Records destruction insurance
Rental insurance
Repair and replace insurance
Riot
Rising water
Robbery

Safe burglary
Safe deposit boxes
Safe depository liability
Service station liability
Smoke damage
Sports liability
Sprinkler leakage
Steam boiler insurance
Stored goods
Strikers, damage from
Surety bonds
Surgeon's liability policy

Team's liability
Tenant's liability
Theft insurance
Third party liability
Title insurance
Tornado
Tourists' baggage floater
Transportation floater

Unoccupied buildings
Use and occupancy

Vandalism

Warehouseman's liability
War risk
Water damage
Windstorm
Worker's compensation

Insurance, office duties. *The secretary's duties.* The secretary's duties with respect to insurance carried by an employer are as follows:

1. Check insurance policies as received.
2. *Maintain adequate records.* (See INSURANCE RECORDS.)
3. Cancel policies when necessary.
4. Report claim. (See CLAIMS, INSURANCE.)
5. Suggest insurance action as new needs develop.

New policies. When new policies are received, check whether all information is correct. For example, a policy on property must be in the name of the person or company or subsidiary that owns it or in the names of the joint owners. Note whether the policy protects the insured when traveling by air on both

scheduled and unscheduled flights. Check all such details and report anything that appears questionable.

Insurance action. Be alert to situations that call for insurance action, just as the insurance agent or broker would be if he or she were present to observe what is taking place. For example, remind your employer of changes that might be needed in existing policies and suggest that it might be advisable to ask the insurance agent or broker about insurance to meet particular situations. The employer may move his or her residence, buy a new car, sell an old car, put a car away for the season, invest in a building, plan a trip, buy his or her spouse a valuable gift—these and many other situations call for insurance action. Information on available coverages can be obtained from the insurance AGENT (see AGENT, INSURANCE) or BROKER. Some of the general insurance coverages available to an individual are listed here. Some of these coverages would typically be combined in a single policy. Others might each represent a separate policy. The list does not specifically include business insurance (see INSURANCE, BUSINESS), because responsibility for such insurance usually rests with someone other than the secretary.

Accident
Air travel
All-risk
Automobile
Blanket policy
Extended coverage endorsement
Fire
Homeowners

Hospital, medical, surgical, etc.
Liability
Life
Moving
Property floaters
Rent and rental value
Theft
Worker's compensation

Cancellation of policies. When the protection offered by an insurance policy is no longer needed, the policy should be returned for cancellation and a return premium obtained for the unexpired period. A secretary acts on instruction but should bring the need for cancellation to the employer's attention. The secretary then notifies the agent or broker and returns the policy. He or she should also make a note that a return premium is expected, if that is the case, and follow up if it is not received.

Insurance companies. State laws require that certain kinds of insurance shall be written only by a certain type of company. The following is a general classification of companies according to kind of insurance written: (1) *Life insurance companies* write life insurance, annuities, and accident and health. Those that write accident and health, as well as life, are sometimes known as *life and accident companies. Fraternal societies* write life insurance or accident and health. (2) *Accident and health insurance companies* write accident insurance only or accident and health. (3) *Fire insurance companies* write fire insurance and miscellaneous property insurance, such as windstorm, riot, explosion, collision, and water damage insurance. (4) *Marine insur-* ance companies write marine insurance, both ocean and inland marine. (5) *Fire and marine insurance companies* are fire insurance companies that also transact a marine insurance business. (6) *Casualty insurance companies* write theft, glass, boiler and machinery, elevator, animal, personal injury liability, worker's compensation and employer's liability, and credit insurance. They may also write accident and health insurance, water damage, and collision insurance. A casualty company that also writes fidelity and surety bonds is a *casualty and surety company.* (7) *Surety companies* write fidelity bonds and surety bonds. They also sometimes write burglary, robbery, and forgery insurance. (8) *Property depreciation insurance companies* insure against the depreciation of buildings and machinery that results from ordinary wear and tear. (9) *Title insurance companies* guarantee the right to real property. (10) *Multiple-line companies* write all lines of insurance except life insurance.

Insurance companies are also classified according to method of organization. A company may be organized as a MUTUAL INSURANCE COMPANY or a stock insurance company. Resembling a mutual insurance company in many ways is the *reciprocal* insurer, which is a kind of unincorporated consumer cooperative insurer. The subscribers are insurers as well as the insured, each subscriber being liable for a proportionate share of every risk pooled except his own. See Chapter 10/STOCK INSURANCE COMPANY.

Insurance contract. A contract of insurance is an agreement by which one party, for a consideration known as a *premium*, which is usually paid in money either in one sum or at different times during the continuance of the risk, promises to make a certain payment of money on the destruction or injury of something by which the other party will have a loss. (See INSURABLE INTEREST.) In fire and marine insurance, the thing is property; in life, health, or accident insurance, it is the life or health of a person. All that is requisite to constitute such a contract is the payment of the consideration by the one and the promise of the other to pay the amount of the insurance upon the happening of injury to the subject by the contingency contemplated in the contract.

Contracts have numerous clauses and provisions. *Declarations* are the insured's statements concerning matters such as occupation and age. *Agreements* concern the definition of perils insured against, losses covered, limits of liability, and other terms of the contract. *Exclusions* state what is not covered. *Conditions* state what must occur for a claim to be paid. *Renewal certificates* are simplified versions of the original contract sent when premiums are due, when a policy is continuous. See DEDUCTIBLE; DOUBLE INDEMNITY RIDER; ENDORSEMENT.

Insurance records. *Life insurance.* Secretaries should keep two classes of life insurance records: (1) a reminder of premium dates and (2) a description of the policies. A premium distribution record might also be desirable.

1. A card tickler file should be kept as a reminder of premium dates. (See Chapter 1/TICKLER FILE.) The card should show (1) due dates of the premiums; (2) amount of premium; (3) to whom the premium is payable (checks are made to the company, agent, or broker who bills the insured); (4) where to mail the check; (5) policy number; (6) name of company issuing the policy; and (7) name of insured. If dividends are to be applied as part payment of the premium, a note to that effect should be made on the tickler card. If the secretary handles more than one bank account, the tickler card should also show the name of the bank account on which the payment check should be drawn. Some secretaries note on the tickler card the dates the premiums are paid.

2. The secretary should maintain a record describing the life insurance policies carried by his or her employer and by each member of the family (if the secretary is responsible for those policies). A desirable form for this purpose is a sheet record, which shows at a glance the entire life insurance program. (See Figure 1.) A separate record should be kept of the policies carried by each person.

3. Executives who carry a heavy life insurance program are interested in knowing how the premiums are distributed throughout the year. Figure 2 is a form that may be used for that purpose. The day of the month on which the premium is due is entered in the "Day of Mo. Due" column, and the amount of the premium is entered opposite the

INSURANCE RECORDS: FIGURE 1: Sheet record of life insurance policies

POLICY RECORD										
					AGE	GROSS	DISABILITY		DOUBLE	
COMPANY	NUMBER	AMOUNT	TYPE	DATE OF ISSUE	AT ISSUE	YEARLY PREMIUM	PREMIUM WAVER	MONTHLY INCOME	INDEMNITY	BENEFICIARY

INSURANCE RECORDS: FIGURE 2: Life insurance premium distribution record

Policy Number	Day of Mo. Due	DISTRIBUTION OF LIFE INSURANCE PREMIUM PAYMENTS												
		Jan.	Feb.	Mar.	Apr.	May	June	July	Aug.	Sept.	Oct.	Nov.	Dec.	Total
397456	6			$100						$100				$200
497653	15						$150							$150
909634	30										$75			$75
				$100			$150			$100	$75			$425

policy number in the column for the appropriate month. The record shows the totals for each month and for the year.

This record may be used in either of two ways: (1) to show the distribution of premiums for the forthcoming year or (2) to enter payments as they are made, thus providing a running record of all premiums paid in a given year. This record is kept in addition to, and not as a substitute for, the reminder of premium dates and description of the policies.

Insurance other than life. The records the secretary should keep for insurance other than life are determined by the extent of the insurance program. A reminder of expiration dates must be kept. The other records described below are desirable.

1. Whenever a policy or certificate is received, whether as a first contract or as a renewal of an expiring con-

tract, the secretary should make up a three-by-five-inch tickler card as a reminder of the expiration date. Entries on the card will vary with the type of policy. The following, however, are the minimum essentials to be noted: (1) type of coverage and expiration date, (2) identification by company and policy number, (3) agent's name, (4) insured, (5) property covered, (6) amount of premium. There is no need for a tickler card for the premium due date because a bill ordinarily accompanies the new policy. The bill is the reminder that a premium payment is due.

2. The form shown in Figure 3 provides for a *detailed description* of policies other than life insurance policies. A separate sheet is kept for each kind of insurance on each piece of property. The entry showing value of the property is particularly useful for reference when market values fluctuate and the insured wants to check on whether he or she is fully insured or overinsured.

3. A form similar to the one shown in Figure 2 for distribution of life insurance premiums may be used to show a distribution of premiums for general insurance. The premium distribution for all general and life insurance may be kept on the same sheet.

Insured. The person, partnership, corporation, or association in whose name an insurance policy is written.

Level premium. A life insurance premium that remains the same—a level amount—through all of the

years that premiums are paid. The level premium is distinguished from the NATURAL PREMIUM, which increases each year with the age of the policyholder.

Liability insurance. Protects against unforeseen financial losses resulting from damage to others for which the insured is responsible. When the negligence of one party is responsible for a loss suffered by another, the injured party is entitled to recover damages from the party causing the loss. Although theoretically the damage must be caused by negligence, the legal definition and interpretation of negligence are extremely broad. See CONTRIBUTORY NEGLIGENCE.

Vicarious liability is indirect liability, such as an employer's responsibility for an employee's acts. *Absolute liability* means one is liable for damages regardless of negligence. *Contractual liability* concerns an agreement to indemnify someone for damages, for example, to satisfy a buyer if a product is damaged or to indemnify a landlord if a leased apartment is damaged.

Life insurance. For definition, see INSURANCE CONTRACT. A life insurance policy may have provisions limiting the liability of the company to a reduced amount in the case of death (1) from certain designated causes, such as violation of law, suicide, or a pulmonary disease; (2) within a certain time after the inception of the policy; and (3) while the insured is in naval or military service. Various deductions may be made in

INSURANCE RECORDS: FIGURE 3: Detailed description of policies other than life insurance

INSURANCE (OTHER THAN LIFE)

KIND OF INSURANCE

PROPERTY INSURED

LOCATION OF PROPERTY

AMOUNT PAID FOR PROPERTY

DATE PROPERTY PURCHASED

PURCHASED FROM

PURCHASED THROUGH

SUBSEQUENT IMPROVEMENTS

REMARKS

DATE OF ISSUE	DATE OF EXPIRATION	NAME OF COMPANY	NAME OF AGENT	POLICY NUMBER	POLICY PAYABLE TO	AMOUNT OF INSURANCE	AMOUNT OF PREMIUM	AMOUNT OF DIVIDEND	RATE OF DIV	NET PREMIUM	DATE CANCELLED	AMOUNT RETURN PREMIUM
					TOTAL BROUGHT FORWARD							
					TOTALS CARRIED FORWARD							

the amount payable under a life insurance policy. For example, if the insured's age is greater than stated, the amount of insurance payable is reduced to the amount that the premiums paid could have bought at his or her correct age. Also, deductions in the amount payable under policies may be made for unpaid premiums.

Life insurance policies differ in (1) terms of purchase and (2) terms of settlement. (See Ordinary life insurance; Term insurance; Single-premium insurance; Limited-payment insurance; Endowment insurance.

As business safeguard. The use of life insurance to protect the family is well known. In business, it may be used with the following objectives:

1. Life insurance strengthens credit: policies are used as collateral.

2. Insurance on the life of an important executive or key employee offsets loss during the period of readjustment immediately following death of the valuable executive or employee. Close corporations and partnerships make extensive use of life insurance for this purpose.

3. Life insurance provides a retirement fund for officers or employees.

4. Life insurance may be used as a funding arrangement to support a deferred-compensation agreement. See Chapter 12/Deferred-compensation agreement.

5. A life insurance policy on the life of a sole proprietor for use with a purchase and sale agreement enables one or more key employees to pur-

chase the business at the proprietor's death. Under the agreement, the proprietor binds himself or herself and his or her estate to sell the business to the employee or employees upon the proprietor's death, and the employee or employees agree to buy the business upon the owner's death at the stipulated price and to pay the premium on insurance on the life of the proprietor in an amount equal to the purchase price.

6. Life insurance is used to insure uninterrupted continuance of the business of a partnership. A purchase and sale agreement financed by life insurance provides that on the death of a partner the surviving partner will buy the deceased's interest in the firm at a stipulated price, and that life insurance will be carried on each partner to furnish the purchase money. Although the original partnership is dissolved, the surviving partners do not have to liquidate their business and jobs, and the deceased's estate receives prompt payment in cash for the full value of the deceased's interest in the firm.

7. Life insurance is used to finance a purchase and sale agreement by which the survivors, upon the death of a close corporation stockholder, acquire ownership and control of the corporation, and the family of the deceased stockholder receives full value for his or her stock. The arrangement includes an insurance policy on the life of each stockholder in the amount of his or her interest.

Limited-payment insurance. Life insurance for which the insured makes payments for a definite number of years, usually twenty or thirty, after which no more payments are required. The policy remains in force for life and affords the same protection as ORDINARY LIFE INSURANCE. The premiums are higher than the premiums on ordinary life insurance. If the insured dies shortly after the policy is issued, he or she has paid more for protection than under the ordinary life plan; if the insured lives beyond the usual life span, he or she has paid less.

Lloyd's. Lloyd's of London's membership includes thousands of underwriters who operate through syndicates of all sizes. This incorporated body is known mostly for its lending position in marine insurance, although it is also recognized for its importance in other areas (except life).

Lloyd's in the United States consists of unincorporated associations of individuals who write insurance. Most of the insurance handled by these Lloyd's associations is for automobile physical damage.

Loan insurance. A form of coverage for loans that meets certain governmental requirements in areas such as housing projects. Such loans are guaranteed and thus insured by the lenders.

Marine insurance contracts. Hull, cargo, freight, and liability contracts for marine interests. Marine insurance, the oldest branch of the insurance business, is subject to marine-insurance laws.

Medicaid. The common name for Title XIX of the Social Security Act pertaining to comprehensive care and services for the needy and for those specifically in need of financial aid for medical expenses. Under the provisions of this act, the federal government pays a percentage of administrative costs and payments made under state programs to doctors, hospitals, and other vendors of medical care.

Medicare. The common name for hospital insurance and supplementary medical insurance for persons aged sixty-five and over, as well as for persons who are qualified as disabled, as provided by amendments to the Social Security Act. The hospital insurance program automatically pays a percentage of hospital costs, extended-care facility costs, and home health-services cost. The supplementary medical insurance program is voluntary. Participants, who pay a small monthly premium, receive medical services, supplies (such as artificial limbs), and home health services. Patients need not be hospitalized to receive supplementary services under this part of the Medicare program.

Merit rating. *Insurance.* For large businesses, a pricing system called "merit rating" is used to determine premiums. More complex than the CLASS RATING, this is a system that measures how a specific risk differs from some standard so that the rate for that risk can be adjusted accordingly.

Mortality table. A table based on the experiences of life insurance companies, showing the probable number of years any man or woman of a given age and race may be expected to live. Mortality tables form the basis of the theory and practice of life insurance.

Mutual insurance company. An insurance company in which each policyholder is a part owner, and the net earnings are distributed to the policyholders in the form of dividends calculated as a percentage of the premium paid. For other types of insurers, see INSURANCE COMPANIES.

Named-perils contract. See ALL-RISK INSURANCE.

Natural premium. A life insurance premium collected each year that is just large enough to pay for the current year's protection. The premium is increased each year as the policyholder gets older. An insurance policy on the basis of a natural premium is a one-year term policy. See TERM INSURANCE.

No-fault insurance. See AUTOMOBILE INSURANCE, *No-fault automobile insurance*.

Nonownership liability insurance. LIABILITY INSURANCE, sometimes called *contingent liability*, that protects an employer against claims arising out of the operation of an automobile by an employee or others in connection with the employer's business, provided the automobile is not owned or hired, loaned to, or registered in the name of the employer. This insurance is necessary because the law of AGENCY (see AGENT, INSURANCE) holds the principal responsible for the acts of his or her agent.

Nuclear-energy loss insurance. Coverage provided by insurers for loss of property or injury to persons caused by nuclear hazard.

Old age, survivors, and disability insurance (OASDI). See Chapter 12/SOCIAL SECURITY TAXES.

Omnibus clause. See AUTOMOBILE INSURANCE, *Definition of insured (omnibus clause)*.

Ordinary life insurance. Insurance for which the policyholder pays a definite sum every year until death. The proceeds are payable at death to his or her beneficiary or estate. In addition, the policy also contains a small investment or savings feature, whereby dividends may be applied to reduce the premiums or increase the insurance. See DIVIDENDS.

Owners', landlords', and tenants' public liability (OL&T) insurance. Protection against legal liability for accidents resulting in bodily injuries or death arising out of ownership, occupation, or use of premises. This type of INSURANCE is available to owners or tenants of private residences, apartments, office and public buildings, and stores. Lessor (landlord) and lessee (tenant) under a lease (See Chapter 15/LEASE) can protect themselves against liability for injuries sustained upon alleged failure to make necessary repairs of leased premises by taking out OL&T insurance. The insurance policy will cover any judgment against the insured within the limit of coverage and will obligate the insurance company to defend the insured even if claims are groundless.

Paid-up life insurance policy. A life insurance policy on which the required premiums have been fully paid. A ten-payment or twenty payment policy becomes a paid-up policy at the expiration of the period. A single-premium policy (see SINGLE-PREMIUM INSURANCE) becomes a paid-up policy after the premium is paid. Life insurance policies and some state laws provide that, on default in premium payments, the insured is entitled to paid-up policy for the amount of insurance that the premiums paid will purchase.

Participating and nonparticipating insurance. *Participating insurance* is a plan of insurance under which the policyholder receives DIVIDENDS from the insurance company. The dividends are actually a refund arising out of the savings, economies, and efficient management of the company. A *nonparticipating contract* is one with a fixed premium rate guaranteed throughout the term of the policy. Mutual companies issue participating contracts; stock companies generally issue nonparticipating contracts but may also issue participating policies if the state law does not forbid this.

Pension plans. An arrangement whereby a percentage of an employee's salaries or wages is accumulated in a fund to be released in periodic payments upon the employee's retirement. Employers sometimes handle GROUP INSURANCE and pension plans together as part of an overall benefits program.

Plate glass insurance. An insurance that indemnifies the insured against loss by reason of breakage of glass. The cost of lettering and ornamentation may also be insured. The service performed by the insurance company in this field of insurance is the prompt replacement of broken glass.

Policy, insurance. The documentary evidence of an INSURANCE CONTRACT.

Premium. *Insurance.* The consideration of money the insurer receives for the assumption of the liability or risk or hazard insured against. For various types of life insurance premiums, see SINGLE-PREMIUM INSURANCE; LEVEL PREMIUM; NATURAL PREMIUM.

Property damage liability insurance. See AUTOMOBILE INSURANCE.

Public liability insurance. See AUTOMOBILE INSURANCE.

Real estate records. *For insurance purposes.* See INSURANCE RECORDS, *insurance other than life.*

Reinsurance. Insurance coverage for the insurer, rather than the insured. An insurance company requires reinsurance to protect itself when it writes a larger amount on a single insured party or in a single region than it can adequately handle should an excessive claim or an excessive group of claims arise. See also CATASTROPHIC INSURANCE, *Catastrophic reinsurance*.

Rent and rental-value insurance. Property damage policies cover the damage to the physical property by fire or other causes, but since an interval must elapse for repair of the property, its use or income from it is lost during this interval. Rental and rental-value insurance protects the insured from the loss of use of property or income from it while the property is not usable. The policy can be written to cover the rent that the owner of the premises would have to pay for other quarters after his or her own property has become uninhabitable through damage.

Renter's insurance. Also known as "leasehold interest insurance." This type of insurance provides payment to a lessee whose premises have become uninhabitable because of an insured risk. If a new property must be occupied at a higher rental, the difference between the value of the lost lease and the new rental is paid. See also HOMEOWNER'S INSURANCE.

Replacement insurance. A contract designed to cover the cost of replacing the lost property, as opposed to paying on the basis of actual cash value or depreciated value. See DEPRECIATION INSURANCE.

Reporting insurance policy. See GENERAL COVER CONTRACT.

Retirement plans. A form of insurance that provides insurance for a specified period or up to a designated age and after that provides one or more payments to the insured. ENDOWMENT INSURANCE, for example, is payable at its face value at the end of the endowment period if the insured is alive. A retirement income annuity, on the other hand, provides a guaranteed number of payments beginning at a specified age. See also PENSION PLANS; Chapter 13/RETIREMENT PLANS.

Rider. An ENDORSEMENT on an insurance policy.

Risk. In regard to loss, risk involves uncertainty about the outcome of an event. When two or more possibilities exist, risk is highest when each of the two possibilities is equally likely. But not all possible outcomes are as uncertain as others. Although all may involve risk, the degree of probability for each outcome may be markedly different.

A variety of tools is necessary for objective measurement of risk. *Probability* is one of the more important analytical tools used in the insurance field. There are two main types. The first, which relies on deductive reasoning from the nature of the case and without observation, is known as *a priori*. To determine risk in this way, there must be a number of equally likely results, a certain proportion of which represent the particular result that is under determination. In most cases probability cannot be determined in this way. If it cannot be analyzed in terms of equally likely results, it can be estimated *a posteriori* if the frequency of the type of case under review is known. The event must be repeatable to apply this relative-frequency definition of probability. Then one can speak of the proportion of outcomes "in the long run." The relative-frequency definition is sometimes called "objective probability." Under a definition known as "subjective probability," it is interpreted as the degree of belief or judgment rather than the thing or events to which it refers.

Salvage. What is left of property after it has been damaged by fire or other perils. Salvage applies to money or property available to an insurer to reimburse itself after a loss that has been paid. In marine insurance, salvage is a right that, for example, a rescuing ship has against the owners of wrecked ship. In this sense, salvage is not property.

Self-insurance. See WORKER'S COMPENSATION.

Single-premium insurance. A life insurance contract on which the premium is paid in one sum. A premium of this kind is necessarily very large, but if the insured lives to an old age, the single premium is less than the sum he or she would have paid in annual premiums.

Subrogation. The substitution of one person in another's place.

EXAMPLE

A's car is insured by an insurance company against collision. *A*'s car is negligently damaged by *B*. The insurance company pays two thousand dollars for repairs to *A*'s car. The insurance company is subrogated to *A*'s position and may prosecute the claim for damages against *B*.

Supplemental insurance. This insurance aims to cover the policyholder after the benefits of the basic hospital contract have been used up. It can sometimes involve the use of a *corridor deductible.* That term refers to the interim period between policies during which the insured is required to pay some of his or her expenses (e.g., one hundred dollars) before protection from a supplemental insurance will begin.

Term insurance. Temporary life insurance obtainable for various periods. The insurance company agrees to pay a stipulated sum upon death, provided death occurs within an agreed-upon period—one, five, ten, twenty or more years. If the insured outlives the period, he or she receives nothing. At the younger ages, the type of policy is lower in cost than any other, but the price increases rapidly with age.

Title insurance. A contract (see Chapter 9/CONTRACTS) by a title insurance company guaranteeing to make good to the beneficiary any loss, up to a fixed amount, sustained through defects in title to real property. (See Chapter 15/REAL PROPERTY; TITLE.) Title insurance is also known in some localities as *title insurance policy, title guaranty policy,* and *guaranty title policy.* A title company issuing its policy of insurance agrees to indemnify the beneficiary against any loss he or she may sustain by reason of any defects in title not enumerated as "exceptions" in the policy. These defects may be (1) discoverable defects disclosed by the public records or (2) hidden defects, such as forgery of a deed (see Chapter 15/DEED) in the chain of title. Some title insurance also guarantees that the title is marketable, and the title insurance company agrees to defend, at its own expense, any action attacking the title based on a defect in the title insured. See Chapter 15/MARKETABLE TITLE.

Underwriter. A key employee of an insurance company whose duty it is to determine the acceptability of risks. In a broader sense, an underwriter is the home office of the insurance company that classifies and finally accepts the risk. In life insurance, the term *life underwriter* is often used in referring to a life insurance agent.

Underwriting. *Insurance.* The function of assuming a risk for another in return for a premium. Underwriting departments have various selection procedures designed (1) to spread their risk over a sufficient number and type of insured parties and (2) to achieve profitable distribution of risks.

Unemployment insurance. See WORKER'S COMPENSATION INSURANCE.

Whole-life contracts. Coverage extending over the entire life of the insured, at a fixed premium. The premium may or may not be payable throughout life. See LIMITED-PAYMENT INSURANCE; SINGLE-PREMIUM INSURANCE; TERM INSURANCE.

Worker's compensation insurance.
Covers an employer's liability to his or her employees under worker's compensation laws, which have been enacted in all states. Generally, these laws provide that every employee is entitled to recover from his or her employer certain prescribed amounts for injury sustained in the course of employment. Since the amount of payments an employer may be required to make within any one year is subject to wide fluctuation, most employers prefer to transfer to an insurance company the obligation to compensate injured employees. Such a transfer is effected by the purchase of worker's compensation insurance.

The methods the employer may use to meet the liabilities imposed by the various worker's compensation insurance laws depend upon the law of the state in which the employer conducts his or her business. In a majority of the states, the employer has a choice from among several methods:

1. *Insurance in a state fund.*

2. *Insurance with a private insurance company.*

3. *Self-insurance.* Self-insurance of the worker's compensation risk, on proof of solvency, is permitted in most of the states. Self-insurance is not generally advisable unless a minimum of two hundred employees are employed regularly.

4. *Partial self-insurance.* Under this system, the employer assumes the liability for all losses under a specified amount, and the excess risk is placed with a private insurance company.

PART VI

REFERENCE SECTION

CHAPTER 17

TABLES, WEIGHTS, AND MEASURES

Birthstones.

January	Garnet
February	Amethyst
March	Bloodstone or Aquamarine
April	Diamond
May	Emerald
June	Pearl
July	Ruby
August	Sardonyx or Peridot
September	Sapphire
October	Opal
November	Topaz
December	Turquoise

Flower calendar.

January	Carnation or Snowdrop
February	Primrose
March	Violet or Daffodil
April	Daisy or lily
May	Hawthorne or Lily of the valley
June	Rose
July	Water lily or Larkspur
August	Poppy
September	Dahlia or Morning Glory
October	Begonia or Calendula
November	Chrysanthemum
December	Poinsettia or Holly

Note: See appropriate entries throughout the individual chapters for additional tables. For example, if you are looking for interest tables, refer to Chapter 13, "Business Mathematics, Investments, and Finance," for the entry, INTEREST.

Wedding anniversary presents.

Anniversary	Traditional	Modern
First	Paper	Clock
Second	Cotton	China
Third	Leather	Crystal/Glass
Fourth	Linen/Fruit/Flower	Appliance
Fifth	Wood/Candy	Silverware
Sixth	Candy/Iron	Wood
Seventh	Wool/Copper	Desk set
Eighth	Bronze/Pottery	Linen/Lace
Ninth	Pottery/Willow	Leather
Tenth	Tin/Aluminum	Diamond jewelry
Eleventh	Steel	Fashion jewelry
Twelfth	Silk/Linen	Pearl
Thirteenth	Lace	Textile/Fur
Fourteenth	Ivory	Gold jewelry
Fifteenth	Crystal	Watch
Twentieth	China	Platinum
Twenty-fifth	Silver	Silver
Thirtieth	Pearl	Diamond
Thirty-fifth	Coral	Jade
Fortieth	Ruby	Ruby
Forty-fifth	Sapphire	Sapphire
Fiftieth	Gold	Gold
Fifty-fifth	Emerald	Emerald
Sixtieth	Diamond	Diamond
Seventieth	Diamond	Diamond

Note: Merchants' associations revise the list from time to time.

State information. The following table gives, for each state, the official abbreviation (see Chapter 2/POSTAL SERVICE; Figure 1, for two-letter postal abbreviations), the legislative body, state capitol, state flower, and state nickname.

State	Official Abbrev.	Legislative Body	Capital	Flower	Nickname
Alabama, State of	Ala.	Legislature	Montgomery	Camellia	Cotton State, Yellow-hammer State
Alaska, State of	Alaska	Legislature	Juneau	Forget-me-not	The Last Frontier
Arizona, State of	Ariz.	Legislature	Phoenix	Saguaro Cactus	Grand Canyon State
Arkansas, State of	Ark.	General Assembly	Little Rock	Apple Blossom	Land of Opportunity
California, State of	Calif.	Legislature	Sacramento	Golden Poppy	Golden State
Colorado, State of	Colo.	General Assembly	Denver	Columbine	Centennial State
Connecticut, State of	Conn.	General Assembly	Hartford	Mountain Laurel	Constitution State, Nutmeg State
Delaware, State of	Del.	General Assembly	Dover	Peach Blossom	Diamond State, The First State
Florida, State of	Fla.	Legislature	Tallahassee	Orange Blossom	Sunshine State
Georgia, State of	Ga.	General Assembly	Atlanta	Cherokee Rose	Peach State, Empire State of the South
Hawaii, State of	Hawaii	Legislature	Honolulu	Hibiscus	Aloha State
Idaho, State of	Idaho	Legislature	Boise	Syringa	Gem State
Illinois, State of	Ill.	General Assembly	Springfield	Violet	Prairie State
Indiana, State of	Ind.	General Assembly	Indianapolis	Peony	Hoosier State
Iowa, State of	Iowa	General Assembly	Des Moines	Wild Rose	Hawkeye State, Corn State
Kansas, State of	Kans.	Legislature	Topeka	Sunflower	Sunflower State, Jayhawker State
Kentucky, Commonwealth of	Ky.	General Assembly	Frankfort	Goldenrod	Bluegrass State
Louisiana, State of	La.	Legislature	Baton Rouge	Magnolia	Pelican State, Creole State, Sugar State
Maine, State of	Maine	Legislature	Augusta	Pine Cone and Tassel	Pine Tree State
Maryland, State of	Md.	General Assembly	Annapolis	Blackeyed Susan	Old Line State, Free State
Massachusetts, Commonwealth of	Mass.	General Court	Boston	Mayflower	Bay State, Old Colony State

State	Official Abbrev.	Legislative Body	Capital	Flower	Nickname
Michigan, State of	Mich.	Legislature	Lansing	Apple Blossom	Wolverine State
Minnesota, State of	Minn.	Legislature	St. Paul	Pink and White Lady's Slipper	Gopher State, North Star State
Mississippi, State of	Miss.	Legislature	Jackson	Magnolia	Magnolia State
Missouri, State of	Mo.	General Assembly	Jefferson City	Hawthorn	Show Me State
Montana, State of	Mont.	Legislative Assembly	Helena	Bitterroot	Treasure State, Big Sky Country
Nebraska, State of	Nebr.	Legislature	Lincoln	Goldenrod	Cornhusker State, Beef State
Nevada, State of	Nev.	Legislature	Carson City	Sagebrush	Silver State, Sagebrush State, Battle Born State
New Hampshire, State of	N.H.	General Court	Concord	Purple Lilac	Granite State
New Jersey, State of	N.J.	Legislature	Trenton	Violet	Garden State
New Mexico, State of	N. Mex.	Legislature	Santa Fe	Yucca	Land of Enchantment, Sunshine State
New York, State of	N.Y.	Legislature	Albany	Rose	Empire State
North Carolina, State of	N.C.	General Assembly	Raleigh	Dogwood	Tar Heel State, Old North State
North Dakota, State of	N.Dak.	Legislative Assembly	Bismarck	Wild Prairie Rose	Flickertail State, Sioux State
Ohio, State of	Ohio	General Assembly	Columbus	Scarlet Carnation	Buckeye State
Oklahoma, State of	Okla.	Legislature	Oklahoma City	Mistletoe	Sooner State
Oregon, State of	Oreg.	Legislative Assembly	Salem	Oregon Grape	Beaver State
Pennsylvania, Commonwealth of	Pa.	General Assembly	Harrisburg	Mountain Laurel	Keystone State
Rhode Island, State of	R.I.	General Assembly	Providence	Violet	Little Rhody, Plantation State
South Carolina, State of	S.C.	General Assembly	Columbia	Yellow Jessamine	Palmetto State

563

State	Official Abbrev.	Legislative Body	Capital	Flower	Nickname
South Dakota, State of	S.Dak.	Legislature	Pierre	Pasqueflower	Coyote State, Sunshine State
Tennessee, State of	Tenn.	General Assembly	Nashville	Iris	Volunteer State
Texas, State of	Tex.	Legislature	Austin	Bluebonnet	Lone Star State
Utah, State of	Utah	Legislature	Salt Lake City	Sego Lily	Beehive State
Vermont, State of	Vt.	General Assembly	Montpelier	Red Clover	Green Mountain State
Virginia, Commonwealth of	Va.	General Assembly	Richmond	Dogwood	Old Dominion, Mother of Presidents
Washington, State of	Wash.	Legislature	Olympia	Western Rhododendron	Evergreen State, Chinook State
West Virginia, State of	W. Va.	Legislature	Charleston	Big Rhododendron	Mountain State
Wisconsin, State of	Wis.	Legislature	Madison	Wood Violet	Badger State
Wyoming, State of	Wyo.	Legislature	Cheyenne	Indian Paintbrush	Equality State

Greek Alphabet

NAME OF LETTER	GREEK ALPHABET	
Alpha	A	$a\ \alpha^1$
Beta	B	β
Gamma	Γ	γ
Delta	Δ	$\delta\ \partial^1$
Epsilon	E	ε
Zeta	Z	ζ
Eta	H	η
Theta	Θ	$\theta\ \vartheta^1$
Iota	I	ι
Kappa	K	κ
Lambda	Λ	λ
Mu	M	μ
Nu	N	ν
Xi	Ξ	ξ
Omicron	O	o
Pi	Π	π
Rho	P	ρ
Sigma	Σ	$\sigma\ \varsigma^2$
Tau	T	τ
Upsilon	Y	υ
Phi	Φ	ϕ
Chi	X	χ
Psi	Ψ	ψ
Omega	Ω	ω

1. Old style character.

2. Final letter.

Metric system of weights and measures. The fundamental units of the metric system are the meter—the unit of length—and the kilogram—the unit of mass.

The *liter* is defined as the volume of a kilogram of water at the temperature of its maximum density, 4° centigrade. All other units are the decimal subdivisions or multiples of these figures. The three units are simply related. For example, for all practical purposes, 1 cubic decimeter equals 1 liter, and 1 liter of water weighs 1 kilogram.

The metric tables are formed by combining the words *meter, gram,* and *liter* with six numerical prefixes: the Latin prefixes *milli-, centi-,* and *deci-;* and the Greek prefixes *deka-, hecto-,* and *kilo-.*

The metric system of weights and measures is used throughout the world with few exceptions.

TABLES OF METRIC WEIGHTS, MEASURES, and VALUES

Metric Prefixes and Multiplication Factors

1 *deka*gram	=	10 grams
1 gram	=	1 gram
1 *deci*gram	=	0.1 gram
1 *centi*gram	=	0.01 gram
1 *milli*gram	=	0.001 gram

Length

1 *kilo*meter	=	1,000 meters
1 *hecto*meter	=	100 meters
1 *deka*meter	=	10 meters
1 meter	=	1 meter
1 *deci*meter	=	0.1 meter
1 *centi*meter	=	0.01 meter
1 *milli*meter	=	0.001 meter

Volume

1 *hecto*liter	=	100 liters
1 *deka*liter	=	10 liters
1 liter	=	1 liter
1 *centi*liter	=	0.01 liter
1 *milli*liter	=	0.001 liter

Weight

1 *kilo*gram	=	1,000 grams
1 *hecto*gram	=	100 grams

METRIC MEASUREMENT CONVERSIONS

When You Know	Multiply by	To Find
Length		
inches (in.)	2.54	centimeters (cm)
feet (ft.)	30.00	centimeters (cm)
yards (yd.)	0.90	meters (m)
miles (mi.)	1.60	kilometers (km)
millimeters (mm)	0.04	inches (in.)
centimeters (cm)	0.40	inches (in.)
meters (m)	3.30	feet (ft.)

METRIC MEASUREMENT CONVERSIONS (*continued*)

When You Know	Multiply by	To Find
Length (*continued*)		
meters (m)	1.10	yards (yd.)
kilometers (km)	0.60	miles (mi.)
Area		
square inches (in.^{2})	6.50	square centimeters (cm^2)
square feet (ft.^{2})	0.09	square meters (m^2)
square yards (yd.^{2})	0.80	square meters (m^2)
square miles (mi.^{2})	2.60	square kilometers (km^2)
acres	0.40	hectares (ha)
square centimeters (cm^2)	0.16	square inches (in.^{2})
square meters (m^2)	1.20	square yards (yd.^{2})
square kilometers (km^2)	0.40	square miles (mi.^{2})
hectares (ha) (10,000 m^2)	2.50	acres
Weight		
ounces (oz.)	28.00	grams (g)
pounds (lb.)	0.45	kilograms (kg)
short tons (2,000 lbs.)	0.90	tonnes (t)
long tons (2,240 lbs.)	1.01	tonnes (t)
grams (g)	0.035	ounce (oz.)
kilograms (kg)	2.20	pounds (lb.)
tonnes (1,000 kg)	1.10	short tons
tonnes (1,000 kg)	0.98	long tons
Volume		
teaspoons (tsp.)	5.00	milliliters (ml)
tablespoons (tbsp.)	15.00	milliliters (ml)
fluid ounces (fl. oz.)	30.00	milliliters (ml)
cups (c)	0.24	liters (l)
pints (pt.)	0.47	liters (l)
quarts (qt.)	0.95	liters (l)
gallons, U.S. (gal.)	3.80	liters (l)

METRIC MEASUREMENT CONVERSIONS (*continued*)

When You Know	Multiply by	To Find
Volume (continued)		
gallons, Imp. (gal.)	4.50	liters (l)
cubic feet (ft.^{3})	0.028	cubic meters (m^3)
cubic yards (yd.^{3})	0.76	cubic meters (m^3)
milliliters (ml)	0.03	fluid ounces (fl. oz.)
liters (l)	2.10	pints (pt.)
liters (l)	1.06	quarts (qt.)
liters (l)	0.26	gallons, U.S. (gal.)
liters (l)	0.22	gallons, Imp. (gal.)
cubic meters (m^3)	35.00	cubic feet (ft.^{3})
cubic meters (m^3)	1.30	cubic yards (yd.^{3})

Temperature

$$°C = (°F - 32) \cdot 0.555$$
$$°F = (°C \cdot 1.8) + 32$$

METRIC EQUIVALENTS

Linear Measure

1 centimeter	0.3937	inches	
1 inch	2.54	centimeters	
1 decimeter	3.937	inches	0.328 foot
1 foot	3.048	decimeters	
1 meter	39.37	inches	1.0936 yards
1 yard	0.9144	meter	
1 dekameter	1.9884	rods	
1 rod	0.5029	dekameter	
1 kilometer	0.62137	mile	
1 mile	1.6093	kilometers	

Square Measure

1 square centimeter	0.1550	square inches
1 square inch	6,452	square centimeters

METRIC EQUIVALENTS (*continued*)

Square Measure (continued)

1 square decimeter	0.1076	square foot	
1 square foot	9.2903	square decimeter	
1 square meter	1.196	square yards	
1 square yard	0.8361	square meter	
1 acre	160	square rods	
1 square rod	0.00625	acre	
1 hectare	2.47	acres	
1 acre	0.4047	hectare	
1 square kilometer	0.386	square mile	
1 square mile	2.59	square kilometers	

Volume

1 cubic centimeter	0.061	cubic inch	
1 cubic inch	16.39	cubic centimeters	
1 cubic decimeter	0.0353	cubic foot	
1 cubic foot	28.317	cubic yards	
1 cubic yard	0.7646	cubic meter	
1 stere	0.2759	cord	
1 cord	3.624	steres	
1 liter	0.908	quart dry	1.0567 quarts liquid
1 quart dry	1.101	liters	
1 quart liquid	0.9463	liter	
1 dekaliter	2.6417	gallons	1.135 pecks
1 gallon	0.3785	dekaliter	
1 peck	0.881	dekaliter	
1 hektoliter	2.8375	bushels	
1 bushel	0.3524	hektoliter	

Weights

1 gram	0.03527	ounce
1 ounce	28.35	grams
1 kilogram	2.2046	pounds
1 pound	0.4536	kilogram
1 metric ton	0.98421	English ton
1 English ton	1.016	metric ton

METRIC EQUIVALENTS (*continued*)

Approximate Metric Equivalents

1 decimeter	4	inches	
1 liter	1.06	quarts liquid	0.9 quarts dry
1 meter	1.1	yards	
1 kilometer	0.625	mile	
1 hektoliter	2.625	bushels	
1 hectare	2.5	acres	
1 kilogram	2.20	pounds	
1 stere, or cubic meter	0.25	cord	
1 metric ton	2,200	pounds	

Tables of weights, measures, and values.
(United States Standard)

LONG MEASURE

12 inches . .	1 foot
3 feet	1 yard
5½ yards, or 16½ feet . .	1 rod
320 rods, or 5,280 feet . .	1 mile
1,760 yards . . .	1 mile
40 rods	1 furlong
8 furlongs .	1 statute mile
6,076 feet	1 international nautical mile
3 miles . . .	1 league

SQUARE MEASURE

144 square inches .	1 square foot
9 square feet . . .	1 square yard
30¼ square yards .	1 square rod
272¼ square feet . . .	1 square rod
40 square rods . .	1 British rood
4 rods	1 acre
160 square rods . .	1 acre
640 acres	1 square mile
43,560 square feet . . .	1 acre
4,840 square yards .	1 acre

SOLID OR CUBIC MEASURE (VOLUME)

1,728 cubic in. .	1 cubic foot
27 cubic feet .	1 cubic yard
128 cubic feet .	1 cord of wood
24.75 cubic feet .	1 perch of stone
2,150.42 cubic in. .	1 standard bushel
231 cubic in. .	1 standard gallon
40 cubic feet .	1 ton (shipping)

DRY MEASURE

2 pints	1 quart
8 quarts	1 peck
4 pecks	1 bushel
2,150.42 cubic inches .	1 bushel
1.2445 cubic feet . . .	1 bushel

LIQUID MEASURE (CAPACITY)

4 gills	1 pint
2 pints	1 quart
4 quarts	1 gallon
31.5 gallons	1 barrel
2 barrels	1 hogshead
1 gallon	231 cubic inches
7.4805 gallons	1 cubic foot
16 fluid ounces .	1 pint
1 fluid ounce .	1.805 cubic inches

MARINERS' MEASURE

6 feet	1 fathom
100 fathoms	1 cable's length as applied to distances or intervals between ships
120 fathoms	1 cable's length as applied to marine wire cable
7.50 cable lengths	1 mile
5,280 feet	1 statute mile
6,080 feet	1 nautical mile
1.15266 statute miles	1 nautical or geographical mile
3 geographical miles	1 league
60 geographical miles, or 69.16 statute miles	1 degree of longitude on the equator, or 1 degree of meridian
360 degrees	1 circumference

Note: A knot is not a measure of distance but a measure of speed. Current usage makes a knot equivalent to a nautical mile per hour (properly it is $\frac{1}{120}$ of a nautical mile). Hence when the speed of vessels at sea is being measured, a knot is equal to a nautical mile, or 6,080 feet, or 2,026.66 yards, *per hour*.

UNITED STATES AND BRITISH WEIGHTS AND MEASURES COMPARED

1 British bushel	1.0326 United States (Winchester) bushels
1 United States bushel	0.96894 British Imperial bushel
1 British quart	1.03206 United States dry quarts
1 United States dry quart	0.96894 British quart
1 British quart (or gallon)	1.20095 United States liquid quarts (or gallons)
1 United States liquid quart (or gallon)	0.83267 British quart (or gallon)

AVOIRDUPOIS MEASURE (WEIGHT)

(Used for weighing all ordinary substances except precious metals, jewels, and drugs)

27.343 grains	1 dram
16 drams	1 ounce
16 ounces	1 pound
25 pounds	1 quarter
4 quarts	1 hundredweight
100 pounds	1 hundredweight
20 hundredweight	1 ton
2,000 pounds	1 short ton
2,240 pounds	1 long ton

TROY MEASURE (WEIGHT)

(Used for weighing gold, silver, and jewels)

24 grains	1 pennyweight
20 pennyweights .	1 ounce
12 ounces	1 pound

Comparison of Avoirdupois and Troy Measures

1 pound troy	5,760 grains
1 pound avoirdupois .	7,000 grains
1 ounce troy	480 grains
1 ounce avoirdupois .	437.5 grains
1 carat or karat	3.2 troy grains
24 carat gold	pure gold

COMMON METRIC EQUIVALENTS

Long Measure

inch	2.540 centimeters
foot	30.480 centimeters
yard	0.914 meters
rod	5.029 meters
mile	1.609 kilometers

Square Measure

square inch	6.452 square centimeters
square foot	0.093 square meters
square yard	0.836 square meters
square rod	25.293 square meters
square mile	2.590 square kilometers

Cubic Measure

cubic inch	16.387 cubic centimeters
cubic foot	0.028 cubic meters
cubic yard	0.765 cubic meters

Dry Measure

pint	0.551 liters
quart	1.101 liters
peck	8.810 liters
bushel	35.239 liters

Liquid Measure

fluid ounce	29.574 milliliters
gill	118.291 milliliters
pint	0.473 liters
quart	0.946 liters
gallon	3.785 liters

Avoirdupois Weight

grain	0.0648 grams
dram	1.772 grams
ounce	28.350 grams
pound	0.454 kilograms
hundredweight	
short	45.359 kilograms
long	50.802 kilograms
ton	
short	0.907 metric tons
long	1.016 metric tons

Troy Weight

grain	0.0648 grams
pennyweight	1.555 grams
ounce	31.103 grams
pound	0.373 kilograms

Apothecaries' Weight

grain	0.0648 grams
scruple	1.296 grams
dram	3.888 grams
ounce	31.103 grams
pound	0.373 kilograms

Note: See also METRIC SYSTEM OF WEIGHTS AND MEASURES.

SURVEYORS' LONG MEASURE

7.92 inches	1 link
25 links	1 rod
4 rods, or 100 links	1 chain
80 chains	1 mile

SURVEYORS' SQUARE MEASURE

625 square links	1 square rod
16 square rods	1 square chain
10 square chains	1 acre
640 acres	1 square mile
36 square miles	1 township

CIRCULAR OR ANGULAR MEASURE

60 seconds (60″)	1 minute (′)
60 minutes (60′)	1 degree (1°)
30 degrees	1 sign
90 degrees	1 right angle or quadrant
180 degrees	1 straight angle
360 degrees	1 circumference

Note: One degree at the equator is approximately 60 nautical miles.

COUNTING

12 units or things	1 dozen
12 dozen, or 144 units	1 gross
12 gross	1 great gross
20 units	1 score

PAPER MEASURE

24 sheets	1 quire
20 quires	1 ream
2 reams	1 bundle
5 bundles	1 bale

Note: Although a ream contains 480 sheets, 500 sheets are usually sold as a ream.

UNITED STATES MONEY

10 mills	1 cent
10 cents	1 dime
10 dimes	1 dollar
10 dollars	1 eagle

APOTHECARIES' FLUID MEASURE (CAPACITY)

60 minims	1 fluid dram
8 fluid drams	1 fluid ounce
16 fluid ounces	1 pint
2 pints	1 quart
4 quarts	1 gallon

APOTHECARIES' MEASURE (WEIGHT)

20 grains	1 scruple
3 scruples	1 dram
8 drams	1 ounce
12 ounces	1 pound

Index